Philological and Historical Commentary on
Ammianus Marcellinus XXIII

Philological and Historical Commentary on Ammianus Marcellinus XXIII

by

J. den Boeft, J.W. Drijvers
D. den Hengst, H.C. Teitler

Groningen
Egbert Forsten
1998

© Copyright 1998 Egbert Forsten Groningen, The Netherlands

All rights reserved. No part of this book may be reproduced or translated in any form, by print, photoprint, microfilm or any other means without written permission from the publisher.

This book was printed with financial support from the Netherlands Organization for Scientific Research (NWO)

This book meets the requirements of ISO 9706:1994
Information and documentation
Paper for documents-requirements for permanence

ISBN 90 6980 120 5

Printed by Scholma Druk, Bedum, The Netherlands

Contents

Preface	vii
Introduction	ix
Ammianus' sources for Julian's expedition	xii
A note on chronology	xv
Legenda	xxi
Commentary	1
Maps and drawings	after 80
Bibliography	235
Indices	255

Preface

In preparing the commentary on book 23, we were able to benefit from the studies of the late Dr M.F.A. Brok on Julian's Persian campaign and the digression on siege engines. These studies were already put to good use by Professor Fontaine in the bilingual edition of books 23–25 in the *Collection des universités de France* and the volume of notes accompanying it. We gratefully used the material which is available in the work of our immediate predecessors. As the reader may have gathered from our commentaries on books 20, 21 and 22, we aim at the integration of a wide variety of evidence and observations. It is our firm conviction that only by making the widest possible use of both philological and historical research, can one reach an adequate understanding of the author's account and of his guiding principles. In other words our purpose is to elucidate what Ammianus Marcellinus is saying, how he says it and, last but not least, why he says what he does in a particular way.

We thank the friends and colleagues who helped us with their advice. Drs. K.J.F. van de Wetering corrected our English. Drs. J. Lendering made drawings of some war-machines according to our assessment of their description in chapter 4. In cooperation with him Ms. T. Hersbach drew the necessary maps. Dr R. Barkhuis prepared our manuscript for the printer with meticulous care. Thanks are due to the Netherlands Organization for Scientific Research (NWO), which subsidized the correction and publication of the book. As usual, the cooperation with our publisher, Mr. Egbert Forsten, was efficient.

J. den Boeft
J.W. Drijvers
D. den Hengst
H.C. Teitler

Introduction

Book 23 is the first part of the trilogy on the Persian expedition. Its tragic protagonist was the man whom Ammianus admired, though aware of the flaws in his character and the failings in his behaviour. The book's primary function is to impress on the reader the enormity of Julian's project so that he is thus in the right state of mind to appreciate the expedition's progress in book 24 and its terrible demise in book 25.

In book 23 Ammianus reports the final stages of Julian's preparations and the beginning of the campaign itself. At first sight the book seems badly constructed, since almost two thirds of it are taken up by two digressions, a lengthy and intricate description of various types of artillery in ch. 4 and a vast survey of the Persian empire in ch. 6. Modern readers who would prefer to concentrate on the exciting events might feel their patience tried by the ballistic technicalities or the dry lists of towns and rivers in Persia. But ancient readers were far more interested in the well-wrought expatiations of encyclopaedical learning which they expected to encounter in historiography. This holds true especially when such information was directly functional for the historian's reports, as is specifically the case in book 23. For Julian, the Persian campaign was not merely one of his notable exploits, but also a grand and much needed expedition to solve the problems on the eastern borders once and for all. As he said to his soldiers shortly after the invasion of the enemy's territory, *abolenda nobis natio molestissima* (23.5.19). He aimed at nothing less than the annihilation of Persian power.

The size of this project calls for an adequate treatment by the historian, whose principal aim in book 23 consists precisely in making its daring and breathtaking dimensions fully clear to his readers. They had to realize the need for large, but efficient war machines and gain an understanding of their workings, and they needed a detailed knowledge of the vast empire Julian was going to attack in order to grasp fully the greatness of the campaign. In fact, the digression on artillery is well placed between the twenty-four sections of ch. 1–3, in which Julian's last acts in Antioch and the first stages of the eastward march up to the invasion proper are reported, and the twenty-five sections of ch. 5, which deal with the first actions within the enemy's borders. Next, before continuing with further manoeuvres, Ammianus first deemed it necessary to provide a sufficiently extensive sketch of the territory and of the mental and economic resources of the Persian empire. Admittedly, the desire to vie with renowned geographers led him to include regions in the eastern world far outside that empire, but, viewed from the practice of ancient historiography, there is hardly another place in the *Res Gestae* more apt for the purpose.

The structure is, however, somewhat more complicated in that the historian understandably imposed upon himself the task to provide the reader with a historical survey of Roman dealings with the Persians. Such a survey was even indispensable in order to judge the practicability of Julian's undertaking. However, a third lengthy digression would have been excessive and the author contrived an excellent solution by putting the information into the emperor's own mouth as part of the speech meant to inspire his soldiers (23.5.16–23). This brought an added advantage in that the campaign's bold aim was now worded by its leader himself, who proved able to rouse his men to combativeness. History itself taught them that the Persians should and could be firmly held at bay. Singularly, in contrast to the heroic stance ascribed to Julian in this chapter, in the elogium Ammianus strikes an apologetic note. Constantine's provocation of the Persians had wrought havoc and Julian had to face the consequences: *docente veritate perspicue non Iulianum, sed Constantinum ardores Parthicos succendisse, cum Metrodori mendaciis avidius acquiescit* (25.4.23).

These considerations lead to the verdict that the structure of book 23 is not haphazard. All the information needed to judge the concept of the Persian expedition is being put at the reader's disposal. He is bound to be faced by the question whether the emperor was not over-estimating his possible options. Were not his *obtrectatores* at Antioch rightly pleading postponement, *studium omne in differendo procinctu ponentes* (22.12.3)? And what were the gods' thoughts about it? Exactly these doubts form the second characteristic of book 23. Right from the start it contains a number of *omina* of all kinds, such as the failure of the plan to rebuild the temple at Jerusalem, the sudden death of important people, the fatal collapse of a building or a pile, the fall of the emperor's horse. It seems quite impossible that anyone could overlook these clear warnings, yet the protagonist turned out to be the only person of authority who waved away the obvious meaning. In this he was supported by the philosophers in his entourage, who even had the arrogance to neglect simple historical facts in their optimistic interpretations of ominous events (23.5.11).

Ammianus' persistent report of *omina* can only be fully appreciated when the digression on divination (*doctrinae genus haud leve*) in 21.1.7–14 is taken into account. There the author had defended divination in its various forms against unsympathetic opponents, winding up the digression by dealing with examples of human failure to appreciate the true meaning of divinely sent signs. Julian is the most pathetic instance of this, with disastrous results. And so the expedition which was thought out well in the eyes of the author, met with a terrible end. If only its leader had listened to the advice of men and heeded the signs from heaven which suggested postponement, history would have taken a different course. As the author says in the elogium, *adortus est Persas triumphum exinde relaturus et cognomentum, si consiliis eius et factis illustribus decreta caelestia congruissent* (25.4.26). Tragically, Julian failed in the domain of his own predilection: overzealous in the cult of the gods by his sacrificial excesses, he fell prey to superstition; neglecting the obvious lessons of divination, he prepared his own downfall. In the early days of 363 the emperor *terrebatur omine quodam, ut docuit exitus, praesentissimo* (23.1.5), but his fear was entirely cast aside by the same optimism as that of his soldiers: *spe prosperorum elatior* (23.5.24).

When read with due respect for its purpose, book 23 is functional. It serves to emphasize that Julian had taken on a tremendous task, which in itself should have induced him to heed the *omina*. Failure to do so was like playing with fire. Alas, he was driven *flagranti studio* (23.1.2) and *speciosa fiducia* (23.2.1), and two disasters, each costing the lives of fifty men, made him sad (*maestus*, 23.3.1), but did not make him wonder whether he was acting rightly, although there was a rumour that he had urged Procopius to grasp the purple, *si se interisse didicerit apud Parthos* (23.3.2).

Ammianus was himself an eye-witness of the Persian expedition. He probably joined it in Cercusium at the beginning of April 363, since in 23.5.7 *Profecti exinde* (from Cercusium) *Zaitham venimus* the first person plural is used for the first time. Presumably Ammianus was not in a position to observe the proceedings from within Julian's inner circle. For this he will have relied on those who had access to that circle and whom he may have already interviewed at the time. In any case, *visa* must have provided both the framework and a large part of his evidence. It is more difficult to ascertain to which degree *lecta* contributed to his material. In his report there are some parallels with the historians Magnus and Zosimus, but these are too slight to come to any conclusions. It is not impossible that, either directly or indirectly, he derived some information from a ὑπόμνημα of Julian's deeds which Oribasius had composed for Eunapius' history. To summarize, the present state of our knowledge cannot but entail a *non liquet* concerning any written sources used by the author for his account of the Persian expedition. Ammianus' achievement has to be judged by a careful analysis of his text, which contains the only clues available for assessing his personal handling of the material he had gathered. If read and scrutinized in a prudent manner, his own words will reveal the author's choices and interpretations: *secuturus aperiet textus* (15.1.1).

Ammianus' sources for Julian's expedition

There can hardly be any doubt that Ammianus Marcellinus participated in Julian's Persian expedition, pace Mommsen, 1909, 428 ("so erscheint seine eigene Betheiligung in hohem Grade zweifelhaft"). Amm. must have joined Julian's forces in Cercusium, at the beginning of April 363 (the occurrence of the first person plural in the narrative from 23.5.7 onwards is a clear indication for this). From Cercusium he marched with the rest of the army southwards to Ctesiphon, went through the fatal outcome of the campaign and then, under the new emperor Jovian, returned to Antioch, where he apparently stayed behind while Jovian moved on (the use of the first person plural ends in 25.10.1).

As an officer in Julian's army Amm. was in an excellent position to gather information about the Persian expedition, both by keeping his own eyes wide open and by interviewing other participants (of course, he could not be in two places at the same time nor is it probable that he would have known without help what was going on in the emperor's inner circle of advisers). Therefore Amm. must already have started the process which later enabled him to write its history during the Persian campaign. Or, as he himself says in the opening sentence of book 15 of his *Res Gestae*, which is totally applicable to books 23–25: *Utcumque potui veritatem scrutari, ea, quae videre licuit per aetatem vel perplexe interrogando versatos in medio scire, narravimus ordine casuum exposito diversorum.*

As to *perplexe interrogando*, it seems reasonable to assume that Amm. in person questioned *versatos in medio* while the expedition was under way, and that after the campaign had ended he tried to contact possible informants both orally and in writing. One can compare Libanius' method of gathering news about Julian's Persian war. The sophist on the one hand exchanged letters with Julian himself (Lib. *Ep.* 802 and 811, Jul. *Ep.* 98), and, after the emperor's death, with his friends Philagrius and Seleucus (*Ep.* 1434.2–6 and 1508.6–7, cf. 802.8). On the other hand, he also heard details from soldiers who were unknown to him before the war and whom he apparently had approached in person after they had come back to Antioch (*Ep.* 1220.7–9, cf. 1402.3).

We can only speculate about the number and the identity of those whom Amm. questioned. For example, we do not even know with certainty if Amm., like Libanius, interviewed Philagrius and Seleucus, although this does seem probable. It would seem that at least Philagrius was known to Amm. and had been his source for the Vadomarius-episode in 21.4 (cf. Sabbah 226–7 and Matthews 376–7). Both men must have been very valuable sources of information indeed, due to their former proximity to the emperor. They had held posts at Julian's court, Philagrius as a *notarius* (21.4.2), Seleucus in an unknown function (Lib. *Ep.* 734). Philagrius, moreover, had made extensive notes on the Persian campaign (Lib. *Ep.* 1434.2–6), while Seleucus even intended to write its history (Lib. *Ep.* 1508.6–7).

Of Seleucus' history nothing more is heard, and it is doubtful whether it was ever written. But there were other participants in the expedition who did commit their experience to writing. The *protector domesticus* Callistus, for example, wrote an epic poem about Julian (Socr. *HE* 3.21.14), while Julian's doctor and close friend Oribasius was the author of a detailed memorandum, which he made available for use to a somewhat younger contemporary, the sophist and historian Eunapius (Eun. *fr.* 15 Blockley). We also know of some historians in Julian's army, Eutropius (cf. *Brev.* 10.16 *cui expeditioni ego quoque interfui*), Magnus of Carrhae and Eutychianus (fragments of the accounts of the latter two authors are quoted by John Malalas, p. 328–30 Bonn = *FrGrHist* 225 F 1 and 226 F 1, respectively). The possibility that these men were amongst those to whom Amm. talked about Julian's Persian campaign cannot be excluded. But did he use their writings as a source for his own history?

Since Amm. is nowhere explicit about his sources, this question can only be answered indirectly, by comparing Amm.'s text with those of the authors just mentioned (in what follows, this is only outlined; for more detailed treatments see most recently Matthews 161 ff. and Fornara, 1991). A complication is caused by the fact that the works of Oribasius and Magnus are not preserved integrally – we can leave the others aside: Callistus' epic is completely lost; the few words devoted to Julian's Persian war in Eutropius' *Breviarium* cannot, if read by Amm., have taught him anything new; and the fragment of Eutychianus preserved by Malalas is too short to build a theory on (pace Seeck, 1906, 538–9).

Malalas' quotation from the history of Magnus is not very long either, but we can at least set parts of it alongside some passages of Amm. Compare for instance 23.5.1–2 *Cercusium... cuius moenia Abora et Euphrates ambiunt flumina velut spatium insulare fingentes. quod Diocletianus exiguum ante hoc et suspectum muris turribusque circumdedit celsis* with τὸ ῾Ρωμαικὸν κάστρον τὸ λεγόμενον Κιρκήσιον, κείμενον εἰς τὸ μέσον τῶν δύο ποταμῶν τοῦ Εὐφράτου καὶ τοῦ ᾿Αββορᾶ, ὅπερ ἔκτισε Διοκλητιανὸς βασιλεὺς ῾Ρωμαίων (*FrGrHist* 225 F 1, 13–15). There is a certain similarity between the two passages. However, the resemblance is hardly enough to conclude, with Klein, 1914, 64–5, that Amm. here copied Magnus. Moreover, the significant detail *ambiunt flumina velut spatium insulare fingentes* is absent in Magnus. It is in general hazardous to conclude from the meagre fragment of Magnus in Malalas, a mere sevenhundred words, that for books 23–5 Magnus was Amm.'s source, let alone his only source (so Klein, 1914, 30 ff.; Klotz believed that, apart from on Magnus, Amm. drew on another written account "die uns in die nächste Umgebung des Kaisers führt" [1916, 506]).

Amm.'s 23.5.1–2 not only has certain points in common with the text of

Magnus just quoted, but also with the following passage in Zosimus (3.12.3): Κιρχησίου (φρούριον δὲ τοῦτο κυκλούμενον ὑπό τε τοῦ Ἀβώρα ποταμοῦ καὶ αὐτοῦ τοῦ Εὐφράτου, τοῖς δὲ Ἀσσυρίων ὁρίοις συναπτόμενον). For some scholars the explanation of the similarity is obvious. Zosimus and Amm. had used the same written source or sources: either Magnus of Carrhae (so e.g. Klein, 1914, following Mendelsohn, 1887) or Magnus and another, anonymous, author (so Klotz, 1916). However, the inference is not cogent. Apart from the fact that the points in common between Amm., Zosimus and Magnus are not striking to such a degree that it makes the thought of literary affiliation inescapable, there is another author who, rather than Magnus, deserves to be considered as Zosimus' source: Eunapius of Sardis.

According to the explicit statement of the ninth-century patriarch Photius (Codex 98 Henry 84 b 27 ff.), Eunapius was the author whom Zosimus almost slavishly had followed. If Photius was right (and there is no reason not to believe him), and if Eunapius in his turn relied on the memoir of Oribasius which Julian's doctor had personally placed at his disposal (Eun. *fr.* 15 Blockley), it would seem that ultimately Zosimus' *New History* was based on Oribasius' memorandum. If so, and if "a literary relationship must be inferred" (Barnes, 1978, 117), then the similarities between Amm. and Zosimus can be explained by assuming either that Amm. had also consulted Oribasius' memoir (so e.g. Paschoud, 1976, 177–9) or that he had read Eunapius (so e.g. Chalmers, 1960, 152 ff., Barnes, 1978, 117 ff., Bowersock, 1978, 7–8 and Matthews 175) – less plausible are other possibilities, such as the reverse conjecture that "Eunapius had direct or more probably indirect access to Ammianus' work" (Thompson, 1947, 136–7), that Zosimus may have used Amm. (Norman, 1957, 129 ff.) or that Amm. and Zosimus had a common source other than Eunapius/Oribasius (e.g. Magnus, see above), and these should be rejected (cf. Matthews 172 with n. 86, Fornara, 1991, 6–8).

A comparison between Amm. and Zosimus shows, apart from some similarities, many differences. To name only a few: the spelling of place-names (e.g. *Zaithan...locum*, 23.5.7, χωρίον Ζαυθὰ, Zos. 3.14.2); the location of the tomb of Gordianus (near Zaitha in 23.5.7, near Dura in Zos. 3.14.2); the sending of an embassy from Edessa with an invitation for Julian to come to this city (Zos. 3.12.2, not in Amm.). These and other differences make it clear that Amm. did not totally depend upon Oribasius' memoir or Eunapius' history, if in fact he consulted these works at all. Even less so if he did not: "it is easier to believe that the similar but often divergent accounts in Ammianus and Zosimus ultimately derive from the autopsy of the two eyewitnesses, Ammianus and Oribasius, than from any literary interdependency between Ammianus and Eunapius" (Fornara, 1991, 13). It was only to be expected from an author whose first and foremost methods of gathering information for his contemporary history were, to refer once again to his own words, personal inspection and interviews (15.1.1).

A note on chronology

In 23.2.6 we find the first of the five passages in book 23 which furnish precise chronological data about Julian's march from Antioch to the east (the other four are 3.3, 3.7, 5.1 and 5.12). Based on these data and with the help of an occasional remark of Zosimus and of Julian himself, an approximately correct reconstruction of the order of events can be made. Some details, however, remain uncertain.

From Antioch to Hierapolis

Julian set out from Antioch on the fifth of March 363 (*tertium nonas Martias profectus*, 23.2.6) and took the usual route to Hierapolis (*Hierapolim solitis itineribus venit*). According to Zosimus he arrived there on the fifth day after he had left Antioch (πέμπτῃ δὲ τὴν Ἱεράπολιν ἡμέρᾳ καταλαβών, 3.12.1). If we combine these data, as has been done so far by all scholars who have commented upon these texts, it would seem that Julian arrived in Hierapolis on March, 9. There is, however, reason to doubt the correctness of this conclusion in view of the contents of Jul. *Ep.* 98.

In Julian's letter, addressed to Libanius, we find a rather detailed description of Julian's journey to Hierapolis (apart from the words quoted above neither Amm. nor Zos. gives any further information). Three halting places where Julian called are explicitly mentioned, viz. Litarba, Beroea and Batnae. The distance between Antioch and Litarba is approximately 55 km (Fontaine's "à 80 km. à l'est de la capitale" in his n. 39 must be a slip), between Litarba and Beroea 34 km, between Beroea and Batnae 45 km and between Batnae and Hierapolis 26 km. As to the journey from Antioch to Litarba (modern El-Terib), it is generally assumed that Julian arrived there on the very same day on which he had left Antioch, i.e. on the fifth of March (cf. e.g. the chronological survey of Brok, 1959, 257 and his commentary ad 23.2.6 *solitis itineribus*).

However, Litarba is at quite a distance, 55 km, from Antioch – this fact is mentioned by Brok, 1959, 44 without further comment, although on p. 45 he himself observes that 30 km a day was the maximum an army covered in normal circumstances (cf. Elton, 1996, 245: "A day's march obviously varied in length, but seems to have averaged 20 km"). Moreover, at the time when Julian took the road which led from Antioch eastwards it was rather rough, consisting of part swamps, part hills (Jul. *Ep.* 98, 399 b; cf. Lib. *Ep.* 802.1). As Julian writes, especially the swamp caused difficulties. One wonders therefore if these circumstances, the distance of 55 km and the condition of the road, did not hinder Julian and his army from reaching Litarba on the same day as that on which he left Antioch. And there is more.

In his letter to Libanius Julian writes that, after he had passed over the swamp, he arrived at his first halting place at about the ninth hour of the day (Ἐπεὶ δὲ διαβὰς μόλις ἦλθον εἰς τὸν πρῶτον σταθμόν, ἐννέα που σχεδὸν ἦσαν ὧραι) and received there a delegation of the Antiochene council (καὶ ἐδεξάμην εἴσω τῆς αὐλῆς τὸ πλεῖστον τῆς παρ' ὑμῖν βουλῆς, *Ep.* 98, 399 c). This reference to the first σταθμός and to the ninth hour (i.e. early in the afternoon, cf. Bidez, 1924, 180 n. 4: "entre deux et trois heures de l'après-midi" and Bickerman, 1968, 15) is crucial for the interpretation of the point under discussion. Scholarly literature unanimously identifies this first halting place with Litarba (see e.g. Cumont, 1917, 6; Wright, 1923, xxv; Bidez, 1924, 115; Brok, 1959, 44, Weis, 1973, 267; Fontaine, 1977, 22 n. 39; Matthews 144 and Dodgeon-Lieu, 1991, 231). However, this would imply that Julian's army, in order to arrive in Litarba at about the ninth hour, had covered the distance of 55 km over a rough road at an amazingly fast pace.

It is true that the swiftness of Julian's operations is stressed in the sources more than once (cf. the note ad 21.9.6). In the present context, however, there is no indication that he was in a hurry. On the contrary, he himself tells us (*Ep.* 98, 399 d) that, when he had reached Beroea, he felt free to stay there for a day instead of immediately passing through. Moreover, it is worth stressing that the emperor did not travel alone. He was leading an army. Procopius, speaking in *Pers.* 2.7.2–4 of the same route, albeit in the opposite direction, notes that an unencumbered traveller, Megas, bishop of Beroea, was able to cover the distance between Hierapolis and Antioch (i.e. 160 km) in four days, but that Chosroes and the Persian army were accomplishing only one half of the distance which Megas travelled each day (Βέροια δὲ Ἀντιοχείας μὲν καὶ Ἱεραπόλεως μεταξὺ κεῖται, δυοῖν δὲ ἡμερῶν ὁδῷ εὐζώνῳ ἀνδρὶ ἑκατέρας διέχει. ὁ μὲν οὖν Μέγας ἅτε ξὺν ὀλίγοις τισὶ πορευόμενος ὀξύτερον ᾔει, ὁ δὲ Περσῶν στρατὸς μοῖραν ἀεὶ τὴν ἡμίσειαν τῆς ὁδοῦ ἤνυε).

Is it in view of these considerations correct to identify Julian's first halting place as Litarba? Does the text of Julian's *Ep.* 98 indeed unequivocally say so, as modern interpreters apparently assume? We think not. The emperor, it is true, opens his letter with the statement that he went to Litarba: Μέχρι τῶν Λιτάρβων ἦλθον (ἔστι δὲ ἡ κώμη Χαλκίδος). But then he gives details concerning the road he had followed: it still had the remains of a winter camp (καὶ ἐνέτυχον ὁδῷ λείψανα ἐχούσῃ χειμαδίων Ἀντιοχικῶν), it was fairly rough (ἦν δὲ αὐτῆς, οἶμαι, τὸ μὲν τέλμα τὸ δὲ ὄρος, τραχεῖα δὲ πᾶσα) and it had only been possible to pass over it thanks to stones lying in the swampy part of the road. After these observations follows the phrase, already quoted, about the σταθμός where he arrived early in the afternoon and received the Antiochene senators.

Since Julian does not explicitly give the name of the σταθμός, the possibility that with this word he referred not to the village of Litarba for which he was heading, but to some less known halting place half way between Antioch and

Litarba, the name of which he did not regard worth mentioning, cannot be excluded. Was this σταθμός perhaps the spot where Julian (*Ep.* 98, 399 b) had found the remains of a winter camp, identified by Cumont, 1917, 7 with modern El-'Amk half way between Antioch and Litarba? The geographical condition of the area there ("la plaine marécageuse d'Amyce – aujourd'hui El-'Amk") is certainly in favour of this hypothesis, which is more than can be said in support of the theory that the first halting place has to be identified with Litarba, for the area near El-Terib is not and never was swampy. Against it speaks the fact that Julian in the rest of his letter, contrary to what one would expect, does not say a word about his stay in Litarba at all. After an additional remark addressed to Libanius ("You are perhaps informed already about the talks at the meeting with your fellow Antiochenes"), he merely says that from Litarba he proceeded to Beroea (Ἀπὸ τῶν Λιτάρβων εἰς τὴν Βέρροιαν ἐπορευόμην). On the other hand, our suggestion would deal with the objections which can be raised against the traditional identification of the σταθμός with Litarba (the distance of 55 km between Antioch and Litarba, the condition of the road, and the fact that Julian arrived at his first halting place early in the afternoon).

All things considered it would seem that Julian did not arrive in Litarba on the same day as that on which he left Antioch. It is more likely that he left Antioch on March, 5, stayed the night in a σταθμός (presumably modern El-'Amk) some 25 km away from Antioch, received the Antiochene delegates there and travelled the next day, the sixth of March, to Litarba.

From Litarba Julian marched to Beroea (ἀπὸ τῶν Λιτάρβων εἰς τὴν Βέρροιαν ἐπορευόμην, Jul. *Ep.* 98, 399 d), where he stayed one day (ἐπιμείνας δὲ ἡμέραν ἐκεῖ, ibid.) and then went to Batnae (Ἔνθεν ὑποδέχονταί με Βάτναι, 400 a). The following day, after having made a sacrifice at dawn, as he had done the previous evening, the emperor went from Batnae to Hierapolis (ἔθυσα δείλης, εἶτ᾽ ὄρθρου βαθέος... Ἐπεὶ δὲ ἦν καλὰ τὰ ἱερά, τῆς Ἱερᾶς πόλεως εἰχόμεθα, 401 b), where he arrived, according to Zosimus, on the fifth day of his journey (πέμπτῃ δὲ τὴν Ἱεράπολιν ἡμέρᾳ καταλαβών, 3.12.1), i.e. on the ninth of March, if Zosimus were to be believed, or on the tenth of March, if the interpretation of Julian's *Ep.* 98 as given above is accepted. In the following diagram the latter alternative is adopted:

March, 5	From Antioch to the first σταθμός
March, 6	From this σταθμός to Litarba
March, 7	From Litarba to Beroea
March, 8	Stay in Beroea
March, 9	From Beroea to Batnae
March, 10	Arrival in Hierapolis

From Hierapolis to Carrhae

According to Zosimus Julian stayed in Hierapolis for only three days (3.12.2 τρεῖς ἐπιμείνας τῇ Ἱεραπόλει μόνας ἡμέρας). If this is correct and if Zosimus included in his enumeration, as would have been normal, the days of arrival and departure, it would seem that Julian stayed in Hierapolis March, 10, 11 and 12, leaving the city on the twelfth. He then headed for Batnae in Osdroena (*unde* sc. Hierapoli... *propere signa commovit... denique cum exercitu et Scytharum auxiliis Euphrate navali ponte transmisso venit ad Batnas, municipium Osdroenae*, 23.2.7). Since Hierapolis and Osdroenean Batnae are approximately 80 km apart from one another, in order to cover this distance the army must have marched for three to four days (if we take some 20 to 30 km for a day's march, cf. Brok, 1959, 45 and Elton, 1996, 245), four days being the more likely, in view of the fact that the Euphrates had to be crossed (*Euphrate navali ponte transmisso*, 23.3.7; cf. however Lib. *Or.* 18.214, suggesting that the Euphrates was crossed at speed). If this assumption is correct, it would mean that Julian arrived at Batnae on March, 15.

The next halting-place mentioned by Amm. was Carrhae (*exinde* sc. Batnae *digressus venit cursu propero Carrhas*, 23.3.1), which lies at a distance of some 60 km from Batnae. If we assume that this march took two or three days, it would seem that Carrhae was reached on March, 17 or 18. To sum up:

March, 12	Departure from Hierapolis
March, 15	Arrival in Batnae in Osdroena
March, 16	Departure from Batnae
March, 17 or 18	Arrival in Carrhae

From Carrhae to Callinicum

Julian stayed at Carrhae a couple of days (*ibi moratus aliquot dies*, 23.3.2), including the 19th of March (*diem... qui erat quartum decimum kalendas Apriles*, 23.3.3). On leaving Carrhae (the exact date has not come down to us), after a quiet last night (*quieta nocte emensa*, 23.3.6), he set out for Davana, but was delayed for a while in order to make a sacrifice to confirm the *omen* caused by the death of his horse Babylonius (*paulisper detentus, ut omen per hostias litando firmaret, Davanam venit*, 23.3.7). After a stop in Davana (*hic corporibus cibo curatis et quiete*, 23.3.7), he reached Callinicum the next day (*postridie ventum est ad Callinicum*, 23.3.7). There he celebrated in the ancient fashion the rites for the Mother of the Gods on the 27th of March (*ubi... diem sextum kalendas... sacrorum sollemnitate prisco more completa*, 23.3.7).

It is clear from Amm.'s account that the terminus post quem for Julian's departure from Carrhae is March, 19 and the terminus ante quem for his arrival in Callinicum March, 27. In other words, he left Carrhae on March, 20 at the earliest and he reached Callinicum on March, 26 at the latest (on March, 23 *Cod. Theod.* 11.30.31 was issued, but where this was done is unfortunately not known). To cover the distance of the approximetely 100 kilometers between Carrhae and Callinicum about four or five days were needed. It would follow, then, that the army arrived in Callinicum on the 23rd or 24th at the earliest, and on the 25th or 26th at the latest (for the arrival in Davana the dates would be the 22nd or 23rd and the 24th or 25th, respectively). However, of these possibilities the one which would imply that Julian arrived in Callinicum on March, 26, only just in time to celebrate on the following day the feast in honour of the Mater Deorum, seems less likely. Therefore this date is omitted in the following diagram.

    March, 20 or 21   Departure from Carrhae
    March, 22 or 23 or 24   Arrival at Davana
    March, 23 or 24 or 25   From Davana to Callinicum

From Callinicum to Dura

In Callinicum Julian celebrated the rites for the Mater Deorum on March, 27 (*diem sextum kalendas*, 23.3.7), after which he spent a peaceful night (*exsultans pernoctavit et laetus*, 23.3.7) and left the city on the following day (*luce vero secuta profectus exinde*, 23.3.8), i.e. on March, 28. He then marched speedily southwards along the high bank of the Euphrates, to arrive in Cercusium at the beginning of April (*agili gradu Cercusium principio mensis Aprilis ingressus est*, 23.5.1). On his way he stayed in at least one outpost: *in statione quadam sub pellibus mansit* (23.3.8). Since, however, the distance between Callinicum and Cercusium measured 165 km, there must have been more of such intermediate halting places.

To cover a distance of 165 km the army needed some five to eight days, which would imply that Julian arrived in Cercusium between April, 1 and April, 4 – the earliest date seems preferable, in view of *agili gradu* in 23.5.1 (for *principio mensis Aprilis* as synonymous with *kalendis Aprilis* cf. Ov. *Fast.* 2.55–8).

At Cercusium Julian stayed some days (how many is not stated, but see below), i.a. to cross the river Abora (*Iulianus...moratur apud Cercusium, ut per navalem Aborae pontem exercitus et omnes sequellae transirent... statimque transgressus pontem avelli praecepit*, 23.5.4–5) and to wait for a fleet with supplies (*alia classis abunde vehens annonam*, 23.5.6). It was probably at Cercusium that Ammianus joined Julian's army. This can be inferred from the sudden appearance of the first person plural in 23.5.7, where it is said that 'we' reached Zaitha: *Profecti exinde* (sc. Cercusium) *Zaithan venimus locum* (this 'we' is to be taken in the sense of 'I and the rest of the army', not as "a 'high-level' reconnaissance group led by Julian himself in which Ammianus was included", as Chalmers, 1959, 185 would have it).

Via the village of Zaitha, some ten kilometers away from Cercusium, where the emperor Gordianus' tomb was visited (*hic Gordiani imperatoris longe conspicuum vidimus tumulum*, 23.5.7), the route led in the direction of Dura (*ad Duram*, 23.5.8) – the actual arrival in Dura, or rather off Dura (which lay at a distance of approximately fifty kilometers from Cercusium on the other bank of the Euphrates), after a two days' march, is not mentioned here, but in the next book: *Emenso itaque itinere bidui prope civitatem venimus Duram*, 24.1.5. During the journey towards Dura two striking and ominous incidents occurred, first of all the presentation of a slain lion to Julian (23.5.8) and secondly, on the next day, the death of a soldier named Iovianus, who was struck by a bolt of lightning. Of the latter event Amm. gives the precise date, April 7 (*secuto itidem die, qui erat septimum idus Apriles, sole vergente iam in occasum*, 23.5.12).

23.5.12 is the last of the five passages in book 23 which furnish precise chronological data about Julian's march. It helps to reconstruct the chronological order of events from the arrival in Cercusium onwards: since the army, at a speed of 20 to 30 km a day, would have needed two days for the approximately fifty kilometers from Cercusium to Dura and in fact did cover this distance in two days (cf. *itinere bidui* in 24.1.5) and since the second day of this march fell on April, 7, it would follow that Julian's soldiers left Cercusium on April, 6, having stayed there since April, 1. In short:

March, 28	Departure from Callinicum
April, 1	Arrival in Cercusium
April, 1–5	Stay in Cercusium
April, 6	From Cercusium via Zaitha southwards
April, 7	Off Dura

Legenda

1. Whereas Dr. De Jonge used the edition of C.U. Clark (Berlin 1910-1915) as the basic text for his commentaries, in our case the lemmata are taken from W. Seyfarth's Teubner-edition (Leipzig 1978), with one alteration: consonantial *u* is always printed as *v* (*venit* instead of *uenit*).
2. For references to Greek authors we follow the abbreviations and indications of books and chapters in H.G. Liddell and R. Scott, *A Greek-English Lexicon*. Passages in Latin authors are indicated according to the system of the *Oxford Latin Dictionary*. For later and Christian authors we follow the *Thesaurus Linguae Latinae*.
   Some exceptions to these rules:
   - In the case of Caesar, Sallust and Tacitus the division of the chapters in sections in the Teubner-editions has also been taken into account.
   - Seneca's *Dialogi* are referred to with the title of the individual works.
   - For the Panegyrici Latini Mynors' OCT-edition has been used.
   - Calcidius is referred to with Chalcid. and quoted from Waszink's edition.
   - The Letters of Julian are quoted from Bidez' edition in the Budé-series.
   - Eunapius' *History* is quoted from Blockley's edition (*The Fragmentary Classicising Historians of the Later Roman Empire*, vol. II, Liverpool 1983)
3. As to secondary literature the following rules are observed:
   - References to the six volumes of De Jonge's commentaries and to our commentaries on books 20, 21 and 22 are usually given with 'see (the note) ad...' or 'q.v.'.
   - Books or articles are normally referred to with the name of the author(s), the year of publication and the page(s). The full titles can be found in the bibliography; e.g. with Hagendahl, 1921, 64 is meant H. Hagendahl, *Studia Ammianea*, Uppsala 1921, page 64.
   - Occasionally reference is made to commentaries on other authors, e.g. Austin's on Vergil and Koestermann's on Tacitus, or to well-known editions like those in the Budé-series. As a rule these works are omitted from the bibliography.
   - Of the following books, which are referred to quite frequently, only the name of the author and the page(s) are given:
     Bitter = N. Bitter, *Kampfschilderungen bei Ammianus Marcellinus*, Bonn 1976.
     Blomgren = S. Blomgren, *De sermone Ammiani Marcellini quaestiones variae*, Diss. Uppsala 1937.

Brok	= M.F.A. Brok, *De Perzische expeditie van keizer Julianus volgens Ammianus Marcellinus*, Groningen 1959.
Ehrismann	= H. Ehrismann, *De temporum et modorum usu Ammianeo*, Diss. Strasbourg 1886.
Fesser	= H. Fesser, *Sprachliche Beobachtungen zu Ammianus Marcellinus*, Diss. Breslau 1932.
Fontaine	= J. Fontaine, *Ammien Marcellin, Histoire, IV (Livres XXIII–XXV)*, 2 vols., Paris 1977.
Harmon	= A.M. Harmon, *The Clausula in Ammianus Marcellinus*, New Haven 1910 (Transactions of the Connecticut Academy of Arts and Sciences, 16, 117–245).
Hassenstein	= G. Hassenstein, *De syntaxi Ammiani Marcellini*, Diss. Königsberg 1877.
Hoffmann	= D. Hoffmann, *Das spätrömische Bewegungsheer und die Notitia Dignitatum*, 2 vols., Düsseldorf 1969.
Jones	= A.H.M. Jones, *The Later Roman Empire 284–602. A Social Economic and Administrative Survey*, Oxford 1964 (repr. 1986).
Kühner-Stegmann	= R. Kühner and C. Stegmann, *Ausführliche Grammatik der lateinischen Sprache*, II, Satzlehre, 2 vols., Hannover 1955^4, 1976^5.
Leumann	= M. Leumann, *Lateinische Laut- und Formenlehre*, Munich 1977.
Matthews	= Matthews, J.F., *The Roman Empire of Ammianus*, London 1989.
Sabbah	= G. Sabbah, *La méthode d'Ammien Marcellin. Recherches sur la construction du discours historique dans les Res Gestae*, Paris 1978.
Seager	= R. Seager, *Ammianus Marcellinus. Seven Studies in his Language and Thought*, Columbia 1986.
Szantyr	= J.B. Hofmann and A. Szantyr, *Lateinische Syntax und Stilistik*, Munich 1965 (repr. 1972).
Wagner	= J.A. Wagner, *Ammiani Marcellini quae supersunt*, cum notis integris Frid. Lindenbrogii, Henr. et Hadr. Valesiorum et Iac. Gronovii, quibus Thom. Reinesii quasdam et suas adiecit, editionem absolvit Car. Gottl. Aug. Er-

furdt, 3 vols., Leipzig 1808 (repr. in 2 vols., Hildesheim 1975).

The following translations are often referred to with the name of the translator only:

Caltabiano	= M. Caltabiano, *Ammiano Marcellino. Storie*, Milan 1989.
Hamilton	= W. Hamilton and A. Wallace-Hadrill, *Ammianus Marcellinus: the Later Roman Empire (AD 354–378)*, Harmondsworth 1986.
Rolfe	= J.C. Rolfe, *Ammianus Marcellinus*, with an English translation, 3 vols., London-Cambridge Mass. 1935–1939 (repr. 1971–1972).
Selem	= A. Selem, *Le Storie di Ammiano Marcellino. Testo e Traduzione*, Turin 1965 (repr. 1973).
Seyfarth	= W. Seyfarth, *Ammianus Marcellinus, Römische Geschichte. Lateinisch und Deutsch und mit einem Kommentar versehen*, II, Berlin 1983^5 and III, Berlin 1986^3.
Veh	= O. Veh, *Ammianus Marcellinus. Das römische Weltreich vor dem Untergang*, übersetzt von Veh, eingeleitet und erläutert von G. Wirth, Zurich-Munich 1974.

4. In cases where this is helpful for the reader or relevant for the interpretation the cursus is indicated as follows:
   – *revocávit in státum* : cursus planus
   – *sublátius éminens* : cursus tardus
   – *fécit et vectigáles* : cursus velox

Chapter 1

Book 23 opens with the report that Julian in his fourth consulship chose a *privatus*, i.e. a man who did not belong to the imperial family, as his colleague (A.D. 363). By doing so, he gave proof, not for the first time, of his *civilitas* (§ 1). Despite his numerous administrative obligations and the complicated preparations for the Persian campaign, Julian launched an ambitious plan to rebuild the temple in Jerusalem, according to Amm. in order to perpetuate the memory of his reign by great works (§ 2). In the introduction to this section the different versions of this controversial plan and Julian's motives will be discussed. The project ended in disaster as a result of supernatural events (§ 3). The gloomy atmosphere created by this episode is deepened in sections 5–7, which deal with a series of adverse *omina* of various kinds. The ultimate failure of the Persian campaign could not have been indicated more clearly. Even the Sibylline Books, consulted in Rome, counselled against Julian's crossing the borders of the Empire. Amm., who earlier, in 22.12.3, had dismissed the opponents to the campaign as *obtrectatores desides et maligni*, here shows himself impressed with the number and the seriousness of the *omina* that warned against Julian's military adventure.

In section 4 Amm. reports a series of appointments by Julian of persons of high moral quality, whereby the emperor lived up to the promise he made on taking the purple, that personal merit would be his only criterion when promoting civil servants and military men.

Haec eo anno...agebantur As Amm. had announced at the conclusion of his long digression on Egypt (22.16.24), he returns to the narrative proper. Similar transitional phrases are found throughout the work. As a rule, they indicate an unfinished series of events, which the author leaves aside for the moment in order to switch to another scene, as in 14.5.1 *Dum haec in oriente aguntur, Arelate hiemem agens Constantius* e.q.s., 16.1.1 *Haec per orbem Romanum fatorum ordine contexto versante Caesar apud Viennam in collegium fastorum...ascitus*, 30.4.1 *Haec per Gallias et latus agebantur arctoum. at in eois partibus* e.q.s. In the less numerous cases where Amm. uses the perfect tense, e.g. 15.8.17 *Haec diem octavum iduum Novembrium gesta sunt*, 20.8.1 *Haec eo anno intra Tigrim gesta sunt et Euphraten*, 21.12.20 and 30.2.1, the series of events is presented, in conformity with classical usage, as completed. The present sentence is anomalous in that it combines an ablative indicating the period within which a finished series of events took place (*eo anno*) with the imperfect *agebantur*. One gets the impression that the use of the tenses is influenced by the verb chosen, since Amm. never writes *gerebantur* nor, on the other hand, *acta sunt*.

1.1

1

Iulianus vero The year referred to is 362. Amm. might have mentioned in this section the publication of the *Misopogon*, which came out in January or February 363. However, he had already mentioned this in Book 22, which deals with the events of 362. From a chronological point of view the reference to the *Misopogon* in 22.14.2 is incorrect, but it is functional from a literary point of view; see the note ad loc.

ut praetereamus negotiorum minutias The assertion that the author will concentrate on important facts and leave out petty details is a topos in historical prefaces, formulated succinctly in Xen. *HG* 4.8.1: τῶν πράξεων τὰς μὲν ἀξιομνημονεύτους γράψω, τὰς δὲ μὴ ἀξίας λόγου παρήσω. For a survey of the topos see Avenarius, 1956, 127–30, Herkommer, 1968, 155 and the note ad 22.15.28. Amm. touches on the subject in his prefatory remarks to Books 15 and 26, for which see Fornara, 1990. In the former he defends himself against those who might criticize the lack of *brevitas* in what is to follow (*nihil obtrectatores longi, ut putant, operis formidantes*). In the latter he argues, against those who would insist on a more detailed treatment of recent events (*strepentes ut laesos, si praeteritum sit, quod locutus est imperator in cena*, e.q.s.), that it is the task of the historian to *discurrere per negotiorum celsitudines... non humilium minutias indagare causarum*. There is a striking similarity between this passage and the preface to the Life of Opilius Macrinus in the *Historia Augusta* (*HA OM* 1.4): *quasi vel de Traiano aut Pio aut Marco sciendum sit, quotiens processerit, quando cibos variaverit et quando vestem mutaverit et quos quando promoverit*, subjects, the author continues, which should properly be called *mythistoriae*. Ensslin, 1923, 15 interpreted Amm.'s repeated defense of what Dio called τῆς ἱστορίας ὄγκος (66.9.4) as an effort to distinguish serious historiography from the *curiositas* of biography.

iam ter consul I.e. 'who had already been consul three times', which is not quite comparable to 16.11.1 *Augusto novies* ('for the ninth time') *seque iterum consule*. A good parallel for the present expression is the use of *septiens* in Vell. 2.26.1 *Deinde consules Carbo tertium et C. Marius, septiens consulis filius*. See the note ad 20.1.1 *consulatu... Constantii deciens* and Szantyr 214. In spite of these parallels Heraeus' *tertio* is very attractive for metrical reasons. Julian had already been consul in 356, 357 and 360, in each case together with Constantius II; 16.1.1, 16.11.1, 21.1.1. See also Bagnall e.a., 1987, 246–9, 254–5.

ascito in collegium trabeae The *trabea* is the official attire of the consuls in Late Antiquity; Claud. *in Eutr.* 2.10, *Cons. Stil.* 2.340, Symm. *epist.* 9.112. For *trabea* see also 14.11.27, 16.10.12 q.v., 25.10.16, 30.3.1. See the note ad 22.7.1 for the various expressions used by Amm. for the appointment of consuls.

Sallustio Flavius Sallustius was possibly of Spanish origin (*CIL* 6.1729). Like Julian he was a pagan. He was praetorian prefect of Gaul from the spring of 361 till September of 363; see 21.8.1 and the note ad loc. According to Lib. *Or.* 17.22 he was already an old man in 363. He clearly belonged to the inner circle of Julian and the two men were good friends. Sallustius' nomination may be considered as an expression of Julian's esteem and appreciation. Sallustius' consulate was celebrated by Alcimus Alethius, a rhetor from Bordeaux, as Aus. *Prof.* 2.23 states: *Sallustio plus conferent libri tui / quam consulatus addidit*. He is also mentioned in 23.1.6. In 23.5.4 Amm. mentions that Sallustius tried to dissuade Julian from the Persian campaign: *Iulianus. . . litteras tristes Sallusti Galliarum praefecti suscepit orantis suspendi expeditionem in Parthos*. For his consulate see Bagnall e.a. 1987, 260–1. See also *PLRE* I, Flavius Sallustius 5. There is some discussion whether or not Sallustius is the author of the Neoplatonic treatise Περὶ θεῶν καὶ κόσμου; see the note ad 22.3.1.

quater ipse amplissimum iníerat magistrátum The pluperfect may have its proper meaning in providing the background to the measures Julian is going to take as consul. This was Julian's first consulate since he became Augustus. Normally new Augusti became consuls on the first of January after their elevation (Bagnall e.a., 1987, 23). However, the previous year (362) Nevitta and Claudius Mamertinus had already been nominated for the consulate to make Julian's subjects feel more confident; 21.12.25 and the note ad loc.

et videbatur novum Amm. frequently opens a new sentence with *et*, elaborating on the preceding sentence, e.g. 22.3.2–3 *causas vehementius aequo bonoque spectaverunt. . . et Palladium. . . in Britannos exterminarunt*. See also 14.5.9, 14.6.26, 15.5.19, 17.9.6, 19.12.17 and 22.10.6. For this use of *et* with the connotation 'and indeed' see TLL V 2.892.70–893.3.

adiunctum esse Augusto privatum In this context a *privatus* is to be interpreted as someone not belonging to the imperial family. Ammianus does not mention here the consulate of the *privatus* Pomponius Ianuarianus, who was consul in 288 together with the Augustus Maximian; Bagnall e.a., 1987, 110–1; *PLRE* I, Ianuarianus 2 + Martindale, 1980, 486. Barnes, 1992, 2 is probably right in thinking that this cannot be just an oversight. He supposes that Amm. did not want to mention Maximian since he preferred to associate Julian with Diocletian and not with Maximian. That is probably also why Aristobulus is only referred to as consular colleague of Diocletian whereas he was in fact appointed by Diocletian's predecessor Carinus. Julian's predecessors Constantine and Constantius II had not elevated a 'private person' to the consulate and had shared the consulship with co-emperors. Therefore, Julian's nomination of Sallustius is a break with tradition. Six years after Julian's reign private persons became consul in 369 (Fl. Victor), 371 (Sex. Cl. Petronius Probus) and

374 (Fl. Equitius). Julian's nomination of a private person for the consulate is according to Amm. a sign of the emperor's modesty, as becomes obvious from 16.10.12 where Constantius' not sharing the consulate with a *privatus* is considered an act of conceit: *nec in trabea socium privatum adscivit, ut fecere principes consecrati, et similia multa elatus in arduum supercilium*; also Lib. *Or.* 12.96: ἐπεὶ καὶ τοῦτο γενναῖον καὶ μεγαλόψυχον τὸ πολὺ τῇ τύχῃ λειπόμενον προελάσθαι τὸν ὁμόζυγα. According to Barnes, 1992, 3 Julian's assumption of the consulate with a *privatus* as his colleague enhances "Ammianus' presentation of Julian as a hero possessing the *civilitas* which was one of the traditional virtues of a pagan Roman emperor". For Julian's *civilitas* see the notes ad 21.16.1 and 21.16.9.

Aristobulus T. Cl. Aurelius Aristobulus was consul in 285, first with the emperor Carinus and after the latter's death with Diocletian. He was also praetorian prefect; see Aur. Vict. *Caes.* 39.14 ff. Afterwards he became *proconsul Africae* (290–4). He was *praefectus urbis Romae* from 295 to 296; Chastagnol, 1962, 21–5. For his consulate see Bagnall e.a., 1987, 104–5; see in general *PLRE* I, Aristobulus + Criniti, 1974, 140.

nullus In Late Latin *nullus* supersedes *nemo* completely. See De Jonge ad 14.7.5 and Szantyr 204–5.

1.2 The restoration of the temple, which is the subject of sections 2 and 3, is to be considered as one of the main events of Julian's reign. The attempt to rebuild the temple made a great impact and exercised great influence on what Julian's contemporaries as well as later generations thought of his reign. All studies on Julian treat the subject extensively. The source material on the subject is vast. However, most of the sources are of Christian signature; the first Jewish text referring to it only dates from the 16th century and remarkably enough Ammianus is the only pagan source which mentions the event; see for an overview of the sources Blanchetière, 1980 and especially Levenson, 1990, who also refers to the latest and most important literature.
Julian had barely died when the first Christian invectives against his reign appeared: Ephraem Syrus' Hymns against Julian and Gregory of Nazianzus' Orations against Julian. Both Ephraem and Gregory refer to the story; Ephraem Syr. *HcJul.* 4.18–23, Greg. Naz. *Or.* 5.3–4. These two sources have set the trend for later 4th- and 5th-century Christian stories; Joh. Chrys., *Jud.* 5.11, *Jud. et gent.* 16, *pan. Bab.* 2.22, *De Laud. Pauli* 4, *Exp. in Ps.* 110.4, *Hom. in Mt.* 4, *Hom. in Acta Apost.* 41.3 (see for Chrysostom on the rebuilding of the temple, Wilken 1983, 128 ff.), Ambr. *epist.* 40.12, Rufin. *hist.* 10.38–40 (see Thélamon, 1981, 296–309), Philost. *HE* 7.9, Socr. *HE* 3.20, Soz. *HE* 5.22, Thdt. *HE* 3.20. The Christian accounts concerning the event greatly resemble each other and are far more elaborate and fantastic than Ammianus' report.

Their main elements are: the great enthusiasm of the Jews for the restoration, the reference to Daniel 9.26–7 and Matthew 24.1–2 that the temple site would remain desolate, Julian's intention to give the Jews the opportunity again to sacrifice, Julian's provision of financial aid and a functionary to supervise the project, the failure of the project caused by storms, earthquakes and fire resulting in the death of many Jews, the appearance of a celestial cross above Jerusalem and a cross on the clothing of the Jews, and the ultimate recognition by the Jews of the omnipotence of the Christian God.

Unlike Ammianus, the Christian authors consider the rebuilding of the temple first and foremost as an anti-Christian act of Julian's. He had supported the Jews with the intention to harm Christianity and wished to prove false Jesus' prophecy in Matthew 24.2 that not one stone of the temple would be left upon another. This motive met with response in modern literature; e.g. Geffcken, 1914, 110; Bidez, 1930, 305; Browning, 1975, 176; Avi-Yonah, 1976, 192–3, Bowersock, 1978, 88–9; Wilken, 1983, 143; Lewy, 1983, 72 f. A second motive mentioned in scholarly works is Julian's wish to make Jerusalem a Jewish city again after Constantine the Great had made it a Christian city; Linder, 1976, 1034, Wilken, 1983, 143. A third alleged motive was to gain the support of the Jewish communities in Mesopotamia for the Persian campaign; Avi-Yonah, 1976, 188–9, Head, 1976, 146. Presumably, there were anti-Christian and political dimensions to the emperor's plan. It is, however, questionable whether these were his main motives. Julian himself has never explained in his writings why he wanted to rebuild the temple. In his *Contra Galilaeos* he is critical about Judaism and considers the Jewish faith inferior to the Hellenic cults and gods. He thinks of the Jewish god as a national deity and not as the god of the whole universe (*Gal.* 100 c, 148 c); for Julian on the Jews, see e.g. Adler, 1978; Vogt, 1939, 34–45; Aziza, 1978; Lewy, 1983, 78–83; Stemberger, 1987, 160–3. In spite of his criticisms, it is obvious that Julian considered the Jewish god to be a powerful deity; Jul. *Ep.* 89a, 89b. It is also evident that, despite the fact that the Jews believed in their one god, Julian must have felt a kind of sympathy towards the Jews and thought of the Jews as his natural allies since they, like the pagans, offered animal sacrifices; *Gal.* 306 a, 306 b, 351 d. In *Ep.* 204, 397 d–398, the so-called letter 'To the Community of the Jews' – the authenticity of this letter is in dispute – Julian expresses his sympathy by declaring that he wanted to make Jerusalem a Jewish city again. Julian as a Neoplatonist of the school of Iamblichus believed that sacrifices were essential to religion; it is therefore only logical that he wanted to repair the Jewish temple just as he restored pagan temples that had been abandoned and fallen into disrepair. Hence the restoration of the Jewish temple fits perfectly into his overall religious policy. It is remarkable that Ammianus does not mention this motive and only remarks that Julian rebuilt the temple *imperiique sui memoriam magnitudine operum gestiens propagare*; see Matthews 110–2. Or is the *magnitudo operum* to be interpreted more broadly as the reopening of temples and the reintroduction of sacrificial ceremonies? See Drijvers, 1992, 25–6.

Julian attached great importance to the restoration of the temple as is obvious from the large sum of money he furnished for the project and the appointment of Alypius, a close friend of his. Like the other nominations mentioned in this chapter, his appointment took place in January. In the same month Julian must have decided to have the temple rebuilt. Apart from Amm. this may also be deduced from Julian's letters *Ep.* 89a (453 c–454 a) and 89b (295 c). Both letters were written according to Bidez, 102 "vers le mois de janvier 363". In the fragmentarily preserved *Ep.* 134 Julian informed the Jews about his plan: "For I am rebuilding with all my zeal the temple of the Most High God". The date of this letter is not known for sure; Joh. Lyd. *Mens.* IV p. 110, 4 (ed. Wünsch) mentions that it was written during the Persian campaign, but the reliability of this information may be questioned. It is not clear to what extent the Jewish community of Antioch as well as the Jewish Patriarch exerted influence on Julian's decision, as has sometimes been supposed; e.g. Avi-Yonah, 1976, 193–4.

Amm. does not inform us when the project actually started and when it was given up. His implied chronology, i.e. that the project started and ended in January, should not be taken seriously. According to Matthews 495, n. 44 the chronology may serve a dramatic function, or Amm. may not have wanted to interrupt his narrative of the Persian campaign by referring to the failure of the project. Most likely Julian issued the order to rebuild the temple in January whereas the actual restoration started later when the necessary preparations had been made. At the end of the last century Adler, 1893 (=1978), 71–2 argued that the actual restoration never started, but this view has not found adherents. Avi Yonah, 1976, 198, 200 argues that the project started before Julian left for Persia on 5 March and ended on 27 May. This latter date is based by Avi-Yonah on an Abyssinian menology (*PO* I, 533) and a Syriac chronicle (*CSCO SS* III, iv, *Chron.* ad a. 724, ed. Brooks, p. 104). Bowersock, 1978, Appendix I, contests Avi-Yonah's view and dates the beginning and failure of the restoration in the first months of 363 when Julian was still in Antioch. He considers Amm.'s *isdem diebus* (23.1.4) and Julian's own words ἀναστήσασθαι διενοήθην (*Ep.* 89b, 295 c) as strong evidence that the project was started and abandoned before Julian left Antioch on 5 March; cf. Stemberger, 1987, 173. An unauthentic letter by Cyril of Jerusalem in Syriac, which is dated c. 400, mentions that the project started on Sunday 18 May and ended already on Monday 19 May on account of earthquakes; see Brock, 1976 and 1977. In spite of the fact that this letter as a whole is not genuine it contains, according to Brock, authentic elements and he considers the mentioned dates reliable. Nevertheless, it seems there is no trustworthy information to establish beginning and end of the restoration project. It is likely, however, that the whole project had barely started when it had to be stopped.

The reason for ending the restoration is not quite clear; according to Amm. fires near the foundations of the temple stopped the enterprise. Gregory, *Or.* 5.4 and the other Christian authors mention divine intervention in the form of storms, trembling of the earth and fires as the causes for the termination of the rebuilding. It is not unlikely that earthquakes – mentioned in Cyril's Syriac letter – causing fires were responsible for ending the project; see Avi-Yonah, 1976, 201 and Russell, 1980.

Although the Christian sources, obviously for propagandistic reasons, refer to the great enthusiasm among the Jews for Julian's plan, it is debatable whether the Jews were as enthusiastic as Gregory and his followers want us to believe. The fact that in Jewish sources of the time no clear reference to the project can be found, is telling in this respect; e.g. Stemberger, 1987, 167–8; cf. Bacher, 1898 and Avi-Yonah, 1976, 197–8.

Amm.'s source for his description of the events in Jerusalem is uncertain. Adler, 1978, 80 has suggested that Gregory was his source. Avi-Yonah, 1976, 201 prefers an official report, possibly the one written by Alypius. Sabbah 220–1 supports this, as well as Levenson, 1990, 266 who writes: "Ammianus' account of the events in Jerusalem might well derive directly or indirectly from Alypius, his fellow Antiochene, whom Julian placed in charge of the project."

In comparison with the Christian sources, which come closer to legend than to a historical report, Amm. treats the events in Jerusalem soberly. Perhaps too soberly, since he does not make mention of the religious and political consequences which the rebuilding of the temple had for the Christians. At least his report is impartial. Miraculous events, like the appearance of a celestial cross, mentioned by the Christian authors are no part of Amm.'s report; this in spite of the fact that he probably knew the stories about divine miracles, from e.g. Gregory's invective against Julian. Although it is not known what exactly happened on the temple site in Jerusalem, Amm.'s report makes a more trustworthy impression than those of the Christian authors. He is probably right about Julian's main motive for rebuilding the temple – his eagerness to extend the memory of his reign by great works –, he does not refer to the Jews who may not have been that enthusiastic about the enterprise, and leaves out legendary and miraculous events; for Amm.'s reliability, see Avi-Yonah, 1976, 201; Levenson, 1990, 264 n. 14; Drijvers, 1992, 26.

accidentium varietatem sollicita mente praecipiens In this characteristically overloaded sentence Amm. distinguishes between the various activities in which Julian was engaged. His main concern was the preparation of the Persian campaign; at the same time he had to pay attention to the day-to-day business of administration and finally he tried to provide for the future reputation of his reign. For substantivized *accidentia* see the note ad 21.2.3 *incidentia* and for the meaning of *accidere* the note ad 22.1.1 *avesque suspiciens*. *Sollicita mente* together with the following *flagranti studio* describes the restless activity that seems to have been a typical characteristic of Julian. When he is seen to act quietly, it is the result of a conscious effort on his part, as in 22.10.1 *per speciem quietis iudicialibus causis intentus non minus quam arduis bellicisque* e.q.s. Apart from the present sentence, *praecipere* is always used by Amm. in the meaning 'to order', mostly with the emperor as its subject. Here it is the equivalent of *antecapere*. Julian, with his quick intelligence, anticipates the problems that may arise. This is typical of a gifted man, according to Cic. *Off*. 1.81 *illud... ingenii magni est, praecipere cogitatione futura et aliquanto ante constituere, quid accidere possit*. Cf. 21.5.1 *nihilque tam convenire conatibus subitis quam celeritatem sagaci praevidens mente*.

multiplicatos expeditionis apparatus Amm. refers not only here but also in 22.10.1 and 22.12.1 to the preparations for the Persian campaign; see the notes ad loc. Unfortunately Amm. is not very specific about these preparations. It is likely that Julian spent most of his time in Antioch preparing the expedition. He had to gather the resources to finance the campaign and to prepare his troops, in particular the soldiers who had served under Constantius and whose morale seems to have been low; see the note ad 22.10.1. We know that Julian ordered the Armenian king Arsaces to muster troops and await further orders; 23.2.2: *solum Arsacem monuerat, Armeniae regem, ut collectis copiis validis iubenda opperiretur, quo tenderet, quid deberet urguere, propere cogniturus*; cf. Lib. *Or.* 18.215, Soz. *HE* 6.1.2. Julian's letter to Arsaces in Wright's edition of Julian's works (*Ep.* 57) is generally considered unauthentic; see the note ad 23.2.2. The emperor sent messages to the troops in all parts of the Roman East to assemble from their winter quarters at various postings and wait for further orders; 23.2.3: *dispersi per stationes varias adventum principis expectabant*. According to Malalas, *Chron.* 13.328–9, Julian gave orders to build ships in Samosata. Julian's enquiries at famous oracles, recorded by Thdt. *HE* 3.21.1–4, also formed part of the preparations. Some scholars consider the rebuilding of the temple as part of the preparations for the Persian campaign; in their view one of Julian's motives for restoring the temple was to get the support of the Jewish communities in Persia; e.g. Vogt, 1939, 49; Avi-Yonah, 1976, 188–9; Head, 1976, 146. Matthews 145 is not convinced.

diligentiam tamen ubique dividens Valesius' *dividens* for V's *diffidens* seems superior to Bentley's *diffundens* in view of 16.5.4 *Hinc contingebat, ut noctes ad officia divideret tripertita, quietis et publicae rei et Musarum* and 22.7.8 q.v. (after an enumeration of measures taken by Julian) *quae cum ita divideret*. *Diffundere* with the meaning required here is not found in Amm.

imperiique sui memoriam magnitudine operum gestiens propagare The same considerations may have inspired Julian's building activities in Constantinople, on which see the note ad 22.9.2 *incrementis maximis fultam*. For *gestire* see the note ad 20.5.10.

ambitiosum quondam... templum There are notes on *ambitiosus* ad 14.7.6 and 20.5.1. It is used of buildings in 22.13.2 and 22.16.12. According to Flavius Josephus *AJ* 15.380–425 and *BJ* 6.267 the (second) Jewish temple was of great architectural beauty and of very large size. The first temple, destroyed in 586 B.C., seems to have been a magnificent building as well; J. *AJ* 8.63–98. The oppression of the Jewish revolt against the Romans from 66–70 was first led by Vespasian; Suet. *Ves.* 4.5, J. *BJ* 3.7. Vespasian was assisted by his son Titus, who took over the command when Vespasian was declared emperor on 1 July 69 by the prefect of Egypt; Tac. *Hist.* 2.79–81. Titus completed the conquest of Judaea and had the temple burnt down; Suet. *Tit.* 5, Tac. *Hist.* 5.1, 5.11 ff., J. *BJ* 6.220–70, D.C. 66.4–7. See for a precise and elaborate account of the capture of Jerusalem and the destruction of the temple, Price, 1992, 162–74.

aegre est oppugnatum The distinction between *oppugnare* and *expugnare* seems to be lost here. See for parallels Löfstedt, 1911, 262–3 and the observations in TLL V 2.1810.54–7 and IX 2.802.12–4. Gelenius' *expugnatum* is probably a specimen of his classicizing tendency.

sumptibus... immodicis Christian authors – Rufin. *hist.* 10.38–40, Socr. *HE* 3.20, Soz. *HE* 5.22, Thdt. *HE* 3.20, Philost. *HE* 7.9 – mention the provision of financial aid by Julian but do not call this support excessive. According to Sozomen and Gregory of Nazianzus (*Or.* 5.4) Jewish women also helped to finance the operation by parting with their jewellery. From the use of the word *immodicus* it can be inferred that Amm. was critical about the enormous amount of money which Julian furnished for the restoration project. In general Amm. seems to have had difficulties with Julian's lavish and extravagant religious policy; e.g. 22.12.7. Note also the speed with which Julian ordered the project to be carried out according to Amm. expressed by *maturandum... dederat* and Alypius' devotion to his task: *cum... fortiter instaret* (§ 3).

Alypio... Antiochensi, qui olim Britannias curaverat pro praefectis Alypius belonged to the inner circle of Julian. He was a pagan and well educated; Lib. *Ep.* 1395, Jul. *Ep.* 10. He studied in Antioch (Lib. *Ep.* 324). It is not clear why the *PLRE* I, Alypius 4, calls him "possibly a Cilician". Sabbah 220–1 calls Alypius "Antiochéen" but does not consider him Antiochene by birth. The possibility that he was Antiochene by birth, as Amm. says, should not be excluded; see also Brok, 1959, 23. Amm. calls him in 29.1.44 a *placiditatis homo iucundae*. Alypius was probably with Julian during the campaigns in Gaul before he became *vicarius Britanniarum* in 358; Lib. *Ep.* 324, *PLRE* I Alypius 4. Amm. does not call him *vicarius* in this section but he does so in 29.1.44: *Alypius quoque ex vicario Britanniarum*. Probably during his time in Britain Alypius received Julian's letters 9 and 10. These letters are written in a cordial tone. It is unclear for how long Alypius remained in Britain but from Julian's *Ep.* 10 it may be inferred that he returned to Gaul in 360. He was apparently available in 363 to supervise the restoration of the Jewish temple. That he received the title of *comes* is known from Rufin. *hist.* 10.38. After Julian's death Alypius probably returned to private life. Together with his son Hierocles he was tried for poisoning in 371/2 in Antioch and condemned to exile after the confiscation of his goods; 29.1.44.

1.3 *idem...Alypius* On anaphoric *idem* see the note ad 20.4.5.

provinciae rector In 358 Palestine was divided into two provinces: *Palaestina* and *Palaestina salutaris*; Lib. *Ep.* 334 and 335. Of the latter province Petra was the capital, whereas Caesarea was the capital of the first. By 409 three Palestinian provinces had been created; *Cod. Theod.* 7.4.30, *Cod. Iust.* 12.37.13. See Eadie, 1967, 157-8. In his work Amm. only refers to one *Palaestina*; 14.8.11, 19.12.8, 22.5.5 (and the note ad loc.). The provincial governor of Palestine bore the title of *consularis*. Although it is not known who the governor was at the time of the rebuilding of the temple (*PLRE* I, Anonymus 132), it may have been a certain Leontius. *Cod. Theod.* 12.1.55 of 1 March 363 by Julian is directed to *Leontio consul(ari) Palaestinae*. Possibly this *consularis* by the name of Leontius is the same as Amm.'s *rector provinciae*. For Leontius see *PLRE* I, Leontius 9; the authors of the *PLRE* do not identify him as Amm.'s *rector*.

metuendi globi flammarum...crebris assultibus erumpentes Balls of fire are normally meteoric phenomena, described e.g. in Cic. *Div.* 1.97 and Sen. *Nat.* 1.1.5 as ominous events. More examples are listed in TLL VI 2052.53-69. Amm.'s description calls to mind the fourth type of earthquake mentioned in 17.7.14 *mycematiae sonitu audiuntur minaci, cum dissolutis elementa compagibus ultro assiliunt (cf. assultibus) vel relabuntur considentibus terris*, apart from the roar which is characteristic of this kind of earthquake. For *assultus* see the note ad 20.8.10. Adjectival *metuendus* is found no less than 17 times in Amm., much more frequently than in other authors; TLL VIII 906.47-70.

elemento destinatius repellente In this remarkable personification the balls of fire are described as defenders of a city, *repellere* being the normal verb for driving away an assailant, as in 14.2.11 *pavore vique repellente extrusi* and 14.2.5 *et quisque serpentes latius pro viribus repellere moliens*. See also 14.3.1, 14.8.13, 17.6.2, 18.8.1, 20.11.17, 25.3.17 and 31.10.3. For *destinatius* see the note ad 20.4.14.

isdem diebus I.e. in the first days of January 363. The vague temporal clause *isdem diebus* is much used by Amm.: e.g. 15.2.10, 16.7.1, 16.11.8, 17.7.1, 22.4.9, 22.9.15, 22.11.1 q.v., 31.10.21.

1.4

legatos ad se missos ab urbe aeterna In view of V's *adiemmissos* it seems preferable to read *ad eum missos* rather than *ad se missos*, which looks like a classicizing correction by Gelenius. For the use of the oblique cases of *is* instead of *sibi, se* cf. the note ad 20.4.8 *ei provinciarum interitum* and Szantyr 175. *Ab urbe aeterna* is best taken as 'from', instead of 'by the eternal city', as Fontaine translates it ("que lui avait députés la Ville éternelle"). The delegates were sent by the senate, not by the city as a whole. Cf. 21.12.24 *senatores conspicuos, a nobilitate legatos ad Constantium missos*, where there is also a note on *urbs aeterna*.

During his march against Constantius in 361 Julian had sent several letters to cities and governing bodies to justify his rising against the lawful Augustus. The Roman senate also received a letter: *orationem acrem et invectivam probra quaedam in eum explanantem et vitia scripserat ad senatum*; 21.10.7 and note ad loc. The senate's reaction was not positive for Julian. The senators remained on Constantius' side and also asked Julian to remain loyal to Constantius: *auctori tuo reverentiam rogamus* (21.10.7). Several arguments can be produced for the senate's loyalty: Constantius' visit to Rome in 357 (16.10) and the setting up of an obelisk in the Circus Maximus by order of the Augustus (17.3). The senate's main motive for remaining on Constantius' side was the fact that the emperor had Italy blockaded (21.7.4–5). This blockade gave Constantius control over Rome's food supply. After he had become emperor Julian only gradually gained the support of the Roman senators, e.g. by a swift food supply; Mamertinus, *Pan*. 3.14.1–2. This embassy of distinguished and noble Roman senators was, as far as is known, the first official delegation of Rome to pay respects to Julian. Symmachus' and Maximus' meeting with Julian in Naissus in 361 may not be considered as such; 21.12.24 and note ad loc.

clare natos meritisque probabilis vitae compertos The wording of this fulsome praise is unconventional. *Clare nati* is found only in 20.11.7 (q.v.) and is without parallel in other authors (TLL III 1277.67–8). For *compertus* = *spectatus* see the note ad 22.4.2. Note Amm.'s insistence on the moral qualities of those elected by Julian for high offices, in accordance with the emperor's promise on taking the purple that he would only promote people for their personal merits (20.5.7).

imperator honoribus diversis affecit From Amm.'s text it can be concluded that all four senatorial appointments mentioned in this section were made in January 363. However, Seeck, 1919, 476, Chastagnol, 1962, 156–9 and *PLRE* I, Apronianus 10, report that Apronianus was already in office on 9 December 362. As Barnes, 1992, 5–6 has observed, this date is based on an unlikely emendation of the date of *Cod. Theod.* 14.4.3: *dat(a) V id(us) Decemb(res) Antiochiae d.n. Iuliano A. IIII et Sallust(io) cons(ulibu)s*. There is no direct evidence for the date of appointment of Octavianus and Venustus. Their dates of appointment are deduced by the *PLRE* from Apronianus' alleged date of nomination. In the case of Octavianus a date late in December 362 or early January 363 is reported (*PLRE* I, Octavianus 2: "a. 362/3"). With respect to Venustus' date of appointment it is argued that "the date must be late in 362 since Venustus' fellow-ambassador Apronianus, who was made *praefectus urbis Romae*, was in office before the end of 362" (*PLRE* I, Venustus 5). Aradius Rufinus' nomination is to be dated after the death of Julian's uncle Iulianus; since he probably died at the end of December or the beginning of January (see lemma below), Rufinus was appointed in January. There is, therefore, no reason to think that Amm. was wrong. "...Julian made all the four senatorial appointments which Ammianus records in the opening chapter of Book 23 exactly when Ammianus states that he made them – in January 363" (Barnes, 1992, 7). It is of some interest with respect to the emperor's religious policy to know that all four men were pagans when appointed by Julian.

Apronianum Romae decrevit esse praefectum L. Turcius Apronianus Asterius (*PLRE* I, Apronianus 10). During his prefecture, on 19 March 363, the temple of Apollo on the Palatine burnt down; 23.3.3. His prefecture is characterized by Amm. in 26.3. Amm. calls him a *iudex integer et severus* (26.3.1). He is known for his regulation of Rome's food supply and during his prefecture there was an abundance of food in Rome (26.3.6). He was succeeded by Symmachus (27.3.3 and *PLRE* I, Symmachus 3). Apronianus was a pagan; Von Haehling, 1978, 377. For his prefecture see Chastagnol, 1962, 156–9; Van de Wiel, 1989, 52 ff.
The use of the AcI-construction after *decernere*, which, according to Pinkster, 1990, 129–30 is restricted to declarative sentences, is found in Amm. also in imperative sentences like the one under consideration. Cf. 16.5.12 *aditus a parentibus virginis raptae eum, qui violarat, convictum relegari decrevit*, 19.1.6 *leni summatum petitione placatus postridie quoque super deditione moneri decreverat defensores*. According to TLL V 1 145.10–20 *decernere* + AcI in sentences of this type is found especially in juridical literature.

Octavianum proconsulem Africae Clodius Octavianus (*PLRE* I, Octavianus 2) had been *pontifex maior, consularis Pannoniae Secundae, vicarius urbis*

Romae and *comes ordinis primi* before he became governor of Africa; *CIL* 9. 2566 (= *ILS* 1253), cf. *CIL* 8.24609. The proconsul of Africa was not subject to the vicar of Africa or the praetorian prefect, and stood therefore outside the official hierarchy; Jones 47 and 375. The proconsulate of Africa and the urban prefecture of Rome belonged to the ancient offices of high prestige held by senators. The turnover of proconsuls of Africa and prefects of Rome was rapid; the average tenure was less than a year; Jones 381 and 385. Octavianus was a pagan; Von Haehling, 1978, 424. Under Valentinian he fell out of favour and went into hiding: *presbyter Sirmii iniquissime decollatur, quod Octavianum ex proconsule apud se latitantem prodere noluisset* (Hier. *Chron.* s.a. 371). He is also mentioned in 29.3.4.

Venusto vicariam commisit Hispaniae Volusius Venustus (*PLRE* I, Venustus 5). Before he became *vicarius Hispaniae* he was *corrector Apuliae et Calabriae* (*CIL* 9. 329 = *ILS* 5557^a) and *consularis Siciliae* (Symm. *epist.* 4.71). According to the *PLRE* he was nominated vicar of Spain late in 362, but see above. He was legatus again to Valentinian in 368 together with Praetextatus and Minervius; 28.1.24. His son was the fervent pagan Virius Nicomachus Flavianus; Macr. *Sat.* 1.5.13: *Flavianum qui, quantum sit mirando viro Venusto patre praestantior, non minus ornatu morum gravitatique vitae quam copia profundae eruditionis adseruit*. Flavianus committed suicide in 394 after Eugenius' defeat by Theodosius at the Frigidus. Brok, 1959, 27 – referring to Ensslin, 1955 – is of the opinion that during his stay in Rome Amm. moved in circles where Venustus was a trend-setter. However, clear evidence for this view is lacking.

Rufinum Aradium comitem orientis Rufinus Aradius (*PLRE* I, Aradius Rufinus 11) was born in Rome; Lib. *Ep.* 1493. After his nomination as *comes orientis* he went with Julian on the Persian campaign; Lib. *Ep.* 1343, 1379, 1398, 1400. He was still in office in the spring of 364; Lib. *Ep.* 1219. Libanius composed a panegyric for him which has not survived; Lib. *Ep.* 1124, 1135. He was prefect of Rome in 376. He is generally considered a pagan, based on Lib. *Ep.* 825 and 1374. However, it is not unlikely that he later converted to Christianity; he seems to have been a Christian when he was *praefectus urbis*; see Von Haehling, 1978, 382–4. He was dead by 401/2; Symm. *epist.* 7.126. Rufinus was a man of culture; Libanius corresponded regularly with him (Lib. *Ep.* 825, 1365, 1379, 1380, 1493).
Under Constantine the vicar of the recently created diocese Oriens, which comprised Asia Minor, was replaced permanently by a *comes*. The *comes Orientis* ranked higher than a vicar but was subordinate to the praetorian prefect of the East; Jones 105.

in locum avunculi sui Iuliani recens defuncti provexit Iulianus (*PLRE* I, Iulianus 12 + Martindale, 1974, 249) was a brother of the emperor's mother Basilinna. He turned pagan to support Julian; Philost. *HE* 7.10. Julian's *Ep.* 28 and 80 (on the repair of the Apollo temple in Daphne) are addressed to his uncle. He was nominated *comes orientis* before July 362; before that he was governor of Phrygia; Lib. *Ep.* 764. He died of a painful disease. The Christian enemies of Julian considered Iulianus' death as an act of divine retribution – Ephr. Syr. *HcJul.* 4.3, Thdt. *HE* 3.9, Soz. *HE* 5.8 – since together with Felix (23.1.5) and Helpidius he had seized the property of the church of Antioch; e.g. Greg. Naz. *Or.* 5.2, Thdt. *HE* 3.11–3, Philost. *HE* 7.10. The date of his death has recently been queried by Barnes, 1992. Seeck, 1919, 466 and *PLRE* consider Iulianus still in office in February 363 so that he would have died after this date. However this consideration is based on an incorrectly emended date by Seeck of *Cod. Iust.* 8.35.12. Remarks in the *Misopogon* (340 a and 365 c) clearly indicate that Iulianus had already died when this pamphlet was written. Since it is not unlikely that the *Misopogon* was composed at the beginning of the new year – cf. the note ad 22.14.2 where January or February 363 are mentioned as dates of appearance for the *Misopogon* – "Iulianus must have died between 6 December 362, when he is unambiguously attested in office (*Cod. Theod.* 3.1.3) and a date well before the end of January 363" (Barnes, 1992, 6); see also Prato-Marcone, 1987, 346. It can be concluded from this that Aradius Rufinus' nomination as *comes Orientis* took place in January, just as Amm. reports.

1.5 *quibus, ut convenerat, ordinatis* With this phrase cf. e.g. 24.4.23 *quibus ita, ut convenerat, ordinatis*, 30.1.15 *quibus ita utiliter ordinatis*, 21.7.6 and 23.3.6. In all these cases *quibus* or *his* refers to measures taken by the emperor. For that reason it seems best to interpret *quibus* here also as *quibus rebus* rather than taking the Roman envoys as the antecedent of *quibus*, as does Seyfarth ("Nach der ordnungsgemäss erfolgten Einsetzung in ihre Ämter"). On *ordinare* see the notes ad 20.9.8 and 22.11.4.

terrebatur omine...praesentissimo The imperfect may be explained as describing the state of mind Julian was in as a result of his frightening experience. Note moreover that Amm. avoids finite forms of the passive perfect of *terrere*. For *praesens* cf. 22.1.2 with the note. The imperfect *pronuntiabat* at the end of this section is best taken as iterative.

Felice...largitionum comite For Felix see *PLRE* I, Felix 3 and the note ad 20.9.5. He was converted to paganism by Julian; Lib. *Or.* 14.36. When, together with Julian, he entered the Great Church in Antioch, he is said to have commented sarcastically on the sacred vessels which Constantine and Constantius had donated to the church; Thdt. *HE* 3.12. As in the case of

Iulianus (see above) Felix' sudden death was already in 363 regarded by Christians as a punishment of God. It is to be noted that Amm. makes no reference to this widely accepted Christian opinion; e.g. Greg. Naz. *Or.* 5.2, Thdt. *HE* 3.12–3, Soz. *HE* 5.8.4, Philost. *HE* 7.10. Felix was *comes sacrarum largitionum*. As such he administered the *aerarium publicum*. Amm. never uses the full title but always speaks of *comes largitionum*; 14.7.9, 16.8.5, 20.11.5, 22.3.7 and the note.

profluvio sanguinis Thdt. *HE* 3.13.14 gives the same cause: ὁ δὲ Φίλιξ ἐξαπίνης θεήλατον καὶ αὐτὸς δεξάμενος μάστιγα αἷμα πανημέριον τε καὶ παννύχιον ἐκ τοῦ στόματος ἔφερε, τῶν ἀγγείων τοῦ σώματος πάντοθεν εἰς τοῦτο συρρεόντων τὸ μόριον. οὕτω δὲ παντὸς δαπανηθέντος τοῦ αἵματος, ἀπέσβη καὶ οὗτος καὶ τῷ αἰωνίῳ παρεπέμφθη θανάτῳ.

vulgus publicos contuens titulos Felicem Iulianum Augustumque pronuntiabat Julian's full name in offical inscriptions was Claudius Iulianus Pius Felix Augustus; e.g. *CIL* 3. 7088 = *ILS* 751, *CIL* 3. 12333 = *ILS* 8945, *CIL* 5. 8024 = *ILS* 753. By adding *-que* (*Augustumque*) the people of Antioch expressed the expectation and, perhaps, even the desire that Julian should follow his uncle and Felix into death. See 22.14.2–3 for the Antiochenes' sarcastic attitude towards Julian. For *tituli* 'inscriptions' cf. 21.16.15, 22.9.1 and Suet. *Cl.* 41.3 *extat talis scriptura in plerisque libris ac diurnis titulisque operum.*

praecesserat aliud saevum V's *processerat*, if not altogether impossible, is certainly inferior to *praecesserat* (Em2). *Procedere* in the sense of *accidere* is not found elsewhere in Amm. As well as mentioning the date on which the *omen* occurred, *praecesserat* emphasizes that Amm. goes back to the time before the death of the comes orientis Iulianus. *Saevus* is not normally used of omina, but may be understood by analogy with expressions like Verg. *A.* 11.896–7 *saevissimus...nuntius* or Tac. *Hist.* 1.2.1 *opus...ipsa etiam pace saevom*. Amm. needed a striking adjective to balance the frightening *omen* mentioned before. Brakman's *scaevum* is neat, but Amm. uses *scaevus* only with the meaning 'misguided' (28.2.9, 29.3.1).

1.6

kalendis ipsis Ianuariis The day on which the consuls officially took up their duties; see the note ad 22.7.1. Whereas in Rome this ceremony took place on the Capitol in front of the temple of Jupiter, in Antioch this official ceremony was apparently performed at the temple of the Genius. Libanius delivered an oration (*Or.* 12) before Julian upon entering his consulship; the oration was commissioned by Julian himself (see for *Or.* 12 in the first place Wiemer, 1995, 151–88). It is improbable that Sallustius was present since he, being consul as well as praetorian prefect of Gaul, had duties to perform in the western part of the Empire. An interesting theory of Alföldi connects the issuing of a special type of contorniate medallions with the date under discussion. Alföldi compared a contorniate in the archaeological museum of Florence, showing a portrait of Julian (Alföldi, 1978, fig. III 6), with similar medallions (e.g. his fig. III 5, from Berlin), which show the head of Alexander the Great and argued that the Florence-type probably was distributed in Antioch on the first day of January 363. Cf. Lane Fox, 1997, 250, but note that Lévêque, 1978, 312–4 pointed to some flaws in Alföldi's reasoning.

gradile Genii templum This is an unparalleled periphrasis for *gradus... templi*, possibly chosen by Amm. in order to avoid the repetition of the ending *-i(i)*. Normally, the adjective *gradilis* refers to bread distributed daily by the local authorities; TLL VI.2137.20–30. The temple of Tyche, τὸ τῆς Τύχης ἱερόν (*Mis.* 346 b), honoured the protecting goddess of the city. Apparently Amm. equates Tyche with the Genius; see also 22.11.7 for a *Genii templum* in Alexandria and the note ad loc. The temple had a statue of Tyche made by Eutychides of Sicyon, a pupil of Lysippus; this bronze statue was set up when Seleucus I reigned, probably during the years 296–293 B.C.; Paus. 6.2.7; see Downey, 1961, 73–5. The statue itself, described by Malalas *Chron.* 8.13–4 and 11.9, has gone lost, but there are several copies of it; see Dohrn, 1960. In 359, during the reign of Constantius, the temple was taken away from the pagans (Lib. *Ep.* 88; Petit, 1955, 197) but restored again by Julian. Evagrius *HE* 1.16 reports that τὸ Τυχαῖον under Theodosius II was turned into a church containing the relics of the martyr Ignatius of Antioch. Fontaine n. 26 refers to a coin minted in Antioch c. 313 which has on the one side the legend *Genio Antiochensi* and on the other side a Tyche. The coin, however, is not mentioned in *RIC*.

quidam ceteris diuturnior nullo pulsante repente concidit A similar incident occurred on January 1st, 43 B.C., when consul Vibius Pansa was offering to the gods: τοῦ Οὐιβίου τὰ ἐσιτήρια τῇ νουμηνίᾳ θύοντος ῥαβδοῦχός τις αὐτοῦ ἔπεσεν ἐξαίφνης καὶ ἀπέθανε (D.C. 45.17.9). For *diuturnus* used of a human being see TLL V 1.1646.67–1647.3. Amm. emphatically insists that the fall of the old priest was fortuitous and therefore not without significance (*nullo pulsante, repente, insperato casu*).

per imperitiam The injudicious interpretations of *omina* by persons in the entourage of Julian are also mentioned in 22.12.7 *iuxta imperitus et docilis*.

1.7 *alia quoque minora signa* Cf. for the many portentous events described in this chapter Liebeschuez, 1988 and Meulder, 1991.

subinde, quod acciderat, ostendebant This sentence illustrates clearly how Amm. blurs the distinction between the pluperfect and the perfect tenses . He means to say that some minor events indicated what actually came to pass afterwards (with hyperbaton of *subinde*). In other words *acciderat* does not precede *ostendebant*, as Fontaine seems to take it ("manifestèrent à plusieurs reprises la signification de cet accident"), but it precedes the moment of writing. In such a case, the perfect tense is of course 'de rigueur' in classical Latin, and indeed, in 25.10.11 Amm. writes about the infant Varronianus, son of Jovian: *cuius vagitus pertinaciter reluctantis, ne in curuli sella veheretur ex more, id, quod mox accidit, portendebat*. In 25.5.6 *suspicati, quod acciderat* and 29.4.5 *idque, quod acciderat, suspecti* the classical rules are also respected, since there *acciderat* precedes the verb to which it is subordinated.

The regular meaning of *subinde* in Amm. is 'repeatedly', but in 16.7.7 (q.v.), 21.3.4 and 21.10.4 it is found with the meaning 'afterwards'.

procinctus Parthici disponendi For *procinctus* 'campaign' see the note ad 20.1.3 and for *disponere* ad 20.4.9. For *Parthicus* see the note ad *Parthos* in 23.3.2.

Constantinopolim terrae pulsu vibratam The unusual expression *terrae pulsus* instead of *terrae motus* also occurs in the opening phrase of Amm.'s digression on earthquakes, 17.7.9 *Adesse tempus existimo pauca dicere, quae de terrae pulsibus coniectura veteres collegerunt*. For *vibrare* cf. Plin. *Nat.* 2.194 *Nec simplici modo quatitur* (terra) *umquam, sed tremit vibratque*, where the verb is used intransitively. The Romans considered earthquakes to be unfavourable signs from the gods; see e.g. Cic. *Div.* 1.78, with the commentary by Pease, and Herrmann, 1962. Amm. too, saw the trembling of the earth as a bad sign; 17.7.3, 22.13.5 q.v. and 26.10.15–16. The earthquake is also referred to by Libanius in his *Or.* 18.177: ἔσειε μὲν ὁ Ποσειδῶν τὴν μεγάλην ἐν Θρᾴκῃ πόλιν.

horum periti Amm. means the *haruspices*. Julian had them in his retinue; 23.5.10 q.v., 25.6.1. The books of these originally Etruscan interpreters of signs were translated into Latin by M. Tarquitius Priscus at the end of the Republican period; cf. 25.2.7: *ex Tarquitianis libris*, see Latte, 1960, 396 and Montero, 1991, 102. In 319 Constantine had forbidden the consultation of *haruspices* by private persons; *Cod. Theod.* 9.16.1. A total prohibition was issued by Constantius in 359; *Cod. Theod.* 9.16.4. Julian lifted the prohibitions against *divinatio* (22.12.7) and practised it himself on a large scale; 21.2.4, 22.1.1, 22.12.6, 25.4.17. Amm. took the *haruspices*' explanations seriously: *Extis itidem pecudum attenti faticidis in species converti suetis innumeras accidentia sciunt*; 21.1.10 and the note ad loc. Throughout his work he pays great attention to their judgements; 23.5.10–12. 25.2.7, 25.10.1. Amm. displays a certain knowledge as to how *haruspices* arrived at their pronouncements; this becomes clear from the use of technical terms: *libri Tagetici vel Vego-*

nici (17.10.2, 21.1.10), *Tarquitiani libri* (25.2.7), *libri exercituales* (23.5.10, q.v.), *libri fulgurales* (23.5.13), *libri rituales* (17.7.10), *fulmen consiliarium* (23.5.13). He refers to only one *haruspex* by name, i.e. Aprunculus Gallus: *haruspicinae peritus Aprunculus Gallus orator*, 22.1.2.

intempestivo conatu desistere suadebant In 22.12.3 those who opposed the Persian campaign were criticized as *obtrectatores desides et maligni*. Here, Amm. does not distance himself explicitly from these advisers. The reason may be that he was convinced by the *omina* that it would indeed be wiser not to invade Persia, whereas he resented opposition inspired by lack of energy or cowardice. It is significant that Amm. stresses the competence of the haruspices (*horum periti*). Moreover, it is to be noted that the opposition, here and in 22.12, does not reject the expedition per se, but argues that it should be postponed (22.12.3 *studium omne in differendo procinctu ponentes*). Both here and in 22.12.3 the venture is called *intempestivum*, for which see the note ad 22.7.3.

ita demum...firmantes, cum For *ita demum* 'only' cf. TLL V 517.1–29. Normally, it is followed by *si*, but cf. Sen. *Ep.* 118.9 *ita demum petendum est, cum coepit esse expetendum bonum*. Amm. prefers *cum* also in 20.3.7 and 24.1.14. For *firmare* as simplex pro composito *affirmare* see the note ad 20.8.15.

lex una sit et perpetua The natural right to defend oneself under attack is expressed by several authors. Valesius quotes *dig.* 43.16.1.27 (Ulpian) *Vim vi repellere licere Cassius scribit, idque ius natura comparatur*. Amm. may have had in mind the famous passage in Cic. *Mil.* 10: *Est igitur haec, iudices, non scripta, est nata lex...ut, si vita nostra in aliquas insidias, si in vim et in tela aut latronum aut inimicorum incidisset, omnis honesta ratio esset expediendae salutis*. Cf. also Cic. *Rep.* 1.1 and *Off.* 1.81.

nihil remittente vi moris Attempts to make sense of V's reading *vimoris* do not carry conviction. See e.g. Fontaine, who is forced to interpret *mos* as "une forme abrégée, une allusion méliorative" of *mos maiorum* and *vis* as "l'énergie qu'il (*mos*) a toujours inspirée." Lindenbrog's *vi mortis* calls for even more specious verbal acrobatics. The point of departure for any emendation should be the expressions with *remittere* found in Amm. himself. He uses the verb both transitively (as in 16.12.18 *nec de rigore animorum quidquam remittebant*) and intransitively (as in 16.2.2 *nihil...remittentibus curis* = 21.4.7, q.v.). Madvig's *nihil remittentem vigoris* is plausible, although in view of the instance quoted, *rigoris* would seem slightly better.

nuntiatum est ei... Romae super hoc bello libros Sibyllae consultos As Rzach, 1923, 2116 has observed, this is the last reference to a consultation of the Sibylline Books that is on record. These books were originally under the custody of Jupiter Capitolinus; since 28 B.C., however, as a consequence of the reforms of Octavian, they were kept in the temple of Apollo on the Palatine in Rome. On 19 March 363 they were barely saved when the Apollo temple caught fire; 23.3.3. At the beginning of the 5th century the books were destroyed on the order of Stilicho; Rut. Nam. 2.52. Shortly after their destruction Prudentius, *apoth.* 439–40, was able to boast that the *libri Sibyllini* could no longer be consulted. In Julian's time the *quindecimviri sacris faciundis*, the college that was allowed to consult the Sibylline books, was still in existence; Apronianus, mentioned in 23.1.4, was one of its members (*CIL* 6.1698 = *ILS* 1257). It is likely that with the destruction of the Sibylline books, the college of quindecimvirs ceased to exist. See in gen. for the *libri Sibyllini*, Parke 1988 and Potter, 1990, 95–140. The advice to Julian not to cross the frontier may well have been influenced by the opposition in the western part of the empire against the war with Persia; Conduché, 1965, 370.

a limitibus suis For *limes* see the note ad 23.3.4.

Chapter 2

Despite the numerous unfavourable *omina* Julian decides in the beginning of the spring of the year 363 to invade Persian territory. In this chapter we are told first how Julian declines offers of military assistance from foreign nations. As we will see in the next chapter, where the participation of Scythians and Saracenes in the Persian campaign is mentioned in passing, this is not completely in accordance with the facts. It seems that Amm. intends this half truth to demonstrate Julian's self-assurance and the contrast with his predecessor Constantius, who had more than once accepted, and even sollicited, help from foreign allies.

Julian's farewell to Antioch, described in sections 3 and 4, shows that the wounds, inflicted by the sarcasms of the Antiochenes, were far from healed. Indeed, Julian told the delegates who escorted him from the city, that he wished to spend the winter months after the campaign in Tarsus. This, as Amm. wrily reminds us, is exactly what happened, be it in a very different way from what Julian intended, since Tarsus was the city in which he was to be buried. In these chapters full of unfavourable *omina*, this declaration of Julian himself is another unmistakable hint of what the outcome of the campaign is going to be.

The first stages of the campaign bring Julian to Hierapolis and Batnae. In both cities there are unfortunate accidents, both of which cost the lives of fifty of Julian's men. Small wonder then that the next chapter opens with the qualification *maestus* for Julian.

2.1 *Inter haec tamen legationes gentium plurimarum auxilia pollicentium* On the weakened force of *tamen* see the note ad 20.5.1. Of these embassies some perhaps came from the kings and satraps beyond the Tigris, to whom Constantius had sent envoys (21.6.7–8). If so, then those coming to Antioch and offering to send auxiliary troops went further than the Transtigritanians mentioned in 22.7.10, who, together with Armenians, Indian Divi and Serendivi, Mauri and Bosporani, had come to Julian in Constantinople to beg for peace.

liberaliter susceptae A traditional formula, cf. 20.4.13 *qui liberaliter... suscepti* (with the note), 20.11.1 *summaque liberalitate susceptum* and 30.2.6 *quo suscepto liberaliter et magnifice*.

speciosa fiducia principe respondente nequaquam decere adventiciis adiumentis rem vindicari Romanam 'Splendid confidence'; see the note ad 21.10.7. In classical usage *speciosus* often implies criticism contrasting fine-sounding words with a less dignified reality, as e.g. Ov. *Met.* 7.69–70 *coniugium putas speciosaque nomina culpae / imponis, Medea, tuae?* or Tac. *Ann.* 1.81.4 *speciosa verbis, re inania aut subdola*. Here, however, it is used to express admiration for Julian's self-confidence.

Note the contrast with Constantius, who, according to Amm. in 20.8.1, asked the Scythians for auxiliaries: *auxilia super his Scytharum poscebat mercede vel gratia*. Libanius (*Or.* 18.169) also states that Julian did not think it necessary to make an appeal to foreign troops (οὐ γὰρ ᾤετο δεῖν ὁ βασιλεὺς Σκύθας καλεῖν εἰς ἐπικουρίαν οὐδὲ ὄχλον ἀθροίζειν). Such troops, he explains, would do harm by their very numbers and raise many problems (βλάψοντα τῷ πλήθει καὶ πολλὰς ἐμποιήσοντα τὰς ἀπορίας). However, the facts contradict these statements. Julian did have auxiliaries, of 'Scythians' (cf. 23.2.7 *cum exercitu et Scytharum auxiliis Euphrate navali ponte transmisso venit ad Batnas*) and of Saracens (cf. 23.5.1 *ascitis Saracenorum auxiliis*). The latter were, according to Amm., gladly received when they offered their help (*suscepti gratanter ut ad furta bellorum appositi*, 23.3.8). As to these Saracens, Julian sent for them when he stayed in Hierapolis (see § 6 below): πρὸς τοὺς Σαρακηνοὺς ἔπεμψα πρέσβεις, ὑπομιμνήσκων αὐτοὺς ἥκειν, εἰ βούλοιντο (Jul. *Ep.* 98, 401 d).

For *nequaquam* see the note ad 19.12.12. It is used sparingly by Amm. (eight times), mostly, as here, in reported speech. *Adventicius* 'from outside' is used of imported articles in 14.2.4, 15.11.4, 23.6.68. Cf. also 31.13.8 *ni desertus ab armigeris princeps saltim adventicio tegeretur auxilio*.

solum Arsacem monuerat, Armeniae regem The pluperfect probably has its proper force, since there had been regular contacts with Arsaces even before the preparations for the Persian campaign (20.11.1). See for the chronological and other problems concerning Arsaces (*PLRE* I, Arsaces III) and his kingdom the notes ad 20.11.1. Despite various attempts of the Persians to bring Arsaces over to their side, the king remained a loyal supporter of Rome (*amico nobis semper et fido*, 25.7.12) – but he failed to arrive in time with his auxiliaries to aid Julian at Ctesiphon (24.7.8).

There is a curious remark of Sozomenus pertaining to Julian's appeal to Arsaces. The church historian reports (*HE* 6.1.2–3) that Julian wrote a letter to the Armenian king (Ἀρσακίῳ δὲ τῷ Ἀρμενίων ἡγουμένῳ συμμαχοῦντι Ῥωμαίοις ἔγραψε συμμῖξαι περὶ τὴν πολεμίαν), which was full of unbounded arrogance and threats (ἀπαυθαδιασάμενός τε πέρα τοῦ μέτρου ἐν τῇ ἐπιστολῇ... ὑβριστικῶς μάλα ἠπείλησεν αὐτῷ). It is hard to believe, however, that Julian really addressed a faithful ally so brusquely, even had he suspected him of intended treachery. Sozomenus' report (not found in Socrates, by the way) should therefore be rejected. It probably caused the writing of a letter (*Ep.* 57 Wright), purported to be written by Julian and addressed to Arsacius, which breathes the same tone as Sozomenus' account.

2.2

Almost all editors rightly bracket this letter as spurious (but see Wright, 1923, xxxvi-xxxvii).

ut collectis copiis validis iubenda opperiretur   See the note ad 20.11.24 on the future force of substantivated *iubenda* (= *quae iuberetur*). Szantyr 374 quotes as an example of this use of the gerund *Pan.* 2.31.4 *colligamus gerenda de gestis.*

quo tenderet, quid deberet urguere   Amm. has a comparable asyndeton in 18.2.1-2, where the beginning of Julian's campaign against the Alamanni is described in terms closely resembling the present passage: *haerebat anxius, qua vi qua celeritate, cum primum ratio copiam tribuisset, rumore praecurso terras eorum invaderet repentinus,* so Blomgren 45 is probably right in rejecting Petschenig's *tendere et.* For *urguere* 'to press in attack' cf. e.g. 16.12.16 *tripertito exitio premebantur imperatore urgente per Raetias* e.q.s. In 23.3.5 q.v. we catch a glimpse of what Arsaces was supposed to do: Julian ordered Procopius and Sebastianus to join the king, march with him through Corduene and Moxoene, lay waste in passing various places in Media and finally meet Julian in Assyria, in order to reinforce the emperor if he needed help.

cum primam consultae rationes copiam praebuissent   Amm. stresses at the same time the swiftness with which Julian acts and his careful planning. For *consultus* 'well-considered' see the note ad 20.5.9. The passage 18.2.1-2 quoted above and 21.9.8 *cum primitus visus adorandae purpurae datam sibi copiam advertisset* suggest that *cum primum* should be read here.

rumore praecurso hostiles occupare properans terras   According to TLL X 2.516.41 here and in 18.2.1-2, just quoted, *praecurrere* with its literal meaning 'to run in front of' is used transitively. Cf. also Sen. *Ep.* 123.7 *ut illos Numidarum praecurrat equitatus.* Julian knew the great advantages of secrecy when he prepared his campaign. He himself testifies to this policy in the letter he wrote from Hierapolis (cf. § 6 below) to Libanius: λίαν ἐγρηγορότας ὡς ἐνεδέχετο τοὺς παραφυλάξοντας ἐξέπεμψα, μή τις ἐνθένδε πρὸς τοὺς πολεμίους ἀπέλθῃ λαθών, ἐσόμενος αὐτοῖς ὡς κεκινήμεθα μηνυτής, "I despatched men as wide-awake as I could obtain that they might guard against anyone's leaving here secretly to go to the enemy and inform them that we are on the move" (Jul. *Ep.* 98, 402 a, transl. Wright). Cf. Libanius *Or.* 18.213: μεγάλην οὖσαν εἰδὼς ἐν ἀπορρήτοις ῥοπήν, ὃ γὰρ οὐδὲν ἂν ὀνῆσαι προρρηθὲν μέγα ἂν ὠφελῆσαι κρυφθέν, οὐχ εἰσόδου χρόνον, οὐχ εἰσβολῆς ὁδόν, οὐ μηχανημάτων τρόπον, οὐδὲν ὧν ἔστρεφεν ἐπὶ τῆς ψυχῆς ἐξήνεγκεν εἰδὼς ὅτι πᾶν ἐκλαληθὲν εὐθύς ἐστιν ἐν ὠσὶ κατασκόπων ("he knew the great advantages of secrecy; the broadcasting of information is valueless, whereas its concealment can be of great assistance; and so he did not reveal the time of his invasion, its proposed route, or his tactics. In fact, he disclosed nothing of what he had in mind, for he was well aware that news once blurted out is picked up by spies", Norman). As to his love for speedy action, see e.g. 21.5.1, 21.5.13, 21.9.6 (q.v.) and 22.2.2. A specific reason for haste at this particular moment is given by Socrates (*HE* 3.21.1). According to him the emperor had learnt that the Persians were greatly enfeebled and totally spiritless in winter: Κρυμὸν γὰρ μὴ φέροντες ἀπόμαχοι μένουσι κατὰ τόνδε τὸν χρόνον. ἀλλ' οὐδὲ χεῖρα, τὸ τοῦ λόγου, βάλλοι ἂν τότε ἔξω τοῦ φάρους Μῆδος ἀνήρ. Cf. further below, ad § 7 *fama de se nulla praeversa*.

nondum adulto vere Servius notes ad *G* 1.43 that Sallust distinguished the three months of every season, as *novus, adultus* and *praeceps*. See the note ad 14.2.9 *nocte adulta*. The normal practice is described by Tacitus: *legionibus intra castra habitis, donec ver adolesceret* (*Ann.* 13.36.1). In § 6 we get more precise information: Julian left Antioch *apricante caelo tertium nonas Martias*. Cf. also Zos. 3.12.1 (λήγοντος δὲ ἤδη τοῦ χειμῶνος), Socr. *HE* 3.21.1 (μικρὸν πρὸ τοῦ ἔαρος) and Soz. *HE* 6.1.1 (ἅμα δὲ ἦρι ἀρχομένῳ).

missa per militares numeros expeditionali tessera See for *tessera* (in military language a tablet on which the watchword or an order was written) and *numeri* (in the fourth century a general term for military units of all kinds) the notes ad 21.5.13 and 20.1.3, respectively.

cunctos transire iussit Euphraten Some difficulty is caused by *cunctos*. Klein, 1914, 60 took the word quite literally ("Julian habe alle Soldaten über den Eufrat vorangeschickt, wo sie ihn erwarten sollten") and therefore saw a discrepancy between Amm.'s statement here and his remark in § 6 that the whole army was meeting at Hierapolis west of the river. However, the problem disappears if one takes *cunctos* in the pregnant sense of 'all the units that were quartered in Syria east of the Euphrates'. These troops had to leave their winter quarters in order to join the rest of the army in Hierapolis. So e.g. Brok, 1959, 37–8.

omnes evolant ex hibernis The verb expresses the alacrity with which the campaign is started. Cf. the vigorous action of Valentinian in 30.3.2 *evolare protinus festinarat...barbaros primo fragore...oppressurus armorum. Evolare* is used in this sense also by Caesar: *ex omnibus partibus silvae evolaverunt et in nostros impetum fecerunt* (*Gal.* 3.28.3). As was pointed out ad 22.12.6 *ad sua diversoria*, several inscriptions in Syria attest to the construction of military inns, apparently built to spare the civilian population the nuisance of compulsory billeting (for this problem see the note ad 22.4.6 *aedes marmoreae*). Apart from these lodgings there must also have been the ususal military winter camps. Cf. Isaac, 1992[2], 136 and 178.

2.3

ut textus docebat scriptorum A reference to the *expeditionalis tessera* of § 2.

dispersi per stationes varias Cf. 20.4.9 (q.v.) *e stationibus... in quibus hiemabant* and the note ad 21.15.2. Among the *stationes* referred to must have been Litarba, Chalcis, Beroea and Batnae, mentioned in Jul. *Ep.* 98 (see below, ad § 6). On his march from Antioch to Hierapolis Julian found the remains of what he regarded as another winter camp, apparently not in use anymore near Litarba (λείψανα... χειμαδίων Ἀντιοχικῶν, Jul. *Ep.* 98, 399 b).

Heliopoliten quendam Alexandrum Syriacae iurisdictioni praefecit, turbulentum et saevum Alexander (*PLRE*, I Alexander 5) hailed from Heliopolis in Phoenice (now Baalbek in Lebanon), but became a citizen of Constantinople (Lib. *Ep.* 1456 πολίτης δέ ἐστι τῆς μεγάλης πόλεως, with Petit, 1983, 215–6). The addition of *quendam* proves that he was not a high-ranking official, which is confirmed by Julian's remark *non illum meruisse*. Amm.'s verdict on Alexander *turbulentus et saevus*, for which cf. the note ad 20.4.20 and Seager 54–5, is harsh and the more striking because in general he is very positive about Julian's appointments. In his capacity of governor of Syria – he bore the title of *consularis* (cf. 14.7.5, 15.13.2 and in general Downey, 1939) – Alexander received several letters from Libanius (cf. Wiemer, 1995, 64). In *Ep.* 838 Lib. urged him to greater leniency towards the people of Antioch, where he had his residence (cf. Pack, 1953, 82; for some literature on the capital of Syria see the note ad 22.9.14). Libanius admitted, however, that Alexander's severe administration proved successful: Ἐγὼ τὴν ἀρχὴν τὴν Ἀλεξάνδρου τὸ πρῶτον ἐδυσχέραινον, ὁμολογῶ... νῦν δὲ ὁ καρπός τε ἀνεδόθη τῆς τραχύτητος καὶ ᾄδω παλινῳδίαν (Lib. *Ep.* 811) and ἔσωσε μὲν Ἀλέξανδρος τὴν πόλιν, ἔσωσεν, οὐκ ἂν ἄλλως φαίην, ἀλλὰ μετὰ πικρῶν ῥημάτων (*Or.* 15.74). After Julian had died Alexander soon left office. Subsequently he was arrested and accused of excesses, but he was acquitted (Lib. *Ep.* 1256, 1294, 1456).

Already classical authors use *iurisdictio* as a terminus for the province of a governor, e.g. Tac. *Ann.* 1.80.1 *plerosque ad finem vitae in isdem exercitibus aut iurisdictionibus habere*. See also the note ad 15.11.6.

Antiochensibus avaris et contumeliosis Julian refers to the greed of the rich in Antioch in his *Mis.* 368 d: ὑπ' ἀπληστίας τῶν κεκτημένων, see the note ad 22.14.1. For the witticisms of the Antiochenes to which Julian had been exposed see 22.14.3 with the notes. Amm. mentions them in the next section: *nondum ira, quam ex compellationibus et probris conceperat, emollita*.

huiusmodi iudicem See for *iudex* in the sense of 'official' the note ad 20.5.7.

cumque eum profecturum deduceret multitudo promiscua... loquebatur as- 2.4
perius The adjective means that persons from all walks of life were represented, as is stated more explicitly e.g. in 14.3.3 *magna promiscae fortunae convenit multitudo* and 15.13.2 *Theophili Syriae consularis... impetu plebis promiscae discerpti*, where *multitudo* is subsequently divided up into *pauperes* and *divites*. Julian's staunch supporter Libanius was among the crowd which escorted the emperor, and begged that they might be forgiven (προπεμπούσης δὲ τῆς βουλῆς καὶ δεομένων ἀφεῖσθαι τὰ ἐγκλήματα, Lib. *Or.* 1.132; note that Libanius speaks of the city council, but no doubt alludes to the same *multitudo* as Amm. does). Libanius, like Amm., relates that in their attempt to bring about a reconciliation (for another try see below, ad § 6), the Antiochenes found Julian unrelenting, and adds that he himself was in tears, while the emperor was not (ἀσπασάμενος δή με δακρύοντα οὐ δακρύων, *Or.* 1.132). He further narrates, with scarcely concealed pride, that Julian predicted on that occasion that later on the Antiochenes would have recourse to him, Libanius, as an intermediary. "The result was *Oration* 16, addressed to the Antiochenes, upbraiding them for their misconduct, and urging them to earn the emperor's pardon by conforming to his policies, and a companion piece, *Oration* 15, addressed to the emperor, constituting a plea for forgiveness and an assurance to the emperor of the city's contrition. Neither oration was actually delivered" (Norman, 1969, xxxii; cf. Lib. *Or.* 17.37 and Socr. *HE* 3.17.7–8).

itum felicem reditumque gloriosum exoptans V reads *promis quantum*. The reading *promiscua itum* adopted by Seyfarth, based on Gelenius' edition, is certainly correct, since this is the traditional formula for the *vota pro itu et reditu* of the emperor. It is found in literary texts as e.g. Suet. *Tib.* 38 *vota pro itu et reditu suo suscipi passus*, Sidon. *epist.* 1.5.2 (not about an emperor this time) *amicorum multitudo, quae mihi... itum reditumque felicem... conprecabatur*, but also in the *Acta of the Arval Brethren* (105 II 41), and on numerous inscriptions and coins. See TLL VII 2.569.35–50. Later, when it was reported in Antioch that Julian had died and was never to return, people danced for joy, not only in the Christian churches and on the burial-places of the martyrs, but in the theatres as well. Cf. Lib. *Ep.* 1220.2 and Thdt. *HE* 3.28.1.

nondum ira, quam ex compellationibus et probris conceperat, emollita loquebatur asperius Cf. for the first symptoms of Julian's anger 22.14.2–3 *multa in se facete dicta comperiens coactus dissimulare pro tempore ira sufflabatur interna* e.q.s. Note that Libanius' *Or.* 16 is called Πρὸς Ἀντιοχέας περὶ τῆς τοῦ βασιλέως ὀργῆς. See Seager 21 for general remarks on *asperitas* in emperors.

disposuisse enim aiebat... Tarsum Ciliciae reversurum For *disponere* see the 2.5
note ad 20.4.9. In *Or.* 1.132 Libanius refers thus to Julian's parting words on

leaving Antioch: Ταρσοῖς, πόλει Κιλίκων δώσειν αὐτὸν εἰπὼν ἦν ὁ θεὸς ἀποσώζῃ. Julian himself had already alluded to his plans to keep away from the Syrian capital in *Mis.* 364 d and 370 b-c, without, however, mentioning Tarsus. Cf. further Lib. *Or.* 15.86, 16.53 (φησιν ἐν Ταρσοῖς τῆς Κιλικίας χειμάσειν) and Socr. *HE* 3.17.6, where the plan to go to Tarsus is said to have been made immediately after the first clashes between Julian and the people of Antioch had emerged: Ἐκ τούτων δὴ τῶν σκωμμάτων εἰς ὀργὴν ἐκπεσὼν ὁ βασιλεὺς διηπείλει πᾶν ποιῆσαι κακὸν τῇ Ἀντιοχέων πόλει καὶ ἐπὶ Ταρσὸν τῆς Κιλικίας ἐξυποστρέφειν. See for Tarsus and Cilicia the notes ad 14.8.3, 21.15.2 and 22.9.13.

hiemandi gratia An indication of Julian's optimism: he hoped to finish his Persian expedition within a year.

per compendiariam viam Coming from Persian territory there were several possibilities to avoid Antioch, depending on where one left the Euphrates area. If the *solita itinera* were taken (cf. § 6), one should, coming from Hierapolis, turn off at Beroea and choose the road which led via Cyrrhus to Nicopolis and from there to Tarsus. However, it was perhaps more convenient to march from Hierapolis north, up to Zeugma, before heading west in the direction of Doliche and Tarsus (there is a fine map showing the Roman roads in northern Syria in Mouterde-Poidebard, 1945, facing the front-page; cf. Dodgeon-Lieu, 1991, 140 and in general Dillemann, 1962, 129 ff.).

consummato procinctu Cf. 18.9.3 *post consummatos civiles procinctus*. The phrase again reveals Julian's confidence that he will be able to bring the expedition to an end in one campaigning season.

ad Memorium praesidem Successor of Celsus (22.9.13 q.v.) as *praeses* of Cilicia (see for the different titles of governors the note ad 21.10.6 and for *praeses* Ensslin, 1956). Memorius (*PLRE* I, Memorius 1) was, like Celsus, a friend of both Julian and Libanius (Jul. *Or.* 7.223 b, Lib. *Ep.* 836 and 1386).

cuncta usui congrua On *congruus* see the notes ad 20.6.1 and 22.12.4.

et hoc haud diu postea contigit With this laconic phrase Amm. anticipates the tragic end of the Persian campaign, for which he had prepared the reader by the enumeration of the bad omens that had attended the preparations.

corpus namque eius illuc relatum... ut ipse mandarat Cf. 25.9.12 *cum Iuliani supremis Procopius mittitur ea, ut superstes ille mandarat, humaturus in suburbano Tarsensi* and 25.10.4–5, with Fontaine n. 708.

exsequiarum humili pompa Julian's burial is merely touched upon in 25.9.12–13, where it is reported that Procopius, who was in charge of the procedures, left immediately afterwards. In 25.10.5, a passage full of pathos, Amm. bewails this undignified end to the life of Julian, who had deserved to be buried on the banks of the Tiber. Greg. Naz. *Or.* 5.19 maliciously insists on his burial place as a τέμενος ἄτιμον.

Iamque apricante caelo This expression is found only here. 2.6

tertium nonas Martias profectus March 5, 363. Gelenius' *Martias* is to be preferred to V's *maias* in view of 23.3.3 *quartum decimum kalendas Apriles* and 23.5.12 *septimum idus Apriles*.

Hierapolim solitis itineribus venit Zosimus tells us that Julian arrived at Hierapolis on the fifth day after he had left Antioch (πέμπτῃ δὲ τὴν Ἱεράπολιν ἡμέρᾳ καταλαβών, 3.12.1), i.e. on March, 9, but see the Note on Chronology. Julian's *Ep.* 98, addressed to Libanius, gives a detailed description of the journey to this city (cf. Cumont, 1917, who followed Julian's footsteps, Poidebard, 1929, Mouterde-Poidebard, 1945, I, 18 and French, 1993. Malalas, *Chron.* 13.328, is wrong in suggesting that Julian passed through Cyrrhus. According to *Ep.* 98 the emperor headed first for Litarba (now El-Terib), a village of Chalcis (ἔστι δὲ ἡ κώμη Χαλκίδος; cf. *IGLS* 2. 354), at a distance of 55 km. from Antioch – Chalcis does, but Litarba does not figure on *Tab. Peut.* IX 5–X 1, where the following stopping-places between Antioch and Hierapolis are enumerated: Emma, Chalcis, Beroea, Banna, Thiltauri and Bathna. On his way to Litarba Julien received a delegation of the Antiochene council (cf. the Note on Chronology), which no doubt tried again (cf. above § 4) to mollify him. Initially Libanius too had been one of the delegates, but he had returned to Antioch before the embassy met Julian (Lib. *Ep.* 802).
From Litarba Julian proceeded to Beroea (modern Aleppo), where he received auspicious omens (ὁ Ζεὺς αἴσια πάντα ἐσήμηνεν, ἐναργῆ δείξας τὴν διοσημίαν, *Ep.* 98, 399 d). He stayed there for a day and observed that the inhabitants of this city were reluctant to show their true religious feelings. In this respect the population of the next stop, Batnae, was more to his liking, although it seemed that the zeal of the Batnaeans was excessive and not an appropriate form of reverence to the gods. Charming Batnae (now Tell Batnân) lay 45 km. east of Beroea (it is not to be confused with Batnae in Osdroene, mentioned by Amm. in the next section). In Batnae too Julian received favourable omens (ἦν καλὰ τὰ ἱερά, *Ep.* 98, 401 b).
On his arrival in Hierapolis, where he was cordially received by the son-in-law of the Neoplatonist philosopher Sopater (*ibid.*), Julian took the military and political measures which he deemed necessary. In his aforementioned letter to Libanius (*Ep.* 98, 401 d–402 b) he gives a summary account of these

arrangements: 1. he sent envoys to the Saracens, asking them to come if they wished (cf. for this the note ad 23.2.1); 2. he tried to prevent anyone from secretly going to the Persians and informing the enemy that the Roman army was on the move (cf. above, ad 23.2.2 *rumore praecurso* and below, ad 23.2.7 *fama de se nulla praeversa*); 3. he held a court martial; 4. he gathered together a great number of horses and mules and inspected his army, now concentrated in the same place: τὸ στρατόπεδον εἰς ταὐτὸ συναγαγών (cf. § 2 *cunctos transire iussit Euphraten*, q.v. and § 7 *contractis copiis omnibus*); 5. he ordered that the boats to be used on the Euphrates were to be laden with baked bread and sour wine (Magnus of Carrhae, cited by Malalas, *Chron.* 13.328, informs us that Julian had ordered ships to be built in Samosata; cf. Lib. *Or.* 18.214 and note that in Amm. a reference to the fleet does not occur before 23.3.9). Julian's order concerning the boats on the Euphrates may ultimately have been based on a statement found in Zos. 3.12.1 which is usually seen as an error of the sixth-century historian (so e.g. Ridley, 1973, 318 and Paschoud n. 31). After having related that Julian had arrived in Hierapolis, Zosimus says that there (ἔνθα) all the ships were bound to come together, both the warships and the transportships (ἔνθα ἔδει τὰ πλοῖα πάντα συνδραμεῖν στρατιωτικά τε καὶ φορτηγά, ἔκ τε Σαμοσάτων καὶ ἐξ ἄλλων τὸν Εὐφράτην καταπλέοντα τόπων). Since Hierapolis was about 30 km. west of the Euphrates, Zos. is either wrong or he uses ἔνθα loosely, in the sense of 'near this city', 'off Hierapolis' (note that there was no other city directly on the borders of the Euphrates on a par with Hierapolis and cf. Procop. *Pers.* 1.13.11 ἐν Ἱεραπόλει τῇ πρὸς τῷ Εὐφράτῃ ποταμῷ and 1.17.22).

Hierapolis, modern Membidj, in the province of Euphratensis, formerly Commagene, was, according to Amm. 14.8.7, in former days called Ninus (cf. Philostr. *VA* 1.19 and 3.58). Strabo 16.1.27 (748C) mentions still other names: Bambyce and Edessa (cf. the note ad 21.13.8). In this city there was i.a. a temple of Atargatis, made famous by the *De Dea Syria* attributed to Lucian. For further information see Honigmann, 1924 and Goossens, 1943.

ubi cum introiret civitatis capacissimae portas Seyfarth is probably right in rejecting V's *introierit*, which was defended by Ehrismann. Undeniably, Amm. often uses the perfect subjunctive where classical Latin would have preferred either the imperfect or the pluperfect. To quote a few examples: 14.3.1 *Nohodares quidam nomine e numero optimatum incursare Mesopotamiam, quotiens cópia déderit, ordinatus explorabat nostra sollicite,* 16.10.6 *unde cum se vertisset ad plebem, stupebat, qua celeritate omne, quod ubique est, hominum genus, conflúxerit Rómam,* 21.13.7 *quo cognito maerore offusus Constantius solacio uno sustentabatur, quod intestinos semper superáverit mótus,* 21.14.2 *post haec confessus est iunctioribus proximis, quod tamquam desolatus secretum aliquid videre desierit,* 22.2.1 *inter quae tam suspensa advenere subito missi ad eum legati Theolaifus atque Aligildus defunctum*

Constantium nuntiantes addentesque, quod eum voce suprema successorem suae fécerit potestátis, 23.2.1 *cuius opibus foveri conveniret amicos et socios, si auxilium eos adegerit necessitas implorare*. Ehrismann 16–22 interprets this use of the perfect subjunctive in imbedded sentences as a form of *repraesentatio*. That may be correct, but at the same time it is clear that, as in most cases where the pluperfect is substituted for the perfect tense, the choice of the tenses is dictated by the cursus. Nevertheless, in the other phrases introduced by *ubi cum* Amm. follows classical usage: 23.5.8 *ubi cum pro ingenita pietate consecrato principi parentasset pergeretque ad Duram,* 26.7.15 *ubi cum legiones iam pugnaturae congrederentur,* 27.9.7 *ubi cum eis nec quiescendi nec inveniendi ad victum utilia copia laxaretur... pacem sibi tribui poposcerunt* and for that reason *introiret* should be preferred here too.

According to TLL III 300.82–301.11, Amm. is the only author to use *capax* for a fortress or a town, cf. 19.6.1 where he calls the *castellum* Ziata *locum capacissimum et munitum*. See, however, Ovid's description of the city of Dis in *Met.* 4.439–40 *mille capax aditus et apertas undique portas / urbs habet*.

subter tendentes quinquaginta milites The same round number is stated for the accident at Batnae reported in section 8. For *tendere* 'to encamp' cf. 16.12.62 *invitissimus miles prope supercilia Rheni tendebat*, 19.9.1, 21.7.6 and 31.7.5. The other meanings of *tendere* in Amm. are 1. 'to stretch out', 'to direct' 16.10.10 *rectam aciem luminum tendens*, 25.1.13 *tendebant divaricatis bracchiis flexiles arcus*; 2. 'to proceed' 14.2.11 *quo tenderet ambigentes,* 14.11.12 *prorsus ire tendebat*, 19.1.7 *Grumbates fidenter... tendebat ad moenia*, occasionally without mention of the direction, as in 21.5.6 *impraepedito cursu tendentes Daciarum interim fines extimos occupemus* and 23.5.1 (q.v.); 3. 'to strive' 14.6.8 *ad ascensus verae gloriae tendere longos et arduos*, 16.8.13 *quorum aemulationem posteritas tendens satiari numquam potuit cum possessione multo maiore*. 4. The passive is used intransitively in geographical descriptions, e.g. 27.4.7, 29.6.18.

exceptis plurimis vulneratis This use of *exceptus* is already classical. Antonius writes in Cic. *Att.* 10.8a.1 *mihi neminem esse cariorem te excepto Caesare meo*.

unde contractis copiis omnibus Mesopotamiam propere signa commovit The **2.7** accusative of Goal without a preposition is occasionally used with the name of a country in classical authors, e.g. Caes. *Civ.* 3.106.1 *coniectans eum Aegyptum iter habere*. Possibly under the influence of Vergil (*Italiam fato profugus Laviniaque venit / litora, A* 1.2–3) this becomes more frequent in later authors such as Suetonius and Tacitus; Szantyr 50. See also De Jonge's note ad 14.11.6.

In Hierapolis, where he had assembled his army (cf. § 2 *cunctos transire iussit Euphraten* with the note and Jul. *Ep.* 98, 402 a, quoted above), Julian stayed only three days, according to Zosimus (3.12.2 τρεῖς ἐπιμείνας τῇ Ἱεραπόλει μόνας ἡμέρας). This tallies with Amm.'s *propere.* Cf. also Lib. *Or.* 18.214, where it is remarked that Julian surprised everyone by crossing the Euphrates at speed (ὑπερβὰς τὰς ἁπάντων ἐλπίδας καὶ κατὰ τάχος διαβὰς τὸν ποταμόν).

When Amm. employs the term *Mesopotamia* he usually means the Roman province, with its capital Nisibis, and not 'all the land between the rivers Euphrates and Tigris' (see the notes ad 14.3.1 and 17.5.6 and cf. Jones 1458; Amm. had described the province in the lost books, as can be deduced from 14.7.21). Probably here too Amm. adheres to his normal practice. However, note that Julian, after crossing the Euphrates and before reaching the province of Mesopotamia, had to march through Osdroena first: *venit ad Batnas, municipium Osdroenae.*

fama de se nulla praeversa – id enim curatius observarat See above, the note ad § 2 *rumore praecurso* and cf. 26.8.3 *rumore quodam praeverso.* As is remarked in TLL X 2.1107.23 sqq., the deponential use of the verb is found from Plautus onward. A good parallel to the present phrase is Dict. 2.37 *Achilles praeverso de se nuntio...intemptato negotio ad tentoria regreditur.* The adverb *curate* 'carefully' is but rarely found in the positive degree, as in 19.1.10 *figmenta...hominum mortuorum ita curate pollincta,* more often in the comparative, for which Tacitus may have provided the model: *Ann.* 2.27.1 *finem curatius disseram* and 16.22.3 *diurna populi Romani...curatius leguntur.*

At this stage of Julian's campaign the Persians could only guess at the emperor's plans. Having assembled his army at Hierapolis it was by no means clear whether Julian would march south along the Euphrates into Persian Mesopotamia or would advance north-eastwards in order to recapture for instance Amida. Cf. Libanius in *Ep.* 1402 to Aristophanes, written while news of Julian's death had not yet reached him: ὡς γὰρ ἐνέβαλε βασιλεὺς ἅμα ἦρι ᾗ οὐκ ᾤοντο, εἴχοντο εὐθὺς Ἀσσύριοι ("As soon as the emperor invaded early in the spring by a route which surprised them, the Assyrians were taken straightaway", Norman).

Assyrios Amm. distinguishes between Assyria in the narrower sense, denoting a specific part of the Persian kingdom, and Assyria in the wider sense, viz. 'all of Persian territory between the Euphrates and Tigris'. We find the first meaning e.g. in Amm.'s description of the Persian kingdom in chapter 6 of this book, where he mentions *Assyria* first among the *regiones* into which Persia was divided (23.6.14) and says that this region was nearest to Roman territory: *Citra omnes propinqua est nobis Assyria* (23.6.15 q.v.). The second meaning is attested in 24.1.1 *Assyrios fines ingressus* and, it would seem, in the present text, where *Assyrios* is almost equivalent to *Persas*. Cf. also De Jonge ad 14.4.3 and 18.8.5.

cum exercitu et Scytharum auxiliis As was argued in the note ad 20.8.1 *auxilia... Scytharum*, in the sources for the history of the later Roman empire *Scythae* is a general term for the nomadic tribes of the north of Europe and Asia, beyond the Black Sea. Often Goths must have been meant (see e.g. Wolfram, 1979, 21 ff. and Heather, 1991, 44–5). Although it is by no means certain that Amm. always used 'Scythae' for 'Goths' (see the note ad 20.8.1), it is likely that in the present text he did, for the Γότθοι of Zos. 3.25.6 are almost certainly to be identified with Amm.'s *Scythae* here (cf. Paschoud n. 71). See for Libanius' denial that Julian used 'Scythian' auxiliaries above, ad 23.2.1 and for *Scythia* as part of the Persian empire below, ad 23.6.14.

Euphrate navali ponte transmisso It is not absolutely certain where precisely Julian's army crossed the river on a bridge of boats (for this type of bridge see the note ad 21.7.7 and for bridges in general O'Connor, 1993; cf. also Desnier, 1995, and Mary, 1992). From *Tab. Peut.* X 2 it can be deduced that there was a crossing at Caeciliana, but unfortunately this Caeciliana has not been identified (Dillemann, 1962, 180). Perhaps we may infer from *Itin. Eger.* 18.2–3 that the crossing was in the neighbourhood of modern Tell-Ahmar. Egeria in 385, like Julian in 363, had to cross the Euphrates on her journey from Antioch via Hierapolis to Batnae and beyond, and she is said to have done so at a point which lay fifteen miles away from Hierapolis (*Itaque ergo proficiscens de Ierapolim in quintodecimo miliario in nomine Dei perveni ad fluvium Eufraten... Itaque ergo quoniam necesse erat eum navibus transire, et navibus nonnisi maioribus, ac sic immorata sum ibi forsitan plus media die, et inde in nomine Dei transito flumine Eufraten ingressa sum fines Mesopotamiae Syriae*). As Cumont, 1917, 26–9, following older authorities, has pointed out there is only one crossing which Egeria (and presumably Julian too) can have used if the words *in quintodecimo miliario* are correctly transmitted, viz. the one near modern Tell-Ahmar, which lies on the east bank of the river, just south of the spot, some fifteen miles from Membidj = Hierapolis, where the Sadjour flows out into the Euphrates.

According to a rather unlikely story in John Chrysostom (*pan. Bab.* 2.121), Julian, when on the verge of crossing the Euphrates (τὸν Εὐφράτην διαβαίνειν μέλλων), tried to convert his soldiers to paganism. The majority refused (Gabba, 1974, 104–6, argues that, on the contrary, most of Julian's soldiers were still pagans or were ready to abandon Christianity), whereupon Julian gave up the attempt, afraid to weaken his army. Even if the story were true, its setting at the borders of the Euphrates seems odd. Hierapolis would have been a more suitable place for such an attempt (as indeed has been suggested; cf. for this Schatkin ad loc.)

venit ad Batnas, municipium Osdroenae In the so-called Syriac Julian romance, a fictional work about Julian, a meeting between the pagan emperor and Jews from Edessa in Batnae is described; see Gollancz, 1928, 143-6. This Batnae in Osdroena, modern Seruj, is not to be confused with Syrian Batnae, mentioned in Julian's *Ep.* 98 (cf. the note ad § 6 above). In 14.3.3 (q.v.) Amm. had mentioned an unsuccessful attempt by the Persians to capture the city (for *municipium* see the note ad 20.7.1), which had been founded by Macedonians and was an important centre of trade (*Batnae municipium in Anthemusia conditum Macedonum manu priscorum ab Euphrate flumine brevi spatio disparatur refertum mercatoribus opulentis, ubi annua sollemnitate prope Septembris initium mensis ad nundinas magna promiscae fortunae convenit multitudo ad commercanda, quae Indi mittunt et Seres, alia plurima vehi terra marique consueta*; cf. *Itin. Eger.* 19.1 *civitas habundans multitudine hominum*).

In *Itin. Anton.* p. 26 (Cuntz) the distance between Hierapolis and Batnae is given as 53 Roman miles, i.e. approximately 80 kilometers (but cf. Dillemann, 1962, 180: "En réalité, il y a 65 km. de Membidj à Seroudj, soit xxxxiiii m.p."), and mention is made of an intermediate station at Thilaticomum (sometimes identified with Arslan Tash, but this identification is rejected by Dillemann, 1962, 182).

As to Osdroena ("der Name war wohl eigentlich Orrhoëne", Krückmann, 1942, 1589), cf. the note ad 14.3.2. See also Dillemann, 1962, 105 ff. and Wagner, 1983. Its description by Amm. is lost (cf. 14.7.21 and 14.8.7 *Et prima post Osdroenam, quam, ut dictum est, ab hac descriptione discrevimus, Commagena*). In 24.1.2 the *Osdroenae dux* Secundinus is mentioned.

According to Zos. 3.12.2 an embassy from Edessa came to Julian while he stayed in Batnae, offering him a crown and inviting him to come to their city; the emperor accepted the invitation and, before going to Carrhae, visited Edessa: Αὐτὸς δὲ τρεῖς ἐπιμείνας τῇ Ἱεραπόλει μόνας ἡμέρας ἐπὶ Βάτνας τῆς Ὀσδροηνῆς πολίχνιον τι προῄει, οὗ δὴ ὑπαντήσαντες Ἐδεσηνοὶ πανδημεὶ στέφανόν τε προσέφερον καὶ μετ' εὐφημίας εἰς τὴν σφῶν πόλιν ἐκάλουν. ὁ δὲ ἀποδεξάμενος καὶ ἐπιστὰς τῇ πόλει, καὶ ὅσα ἔδει χρηματίσας, ἐπὶ Κάρρας ἐβάδιζε. However, since Lib. *Or.* 18.214 (διαβὰς τὸν ποταμὸν οὐκ ἐπὶ τὴν πλησίον μεγάλην τε καὶ πολυάνθρωπον πόλιν [= Edessa] ἦλθεν ὡς ἴδοι τε καὶ ὀφθείη καὶ τὰ εἰωθότα τοῖς βασιλεῦσι τιμηθείη, ἀλλ' ὀξύτητος δεῖσθαι τὸν καιρὸν εἰδὼς ᾖκε μὲν εἰς πόλιν [= Carrhae] ἔχουσαν μέγα Διὸς ἱερὸν ἀρχαῖον; cf. also Soz. *HE* 6.1.1 and Thdt. *HE* 3.26.2) flatly contradicts this story, it would seem that Zos. is either simply wrong or his text is faultily transmitted (cf. Paschoud n. 32).

ibique illaetabile portentum offendit Cf. 23.5.6 *hic quoque omen illaetabile visum est* with the note ad loc. The adjective is rare (TLL VII 1.337.35 sqq.), but it occurs in Verg. *A.* 3.707 *Drepani portus et illaetabilis ora*. For *offendere* 'to be faced with' cf. the note ad 21.8.2 *inter subita* and Amm.'s personal experience described in 19.8.6 *offendi dirum aspectum*.

calonum frequens multitudo   According to Schol. Hor. *S.* 1.2.44 *calones sunt ministri militum, liberi homines, lixae vero servi eorundem*. This tallies with 18.2.13 *lixas vero vel servos, qui eos pedibus sequebantur. . . occiderunt*. Traditionally, the *lixae* look after the food for the soldiers, whereas the *calones* are stable-boys. That explains why they are standing here near the hay-stacks. On *calones* see further the note ad 18.8.10. *Palea* is regularly used as horse fodder (cf. Plin. *Nat.* 18.99 *si vero in area teritur cum stipula palea* (vocatur), *in maiore terrarum parte ad pabula iumentorum*) or as straw for the stables (Plin. *Nat.* 18.297 *ubi foeni inopia est stramento paleam quaerunt*).

2.8

ad suscipiendum consuete pabulum   The adverb is extremely rare. TLL IV 552.76–84 quotes Filastr. 120.7 *ius coniugii. . . laudatur cotidie ac benedicitur consuete*.

prope acervum palearum. . . impendio celsum   In order to make sense of the story, we must suppose that the chaff had been compressed into bales that had been piled high, and that the hayrick thus formed began to totter when the *calones* started to pull out bales from below.

tales species   For this use of the plural *species*, 'goods', 'wares', which is not found before the fourth century, cf. 27.3.10 *sed si ferrum quaerebatur aut plumbum aut aes aut quidquam simile, apparitores immittebantur, qui velut ementes diversas raperent species*.

quassata congeries   Amm. uses the verb *quassare* only rarely in its literal sense, e.g. 19.8.2 *moles illa nostrorum velut terrae quodam tremore quassata procubuit*. In the majority of cases *quassare* is used figuratively: 24.3.9 *ita quassatum recrearet orbem Romanum*, 27.6.1 *Valentiniano magnitudine quassato morborum*.

mole maxima ruinarum   As Fontaine observes in note 528, there is a striking resemblance between the ominous events reported in this chapter, and Amm.'s description of Julian's death on the battle-field. When Julian rushed out into the mêlée, his body-guards warned him *ut fugientium molem tamquam ruinam male compositi culminis declinaret*.

Chapter 3

This chapter relates the advance of Julian's army along the left bank of the Euphrates. The first stop is made in the ancient city of Carrhae, where Julian honours the local Moon-god (§ 1). It was here that Julian, according to unconfirmed rumours, appointed Procopius as his successor in case anything should happen to him during the campaign (§ 2). In § 3 Julian is warned by a bad dream not to proceed on the 19th of March. Later it turned out, as Amm. adds, that during the night in which Julian had the dream, the temple of Apollo on the Palatine had burned down and that the Sibylline books had only just been saved.

In sections 4 and 5 we are told that a Persian cavalry unit had crossed the Tigris and raided Roman border territory. This induced Julian to order Procopius and Sebastianus to strengthen the Tigris border with an army corps of 30.000 men. Amm. emphasizes that this was not an impromptu measure, but that it was part of a plan Julian had developed long before. This strategy implied a two-pronged attack on Persia. The army corps under Procopius and Sebastianus was to wait in the Tigris area for king Arsaces, and after they had united their forces with the king, they were to join Julian himself to assist him in the hour of need.

Section 6 is devoted to another portentous event: the fall of the emperor's horse Babylonius. This was in itself a very bad *omen*, but Julian turned it into a positive sign by interpreting it as a prediction of the fall of Babylon. The army marches next to Callinicum by way of Davana (§ 7), where the emperor on the 27th of March celebrated the *Lavatio*, the ritual bath of Cybele's chariot. Amm. stresses Julian's devotion to the Mother of the gods. It is significant that Amm., using the present tense, remarks in passing that on that day the *Lavatio* is celebrated at Rome, since we know that the cult of Cybele played an important part during the short-lived reign of the usurper Eugenius and that it was abolished soon afterwards by Theodosius and his sons. Julian, so Amm. tells us, shared the festive mood at the end of the festival, which marked the beginning of spring. At the end of his Εἰς τὴν μητέρα τῶν θεῶν (20, 180 a-b) Julian had prayed to the goddess for help in washing away from the world the stain of impiety, and in saving the empire for thousands of years to come. Amm.'s emphasis on Julian's worship of Cybele therefore has a considerable ideological significance.

In the last two sections Amm. reports the arrival of Saracene auxiliaries and a huge fleet carrying food supplies and the siege-engines, to which the following chapter is devoted.

venit cursu propero Carrhas The phrase *cursu propero* is found nowhere 3.1
else in Amm., who prefers *celeri cursu* (16.12.45 and often). For the event cf.
Zos. 3.12.2. Carrhae, or Harran (modern Altinbasak), was a very old city and
was especially known for its Moon cult (Sîn). There are several near-eastern
sources which mention the city and its cult, the oldest of which is a tablet
from Mari, of about 2000 B.C.; it records a treaty sealed in the temple of Sîn
in Carrhae; Lloyd-Brice, 1951, 87 ff. The town is mentioned in Gen. 11.31,
24.4, 28.2 as the residence of Abraham. For that reason the Christian pilgrim
Egeria visited the place c. 385. She reports that Carrhae had a bishop and a
few clergy, but that absolutely no Christians lived in the city (*Itin. Eger.* 20.8).
However, in the desert around the city there lived many monks and ascetics.
Carrhae's church was at the site where originally Abraham's house was said
to have been. Carrhae was hardly fortified in Ammianus' days: *Carrhas,
oppidum invalidis circumdatum muris* (18.7.3). Zos. 3.13.1 is wrong when he
says that Carrhae marked the boundary between Roman and Persian territory:
ἡ δὲ πόλις διορίζει Ῥωμαίους καὶ Ἀσσυρίους; see Paschoud n. 34. See for
Carrhae/Harran, Mez, 1892; Weissbach, 1919; Lloyd-Brice, 1951; Cramer,
1986 and the note ad 18.7.3.
Dillemann, 1962, 179–80 referring to the *Tab. Peut.* X 3 and *Itin. Anton.* p. 86
(Cuntz), gives as the distance between Batnae en Carrhae 30 Roman miles.
Brok, 1959, 49 following Regling, 1902 notes that according to the *Tab. Peut.*
the distance between the two towns is 39 miles. This seems more likely since,
according to Dillemann, 1962, 180 the distance, as the crow flies, is 56 km.,
which is more in line with 39 than with 30 Roman miles. As to the the question
whether or not Julian visited Edessa see the note ad 23.2.7.

Crassorum et Romani exercitus aerumnis insigne On 9 June 53 B.C. M.
Licinius Crassus was defeated by the Parthians near Carrhae; Plut. *Crass.* 19
ff., D.C. 40.17 ff. His son Publius was killed in battle; Crassus himself was
killed during his retreat to Syria. In 20 B.C. the captured trophies were returned
to Augustus by the Parthian king Phraates IV; Aug. *Anc.* 29.2. Furthermore,
Carrhae was known to the Romans because Caracalla was murdered nearby
on 8 April 217; D.C. 78.4–5 and Hdn. 4.13. For *aerumnae* see the note ad
20.7.7.

duae... viae regiae Cf. Zos. 3.12.3 with Paschoud n. 33: Δυοῖν τοίνυν
ἐντεῦθεν ὁδοῖν προχειμέναιν, τῆς μὲν διὰ τοῦ ποταμοῦ Τίγρητος καὶ
πόλεως Νισίβιος ταῖς Ἀδιαβηνῆς σατραπείαις ἐμβαλλούσης, τῆς δὲ διὰ
τοῦ Εὐφράτου καὶ τοῦ Κιρχησίου (φρούριον δὲ τοῦτο κυκλούμενον ὑπό τε
τοῦ Ἀβώρα ποταμοῦ καὶ αὐτοῦ τοῦ Εὐφράτου, τοῖς δὲ Ἀσσυρίων ὁρίοις
συναπτόμενον) σκεπτομένου τε τοῦ βασιλέως ποτέρα τούτων χρήσασθαι
δέοι πρὸς τὴν διάβασιν...; Malalas, *Chron.* 13.329: κἀκεῖθεν εὗρε δύο
ὁδούς, μίαν ἀπάγουσαν εἰς τὴν Νίσιβιν πόλιν...καὶ ἄλλην ἐπὶ τὸ Ῥω-

μαικὸν κάστρον τὸ λεγόμενον Κιρκήσιον, κείμενον εἰς τὸ μέσον τῶν δύο ποταμῶν τοῦ Εὐφράτου καὶ τοῦ Ἀβορρᾶ. See for a discussion of the passages of Ammianus, Zosimus and Malalas Paschoud, n. 33, and Matthews 169 f. for a discussion about the interdependence of these passages. At least six routes in Mesopotamia, giving access to the heartland of Persia, can be reconstructed; see Dillemann, 1962, 147 ff. and for "la route de l'Euphrate d'Isidore à Julien", Gawlikowski, 1990. The *viae regiae* mentioned here are the old Parthian Royal Roads. Amm. and Malalas nowhere report explicitly that Julian opted for the route *dextra per Assyrios et Euphraten*. Zos. 3.13.3 thinks that Julian when at Carrhae still had a choice between the two roads. In fact, at this stage he had no choice since all preparations, especially those for the fleet, were intended for the route along the Euphrates; see the note ad 23.3.5.

per Adiabenam Adiabene, which since the first century A.D. was ruled by its own kings under Parthian domination, was regularly involved in the Roman-Parthian conflicts; J. *AJ* 20.35, Tac. *Ann*. 12.13.1, D.C. 62.20, 68.28; cf. Teixidor, 1967/8. In 116 Trajan conquered the region and may have transformed it into the Roman province of Assyria, although the fact that there are only two late antique sources – Eutr. 8.3.2 and Ruf. Fest. 14 and 20 – which mention a province of Assyria is reason for serious doubt that there ever was such a province; Millar, 1993, 101. See for Adiabene furthermore Str. 11.4.8 (530C), 11.14.13 (530C), 16.1.1 (736C), 16.1.19 (745C); Plin. *Nat*. 5.66, Ptol. 6.1.2 and Dillemann, 1962, passim. In 23.6.20 and 21 Amm. gives two explanations for the name of Adiabene. According to the first explanation Adiabene was first called Assyria; however, it changed to Adiabene since it was lying between two rivers and could not be approached by a ford: *Intra hunc circumitum Adiabene est Assyria priscis temporibus vocitata longaque assuetudine ad hoc translata vocabulum ea re, quod inter Onam et Tigridem sita navigeros fluvios adiri vado numquam potuit; transire enim diabenin dicimus Graeci* (23.6.20). The second explanation, i.e. that Adiabene was named after the rivers Diabas and Adiabas, is considered by Amm. more probable: *nos autem didicimus, quod in his terris amnes sunt duo perpetui, quos transiimus, Diabas et Adiabas, iunctis navalibus pontibus, ideoque intellegi Adiabenam cognominatam...* (23.6.21). From these words one might conclude that Amm. had visited Adiabene, pace Dillemann, 1961, 141 and 1962, 306–8.

Assyrios I.e. Assyria in the narrower sense; cf. the note ad 23.2.7 above.

3.2 *ibi moratus aliquot dies, dum necessaria parat* Here he divided his forces; 23.3.5, Zos. 3.12.5, Soz. *HE* 6.1.2; Malalas, *Chron*. 13.329. In 3.13.1 Zosimus mentions a parade which took place in or near Carrhae: Ταῦτα ἐν Κάρραις διαθείς... ἠβουλήθη τὸ στρατόπεδον ἐξ ἀπόπτου τινὸς θεωρῆσαι χωρίου, ἄγασθαι δὲ τὰ πεζικὰ τάγματα καὶ τὰς τῶν ἱππέων ἴλας. Dillemann, 1961, 146 followed by Blockley, 1992, 176 n. 68 thinks that the parade was not held in Carrhae but in Cercusium: "La revue de Carrhes, dont Zosime est seul à parler, doit être un dédoublement de la présentation des troupes à Circesium" (Paschoud n. 34 considers this suggestion "ingénieuse et séduisante, mais non contraignante"). Matthews 167 is of the opinion that Eunapius, on whom Zos. 3.13.1 is based, introduced this episode as "a rhetorical fabrication to enable (him) to describe the army".

Lunae, quae religiose per eos colitur tractus, ritu locorum fert sacra Cf. 15.10.7 *manesque eius* (king Cottius)... *religiose coluntur* and Cic. *N.D.* 3.48 *Circen quoque coloni nostri Cerceienses religiose colunt.* For *ritu* "according to a given rite" (OLD) with genitive cf. 19.1.10 *iuvenis... ritu nationis propriae lugebatur*, 28.1.20 *obsecrato ritu sacrorum sollemnium numine.* In classical Latin it normally means 'in the manner of', 'like', but cf. Stat. *Theb.* 1.718 *gentis Achaemeniae ritu.*
According to Lib. *Or.* 18.214 and Soz. *HE* 6.1.1 Julian (also?) visited the temple of Zeus in Carrhae. The Moon-god Sîn was venerated in Carrhae since c. 2000 B.C.; see for his cult, Weissbach, 1919, 2018–20; Segal, 1953, 107–12; Drijvers, 1980, 122 ff. Ancient and Arabic sources indicate that there were probably three temples dedicated to the moon in and near Carrhae: 1. a shrine of Sîn at 'Ain-al-'Anus, to the south of Carrhae; 2. a temple at Aşagi Yarimca some 5 km. to the north-west of Carrhae on the road to Edessa; 3. a temple at Carrhae itself at the site of the present ruins of the citadel. See for an extensive discussion of the various temples and their location, Lloyd-Brice, 1951, 87–96. Julian presumably sacrificed in front of the temple in Carrhae itself, since Amm. does not say that Julian left the town to perform his sacrificial duties. Nothing is known with regard to the nature of the rites. Thdt. *HE* 3.26.2 f., however, tells the improbable story that Julian did an *extispicium* on a woman during his sacrifice. Whereas Amm. speaks of *Luna*, HA *Cc* 6.6 speaks of *Lunus* when reporting the murder of Caracalla (*hibernaret Edessae atque inde Carrhas Luni dei gratia venisset*) and in *Cc.* 7.3–5 offers a fanciful explanation for the occurrence of *Luna* as well as *Lunus*, saying that whoever believes that the deity should be called *Luna* is subordinate to women whereas he who believes the god is male dominates his wife and is not caught by any woman's wiles.

nullo arbitrorum admisso Amm. probably writes *arbitrorum* instead of *arbitro* for euphonic and metrical reasons, since the *arbitri* do not form a class such as the *clarissimi* and the *potentes* in the following examples: 26.6.18 *nullo clarissimorum, sed ignobilium paucitate reperta* and 27.10.10 *nullo potentium in conscientiam arcani adhibito.*

dicitur... paludamentum purpureum propinquo suo tradidisse Procopio For the purple cloak as one of the emperor's *insignia* see the notes ad 20.5.4 and 22.9.10. The story about Julian's appointment of Procopius as his successor is clearly based on rumour as Amm. himself indicates in 26.6.2 (*obscurior fama*). The only other source which mentions the story is Zos. 4.4.2. Thompson, 1947, 38 considers this episode as progaganda put about by Procopius himself, whereas Sabbah 411–3 thinks that the rumour was spread by adversaries of Procopius. See also Béranger, 1972, 88–90 who thinks that the story about Procopius' appointment is true. For Procopius, see *PLRE* I, Procopius 4 + Lippold, 1974, 270 and the comprehensive note ad 17.14.3. For Procopius' usurpation in 366 under Valentinian and Valens, which eventually led to his death, see 25.7.10 and 26.6.12 ff.; cf. e.g. Blockley, 1975, 55–61; Matthews 191 ff.

mandasseque arripere fidentius principatum For *mandare* with inf. cf. Tac. Ann. 15.2.4 *mandavitque Tigranen Armenia exturbare.* As was stated in the note ad 20.8.19 *fidenter* does not imply any disapproval. It does mean that Procopius is explicitly authorized by Julian to take the purple, should anything happen to himself.

si se interisse didicerit See the note ad 23.2.6 for more examples of the perfect instead of the pluperfect subjunctive.

Parthos Amm. uses *Parthi* as well as *Persae* to designate the Persians (e.g. 20.7.5 *Persarum*, 20.7.6 *Parthorum*, 25.1.18 *Persis... Parthis*; see the notes ad 15.1.2 and 20.4.2; Brok, 1959, 54 and Chauvot, 1992, 121–5), but *Persae* occurs far more often than *Parthi*. The Persian kingdom was named Parthia since Arsaces (c. 240 B.C.): *Hoc regnum quondam exiguum multisque antea nominibus appellatum... in vocabulum Parthi concessit Arsacis* (23.6.2). The Romans apparently did not distinguish, as modern historians do, between Persia ruled by the Parthian dynasty and Persia under the Sasanian dynasty, although they knew about the change of power from the one dynasty to the other; Hdn. 6.2. Amm. nowhere in his work speaks of Sasanians.

3.3 *animus agitatus insomniis* Cf. Liv. 25.38.5 *Scipiones me ambo dies noctesque curis insomniisque agitant et excitant saepe somno.*

eventurum triste aliquid praesagibat Concerning the vacillation between *-ibat* and *-iebat* see TLL X 2.810.14–6. As was remarked in the note ad 20.8.20, expressions denoting forebodings are regularly mitigated by *velut*. The cumulation of bad omens does not allow such a qualification here.

et ipse Apparently Julian himself was able to interpret dreams, just as he was able to understand *praesagia* (21.1.6).

visorum interpretes I.e. *somniorum interpretes*. Amm. also uses the terms *ratiocinantes* (21.1.12) and *interpretantes* (21.14.1) for interpreters of dreams. According to Rike, 1987, 65 Oribasius may have been one of the *visorum interpretes*.

praesentia contemplantes It is not at all clear what exactly Amm. means by this. *Praesentia* can hardly refer to the appointment of Procopius as Julian's successor, as Fontaine's translation "en considération de ces événements" seems to suggest. On the contrary, that decision would have followed more naturally after Julian's dreams had been mentioned. So *praesentia* should refer more generally to the situation at the outset of the campaign, implying that there were plenty of reasons for anxiety.

diem secutum... observari debere pronuntiabant The words must mean that no action should be undertaken on that day, but there are no clear parallels for this use of *observare*.

quartum decimum kalendas Apriles I.e. 19 March.

Palatini Apollinis templum praefecturam regente Aproniano in urbe conflagravit aeterna For Apronianus, see the note ad 23.1.4. For the destruction of the Apollo temple, which was originally part of Augustus' house on the Palatine (Suet. *Aug.* 29.3), see the note ad 23.1.7. Rike, 1987, 27 rightly connects the report on the fire in the temple of Apollo on the Palatine with the burning down of the Apollo temple in Daphne (22.13.1–3) and the unfavourable reply of the Sibylline Books when they were consulted about Julian's plans (23.1.7).

Cumana carmina consumpserat magnitudo flammarum Since the time of Augustus the Sibylline books were kept in the pedestal of Apollo's statue in his temple; Suet. *Aug.* 31.1. For the indicative in the apodosis of an unreal condition see the notes ad 14.3.2 and 22.10.4.

Post quae ita digesta The only close parallel for this transition formula is 15.5.22 *post haec ita digesta*.

3.4

agmina et commeatus... disponenti imperatori procursatorum adventu... indicatur The Teubner text is a combination of conjectures by Lindenbrog (*disponenti* for V's *disponendi*) and Petschenig (*imperatori procursatorum* for V's *perparo cursatorum*). Fontaine conjectured *propere procursatorum*, which is paleographically superior. He takes the adverb, however, with *indicatur*, which seems otiose next to *anhelantium etiam tum*. If taken with *disponenti* it is in accordance with Amm.'s repeated remarks about Julian's swift and decisive actions, e.g. 22.2.2 *motis propere signis* and 23.2.7 *propere signa commovit*.

Julian both issues the battle orders and takes care that there wil be sufficient supplies along the march route. Such precautions were essential. As Vegetius remarks in his chapter on the *commeatus* (*mil*. 3.3): *saepius... penuria quam pugna consumit exercitum et ferro saevior fames est*. He also stresses the necessity to keep the *commeatus* in safe places: *in opportunis ad rem gerendam ac munitissimis locis amplior semper modus quam sufficit adgregetur*. Once Julian's army was in enemy territory, the Persians practiced a scorched-earth policy with disastrous results: 25.2.1 *commeatibus nos destitutos inedia cruciabat iam non ferenda*. The *agmina* are smaller separate units of the army, as in 17.13.6 *in agmina plurima clam distributo exercitu* and 17.13.28 *in agmina nobilium legionum*.

The *procursatores* were units of light cavalry; 24.1.10, 24.3.1, 24.5.5. Amm. also uses *excursatores* (24.1.2) and *proculcatores* (27.10.10) for these army units. It appears from Amm.'s work that their duties included gathering tactical intelligence (16.12.8 with note, 25.8.4, 27.10.8, 31.12.3) as well as some fighting (24.3.1, 24.5.5). See Austin, 1979, 125–7. Lee, 1993, 171 suggests that if one takes *speculationes* to be the reports of *speculatores*, then Amm. sometimes uses this term for people who undertake work of a tactical, scouting nature (e.g. 14.2.15, 27.2.2).

anhelantium etiamtum The verb *anhelare* and the adjective *anhelus* are found in Amm. with the connotation of haste, as here and in 16.12.59 *statim anhelo cursu cohors... secuta*, distress, as in 16.5.14 *anhelantibus extrema paenuria Galliis* and, in combination with *altius* or *celsius,* pride, as in 15.5.27 *anhelantem celsius*.

indicatur equestres hostium turmas... avertisse subito praedas The word *turma* – with or without *equestris* or *equitum* – usually has, like in this passage, the meaning of cavalry unit in Amm. (e.g. 15.4.10, 18.6.16, 21.6.6 q.v.), but it can also have the more general meaning of unit or group (15.4.9, 18.9.3, 19.2.2, 26.8.5, 27.1.4, 29.1.3, 31.13.5). From Varro, *L* 5.91, it may be concluded that the *turma* originated in early Roman times as part of the Roman army; Varro speaks of a unit of 30 men: *Turma terima (E in U abiit), quod ter deni equites ex tribus tribubus Titiensium, Ramnium, Lucerum fiebant*; cf. Plb. 6.25.1–2. Veg. *mil.* 2.14 reports that a *turma* consisted of 32 men, commanded by a *decurio*: *Quemadmodum inter pedites centuria vel manipulus appellatur, ita inter equites turma dicitur; et habet una turma equites XXXII. Huic qui praeest decurio nominatur.* Apparently *turmae* could also consist of many more men in the late Roman army; Amm. 18.8.2 mentions c. 350 (*duarum turmarum equites circiter septingenti*). These larger units were commanded by *tribuni*; 16.11.6, 16.12.39, 21.11.2, 24.3.1–2. As to the Persian raid Zos. 3.12.4 differs from Amm.'s report; according to Zosimus Julian realised that the invaders were not Persian cavalry but merely robbers: μαθὼν δὲ ὁ βασιλεὺς λῃστὰς εἶναι μᾶλλον, οἳ διαρπάσαντες τὰ ἐν ποσὶν ἀνεχώρησαν.

vicino limite quodam perrupto The same expression is found in 17.13.1 *tempus aptissimum nancti limitem perrupere Romanum*. *Limes* refers either to the actual borderline, as in 14.8.5 *Orientis vero limes... ab Euphratis fluminis ripis ad usque supercilia porrigitur Nili*, or to border territory, for which compare e.g. 23.6.55 *proximos his limites possident Bactriani*. The singular and the addition of *quodam* 'at a certain point' would seem to favour the former meaning. For a full discussion of the term *limes* in Amm. and in the other ancient sources see Isaac, 1988 and 1992², 408–10. In both cases *perrumpere* can be used. For its meaning 'to overrun' see the note ad 21.7.2 *ne Africa absente eo perrumperetur*. *Vicinus* does not necessarily imply that the border was at a short distance, but only that it was nearest to the army of Julian. In fact, from Carrhae it was a long distance to the frontier. The whole of northern Mesopotamia was still Roman territory and at this time the Tigris demarcated the frontier between the Roman and Sasanian empires; see Dillemann, 1962, 211–6 and esp. fig. XXIX. There were various strongholds at strategic places on the Roman side of the Tigris. These strongholds were connected to one another by roads. This system of defense – commonly referred to as defense-in-depth – was initiated by Diocletian (cf. also 23.5.2) and extended by Constantine; see Poidebard, 1934; Luttwak, 1978², ch. 3. Cf. now Isaac, 1992², ch. IX ('Frontier Policy – Grand Strategy?') for a critical approach to the theory of defense-in-depth and Nicasie, 1997, 117–84. Possibly the Persian cavalry unit attacked one of these strongholds.

cuius atrocitate mali perculsus This is strong language, used elsewhere by Amm. for the report of a revolt, cf. 21.13.7 and 26.7.13. Zosimus 3.12.4 has a comparable phrase: καὶ συνταραχθῆναι μὲν ἐκ τούτου τῷ στρατοπέδῳ συνέβη. 3.5

ilico, ut ante cogitaverat In Amm.'s version of the events, the army corps under Procopius and Sebastianus was not sent as a defensive measure against the enemy attack reported above, but as part of Julian's plan of campaign. *Ilico* emphasizes that the marching orders had been dispatched with haste because of this incident. Julian had already planned the division of his forces as part of his strategy for a combined attack on Persia from both the Tigris and the Euphrates; cf. Lib. *Or.* 18.214, Ridley, 1973, 318–9; Austin, 1979, 94–6; Matthews 138–9; see also the note ad 23.3.1. The intention of Julian's strategy was to occupy Sapor in northern Mesopotamia in order that the main force should reach Ctesiphon quickly and without opposition. Malalas, *Chron.* 13.331, relates that Sapor realised only later that he had been misled. Zos.

3.12.4 also reports that the division of the army was meant to protect the regions near the Tigris. In his account of Julian's campaign, Amm. has very little to say about the army commanded by Procopius and Sebastianus.

triginta milia lectorum militum   The sources are not unanimous as to the number of Procopius' and Sebastianus' force; Lib. *Or.* 18.214 and Soz. *HE* 6.1.2: 20.000; Malalas, *Chron.* 13.329: 16.000; Zos. 3.12.5: 18.000. Brok, 1959, 252 believes that the number given by Amm. may well be right; Paschoud n. 34 thinks that 20.000 is a more likely number. As to the total number of Julian's army Eutr. 10.16.1 speaks of *ingenti apparatu*; cf. Ruf. Fest. 28. Only two sources provide more exact information. Joh. Lyd. *Mens.* 4.118 mentions 170.000, but that number is generally considered too high. Zos. 3.13.1, in describing Julian's inspection of his troops (on this see the note ad 23.3.2 *ibi moratus aliquot dies*) mentions the number of 65.000: ἦσαν δὲ ἅπαντες ἄνδρες πεντακισχίλιοι καὶ ἑξακισμύριοι. It is probable that the troops under the command of Procopius and Sebastianus are not included in this number, which means that at least 16.000 men (Malalas' number) or the 18.000 given by Zosimus, and probably even more, have to be added to the 65.000. It is also known that c. 20.000 men were employed in the fleet (24.7.4). This leads to the conclusion that Julian's total army numbered more than 100.000 men. See for a full discussion of the size of Julian's army: Brok, 1959, 251–2 and Paschoud n. 34.

eidem commisit Procopio   For the anaphoric use of *idem* see the note ad 20.4.5. On Procopius see the note ad 23.3.2.

ad parilem potestatem   There is a note on *parilis* ad 20.7.11. It was not a happy decision of Julian's to divide the command between Procopius, who had thus far only performed civil duties, and Sebastianus, who was a military man, since the cooperation between the two men left much to be desired; Lib. *Or.* 18.260: καὶ ἅμα ἡ τῶν ἡγεμόνων πρὸς ἀλλήλους φιλονεικία ῥαθυμεῖν τοῖς ἀρχομένοις ἐπέτρεπεν. ὁπότε γὰρ ἅτερος κινοίη, μένειν ἅτερος παραινῶν χαριζόμενος ἔπειθεν.

Sebastiano comite ex duce Aegypti   For Sebastianus, see *PLRE* I, Sebastianus 2. He was *dux Aegypti* between 356–8 (for this function see the note ad 22.16.6). He supported George, bishop of Alexandria, against the adherents of Athanasius and expelled them from the churches; *Hist. Aceph.* 6. He was called a Manichee; e.g. Athan. *Hist. Ar.* 59 (τὸν δοῦκα Σεβαστιανὸν Μανιχαῖον ὄντα καὶ ἀσελγῆ νεώτερον), Socr. *HE* 2.28.6, Thdt. *HE* 2.13–4. He was *comes rei militaris* in 363–8; see 25.8.7, 25.8.16, 26.6.2; Zos. 3.12.5, 4.4.2; Lib. *Or.* 18.214, 260; see for the title of *comes* the note ad 20.4.18. Sebastianus assisted Valentinian I in his campaign against the Alamanni; 27.10.6.

In 375 he accompanied Merobaudes on his expedition against the Quadi (30.5.13: *comite adiuncto Sebastiano*). However, Merobaudes dismissed him on receiving news of Valentinian's death because of Sebastianus' popularity with the soldiers: *Sebastianum principis adhuc ignorantem excessum, longius amendavit, quietum quidem virum et placidum sed militari favore sublatum, ideo maxime tunc cavendum* (30.10.3). In 378 Valens appointed him *magister peditum* and as such he fought in Thrace against the Goths: 31.11.1 ff., Zos. 4.23.1 f., Eun. fr. 44 (Blockley). He was killed at Adrianople: *In hac multiplici virorum illustrium clade Traiani mors eminuit et Sebastiani* (31.13.18). He was an outstanding general (31.11.1: *Sebastiano... vigilantiae notae ductori*). He was not only known for his military qualities but also for his contempt of wealth; Eun. fr. 44 (Blockley).

ut intra Tigridem interim agerent Procopius and Sebastianus are ordered to guard the west bank of the Tigris for the time being (*interim*; cf. the note ad 22.15.21), i.e. until they will have joined forces with Arsaces.

vigilanter omnia servaturi The verb is used with the meaning 'to keep under observation' (OLD 2), as in 18.2.14 *qui pontem ne strueretur studio servabant intento*.

ex incauto latere Amm. uses *incautus* both with active force ('off one's guard': *incautum rectorem* (equi) *praecipitem agere*, 16.12.22) and passively ('unguarded': *invasere Lugdunum incautam*, 16.11.4).

mandabatque According to Zos. 3.12.4 the assignment was only to guard the Tigris districts. In 4.4.2, however, Zosimus' report is more in line with that of Ammianus: τούτῳ (sc. Προκοπίῳ) γὰρ Ἰουλιανὸς... ἐκέλευσεν ἅμα Σευαστιανῷ διὰ τῆς Ἀδιαβηνῆς χωροῦντι ἀπαντῆσαί οἱ δι' ἑτέρας ὁδοῦ κατὰ τῶν πολεμίων ἰόντι. Lib. *Or.* 18.214 tells us that the army under Procopius and Sebastianus was to cover the Tigris area and to support Julian if he summoned them, should the occasion demand it. Neither Zosimus nor Libanius mention Arsaces in this respect, although Lib. *Or.* 18.215 reports that the Armenians had to perform similar duties as commisioned to Procopius and Sebastianus.

si fieri potius posset No real parallel can be found for this use of *potius* in Amm., nor indeed in the TLL or in the lengthy article on *potius* in Handius, 1829–45, t. 4, 512–9. Translators vary in their attempts to render it. Seyfarth writes "so schnell wie möglich", Rolfe "if it could be done to greater advantage". For an interpretation we may take as a starting point the elliptical use of *potius* "ut vergat hic illic in notionem q.e. potissimum, praecipue, e.g. Amm." (TLL X 2 350.6–30), as in 20.11.3 *inter quas illud potius excellebat, quod* and 26.6.17 *ea re potius incitante, quod*. In the present phrase *potius* might emphasize the desirability of the envisaged encounter with Arsaces' forces and could be translated 'if it was in any way possible'.

Arsaci See the note ad 23.2.2.

Corduenam Corduene was situated east of the Tigris; its northern border was the river Centrites (modern Buhtan); see Dillemann, 1962, fig. IV. It is more or less identical with modern Kurdistan (see the extensive note ad 18.6.20). It belonged to the five *regiones Transtigritanae* which in 298/9 (Barnes, 1982, 63) were brought under Roman supremacy by Galerius, but not incorporated as provinces into the Roman Empire. The regions had to be returned by Jovian in 363: *Petebat autem rex... sua dudum a Maximiano erepta... quinque regiones Transtigritanas: Arzanenam et Moxoenam et Zabdicenam itidemque Rehimenam et Corduenam* (25.7.9); see for the *regiones Transtigritanae*, Dillemann, 1962, 210 ff.; Blockley, 1984; Winter, 1989 and the note ad 21.6.7. Amm. knew the region personally since he visited it in 359 (18.6.20); for Ammianus on the North-East frontier, see Matthews 48–57. At that time Corduene was no longer part of the Roman territory: *Erat eo tempore satrapa Corduenae, quae obtemperabat potestati Persarum, Iovinianus nomine appellatus in solo Romano, adolescens nobiscum occulte sentiens* (18.6.20). However, during Julian's reign the region was again under Roman domination: *Corduenae, uberis regionis et nostrae* (25.7.8; see also 25.7.9). When Julian realised that his campaign against Persia would not be successful, he decided to return by way of Corduene (24.8.4–5).

Moxoenam Like Corduene it was one of the five *regiones Transtigritanae*. In 298/9 it came under Roman domination but was lost again in 363 (25.7.9). It was situated north of Corduene of which it originally may have been a part; see Schachermeyr, 1935 and Dillemann, 1962, fig. IV. It was not situated in Armenia, as Rolfe thinks.

Chiliocomo uberi Mediae tractu Chiliocomum ('thousand villages') near Corduene (24.8.4: *Chiliocomum prope Corduenam situm*) was Persian territory. As to its precise location opinions differ; cf. Tomaschek, 1899, TLL, s.v., Brok, 1959, 59 and Seyfarth n. 23 in his bilingual edition, but Dillemann, 1962, 300–2 (see also Fontaine n. 58) rather convincingly argues that Chiliocomum was part of Media Atropatene and may be identified with the plain of Salmas, just north of Lake Ulmia. It should not be confused with τὸ Χιλιόκωμον καλούμενον πεδίον mentioned by Strabo 12.3.39 (516C); this Chiliocomum was situated near Amaseia.

praestricto cursu 'In a lightning attack', a unique phrase according to TLL X 2.943.24–9. There are notes on *praestringere* ad 14.7.10, 20.3.4 and 21.7.2.

vastatis It was in fact Arsaces who devastated Chiliocomum: *homo (sc. Arsaces), qui Chiliocomum mandatu vastaverat principis* (25.7.12).

apud Assyrios Cf. the note ad 23.2.7.

sibi concurrerent The forces of Procopius, Sebastianus and Arsaces never reached Ctesiphon, although they were expected there: *nec adminicula, quae praestolabamur, cum Arsace et nostris ducibus apparebant ob causas...praedictas* (24.7.8); *quidam arbitrabantur Arsacen ac duces adventare iam nostros rumoribus percitos, quod imperator Ctesiphonta magnis viribus oppugnaret* (24.8.6). As to the *causas praedictas*, Amm. had probably mentioned them in a lost passage in 24.7.2. Lib. *Or.* 18.260 gives as reasons 1. treason of Arsaces, 2. Roman soldiers fighting natives instead of the Persian army, 3. rivalry between Procopius and Sebastianus. However, Brok, 1959, 165 is probably right in seeing the real reason for their not reaching Ctesiphon in the relative weakness of the army in combination with the fact that Sapor lingered on in the Tigris area.

necessitatum articulis affuturi 'At the crucial moment', see the note ad 20.11.22 on both *necessitas* and *articulus*.

exitu simulato None of the other sources mentions this strategic trick. It is possible that Lib. *Ep.* 1402.2 refers to it: ὡς γὰρ ἐνέβαλε βασιλεὺς ἅμα ἦρι, ἢ οὐκ ᾤοντο. The fact that Julian had ordered supplies to be prepared for the route along the Tigris (*quod iter etiam re cibaria de industria iusserat instrui*), is another argument in favour of the conclusion that the emperor intended a two-way attack on Persia; see also the notes ad 23.3.1 and 23.3.5.

3.6

quod iter etiam re cibaria de industria iusserat instrui On *res cibaria* see the note ad 20.11.4. Rolfe's translation of this sentence ("an expedition for which he had also ordered supplies to be carefully prepared") does not do justice to *de industria*, which means that Julian, as part of his plan to mislead the enemy, had even 'deliberately' built up these corn supplies.

flexit dextrorsus Instead of following the route along the Tigris, Julian went from Carrhae southwards, marching along the river Belias (modern Balikh) to Callinicum. The distance from Carrhae to Callinicum is c. 100 km. The route followed by Julian was the so-called Parthian Royal Road, which was already described at the beginning of our era by Isidorus of Charax (*GGM* I, 246–7); see also Poidebard, 1934, carte 1 and Dillemann, 1962, 178–9. Zos.

3.13.1 mentions that there were fortifications along this route. These are not mentioned by Amm., but this does not mean that there were no Roman forts there in his time; Millar, 1993, 181.

quieta nocte emensa The adjective indicates that it was a night without bad dreams, such as he had at Carrhae (23.3.3). On the passive use of the ptc. *emensus* see the note ad 22.13.3.

iumentum, quo veheretur, ex usu poposcit 'His horse' or 'a horse'? The former is a priori more likely, and *ex usu* certainly goes with *poposcit*. In that case, the subjunctive is best taken in a frequentative sense. Some examples of this use in relative clauses are given in Ehrismann 170, but they are not strictly parallel to the present phrase, as they are without exception introduced by *quisquis, quicumque* and have therefore generalizing force. If this is what Amm. meant, the absence of any attribute to make clear that this was the horse the emperor always rode on is rather odd. Alternatively, the relative clause may have a final meaning, in which case it would suggest that the emperor was given a horse for that particular day. The vagueness on this point may betray that the story is made up for the sake of adding another *omen*. The fact that a horse is involved in this and other *omina* (cf. 23.5.13 *cum bellatoriis iumentis* with the note ad loc.) is one of the reasons for Meulder to see in Julian a specimen of the genus of the 'impious warrior': "Pour nous, le portrait de Julien l'Apostat que trace Ammien Marcellin, du moins dans la guerre contre les Parthes [sic!] ... relèverait en très grande partie de celui que l'idéologie politico-religieuse dresse du Guerrier Impie" (Meulder, 1991, 458). For those who do not adhere to the theories of Dumézil, Meulder's article has little to offer. However, it does comprise some interesting observations. Meulder on p. 462 for instance rightly points to the fact that Amm.'s Julian in 22.1.2 had been able to predict the death of Constantius because of an *omen* (incidentally, in this case too a horse was involved: *lapso milite, qui se insessurum equo dextra manu erexit, humique prostrato*; but see the note ad 23.5.13), while in the present text he fails to draw the correct conclusion as regards his own death from a similar *omen*.

equus Babylonius nomine Toynbee, 1973, 179 gives a list of horses' names taken from cities, countries etc. like *Corinthus, Euphrates, Macedo, Gallus*.

ictu torminis consternatus The normal term used for a colic is *tormina*; hence Bentley's *torminum*. The singular is exceedingly rare. V's *tormini* slightly favours *torminis*. Julian's horse suffered a griping of the bowels, a colic; cf. e.g. Cels. 4.22.1 (*intestinorum mala tormina esse consueverunt*); Cato *R.R.* 156.5, 157.9; Cic. *Tusc.* 2.45 (Rolfe's translation that the horse 'was laid low by a missile from the artillery' is incorrect). Seyfarth seems to be unduly credulous in saying that this story "beweist, dass Ammians Hauptquelle in unmittelbarer Nähe des Kaisers zu suchen ist." Amm.'s addiction to *omina*, especially in this part of his narrative, and the fact that the name of the horse is altogether too apt, call for scepticism.

auro lapillisque ornamenta distincta conspersit Such breastplates or *phalerae* are mentioned by App. *Mith*. 115 as belonging to the treasure of Mithridates: ἵππων χαλινοὶ καὶ προστερνίδια καὶ ἐπωμίδια, πάντα ὁμοίως διάλιθα καὶ κατάχρυσα. According to TLL IV 494.73–5 *conspergere* is here the equivalent of *dispergere; erat enim arduum sequi per diversa conspersos* (17.13.19) is quoted as a parallel. Cf. also 30.1.22 about a guest murdered at the table of his host: *peregrinus cruor in ambitiosa lintea conspersus*. On the other hand, in 23.4.15 it is said of a fire-dart that *aquis... conspersa acriores excitat aestus incendiorum*, where *conspergere* means 'to pour upon'. In the absence of a complement in the ablative it seems best to accept the former meaning 'to scatter'.

quo ostento laetior exclamavit Another example of Julian's alertness to turn bad *omina* into positive signs; see also 21.2.2, 22.1.2 and the notes ad loc. Plut. *Crass*. 19.8 relates a similar story about Crassus. When during his ill-fated Parthian campaign a victim's entrails were given to him, they fell out of his hands, whereupon he reacted: 'Τοιοῦτον', ἔφη, 'τὸ γῆρας; ἀλλὰ τῶν γ' ὅπλων οὐδὲν ἂν ἐκφύγοι τὰς χεῖρας'.
Fontaine in n. 60 defends the reading of V *extento*, comparing 23.5.6 *apparitoris cuiusdam cadaver extentum*. There, however, *extentus* is used of a dead man stretched out at the side of the road. The word does not fit a horse rolling on the ground in pain.

Babylona Babylon stands of course for the Persian empire (see for the town of Babylon the note ad 23.6.23). Although coins, medaillons, diptycha and plates show emperors' horses which are richly adorned (see e.g. MacCormack, 1981, Pls. 16, 22, 23, 51 and Weitzmann, 1979, 34, 43, 45, 61, 63), here the mentioning of a horse adorned with gold and precious stones may have a symbolic meaning and refer to the proverbial wealth of the Persians.

paulisper detentus, ut omen per hostias litando firmaret On the different 3.7
grammatical constructions of *litare* see the note ad 22.9.8. For *omen firmare* cf. Cic. *div*. 1.106, where the favourable omen of an eagle is said to be confirmed by thunder: *sic aquilae clarum firmavit Iuppiter omen*. See Pease ad loc., who remarks ad 1.97 *congruebant*: "The practice of verifying the truth of one form of prediction by its agreement with that of another seems to have been not infrequent", quoting a number of parallels from Greek and Latin authors, to which may be added Verg. *A*. 2.691 (Anchises prays for

confirmation of an *omen oblativum*, the tongue of fire above Iulus' head, by an *omen impetrativum): da deinde auxilium, pater, atque haec omina firma.* Servius remarks ad loc. *secundum Romanum morem petit ut visa firmentur. non enim unum augurium vidisse sufficit, nisi confirmetur ex simili.*

Davanam... unde ortus Belias fluvius The location of Davana is not clear yet but it can only have been a day's march (c. 30 km.) north of Callinicum where the army arrived on the day it left Davana. In the past modern Ras-el-Ain-el-Khalil and Karayer have been suggested as the sites of ancient Davana, but the first is some 70 km. and the latter some 50 km. remote from Callinicum; they have therefore been rejected by Brok, 1959, 60–1. Dillemann, 1962, 168 n. 2 and carte xxiii (p. 178) suggests situating Davana near Aïn-el-Arous, a suggestion with which Fontaine n. 61 agrees. The suggestion is attractive since (as Amm. notes) the Belias had its source here; against it speaks the fact that Aïn-el-Arous is far more than a day's march away from Callinicum and the observation of Brok, 1959, 60–1 that the Belias had many sources.
The river Belias is the modern Balikh; Isidorus of Charax (*GGM* I, 246) calls it Βίληχα and Plut. *Crass.* 23.4 Βασιλισσός. Poidebard, 1934, 129 f.; Dillemann, 1962, 177–9. Near Callinicum the Belias joins the Euphrates. See for the course of the river Dillemann, 1962, fig. xxiii (p. 178).

castra praesidiaria See De Jonge ad 18.7.10. *Castra praesidiaria* were garrisoned fortifications in the border districts; also mentioned in 28.2.4, 28.3.7, 29.6.2.

corporibus cibo curatis et quiete Cf. 21.12.5 *curatis utrubique cibo somnoque corporibus* with the note.

Callinicum Formerly called Nicephorium. According to Plin. *Nat.* 6.119 and Isid. Char. (*GGM* I, 247) it was founded by Alexander the Great. App. *Syr.* 57 mentions Seleucus I Nicator as its founder. Although it seems obvious to suppose that the place was named after Seleucus II Callinicus, Lib. *Ep.* 21 reports that during the reign of Gallienus (260–8) the town received the name Callinicus after the sophist Callinicus Sutorius: σταθμός τίς ἐστι περὶ τὸν Εὐφράτην, Καλλίνικος ὄνομα αὐτῷ. Καλλινίκου γὰρ ἐνταῦθα ἀποσφαγέντος ὁ σοφιστὴς γίνεται προσηγορία τῷ τόπῳ. Libanius also mentions that Callinicum had a standing garrison (*Ep.* 21: τοῦτο δὴ τὸ χωρίον ἔχει στρατιὰν ἱδρυμένην). The place is to be located near modern Al Raqqah; see Weidner, 1937 and Al-Khalaf-Kohlmeyer, 1985. The town is also known because of the so-called Callinicum affair in 388. In that year a Christian gang, led by the bishop, destroyed Callinicum's synagogue; the violence was brought to the notice of the emperor (Theodosius I), who gave orders to have the synagogue repaired at the cost of the bishop. This order induced Ambrose to write his famous *epist.* 40, in which he i.a. argued that the bishop would betray his faith if he was forced to rebuild the synagogue.

munimentum robustum et commercandi opimitate gratissimum 'Strong and very attractive on account of its well-stocked market'. This is the only instance of *robustus* in connection with a town in the *Res Gestae*. Elsewhere it is found of human qualities (e.g. 15.8.14 *robusta constantia*, 16.12.9, 29.1.36) and physical strength 16.12.47 *Alamanni robusti et celsiores*, 20.6.5, 23.4.4, 23.6.85, 26.8.8, 26.9.1 and 31.7.12). Amm. uses the otherwise rare *opimitas* (TLL IX 2.707.84–708.1) in 24.3.4 about the Persians (*opimitas gentis*) and in 16.11.9 (q.v.), 17.2.1 and 19.11.2 in connection with *praedarum*.
Callinicum was one of the towns where goods were traded between Romans and Persians, like for instance Batnae (14.3.3). A law from the year 408/9 specifies Callinicum as one of the three places – the others are Nisibis and Artaxata – where Roman and Persian merchants were permitted to conduct business; *Cod. Iust.* 4.63.4. See also Lee, 1993, 61 ff.

diem sextum kalendas, quo Romae Matri deorum pompae celebrantur annales Lindenbrog thought it necessary to add *Apriles*. It is true that Amm. always supplies the name of the month after *Kalendae*, *Nonae* and *Idus*, but since the date is unambiguous after *quartum decimum kalendas Apriles* in section 3, and every reader knows that the festival of Cybele fell in March, the text may be left as it stands (as was already argued by J. Rougé in *REL* 56 (1978) 471). It is remarkable that Amm. draws attention to the festivities in honour of the Mother of the gods at Rome. In this narrative of the Persian campaign it would have been quite sufficient to mention Julian's celebration of the Cybele festival as proof of his devotion to this goddess, if proof were needed in the case of the author of Εἰς τὴν μητέρα τῶν θεῶν (Jul. *Or.* 8). See for this aspect of Julian's religious beliefs the notes ad 22.9.5–6 and Smith, 1995, 177–8. The present tense *celebrantur* also deserves attention. It confirms what we know from other sources, both literary and epigraphical, about the vitality of the Cybele cult in aristocratic circles in the capital during the second half of the fourth century (Bloch, 1960, 204–6; Matthews, 1973; Thomas, 1984, 1533–4; Chuvin, 1990, 222–8; Thrams, 1992, 74–87). In the *Phrygianum* on the Vatican hill, the centre of the cult of Mater Magna and Attis, a number of inscriptions have been found recording the initiation into the mysteries of Cybele of members of the senatorial aristocracy (Vermaseren, 1977).
Amm.'s reference to the cult of Cybele is therefore of topical interest, the more so if one takes into account that the cult of Cybele flourished again and for the last time during the usurpation of Eugenius (392–4), provided that Mommsen's interpretation of the *Carmen contra paganos* as referring to the events of those years is correct (it is upheld by Matthews, 1970; for an alternative dating see Cracco Ruggini, 1979). In that poem (*Anth. Lat.* I 1

Shackleton-Bailey, 103–9) the unnamed *praefectus* and other aristocrats are ridiculed for their participation in the rites of Cybele and mention is made of the chariot of Cybele, the procession of the sacred tree through the city of Rome, and Attis, whose resurrection symbolizes the beginning of spring after the vernal equinox.

After the defeat of Eugenius in 394 the anti-pagan legislation of Theodosius ended the public cult of the Mater Magna. All privileges granted to pagan priests were withdrawn in *Cod. Theod.* 16.10.14. *Cod. Theod.* 16.10.20 of A.D. 415 specifically orders the confiscation of land and other belongings of among others the priests of Cybele, the Dendrophori.

The appeal and the tenacity of the cult is evident from the number and vehemence of the attacks by Christian authors on the Great Mother, *mater daemoniorum*, as she is called in Hier. *adv. Iovin.* 2.17. See e.g. Ambr. *epist.* 18.30; Prud. *Perist.* 10.153 ff., 1006 ff., 1061 ff.; Arnob. *c. Gent.* 7.49; August. *C.D.* 2.4 (Graillot, 1912, 534–60). As he had done earlier, e.g. in his digressions on *divinatio* (21.1.7–14), the *genius* (21.14.5–5) and Egypt (22.15 and 16) in a seemingly innocuous and matter-of-fact aside, Amm. draws attention to the continuing existence of pagan cults and beliefs despite the legislation of the emperor Theodosius, during whose reign he wrote his *Res Gestae*.

carpentum, quo vehitur simulacrum, Almonis undis ablui perhibetur A fine description of the procession from the Palatine to the rivulet (*cursu brevissimus*, Ov. *Met.* 14.329) on the Via Appia is given by Graillot, 1912, 139–40, who quotes a long list of testimonia on p. 137 n. 5 for the ritual cleansing of the *carpentum* itself as well as the idols and the knives used by the *Galli*. The *carpentum* was a two-wheeled carriage drawn by two horses or mules; it could have a (removable) top of either canvas or leather. See Mau, 1899. For a picture: Daremberg-Saglio I, 927. See also the note ad 17.10.9. *Perhibetur* seems to imply that Amm. had not himself attended the ceremony. The verb is rare in Amm. Apart from 24.6.15, where it is used actively, it occurs only in 23.6.10 *Persicum... mare, cuius ostia... esse perhibentur angusta*.

sacrorum sollemnitate prisco more completa March 27th (*diem sextum kalendas*) was the last day of the great week (22–27 March) of festivities in honour of Cybele/Magna Mater, which were celebrated in Rome. On this day the so-called *Lavatio* took place, the ritual washing of the goddess' image in the Almo. It cannot be ruled out that a formal *Lavatio* took place at Callinicum, as Fontaine believes: "Le passage invite à supposer l'existence d'un sanctuaire de la Grand Mère dans la ville de Callinicum", n. 65. Graillot, 1912, 137 n. 5 mentions *lavationes* in Carthage (August. *C.D.* 2.4), Autun (Greg. Tur. *glor. conf.* 76) and Ancyra (*Passio S. Theodoti, BHG*^{3}, 1782). Indeed, *prisco more* following the reference to the *lavatio* at Rome would suggest that the complete ritual took place at Callinicum. Brok, 1959, 62 interprets *prisco more* as a reference to the *mysteries* of Cybele/Magna Mater into which Julian had been initiated.

exsultans pernoctavit et laetus Julian shares the festive mood that used to attend the *lavatio*. There could have been no preparation more apt for the Persian campaign than this festival of Mater Magna, to whom Julian had prayed at the end of his hymn (*Or.* 8.20, 180 b): ἐμοὶ δὲ (δίδου)... πάντων ἔργων, οἷς προσερχόμεθα περὶ τὰς πολιτικὰς καὶ στρατιωτικὰς τάξεις ἀρέτην μετὰ τῆς Ἀγαθῆς Τύχης.

profectus exinde per supercilia riparum fluvialium On *supercilia* to denote 3.8 the banks of a river see the note ad 22.8.8. From Callinicum Julian and his army marched to Cercusium (Zos. 3.13.1: Καλλινίχον, κἀκεῖθεν ἐλθὼν ἐπὶ τὸ Κιρχήσιον), a distance of approximately 165 km., where they arrived *principio mensis Aprilis* (23.5.1, and the notes ad loc.). They followed the route along the left bank of the Euphrates which was part of the fortified road system of the frontier district and was, in fact, the old Parthian Royal Road; Poidebard, 1934, 88–90 and carte I. The route is described by Isid. Char. 3 (*GGM* I, 246–7) and Ptol. 5.18.6. Contrary to Amm., Isidorus and Ptolemy mention various *stationes* along the route. Amm. does not inform us as to how Julian's army crossed the Belias/Balikh. One can only imagine that this was done by way of a bridge of boats as suggested by Brok, 1959, 63 and Fontaine n. 66.

aquis adolescentibus undique convenis Cf. 22.8.40 about the Borysthenes *concursuque multorum amnium adolescens* with the note ad loc. Amm. probably means to say that the volume of water in the Euphrates had been increased by a number of tributaries and that the high water level forced the army to follow the *supercilia*.

cum armigera gradiens manu As in 24.3.2 the *armigera manus* is Amm.'s term for the imperial *cohors*. Individual members of the guard are called *armigeri*, as in 24.5.6 *vulnerato armigero, qui lateri eius haerebat*. Cf. also 27.5.9, 31.10.3, 31.10.21 and 31.13.8. *Armiger* is already found in this sense in Suet. *Aug.* 49.1 *dimissa...Germanorum* (manu)*, quam usque ad cladem Varianam inter armigeros circa se habuerat.*

in statione quadam sub pellibus mansit 'Under canvas' (OLD 2d). See the note ad 20.6.9. This is the only time that Amm. mentions a *statio* on the route from Callinicum to Cercusium. However, the reference is so vague that it cannot be determined where this *statio* is to be located.

Saracenarum reguli gentium Although Amm. had said in 23.2.1 that Julian refused the help of non-Roman troops (but see the note ad loc.), he seems to correct himself here. The Saracens' experience with guerilla warfare (*ut ad furta bellorum appositi*) made them very useful auxiliaries. As to their activities in Julian's army, see e.g. 24.1.10. Saracens did not only fight at the Roman side but also in the Persian army. As appears from 25.6.10 they offered their help to the highest bidder. From the Saracens on the Persian side the Romans experienced a lot of difficulties; 25.1.3, 25.6.8–10, 25.8.1; Zos. 3.27.1. For the Saracens in general, see the note ad 22.15.2.

genibus supplices nixi This seems to be a standard element in descriptions of foreign kings offering homage to the Roman emperor (or his representative), cf. 17.10.3 q.v. (the Alamannic king Suomarius) *pacem genibus curvatis oravit* and 17.12.10 (Zizais, prince of the Quadi) *iussusque exsurgere genibus nixus... concessionem delictorum sibi tribui supplicavit*.

oblata ex auro corona According to Mommsen, 1889, 219 Amm. means the *annua sollemnia*; cf. 22.7.10 and the note ad loc., as well as *Cod. Theod.* 12.13.6 (14 June 387): *secundum consuetudinem moris antiqui omnes satrapae pro devotione, quae Romano debetur imperio, coronam ex propriis facultatibus faciant serenitati nostrae sollemniter offerendam*.

tamquam mundi nationumque suarum dominum adorarunt suscepti gratanter For *adorare* to denote the προσκύνησις see TLL I 820.18–30. In 15.5.18 Amm. names Diocletian as the first Roman emperor to introduce this ritual. It is also mentioned in 15.5.27, 21.6.2 (q.v.), 21.9.8 and 22.9.16. Its history is described in Alföldi, 1980³, 45–59. The sentence as a whole is a clear illustration of Amm.'s tendency to accumulate participle constructions, for which cf. Blomgren 61, Szantyr 738 and Den Boeft, 1992, 14. *Suscepti*, following the main verb, is best taken as an expression of attendant circumstance, not referring to a state of affairs preceding the action of the main verb, but preceding the moment of writing, just as *iuncto ad parilem potestatem Sebastiano* in section 5 does not precede *commisit*. There are parallels for this use in Tacitus, e.g. *Hist.* 4.34.2 *ostentati* (sunt) *etiam captivi, ex quibus unus, egregium facinus ausus clara voce gesta patefecit, confossus ilico a Germanis* and *Ann.* 6.3.3 *hoc pretium Gallio meditatae adulationis tulit, statim curia, deinde Italia exactus*. See Koestermann's note ad loc., who calls this an "aoristisches PPP." More examples are to be found in Weissenborn-Müller ad Liv. 21.1.5 and Kühner-Stegmann II 759.

ad furta bellorum appositi For this term indicating guerilla warfare cf. 16.11.4 *Laeti barbari ad tempestiva furta sollertes* and 31.16.5 (Saracenorum cuneus) *ad furta magis expeditionalium rerum quam ad concursatorias habiles pugnas*.

dumque hos alloquitur... classis advenit According to Amm. the fleet and the army met before reaching Cercusium, whereas Zos. 3.13.2 states that the fleet was already at Cercusium when Julian and the army arrived there.

3.9

Xerxis... instar classis Cf. 18.6.23 and 22.8.4 *Abydon* q.v. for other references to Xerxes' army. Its size also serves as a point of reference in 31.4.7. Amm. refers here to the gigantic army and fleet which Xerxes assembled at Doriscus to launch his attack on Greece; Hdt. 7.59 and 7.89–100. Evidently, the comparison is made to underline the power of Julian's force. See for allusions to Xerxes' expedition also 22.8.4 and the note ad loc., as well as 23.6.8. In 18.6.23 Amm. is sceptical about Herodotus' story (*quo usque nobis Doriscum... et agminatim intra consaepta exercitus recensetos, Graecia fabulosa, narrabis?*), whereas in 31.4.7-8 he is not. For *instar* see the note ad 20.3.12 *rerumque magnitudini*.

tribuno Constantiano For tribunes, see the note ad 22.11.2. In the present passage the tribune is a military officer who leads the soldiers in battle (cf. e.g. 15.4.10, 16.12.55, 18.2.11). Nearly every part of the army could be led by a tribune: legions (19.5.3, 19.6.3, 22.3.2, 30.1.7), *auxilia* (16.11.9, 16.12.63, 25.6.3, 27.2.9), *sagittarii* (29.5.4), cavalry (16.11.6, 16.12.39, 21.11.2, 24.3.2, 25.1.8, 25.1.9), *scutarii* (14.11.11, 16.11.6, 17.10.5), *protectores* (18.3.5) and *armaturae* (14.11.21, 15.5.6, 27.2.6). There were also civilian tribunes: *tribunus stabuli* (14.10.8, 20.4.3 q.v., 20.4.5, 26.4.2, 28.2.10) *tribunus et notarius* (17.5.15, 19.9.9, 20.4.2 q.v., 26.6.1, 28.6.12) and *tribunus fabricarum* (14.7.18, 15.9.4, 15.5.9); see further Brok, 1959, 63–4. For Constantianus, see *PLRE* I, Constantianus 1. Zos. 3.13.3 calls him Constantius: κατέστησαν δὲ ναύαρχοι Λουκιανὸς καὶ Κωνστάντιος (note that by using the term ναύαρχοι Zosimus is imprecise as to the different ranks – tribune and comes – of the two men). He is probably the same one as the *tribunus stabuli* and relative of the emperor Valentinian mentioned in 28.2.10 who was killed by brigands in 369: *denique praeter complures alios, quos absumpserunt insidiae tales, Constantianus tribunus stabuli impetu est clandestino exceptus moxque interfectus, Valentiniani affinis, Cerialis et Iustinae germanus*.

comite Lucilliano In Zos. 3.12.1 one Hierius is mentioned as a commander of this fleet; see Paschoud n. 31. For Lucillianus, see *PLRE* I, Lucillianus 2. Zos. 3.13.3 calls him Λουκιανός – as does Malalas (Magnus?), *Chron.* 13.330 – but elsewhere Λουκιλλιανός. He was probably a *comes rei militaris*; Jones 525, 543. Julian sent him ahead with 1500 light-armed scouts during the march from Cercusium to Zaitha and thence to Dura; 24.1.6–8; Zos. 3.14.1 (who alone records that Lucillianus led these troops). According to Malalas, *Chron.* 13.330, these scouts belonged to the brigades of the Lanciarii and the Mattiarii; it seems therefore plausible to consider Lucillianus as the comes of these units. He was sent ahead with 1000 light-armed soldiers to capture the fortress of Anatha; 24.1.6; Zos. 3.14.2–3. Near Pirisabora Julian ordered Lucillianus to cross a canal with his 1500 scouts and to attack the Persians from the rear; 24.2.8, Zos. 3.16.1–17.2. He should not be confused with Lucillianus, the father-in-law of the emperor Jovian (*PLRE* I, Lucillianus 3), who is often mentioned by Amm.

quae latissimum flumen Euphraten artabant This poetic expression is found e.g. in Luc. 9.35 *pelagus victas artasse carinas* and Stat. *Th.* 8.413 *iaculis artatus... aer.* For the Euphrates, see the note ad 23.6.25. The pilgrim Egeria, who in the 380s crossed the Euphrates near Hierapolis, remarks that it is very big, bigger than the Rhône, that it flows very fast and that she had to cross it in a large ship (*Itin. Eger.* 18.2–3).

in qua mille erant onerariae naves ex diversa trabe confectae... quinquaginta aliae bellatrices totidemque ad compaginandos necessariae pontes V has *contectae*, G *contextae*; *confectae* is a conjecture by Mommsen, rightly rejected by Fontaine. The verb *conficere* is rarely used for the building of ships. There is only one instance in TLL IV 199.28–33, from *B. Alex.* 13.4: *quinqueremes v confecerunt.* In view of Tac. *Hist.* 2.34.2 *naves... validis utrimque trabibus conexae* and *Ann.* 15.3.1 *naves... conexas trabibus ac turribus auctas*, it is tempting to read *conexae. Conectere,* however, is used there of boats forming a shipbridge. It is used in a comparable way by Amm. himself in 21.12.9 *navibus valide sibi conexis*, where see the note. The best reading certainly is *contextae* (not in V, as Fontaine has it in note 71). Cf. e.g. 31.5.3 *ratibus... male contextis* and 14.2.10 *innare temere contexti ratibus* and see TLL IV 691.62–76. Veg. *mil.* 4.34 *ex cupresso... et pinu... praecipue liburna contexitur* reads like a commentary on the expression used here by Amm. For *diversa trabe* cf. 29.1.30 *ex diversis metallicis materiis fabrefacta* and see the note ad 21.4.3.
Julian, like Trajan (D.C. 75.9), Septimius Severus (Hdn. 3.9) and, Gordian, if we may believe the Historia Augusta (*Gd* 29.2), used a fleet for the transport of equipment and provisions. The number of vessels of Julian's fleet differs in the various sources. Zos. 3.13.2–3 mentions 600 vessels made of timber, 500 constructed of skins, 50 warships and vessels for making bridges to cross rivers. Furthermore, Zosimus mentions ἄλλα πάμπολλα πλοῖα for the transport of supplies, materials for constructing war machinery and machinery already constructed. Malalas (Magnus?), *Chron.* 13.329 mentions 1250 vessels in total, both made of timber and skins. Zon. 13.13.8, when relating the episode about the burning of the ships near Ctesiphon (cf. 24.7.4), speaks of 700 triremes and 400 cargo-carriers. See for a discussion of the number of ships, e.g. Brok, 1959, 65–6; Paschoud n. 35; Ridley, 1973, 319–20. As to the types of ship of which Julian's fleet consisted, Dillemann, 1961, 151–2 suggests

that ships comparable to the modern *kellek*, which is made of hides, and the modern *chakhtour*, which is constructed of timber, were used. Both types could only be used for going downstream and were demolished when they had fulfilled their purpose. Most of the fleet was especially constructed for this campaign; Brok, 1959, 66 and Fontaine n. 71 have suggested, that the 50 war vessels belonged to a permanent Euphrates fleet. There was, however, no permanent military fleet on the Euphrates, because, besides being hardly navigable upriver, it was not considered a *limes*; Reddé, 1986. The fleet was assembled at the upper course of the Euphrates (Lib. *Or.* 18.214). It might be that Julian, while in Hierapolis (see the note ad 23.2.6), gave the last orders to the PPO – he was ultimately responsible for the necessary supplies for the troops (see 17.3.4, 18.2.4, 20.4.6 and the note) – for the provisions to be taken on the fleet; Jul. *Ep*. 98, 402 b: ναῦς πληροῦνται ποτάμιαι πυροῦ, μᾶλλον δὲ ἄρτων ξηρῶν καὶ ὄξους. As to the food and beverage for the soldiers, *Cod. Theod.* 7.4.6 (= *Cod. Iust.* 12.37.1), issued by Constantius II on 17 May 360 and addressed to Julian and Helpidius, gives some interesting information: *Repetita consuetudo monstravit expeditionis tempore buccellatum ac panem, vinum quoque atque acetum, sed et laridum, carnem verbecinam etiam, milites nostros ita solere percipere: biduo buccellatum, tertio die panem; uno die vinum, alio die acetum; uno die laridum, biduo carnem verbecinam.* For the diet of Roman soldiers, see also Davies, 1989.

obsidionales machinas Cf. 20.7.18. Amm. introduces here the subject of the digression in the next chapter, described in 21.12.8 as *instrumenta obsidionalium artium*.

ad compaginandos...pontes For *compaginare* cf. the note ad 21.12.9.

Chapter 4

In studies on Roman warfare Ammianus figures prominently. As a former army officer Amm. shows a lively interest in and a detailed knowledge of military matters. The following digression concerning siege-engines serves to provide the necessary background information for the account of Julian's Persian campaign. Military conflicts between Romans and Persians in Mesopotamia invariably took on the character of siege wars, in which these engines played a crucial role. That explains why Amm. places this digression here, although in his preceding accounts of the sieges of Amida (19.7), Bezabde (20.11) and Aquileia (21.12) he had mentioned these engines several times already. The immediate cause for the digression is the remark about the large number of *obsidionales machinae* that Julian had shipped by way of the Euphrates to Callinicum (23.3.9).

From a military man like Amm. one might expect a description based on personal observation, but, as in his digressions on countries he had visited himself, both the vagueness of his account and the similarities to the descriptions found in other historians suggest that his knowledge, or at least his way of presenting the material, stems primarily from book-learning.

Earlier descriptions in Greek and Latin authors are of two kinds. There are technical treatises in which the construction of these engines is explained in great detail, with exact measures for their various parts; these treatises, by Greek authors like Heron, Philon and Biton and in Latin by Vitruvius in the tenth book of his *De architectura*, which date from the second century B.C. to the first century A.D., are collected, translated and expertly commented upon in Marsden, 1971. On the other hand we find less technical descriptions of siege-engines in the works of historians like Josephus, Procopius, Eusebius (*FGrHist* 101) and military authors like Vegetius and the Anonymus *de rebus bellicis*. The similarities between the descriptions in these Greek historians and in Ammianus suggest a common model, which it seems impossible to identify.

In this digression Amm. treats successively the *ballista* (§ 2–3), the *scorpio* or *onager* (§ 4–7), the *aries* (§ 8–9), the *helepolis* (§ 10–13) and the *malleolus* (§ 14–15). Properly speaking, the last item does not belong in the series, because, as Amm. tells us himself, the *malleolus* is *teli genus*, not a siege-engine. The descriptions have in common that Amm. begins with the material from which the engines are made. Next, he describes them not as finished products, but as they are put together: *ferrum... compaginatur* (§ 2), *dolantur axes duo quernei* (§ 4), *eligitur abies... cuius summitas duro ferro concluditur* (§ 8), *aedificatur... hoc modo* (§ 11), *sagitta... concavatur ventre* (§ 14). In this respect Amm.'s descriptions resemble the technical treatises of Philon, Bito and Vitruvius. It would be as difficult, however, to construct these engines following Amm.'s instructions as to make a living as a farmer using only Vergil's *Georgics* for one's manual. In comparison with the technical treatises mentioned above Amm.'s descripton is hopelessly lacking in precision and unsatisfactory even with regard to essential parts of the engines. It is clear that Amm. supposed his readers to have some idea of how these engines looked and worked, and that his aim differs completely from that of the technical authors in that his digression is first of all a literary tour de force on a forbidding subject. This is evident also from the vividness with which, at the end of every single description, he relates the deadly effects of these weapons. The flowery style Amm. favours for his digressions makes the interpretation of this thorny passage even more difficult.

If we look at the engines one by one, it turns out that in every single case there remain problems. In order to understand how the *ballista* works it is essential to know that it is a torsion engine and that the motive power for the arrow is provided by the sinew-springs. This is only implicitly touched upon by Amm. Furthermore the reader must know the difference between the fixed stock (*ferrum*) and the slider (*stilus* or *temo*). Unlike Procopius in the parallel passage quoted in the commentary (§ 2 *ferrum inter axiculos*), Amm. does not distinguish clearly between the two. His account of the *scorpio* is much easier to understand, but the comparison to the frame-saw (*serratoria machina*, § 4) remains problematic, as do his remarks about the position of the buffer (*fulmentum*, § 5), the meaning of *sublimis* and the way in which the artillerist releases the trigger (§ 6). In the description of the *aries* it is not clear how the battering ram is suspended from the horizontal beams mentioned in § 8. The *helepolis* is the most puzzling of them all in that Amm. describes it as a cross between a *helepolis* or giant mobile tower used to gain superior height for the attackers and a kind of *falx muralis* for tearing a wall apart. Lendle, 1983, 58 n. 71, qualifies Amm.'s description rightly as a 'phantasievolle Darstellung', which cannot be used as a source of information about this engine. This confusion is all the more amazing since in 24.2.19 Amm. describes a normal *helepolis* in action during the siege of Pirisabora, where the sight of this *moles ingens superatura celsarum turrium minas* causes the defenders to surrender. In the description of the *malleolus*, Amm. fails to specify the incendiary material, which makes it difficult to understand the effect of the fire-dart.

Further literature on this digression and related subjects in Amm. is to be found in Schramm, 1918; Marsden, 1969 and 1971; Crump, 1975, 97–113; Brok, 1975, 1977, 1978; Austin, 1979, 141–51 and Matthews 291–4. The technical vocabulary in the translations of the *lemmata* is based on Marsden, 1971, with occasional variations due to differences in interpretation of the text.

4.1 *Re ipsa admoneor* Amm. likes to stress that his digressions are necessary for a correct understanding of his narration, or *res*, cf. 16.7.4 *Res monuit* e.q.s. and 23.6.1 *Res adigit huc prolapsa,* 31.2.12 *quoniam huc prolapsa res est.* For other expressions of suitability see Emmett, 1981, 18–9, who points to parallels in among others Sallust, such as *Jug.* 17.1 *res postulare videtur* or *Jug.* 79.1 *locus admonuit.*

breviter, quantum mediocre potest ingenium, ... monstrare The *quantum*-clause qualifies *monstrare*, not *breviter*, as Rolfe's translation suggests ("as briefly as my modest ability permits"). Other promises of *brevitas* at the outset of digressions are quoted by Emmett, 1981, 19–20. A declaration of modesty is also found at the beginning of Amm.'s report of Julian's heroic deeds in 16.1.2: *singula serie progrediente monstrabo instrumenta omnia mediocris ingenii, si suffecerint, commoturus.* In other cases, such as 27.11.1 *iuste an secus, non iudicioli est nostri* and 28.4.14 *quam ob causam non iudicioli est nostri,* Amm. hides behind his modesty in order to withhold his personal judgment. On declarations of modesty in Amm. see further Sabbah 528–31. Unlike many other digressions of a scientific or technical nature, this one does not refer to the studies of specialists in a particular field, such as *physici* (17.7.9, 21.1.11, 25.10.2), *theologi* (21.1.8, 21.14.3), *periti mundani motus et siderum* (i.e. astronomers, 26.1.8). It would, however, be rash to conclude from this that the following digression is based entirely on Amm.'s own observations. As has been said in the introduction to this chapter, his digressions seem to be primarily the product of book-learning.

ignorantibus circumscripte monstrare Amm. is aware that most of his readers are unfamiliar with this technical subject: *ignorantibus* does not imply criticism. The case is different at the beginning of a short digression on earlier Roman defeats in 31.5.11: *negant antiquitatum ignari... sed falluntur.* At the outset of the digression on earthquakes (17.7.9) Amm. includes himself among the uninformed: *haec nostra vulgaris inscitia. Circumscripte* is found only here in Amm. It means 'in outline', i.e. without entering into details, as in Cic. *de Orat.* 1.189 *est enim definitio rerum earum quae sunt eius rei propriae quam definire volumus brevis et circumscripta quaedam explicatio.* It is combined with *breviter* also in Lact. *inst.* 5.9.20 and 5.14.8. *Circumscripte* has the same function as *summatim* or *carptim* in other digressions, such as 14.6.2 and 16.7.4.

4.2 *et ballistae figura docebitur prima* As the following description will show, Amm.'s *ballista* is an arrow-shooting engine. In the most detailed description of artillery that is preserved in Latin, Vitr. 10.10–2, the *ballista* is a stone thrower, which Amm. calls *scorpio* or *onager*, whereas the arrow-shooting engine is called *catapulta* by Vitruvius. The new terminology is also used in

20.7.10: *nec ballistae tamen cessavere nec scorpiones, illae tela torquentes, hi lapides crebros.* The change in terminology is explained by Fleury, 1993, 226–39 and 1996, 52–4 as the consequence of a technical innovation in the construction of the arrow-shooter, illustrated by the tombstone of Vedennius and Trajan's Column (see plates 1 and 9–13 in Marsden, 1969). The mechanics of the new type of arrow-shooter closely resembled those of the stone throwing *ballista* with the result that this name came to be used also for the newly developed piece of artillery.

ferrum inter axiculos duo firmum compaginatur et vastum 'An iron beam, strong and large, is fixed firmly between two little posts'. Marsden, 1971, 238 identifies the *ferrum* with the 'little ladder', or χλιμάκιον of Hero's χειροβαλλίστρα (if Hero is the author of the treatise), a strut to the centre of which the stock is attached. It is, however, a priori unlikely that Amm. would open his description of the *ballista* with a relatively minor component of the engine instead of its most prominent part, the stock. Moreover, despite the fact that the χλιμάκιον keeps the spring frames "much further apart than they were in the earlier catapults, e.g. those of Vitruvius" (ibid. n. 2), this does not seem to do justice to the qualifications *vastum* and *in modum regulae maioris extentum*, which fit the stock itself much better, projecting as it does from between (*ex-tentum*) the field frames holding the cylinders with the sinew-springs. This is how Brok, 1977, 343–5 and Fontaine n. 73 interpret the *ferrum*. See the drawing of the *ballista*. The word *ferrum* for the stock is compared by Brok with Procop. *Goth.* 1.21.14. In this report of the siege of Rome by the Goths, Procopius describes the *ballistae* put into place by Belisarius as follows: Βελισάριος δὲ μηχανὰς μὲν ἐς τοὺς πύργους ἐτίθετο, ἃς καλοῦσι βαλλίστρας. τόξου δὲ σχῆμα ἔχουσιν αἱ μηχαναὶ αὗται, ἔνερθέν τε αὐτοῦ κοίλη τις ξυλίνη κεραία ('a hollow wooden beam') προύχει, αὐτὴ μὲν χαλαρὰ ἠρτημένη ('moving freely'), σιδηρᾷ δὲ εὐθείᾳ ('a straight iron beam') τινὶ ἐπικειμένη, where the σιδηρὰ εὐθεῖα (sc. κεραία) corresponds to Amm.'s *ferrum*, and the ξυλίνη κεραία to his *stilus* or *temo*.

The *axiculi* are the horizontal struts holding the two cylinders with the sinew-springs. It is typical of Amm.'s somewhat impressionistic description that he does not explain the construction of the frame of which the *axiculi* are a part, and it is downright amazing that the cylinders with the sinew-strings, the motive power for firing the arrow, are only mentioned in passing. Frames for *ballistae* have been found in Rumania and Britain. For photographs see Bishop and Coulston, 1993, 166. *Compaginare* is Amm.'s standard term for the construction of bridges, see the note ad 21.12.9.

in modum regulae maioris extentum 'Stretching out like a large ruler'. The only other instance in Amm. of *regula* is to be found in the description of the Scythian bow, 22.8.37 (q.v.), where *regula* is the term for the handle separating the two halves of the bow. In Vitruvius' chapter on the catapult the term *regula* indicates the strips to the right and left of the case forming the groove (*canalis*) in which the slider moves, in other words as components of Amm.'s *ferrum*. The phrase *in modum regulae* not only emphasizes the straightness of the stock, but also its function in guiding the arrow. *In modum* might thus be paraphrased 'to serve as', cf. 16.11.9 *scutis in modum alveorum suppositis nando ad insulam venere*.

cuius ex volumine tereti. . . quadratus eminet stilus extentius 'A rectangular beam sticks out rather far from a cylindrical groove in this beam.' Amm. uses *volumen* usually for a book-roll (20.9.6, 28.4.14, 29.1.10). *Teres* is the normal adjective for cylindrical objects, such as stakes, as in Caes. *Gal*. 7.73.6 *teretes stipites*, or the shaft of a spear, as in Liv. 21.8.10 *hastili. . . tereti*, so *volumen teres* is an appropriate expression for the longitudinal semi-cylindrical groove in the case (*ferrum*), into which the underside of the slider is dovetailed and in which it moves backward when it is pulled by the windlass and shoots forward when it is released. Since Amm. tells us that the *stilus* itself is also provided with a narrow groove (*recto canalis angusti meatu*) into which the arrow is placed, the *stilus* must be identified with the slider. It is called *quadratus* in contrast with the semi-cylindrical groove in which it moves. The choice of the word *stilus* for the slider is surprising, because it is used nowhere else for this part of the engine, for which the t.t. in Vitruvius is *canalis fundus* or *chelonium* (10.11.7). The primary meaning of *stilus* being 'spike', the word indicates much more naturally the wooden arm of the *onager* (§ 5) than the slider of the *ballista*. In any case, it should be pictured as protruding considerably (*eminet extentius*) from the *ferrum*. Strange though the choice of *stilus* for this part may seem, it corresponds exactly to the Greek term κεραία found in Procopius' description of the *ballista* quoted above to indicate the slider, just as προύχει in Procopius' text matches *eminet*.

quod in medio pars polita componit 'Which is formed by a well-polished central component (of the stock).' The reading *pars* was conjectured by Wagner for V's *ars*. As it is a priori unlikely that in a technical description like this *politus* should have any but its literal meaning 'polished', 'finished', Fontaine's defence of *ars polita* as meaning "une technique raffinée" is unconvincing. Moreover, *pars polita* may well be a reminiscence of Verg. *A*. 8.426–8 *iam parte polita. . . pars imperfecta manebat*. The question is then what is meant by this exasperatingly vague phrase, a perfect illustration of Horace's *brevis esse laboro, obscurus fio*. If *componere* is taken in its literal meaning 'to put together', the phrase could mean that the semi-cylindrical groove within which the slider moves is part of a well-polished central component of the stock, stuck between two other components to its right and left, which, incidentally, would simplify the construction of such a groove considerably. It is to be noted that in Vitruvius' description of the arrow-shooting *catapulta* quoted above (10.10.4), the groove for the slider is constructed by fastening two strips (the *regulae*) to the case, leaving room in between to serve as the female dovetail into which the male dovetail of the slider is inserted. If this interpretation of *componere* is correct, *pars polita* refers to the polished central part of the stock. The translation would be: '(the groove) which is formed in its middle (*in medio* sc. *ferro*) by the polished part (of the same *ferrum*).'

recto canalis angusti meatu cavatus 'Fitted with a straight narrow-channelled groove.' The same detail is expressed by the simple κοίλη in Procopius' description. *Canalis angustus* does not indicate the female dovetail of the case, as Marsden, 1971, 239 would have it, but the groove into which the arrow is placed, just as in Anon. *de mach. bell.* 18.1 *supra canalem quo sagitta exprimitur. Canalis* is a gen. identitatis, a convenient stylistic feature if one wishes to add two qualifications to one constituent, one of which is attached to the Head, the other to the Attribute. It could be translated 'a straight, hollow groove.'

et hac multiplici chorda nervorum tortilium illigatus 'And attached to this complex cordage of twisted sinews.' There are two problems here: a. *hac* has no direct reference and b. *illigatus* is without a complement indicating what the slider was attached to. For the first problem cf. *ab hac medietate restium* in § 5, where *hac* is used despite the fact that *medietas* has not been used before. There, however, it can easily be understood to refer to *funes* (= *restes*) in the preceding sentence. A better parallel is 20.5.8 *hac fiducia spei melioris animatus*, where *hac* refers to the preceding speech of Julian: 'the confidence caused by these words'. In the present phrase *hac* could just possibly be interpreted as 'belonging to this engine', but it looks as if there is something wrong with the text here. Brok, 1977, 340 n. 22 pointed out that both in Procop. *Goth.* 1.21.14 and in the Anon. *de mach. bell.* 18 the τόξον or *arcus* is mentioned, by which these authors mean the arms of the bow, which are fastened at one end to the cylinders with the sinew-springs, at the other to the bow strings and the slider. The two difficulties signalled above would, he suggests, disappear simultaneously if, instead of *hac*, we would read *arcu* (dative). In support of this hypothesis he lists a number of corruptions of *hic* in the text of Ammianus in n. 21 on p. 340. Alternatively, *hac* might be considered a corruption of *ac*, the loss of which was subsequently compensated by adding *et*. The second problem may be less serious. In classical usage *illigare* 'to attach by tying' has its complement in the dative; TLL VII 1.379.72–7. In Amm. we find three comparable phrases: 16.10.7 *dracones hastarum aureis gemmatisque summitatibus illigati*, 19.8.7 *habenam...sinistra manu artius illigavit* and 25.1.15 *quibus insidentes magistri manubriatos cultros dexteris manibus illigatos gestabant*. In 19.8.7, the only unambiguous case, it is clear that Amm. uses the ablative in such a connection. So *chorda* may be seen as the component to which the slider is attached. In the phrase *multiplex chorda nervorum tortilium, nervorum tortilium* is a defining genitive, which may well have been inspired by Luc. 6.198–9 *hunc aut tortilibus vibrata phalarica nervis/obruat*, which in its turn echoes Verg. A. 9.705–6 *sed magnum stridens contorta phalarica venit/fulminis acta modo*. The *multiplex chorda nervorum tortilium* is probably Amm.'s term both for the sinew-springs and the bow-strings, to which the slider is attached.

eique cochleae duo ligneae coniunguntur aptissime 'To it two wooden rollers are fittingly joined.' The *cochleae* are the rollers fixed right and left of the case (so *ei* refers to the case, not to the slider, as Marsden, 1971, 239 says). They turn the windlass, thus drawing back the slider. Mommsen's conjecture *artissime* is certainly no improvement, on the contrary, if the rollers were fixed tightly to the case, they would be difficult to handle. Brok, 1977, 342 translates *aptissime* "an der meist geeigneten Stelle", which in itself makes excellent sense. In Amm.'s flowery prose, however, the verb form *coniunguntur* could hardly be used without a qualification which emphasizes the meaning of the verb in the same way as Attributes in the genitive do in phrases like *caerimoniarum ritus* (22.12.7) or *diversis genitalium notarum figuris* (22.14.7). Cf. e.g. 16.10.8 *iunctura cohaerenter aptata* and, for another possible parallel, *patentius perforati* in § 4.

quarum prope unam assistit artifex contemplabilis 'Beside one of which stands the artilleryman taking aim.' Amm. uses *artifex* for professionals like wrestlers *(artifices palaestritae*, 15.2.24) or surgeons *(medellarum artifices* 17.5.7). The *artifex contemplabilis* is an artillerist, more specifically the marksman. He is called *contemplator* in 19.1.7 *quem* (Grumbatem) *ubi venientem iam telo forte contiguum contemplator peritissimus advertisset, contorta ballista filium eius...perfodit*. In 24.4.28 the context is sufficiently clear for Amm. to call him just *artifex*. The technical meaning of *contemplor* and its derivatives is evident also in 20.7.9 *intuta loca...contemplabiliter machinae feriebant hostiles*, q.v.

subtiliter apponit in temonis cavamine sagittam The adverb stresses again the delicate technique needed for artillery matters. Amm. uses *subtiliter* also in his description of the *malleolus* in section 14 below and *arte subtili* for the defensive measures against the battering-ram in 20.11.15. The *temonis cavamen* is identical with the *canalis angustus* mentioned before, so *temo* must be synonymous with *stilus*. Fontaine's translation is correct, but in his drawing the *temo* is mistakenly identified with the *ferrum*. *Temo* is used with its normal meaning 'pole' in the description of the *scorpio* (§ 5) in a comparison to explain the position of the *stilus*: *ligneus stilus exsurgens obliquus et in modum iugalis temonis erectus.*

spiculo maiore conglutinatam For photographs of such large arrow-heads see Bishop and Coulston, 1993, 247.

hinc inde validi iuvenes versant agiliter rotabilem flexum 'Energetically turn a rotating winch.' Cf. Procop. *Goth.* 1.21.17 σφίγγουσι τε σθένει πολλῷ οἱ ἀμφοτέρωθεν μηχαναῖς τισί. These men are called *tortores* in 19.7.7 *ballistae earumque tortores.* *Rotabilis flexus* is the circular movement of the rollers turning the windlass that draws back the slider. It is a laboured phrase, comparable to *gradile templum* in 23.1.6 in that in both cases the adjective is substituted for a constituent in the ablative.

cum ad extremitatem nervorum acumen venerit summum 'When its extreme tip comes opposite the outer edge of the sinews.' Since Amm. does not tell us at which point the *stilus* is connected to the bowstrings, nor where it is attached to the windlass, this phrase cannot be interpreted with absolute certainty. If we identify the *nervi* with the *nervi tortiles* in the preceding section, as seems necessary, the *extremitates* are either the ends at the right and left tip of the bow, or the ends that are attached to the *stilus*. In the latter case, the distance between the *acumen* and the *extremitates* remains constant when the *stilus* is drawn backward, so that the arrow cannot be said to 'come to' the ends of the strings. If, however, the *extremitates* at the right and left of the bow are meant, the distance between the *acumen* and the *extremitates* does become shorter as the arms of the bow are drawn backward and inward. This would tally with the use of *extremitates* in the description of the Scythian bow (22.8.13), where the *extremitates arcus* are the tips of the arms of the bow. For *acumen* cf. 31.2.9 about the arrow-heads used by the Goths *acutis ossibus pro spiculorum acumine. . . coagmentatis.*

4.3

percita interno pulsu a ballista Amm. seems to forget that the subject was *acumen* instead of *sagitta*. For a similar shift cf. 22.15.22, where *repertum* agrees with an unexpressed subject *animal*, although in the preceding phrase *belua* was the subject. For *percitus* see the notes ad 20.11.5 and 21.9.5. This is the only occurrence where it has its literal meaning. *Interno pulsu* marks the difference between the arrow-shooting engine and the handbow. *Interno* contrasts with *digitorum* in the description of the Persian bow in 24.2.13 *nervi digitorum acti pulsibus violentis* 'the strings set in violent motion by the fingers' and 25.1.13 *digitorum pulsibus argutum sonantes harundines evolabant.* In accordance with his announcement that he will describe these engines *circumscripte*, Amm. refrains from explaining the trigger mechanism by which the arrow is released. Vitruvius in his far more technical description does mention the trigger (*manucla*, σχαστηρία). See Marsden, 1971, 48, fig. 4, 195, 219–20 for further details.

nimio ardore scintillans Amm. probably explained these sparks resulting from friction, as in the case of comets. Cf. 25.2.6 *scintillas... ab aetherio candentes vigore* and Sen. *Nat.* 1.1.5 *eiusmodi ignes existere aere vehementius trito*. In 30.1.7 the tertium comparationis between sparks and arrows is their number: *fundensque in modum scintillarum sagittas*.

antequam telum cernatur, dolor letale vulnus agnoscat For *antequam* with subjunctive see the note ad 20.9.5. The sudden impact of the arrow is brought out well by the personification *dolor... agnoscat*, expressing how the arrow is felt before it is seen. The power with which these bolts hit their targets can be illustrated by the anecdote of the killing of Grumbates' son in 19.1.7 *thorace cum pectore perforato* and the fact that it was possible to kill two men with one shot: 19.5.6 *leviores quinque ballistae..., quae ocius lignea tela fundentes nonnumquam et binos forabant*. Southern and Dixon, 1996, 156 quote Procop. *Goth.* 1.23.9–12 about a Goth hit by such a bolt: διαβὰν δὲ τόν τε θώρακα καὶ τὸ τοῦ ἀνθρώπου σῶμα τὸ βέλος ὑπὲρ ἥμισυ ἐς τὸ δένδρον ἔδυ (§ 11). The range of these engineswas therefore enormous: *ut etiam Danubii, famosi pro magnitudine fluminis, latitudinem valeat penetrare* (Anon. *de mach. bell.* 18.5).

4.4 *Scorpionis autem, quem appellant nunc onagrum* The latter term seems to be more modern and less dignified, cf. § 7 below *cui etiam onagri vocabulum indidit aetas novella* and 31.15.12 *quem onagrum sermo vulgaris appellat*. In Veg. *mil.* 4.22.4 *onager* is the normal term for a stone-throwing engine: *onager autem dirigit lapides*. His remark in the same section about the *scorpio* shows the changed meaning of that term (for which see above the note ad § 2 *et ballistae figura docebitur prima*): *scorpiones dicebant, quas nunc manuballistas vocant*.

dolantur axes duo... curvanturque mediocriter, ut prominere videantur in gibbas 'Two beams of oak or holm-oak are fashioned and given a moderate curvature, so that they seem to bulge into humps.' The first stage in constructing the *onager* consists in fashioning two beams that form the bottom sides of the engine. For *gibba* 'hump' cf. Suet. *Dom.* 23.2 *Domitianum ferunt somniasse gibbam sibi pone cervicem auream enatam*. In all other cases *gibbus* seems to be preferred (TLL VI 2.1975.20–6). In 20.3.11 *utrimque prominentibus gibbis* it is not clear which word Amm. had in mind.

in modum serratoriae machinae conectuntur 'They are connected as in a frame-saw.' See Marsden, 1971, 251 and his fig. 2 on p. 252 reproduced below. In Marsden's words: "if you imagine that the strut *A*, in fig. 2, is placed where the tightening rope *B* is, and that the rope *B* is fastened where the strut *A* has just been, the arrangement will very closely resemble the ground framework of the *onager*". This is an ingenious explanation, which also helps to understand the obscure phrase *compagem, ne dissiliat, continentes*, as we shall see. The side beams of the frame are joined together by cross-beams. In Marsden's reconstruction there are two cross-beams at either end of the side beams and two in the middle, on either side of the spring.

ex utroque latere patentius perforati 'Having quite large holes bored in both sides.' Into the side-beams the spring-holes are drilled. Amm. does not express himself very exactly here, since *ex utroque latere* must apply to the frame as a whole, not to the side-beams themselves. *Patentius* may be understood literally, as the ropes that pass through these holes will have to be thick. It is equally possible, however, that *patentius perforati* is an expressive pleonasm like *coniunguntur aptissime* in section 2. Vitruvius opens his description of what he calls the *ballista* with the sentence *Nam quae fiunt in capitibus* ('frames') *foramina, per quorum spatia contenduntur capillo maxime muliebri vel nervo funes* e.q.s. ('ropes mostly of women's hair or sinews', 10.11.2).

quos inter per cavernas funes colligantur robusti 'Between these beams, through the holes, powerful ropes are tied.' For the anastrophe see Szantyr 216, who observes that it is not rare in Sallust and frequent in Tacitus. The *cavernae* are the holes drilled through the side-beams. *Caverna* is found with the meaning 'hole', 'aperture' in Ital. *Marc*. 10.25 *camellum per cavernam acus introire*, Tert. *anim*. 14.5 *flatus in calamo per cavernas*, TLL III 646.25–39. Amm. does not tell us how the ropes are attached. Marsden's translation of *colligantur* "are stretched" is in fact an improvement on Amm.'s text.

compagem, ne dissiliat, continentes 'Preventing the structure from falling apart.' Amm.'s comparison of the frame of the *onager* to a frame-saw may have led him astray. In a saw of the type shown in the drawing above the ropes hold the *serratoria machina* together and stretch the blade. The *onager* is not held together by the ropes, but by the cross-beams. The whole passage is misunderstood by Fontaine (n. 81 and fig. 2). He takes Amm. at his word in interpreting the *funes* as ropes that hold the *onager* together while at the same time following Marsden in rejecting the phrase under discussion as a clear mistake. As a consequence, he fails to see that the *funes robusti* serve as the spring of the *onager*, so that in his interpretation the spring makes its appearance only in the next sentence, with the words *ab hac medietate restium*, in which case *hac* does not make any sense at all.

ab hac medietate restium 'From the middle of these ropes.' This use of the **4.5** demonstrative *hac* is less surprising than in *hac multiplici chorda* in section 2 in so far as the *restes* are identical with the *funes* which have been mentioned in the preceding sentence. The present phrase might be called a form of hypallage for *a medietate harum restium*. For *medietas* see the note ad 22.13.3 and Wölfflin, 1886.

ligneus stilus exsurgens obliquus 'A wooden arm rising at an angle.' On *obliquus* see the note ad 22.7.5. Bentley probably wanted an adverb with *exsurgere* and for that reason suggested *obliquius*, but cf. 17.7.13 about a type of earthquake: *climatiae, qui limes ruentes et obliqui* e.q.s.

in modum iugalis temonis erectus 'Set upright in the manner of a yoke-pole.' Again, as in the description of the *ballista*, the words *stilus* and *temo* are found together. Here, however, *temo* is not the equivalent of *stilus*, but serves as a comparison.

ita nervorum nodulis implicatur, ut altius tolli possit et inclinari 'It is so inserted in the twists of sinew that it can both be raised and lowered.' Note that Amm. has three words for the strings in this passage: *funes, restes* and *nervi*. The material used for the strings was either sinews or hair. For that reason Veg. *mil.* 4.9.1 insists that these articles should always be in store: *nervorum quoque copiam summo studio expedit colligi, quia onagri et ballistae ceteraque tormenta nisi funibus nervinis intenta nihil prosunt*. The consecutive clause means only that the arm moves vertically. *Inclinari* is the important word, because the arm is drawn down before it is released. For *inclinare* 'to lower' cf. Liv. 36.44.2 *vela contrahit malosque inclinat*.
Nervorum noduli, in which *nervorum* is a gen. inversus, is the equivalent of *nervi tortiles* in section 2; *noduli* emphasizes that the arm is inserted into and connected with the ropes. The diminutive *nodulus* seems out of place in the description of this piece of heavy artillery. A similar incongruity is found in Apul. *met.* 9.40 *inversa vite de vastiore nodulo cerebrum suum diffindere* "he reversed his staff and was using its very large knob to split his skull" (Hijmans et al. in their commentary ad loc.).

summitatique eius unci ferrei copulantur According to Marsden, 1971, 253 "Three hooks will be required at the tip of the arm. The sling, with one end free to fly off at the right moment, is fitted to the end of the arm."

e quibus pendet stuppea vel ferrea funda Fontaine ingeniously defends V's *struppea* as a derivative of *struppus* "a twisted cord" (OLD), but apart from the fact that *struppeus* is not attested in Latin, we need an adjective to match *ferreus*. Amm. may have had in mind Verg. *G.* 1.309 *stuppea torquentem Balearis verbera fundae*.

cui ligno fulmentum prosternitur ingens 'A huge buffer is placed in front of this arm.' The buffer (*fulmentum*) stops the arm (*lignum*) after it has been released. Because of the enormous power of the *scorpio* (see the end of this section), this is a vital part of the engine. *Prosternitur* poses a problem. The verb must mean that the buffer is spread out on the ground (which is how it is drawn in Fontaine's fig. 2). The next section, however, states that the shot is projected from the sling when the arm hits the buffer (*stilus... mollitudini offensus cilicii saxum contorquet*), which, of course, should happen well before the arm hits the ground. Experiments carried out by Marsden have shown that the best results are obtained when the buffer is placed in an upright position. See the reconstructions of Schramm and Marsden in Marsden, 1971, 263. In other words the buffer must be above the horizontal frame of the *onager*. It seems to follow that *prosternitur* is corrupt and that a verb meaning 'to stop' or 'to block' should be substituted for it. *Obtendere* (sometimes written *obstendere*, TLL IX 2.273.72–3) "i.q. tendendo obicere, opponere" (TLL) would suit the meaning well. It is found in combination with *cilicium* also in 20.11.9 *sub obtentis ciliciis*, q.v. For the general meaning of *obtendere* cf. e.g. Sil. 13. 341/2 *obtendensque manum solem infervescere fronti arcet*. For *palea* see the note ad 23.2.8.

validis nexibus illigatum Amm. does not state what the *cilicium* is attached to by the 'strong bindings.' Schramm and Marsden plausibly suggest that there was a heavy block of wood behind the *cilicium*.

et locatum super congestos caespites vel latericios aggeres Schneider, 1908, 46, proposed to read *et locatur*, so that *scorpio* could be the subject instead of *fulmentum*. It is, however, not at all impossible that Amm. means the engine as a whole while retaining the neuter form. Similarly, in § 8 Amm., when speaking about the *aries*, retains the feminine form *suspensa* because of the preceding *abies vel ornus*. Marsden, 1971, 253 mentions a platform of the former type in a Roman fort near Hadrian's Wall. Its resilience serves to absorb the shock when the arm hits the buffer. Matthews 292 plausibly supposes that the piles of turf were for temporary use, whereas bonded brick emplacements were for permanent location on city walls.

nam muro saxeo huiusmodi moles imposita disiectat The adj. *saxeus* contrasts with *latericius*. A similar contrast is found in Suet. *Aug.* 28.3 *marmoream se relinquere* (urbem) *quam latericiam accepisset*. The hyperbaton of *muro saxeo* emphasizes this opposition.

quidquid invenerit, subter concussione violenta, non pondere The adverb *subter* goes with *invenerit*, so the semicolon should be put after it. For *invenire* with non-human subject cf. TLL VII 2.136.84–137.18, where the following parallels are given: Sen. *Nat.* 3.7.3 *putei in altum acti...inveniunt aquarum uberes venas* and Vulg. *lev.* 7.17 *quidquid...tertius invenerit dies, ignis absumet.*

4.6 *cum...ad concertationem ventum fuerit* For *concertatio* see the note ad 21.11.3. The subj. is iterative, cf. De Jonge ad 14.2.7 and Szantyr 624. For perfect passive forms with *fui* see the note ad 20.11.19 (where (plu)perfect should be read).

repagula, quibus incorporati sunt funes, explicantes retrorsus Both in 16.12.38 and in 19.6.4 *repagulum* is a bar that keeps in check horsemen and wild beasts respectively. At first sight it is not clear what the function is of the *repagula* and the *funes*. Since the effect of the action described is that the *stilus* is drawn down, Marsden must be right in thinking that the *iuvenes* are "pulling rearwards the bars to which the withdrawal ropes are connected." These *funes* therefore are not identical with those in § 4, which formed the spring of the engine. *Explicare* is convincingly explained in TLL V 2.1728.78–81 as "i.q. torquere, rotare." The eight *iuvenes* have the same task as the *validi iuvenes* of § 2, just as the *repagula* correspond to the *cochleae* mentioned there. *Incorporare* is post-classical, found for the first time in Sol. 22.12 (TLL VII 1.1029.17).

stilum paene supinum inclinant For *inclinare* see the preceding section. *Supinum* means 'to a horizontal position.'

itaque demum sublimis astans magister claustrum...reserat The climax of the description is introduced by *itaque demum* and reached by the vivid picture of the artillery officer bringing down his hammer. Matthews 293, n. 17 rightly rejects Marsden's interpretation of *sublimis* as referring to the rank of the officer ("standing loftily"). He himself supposes that the operator "had in some way to stand 'above' the mechanism." It seems preferable, however, to take *sublimis* in its meaning "drawing himself up to his full height" (OLD *sublimis* 6b). There may be an echo of Vergil here, cf. *A.* 12.788 *olli sublimes armis animisque refecti.*
Itaque demum is best interpreted as *et ita demum*, cf. 20.3.7 *apertum et evidentem ita demum sustinet luna defectum*, 23.1.7, 24.1.14. Again, we are not told exactly how the trigger is released by the *magister*. For a plausible reconstruction of the mechanism see Marsden, 1971, 260–1.

quod totius operis continet vincula With the *vincula* both the spring and the withdrawal ropes are meant, which will unwind as soon as the trigger is released. Tacitus has *vincula* in the same meaning in *Hist.* 3.23.2 *ni duo milites...vincla ac libramenta tormentorum abscidissent.*

saxum contorquet, quidquid incurrerit, collisurum For the enormous power of the *onager* see the anecdote in 24.4.28 about the artillery officer who was killed by his own engine: *nostrae partis architectus...post machinam scorpionis forte assistens reverberato lapide, quem artifex titubanter* (the opposite of *subtiliter!*) *aptaverat fundae, obliso pectore supinatus profudit animam disiecta compage membrorum adeo, ut ne signa quidem totius corporis noscerentur.* Cf. also Veg. *mil.* 4.22.8 *Saxis tamen gravioribus per onagrum destinatis non solum equi eliduntur et homines, sed etiam hostium machinamenta franguntur.*

tormentum quidem appellatur ex eo, quod omnis explicatio torquetur The **4.7** literal meaning of *explicatio*, viz. 'uncoiling' is exceedingly rare (TLL V 2.1723.9–12). There is only one parallel: Cic. *Div.* 1.127 *rudentis explicatio.* Amm. probably means to say that the ropes by which the arm is drawn down uncoil the moment the trigger is released and that this uncoiling is the effect of torsion. If this interpretation is correct, *torquetur* is the equivalent of *torquendo efficitur. Tormentum* is a generic term that applies also to the *ballista* which operates on the same principle. In 31.15.12 Amm. expresses himself more carefully: *scorpio, genus tormenti*. The *tormentum* in 24.5.6 is certainly a *ballista*. In the classical period too, *tormentum* was used for all torsion engines; see OLD s.v. 2.

scorpio..., quoniam aculeum desuper habet erectum Cf. Cic. *Fin.* 5.42 *cornibus uti videmus boves, nepas* (a kind of scorpion) *aculeis* and Sol. 52.37 (mantichoreae) *cauda velut scorpionis aculeo spiculata.*

cui etiam onagri vocabulum indidit aetas novella See § 4 *quem nunc appellant onagrum*. For *aetas novella* cf. Fro. *Aur.* 2. p. 80 (153N) *nonnihil...elocutione novella parum signatum.*

eminus lapides post terga calcitrando emittunt Both *eminus* and *emittunt* suit a stone-throwing machine better than a wild ass.

capita ipsa displodant For the very rare *displodere* see TLL V 1.1420.43–53. Horace (*S.* 1.8.46) has it for a bursting balloon.

The *aries,* which Amm. describes in the following sections, has been shown in **4.8** action in 20.11.11–15. Two details of that description are repeated here. *Prominentem eius ferream frontem* matches *arietis efficiens prominulam speciem* and *quae re vera formam effingit arietis* has its counterpart in *quae forma huic machinamento vocabulum indidit.* Equally detailed descriptions of the battering-ram are to be found in Vitr. 10.13.1–3, J. *BJ* 3.214–7 and Procop.

Goth. 1.21.5-12. The resemblance between the passages in Josephus and Ammianus is especially striking.

cuius summitas duro ferro concluditur et prolixo, arietis efficiens prominulam speciem 'The end of which is fitted with a pointed head of hard iron.' Cf. J. *BJ* 3.214 ἐστόμωται ('is fitted') δὲ παχεῖ σιδήρῳ κατ' ἄκρον εἰς κριοῦ προτομήν ('head'), ἀφ' οὗ καὶ καλεῖται, τετυπωμένῳ and Procop. *Goth.* 1.21.8 ἧς δὴ ὀξεῖαν ποιούμενοι τὴν ἄκραν, σιδήρῳ πολλῷ... καλύπτουσιν.

et sic suspensa utrimque transversis asseribus et ferratis quasi ex lance vinculis trabis alterius continetur 'And so, suspended from horizontal beams, left and right, covered with iron, as from (the arm of a pair of) scales, it is held in its place by ropes from another beam.' The type of ram described by Josephus is less complicated than the *aries* as described by Vitruvius and Procopius. In Josephus the *aries* is suspended from a beam that rests upon two posts fixed in the ground: καταιωρεῖται δὲ κάλοις μέσος... ἑτέρας δοκοῦ σταυροῖς ἑκατέρωθεν ἑδραίοις ὑπεστηριγμένης (§ 215). The construction described in the other two authors consists of a four-sided building (οἴκημα, *varae*), consisting of four upright posts and four horizontal timbers in the middle of which the ram is suspended. From the fact that Amm. mentions two horizontal beams at either side of the ram it follows that his engine belongs to the second, more sophisticated type. Note that Amm. continues with the *abies vel ornus* as the subject, rather than the masculine *aries*.

What is the *aries* suspended from? At first sight the answer would seem to be "from the *transversi asseres*", but that would make it unclear how we should interpret *quasi ex lance vinculis trabis alterius*. The ambiguity in Amm.'s text as to the point to which the ram is attached would vanish if we read *suspensis... asseribus*, but this simplification seems to be precluded by Vitruvius' *in his suspendit arietem* (10.13.2) and Procopius' ἀρτήσαντες in the passage quoted below. The description in Procop. *Goth.* 1.21.8 ἐντὸς δὲ αὐτῆς (sc. μηχανῆς= the οἴκημα) δοκὸν ἑτέραν (sc. the battering-ram) ἄνωθεν ἐγκαρσίαν ('horizontal') ἀρτήσαντες χαλαραῖς ταῖς ἁλύσεσι ('chains', *vincula*) κατὰ μέσην μάλιστα τὴν μηχανὴν ἔχουσιν does not help, because ἄνωθεν might equally well refer to the roof-beams to the right and left of the ram as to a cross-beam between the two. In Josephus' machine the ram is certainly suspended from a beam that is perpendicular to it (ἑτέρα δοκός in the pasage quoted above having a different meaning from that in Procopius). It seems necessary to suppose that in Amm. the ram is fastened to a cross-beam between the two side-beams, which are called here *transversi asseres* (*asseribus* should therefore be taken as an instrumental ablative). That means that in Amm. *trabis alterius* is the equivalent of Josephus' ἑτέρα δοκός, not the one mentioned in Procopius.

We may wonder at this point whether *alterius* serves as the gen. of *altera* or of *alia*. The opposition to *transversi asseres* would suggest the latter, but it cannot be excluded that Amm. had a Greek source in mind in which, as in Procopius and Josephus, the battering-ram is contrasted to the beam(s) from which it is suspended.

The comparison to a balance (*quasi ex lance*) is conventional, cf. Vitr. 10.13.2 *malo statuto ex eo alterum transversum uti trutinam suspendit* and J. *BJ* 3.215 ὥσπερ ἀπὸ πλάστιγγος. Both in Amm. and in Josephus, the *lanx* and the πλάστιγξ are used metonymically for the balance as a whole. If this interpretation is correct, the battering-ram is compared to the horizontal beam of the balance from which the pans of the scales are hung. The *vincula* in Amm. correspond to χαλαραῖς ταῖς ἁλύσεσι in Procop. § 8 (taken, incidentally from Thuc. 2.76.4 ἀφίεσαν τὴν δοκὸν χαλαραῖς ταῖς ἁλύσεσι) and to κάλοις in J. *BJ* 3.215.

eamque quantum mensurae ratio patitur multitudo retro repellens Whatever the precise meaning of *mensurae ratio*, the phrase must be understood as qualifying *repellens*, not *multitudo*. Rolfe translates as if he reads *quantam*: "as great as the length of the pole permits." For *ratio* see the note ad 21.9.5. The case seems to be different here, where *ratio* rather means 'proportion'. The phrase looks like a contamination of *pro ratione mensurae*, as e.g. in Vitr. 5.5.1 *fiant vasa aerea pro magnitudinis ratione theatri* and *quantum mensura patitur*, as in Liv. 9.41.16 *prout loci natura tempusque patiebatur*. Procopius, in his description, adds two fascinating details: § 9–10 ἄνδρες δὲ αὐτὴν οὐχ ἧσσον ἢ κατὰ πεντήκοντα κινοῦσιν ἔνδοθεν. οἳ ἐπειδὰν αὐτὴν τῷ περιβόλῳ ἐρείσωσι, τὴν δοκὸν ἧς δὴ ἄρτι ἐμνήσθην μηχανῇ τινι στρέφοντες ὀπίσω ἀνέλκουσιν. Josephus is again very close to Amm.'s account: § 216 ἀνωθούμενος δὲ ὑπὸ πλήθους ἀνδρῶν εἰς τὸ κατόπιν.

rursus ad obvia quaeque rumpenda protrudit Cf. J. *BJ* § 216 τῶν αὐτῶν ἀθρόως πάλιν εἰς τοὔμπροσθεν ἐπιβρισάντων ('exerted pressure').

ictibus validissimis instar assurgentis et cedentis cornuti Pace Fontaine, V's *armati* seems untenable, since Amm. never uses *armatus* in the singular for *miles*. For the whole phrase cf. 20.11.15 *ne retrogradiens resumeret vires neve ferire muros assultibus densis...posset*, where *aries* is understood as the subject. Josephus § 211 has πλήσσειν..., καθάπερ τῶν προβάτων τὰ ἄρρενα εἴωθε. There is a note on *instar* ad 20.3.12 and on *adsurgere* ad 20.5.8 *hastis feriendo*. Valesius' simple correction *arietis* seems perfectly acceptable and is paleographically much closer to *armati* than Clark's *cornuti*. Cf. Veg. *mil.* 4.14 *et appellatur aries..., quod more arietum retrocedit ut cum impetu vehementius feriat*.

qua crebritate velut reciproci fulminis impetu aedificiis scissis Cf. Verg. *A.* 2.492–3 *labat ariete crebro / ianua*. For the idea that the lightning bounces back after touching the earth see Bailey ad Lucr. 6.86–9 and Beaujeu ad Plin. *Nat.* 2.43. The idea is found also in Cic. *Div.* 2.42–5, Sen. *Nat.* 2.57.4 and Luc. 1.156. There is, therefore, at first sight no reason to read *fluminis* with Petschenig. However, it must be admitted that *reciprocus* is not found as an attribute with *fulmen*, whereas it is the normal adjective for tidal movements, and, moreover, that the notion of repetition (*crebritas*) is brought out more naturally by a comparison with the recurrence of the tides, which would also tally with the preceding words *assurgentis et cedentis*. Ultimately, however, the fierceness of the attacks of the ram favours a comparison with a shaft of lightning.

Aedificium is used here of the walls of the beleaguered city, as in 21.12.9 *aedificii parte convulsa*, 24.2.12 *minae murorum bitumine et coctilibus laterculis fabricatae, quo aedificii genere nihil esse tutius constat* and Greg. Tur. *Franc.* 3.19 *totum...aedificium*. The plural refers either to several parts of the wall or, more probably, it has generalizing force.

4.9 *hoc genere operis, si fuerit exserto vigore discussum* As in § 6, *opus* is the equivalent of *machina*. *Si fuerit...discussum* is syntactically parallel to *cum...ventum fuerit*. *Exserto vigore* 'with great vigour', cf. 31.10.18 *exserta celeritate*. Amm. even says *exsertus bellator* (26.8.9, 27.10.16) meaning 'an excellent warrior'. On *quatio* and its derivatives in connection with battering-rams see the note ad 20.11.15. Damsté, 1930, 5 is certainly right in saying that the impersonal passive *fuerit discussum* is awkward, and that *nudatis defensoribus* needs a non-human subject such as *muris* or *moenibus* (with *defensoribus* as abl. separativus, not as a "complément d'agent", as Fontaine has it in his n. 88). He proposed to read *hoc genere operis <oppidum> si fuerit...discussum, nudatur defensoribus*, which would indeed solve both problems at the same time. Similar expressions are found in e.g. Caes. *Gal.* 2.6.2 (*murus*) *defensoribus nudatus est*, Liv. 38.7.4 *Romani...quatiendo arietibus muros aliquantum urbis nudaverant* and Tac. *Ann.* 13.39.4 *nudati propugnatoribus muri*. Inserting *murus* either after *fuerit* or before *discussum* (changing that to *discussus*) and taking over Damsté's *nudatur* would combine the required elements in a satisfactory way. For *solvere obsidium* see the note ad 21.12.16. There, as here, the besiegers are the Agents and the verb means 'to bring to an end.' The plural is again generic, as in § 8 *aedificiis*. For *recludere* cf. 27.12.7 *reclusis subito portis*.

4.10 In the introduction to this chapter Lendle was quoted, who characterized the following description as a 'phantasievolle Darstellung', which cannot be used as a source. Southern and Dixon, 1996, 161, are of the opinion that the machine of Ammianus should not be confused with the *helepolis* of the Hellenistic period. And indeed, there are indications that the word *helepolis* was used in later times with a less restricted meaning to indicate different types of siegetowers. Hesychius defines *helepoleis* as μηχανήματα, οἱ κριοὶ ἢ οἰαδήποτε δι' ὧν αἱ πόλεις καθαιροῦνται, that is to say he does not distinguish them from battering rams and other siege-engines. The same seems to be the case in Josephus. In his account of the siege of Iotapata he mentions the heroic deeds of one Eleasar, who succeeded in putting the *helepolis* of the Romans out of action: *BJ* 3.230–1 ὑπερμεγέθη πέτραν ἀράμενος ἀφίησιν ἀπὸ τοῦ τείχους ἐπὶ τὴν ἑλέπολιν μετὰ τοσαύτης βίας, ὥστε ἀπορρῆξαι τὴν κεφαλὴν τοῦ μηχανήματος. Later, he dies with the κεφάλη in his arms, § 232: μετὰ τοῦ κριοῦ κατέπεσεν.

Even if we accept that Amm. uses the term *helepolis* with a wider definition, the fact remains that his description of the nature and the function of the *trisulcuae cuspides* is totally unsatisfactory. Brok's ingenuous suggestion, mentioned in Fontaine n. 91, that Amm. may have had in mind the *tichodifros*, sketched in Anon. *de mach. bell.* 8, would not solve the incongruity that Amm. suggests a vast machine (§ 11), whereas the *tichodifros* served only to protect the *ballistae* as they advanced toward the wall. Fontaine praises "la précision d'une chose vue", but the passage gives more the impression *d'une chose lue*, and not quite understood.

The *helepoleis* could be transported in parts and assembled where they were needed, as is evident from the description of the siege of Pirisabora in 24.2. The effect of the *helepolis* must have been devastating. As Vegetius says at the conclusion of his discussion of the engine itself and the possible countermeasures to be taken against it (*mil.* 4.17): *Quid enim auxilii superest, cum hi, qui de murorum altitudine sperabant, repente supra se aspiciunt altiorem hostium murum?*

Pro his arietum meditamentis iam crebritate despectis The reading *meditamentis* is not above suspicion. *Meditamentum* is not found elsewhere in Amm., and is altogether rare (TLL VIII 570.3 sqq.). *Machinamentis*, the reading of BAG, for which cf. § 8 *huic machinamento* (the ram), is closer to *machina*, the usual term for these engines. Cf. μηχανή and μηχάνημα in the Greek treatises on this subject. Tac. *Hist.* 4.26.3 *muniendo vallandoque et ceteris belli meditamentis* is no real parallel, since there *meditamenta* means 'exercises'. On the other hand, *arietum meditamentis*, which is certainly lectio difficilior, can be understood as meaning 'these cleverly constructed rams', so it seems prudent to stick to V's text.

The rams have become a common feature in sieges and for that reason no longer inspire much fear. *Crebritas* is a favourite word in Amm. He uses it no less than 24 times, mostly in periphrastic phrases of the type *sagittarum volantium crebritate* (25.3.11).

conditur machina scriptoribus historicis nota, quam helepolin Graeci cognominamus See the note ad 21.10.6, where Aurelius Victor is described as *scriptor historicus.* In 22.15.28 Herodotus is called just *scriptor.* Amm. may be thinking here of Diodorus Siculus (20.48.2–3, 20.91.2–5) and Plutarch (Plut. *Demetr.* 20.7, 21.1–2 and *Mor.* 183 b), our principal sources for the *helepolis* in connection with the sieges of Demetrius Poliorcetes. That Amm. is thinking of Plutarch in particular is suggested by the fact that Plutarch, in the chapters leading up to the description, pays much attention to Antigonus, the father of Demetrius, whom Amm. explicitly (and unnecessarily) mentions. Also the phrase *opera diuturna* in the next sentence seems to echo Plut. *Demetr.* 20.9 ‛Ρόδιοι δὲ πολὺν χρόνον ὑπ' αὐτοῦ πολιορκηθέντες.

The word ἑλέπολις, used adjectivally for e.g. the 'city-destroying' Helen of Troy in Aeschylus' *Ag.* 689, is first attested in the sense of 'siege-engine', 'giant siege-tower' in Bito's *Construction of War Machines and Artillery*, which dates from "the early years of the reign of Attalus I, 241–197 B.C." (Marsden, 1971, 78). Bito (p. 52–6 Wescher) describes the construction of the machine which 'Posidonius the Macedonian designed for Alexander son of Philip' (p. 52). However, the most famous *helepolis* of Antiquity was the one used by Demetrius Poliorcetes and described by Diodorus and Plutarch. Cf. also Athenaeus Mechanicus (p. 27 Wescher), Ph. *Bel.* p. 95 Thévenot, Vitr. 10.16.4, Ath. 5.206 d and 10.415 a.

Amm. has the Greek term again in 24.2.18 *machinam, quae cognominatur helepolis, iussit expeditius fabricari.* It is used also by Vitruvius in his detailed description of this siege-tower (10.16). The Latin equivalent of the term is *turris ambulatoria (B. Alex.* 2.5, Vitr. 10.13.3, Veg. *mil.* 4.16), *turris mobilis* (Liv. 21.11.7, Curt. 8.10.32) or simply *turris* . For phrases like this, in which the author seems to pride himself on his Greek origins, cf. Den Boeft, 1992.

cuius opera diuturna Demetrius...Poliorcetes est appellatus The sentence is somewhat compressed. *Opera diuturna* must be taken with the abl. abs. *Rhodo aliisque urbibus oppugnatis,* which in its turn explains why Demetrius was given the surname 'the Besieger'. For similar compressed sentences see the note ad 20.3.9 *et tunc lunae Graece synodos dicitur.*

According to Diodorus Siculus (20.48.1–3) Demetrius constructed his first *helepolis* during the siege of Salamis on Cyprus in 307 B.C. It was to no avail, for the *helepolis* and the other engines for siege, were set on fire and destroyed by the besieged (20.48.4–8). Nevertheless, Demetrius continued the siege and finally took possession of Salamis and all other cities on Cyprus (20.53.1).

The next time we hear of Demetrius' *helepolis* is when the Macedonian tried to conquer Rhodes in 305–4 B.C. (cf. D.S. 20.58.1 ff. and Plut. *Demetr.* 20–1); for a modern account of this siege see Berthold, 1984, 67–80 and for Demetrius in general Willrich, 1901 and Elkeles, 1941). In his report of the siege Diodorus (20.91.2–8) gives a detailed description of the engine (which differs in some respects from the one he had given in 20.48.1–3 regarding the *helepolis* used on Cyprus). Plutarch (*Demetr.* 21.1–3) also devotes some words to its manufacturing. To Athenaeus Mechanicus (p. 27 Wescher) and Vitruvius (10.16.4) we owe the name of the engineer who built the machine: Epimachus of Athens (cf. Garlan, 1974, 209).

Despite all his efforts Demetrius failed to capture Rhodes (the use of *oppugnare* in the present passage does not prove that Amm. was aware of this fact; see the note ad 23.1.2 and cf. 24.2.18 *qua* (sc. helepoli), *ut supra docuimus, rex usus Demetrius superatis oppidis pluribus Poliorcetes appellatus est*), but later on he did take other cities, e.g. Sicyon in 303 (D.S. 20.102.2) and Thebes in 291 (Plut. *Demetr.* 39–40), as he had done before (cf. e.g. D.S. 20.45.5 ff. about Munychia and 20.46.3 about Megara; for the cities on Cyprus, see above).

According to Vitruvius (10.16.4) Demetrius owed his surname to his pertinacity (*rex Demetrius, qui propter animi pertinaciam Poliorcetes est appellatus*) – a rather inadequate explanation. Pliny translated *Poliorcetes* with *expugnator* (*rex Demetrius expugnator cognominatus, Nat.* 7.126), but did not give any further comment. Neither did Plutarch (*Demetr.* 1.7 and 42.10). Amm. is more detailed and more to the point. His words tally with what we find in Diodorus: οὐ μόνον γὰρ τὰ μεγέθη τῶν μηχανῶν καὶ τὸ πλῆθος τῆς ἠθροισμένης δυνάμεως ἐξέπληττεν αὐτούς (sc. the Rhodians), ἀλλὰ καὶ τὸ τοῦ βασιλέως βίαιον καὶ φιλότεχνον ἐν ταῖς πολιορκίαις. εὐμήχανος γὰρ ὢν καθ' ὑπερβολὴν ἐν ταῖς ἐπινοίαις καὶ πολλὰ παρὰ τὴν τῶν ἀρχιτεκτόνων τέχνην παρευρίσκων ὠνομάσθη μὲν πολιορκητής (20.92.1–2, cf. 20.103.3). This explanation of *Poliorcetes* as an honorific title is accepted by almost all modern scholars. However, Heckel, 1984, stressing the fact that the siege of Rhodes, although an impressive undertaking, was a complete failure, suggests that originally *Poliorcetes* was a sarcastic nickname, the humour of which was lost on subsequent generations.

testudo compaginatur immanis The choice of the term *testudo* already suggests that the primary function of the *helepolis*, in Amm.'s view, is to offer protection to the attackers, rather than to eliminate the height advantage enjoyed by the defenders. The element of height is dominant e.g. in the description of the sieges of Amida: *turresque fabricabantur frontibus ferratis excelsae* (19.5.1) and Pirisabora: *ad hanc molem ingentem* (of the *helepolis*) *superaturam celsarum turrium minas* (24.2.19). On seeing the *helepolis* the defenders of Pirisabora surrendered immediately. For *compaginare* see the note ad § 2 above.

4.11

axibus roborata longissimis ferreisque clavis aptata For the enormous dimensions of the *helepoleis* in the Hellenistic period see Marsden, 1971, 84. The *ferrei clavi* are mentioned also in Vegetius' description of the mobile siege-tower in 4.46 *utroque capite* (sc. of the *trabes*) *ferrato* and 4.20 *ferratasque trabes*. Presumably, the nails did not only serve to join the wooden beams, but also to reinforce the walls of the tower. Cf. D.S. 20.91.5 τὰς δὲ τρεῖς ἐπιφανεῖς πλευρὰς τῆς μηχανῆς συνεκάλυψε λεπίσι σιδηραῖς καθηλωμέναις ('iron plates nailed on'), 19.5.1 quoted in the preceding note and D.S. 19.7.2 and 19.7.5 where *turres ferratae* are mentioned.

contegitur coriis bubulis virgarumque recenti textura Cf. 20.11.13 *quod umectis scortis* (*coriis* Petschenig) *et centonibus erant opertae materiae plures* with the note and the description of the shields of the defenders of Pirisabora in 24.2.10 *obtecti scutis vimine firmissimo textis et crudorum tergorum densitate vestitis*. In his description of the *testudo arietaria*, Vitr. 10.13.2 has the same detail: *coriisque bubulis texit*. See also Veg. *mil.* 4.17 (*machinamenta*) *ne tantum opus hostili concremetur incendio, diligentissime ex crudis coriis vel centonibus communita*. *Virgarum recens textura* is the equivalent of *virgae recentes inter se contextae*.

atque limo asperguntur eius suprema, ut flammeos detrectet et missiles casus Caesar's detailed description of the construction of a siege-tower in *Civ.* 2.9.4 reads almost like a commentary on this sentence: *eamque contabulationem summam lateribus lutoque constraverunt, ne quid ignis hostium nocere posset, centonesque insuper iniecerunt, ne aut tela tormentis missa tabulationem perfringerent aut saxa ex catapultis latericium discuterent*. In the two other instances of *detrectare* in Amm., 20.4.8 and 28.6.23, the verb has its normal meaning 'to shirk' (one's duty). Here the meaning is 'to be protected from', for which, however, no parallel can be found in TLL V 1.835.26 sqq. An attractive alternative would be to read *deflectat*, for which see TLL V 1.359.24–7 ("i.q. vitare"). For the substitution of the adjectives *flammeus* and *missilis* for *flammarum* and *missilium* see Szantyr 60–1.

4.12   *conseruntur... eius frontalibus trisulcae cuspides praeacutae ponderibus ferreis graves* The Hellenistic *helepolis* had several storeys, no less than 20 in the tower built (or designed) by Diades, the engineer of Alexander the Great, according to Vitr. 10.13.3, which carried artillery, drawbridges and sometimes battering rams. In order to be able to use these the walls had to have openings and indeed Vitr. 10.13.4 says *singulis partibus in ea* (sc. turri) *fenestratis*. Plutarch too mentions θυρίδες: τὸ δὲ πρὸς τοὺς πολεμίους αὐτῆς μέτωπον ἀνέῳκτο... θυρίσιν (*Demetr.* 21.2). See also Veg. *mil.* 4.17. Amm., however, does not mention any storeys here and he depicts the front of the tower as closed with the *trisulcae cuspides* somehow fastened to it. Unfortunately, it is impossible to imagine how these *cuspides* could be put to any use if they were fixed onto such an unwieldy contraption. The function of the *trisulcae cuspides* being to tear down the wall, they must be compared to the *falx muralis* described by Vegetius in the following terms: *Haec* (sc. turris) *intrinsecus accipit trabem, quae... adunco praefigitur ferro et falx vocatur ab eo, quod incurva est, ut de muro extrahat lapides* (mil. 4.14). Caes. *Gal.* 3.14.5 mentions *falces praeacutae insertae adfixaeque longuriis* ('poles'), *non absimili forma muralium falcium*. Presumably they were swung against the wall, which is the only way in which the detail *ponderibus ferreis graves* makes sense. The fact that the *trisulcae cuspides* are an incongruous element in the description of the *helepolis* led Brok, according to Fontaine n. 91, to believe that Amm. may have been thinking of the *tichodifros*, a siege-engine mentioned by Anon. *mach. bell.* 8. Indeed this engine was fitted with *fuscinae* ('tridents') and *lanceae*: § 4 *cuius axium extremitates et frons nec non et superior latitudo fuscinis et lanceis armatur*. Still, the short passage in the Anonymus evokes a small wheeled vehicle serving exclusively to protect *ballistae* approaching a wall. *Frontalibus* is best taken with TLL VI 1365.57–60 as a dative dependent on *conseruntur*. The only parallel for *conserere* with dative is 14.8.13 *Huic Arabia est conserta*; TLL IV 415.42–84.

Trisulcus is not found anywhere else in Amm. Indeed, the choice of the adjective seems to be dictated by the object with which the *cuspis* is compared, *trisulcus* being the preferred adjective for Jupiter's lightning bolt, e.g. in Ov. *Am.* 2.5.51–2 (oscula) *qualia possent / excutere irato tela trisulca Iovi*.

qualia nobis pictores ostendunt fulmina vel fictores For *ostendere* "to represent in art" (OLD s.v. 1e) cf. Plin. *Nat.* 35.73 *patris... voltum velavit, quem digne non poterat ostendere*. Surprisingly, the TLL VI 649.5–75 gives no parallel for the jingle *pictor – fictor*.

aculeis exsertis abrumpat For *aculeus* see the note ad § 7. Here the *aculei* must be the barbed hooks of the trident. *Exsertus* is often found concerning threatening weapons: TLL V 2.1856.70–1857.3.

hanc ita validam molem The adverb recapitulates what has been said about the strengthening of the tower by means of the heavy beams and the iron plates. 4.13

rotis et funibus regens numerosus intrinsecus miles For technical details about the way in which the *helepolis* was moved forward see Marsden, 1971, 88–9 and Lendle, 1983, 48–53. A detailed account is given by D.S. 20.91.7: οἱ δὲ μέλλοντες κινήσειν τὴν μηχανὴν ἐξελέχθησαν... οἱ ταῖς ῥώμαις διαφέροντες ἄνδρες τρισχίλιοι καὶ τετρακόσιοι·(!) τούτων δ' οἱ μὲν ἐντὸς ἀποληφθέντες, οἱ δ' ἐκ τῶν ὄπισθεν μερῶν παριστάμενοι προεώθουν. Caesar tells us that the Atuatuci were flabbergasted to see a siege-tower approaching and surrendered immediately: *non se existimare Romanos sine ope divina bellum gerere, qui tantae altitudinis machinationes tanta celeritate promovere et ex propinquitate pugnare possent (Gal.* 2.31.2).

languidiori murorum parti See TLL VII 2.925.51 for more instances in which *languidus* is used of "res corporeales quasi animatae".

nisi desuper propugnantium valuerint vires The *propugnantes* are the defenders on the wall. Possible counter-measures against the *helepolis* are enumerated in Veg. *mil.* 4.18, the most effective being incendiary materials such as the *malleoli*, which Amm. discusses in the next sections. *Valere* has the connotation of predominance here, for which see OLD s.v. 5.

collisis parietibus aditus patefacit ingentes For *paries* = *murus* see the note ad 20.6.3. *Aditus* 'breach' is found again in 24.4.25 *Tandem nudata reseratis aditibus multis lapsura invaditur civitas* and Curt. 9.5.19 *perfregerunt murum et, qua moliti erant aditum, inrupere in urbem.*

4.14 *Malleoli autem, teli genus, figurantur hac specie* The *malleolus* or 'little hammer' derives its name from its form. It is basically a stick with at its end a round thickening consisting of or filled with incendiary material, which makes it resemble a mallet or a club. The *malleolus* or fire-dart is mentioned for the first time in Latin literature by Sisenna *hist.* 83 *de quibus partim malleolos, partim fasces sarmentorum incensos supra vallum frequentes,* so that it may safely be assumed that this weapon, like the engines mentioned earlier in this digression, dates back to at least Hellenistic times. Apart from the brief mention in Veg. *mil.* 4.18, this is the only description of the fire-dart in Latin. Amm. mentions *malleoli* in his descriptions of the sieges of Singara (20.6.6, q.v.), Bezabde (20.7.10 and 20.11.13), Maozamalcha (24.4.16) and in his account of the riots in Rome against the urban prefect Lampadius (27.3.8). For the opening phrase of this part of the excursus cf. 26.8.9 *quod machinae genus... figuratur hac specie* and 20.11.26 *quae species unde ita figurari est solita, expositio brevis ostendet.*

sagitta est cannea inter spiculum et harundinem multifido ferro coagmentata The *sagitta* is the fire-dart as a whole, of which the *spiculum* ('point') and the *harundo* ('shaft') are the component parts. Between the point and the shaft is the *multifidum ferrum*. The first satisfactory explanation of this puzzling phrase has been given by Brok, 1978. He compared the present description with the following passage from the Greek historian Eusebius (*FGrHist* 101, p. 481.9–21): τὰ δὲ πυρφόρα ταῦτα βέλεα ἦν τοιάδε· ἀντὶ τῆς ἄρδιος τῆς πρὸς τῷ ἄκρῳ τοῦ ὀιστοῦ εἶχε ταῦτα τάπερ μεμηχάνητο ὥστε τὸ πῦρ αὐτὸ ἐπιφέρειν· ταῦτα δὲ ἦν σιδήρεα, ἔχοντα ἔνερθεν ἐκ τοῦ πυθμένος κεραίας ἐπεχεχλημένας. αἱ δὲ κεραῖαι χωρὶς ἐπ' ἑωυτέων ἐλαυνόμεναι, ἔπειτα καμπτόμεναι κατὰ κορυφὴν πρὸς ἀλλήλας ξυνήγοντο.

συναφθεισέων δὲ τούτων ἐς ἄκρον ἀκὶς ἰθείη καὶ ὀξυτάτη ἀπὸ πασέων ἐξῄιε. τῆς δὲ δὴ μεμηχανημένης οὕτως ἔργον ἦν, κατ' ὅτεω ἂν ἐνεχθείη, προσπερονημένην μιν ἐνεστάναι ('these fire-darts were as follows: instead of the point at the end of the arrow it had a part that was construed with a view to carrying fire. It was made of iron and had strips diverging below from the shaft (reading ἐπεχκεχλιμένας with Wescher). These diverging strips then bent back and met at the top. Where they were joined together at the top, a straight and very sharp point projected from all of them. The effect of this construction was that it remained fixed in whatever object it was shot into'). The part of the *malleolus* that carried the fire is described by Eusebius as follows: καμπτόμεναι αἱ κεραῖαι κόλπον κοῖλον, κατὰ τὸν διεστεῶσαι ἦσαν ἀπ' ἀλληλέων, ἐποίεον, οἷον δὴ καὶ τῶν οὕτως ἐχουσέων γυναίκων ἠλακάται, περὶ ἃς δὴ στρέφεται τὸ εἴριον ἔξωθεν περιβαλλόμενον, ἀπ' ὧν δὴ τὸν στήμονα κατάγουσι ('these bending iron strips formed a hollow bosom by the distances between them, like the distaffs of women spinning wool (reading ἐριουργουσέων with Brok), around which wool is wound and from which they draw the thread'). The comparison with the distaff in both authors proves beyond reasonable doubt that they are describing the same weapon, so that Eusebius' text may be used to interpret Amm.'s vague phrase *multifido ferro*, which turns out to refer to an iron container between the point and the shaft.

Hagendahl, 1921, 60 discusses the poeticism *multifidus* which Amm. uses again in 17.1.8 for trenches with several branches *indicio perfugae doctus per subterranea quaedam occulta fossasque multifidas latere plurimos* and the diverging arms of the Euphrates in 24.3.14 *ubi pars maior Euphratis in rivos dividitur multifidos*.

For *coagmentare* see the note ad 22.8.10 *in speciem Scythici arcus*. The present use is correctly explained in TLL III 1377.10–8 as "i.q. instruere".

quae in muliebris coli formam... concavatur ventre subtiliter The relative *quae* refers to the *sagitta* as a whole. The following comparison clearly illustrates more specifically a part of the *sagitta*, viz. the *multifidum ferrum*. The distaff is typically a woman's concern, cf. e.g. Tib. 2.1.63 *hinc et femineus labor est, hinc pensa colusque*. *Concavare* is explained by Brok, 1978, 59 n. 16. It does not mean 'to hollow out', but rather 'to give a curved form to', as the OLD has it. Brok gives as parallels Nemes. *ecl.* 3.49 *concavat ille manus palmasque in pocula vertit* and Ov. *Met.* 2.195–6 *in geminos ubi bracchia concavat arcus / Scorpius*. *Concavatur ventre* tallies exactly with Eusebius' κόλπον κοῖλον... ἐποίεον. *Subtiliter* describes the container as sloping outward gently (presumably to reduce the resistance of the air).

plurifariam patens The only other occurrence of this rare adverb in Amm. is 27.8.7 *divisis plurifariam globis*.

79

in alveo ipso ignem cum aliquo suscipit alimento Eusebius is more specific: μεταξὺ τούτου τοῦ κόλπου εἴσω στυππίον ἢ καὶ ξύλα λεπτά, θείου αὐτοῖσι προσπλασσαμένου ἢ καὶ τῷ Μηδείης ἐλαίῳ καλεομένῳ αὐτὰ χρίσαντες, ἐνετίθεσαν ('within this cavity they put hemp smeared with sulphur or rubbed with what is called Medic oil'). For this last substance cf. 23.6.37 *In hac regione oleum conficitur Medicum, quo illitum telum* e.q.s. The rest of that section practically repeats the next section in this digression. However, it is to be noted that Amm. here, where he probably follows a source similar to, if not identical with, that of Eusebius, expresses himself with greater precision than in 23.6.37. Here the incendiary material or *alimentum* is present inside the cavity of the *malleolus*; in the later passage the Medic oil is said to be rubbed onto the fire-dart as a whole.

4.15 *et si emissa lentius arcu invalido... haeserit usquam, tenaciter cremat* In 23.6.37 Amm. varies *arcu invalido* to *laxiore arcu*. In Eusebius this detail is lacking: τοῦ δ' ὧν ἀτράκτου τοξευομένου ἤτοι ὑπὸ μηχανῆς ἢ καὶ τοξοτέων, τὰ ἐνεχόμενα ὑπὸ τῆς ῥύμης ἐξήπτετο καὶ ἀφθέντα φλόγα ἐποίεε ('when the dart was shot either by an engine or by archers, its contents would flare up because of the rush and, having flared up, would start a fire').

arcus ictu enim rapidiore exstinguitur The parallel passage in 23.6.37 – *nam ictu exstinguitur rapido* – makes it practically certain that V's *arcus* before *ictu* should not be accepted. *Enim* moreover occupies the third place in the sentence only in prepositional phrases and after composite verb forms.

aquisque conspersa acriores excitat aestus incendiorum Why this is the case is not explained by Amm. We have to turn to Eusebius and to the parallel passage in 23.6.37 to find the answer. The sulphur and the Medic oil burn even more hotly when they come into contact with water. It is an old trick, already described by Livy in his account of the Bacchanalia, 39.13.12 *matronas Baccharum habitu crinibus sparsis cum ardentibus facibus decurrere ad Tiberim demissasque in aquam faces, quia vivum sulphur cum calce insit, integra flamma efferre.*

nec remedio ullo quam superiacto pulvere consopitur The verb *consopire* is used literally in 29.1.16 *leni quiete post meridiem consopitus,* but more often metaphorically as here and in 22.5.3 *discordiis consopitis*. One is reminded of Vergil's famous verses about ending a war between bees: *hi motus animorum atque haec certamina tanta / pulveris exigui iactu compressa quiescent* (*G.* 4.86–7).

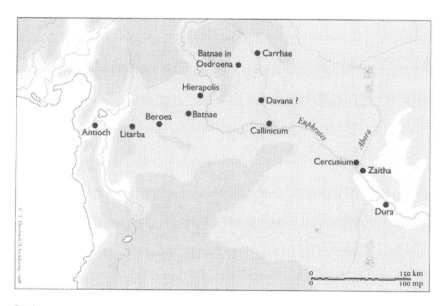

Syria

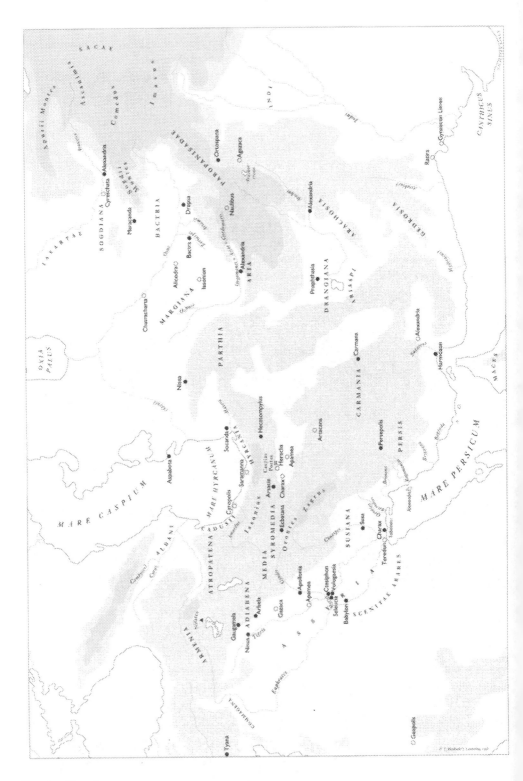

Persian Empire

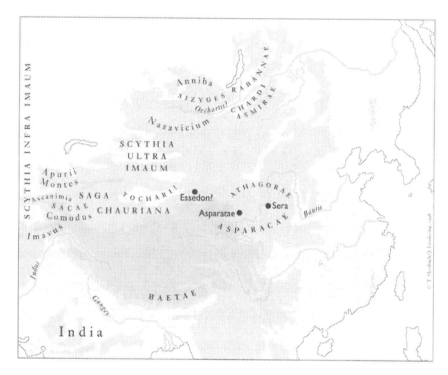

China

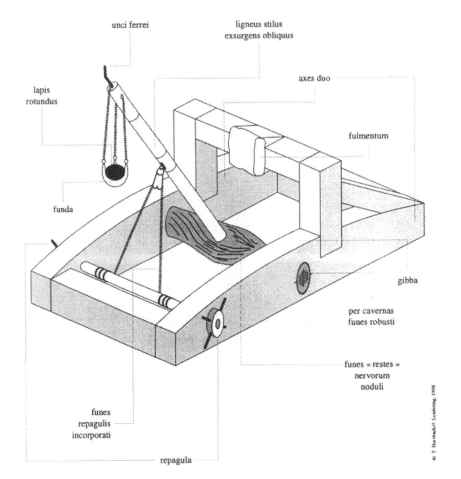

Scorpio

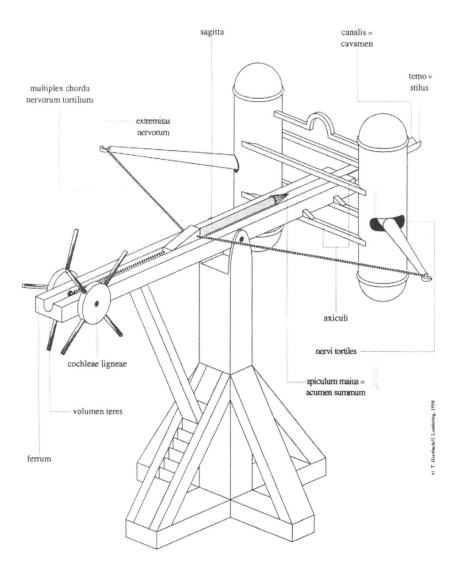

Ballista

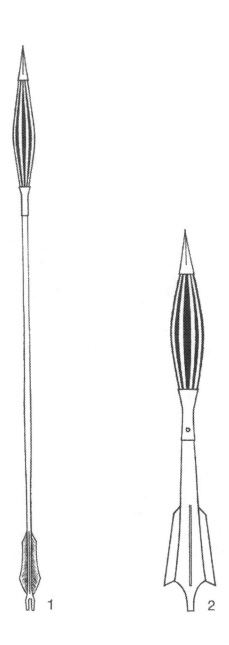

Mallelus (1 bow, 2 ballista)

Chapter 5

This chapter reports the expedition's arrival at Cercusium and the subsequent invasion of Persian territory. As could be expected, the author pays much attention to this momentous phase, emphasizing its importance by introducing a series of reminiscences from history. This begins straightaway in the first sections, where Diocletian's measures against Persian threats are the main point of interest in the description of Cercusium and its geographical position. In the rest of the chapter, past experiences with the Persian empire remain in the foreground, to be incorporated in the wider framework of Roman history in general in Julian's great speech to his soldiers. The author has chosen this device to avoid a further digression by himself, the additional advantage being that the historical reasons for the attack on Persia are given by the protagonist himself. Moreover, the movement forward of the narrative which is precisely caused by history's lessons reaches its high point in Julian's inspired speech. This moving into the future is, however, continuously accompanied by a counterforce which aims at delaying and postponing the actions. At first this is restricted to a negative advice by the PPO of Gaul, but soon more alarming facts appear, viz. the unremitting series of bad *omina*, which had also been a feature in the earlier part of the eastbound march, reported in the first three chapters of book 23. Although these *omina* are rated at their true value by the experts, Julian makes light of their warnings, supported in this by the philosophers in his entourage. In fact, these men made the same wrong assessment of the situation as the soldiers who reacted jubilantly after Julian's speech. They could only imagine the continuation of the successes of the past, just as the philosophers gave a completely wrong interpretation of a warning sign on historical grounds. Thus in the end both the soldiers and Julian's intellectual advisers had *spem magis ipsam quam causam spei* in mind.

To his credit, the historian has brought out clearly the two contrasting forces which he must have experienced as exasperating. The lessons of history demanded the final settlement of the conflicts with Persia: *abolenda nobis natio molestissima* (§ 19) was Julian's conclusion, yet the gods forbade this solution, at least at that particular moment. Julian failed to deal with this tragic dilemma and thus *quod praescripsit fatalis ordo* (§ 5) came to pass.

5.1 *Ascitis Saracenorum auxiliis, quae animis obtulere promptissimis* See for this use of *asciscere*, 'to incorporate in the armed forces', 14.10.14 *ut auxiliatores pro adversariis asciscamus*, 21.13.13 *ascitis in societatem superbam auxiliaribus paucis*. The verbal form *obtulere* can be explained either as a normal example of the historic perf.: 'which they offered (at that moment)', or as one of many cases of Amm.'s use of perf. instead of pluperf. because of the cursus (tardus): 'which they had offered (at the meeting reported in 23.3.8)'. For *animis...promptissimis* cf. *prompta...audacia* (17.12.8) and *animis...promptis* (27.6.5). Sabbah 488 n. 104 aptly remarks that the adjunct is not superfluous, but implicitly anticipates the objections of those who might have taken the grandiloquent phrase in 23.2.1 *nequaquam decere adventiciis adiumentis rem vindicari Romanam* too literally. The Saracens' enthusiasm could not be answered with a rebuff. Amm. fails to mention that Julian himself had sent for the Saracens: Jul. *Ep.* 98, 401 d (cf. above, ad 23.2.1).

tendens imperator agili gradu The verb *tendere*, 'to march', sometimes occurs without explicit reference to direction, e.g. in 21.5.6, 21.15.2, 27.10.8. In the present text, however, *Cercusium* can be regarded as functioning ἀπὸ κοινοῦ as a complement of both *tendens* and *ingressus est*. For *agili gradu*, which occurs only here, see the note ad 20.4.12 on phrases with *gradus*.

Cercusium principio mensis Aprilis ingressus est Julian, leaving Callinicum on March, 28 (cf. 23.3.7–8), had marched speedily southwards along the high bank of the Euphrates to Cercusium, some 165 km away from Callinicum. He arrived in Cercusium *principio mensis Aprilis*. What precisely do these words mean? "At the beginning of the month of April" (thus Rolfe and all other translators) or 'on April, 1' (suggested by Brok, 1959, 63 and 257)?
To cover a distance of 165 km the army needed some five to eight days (if we assume that it marched at an average speed of 20 to 30 km a day; cf. for this the note on chronology), which would imply that Julian arrived in Cercusium between April, 1 and April, 4. In the present case the earliest possible date seems preferable, in view of *agili gradu*. If this is right, then *principio mensis* is synonymous with *kalendis*, for which use an exact parallel can be found in Ov. *Fast.* 2.55–8: *Principio mensis Phrygiae contermina Matri / Sospita delubris dicitur aucta novis. / nunc ubi sint illis, quaeris, sacrata Kalendis / templa deae?*

cuius moenia Abora et Euphrates ambiunt flumina The Roman fortress of Cercusium or Circesium (Eutr. 9.2.3, cf. Κιρκήσιον in e.g. Zos. 3.12.3, 3.13.1 and Procop. *Aed.* 2.6.2, *Pers.* 2.5.2; see for yet other orthographical alternatives Weissbach, 1922, 505), at the confluence of the Euphrates and the Khabur (*cuius moenia Abora et Euphrates ambiunt flumina velut spatium insulare fingentes*), has been identified with the present-day village of Busaira (cf. for a description of its ruins Sarre and Herzfeld, 1911, 172–4). In Julian's time it was a border town: φρούριον δὲ τοῦτο κυκλούμενον ὑπό τε τοῦ Ἀβώρα ποταμοῦ καὶ αὐτοῦ τοῦ Εὐφράτου, τοῖς δὲ Ἀσσυρίων ὁρίοις συναπτόμενον, Zos. 3.12.3. Cf. further Procop. *Pers.* 2.5.2 ἔστι δὲ τοῦ ποταμοῦ ἐπὶ θάτερα Ῥωμαίων φρούριον ἔσχατον ὃ Κιρκήσιον ἐπικαλεῖται, ἐχυρὸν ἐς τὰ μάλιστα ὄν, ἐπεὶ Ἀβόρρας μὲν ποταμὸς μέγας ἐνταῦθα τὰς ἐκβολὰς ἔχων τῷ Εὐφράτῃ ἀναμίγνυται, τὸ δὲ φρούριον τοῦτο πρὸς αὐτῇ που τῇ γωνίᾳ κεῖται ἣν δὴ τοῖν ποταμοῖν ἡ μίξις ποιεῖται. The Abora is called Ἀράξης by Xenophon (*An.* 1.4.19).

Although Magnus of Carrhae, cited by Malalas *Chron.* 13.329, makes Diocletian the founder of the fortress (τὸ Ῥωμαικὸν κάστρον τὸ λεγόμενον Κιρκήσιον, κείμενον εἰς τὸ μέσον τῶν δύο ποταμῶν τοῦ Εὐφράτου καὶ τοῦ Ἀββορᾶ, ὅπερ ἔκτισε Διοκλητιανός, βασιλεὺς Ῥωμαίων, cf. Procop. *Aed.* 2.6.2), Amm. is right in stating that Cercusium already existed before Diocletian as a small and unfortified stronghold, for "it appears on the Ka'ba inscription among the cities captured by Shapur I in the course of his second campaign" (Oppenheimer, 1983, 381, referring to Honigmann-Maricq, 1952, 147, no. 27: krksy'; Κορχουσίωνα). Cf. also Eutropius 9.2.3 and HA *Gd* 34.2, where it is reported that the third century emperor Gordian III was buried not far from the *castrum Circesium*, and *Chron. Pasch.* s.a. 250, which refers to the time of the emperor Decius (but the testimony of these sources, written after Diocletian, is not conclusive; their terminology may be anachronistic). Perhaps Cercusium's name in former times was Phaliga or Phalga (for references see Musil, 1927, 334–5 and Oppenheimer, 1983, 380–1). Cf. in general Weissbach, 1922.

Diocletian's fortification of Cercusium was part of his programme of building and fortifying cities, forts and towers all along the frontiers, especially the eastern one (*Pan.* 5.18.4, Zos. 1.34.1 and Malalas *Chron.* 12.308; cf. Lewin, 1990 and Whittaker, 1994, 134 ff.).

munimentum tutissimum et fabre politum Amm. frequently uses *munimentum* as a synonym of *castellum*. See the note ad 16.12.58. The phrase *fabre politus* also occurs in 19.5.4 (q.v.); cf. also *fabre munitam* (31.13.14). The fortress was not an emergency stronghold, but "bâtie selon toutes les règles de l'art" (Fontaine).

velut spatium insulare Cf. the phrase *ambitu insulari* in 15.11.3 and 24.2.9 and see the note ad 22.8.10.

exiguum ante hoc et suspectum For *exiguus* denoting the small size of a town cf. Verg. *A.* 4.211–2 *urbem exiguam* and 26.1.1 *super exiguis silere castellis*. For *suspectus*, 'exposed to danger', see the note ad 20.8.1. 5.2

cum in ipsis barbarorum confiniis interiores limites ordinaret Millar, 1993, 180–1 rightly explains Amm.'s "puzzling reference to *limites interiores*" (Whittaker, 1994, 137) thus: the expression "should not be taken to imply the idea of a double line of frontier installations, outer and inner. It means 'the border-districts further inland'". Cf. Malavolta, 1982. For *limes* see the note ad 23.3.4.

documento... per Syriam Persae Seyfarth agrees with Clark's assumption of a lacuna, without accepting Heraeus' suggestion for its repair: *(documento) recenti perterritus, ne vagarentur*. Here Heraeus makes use of Gelenius' *ne vagarentur*, which tallies with Amm.'s usage: 18.6.10 *praedatores latius vagabantur*, 19.11.1 *vagarique licentius*. The addition *recenti* seems superfluous in view of *paucis ante annis* in the immediate sequel of the text, but the combination *documentum recens* also occurs in 14.7.6, 26.2.4, 26.5.11, 31.4.8. Češka, 1974, 92–3 proposes a more economical solution, adding only *ne vagarentur* after *documento*. Independently, Sabbah 380 n. 28 defends the same solution. This can best be explained by Češka's rendering: "zur Warnung, damit die Perser nicht durch Syrien streiften". Unfortunately, this translation cannot stand. Indeed, *documentum* often denotes a warning, but is then directly linked to a deterring precedent. Cic. *ad Brut.* 1.15.10 is a good example: *ut... in posterum documentum statuerem ne quis talem amentiam vellet imitari*. Cicero refers to his proposal to take measures against Antonius and Lepidus. Adequate military preparations do not constitute a *documentum*. It should be noted that *ne discurrerent* is proposed by Kiessling, 1874, 6 as an emendation for V's *e documento*, which seems too drastic a measure, although in Gelenius' edition the word *documento* is also missing. The conclusion must be that some words in the spirit of Heraeus' proposal have been lost. The assumption of a lacuna is inevitable.

paucis ante annis   I.e. before Diocletian's measure, not before Julian's arrival. Cf. the final words of § 3 *et haec quidem Gallieni temporibus evenerunt*.

provinciarum   This refers to sing. *Syriam*: the geographical region contained more than one Roman province, as is explained in the note ad 22.10.1.

5.3   The historicity of the incident narrated in this section (for the sources see Felix, 1985, 58–61) is severely questioned by Downey, 1961, 256–7 ("the theater scene might well seem to be merely a literary detail"). Seyfarth, 1962 combats this view, noting, as Brok ad loc. had already done, that another Antiochene, Libanius, refers to the same scene, although with far fewer details: 'we have no reason to fear a disaster as occurred in the days of our ancestors, οἷς ἐν τῷ θεάτρῳ συγκαθημένοις ἐφειστήκεσαν οἱ τοξόται τὸ ὄρος κατειληφότες' (*Or.* 24.38).
Seyfarth is right in observing that the chronology of the episode (see for this below) is so much in dispute that any argument based on it is inconclusive, and that the supposed literary parallel to Macrobius *Sat.* 1.17.25, about an event at the *ludi Apollinares* in Rome, is far from striking (*nam cum ludi Romae Apollini celebrarentur ex vaticinio Marcii vatis carmineque Sibyllino, repentino hostis adventu plebs ad arma excitata occurrit hosti, eoque tempore nubes sagittarum in adversos visa ferri et hostem fugavit et victores Romanos*

ad spectacula dei sospitalis reduxit). However, his own reasoning is not very cogent either. Against Downey's view that it would be odd to suppose that Sapor was able to march through Syria and then lay siege to Antioch without it being noticed by anyone, Seyfarth postulates that Libanius and Amm. confused the reports of two events, one in which the Persians made a quick raid on Antioch but returned empty-handed, another in which they actually took the city after a siege and burnt it.

The reliability of the anecdote is impaired by the fact that it occurs in other ancient authors too. As Valesius already noted, we find it with great similarity of detail in the description by Hegesippus (who lived in the fourth century) of the topography of Antioch, which is brought about by the author's report on Vespasian's arrival in the city in 67 A.D. Expatiating on the mountain which dominates Antioch and offers excellent hiding-places to intruders, the author illustrates the situation with these words: *Denique ferunt, cum ludi scenici in ea urbe celebrarentur, quendam actorem mimorum elevatis oculis ad montem Persas vidisse advenientes, et dixisse continuo: 'Aut somnium video aut magnum periculum. Ecce Persae.'* (3.5.2). And as Baldini, 1989, 154 points out, Eunapius also tells the story, although he dates the event to the reign of Constantius II. Referring to Constantius' fear of an attack by the Persians, Eunapius (*VS* 465) says that the Persian king had laid siege to Antioch once already and had raided it with his bowmen: παρὰ τοῦ Περσῶν βασιλέως ἀνάγκη τις ἐπέχειτο, καὶ τὴν Ἀντιόχειαν ἤδη περιειργασμένου καὶ συντοξεύοντος, ὅς γε τὴν ἄκραν τὴν ὑπερχειμένην τοῦ θεάτρου καταλαβὼν ἀδοκήτως καὶ ἐξαπιναίως, τὸ πολὺ πλῆθος τῶν θεωμένων συνετόξευσε καὶ διέφθειρε.

in alto silentio As is noted ad 21.4.8, the phrase *altum silentium* is quite a common one and occurs seven times in Amm. In view of the context it may denote the undisturbed peace at the time, as in 30.4.1 *alto externorum silentio*, but the absence of any further qualification rather suggests a reference to the utter silence of a crowd intently watching a performance. This tallies well with the evident audibility of the woman's astonished remark.

scaenicis ludis mimus cum uxore immissus Even in classical Latin the expression *scaenici ludi* is not frequent. It can be found in the prologue of Terentius' *Hecyra* (45) and in Cic. *de Orat.* 3.2. Cf. also 14.5.1 *theatrales ludos* (at Arles). The masc. *mimus* occurs only here in Amm. Their female colleagues were very much the rage in Rome, to Amm.'s disgust (14.6.19). The comparison with the art of these performers in 26.6.15 may also express the author's negative verdict. The mime could be acted by a solo performer playing different parts. One can only guess which part of the proceedings Amm. had in mind for the *uxor*. Was she a stage-hand or did she play the female parts in the various pieces? As TLL VII 1. 468.55 suggests, the instances in Cic. *Har.* 22, 25 and 26 imply that *immittere* is a t.t. of the stage, synonymous with *producere*.

e medio sumpta quaedam imitaretur Cf. Cic. *Dom.* 138 *sumpta de medio* with Nisbet's note and see also Brink ad Hor. *Ep.* 2.1.168. The expression is in tune with the general characteristics of the mime, in which scenes from everyday life were brought onto the stage, to amuse a large public of unsophisticated taste. The Antiochenes were fond of it and Julian even noticed that there were μῖμοι... πλείους τῶν πολιτῶν (*Mis.* 342 b). Jerome says that at Alexandria people rioted *propter aurigas et mimos et histriones* (*Comm. in Naum* 3.646). For *imitari* as a theatrical t.t. cf. Ov. *Tr.* 2.515 *imitantes turpia mimos*, Cic. *Q.Rosc.* 20, *de Orat.* 2.34.

populo venustate attonito Quite often *attonitus* is a sign of fright: 18.10.2 *attonitae metu mulieres*, but it can also denote dumbfoundedness caused for varying reasons, or can even mean "speechless with admiration" (OLD s.v. 2d); cf. *attonitis haesere animis* (Verg. *A.* 5.529), *sic attonitus* (Apul. *Met.* 2.2), *mater gaudio stabat adtonita* (Hier. *epist.* 130.5). A clear example in Amm. depicts Constantius II on Trajan's forum in Rome: *haerebat attonitus* (16.10.15). In the present text the word tallies well with *in alto silentio*: the audience was completely enthralled by the charm of the performance.

retortis plebs universa cervicibus Petschenig, *Philologus* 51 (1892) 360 explains the situation: the woman on the stage saw the Persian archers on the mountains behind the rows of seats in the theater. The public had to turn round to see them.

exacerbantia in se tela On the basis of his judgement of the scene, referred to in the preceding note, Petschenig conjectured *ex arce volantia*, on which Novák improved with *ex arce ruentia*. Seyfarth, 1962, 62 will have nothing to do with this: "Die Burg lag 750 m weit vom Theater entfernt", an impossible distance for archers. He believes that V's *exacerbantia* can stand, if it is assumed that Amm. mistakenly regarded *exacerbare* as the equivalent of παροξύνειν with the meaning "(sich) richten auf". This hypothesis of a lexical Grecism seems too speculative. Seyfarth might have strengthened his point in another way, viz. by referring to some curious instances in glossaria: Gloss. IV 68.44 *exacerbauit afflecauit* (= a misspelt *affligauit*), V 292.4 *exacerbauit afflixit*. However, this train of thought does not look very promising either. Fontaine prefers Gelenius' *exacervantia*, but this verb is very weakly attested, as appears from TLL V 2.1133.80–4, and his rendering "qui pleuvaient dru" is too smooth to be true. Novák's conjecture is the most plausible, in spite of Seyfarth's objection to the distance between the citadel and theater. Paschoud,

1989, 42–3 shows how the long-distance view reported in 18.6.22 is also no more than a literary reminiscence.

pacis more palabantur effusius See for this phrase the note ad 22.12.8. As *effuse* would have resulted in a normal cursus, the comparative probably is not simply used pro positivo (see the note ad 20.4.17 *sublatius*), but adds something to the meaning: 'over a very wide area'.

civitate incensa... incensisque locis finitimis et vastatis Antioch had been taken by Sapor I about the middle of the third century (cf. for the date the note ad *haec quidem Gallieni temporibus evenerunt*), as is testified by the list of captured cities in the so-called *Res Gestae Divi Saporis*, the trilingual inscription set up by the Persian king at Naksh i Rustem near Persepolis: Ἀντιόχιαν πόλιν σὺν τῇ περιχώρῳ (l. 15 of the Greek text). In 20.11.11 Amm. alludes to this event when speaking of a ram which the Persians had used during their siege (*molem arietis magnam, quam Persae quondam Antiochia pulsibus eius excisa relatam reliquerant apud Carrhas*). According to Libanius (*Or.* 15.16) the effects of the burning of the city were still apparent in his own days: χάλλη μὲν ἡμῖν οὐχ ἔστιν οἰκοδομημάτων, οὐ γὰρ εἴασεν ἡ πάλαι Περσῶν ὕβρις πῦρ ἐπιφέρουσα τοῖς ἀνθισταμένοις "we may have no noble buildings – the age-old insolence of the Persians that fired all that stood in its path has seen to that", Norman). In *Or.* 60.2–3 Libanius tells us that the Persian king did take and burn Antioch, but refrained from destroying Daphne, because he was checked by Apollo: Τόν τοι βασιλέα Περσῶν τοῦ νῦν τούτου πολεμοῦντος πρόγονον προδοσίᾳ τὸ ἄστυ λαβόντα καὶ ἐμπρήσαντα χωρήσαντα ἐπὶ Δάφνην ὡς τὸ αὐτὸ δράσοντα μετέβαλεν ὁ θεός, καὶ τὴν δᾷδα ῥίψας προσεκύνησε τῷ Ἀπόλλωνι... Ὁ μὲν στρατὸν ἐφ' ἡμᾶς ἀγαγὼν ᾤετο αὐτῷ βέλτιον εἶναι σεσῶσθαι τὸν νεών, καὶ τὸ κάλλος τοῦ ἀγάλματος ἐκράτει θυμοῦ βαρβαρικοῦ.

Sapor's campaign against Syria and his attack on Antioch are further mentioned in *Orac.Sibyll.* 13.125–8, HA *T* 2, Zosimus 1.27.2 (cf. 1.32.2), Malalas *Chron.* 12.295–6, the anonymous Continuator of Dio whose fragments Müller in his *FHG* (4, p. 192) has added to those of Petrus Patricius, Zonaras 12.23 and Syncellus 715–6 (not to mention the Arabic chronicles referred to by Downey, 1961, 592–3 and Potter, 1990, 292–7). More details in the notes below.

ad sua remearunt innoxii A stereotyped phrase; cf. the note ad 21.5.12 and TLL I 67.50–61.

Mariade vivo exusto, qui eos ad suorum interitum civium duxerat inconsulte One could infer from Amm.'s wording that Mariades (*PIR*², M 273), who, like Antoninus and Craugasius in the fourth century (cf. for them the note ad 20.6.1), deserted to the Persians, hailed from Antioch. Malalas (*Chron.* 12.295-6) says that he belonged to the *curiales* of that city, but was expelled from the local senate after having embezzled funds destined to be used for the public horse-races: εἷς τῶν πολιτευομένων Ἀντιοχείας τῆς μεγάλης ὀνόματι Μαριάδης, ἐκβληθεὶς ἐκ τῆς βουλῆς κατὰ συσκευὴν τοῦ παντὸς βουλευτηρίου καὶ τοῦ δήμου, ἐλείπετο γὰρ εἰς τὰ ἱππικά, εἰς οἷον δήποτε μέρος ἐστρατήγησε, μὴ ἀγοράζων ἵππους, ἀλλὰ τὰ τοῦ ἱππικοῦ δημόσια ἀποκερδαίνων, ἀπῆλθεν εἰς τὴν Περσίδα καὶ ἐπηγγείλατο τῷ βασιλεῖ Περσῶν Σάπωρι προδίδοναι αὐτῷ Ἀντιόχειαν τὴν μεγάλην, τὴν ἰδίαν αὐτοῦ πόλιν (on the basis of Malalas' words Gagé, 1952-3 suggested that Mariades was connected with one of the circus factions in Antioch, but this theory has been refuted by Cameron, 1976, 200-1).

Malalas is at variance with Amm. about the manner of Mariades' death. Apart from the fact that in his version of the story the traitor's life is ended by decapitation rather than by the stake, there can be no doubt that Malalas makes the Persian king responsible for the traitor's death: ἀπεκεφάλισε δὲ καὶ τὸν πολιτευόμενον, ὡς προδότην ὄντα πατρίδος ἰδίας (12.296). Amm.'s *Mariade vivo exusto* is ambiguous as to the Agens, although the structure of the sentence suggests the responsibility of the Persians (*hostes*) rather than of the Antiochenes (*suorum civium*) – see for burning alive and other methods of executing the death penalty the literature cited ad 21.12.20 *exustus est vivus*.

There is yet another report of Mariades' death, if, as is generally believed, the Cyriades of HA *T* 2 is to be identified with our man (who is called Μαριάδης by Malalas *Chron.* 12.295 and Μαριάδνος by the Continuator of Dio, *FHG* 4, 192, but Mareades in Amm.'s Fuldensis; why Seyfarth preferred to read Mariades is not clear) – it would seem that the name Mareades is produced by the combination of Marea (derived from the semitic root mr 'lord') with the Greek ending -αδης, and that in the form Cyriades we find a Greek translation (κύριος) of the Semitic part of the name (so Potter, 1990, 269 n. 199; for another view see Stein, 1930, 1744). For the name Cyriades and a possible reference to the Cyriades/Mareades of the texts under discussion one should also consult Bereshit Rabbah (76.6), the rabbinic commentary on Genesis of the first half of the fifth century A.D. With reference to Dan. 7.8 the author mentions a certain QRYDWS (= Cyriades) among three 'horns' who threatened 'the wicked kingdom which imposes levies on all the nations of the world' (= Rome). See for this Potter, 1990, 271 and Swain, 1992, 377-9.

The author of HA *T* 2 states that Cyriades, *dives et nobilis*, joined Sapor after a quarrel with his own father, whom he robbed of an enormous amount of gold and silver. He captured Antioch for Sapor and won for himself the name of Caesar and even of Augustus. He was put to death by the treachery of his followers: *ipse per insidias suorum... occisus est* (*T* 2.3). There is no reason to suppose that a man called Cyriades or Mareades actually was proclaimed Caesar or Augustus in the third century. Nor, given the notorious unreliability of the HA, that all the other details of *T* 2 are historical (e.g. the statement in 2.3 that Cyriades was murdered by his own followers; note that the Anonymus post Dionem alleges, for what it is worth, that most of the common people in Antioch had welcomed Μαριάδνος' action: Καὶ οἱ μὲν φρόνιμοι ἔφυγον τῆς πόλεως, τὸ δὲ πολὺ πλῆθος ἔμεινεν, τοῦτο μὲν φίλοι ὄντες τῷ Μαριάδνῳ, τοῦτο δὲ καὶ τοῖς καινισμοῖς χαίροντες (*FHG* 4, p.192). However, the mere mentioning of Cyriades/Mareades among the *Tyranni Triginta* testifies to the fact that the defection of this Antiochene to the Persians must have been well-known. This may also be concluded from some passages in the thirteenth Sibylline oracle (dating from the third century), if, as has been argued, 'the brigand from Syria, an obscure Roman' (ληστὴς ἐκ Συρίης προφανείς, ῾Ρωμαῖος ἄδηλος) mentioned in verse 90 is identical with Cyriades/Mareades (cf. in the first place Potter, 1990, 268 ff., who i.a. discusses and rejects other suggestions for identification). According to *Orac.Sibyll.* 13.119-28 this ληστής assisted the Persians when they attacked Syria and captured Antioch: ἄρτι δὲ σέ, τλήμων Συρίη, κατοδύρομαι οἰκτρῶς·/ ἥξει καὶ πληγή σοι ἀπ' ἰοβόλων ἀνθρώπων/ δεινή, ἥν τοι οὔποτ' ἐπήλπισας ἥξουσάν σοι./ ἥξει καὶ ῾Ρώμης ὁ φυγάς, μέγα ἔγχος ἀείρας,/ Εὐφράτην διαβὰς πολλαῖς ἅμα μυριάδεσσιν,/ ὅς σε καταφλέξει καὶ πάντα κακῶς διαθήσει,/ τλήμων Ἀντιόχεια, σὲ δὲ πτόλιν οὔποτ' ἐροῦσιν,/ ὁππόταν ἀφροσύνῃσι τεαῖς ὑπὸ δούρασι πίπτῃς·/ πάντα δὲ συλήσας καὶ γυμνώσας σε προλείψει/ ἄστεγον ἀοίκητον· ἄφνω δέ σε κλαύσεθ' ὁρῶν τις. In Potter's translation: "Now for you, wretched Syria, I have lately been piteously lamenting; a blow will befall you from the arrow-shooting men, terrible, which you never thought would come to you. The fugitive of Rome will come, waving a great spear; crossing the Euphrates with many myriads, he will burn you, he will dispose all things evilly. Alas, Antioch, they will never call you a city when you have fallen under the spear in your folly; he will leave you entirely ruined and naked, houseless, uninhabited; anyone seeing you will suddenly break out weeping".

inconsulte This is not a synonym of *temere*, as can be illustrated from Liv. 22.43.1, where it is reported that in the manoeuvring of the armed forces in the days preceding the battle of Cannae Hannibal saw *motos magis inconsulte Romanos quam ad ultimum temere evectos*. Mariades' treachery was not irrational, but ill-considered.

et haec quidem Gallieni temporibus evenerunt Is Amm. right in stating that the capture of Antioch by the Persians occurred during Gallienus' reign? What exactly does he mean by 'the time of Gallienus'? The time during which Gallienus was sole emperor i.e. 260-268? Or (Gallienus was appointed Caesar and shortly thereafter Augustus in 253; cf. for these dates Kienast, 1996[2], 218-20) the period from 253 until 268? When precisely did the capture of Antioch take place? And did Sapor capture Antioch once, twice or even thrice? These questions have been variously answered by modern historians. Alföldi, 1937, 41 ff. believed that Sapor captured Antioch thrice, in 253, 258 (or 259) and 260. Downey, 1961, 587–95 opted for two captures, one in 256 and another in 260. Most scholars argue that the city on the Orontes was captured only once (this seems to be Amm.'s opinion too), in 251 (e.g. Olmstead, 1942, 398 ff.), 252 (e.g. Potter, 1990, 290 ff.), 253 (e.g. Rostovtzeff, 1943, 17 ff. and Baldus, 1971, 244–6), 256 (e.g. Honigmann-Maricq, 1952, 131 ff. and Chaumont, 1973, 669–71) or 260 (e.g. Ensslin, 1949, 92 ff.).

The ancient authors are not very helpful in these matters, as the dissension among modern scholars already leads one to suspect; nor is the numismatic evidence (pace Alföldi, 1937 and Baldus, 1971). Some of the sources do not give any information at all (Libanius, the Continuator of Dio, Zonaras); others are difficult to interpret chronologically (Zosimus, *Orac.Sibyll.*) or, like the Historia Augusta, are suspect on general grounds. HA *T* 2.3 gives as the terminus ante quem for the capture of Antioch A.D. 254 (for it states that Cyriades was slain by his followers 'at the time that Valerian was on his way to the Persian war', *cum Valerianus iam ad bellum Persicum veniret*), but can we trust "the doubtful chronology of a most inaccurate writer" (Gibbon)? The *Res Gestae Divi Saporis* mention two invasions of Syria (but give no date for either), but only one capture of Antioch. Syncellus on the other hand seems to speak of two captures of the city by Sapor, one before and one after Valerian fell into the hands of the Persians (in 260). Malalas contradicts himself (or his text is corrupt): he first places the story of Μαριάδης in the reign of Valerian, Gallienus' father and for the years 253–260 his co-emperor, but later he dates the capture of Antioch in the year 314 of the Antiochene era (χρηματιζούσης τότε τῆς μεγάλης Ἀντιοχείας τιδ'), i.e. AD 265/6, when Gallienus was sole emperor. In view of all this a non liquet seems unavoidable, unless one trusts the so-called Liber Caliphorum, an eighth-century Syriac chronicle, and the thirteenth-century Arabic chronicle of Seert (see for the Arabic chronicles also Downey, 1961, 592–3), as Potter, 1990, 292–7 does in the most recent discussion of the evidence; he opts for 252 as the date of Antioch's capture.

As to Gallienus, see the note ad 21.16.9 on the bad reputation of this emperor in the literary tradition, notably the HA. Whether Amm. is right or wrong in dating the capture of Antioch to Gallienus' reign, the phrase aptly concludes the section, for 'in the times of Gallienus' the Romans frequently had to suffer rough treatment from the Persians; cf. 18.6.3 and 30.8.8.

5.4 *ut per navalem Aborae pontem... transirent* Cf. Malalas *Chron.* 13.328 ἐξῆλθεν ἐκεῖθεν (i.e. Cercusium) καὶ παρῆλθε τὸν Ἀββορὰν ποταμὸν διὰ τῆς γεφύρας, τῶν πλοίων φθασάντων ('having arrived beforehand') εἰς τὸν Εὐφράτην ποταμόν. For such bridges (another one is mentioned in 23.2.7: *Euphrate navali ponte transmisso* (q.v.); cf. also 23.6.21), see the note ad

21.7.7. Speaking of the crossing of the Abora (διαβὰς τὸν Ἀβώραν ποταμὸν), Zosimus mentions the fact that part of Julian's fleet was specifically concerned with building bridges of boats: καὶ ἕτεραι πλατεῖαι (sc. νῆες) συνηχολούθουν, δι' ὧν, εἴ που δεήσειεν, ἔδει γίνεσθαι ζεύγματα πεζῇ διδόντα τῷ στρατοπέδῳ τοὺς ποταμοὺς διαβαίνειν (Zos. 3.13.2). Amm. himself had made reference to such boats when he spoke for the first time of Julian's fleet: *totidemque* (sc. naves) *ad compaginandos necessariae pontes* (23.3.9). See for the bridge over the Abora also the note ad *pontem avelli praecepit* in § 5 below.

omnes sequellae A rare word with the general meaning 'that which follows'. The only other instance in Amm. is 24.2.1. In 24.1.4 Amm. is a little more specific: *sarcinas vero et calones et apparitionem imbellem impedimentorumque genus omne* (that passage can be compared with Zos. 3.14.1 τά τε νωτοφόρα ζῷα, τὰ βαρέα τῶν ὅπλων καὶ τὴν ἄλλην παρασκευὴν φέροντα, καὶ ὅσον ἦν ὑπηρετικόν). Cf. also Fron. *Str.* 2.4.8 *lixas calonesque et omnis generis sequellas*.

litteras tristes Sallusti Galliarum praefecti The precise meaning of *tristes* is difficult to ascertain. Translators tend to choose adjectives expressing distress: "sorrowful" (Rolfe), "gloomy" (Hamilton), "pessimiste" (Fontaine), "pessimistico" (Caltabiano). These seem too passive. The present instance of *tristis* rather belongs to the category listed s.v. 5b in OLD ("grim"). Sallustius wants to get a serious message across. Seyfarth's "ernst" renders it well: it was a stern letter, sent by an important man, highly esteemed by Julian, his colleague as consul (see the note ad 23.1.1) and a close friend; cf. the note ad 21.8.1.

orantis suspendi expeditionem Sallustius pleads adjournment, not cancellation of the project. See TLL IX 2.1041.24–31 for instances of *orare* with a passive infinitive. In Amm. this further occurs in 25.2.8 *orabant haruspices...profectionem differri*, 15.5.6, 21.6.9, 21.13.5.

ita intempestive It seems unlikely that *ita* qualifies *intempestive*, since there is no reference to an earlier relevant statement (cf. the note ad 20.11.5 *ita amarum*). The words mean rather 'in this way, (viz.) untimely', which in its turn is explained by *nondum...exorata*.

nondum pace numinum exorata This can hardly refer to the general attitude of the gods towards the empire and the emperor. In that respect Julian must have been on the right track in Sallustius' eyes. The phrase *pax deum* was deeply rooted in Roman religion, and this peace was prayed for in specific situations, during a storm at sea: *divum pacem votis adit* (Lucr. 5.1229), before consulting an oracle: *exorat pacem divum* (Verg. A. 3.370), after the appearance of evil portents: *pacem deum exposcentium... turba* (Liv. 3.5.14). Here it denotes the gods' approval of the Persian expedition. As was obvious from the *omina*, such approbation had not been acquired. See the following sections in book 23: 1.6, 1.7, 2.6, 2.8 with the relevant notes. One may question whether Sallustius was entirely au courant with all these adverse signs, but for Amm.'s reader the phrase *nondum pace numinum exorata* aptly summarizes the gist of their message. Camus, 1967, 134–6 has shown that Amm. uses *deus* and *numen* as synonyms.

irrevocabile subiret exitium For *exitium* see the note ad 22.11.7. In the absence of the gods' blessing, disaster was beyond recall.

5.5 *posthabito tamen suasore cautissimo* Contrary to reasonable expectations, Julian simply 'paid no attention' to the serious message he received from Gaul. See for this meaning of *posthabere* the note ad 20.11.2. There cannot be any doubt that *cautissimus* has a positive meaning. In his speech to the soldiers at the beginning of his eastward march, Julian calls himself *consideratus et cautus* (21.5.5, q.v.). Tiphys is described as *cautissimus rector* in 22.8.22 (q.v.); "*cautus* is his favorite word of commendation in both politics and particularly military matters" (Seager 69).

fidentius ultra tendebat In the note ad 20.8.19 it is pointed out that *fidenter* normally denotes a justified degree of confidence. As in 22.7.4 (q.v.), the present instance seems a clear exception to this rule. Perhaps the term has to be taken in a purely neutral sense here. The editors change V's *ultro* to *ultra*, which seems a plausible step; cf. Liv. 24.31.4 *si ultra tenderent* and also 36.32.9. Yet one just wonders whether *ultro* could not stand: 'on his own initiative Julian marched on with great confidence', or 'Julian even...' (cf. the note ad 21.12.13). In that case *fidentius* might be taken as a true comparative: 'more confident (than before)'. See below the note ad § 13.

meruisse umquam potuit, ut quod praescripsit fatalis ordo non fiat TLL VIII 807.43–5 lists this among a mere handful of instances in which *merere* is a synonym of *efficere*. The negation must, of course, directly precede *fiat* ('be left undone'). In classical Latin *ne* would have been more usual, but Szantyr 642 notes that "nach *facio, efficio* u.ä. von Anfang an ein Schwanken zwischen konsekutiver und finaler Auffassung besteht". For the background to the thought expressed here see the note ad 21.1.8 *fixa fatali lege decreta*. The failure to take Sallustius' prudent advice clearly illustrates man's helplessness in the face of fate's decrees. The death of some Roman soldiers, when resisting an attack of the Sarmatian Limigantes, was also due to the *ordo fatalis* (19.11.15). However, in that context the phrase is not enlarged upon as in the present text, which, like 21.14.3 *salva firmitate fatali* (q.v.), reveals Amm.'s convictions about the role of fate in human affairs.

statimque transgressus pontem avelli praecepit For literature on bridges see the note ad 23.2.7. The word *avellere* seems rather a strong term to denote the dismantling of a bridge; cf. 17.4.13 *avulsam hanc molem sedibus suis*. However, it is also used in this way in 30.10.2 *avulso ponte*. In classical Latin *praecipere*, 'to enjoin' is seldom used with an inf. praes. pass., but in later Latin this occurs "saepissime" (TLL X 2.449.27 sqq.). Some other examples in Amm.: 15.7.4, 17.1.2, 21.16.11.
Instead of the dismantling of the bridge over the Abora (cf. *fracto igitur, ut ante dictum est, ponte* in 23.5.15) Theodoretus improbably speaks of its burning: διαβὰς γὰρ τὸν ὁρίζοντα ποταμὸν ἀπὸ τῆς Περσῶν τὴν ῾Ρωμαίων ἡγεμονίαν καὶ τὴν στρατιὰν διαβιβάσας, ἐνέπρησε παραυτίκα τὰ σκάφη (*HE* 3.25.1) – he presumably confuses the episode under discussion with the notorious burning of the fleet mentioned in 24.7.4 *et tamquam funesta face Bellonae subiectis ignibus exuri cunctas iusserat naves praeter minores duodecim*.

ne qui militum ab agminibus propriis revertendi fiducia remaneret This testifies to a realistic appraisal of the soldiers' warlike spirit on the part of Julian (there is a nice parallel in Plb. 2.32.9–10, about an episode in the struggle between Romans and Celts in 223 B.C.: ἀνέσπασαν τὰς ἐπὶ τοῦ ῥείθρου γεφύρας, ... ἅμα δὲ μίαν ἑαυτοῖς ἀπολείποντες ἐλπίδα τῆς σωτηρίας τὴν ἐν τῷ νικᾶν, the Romans "demolished the bridges that crossed the stream... to leave themselves no hope of safety except in victory", Paton). It is not necessarily incompatible with *properantem intrepide* in § 15 or the opening of Julian's speech in § 16. The measure narrated in the present text is a sign of long-term prudence. Incidentally, Crassus on his campaign which ended at Carrhae had done the same: Ἔφη γὰρ τὸ ζεῦγμα τοῦ ποταμοῦ διαλύειν, ὅπως μηδεὶς αὐτῶν ἐπανέλθῃ, Plu. *Crass*. 19.7. In the passage just mentioned Theodoretus expresses even less belief in Julian's ability to rouse his soldiers to enthusiasm: πολεμεῖν ἀναγκάζων, οὐ πείθων, τοὺς στρατιώτας. The translators link *ab agminibus propriis* with *remaneret* (e.g. Hamilton: "should lag behind his unit"), but *remanere ab* is an unlikely combination and it is more natural to link *ab agminibus* with *revertendi*, 'to return home from their own ranks'. Valesius *ne cui* is not unattractive. As appears from OLD s.v. *remanere* 4, the verb can very well be used about ideas and the like lingering in the mind. However, Kellerbauer's reference to Julian's warning in § 21 (*si remanserit usquam*) makes the argument for keeping V's *ne qui* and interpreting *fiducia* as an abl. causae conclusive, although in his speech Julian warns against marauding, whereas here he tries to prevent desertion. For *fiducia* meaning 'confident expectation of' see the note ad 21.12.7.

5.6 *pari sorte hic quoque omen illaetabile visum est* Examples in Amm. of *pari sorte* are listed in the note ad 22.3.7. The general sense of the phrase refers to identical conditions: e.g. in 24.2.14 and 31.8.10 a struggle in which honours are even is meant, in 28.2.14 children suffer the same fate as their fathers. Here it emphasizes that the incident, reported in this section, is yet another example in the series of ever-recurring portents, the last of which was mentioned in 23.3.6. Cf. also *illaetabile portentum* (23.2.7, q.v.).

apparitoris cuiusdam cadaver extentum carnificis manu deleti This portent is remarkably similar to the one witnessed by Constantius in a suburb of Antioch: *cadaver hominis interfecti dextra iacens capite avulso* (21.15.2, q.v.). De Jonge rightly notes ad 15.7.3 that in late antiquity both *apparitor* and *officialis* were used as general terms for the clerks and officials in the various offices of the civilian and military dignitaries. Amm. has a predilection for *apparitor*, which he employs thirteen times (and another six times in expressions like *ut apparitor fidus* in 20.8.6). *Officialis* occurs only once (27.7.5). The *apparitor* here, like the one who later saved Salutius' life (25.3.14), served in the prefect's office. He was, in other words, an *apparitor praefectianus* (cf. 17.3.6 *nec praefectianus nec praesidalis apparitor*). Since he was responsible for the supply of additional provisions (*intra praestitutum diem alimentorum augmentum exhibere pollicitus*) he must have been one of the office's principal officials, perhaps its head or *princeps* (cf. 15.3.8 *Rufinum apparitionis praefecturae praetorianae tunc principem*). See in general for the office of the praetorian prefect Stein, 1922, Jones 586–92 and Morosi, 1977.
TLL III 478.9 sqq. provides a long list of instances in which "qui supplicium sumit de condemnatis" is denoted by *carnifex* ('executioner'). The phrase *carnificis manu* also occurs in 27.3.2, 28.1.26 and 30.5.11. For *delere*, 'to execute', cf. 22.11.2 *publica deletus est morte*, 28.2.14 *suboles...pari sorte deletus est morte*.

quem praefectus Salutius praesens...supplicio capitali damnarat See concerning Salutius, one of the pillars of the Julianic establishment, the note ad 22.3.1 and for his office the note ad 21.6.5. Cf. now also Barnes, 1992, esp. p. 249: "Salutius Secundus was not praetorian prefect of the East (as is often assumed), but an old-style prefect who accompanied the emperor wherever he went: Ammianus styles him pointedly and correctly 'praefectus Salutius praesens', 23.5.6". For the death penalty in Amm. see Arce, 1974 and in general the articles collected in *Du châtiment dans la cité*, 1984.

alimentorum augmentum exhibere pollicitus In ch. 3 it was reported that the food supply was perfectly in order: *mille erant onerariae naves...commeatus abunde ferentes* (§ 9), but now it indirectly becomes clear that it caused grave concern to those in charge, with an experienced man as Salutius even losing his nerve. The necessity of an *augmentum* contradicts the report in 23.3.9. For *exhibere*, 'to supply', see the note ad 21.4.6. The food supply of the army was one of the responsibilities of a praetorian prefect (cf. the note ad 20.4.6) and, as appears from Lib. *Or*. 18.214, Salutius had been entrusted to transport it via the Euphrates (πλοίων ἐμπλῆσαι τὸν Εὐφράτην καὶ τροφῆς τὰ πλοῖα πρὸς τὸν ὕπαρχον εἴρητο).

casu impediente frustratus est Curiously, a whim of fortune, which played the piteous *apparitor* false, now serves as a further sign of what the *fatalis ordo* had in store. See for the passive meaning of *frustratus est* the note ad 22.6.4.

postridie advenit, ut ille promiserat, alia classis Salutius' severe measure proved to be entirely unwarranted. Amm.'s words express compassion for the victim (*miserando homine*), but contain also a veiled criticism of Salutius' handling of the affair. Indeed, when compared with the similar incident which befell Constantius (21.15.2), the present omen has a further dimension in that the death of the *apparitor* was the fearful result of a hasty decision, where postponement would have been beneficial.

Amm.'s report on the sequence of events after the army had crossed the river Abora and entered Persian territory, has given rise to considerable scholarly discussion. This is mainly due to the first phrase of § 15 (*Fracto...ponte cunctisque transgressis*), which seems to imply that Amm. is returning to the situation he had indicated at the end of § 5 (*transgressus pontem*). Moreover, in 24.1.1 sqq. Amm. picks up the description of events which he had interrupted at 23.5.25 for the large digression on Persia. At 24.1.5 the arrival at Dura is mentioned, but almost the same point seemed to have been reached in 23.5.8. A solution favoured in earlier scholarship is the assumption of an ill-contrived conflation of two sources. Mommsen, 1909, 427, however, suggests that Amm. merely wanted to introduce Gordian's tomb in Julian's speech (§ 17) and "um dies in der Rede anzubringen, musste der Standort verschoben werden", viz. to the neighbourhood of Dura. Matthews 130–2 also holds literary motives responsible for the arrangement of the events. According to Zos. 3.13.3, Julian addressed his soldiers shortly after the crossing of the Abora, and only then τὴν ἐπὶ Πέρσας εἰσβολὴν ἐποιήσατο, with Zautha as the first stage. In itself an address right at the start of an invasion into a hostile country seems quite plausible. However, Amm. perhaps preferred to pursue a series of bad omens which resulted in several forms of advice to Julian to rethink his ambitious project "continuously into the first days of the march of the monarch into Assyria" (Matthews 178, a view not dissimilar to the one expressed by Dillemann, 1961, 134).

Chalmers, 1959, has tried to save τὰ φαινόμενα by an ingenious explanation: he assumes that the report of § 7 sqq. only concerns a small reconnaissance party led by Julian, in which Amm. himself had taken part (cf. *venimus* in § 7); after this journey the emperor returned to the army. However, the speech was not made at the assembly point, but "at some point between Zaitha and Gordian's tomb", to which Julian refers in § 17 (*cuius monumentum nunc vidimus*), from afar, as Chalmers insists. The objection which can be raised is not that such a course of events is impossible or improbable, but that Amm.'s text does not contain any explicit information about the postulated reconnaisance force. Fornara, [1985]1992 argues that there is nothing wrong with Amm.'s report. In his view, Amm. means to say that the army was marching onwards speedily (*militem...properantem intrepide* in § 15), when Julian decided to address it, somewhere between Zaitha and Dura. The decision was caused by the fact that he had been informed that all his men were now gathered on this side of the Abora (*cunctisque transgressis*). After the speech the army resumed its march and arrived at Dura after two days (24.1.5). If *fracto...ponte cunctisque trangressis* (§ 15) can be interpreted as 'when Julian had received information that all his troops had crossed the Abora and the bridge had been demolished', Fornara's solution is just what the doctor ordered. Unfortunately, this interpretation seems rather forced.

It is difficult not to conclude that by trying to combine too many different pieces of information within one chronological framework, Amm. has produced a somewhat garbled report.

5.7 *Profecti exinde Zaithan venimus locum, qui olea arbor interpretatur* The sudden appearance of the first person plural is remarkable and reminds one of ἐζητήσαμεν in *Acts* 16.10, the first of a number of 'we'-forms in *Acts*. Whatever the precise origin of the information provided in these passages, it points undoubtedly to personal recollection.

There is a remarkable difference between the narratives of Amm. and Zosimus on this matter. According to the latter Julian boarded one of his ships after he had crossed the Abora: διαβὰς τὸν Ἀβώραν ποταμὸν ἔπλει διὰ τοῦ Εὐφράτου, νεὼς ἐπιβάς (3.13.1). Neither here nor anywhere else does Amm. mention this. Malalas *Chron.* 13.329–30 does, and he adds that the army, too, went aboard (Zosimus perhaps implied this, but he did not say it explicitly): καὶ εὐθέως ἐμβαίνειν εἰς τὰ πλοῖα ἐπέτρεψεν, εἰσελθὼν καὶ αὐτὸς ὁ βασιλεὺς εἰς τὸ εὐτρεπισθὲν αὐτῶι πλοῖον. However, in Malalas' version the embarkation occurred after the emperor had held the speech.

In view of the discrepancy between Zosimus and Malalas, and Amm.'s silence, it is difficult to imagine what actually happened (Paschoud, 1979, 112–3, following a suggestion of Dillemann, argues that Julian indeed may have boarded a ship, but that Zosimus wrongly made this happen in Cercusium instead of in Callinicum).

As to Zaitha, Zosimus also mentions the place (although he uses a slightly different orthography). Zosimus informs his readers that Zautha lay at a distance of sixty stades (i.e. some ten kilometers): ἑξήκοντα δὲ προελθὼν σταδίους εἴς τι χωρίον Ζαυθὰ προσαγορευόμενον ἦλθε (3.14.2) – the point of reference must be Cercusium, spoken of by Zos. in 3.13.1. Musil, 1927, 237–8 and 337–8 has suggested that Zaitha or Zautha may be identified with modern al-Merwânijje. He argued that in the eighth century this name, after the caliph Merwân, replaced the former az-Zejtûne, 'the olive tree', which in its turn had been derived from Zaitha (Zautha). If this identification is right (but as yet archaeology has not confirmed the hypothesis), it means that Zosimus is wrong or that his text is faultily transmitted: the settlement of al-Merwânijje is at a distance of 29 (not 10) kilometers from the point where the Abora and the Euphrates flow together. See for Zaitha further the next note.

hic Gordiani imperatoris longe conspicuum vidimus tumulum The phrase seems to indicate quite a distance (*longe conspicuum*) from the place. Usually the adj. means 'notable' (14.11.28 *forma conspicuus bona*), but here and in 16.12.13 its meaning is 'visible'; cf. the Etna's *excelsum cacumen et conspicuum per vasti maris spatia* (Sen. *Ep.* 79.10).

Once again the versions of Amm. and Zosimus diverge. Zosimus locates the tomb of Gordianus (i.e. Gordian III, who died in 244; see below) not in or near Zaitha, as Amm. does (*hic*), but at least a day's march more to the south, in Dura: (ἦλθεν) ἐντεῦθεν εἰς Δοῦρα... οὗ Γορδιανοῦ τοῦ βασιλέως ἐδείκνυτο τάφος, 3.14.2) – Dura lies at a distance of some sixty kilometers from Cercusium.

Until archaeological excavations give a definite answer it seems best to stick to the story of Amm., who, after all, was an eyewitness. The suggestion of Potter ad *Orac.Sibyll.* 13.17, referring to TLL s.v. *locus*, cols. 1581–2, that the name Zaitha indicates a territory rather than a specific town, would solve the problem, but is unconvincing in view of the relative clause *qui olea arbor interpretatur*. In fact, the main reason for Amm. to mention Zaitha at all seems to be that the place was the site of an imperial tomb. Besides, Amm.'s version tallies better with the (admittedly vague) allusions to the location of Gordian's tomb in the other sources. In almost identical words Eutropius (9.2.3) and Festus (22) locate the *tumulus* at a distance of twenty miles from Cercusium (*Miles ei tumulum vicesimo miliario a Circesio, quod castrum nunc Romanorum est Euphratae imminens, aedificavit, exequias Romam revexit, ipsum Divum appellavit* and *Milites ei tumulum in vicensimo miliario a Circensio quod nunc exstat aedificaverunt atque exequias eius Romam cum maxima venerationis reverentia deduxerunt*, respectively). Cf. HA *Gd.* 34.2 *Gordiano sepulchrum milites apud Circesium castrum fecerunt*. According to *Epit.* 27.3 the fact that Gordian's tomb was set up here gave a new name to the place: *Corpus eius prope fines Romani Persicique imperii positum nomen loco dedit Sepulcrum*

Gordiani. Incidentally, from the statements of Eutropius and Festus quoted above it may be inferred that the *tumulus* was a cenotaph, but see Johnson, 1995.

cuius actus a pueritia prima exercituumque felicissimos ductus et insidiosum interitum digessimus tempore competenti In a lost book, of course. Other references to the times of the Gordiani are 14.1.8 (q.v.), 23.5.17 (q.v.) and 26.6.20 (cf. Gilliam, 1972, 138–40 and Stertz, 1980, 507). The phrase *a pueritia prima* (Gordian III was born in Rome on January 20, 225 or 226; cf. for his dates Kienast, 1996², 195–6) cannot be regarded as a corroboration of the idea of Michael, 1880, 18 that Amm.'s report must have been quite detailed. After all, Gordian was only 18 or 19, when he died. *A pueritia prima* also occurs in entirely different contexts (25.6.14, 30.7.2 and 31.2.20).

As to Gordian's Persian campaign, Eutropius 9.2.2 also speaks of its felicitous progress: *Quod quidem feliciter gessit proeliisque ingentibus Persas adflixit*. Other authors are equally jubilant. Cf. e.g. Ruf. Fest. 22 *Sub Gordiano, acri ex iuventatis fiducia principe, rebellantes Parthi ingentibus proeliis contusi sunt*, Aur. Vict. *Caes.* 27.8 *gesto insigniter bello*, HA *Gd.* 26.3 ff. (cf. for the sources Felix, 1985, 47 ff.; for a convenient survey of all the relevant literary sources concerning the Persian expedition of Gordian III translated into English see Dodgeon and Lieu, 1991, 34 ff.).

On the other hand, Gordian's direct opponent Sapor struck a different note (cf. Kettenhofen, 1982 and 1983). In the *Res Gestae Divi Saporis* he did not mention any Roman successes but only recorded that Gordian was killed and the Roman army destroyed in the battle of Mesichise (afterwards renamed Peroz-Sapor or Pirisabora): ἐν τῇ Μησιχίσῃ ἐξ ἐναντίας πόλεμος μέγας γέγονεν καὶ Γορδιανὸς Καῖσαρ ἐπανήρη καὶ ἡμεῖς τὴν στρατείαν τῶν ῾Ρωμαίων ἀνηλώσαμεν (l. 8 of the Greek version of the inscription). On the accompanying reliefs the dead Gordian is shown beneath the feet of Sapor's horse (cf. for these reliefs MacDermot, 1954, Goebl, 1974 and Meyer, 1990). Sapor's representation of Gordian's ultimate fate (accepted as the truth by e.g. Bengtson, 1982³, 408, but rejected as a vainglorious and self-justifying boast by e.g. Oost, 1958 and Stolte, 1970) is clearly at variance with that found in Amm., who here (*insidiosum interitum*) and in 23.5.17 (*redissetque pari splendore...ni factione Philippi praefecti praetorio sceleste iuvantibus paucis in hoc, ubi sepultus est, loco vulnere impio cecidisset*) refers to a treacherous conspiracy hatched by the praetorian prefect Philip and makes Zaitha, not Mesichise the scene of the action. There is yet another tradition about Gordian's end. In this version, found i.a. in Zonaras 12.17, Philippus Arabs had nothing to do with the death of Gordian: the youngest of the Gordiani died in Rome, after he had been injured in the Persian war (according to MacDonald, 1981, this story is compatible with Sapor's version and deserves credence; but see the convincing refutation of this idea by Bleckmann, 1992, 57–60).

In making the future emperor Philippus Arabs responsible for Gordian's death Amm. follows a tradition which is found in most other Greek and Latin authors who speak of the end of Gordian's reign (albeit with differences of detail; Loriot, 1975 distinguishes three varieties in this tradition; see for a discussion also Potter's commentary on the thirteenth Sibylline Oracle) and which is accepted by the greater part of the modern authorities. Cf. e.g. *Orac.Sibyll.* 13.18 ff. Potter πολεμήιος Ἄρης,/ καππέσετ' ἐν τάξει τυφθεὶς αἴθωνι σιδήρῳ/ <ζηλοσύνης> ἕνεκα, καί <γε> προδοθεὶς ὑφ' ἑταίρου, Eutr. 9.2.3 *Rediens haud longe a Romanis finibus interfectus est fraude Philippi, qui post eum imperavit*, Festus 22 *Isque rediens victor de Perside fraude Philippi, qui praefectus praetorio eius erat, occisus est*, Aur. Vict. *Caes.* 27.8 *Marci Philippi praefecti praetorio insidiis periit sexennio imperii, Epit.* 27.2 *Apud Ctesiphontem a Philippo praefecto praetorio accensis in seditionem militibus occiditur anno vitae undevicesimo*, HA *Gd.* 29–33, Zos. 1.18.2–19.1, Zon. 12.18 – one would have expected Orosius also to be in this camp, for in the relevant section of his work he follows, as he himself indicates, Eutropius (*Gordianus admodum puer in orientem ad bellum Parthicum profecturus, sicut Eutropius scribit*, 7.19.4). However, unlike Eutropius Orosius avoids mentioning Philip by name (*igitur Gordianus ingentibus proeliis adversum Parthos prospere gestis suorum fraude haud longe a Circesso super Euphraten interfectus est*, ibid.), presumably because he thought that Philip was a Christian (*primus imperatorum omnium Christianus fuit*, 7.20.1).

Philip's supposed Christianity is already referred to by Eusebius (*HE* 6.34) and may have been influential in colouring the historiographic tradition in the third and fourth centuries: the accounts of Philip's reign are on the whole hostile to him (see, for the image of Philip, York, 1972). It may also have influenced Amm. If so, then the passage under discussion can be seen as a hidden polemic against Christianity. But this is by no means certain. We do not know whether or not Amm. was acquainted with Sapor's version of the story of Gordian's death. If he was, he may have suppressed it because he did not believe it to be true. If he was not, he had no choice but to join the tradition which blamed the death of Gordian on Philip. At any rate, this tradition suited Amm. well. The Persian campaigns of Gordian III and of Julian showed remarkable parallels. One of these was that in both campaigns the Persians would have been defeated, had not the heroic Roman emperors died.

For the *felicitas* of an emperor cf. the note ad 21.5.9; cf. also *felicissimis ductibus* (26.9.5), the only other instance of the plur. of *ductus* in the sense 'command'. According to TLL VII 1898.19–20, the present sentence provides the only instance of *insidiosus* meaning "i.q. insidiis effectus". The expression *tempore competenti* can be parallelled by similar phrases in 16.10.17, 17.9.7,

26.5.15, 30.7.4, which are, however, all concerned with a future treatment of a specific point.

5.8 *pro ingenita pietate* In spite of being recognized as an official virtue of emperors, *pietas* does not often occur in Amm. and never in necrologies or comparable passages. Therefore it is the more remarkable that it is here ascribed to Julian as innately characteristic of him. Moreover, the phrase is put at the beginning of the sentence, presumably in order to lend a tinge of religiosity to an act, which in all probability was primarily intended to emphasize Julian's role as a worthy successor to rulers who had invaded Persia (see below ad § 16 sqq.). It would seem that the suggestion of Meulder, 1991, 466 is too ingenious. According to him Amm. wants his readers to take Julian's offerings to Gordian as "un funeste présage, ou du moins le pressentiment de sa mort". Meulder argues that the death of Julian as reported by some sources (Lib. *Or*. 18.274, Greg. Naz. *Or*. 5.13) was the result of treason and therefore similar to the *insidiosus interitus* of Gordian. However, he overlooks that this version of Julian's death is not found in Amm., who leaves the question of the responsibility of Julian's death open (cf. 25.3.6 *incertum unde*).

consecrato principi parentasset The phrase has a solemn ring: Julian performed the rites of appeasement for the 'deified' emperor. According to Eutr. 9.2.3, *Miles... ipsum Divum appellavit*, and the inscription (otherwise completely fictitious; cf. Gilliam, 1970, 103–7), reported in HA *Gd*. 34.3, begins with *Divo Gordiano*. The deification of Gordian is also attested epigraphically. Although in *CIL* 6. 1638 [*a divo*] *Gordiano* the restoration seems sound, it remains of course a restoration. But the reading can be confirmed by comparison with *AE* 1964.231 (date: 247–248 A.D.), where in l. 23 is written: τοῦτο καὶ θεοῦ Γο[ρδιανοῦ.

pergeretque ad Duram, desertum oppidum Cf. Zos. 3.14.2 καὶ ἐντεῦθεν (sc. Zautha) εἰς Δοῦρα, ἴχνος μὲν ὡς ἄρα ποτὲ πόλις ἦν φέρουσαν, τότε δὲ ἔρημον. Chalmers, 1959, 186 and Fornara, [1985]1992, 32 correctly stress that Amm.'s words signify the march towards Dura, which is situated on the right bank of the river, not the arrival there (not mentioned until 24.1.5 *Emenso itaque itinere bidui prope civitatem venimus Duram desertam marginibus amnis impositam*).

Dura on the Euphrates (not to be confused with Dura on the Tigris, mentioned in 25.6.9), had been established as a Macedonian-Greek settlement by Seleucus I Nicator, who originated from Europos in Macedonia (hence the name Dura-Europos, Babylonian 'duru', meaning 'wall' or 'town'). The town, excavated in the 1920s and 1930s (cf. Hopkins, 1979), was in Roman hands from the 160s until its destruction by the Persians in 256 or 257 A.D. (cf.

James, 1985 and MacDonald, 1986). See Millar, 1993, 445–52 and 467–71, also for further references.

militarem cuneum conspicatus Chalmers is justified in noting this as a curious detail; it seems to tally with his hypothesis that the present passage reports a reconnaissance outing. During the advance of the whole army Julian would have seen 'troops of soldiers' all around; *militaris cuneus* has no specific meaning here; cf. *Francorum validissimos cuneos* (17.2.1), *cum cuneo Persico* (24.5.5).

stetit immobilis This is a stereotyped phrase, which Amm. uses for various situations. It denotes e.g. Ursicinus' undaunted attitude towards slanderers (15.2.3), Constantius' waiting during a speech until the soldiers became silent (15.8.9), the motionless stance of some of the iron-clad Persian forces (25.1.13), and the Goths' attitude of waiting, when they were confronted with ill treatment (31.6.3). In the present text it merely expresses Julian is halting out of curiosity. The perfect tense can be interpreted as 'ingressive' (cf. Szantyr 301, 318, Pinkster, 1990, 232).

dubitanti, quid ferrent This is an instance of *dubitare* in which its meaning "abit in notionem quaerendi" (TLL V1.2086.24–53).

immanissimi corporis leo The superlative of *immanis* already occurs in classical Latin. In 18.7.5 there is a brief digression on lions in Mesopotamia, where *leones vagantur innumeri*. Julian would not often have seen lions in their natural surroundings. Amm.'s other references to lions occur in comparisons (14.9.9, 19.3.3, 29.4.7) and in descriptions of the pastimes of rulers (24.5.2, 31.10.19).

multiplici telorum iactu Cf. *telorum genere multiplici* (15.4.8), a phrase which is, however, somewhat easier to explain: 'all sorts of missiles'. In the present phrase *multiplici* seems a case of enallage: 'by a volley of many missiles'.

certiore iam spe status prosperioris elatus Valesius' brilliant emendation (*spe status* for V's *spectatos*), which was supported by Bentley, is not improved upon by a suggestion put forward by Kiessling, 1874, 6 (*spe elatus prosperiorum*), who refers to 24.1.12 *certiore iam spe provectus* and 16.4.5 *laetiore spe prosperorum*, but, curiously, not to 23.5.24 *speque prosperorum elatior* (*prosperorum* being a correction by Valesius). Cf. also 15.5.23 *ad meliorem statum fortuna revocatur*, 18.1.1 *cum in meliore statu res essent*.

exsultantius cedebat The verb *exsultare* expresses great, and often even excessive, joy, caused by successes and victories; see Seager 44–5. TLL V

2.1953.24–6 plausibly interprets *exsultantius* here as "fere i.q. superbius". In contrast to his bilingual edition, Seyfarth's Teubneriana curiously rejects Accorsi's *incedebat* in favour of V's *cedebat*, defended by Chalmers, 1959, 186, with the surprising translation "began to return", viz. from reconnoitring to the base at the Abora. Such a meaning of *cedere* is, to put it mildly, quite improbable. Fontaine also prints *cedebat*, interpreting it as a (poetical) simplex pro composito, meaning "s'avancer", which seems very doubtful and which moreover would be unique in Amm.

incerto flatu fortunae Kiessling's fine emendation can be illustrated by a reference to 16.1.1 *si affuisset fortuna flatu tandem secundo*, where *fortuna*, however, is an addition by Wagner, not accepted by De Jonge ad loc. Some other examples of the metaphor are A. *Pers.* 602, E. *El.* 1147–8, Liv. 45.8.7, Sen. *Ag.* 247–8; cf. especially Cic. *Off.* 2.19 *cum prospero flatu eius* ('of fortune') *utimur*.

aliorsum prorupit eventus Cf. *summa coepti prudentis aliorsum evasit* (21.12.9, q.v.). The metaphoric use of *prorumpere* is bolder than in e.g. Tac. *Ann.* 6.3.4 *prorupere concepta pridem odia*.

obitus enim regis portendebatur For the royal status of the lion in fables see Babr. 95.16 and cf. Steier, 1927, 985.

5.9 *oracula dubia* Cf. the instances listed in TLL V 1.2110.41–66, in which *dubius* denotes "id quod duplicem accipit interpretationem... saepe de oraculis".

casus discrevere postremi TLL V 1.1305.41–2 lists this instance of *discernere* amongst those in which the verb means "i.q. discernendo sive distinguendo plane cognoscere".

fidem vaticinii Delphici This is a difficult phrase, in which *fides* indicates the 'probabilitas' of the oracle (TLL VI 1.684.73 sqq.); cf. *fatidicarum sortium fidem* (15.7.8). In the present text *fides* seems to be a case of abstractum pro concreto: 'a reliable pronouncement'. In view of the literal quotation from Enn. *Ann.* 167 Sk., it is as good as certain that Amm. has borrowed the very apt examples of Croesus and Pyrrhus from Cic. *Div.* 2.115–6. Both kings made a mistake similar to Julian's: the demise which was correctly forecast turned out to be their own fate. The reference to the famous oracle about the wooden walls of Athens introduces a wholly different type of enigmatic oracle, which needs to be interpreted allegorically.

post Halyn... praedixerat Croesum Pease ad Cic. *Div.* 2.115 provides a long list of ancient references to the famous oracle, reported by Hdt. 1.53.

et aliam... oblique destinaverat mare   According to Hdt. 7.142, this was one of the contemporary interpretations of the Pythia's second oracle to the Athenians, reported in the preceding chapters. See for a list of passages referring to this Fontenrose, 1978, 316–7, who regards the historicity of the oracle as doubtful. For *oblique*, 'in indirect terms', cf. the note ad 20.9.1.

sortemque his posteriorem   For *sors*, 'oracular response', cf. 31.14.8 *eiusdem sortis recordatione*, Verg. A. 7.254 *Fauni... sortem*. Amm.'s use of the plural *his* rules out any suggestion that the inopportune reference to Athens' wooden walls might be a spurious addition to the text.

aio te Aeacida Romanos vincere posse   A list of references is given by Skutsch ad Enn. *Ann.* 167; he complains that Ennius ought to have used the inf. fut. (*victurum*). Amm.'s readers in late antiquity will have had no difficulty in interpreting *vincere posse* precisely in that sense; see the notes ad 21.7.3 and 22.12.2.

Etrusci tamen haruspices   Cf. 25.2.7–8, where it is reported that they were consulted about a shooting star, which worried Julian, but their advice was not followed. Their art is described with considerable respect in 21.1.10 (q.v.). In 320 or 321 Constantine found it normal to consult them in the case of a stroke of lightning (*Cod. Theod.* 16.10.1), but in 357 Constantius ordained: *Nemo haruspicem consulat* (*Cod. Theod.* 9.16.4). After Julian, in 371, Valentinian only objected to a wrong use of *haruspicina* (*Cod. Theod.* 9.16.9), but in the days of Theodosius it was flatly condemned (*Cod. Theod.* 16.10.9, 25 May 385). The mere fact that the art is mentioned in official proclamations proves its persistent continuity. See the note ad 20.5.1 for the loss of the adversative force of *tamen*. **5.10**

qui comitabantur gnaros prodigialium rerum   Pace Liebeschuetz, 1988, 208 n. 27 ("Surely *gnari* of some manuscripts is preferable"), the correctness of Mommsen's emendation (*gnaros* for V's *gnarus*) is proved by 25.10.1 *gnari rerum prodigialium* and 27.3.1 *prodigialium rerum periti*.

cum illis procinctum hunc saepe arcentibus non crederetur   Obviously, some translators think that *illis* refers to the *haruspices*, but it seems more likely that the 'experts in the field of prodigies' are meant. These are continuously trying hard, if in vain, to stop the campaign. In the present case the *haruspices* who are accompanying these experts, are able to contribute a piece of specific lore in support. See the note ad 16.11.6 for *procinctus*, 'campaign'.

libris exercitualibus   The adj. occurs only here in Amm. and the only other author who uses it, is Cassiodorus. Valesius thinks that these books "de ostentis tractabant quae ad expeditiones pertinebant".

signum hoc esse prohibitorium Again a ἅπαξ in Amm. Cf. Plin. *Nat.* 10.37 about a bird of ill omen: *quidam clamatoriam dicunt, Labeo prohibitoriam.*

principique aliena licet iuste invadenti contrarium Cf. *minus laetum...aliena pervadere molienti rectori* (23.1.7, q.v.). It was of course out of the question that Julian's attack on Persia could be deemed unjustified, but the higher powers notified its inopportunity at the present time. For *contrarius*, 'unfavourable', cf. Verg. *G.* 1.286 *nona fugae melior, contraria furtis.*

5.11 *sed calcabantur philosophis refragantibus* Neither the Agens nor the Patiens of *calcabantur* is clear at first sight. As to the latter, TLL III 138.12–3 regards the *Etrusci haruspices* of § 10 as the subject, but Amm.'s figurative use of the verb – of which the meaning is succinctly phrased by Augustine in the following way: *calcari dicitur quidquid contemnitur* (*s.dom.m.* 2.20.68) – always concerns impersonal entities, e.g. *aequitate calcata* (21.13.13). Perhaps it is therefore better to take either the *libri exercituales* or the warnings of the *haruspices* which are implied in the text, as the subject. Amm. not infrequently uses the dat. of the author (see the notes ad 18.4.7, 22.8.24 and 42), so that one could interpret *philosophis refragantibus* as an instance of this particular dat. However, the final responsibility for the misinterpretation of the *omina* lay elsewhere. Amm. is loath to make a clear statement, and opportunely uses the passive form of the verb in order to evade mentioning the Agens. Its tense here denotes a continuing situation: 'The *haruspices'* handbooks were being spurned because of the philosophers' opposition'. Amm. is by no means hostile to philosophy as such. As De Jonge notes ad 17.5.15, "for Amm. *philosophus* is a name of honour"; see also the notes ad 19.4.2 and 22.4.1. However, the philosophers in Julian's entourage were guilty of overestimating their learning and were blind to their own not infrequent errors (*errantium subinde*). Among the philosophers in question were Maximus of Ephesus (*PLRE* I, Maximus 21), whose arrival at Constantinople Amm. had mentioned in 22.7.3 (q.v.), and Priscus (*PLRE* I, Priscus 5). Both were present when Julian died (25.3.23).

quorum reverenda tunc erat auctoritas The adj. is quite forceful: e.g. Cicero is called a *testis reverendus* in 26.1.2; see also the note ad 16.10.5. Obviously Amm. adds this piece of information for the benefit of readers who are not acquainted with the fact that intellectuals exert influence at the imperial court.

etenim ut probabile argumentum...praetendebant Mark the exasperation of the historian who stigmatizes these self-confident experts for their flagrant lack of historical knowledge. See the note ad 20.2.3 for *probabile argumentum*, which also occurs in 15.5.21 and 27.7.4. The phrase *fidem implere* could be a juridical metaphor: cf. *Dig.* 17.1.29.6 and 19.2.19.9. The verb *praetendere*, 'to put forward', per se is a vox media: 28.6.2 *hanc causam praetendentes ut seriam*, but as this example shows, it tends to be used concerning dubious statements. It is a strong term; cf. Tac. *Ann.* 4.2.1 about Sejanus: *praetendebat lascivire militem diductum*; see the note ad loc. on *praetendere* by Martin and Woodman.

Maximiano antehac Caesari cum Narseo... congressuro There are other instances where Amm. refers to the campaigns led by Diocletian's Caesar Maximianus, who later became the emperor Galerius (*PLRE* I, Maximianus 9 + Barnes, 1972, 164), against the Persian king Narses (see for him below). At first he suffered a heavy defeat near Carrhae, which led to his humiliation at the hands of Diocletian (14.11.10, q.v.), but later, in 297 or 298 (cf. for the date e.g. Barnes, 1976, 182 ff. and Kienast, 1996^2, 283–7), he made amends by defeating the Persian king, who had to give up some territory (22.4.8, q.v.), which was returned by Jovian after Julian's death (25.7.9).

leo et aper ingens There is no reference to the *omen* mentioned here in the other sources reporting Galerius' victory over Narses in 297 or 298 (cf. e.g. Lact. *mort.pers.* 9.7, Aur. Vict. *Caes.* 39.35, Eutr. 9.25.1, Ruf. Fest. 14 and 25 and Oros. *hist.* 7.25.10–11). Lindenbrog refers to a similar incident during Septimius Severus' eastern campaign in 198 reported by D.C. 75.9.2: ἀφικόμενος δὲ ἐς τὴν προειρημένην Νίσιβιν ὁ Σεουῆρος ἐνέτυχε συὶ μεγίστῳ. No fewer than 30 soldiers were needed to deal with the animal, after which it τῷ Σεουήρῳ προσεχομίσθη. However, no mention is made of any ominous significance.

illo minime contemplato Sound historical information would have opened the philosophers' eyes to the faultiness of the parallel and would thus convincingly have shown the value of the *omen*. The present participle is by far the most frequent form of *contemplari* in Amm. Its finite forms and the perfect part. are deponential apart from the present case, 16.8.6 (*legibus contemplatis*, which is Valesius' conjecture) and 31.5.9 (*hoc contemplato*). See for this passive use of a deponential verb the note ad 21.5.1 *professa*.

Narseus primus Armeniam Romano iuri obnoxiam occuparat The king's name is spelled *Narses* in Gelenius' edition (and in most books written in English), but the reading of V, *Narseus*, also found in other Latin sources (cf. e.g. Eutr. 9.22.1, Ruf. Fest. 14, HA *Pr.* 17.5, Lact. *mort.pers.* 9.5, Oros. *hist.* 7.25.4), is rightly kept by Seyfarth. In Greek authors we find Ναρσῆς (cf. Agathias 4.25.1 and Zon. 12.31) or Ναρσαῖος (Petrus Patricius, *fr.* 13 and 14).
When Narses (*PLRE* I, Narses 1 + Barnes, 1972, 164 and Martindale, 1980, 489) invaded Armenia in 296 and thus provoked war with the Romans (see

for the outcome above, the note ad *Maximiano... congressuro*), he did so in his capacity as Great King of Persia. He had ascended the Persian throne in 293 (cf. Humbach-Skjarvø, 1978–83 and Felix, 1985, 110 ff.), as successor of Vararanes III (*PLRE* I, Vararanes III).

In the years before his ascension as Great King Narses had been king of Armenia (for how long is not certain, cf. e.g. Chaumont, 1976, 180; see the note ad 20.11.1 for literature about Armenia). This was in accordance with the practice, introduced by Sapor I, to place Persian princes as rulers in various parts of the empire (cf. Frye, 1983, 299). For a couple of years he reigned there as sole king, but at some point in time, probably in 287, the Romans put the Arsacid prince Tiridates (*PLRE* I, Tiridates III) on the throne of western Armenia, leaving the eastern part to Narses. In 293, when Narses began his struggle for the Persian throne, he probably ("the dates and events of the history of Armenia in this period are most uncertain", Frye, 1983, 305) ceded the eastern part of Armenia to Tiridates in exchange for vassal allegiance, but, soon after his accession as Great King, he apparently felt strong enough to try to win back Armenia (cf. Toumanoff, 1969, 262). See in the first place Kettenhofen, 1995.

Since Narses certainly was not the first Persian king to invade Armenia, *primus* here seems to be an instance of superlativus pro comparativo; see Szantyr 162. For *Romano iuri obnoxiam* cf. *Rhodiorum erat obnoxia vectigali* (22.16.10), *dicioni nostrae obnoxiam* (31.5.5) and TLL IX 2.127.36 sqq.

5.12 *secuto itidem die, qui erat septimum idus Apriles* I.e. April 7. This is the last of the five passages in book 23 which furnish precise chronological data about Julian's march early in 363 (see further the note on chronology). The phrase *secuto die* also occurs in 15.4.9 (Clark's conjecture), 20.7.7, 21.15.2, 24.2.14, 24.4.18, 25.6.5, but never with the addition of the precise date in the calendar. See for this 23.3.3 and the note ad loc.

sole vergente iam in occasum Cf. *vergente in vesperam die* (22.13.5, q.v.), the time of the earthquake which destroyed Nicomedia.

aere crassato For other instances of this expression, which is used for various phenomena, see the note ad 20.3.5.

post minacem tonitruum crebritatem et fulgorum As an expert in divination (see 21.1.7 and the note ad loc.), Julian ought to have attached due importance to these phenomena. Their significance is stressed in 21.1.11 (q.v.). See Speyer, 1978, for a complete survey of the ancients' views. Cf. Leumann 83 for *fulgorum* as the gen. plur. of *fulgur*. Löfstedt, 1907, 66–7 interprets *post* as meaning "nach dem Anfang" of a situation or incident. "Denn zweifelsohne will der Verfasser sagen, dass der Soldat während des Gewitters und nicht nach demselben vom Blitz getötet wurde"; cf. the note ad 15.6.1, Szantyr 243.

Iovianus nomine miles ex caelo tactus The theophoric name *Iovianus* was not uncommon, although *Iovinus* seems to have been slightly more frequent, judging from the relevant lists in Kajanto, 1965, Solin-Salomies 1994 and Index II in *ILS*. Presumably, Clark changed Lindenbrog's addition *de* to *ex* on the assumption of haplography, but without any doubt *de caelo tactus* is the normal expression: *Etruria autem de caelo tacta scientissume animadvertit* (Cic. *Div.* 1.92). It often occurs in Livy; cf. also *de caelo tactas... quercus* (Verg. *Ecl.* 1.17), *Iovis ac Minervae aedes de caelo tactae erant* (Tac. *Ann.* 13.24.2).

a flumine The Euphrates, of course, near Dura.

harum rerum interpretes arcessiti interrogatique For the use of *interpres* in the field of divination cf. *deorum autem interpretes sunt* (Cic. *N.D.* 2.12), *somniorum interpretes* (Tac. *Ann.* 2.27.2). Other instances in Amm. are 23.3.3, 28.4.26, 30.4.11. Again the Agens is left unmentioned, but there is of course no doubt about his identity; cf. also *et ipse et visorum interpretes* (23.3.3).

5.13

fidentius affirmabant Cf. the note ad 20.8.19 about *fidenter* denoting a justified degree of confidence. The choice of the comparative may be c.c., but in the context it can also be interpreted as 'quite confident'. See also above the note ad § 5.

fulmen consiliarium Sen. *Nat.* 2.39.1 makes a distinction between different types of lightning in Aulus Caecina's *Etrusca disciplina*: *Genera fulgurum tria esse ait Caecina, consiliarium, auctoritatis et quod status dicitur. Consiliarium ante rem fit sed post cogitationem, cum aliquid in animo versantibus aut suadetur fulminis ictu aut dissuadetur.* This suits the situation excellently; the men consulted proved to be genuine experts.

ita enim appellantur The author's explanatory remark may well derive from the passage in Seneca quoted in the preceding note. Amm. also used the *Naturales Quaestiones* for his digression on Egypt in 22.15 and 16, as has been pointed out in the relevant notes to these chapters.

dissuadent aliquid fieri As appears from TLL V 1. 1507.55 sqq., *dissuadere* with (acc. c.) inf. is quite usual; cf. e.g. *hoc fieri dissuadebant* (August. *C.D.* 1.23).

ideoque hoc nimis cavendum Probably the whole sentence, up to *pronuntiant libri*, expresses the interpretation of the *omen* by the *haruspices*. One is almost tempted to use quotation-marks. For *nimis*, 'to an exceedingly high degree', cf. the note on *nimium cautus* (21.16.3) and Amm.'s description of urgent affairs: *seria, quae nimis urgebant* (20.4.19).

militem celsi nominis The importance of names in divinatory practice is dealt with by Cic. *Div.* 1.102–3; e.g. *Quod idem in dilectu consules observant, ut primus miles fiat bono nomine* (1.102). TLL IX 2.575.70 sqq. lists some examples. Curiously, the well-known phrase *nomen est omen* does not occur in ancient texts; see Woytek ad Pl. *Persa* 625. The fall of the horse *Babylonius* (23.3.6) is another incident where a name proves ominous.

cum bellatoriis iumentis The same phrase is used for the Halani's horses in 31.2.22. In the present text the adj. is of prime importance: the *omen* specifically forbade the continuation of the *war*. In Meulder's view (cf. the note ad 23.3.6) this *omen* "concerne tout particulièrement le Guerrier Impie, puisque le cheval de guerre est présent" (Meulder, 1991, 468). It apparently does not bother him that the horses of the present text were those of the soldier Iovinus and that in 22.1.2 (see above, ad 23.3.6) the horse concerned belonged to Constantius, although on p. 458 of his article he had merely spoken of the horse of the 'impious warrior' himself: "Celles-ci (i.e. les caractéristiques du Guerrier Impie) consistent en des impiétés à l'égard de la divinité, dans le mépris des présages et notamment dans le comportement, que nous qualifions de bizarre, du cheval du guerrier impie, et qui annonce la mort de ce dernier".

et hoc modo contacta loca...fulgurales pronuntiant libri To put it in technical terms, the place had to be furnished as a *bidental* (cf. Pers. 2.27 *evitandumque bidental*) or, more in line with the present text, as a *puteal*, signifying *fulgur conditum publice*, a formula which is well attested epigraphically; "everything scorched by the lightning would be collected and buried" (Courtney ad Juv. 6.587). See also Wissowa, 1912, 123, Latte, 1960, 81, Speyer, 1978, 1127. Obviously the *haruspices* had the relevant handbook of their lore at their disposal. See for these *libri fulgurales* Weinstock, 1951; Cf. TLL VII 2.87.56 sqq. for other late Latin examples of the passive use of *intueri*. It should be noted that in 21.6.2 *intueri lucem* V's first hand wrote *intuere*. TLL VII 2.87.38 lists other active forms of the verb.

5.14 *contra philosophi...nihil significare aiebant* In contrast to the traditional lore of the *haruspices*, the 'philosophers' (see about them above, § 11 *philosophis refragantibus*) advocate a natural explanation for lightning which is, somewhat curiously, denoted as *ignis sacer*. This could be explained either as a sort of quotation by the philosophers ('lightning, which others call sacred fire') or as expressing Amm.'s own conviction: these men dared to suggest that the sudden appearance of the sacred fire had no meaning at all; cf. also *vi ignis divini* (17.4.15). The verb *significare* is here used as a divinatory t.t.; cf. 21.1.11 *multa significant...fulgora et fulmina*, Cic. *Div.* 1.2 *significari futura*, Tac. *Ann.* 6.20.2 *seram ac brevem potentiam significans, scientia Chaldaeorum artis*. The two other instances of *candor* in Amm. also denote heavenly phenomena: 20.3.9 (moon), 31.1.2 (morning light). Amm. was probably not aware that *ignis sacer* as a medical t.t. denotes a skin disease, which is mentioned e.g. in Lucr. 6.660, Verg. *G.* 3.566.

sed esse acrioris spiritus...ad inferiora detrusum Von Scala, 1898, 129 refers to Sen. *Nat.* 2.18-9, where the report of Anaximander's view on lightning is concluded with these words: *Quid est fulmen? Acrioris densiorisque spiritus cursus.* The text then continues: *Anaxagoras* (this is a conjecture) *ait omnia ista sic fieri ut ex aethere aliqua vis in inferiora descendat.* Although it is obvious that Amm. uses these phrases when summarizing the philosophers' scientific explanation, this does not imply that the philosophers did not actually offer interpretations of this kind, but only that the author borrowed some useful formulas from Seneca's treatise with which he was familiar.

si exinde praenoscitur aliquid In classical Latin, apart from the fact that a potential subjunctive might have been expected, the subjunctive is normal in subordinate clauses of oratio obliqua. However, as Szantyr 548 notes, especially in archaic and late Latin this rule is not at all followed rigidly. See also the notes ad 16.10.17 and 20.4.12. The use of *aliquid* in a *si*-clause is caused by "Fernstellung" (Szantyr 194); cf. 22.11.11 *si deinde temptatum fuerit aliquid*.

incrementa claritudinis As is noted ad 22.7.9, *incrementum* here means 'increase'. The use of *claritudo* is quite apt. Here it means 'renown', a meaning which is already common in classical Latin: Sal. *Jug.* 7.4 *in tantam claritudinem brevi pervenerat*; cf. 31.4.9 *claritudine gestarum rerum notissimos*. Amm. also uses the word to denote bright light: 16.10.6 *fulgenti claritudine lapidum variorum*, 20.11.28 *solis obnoxia claritudini*. The philosophers suggest that the 'brightness' of the lightning indicates the emperor's 'renown'.

cum constet...convolare As in 22.8.47 and 24.2.12, "*constare* exprime l'évidence objective, la règle établie scientifiquement, par l'observation ou l'expérience, donc indiscutable" (Sabbah 398). Again Amm. seems to rely on Sen. *Nat.*: *Ignis enim natura in verticem surgit et, si nihil illum prohibet, ascendit* (2.24), *nullo obstante* being Amm.'s version of *si nihil illum prohibet*. Amm. refrains from commenting on the philosophers' alternative explanation, in which a compromise between science and divination is sought.

5.15 *Fracto igitur, ut ante dictum est, ponte cunctisque transgressis* V's *praetor* is inexplicable. Two of Amm.'s other instances denote the Roman *magistratus* in question (26.1.1, 27.3.6). The third one, 30.8.5, concerns a 'general' from Praeneste in the time of the Roman republic (cf. Liv. 9.16.17, Plin. *Nat.* 17.81). Moreover, the text obviously lacks a participle in the abl. to go with *ponte*. It could just be that *praetor* contains this participle. On account of the parenthesis *ut ante dictum est*, which can only refer to § 5, Mommsen's *fracto* seems unassailable. Other conjectures (*parato, peracto, perfecto*) aim at evading the hysteron proteron involved, which is unnecessary. Besides, it is by no means certain that the bridge across the Abora (§ 4) did not already exist beforehand. Novák, 1911, 318 notes that Amm. has no other instances of *pontem frangere*. Indeed, the only other example of this phrase seems to be Tac. *Hist*. 3.17.1 *fracto interfluentis rivi ponte*. Cf. further the note ad 5.6 *postridie advenit*.

antiquissimum omnium ratus est Similar phrases are used in 19.11.13 and 31.6.1; cf. also 30.4.1 *apud quos honestate utilitas erat antiquior*. The meaning 'most important' already occurs in classical Latin, e.g. Liv. 1.32.2 *longe antiquissimum ratus*.

militem alloqui Cf. for Julian's speech to the army also Zos. 3.13.3 (ἀπό τινος βήματος ὁ βασιλεὺς πᾶσιν ὁμοῦ τὰ καθήκοντα προσφωνήσας) and Magnus (*FGrHist* 225 F 1). The latter summarizes the emperor's words thus: ἐπαινῶν αὐτοὺς καὶ προτρεπόμενος προθύμως καὶ σωφρόνως ἀγωνίσασθαι κατὰ Περσῶν. Note that both Zosimus and Magnus place the oration shortly after the crossing of the Abora (cf. the introductory note ad 23.5.7). In all likelihood Amm. was personally present and near enough to the mound of earth on which Julian stood (see below the note ad *aggere glebali assistens*) to have heard the emperor's own words. However, in accordance with the hallowed tradition of ancient historians he wrote the speech himself.

sui rectorisque fiducia properantem intrepide With the exception of *mei* and *sui*, the genitive of a person in whom one has confidence (*fiducia*) is rare. There are no other instances in Amm., and the parallel phrase in 16.12.13 is a further illustration: *fiduciaque sui et fortunati rectoris expertis virtutibus freti*. As was pointed out above ad 5.5 *ne qui militum*, the soldiers' enthusiasm is not necessarily incompatible with the measure reported in that section.

signo itaque per lituos dato The same phrase occurs in 19.2.12, 27.2.3, 31.7.10, where it is the signal for battle. Other such instances of *lituus* are 19.6.10, 22.12.2, 24.1.1. The present text is more closely parallelled by *classico ad contionem exercitu convocato* (21.5.1). See for *lituus*, "an elongated J-shaped instrument with an enlarged mouth-piece" (Webster, 1981[2], 142), apart from the literature cited ad 20.7.6 (q.v.): Behn, 1954, 137–9 and Wille, 1967, 78–84, 90–2.

centuriae omnes et cohortes et manipuli See for this formulaic expression the note ad 21.13.9.

aggere glebali assistens coronaque celsarum circumdatus potestatum Amm.'s imperial *adlocutiones* are dealt with in the introductory note ad 20.5. For the scene in general cf. 14.10.10 about Constantius: *tribunali assistens circumdatus potestatum coetu celsarum*, 15.8.4, 17.13.25, 27.6.5. In 21.5.1 Julian is said to have stood *saxeo suggestu* for his speech to the soldiers. The 'mound of earth' in the present text is unique and may be an exact personal recollection, in contrast to the vague formula in Zos. 3.13.3 ἀπό τινος βήματος and Magnus *FGrH* 225 F 1 ἐν ὑψηλῶι βήματι. Magnus also informs us that among the high-ranking officials were the magister officiorum Anatolius (cf. for him the note ad 20.9.8) and Salutius, the praetorian prefect mentioned in 23.5.6 (q.v.): συναθροίσας τὸν ἴδιον αὐτοῦ στρατόν, ἔχων μεθ' ἑαυτοῦ Ἀνατόλιον μάγιστρον καὶ Σαλούστιον ἔπαρχον πραιτωρίων καὶ τοὺς στρατηλάτας αὐτοῦ.

talia ore sereno disseruit favorabilis studio concordi cunctorum The stereotyped character of the description continues here; cf. 15.8.4 about Constantius: *haec sermone placido peroravit*, 16.12.8 about Julian: *circumsistentes alloquitur genuina placiditate sermonis*, 21.13.9 about Constantius: *haec prosecutus est ad serenitatis speciem et fiduciae vultu formato*. On entering Rome Constantius beheld the senate's pomp *ore sereno* (16.10.5). Indeed, *serenitas* was expected of an emperor after the model of Antoninus Pius (30.8.12). For a similar case of *favorabilis*, 'received with favour', cf. 17.13.25 *ore omnium favorabilis*.

A survey of earlier campaigns against the Persians is of course quite opportune at the very beginning of the invasion proper. Amm. transfers this task to the protagonist, who winds up his rather long review of past invasions with the phrase *haec ut antiquitatum peritus exposui* (§ 21). This qualification is not at variance with the truth, since Julian's oeuvre amply testifies to his interest in history. See for this Bouffartigue, 1992, 436–56. Therefore, his references to relevant experiences in the past are not a priori unlikely. However, the complete absence of any mention of Greek history in general and Alexander the Great in particular strains our credibility (cf. Szidat, 1988, 1025–7 and Lane Fox, 1997, 259). One can hardly imagine that Julian would not have referred to the success of the famous Macedonian king, whom he mentions more than 30 times in his oeuvre, as Bouffartigue, 1992, 444 reports. The

5.16

speech is thus one of the most remarkable specimens of Amm.'s romanization of Julian.

The structure of the speech can be analyzed in this way:

§ 16–19   The historical precedents for the invasion of Persia.
§ 20   Early examples of the annihilation of enemies of Rome.
§ 21–22   The lessons of the past call for the soldiers' correct and valiant behaviour during the actions.
§ 23   Peroratio.

fortissimi milites Amm. is careful in phrasing the appellativa in Julian's speeches to his soldiers: in 16.12.9, before the battle at Strasbourg, he addresses them with *commilitones mei*; in the speech after the pronunciamiento at Paris a pompous phrase is used: *propugnatores mei reique publicae fortes et fidi* (20.5.3); at the start of the eastbound march against Constantius the soldiers are called *magni commilitones* (21.5.2); remarkably, in his indignant and reproachful speech at Pirisabora (24.3.4–7) he refrains from all appellativa. In the present text Julian understandably emphasizes the soldiers' valour.

contionari disposui docturus ratione multiplici For *disponere*, 'to decide', see the notes ad 16.11.4 and 20.4.9. Sabbah 493 n. 117 interprets *docturus* as the introduction of "un exposé didactique et presque pédagogique".

non nunc primitus...Romanos penetrasse regna Persidis The expression *regna Persidis* is used loosely and anachronistically. Armenia was an independent kingdom at the time of Lucullus' invasion (see below) and not part of any Parthian or Persian empire (Amm., as is his wont, cf. the note ad 23.3.2, does not make any distinction between Parthians and Persians in the examples given in § 16 and 17, although of the generals and emperors referred to only Gordianus fought against Persians in the strict sense of that word). However, the Armenian king Tigranes, taking advantage of the weakness of the Parthian dynasty, had annexed parts of Parthia. Moreover, Armenia in later days did become part of the Persian empire (see e.g. the note ad § 11 above). Therefore Amm.'s words, although anachronistic, are perfectly understandable. With *regna Persidis* he means what a modern historian would have put thus: 'the territory which now, in the fourth century, belongs to the Sassanian empire, but which in former days was held by Parthians or Armenians or others'.

ut maledici mussitant In 22.12.3 these criticasters are called *obtrectatores desides et maligni*; see the note ad loc. Disgustingly, they do not openly speak about their objections to the great project, but only in muttering tones. The criticism of Gregory of Nazianzus is of a different kind. In *Or.* 5.8 he chides Julian for his desire to emulate emperors like Trajan and, remarkably in this context, Hadrian, thus neglecting to pay heed to the disasters suffered by Carus and Valerian: πρὸς τοὺς Τραιανοὺς βλέπων ἐκείνους καὶ τοὺς Ἀδριανούς, ὧν οὐχ ἧττον τῆς ἀνδρείας τὸ ἀσφαλὲς ἐθαυμάζετο. Τὸν Κάρον δὲ οὐχ ἐνενόει ἐκεῖνον, οὐδὲ τὸν Οὐαλεριανόν, οἳ δίκην ἔδοσαν ὁρμῆς ἀλογίστου... ἐν Περσῶν ὅροις, ἐν ἀκμῇ τῆς εὐτυχίας καταλυθέντες.

ut Lucullum transeam vel Pompeium Amm.'s Julian quickly disposes of the campaigns in the East which took place in the first century B.C., starting with Lucullus and Pompey. Cf. Julian himself, who in his *Or.* 1 first mentions Roman failures (using, like Amm. a praeteritio: τὶ χρὴ νῦν ὑπομιμνήσκειν, Ἀντωνίου καὶ Κράσσου κτλ, 17 d), only to see sucesses begin in the time of Diocletian. During the third war against Mithridates VI L. Licinius Lucullus (117–56) was 'the first Roman to cross the Taurus with an army' (D.C. 36.16.1). When Mithridates had fled to Armenia and the Armenian king Tigranes had allied himself with him, Lucullus invaded Armenia in 68 and there won 'the greatest victory the sun had ever seen' (Plut. *Luc.* 28.8). In the end however he had limited success, being checked by the weather and a mutiny of his men – despite this he became famous: he took the cherry with him to Europe (22.8.16 *Cerasus, unde advexit huiusmodi poma Lucullus*). See for Lucullus e.g. Eckardt, 1910; Gelzer, 1927; Van Ooteghem, 1959; Keaveney, 1992 and Sherwin-White, 1994.

It was left to Pompey to make Armenia a Roman protectorate and to finish the war against Mithridates. Mithridates was forced to retreat to his Crimean kingdom (cf. 16.7.10 *ingenti proelio superatus a Romanis et Pompeio rex praedictus fugiensque ad regna Colchorum*), where he committed suicide in 63. Tigranes was allowed to retain the core of his kingdom, but he had to cede to the Romans the conquests which he had recently made at the expense of the Parthians (cf. 14.8.10 *has...provincias... Gnaeus Pompeius superato Tigrane regnis Armeniorum abstractas dicioni Romanae coniunxit*), i.a. the regions between the northern Armenian mountains and the Caucasus massif. After the submission of Tigranes Pompey demonstrated Rome's power to the Caucasian peoples, defeated them a few times, and then ended his campaign a few days' march from the Caspian sea, to return to bases in Lesser Armenia and Pontus by the end of 65. See Anderson, 1922 and Sherwin-White, 1994. For Pompey in general e.g. Miltner, 1952, Gelzer, 1959², Seager, 1979 and Greenhalgh, 1980.

per Albanos et Massagetas, quos Alanos nunc appellamus In the accounts of Plutarch (*Pomp.* 34.1–36.1) and Cassius Dio (37.3.3–5), the best sources for Pompey's Caucasian campaign, the Albanians also occur, but the Massagetae, *quos Alanos nunc appellamus* (see for this identification the note ad 22.8.38), are absent. In their place Plutarch mentions the Iberians (see for them e.g. 27.12.17 and the note ad 21.6.8), which is surely nearer to the truth. As to the

Albanians, who dwelled in what is now called Georgia (cf. Braund, 1994), a *rex Albanorum* with a contingent of his people served in the Persian army during Sapor's campaign of 359 (18.6.22, 19.2.3). Cf. further 23.6.13 and 27.12.17.

hac quoque natione perrupta vidit Caspios lacus For *perrumpere*, 'to force a way into', see the note ad 21.7.2. Presumably, *hac natione* denotes the Persians, *hac* being used anaphorically to refer to *regna Persidis*. Elsewhere Amm. has the usual name for the Caspian Sea, viz. *Caspium mare*: 22.8.27, 23.6.26, 40 and 69. According to Plut. *Pomp.* 36.1 Pompey did not reach the Caspian sea, but turned back because of a multitude of deadly reptiles (ὑπὸ πλήθους ἑρπετῶν θανασίμων), when he was only at a three days' march distance from its shores.

Ventidium novimus Antoni legatum strages per hos tractus innumeras edidisse P. Ventidius, probably surnamed Bassus (but not so in contemporary sources), was brought into the senate by Caesar in 47 B.C. In 44 he associated himself with Mark Antony, and as a reward became consul suffectus in 43; after the pact of Brundisium between Antony and Octavian (40) he was sent to the East to fight against the Parthians; having won brilliant victories, i.a. at Mount Amanus in 39 and at Gindarus in 38, he returned to Rome when Antony himself took over the Parthian campaign; he died shortly after he had celebrated a triumph on 27 November 38. Yet even this successful general cannot be said to have 'penetrated the Persian domain' itself. Julian's historical knowledge is suffering from exaggeration.

Deservedly famous for his military exploits (cf. e.g. Liv. *per.* 127–8, Fron. *Str.* 1.1.6 and 2.2.5, Plut. *Ant.* 33-4, Gel. 15.4.4 *eumque primum omnium de Parthis triumphasse*, D.C. 48.39 ff., Eutr. 7.5.2), Ventidius is also known for his rise in social position. According to Gel. 15.4.3 he was *genere et loco humili* and was derided during his consulship for having been a muleteer (cf. Cic. *Fam.* 10.18.3 and Plin. *Nat.* 7.135). Even if this is not taken literally (Syme, 1979 [1958], 396 suggests that Ventidius had been a *publicanus)*, the man certainly was a *homo novus* whose career was spectacular.

For arguments against the often assumed identification of Ventidius and the *mulio celerrimus* of Verg. *Cat.* 10 (8) see e.g. Syme 1979 [1958], 394 ff. and Westendorp Boerma, 1963, 33 ff. Cf. further Gundel, 1958 and Ratti, 1992.

5.17 *ut a vetustate discedam* The vague term *vetustas* may either denote the Roman republic or, as Brok suggests, all history up to the starting point of Amm.'s *Res Gestae* (the principate of Nerva, 31.16.9), which deals with *recens memoria*. Choosing to be silent on the period between Ventidius and Trajan (a period, it is to be noted, in which no major campaigns against the Parthians took place), Amm. accordingly does not pay attention to one of the most memorable feats in the history of the relations between Rome and Parthia, viz. the restitution in 20 B.C. of the standards lost at Carrhae.

Traianus et Verus, Severus Clark accepts Valesius' *et* between *Verus* and *Severus*, but Seyfarth prefers to follow Blomgren 7, who more suo defends V's asyndeton: "Sed Traiano, qui Armeniam et Mesopotamiam provincias primus constituit, apte, nisi fallor, Verus et Severus artius inter se coniuncti opponuntur, qui easdem feliciter defenderunt recuperaruntque". Trajan's campaigns led to the annexation of Armenia and Mesopotamia. His successes were parallelled by Lucius Verus' generals in 163 and 164. Since Amm. refers to the campaigns of Verus' generals in the next chapter, as he apparently had also done in a lost book (23.6.24 *qua* sc. Seleucia *per duces Veri Caesaris, ut ante rettulimus, expulsata* [or *expoliata*, cf. the note ad loc.]), it would seem that athetizing or substituting *Verus* here is an unlikely way of smoothing the text, pace Klotz, 1916, 479 n. 2.

With Trajan's Parthian campaign of 114–117 the policy of conquest in the East was resumed after a period of some 150 years during which the Parthian kingdom had been practically without menace, thanks to skillful diplomacy on the Roman side and internal strife among the Parthians. The reasons for Trajan's decision to reverse the prevailing policy have been much discussed by modern scholars (for some suggestions see e.g. Garzetti, 1960, 363 ff.), but the only explanation to be found in the ancient sources, and one which no doubt played its part, is love of glory (δόξης ἐπιθυμίᾳ, D.C. 68.17.1).

Trajan (98–117) set out from Antioch early in 114 and soon annexed Armenia to the empire (it became a client state again in 117). He then marched through Mesopotamia, captured the Parthian capital Ctesiphon and advanced further to the Persian Gulf. The result was the creation of the short-lived province of Mesopotamia – it is disputed whether there was another new province, Assyria (cf. the note ad 23.3.1 *per Adiabenam*). Meanwhile the Parthians recovered from their initial defeats and a serious insurrection of the Jews broke out in Egypt and Cyrene. This caused the emperor to return whilst leaving the reponsibility for ending the war to Hadrian, whom he invested with the supreme command shortly before he himself died at Selinus in Cilicia (117). For more information on Trajan's Parthian war cf. e.g. Longden, 1931; Guey, 1937; Lepper, 1948; Frankfort, 1955; Angeli Bertinelli, 1976; Lightfoot, 1990 and Millar, 1993, 99–105. See in general Hanslik, 1965; Waters, 1975 and Bennett, 1997.

There are fifteen references to Trajan in Amm. (cf. Gilliam, 1972, 128 n. 10 and Stertz, 1980, 500–1). In most of these he is merely mentioned in passing, but at 16.1.4 he features conspicuously *ita domi forisque colluxit* sc. Iulianus, *ut prudentia Vespasiani filius Titus alter aestimaretur, bellorum gloriosis cursibus Traiani simillimus, clemens ut Antoninus, rectae perfectaeque rationis indagine congruens Marco* (see also 30.9.1 *si reliqua temperasset* sc.

Valentinianus, *vixerat ut Traianus et Marcus*). In 14.8.13 Trajan's Parthian war is mentioned (*cum glorioso Marte Mediam urgeret et Parthos*) and in 25.8.5 he and Septimius Severus are called *principes bellicosi*, when Amm. refers to their unsuccessful attempts to take Hatra, more fully discussed in the lost books (*ut in eorum actibus has quoque digessimus partes*). Both emperors are also mentioned in one breath in 24.6.1. During the reign of Trajan's successor Hadrian (117–138), who abandoned the newly conquered territory, and that of Antoninus Pius (138–161), relations with the Parthians were always tense, but it never came to a war. This changed under Marcus Aurelius (161–180). When Marcus had made his adoptive brother Lucius Verus co-emperor (*principem Marcum, qui Verum adoptivum fratrem absque diminutione aliqua auctoritatis imperatoriae socium fecit*, 27.6.16), he sent him to the East, where the Parthian king Vologaeses IV had started a war by invading Armenia and attacking Syria in 161. At the end of 162 or early in 163 the indolent (but see Lambrechts, 1934) Verus arrived in Antioch, after a slow and leisurely journey. He hardly ever moved from there during the war (which lasted until 166), leaving the fighting to his generals (among them Avidius Cassius, cf. 21.16.11 q.v.). The generals performed splendidly, parallelled Trajan's successes and made it possible for Verus to assume the titles Armeniacus, Parthicus and Medicus. Cf. e.g. Dodd, 1911, Garzetti, 1974, 474 ff., Sartre, 1991, 49–50 and Millar, 1993, 111–4. In his *Caesares* Julian ranks Trajan on a par with Alexander the Great.

During the reign of Marcus Aurelius it was not only Lucius Verus who came to the East, but also Marcus himself. This time the danger had not come from the Parthians, but from Avidius Cassius, one of the generals of Verus, who proclaimed himself Augustus in 175 (cf. 22.5.4–5 with the notes). A similar event forced Septimius Severus (193–211) to leave Rome: Pescennius Niger, legatus of Syria, had proclaimed himself emperor in April 193. Unlike Marcus, however, Severus fought also against Parthia and her allies. After his victory over Niger (cf. 26.8.15) he first campaigned in 194–5 against those Parthian vassals who had helped Niger, and annexed most of Osdroena (cf. Wagner, 1983). In 197, after an intermezzo in the West, where he had to cross swords with his rival Clodius Albinus, he went again to the East, not to return to Rome until 202. During Severus' second Parthian war Ctesiphon was captured (198) and once again a province of Mesopotamia was created. But attempts to take Hatra failed, as Amm. notes in 25.8.5, which is one of the seven times 'the African emperor' is mentioned by him (cf. Gilliam, 1972, 136–7 and Stertz, 1980, 506). See for Severus' campaigns in the East e.g. Rubin, 1975, Kennedy, 1980, Sartre, 1991, 52–3 and Millar, 1993, 121 ff. In general see Birley, 1988².

victores et tropaeati The second term is a ἅπαξ in Amm.; cf. the phrase *post victorias et tropaea* (30.4.6) in another historical survey, and for the bringing home of trophies Tac. *Ann.* 15.18.1 *Romae tropaea de Parthis... sistebantur.*

redissetque pari splendore iunior Gordianus, cuius monumentum nunc vidimus honorate The comparatively large amount of attention devoted to Gordian III is not surprising. The soldiers had seen the emperor's tomb (cf. 23.5.7) and they might jump to the wrong conclusions regarding the outcome of his Persian campaign.

As to the adjective *iunior*, Schlumberger, 1974, 138 n. 32 suggests that Amm. only knew of two emperors with the name Gordianus, the *iunior* of the present text (= Gordian III) and the *superior* of 26.6.20 (= Gordian I). The suggestion is attractive, but see the objections of Bleckmann, 1992, 403 n. 33, who refers to 14.1.8 (*ut in Gordianorum actibus factitasse Maximini illius imperatoris rettulimus coniugem*), "was wohl nur gemeinsam zu Lebzeiten des Maximinus herrschenden Gordiane bezogen werden kann".

The adverb *honorate* means "cum honore, honeste, honorifice" (TLL VI 3.2951.18–31). Wagner has made this more explicit for the present text: "non sine honore memoriae eius debito, reverenter". Indeed, it was not the grave of a man who had miserably failed in his ambitious plans.

apud Resainan superato fugatoque rege Persarum As in the case of Lucius Verus (see above), the successes of Gordian during his campaign were achieved by his generals rather than by the emperor himself, notably the praetorian prefect C. Furius Sabinius Aquila Timesitheus (*PIR*^{2}, III 581), Gordian's father-in-law (called Misitheus in the HA and Timesicles in Greek sources).

Amm. is the only author who explicitly mentions the battle of Resaina. It would seem, however, that Zosimus in 1.18.2–3 (τοῦ δὲ Ῥωμαικοῦ στρατοῦ δόξαντος ἐν τῇ πρώτῃ μάχῃ κεκρατηκέναι... τοῦ βασιλέως περὶ Κάρρας καὶ Νίσιβιν σὺν τῷ στρατῷ διατρίβοντος) and Zonaras in 12.18 (ἥττησέ τε τοὺς ἐναντίους, καὶ Νίσιβιν καὶ Κάρρας Ῥωμαίοις αὖθις ἐπανεσώσατο) refer to the same occasion, since Resaina (later Theodosiopolis, modern Ras el Ain) is situated halfway between Carrhae and Nisibis (cf. Weissbach, 1920).

ni factione Philippi... in hoc, ubi sepultus est, loco vulnere impio cecidisset In view of *Cod. Iust.* 6.10.1 and 3.42.6 Gordian's death must have occurred between 13 January and 14 March 244 (cf. Kienast, 1996^2, 195). Philippus Arabs' foul play is also found in most of the other Greek and Latin authors who speak of Gordian's death (cf. the note ad 23.5.7 *cuius actus*). However, there is a discrepancy in the sources as to the time and place of Gordian's death. Amm. seems to suggest that the young emperor was killed on his outward journey and that he had not been able to penetrate deep into Persia: after his early victory over the Persian king in the battle of Resaina (*apud Resainan superato fugatoque rege Persarum*) Gordian had marched in a southerly direction until he reached Zaitha, there to meet his death on the very same spot where afterwards his tomb was raised (*in hoc, ubi sepultus est, loco*, cf. 23.5.7).

The *Epitome*, on the other hand, reports that Gordian was killed near Ctesiphon (27.2 *apud Ctesiphontem a Philippo praefecto praetorio accensis in seditionem militibus occiditur*), while Eutr. 9.2.2 (*rediens haud longe a Romanis finibus interfectus est*) and Ruf. Fest. 22 (*isque rediens victor de Perside fraude Philippi... occisus est*), although not explicit as to the name of the place where Gordian died, date the event to the return journey (*rediens*), which implies that in their view Gordian must have marched further south than Zaitha; Zosimus' view is not clear and his remark in 3.32.4 that Gordian died ἐν μέσῃ τῇ πολεμίᾳ sheds no further light on the question under discussion. Set alongside the other sources, not to mention the version of the *Res Gestae Divi Saporis*, which reports that Gordian fell in the battle of Mesichise/Pirisabora (cf. the note ad 23.5.7), Amm. must be either wrong or very brachylogic.
In the context of Julian's speech the emphasis laid on the small number of the conspirators (cf. HA *Gd.* 33.5 *novem fuisse dicuntur*) is functional: Gordian's demise was due neither to any large-scale reverse nor to the wrath of the gods, but was caused by a mere handful of criminals.

nec erravere diu manes inulti The ancients were much preoccupied with the revenge to which those who had died a violent death were entitled: ὅ τε διαφθαρείς... ἀδικοῖτ' ἂν ἀτιμώρητος γενόμενος (Antiphon 3.7), *ne inultos imperatores suos iacere sinerent* (Liv. 25.37.10), *ulta virum poenas inimico a fratre recepi* (Verg. A. 4.656), *manet inter umbras impiae caedis mihi/ semper memoria, manibus nostris gravis/ adhuc inultis* ([Sen.] *Oct.* 598–600), *non sine ultionis solacio decessit, ita vivus vindicatus, ut occisi solent* (Plin. *Ep.* 3.14.4), 19.2.1 *nec enim Grumbates inulta unici pignoris umbra ire ultra patiebatur*. See also Wlosok, 1990, 425–8 on the "Rolle der 'Rache' in der Aeneis". Here this idea is combined with the well-known notion of the *biothanati*, who could not find rest until the time of which they had been deprived by their *mors immatura* had passed. Cf. Serv. *ad Aen.* 4.386 *dicunt physici biothanatorum animas non recipi in originem suam, nisi vagantes legitimum tempus fati compleverint*. They were employed by the magicians, as Tertullian reports with disgust in *De anima* 57.1–5 and as can be illustrated from several texts in *PGM* (e.g. IV 1888 and 2578, XII 107); cf. also Amm. 19.12.14 *errantium ibidem animarum ludibria colligens vana*. See Waszink, 1947, 574–80 and Waszink, 1954, 391–4. The present text can be parallelled by 30.2.9 *legatorum Tripoleos manes inultos etiam tum et errantes*.

veluti librante iustitia Amm. likes to personify justice. Men sometimes make her cry on account of their wicked actions (22.3.7, 28.6.1), but she never gives up her strategy of righteous compensation: *inconivus Iustitiae oculus, arbiter et vindex perpetuus rerum, vigilavit attente* (29.2.20), even if in some cases she leaves it rather late: *sempiternus vindicavit Iustitiae vigor, aliquotiens serus, sed scrupulosus quaesitor gestorum recte vel secus* (30.2.9). In the present case her balancing the scales comes more swiftly. A theological reflection of divine justice can be found in the digression 14.11.25–6. See Rike, 1987, 11–2.

omnes, qui in eius... conspiravere Although the addition of *perniciem*, proposed by Novák, 1911, 318, with a reference to *in eius perniciem conspiraret* (14.7.9), is not implausible, Clark and Seyfarth prudently indicate a lacuna, as there are also other possibilities.

cruciabilibus interiere suppliciis Cf. HA *Gd* 33.4 *nam omnes, quicumque illum gladio adpetiverunt (qui novem fuisse dicuntur) postea interemptis Philippis se sua manu suisque gladiis et isdem, quibus illum percusserant interemisse dicuntur;* cf. also Suet. *Jul.* 89 about the death of Caesar's murderers.

ad altiora propensiores V's *propensiore* is a case of haplography, as Petschenig has pointed out. These emperors were 'quite inclined to more lofty enterprises'. For the love of glory attributed to Trajan see above, ad 23.5.17. For the expression *propensior ad* cf. 25.3.18 *ad tranquilliora... propensior*, 28.1.44, 30.6.3. In contrast, Julian and his men were spurred on by their bounden duty.

5.18

subire impulit facinora memoranda Clark was not happy with *subire*, which is understandable in view of Cic. *Phil.* 11.9 *Miserior igitur qui suscipit in se scelus quam is qui alterius facinus subire cogitur*. His tentative suggestion *obire* could be defended by *ad facinus obeundum* (Cic. *Cat.* 1.26). There are, however, some interesting instances of *subire* in Amm.: *ad munia subeunda bellandi* (16.12.41), *subeundae indicium pugnae* (19.5.5). Seyfarth is justified in retaining *subire*.

nos vero miseranda recens captarum urbium et... hortantur The lack of a noun, to go with *miseranda*, has been noticed by many, and this has induced Clark to indicate a lacuna in the text. In his bilingual edition Seyfarth followed suit, but he has since been persuaded by Gronovius' interpretation of *captarum urbium* as a genit. inversus.
In 22.12.1 (q.v.) Julian's motive for the Persian expedition had been expressed thus: *ad ultionem praeteritorum vehementer elatus est sciens et audiens gentem asperrimam per sexaginta ferme annos inussisse orienti caedum et direptionum monumenta saevissima ad internecionem exercitibus nostris saepe deletis*. And in 25.4.24, defending Julian against the accusation that he had ruined the empire by his Persian war, Amm. once again points to the disasters caused by the Persians which had cried out for revenge: *caesi ad indignationem exercitus nostri, capti militares aliquotiens numeri, urbes excisae, rapta munimenta vel diruta, provinciae gravibus impensis exhaustae*. Cf. Lib.

Or. 17.19 τὰ παθήματα τῆς πρὸς τῷ Τίγρητι γῆς...δεδῃωμένης τε καὶ ἐρημωθείσης καὶ πολλὰς ἐμβολὰς ἀνασχομένης.
As to the recently captured cities, one is reminded of the fate of Amida (19.8), Singara (20.6) and Bezabde (20.7).

castrorumque amissiones Petschenig's reference to *amissionem castrorum* (20.7.16) seems a decisive argument for this emendation of V's *carorumque*. See for the loss of the *castella* Reman and Busan 18.10.

votis omnium sociis This emendation is based on 15.8.14 *propera sociis omnium votis*.

ut medeamur praeteritis Cf. *ad ultionem praeteritorum* in 22.12.1.

roborata huius lateris securitate re publica Although Müller, 1873, 352 and Cornelissen, 1886, 274 present *roborata* as an emendation of *honorata* in a very laconic manner, Clark, Seyfarth and Fontaine have all been persuaded to print it in their text. No doubt it makes an excellent sense: 'by strengthening the commonwealth with the safety of this, viz. the eastern, frontier'. But would 'by paying due honour (*honorata*) to the commonwealth in safeguarding its eastern frontier' really be impossible? In any case, a hidden polemic against Constantius' eastern policy can be detected. Nowadays *iustitia librante* this policy has been recognized as far more beneficial than Julian's ill-prepared campaign.

(ut) quae de nobis magnifice loquatur posteritas, relinquamus Cf. 22.12.2 (q.v.), where it is said that Julian longed for war because he was tired of inactivity and wanted to add the title of Parthicus to the glorious record of his victories (*ornamentis illustrium gloriarum inserere Parthici cognomentum ardebat*). See also 21.5.4.

5.19 *adero ubique vobis adiumento numinis sempiterni* The first phrase reminds one of Julian's exhortations on the battlefield at Strasbourg: *hostium terga caesuris adero* (16.12.33). It illustrates Julian's personal involvement, presumably also in contrast to his autocratic predecessor, who *(nec) usquam in necessitatibus summis primus vel inter primos est visus* (16.10.2). Cf. for the 'support' mentioned the pillar on which Rome's eternity rests: *adiumento numinis divini* (26.1.14), the basis of Theodosius' success in Africa: *magni numinis adiumento* (29.5.40) and Gratian's victory over the Lentienses: *sempiterni numinis nutu* (31.10.18). These expressions illustrate the "blasse Deismus" which Nilsson, 1974, 571 detects in Amm. and which nowadays could be better characterized as his version of late antique henotheism. This can also be found in the so-called edict of Milan of 313: *quo quidquid est divinitatis in sede caelesti...placatum ac propitium possit existere* (Lact. *mort.* 48.2), and the famous inscription on the Arch of Constantine: *instinctu divinitatis* (*CIL* 6. 1139).

imperator et antesignanus et conturmalis Julian's presence in the vanguard is often mentioned: 24.1.13 *imperator nunc antesignanus, nunc agminibus cogendis insistens*, 24.5.11 *nusquam ab antesignanis ipse digrediens*, 25.3.3. It is also reported about Gratian in 31.10.13, but personal presence in the thick of the action obviously belonged to Julian's public image: *quasi conturmalis strenuus properabat et rector* (24.6.11); cf. also 17.1.2 and the notes ad 16.12.18 (*antesignanus*) and 16.12.45, where *conturmalis* is rightly rendered with "brother-in-arms".

ut reor Such a modifying parenthesis also occurs in Julian's speech at the start of the campaign against Constantius: *sequimini viam consilii mei salutarem, ut puto* (21.5.6). In the present text it lessens the confidence expressed in the phrase *ominibus secundis*, which is bound to surprise the reader, and at the same time neatly introduces the eventuality of the speaker's own death on the battlefield.

at si fortuna versabilis in pugna me usquam fuderit Amm. often mentions Fortune's whims. See the note ad 22.1.1 on its occurrence at the beginning of books. The present expression can be compared to *versabiles eius motus* (14.11.29) and *fortunarum versabiles casus* (31.10.7). The subject has been thoroughly treated by Naudé, 1964; see especially p. 78 and 83. For *fundere*, 'to slay', cf. *per diversas fuderat pugnas* (19.9.9), *sagittariorum hostilium peritia fundebantur* (20.11.12), *fortissimus quisque e Batavis...funduntur* (Tac. *Hist.* 4.33.4).

pro Romano orbe As is pointed out in the note ad 21.13.13, the expression *orbis Romanus*, which occurs often in Amm., is found from Lucan onwards and is especially frequent in the HA. Most of the instances in Amm. are of a patriotic nature. Roman patriotism in a speech ascribed to Julian is by no means implausible, on the contrary, it tallies well with his own works, as has been pointed out by Bouffartigue, 1992, 658–65 ("Julien ne se voit pas régner sur des Grecs, comme le voudrait Libanios, mais sur des Romains", 663), who opportunely quotes a phrase in Jul. *Ep.* 25b (fr. 4): ἐν τῇ Ῥωμαίων, 'in the Roman world'.

memet vovisse sufficiet ut Curtii Muciique veteres et clara prosapia Deciorum Fontaine aptly refers to August. *C.D.* 4.20, where these Republican heroes are also given as examples, and moreover in the right chronological order: Mucius before Curtius. Compare for such lists e.g. the 'Heldenschau' in book

6 of Vergil's *Aeneis* (we meet there in verse 824 the Decii) and the Roman 'Hall of Fame' on Augustus' forum in Rome, consisting of the statues of some hundred heroes (cf. Kellum, 1982).

Mucius Scaevola's feat is reported in e.g. Liv. 2.12 and V.Max. 3.3.1. The story of M. Curtius, who in 362 B.C. sacrificed himself by jumping into a deep gap in the Forum, can be found in e.g. Liv. 7.6 (cf. Var. *L.* 5.148–9 for other Curtii connected with the lacus Curtius). For the typifying plural cf. Szantyr 19.

The 'famous family of the Decii' refers to the real or alleged *devotiones* (cf. for this ritual Versnel, 1976 and 1981) of father, son and grandson P. Decius Mus, who by their acts of self-sacrifice on the battlefield won victories for Rome. Amm. also had these *devotiones* in mind when he says in 16.10.3 that of earlier emperors *alium ad Deciorum exempla vovisse pro re publica spiritum*.

According to Liv. 8.9–10 P. Decius Mus 'devoted' himself to the gods of the underworld, when fighting against the Latins at Veseris in Campania (in 340 B.C.). In 295 his son did likewise at Sentinum in the Third Samnite War (see D.S. 21.6.1 and Liv. 10.28). The *devotio* at Sentinum is commonly accepted as historical, but the one mentioned first is sometimes seen as an invention, modelled on that of 295 (cf. e.g. Münzer, 1901 and Wissowa, 1905). As to the tradition that consul P. Decius Mus followed the example of his (grand)father in the battle at Asculum Satrianum against Pyrrhus in 279, Cicero (*Fin.* 2.61 and *Tusc.* 1.8) says that he actually did so, while Cassius Dio, preserved by Zonaras 8.5, reports that he only toyed with the idea (see for a supposed Ennian origin of this tradition Skutsch, 1987 and Cornell, 1987). Amm. uses *devovere* as a t.t. for the death of Codrus, the mythical king of Athens, in 22.8.12 (q.v.) and 28.1.4. He justly refrains from it here, since it was a rite of the distant past. Presumably, there is an ellipsis of *voverunt* or *fecerunt* in the *ut*-sentence.

abolenda nobis natio molestissima The demarcation of sections is quite unsatisfactory here. At this point in his speech, Julian reaches the heart of the matter. Having dwelt on previous invasions, the urgent need for retaliation, and finally on his personal devotion, he now presents the main issue in the clearest possible terms; beginning straightway with the essential word: wiping out the arch-enemy, that is the soldiers' task. The Roman successes mentioned in § 16 and 17 were praiseworthy precedents, but now a far more ambitious goal is set. Since the annihilation of an adversary was unprecedented in imperial times, Julian has to dig up some examples of similar actions from ancient history. The choice of adj. is excellent. Words with a more emotional tinge (e.g. 23.6.80 *callidi, superbi, crudeles*) are out of place here, where the 'Realpolitiker' states the facts: the Persians are an obstacle to the well-being of the Roman empire and this obstacle should be removed once and for all.

Sabbah 485 points to the analogy with Cato's famous words *delendam esse Carthaginem* (Flor. *Epit.* 1.31.4, Plin. *Nat.* 15.74).

nostrae propinquitatis For this meaning of *propinquitas* ('kin') cf. 14.11.7 and 23.6.81.

plures absumptae sunt maioribus nostris aetates When used about a period of time, *absumere* means 'to spend', 'to use up', often with the connotation 'wastefully': *quot dies quam frigidis rebus absumpsi* (Plin. *Ep.* 1.9.3). This connotation is, however, not necessarily present: *parandis operibus dies et nox omnis absumpta* (31.15.6). For *aetates*, 'generations', cf. 17.4.16 *secutaeque aetates*, 22.15.4 *posterae...aetates*. In the present text the quoted sentence merely refers to past successes which proved to be the preliminary steps toward the final solution: *ut interirent radicitus, quae vexabant*. The emphasis is entirely on *radicitus*, whilst *quae vexabant* (past) is the equivalent of *molestissima* (present) in § 19.

5.20

devicta est perplexo et diuturno Marte Carthago Amm. uses *Mars* as a worn-out metonymy for warfare often, e.g. *glorioso Marte* (14.8.13), *Marte acerrimo* (19.1.9). The present phrase means, that in Roman history a resounding victory (*devicta est*) after long and complicated campaigns is not necessarily the end of the affair. The complete destruction of the rival powers is first expressed by way of a euphemism (*timuit superesse victoriae*) and is then described three times in a more direct manner (*evertit funditus, subvertit, oppressit*).

sed eam dux inclutus timuit superesse victoriae The 'famous general' can hardly be anyone other than P. Cornelius Scipio Aemilianus Africanus, who is mentioned explicitly in the next sentence as conqueror of Numantia and to whose destruction of both Carthage and Numantia Amm. refers in 17.11.3 (*Aemilianum itidem Scipionem..., cuius impetrabili vigilantia obstinatae in perniciem Romae duae potentissimae sunt urbes excisae*). Cf. Sen. *Cons. Polyb.* 14.5 *Quid referam Aemilianum Scipionem... vir in hoc natus, ne urbi Romanae aut Scipio deesset aut Carthago superesset*. Instances of *timere* with AcI can already be found in classical Latin; see Szantyr 358.

evertit funditus Numantiam Scipio Scipio's treatment of Numantia in 133 was "relentless" and "brutal" (Astin, 1967, 17; cf. 153–5). The taking of the Celtiberian city earned Scipio, who had already added the title 'Africanus' to his name, the (unofficial) surname Numantinus (Ov. *Fast.* 1.59), but Amm. calls him merely Aemilianus Scipio (17.11.3, 24.2.16 and 25.10.13), Aemilianus (24.2.17) or Scipio, as in the present text. For passive *emensus* concerning difficulties cf. 14.10.6 *emensis itaque difficultatibus multis*, 30.7.5 *post periculorum molestias plures... emensas.* It occurs in phrases denoting the passing of time; see the list in a note ad 22.13.3.

Fidenas... valuisse credamus For other examples Julian has to go back to Rome's early wars. A sober critic could rightly remark that the campaigns of that period took place on an entirely different scale compared with the conflict with Persia. According to Liv. 4.34.3 Fidenae was destroyed in 426, because of its alliance with Veii (cf. Flor. *Epit.* 1.6.4 and Eutr. 1.19.1; the latter dates the event to 437). The Faliscans, whose principal city was Falerii, were reduced to submission in 394 (cf. e.g. Liv. 5.27, the famous episode of the Falerian schoolmaster; Livy does not say that the city was subsequently destroyed, but see D.S. 14.96.5). In 241 there was a rebellion, which resulted in (another) destruction of Falerii (cf. e.g. Liv. *per.* 20 Jal). For the capture and devastation of Veii in 396 see e.g. Liv. 5.1–22 (Camillus, the conqueror of Veii, is mentioned by Amm. in 21.16.13).

Valesius refers to the remarkable similarity to Flor. *Epit.* 1.6.12 *laborat annalium fides, ut Veios fuisse credamus.* Since Fidenae and the Falisci are treated in the same chapter of Florus' *Epitome*, it does not seem unlikely that Amm. borrowed his information from this source; cf. Finke, 1904, 31. Amm. also uses the expression *monumentorum veterum fides* in 22.16.13 (q.v.); cf. also 24.4.5 and Cic. *Agr.* 2.88 *hoc perscriptum in monumentis veteribus reperietis.*

5.21 *ut antiquitatum peritus* Julian's fondness of history is often mentioned by Amm.; see 16.5.7, 20.8.17 and the note ad 21.12.1 (add to the literature cited there Bouffartigue, 1992, 436 ff. and see also Sabbah 293 ff.). However, Constantius too refers to history at the end of his speech to the soldiers in 21.13: *docente antiquitate* (§ 13). For *antiquitates*, 'historical works', see 16.7.8–9 (q.v.).

aviditate rapiendi posthabita, quae insidiatrix saepe Romani militis fuit Cf. the similar complaint in 29.4.6 about the lack of discipline of the soldiers, which was often responsible for heavy losses to the Roman state (*intemperantia militis, quae dispendiis gravibus saepe rem Romanam afflixit*). In the previous section Amm. had reported that Valentinian had tried in vain to restrain his soldiers from looting and burning (*quibus assidue mandans, ut rapinis et incendiis abstinerent, impetrare non potuit*, 29.4.5).

Although lack of discipline and rapaciousness was common to soldiers at all times (cf. the note ad 22.4.6 *flagitia disciplinae castrensis*), Amm. specifically accuses the army of Julian's predecessor of having these vices: *ferox erat in suos illis temporibus miles et rapax* (22.4.7). Ironically, according to Lib. *Or.* 18.255 and Ruf. Fest. 28 the eagerness for spoils caused the fact that Julian's own soldiers missed the opportunity to capture Ctesiphon (Amm. 24.6.12 is silent on this). For *posthabere*, 'to renounce', see the note ad 20.11.2. The intrinsic dangers of *aviditas* are denoted by the same metaphor *insidiatrix* in 31.4.10.

agmini cohaerens The absolute necessity for sticking together during the marches is strongly expressed; cf. 26.8.9 *densetis cohaerentes supra capita scutis*.

exsectis cruribus Cf. 17.7.7 *umeris praesectis aut cruribus* about the victims of the earthquake at Nicomedia, 19.6.2 *suris vel suffraginibus relinquebantur exsectis* about men and women made captive by the Persians and not equal to the hardships they had to suffer. According to Julian, such would be the destiny of soldiers falling into the Persians' hands. It was, however, by no means only a Persian habit to hamstring enemies. Cf. 17.13.10 (*succisis poplitibus ideoque adempto fugiendi subsidio*) and 25.3.5 (*Persarum et beluarum suffragines concidebat et dorsa*), where Romans did this in battles against Limigantes and Persians, respectively. Cf. also 31.7.13 (*lapsorum... secando suffragines*), said of both Goths and Romans.

nihil enim praeter dolos et insidias hostium vereor nimium callidorum Romans are brave and fight openly, but the enemies are sly and sneaky: *magis artifices quam fortes* (23.6.80); see also 21.13.4 (q.v.), 24.1.13. Although negative connotations are not necessarily present in *callidus*, *TLL* III 169.57–170.67 provides a long list of cases where it is used "in malam aut ambiguam partem". A remarkable instance is *Jb.* 36.13 where the LXX's ὑποκριταί is rendered by *simulatores et callidi*. In Amm. *callidus* with gen. is used in a neutral way: 15.10.5 *locorum callidi*, 20.7.9 (q.v.), 27.10.7; other cases, however, are negative, with 22.16.11 *femina callida semper in fraudes* as the clearest example.

ad summam In the present context this phrase cannot mean "in short" (OLD s.v. 7c), as in 20.3.4 (q.v.). Rather, it introduces a final reflection "as the crowning touch" (OLD s.v. 8b): the emperor will not only share all the pain and risks on the battlefield, he is also ready to act in a manner diametrically opposed to autocratic rule, which implies that all others render account of their actions to the ruler; instead he is prepared to account for his own deeds to everyone (*universis*). Julian's attention to the times of the Republic has obviously inspired him to play the completely anachronistic role of a republican *magistratus*.

5.22

rebus post haec prospere mitigatis Clark and Fontaine print a comma behind *universis* in order to make clear that this is not an attribute of *rebus*. The verb *mitigare* sometimes expresses the relief of harsh and difficult conditions; Suet. *Tib.* 48.1 *ad mitigandam temporum atrocitatem* is, however, the closest parallel to the present text. Usually *mitigare* in this sense concerns laws, decisions, punishment and the like.

absque omni praerogativa principum For this use of *praerogativa* see TLL X 2.796.5–7: "cum respectu potestatis cuiusdam conlatae vel praesumptae fere i.q. privilegium, ius praecipuum". Although both in theory and in practice an emperor's powers were absolute, there were still "some faint survivals from the days when the emperor had been a republican magistrate" (Jones 321; cf. Demandt, 1989, 212 ff.). As was observed earlier (cf. the notes ad 21.12.23, 21.16.9 and 22.14.1), Julian wanted to be seen as a *civilis princeps*, while his friend Libanius, when addressing Theodosius, remarked that not even an emperor could do entirely as he wished (οὐδὲ σοί πάντα ἔξεστιν, ὦ Βασιλεῦ, *Or.* 50.19).

pro potestate auctoritatis At first sight, one could regard this as a case of gen. explicativus or identitatis, with 29.1.5 *pro potestatis auctoritate* as an illustrative parallel. However, Amm.'s use of the terms is by no means haphazard. In 29.1.5 Procopius is said to act 'in accordance with the prestige of his specific competence', whereas in the present case the 'imperial majesty' is denoted by *auctoritas* (cf. 27.6.16). Julian declares that he intends to refrain from the official power inherent in his imperial authority.

recte consultorum vel secus See for *secus*, 'wrongly', the note ad 20.8.11.

si quis exegerit Cf. the similar idea in 21.5.7 *producturo, si quis exegerit, incorruptam conscientiam meam*. Amm. is consistent in his profile of Julian.

5.23 *erigite iam nunc, quaeso, erigite animos vestros* Cf. 20.8.17 (q.v.) and 28.4.9, the two other instances of pathetic geminatio noted by Hagendahl, 1924, 190. See for the tone of urgency present in *quaeso* the note ad 20.4.16. As is noted ad 21.1.3, *erigere animum* means 'to take courage'; cf. also 21.5.1 *mentibus...erectis*.

multa praesumentes et bona aequata sorte nobiscum This instance of *praesumere* is rightly listed in TLL X 2.963.42 as an example of the meaning "exspectare, pro certo habere". Amm.'s Julian is fully aware of the psychological truth inherent in *inter arma et lituos condicionis aequatio leviora facit pericula* (26.10.10). Caesar had set the example: *aequato omnium periculo* (Gal. 1.25.1).

quidquid occurrerit, difficile The comma behind *occurrerit* is an annoying misprint.

coniectantes aequitati semper solere iungi victoriam For *coniectare* denoting careful judgment see the note ad 21.5.1. Sabbah 519 n. 37 lists the present text as a typical "sentence", like 21.5.2 *plus enim audire quam loqui militem decet*. See also the note ad 21.9.8 on Julian's sayings in the oratio recta. The always victorious *aequitas* has nothing to do with *aequata sorte*. Most often Amm. uses the word in a juridical context, but here it means 'righteousness' in a general sense, though specifically denoting the just cause which Julian was now pursuing. In his letter Sapor had made a comparable claim concerning the past (17.5.3).

Conclusa oratione Only here Amm. uses *concludere* as a rhetorical t.t.; *conclusio* is a synonym of *peroratio* (Martin, 1974, 147); cf. 30.4.19 *in eam conclusionem... desinit*.

5.24

ductoris gloria proeliator miles exsultans Whatever the historical reliability of the version which Amm. gives of Julian's exhortatory speech, in this account the soldiers naturally have little use for the orator's excursions into ancient history or for his sham democratic phrases. What they are interested in is his proven success as a general (cf. the note ad 21.5.9) and his readiness to share their labours and perils. *Proeliator* is also used adjectivally with *miles* in 19.7.8 (q.v.)

speque prosperorum elatior Cf. *affusa laetiore spe prosperorum sublato animo* (16.4.5), *spe prosperorum erectior* (26.8.4). Julian himself was *prosperis... elatior* (22.9.1, q.v.). "Joy and success are the most frequent causes of exultation" (Seager 44). Zosimus gives another reason for the exultation of the soldiers: Julian gave them a considerable sum of money (ἀργυρῶν τε νομισμάτων τριάκοντα καὶ ἑκατὸν τῶν στρατιωτῶν ἕκαστον δόσει τιμήσας, 3.13.3).

sublatis altius scutis The soldiers frequently show approval or dissent with their shields: *hastis feriendo clipeos* (20.5.8, q.v.), *unanimanti consensu voces horrendas immani scutorum fragore miscebat* (21.5.9), *circumclausus horrendo fragore scutorum* (26.6.16). In the present text, however, there is no mention of any noise made by the shields. Brok refers to 29.5.38 *scutaque in formidabilem moventibus gestum* about the combative attitude of Theodosius' soldiers in Africa. The gesture reported in the present text may express the same warlike spirit.

plus sibi laboris quam gregariis indicente During a campaign against the Alamanni in 357, Julian's army was also ready to follow *ducem plus laboris indicere sibi quam militi... assuetum* (17.1.2); see the note ad loc., in which the most likely model for this idea is quoted: *numquam iste plus militi laboris imposuit quam sibi sumpsit* (Cic. *Mur.* 38).

5.25 *maxime omnium id numeri Gallicani...monstrabant* For *numerus* "as a general term covering units of all kinds" see the note ad 20.1.3. The Gallic soldiers were absolutely devoted to Julian, as is clearly expressed in Amm.'s elogium: *exhortatum eum supplici contione militem Gallicanum pruinis assuetum et Rheno peragratis spatiis regionum extentis per tepentem Assyriam ad usque confinia traxisse Medorum* (25.4.13). In the *Misopogon* Julian contrasts the Celts, who loved him (με δι' ὁμοιότητα τρόπων ἠγάπησαν, 360 c) and who were ready to fight for him, with the sophisticated Antiochenes, for whom he was an unsympathetic outsider. But not only the Gallic soldiers were enthusiastic, the whole army was. Apart from the Gallic *numeri* Julian had former soldiers of Constantius among his troops. Under Constantius these men used to become frightened when they merely heard the word 'Persian', according to Libanius (*Or.* 18.211). But their attitude had changed. Thanks to Julian they had gradually recovered the courage they once possessed (ibid. 212).

fremitu laetiore Such a roar can also have a menacing character, e.g. 20.7.5 *acriter minans ac fremens*, 29.5.38. Constantius' announcement of Julian's rise to the position of Caesar was also greeted with loud approval: *vestrum quoque favorem adesse fremitus indicat laetus* (15.8.10).

perque ordines discurrente For *discurrere* denoting a commander's active omnipresence on the battlefield see the note ad 20.6.2.

memores...vidisse For *memor* with (a.c.)i. cf. 16.10.12, 31.4.13. It occurs already in classical Latin: *memor...victoriam datam* (Liv. 5.16.10); see Szantyr 359, Kühner-Stegmann 1.696.

cadentes...supplicantes Brok refers to the battle of Strasbourg (16.12), the successful siege of a large group of Franks (17.2), the defeat of the Juthungi (17.6), and the surrender of the Alamanni (17.1.12) and the Salii (17.8.4) respectively.

Chapter 6

The digression on the Persian provinces, the longest of all digressions in the *Res Gestae*, is functional and indispensable in view of Julian's ambitious project. Matthews 111 deems its size "far exceeding what is needed for Ammianus' purpose" and Sundwall, 1996, 624 remarks that the digression "suits Julian's invasion of Assyria, but the contents ill-fits the immediate context of the chapter". This, of course, depends on the delineation of that purpose and context. If Amm. only wanted to sketch the necessary background for the military operations as they occurred, the digression cannot but be regarded as overstepping its reasonable limits. But it seems more likely that the author intended a more or less complete description of the enemy's empire and its moral and natural resources; in that case the geographic and ethnographic overview as such, apart from some digressions in the second degree and the descriptions of regions like Arabia Felix and Serica which were never part of the Persian territory, is none too extensive. Amm. probably also had another purpose in mind by presenting this digression, i.e. to follow in the footsteps of famous geographers such as Strabo and Ptolemy and to present a description of the whole eastern world (India excepted) as known in his time. One should also bear in mind that digressions offered an author the opportunity to display his knowledge and to rival with his predecessors (Sabbah 525–8). That is what Amm. does when he remarks in the first section of the chapter that few of his predecessors had told the truth and that only barely.

The digression, which comprises the larger part of Book 23, is structured as follows (Signes, 1990, 362 ff.):

- § 1   Author's introduction
- §§ 2–9   Historical survey
- §§ 10–14 Geographical introduction
- §§ 15–74 Description of the Persian provinces
- §§ 75–84 Ethnographical description of the Persians
- §§ 85–88 Excursion on pearls

One would expect that a long digression like this is rounded off by a conclusion, but that is not the case; this, however, is not exceptional for Amm. (Emmett, 1981, 16).

The historical survey mainly deals with the early history of the Parthian Empire and the person of Arsaces I. The Achaemenids are hardly taken into account and the Sasanid Empire is not mentioned at all. There is only a brief reference to Persia's relations with Rome, this subject having been sufficiently treated in Julian's speech (23.5.16–23).

The geographical introduction delineates the general geographical setting of the Persian Empire. The Persian Gulf is central to this setting; furthermore, the border areas of Persia are given. Generally speaking, the large middle part of the digression (15–74) breathes a pragmatic and neutral spirit. In his description of the various provinces Amm. generally proceeds from west to east; after having reached Serica Amm. turns back and describes the remaining regions from east to west. Amm. applies a systematic pattern in his discussion of the Persian regions: in general he characterizes the geography of each district, discusses the condition of its soil, its fertility or infertility, and, if suitable, makes some remarks about its inhabitants, its animals and the products of the land. He always mentions cities and rivers, and occasionally refers to mountain ranges (Brok, 1975, 51; Sundwall, 1996, 628). However, the account of the various regions is rather uneven. Assyria is treated extensively and comprises no less than 11 sections (15–25), whereas other regions are only briefly dealt with. In general the central provinces of the Persian Empire such as Assyria, Media and Persis receive more attention than the less central districts further to the east, i.e. those in Central Asia and Serica. The latter are described succinctly because the author knew little about these regions.

In this long digression Amm. seems to be particularly fond of inserting minor digressions in the second degree. The most important one from a historical point of view is undoubtedly that on the Magi (32–36). Other excursions are those on deadly exhalations (17–19), on the statue of Apollo Cumaeus in Seleucia (24), on Medic oil (37–38), and on the character of the Chinese (67–68, with a reference to silk-making).

The order in which the various districts are described follows that of Book 6 of Ptolemy's *Geography*. This work undoubtedly was one of Amm.'s sources, specifically for structuring the main part of the digression. For factual information on cities, rivers and mountain ranges Amm. probably also consulted Ptolemy (Mommsen, 1881; Dillemann, 1961, 137–8; Signes, 1990, 360–2; pace Brok, 1975). It is, however, unclear which criteria Amm. applied for selecting the material provided by Ptolemy. One sometimes gets the impression that there were no criteria and that he selected his material randomly. This applies especially to the description of the eastern districts, of which he seems hardly to have had an idea. In general Amm. does not add information which could not be found in Ptolemy and other sources, nor does it seem that he critically weighed his sources in order to present a more accurate representation (cf. Sundwall, 1996, 625). Compared to the promise of a *scientia plena* in § 1, the digression falls short of this ambitious goal.

It is well-nigh impossible to establish which other sources Amm. has used, but some remarkable references indicate that Dio Cassius was one of them; the same holds true for Solinus. From the author's introduction it is evident that autopsy played a minor role, in spite of the fact that Amm. knew parts of the Persian Empire by own experience, and that most information was gathered by

Amm. from written sources (*descriptionibus gentium curiose digestis*). The many references to other geographical texts, especially Strabo and the Elder Pliny, in the notes below do not intend to suggest that these texts are direct or indirect sources of Amm. Their purpose is to explain what Amm. is reporting or to enlarge on his information to provide a fuller picture of what ancient geography could offer.

The ethnographical description of the Persians is probably the most interesting part of the digression. In this account, which combines an Herodotean imprint (Barnes, 1990, 70–1) with an implicit Roman feeling of superiority, the 'otherness' of the Persians is emphasized. Especially the Persians' national vices (according to the Greeks and Romans) are receiving the limelight: arrogance, sexual intemperance, cruelty and violence, constant domestic and foreign wars, effeminacy – to mention the most important. Some virtues are mentioned too, like their avoidance of excessive drinking, their moderation and caution. The greatest virtue, however, was their military training and discipline, and their expertise with warfare. The soldier Amm. clearly shows here his admiration for the Persians' military qualities which he himself knew so well from personal experience. The description of these qualities may be seen as a warning for the events to come, i.e. the disaster in which Julian's campaign ended. The Persians' way of dressing with a lot of jewelry and precious stones provides Amm. with the opportunity to end this long digression with yet another digression in the second degree, i.e. that on pearls.

In this interesting introductory section Amm. formulates his own principles for composing geographical digressions, obviously polemicizing against the practice of other writers.

6.1

Res adigit huc prolapsa Petschenig presents his emendation of V *adegit* in an apodictic manner ("XXIII 6, 1 schreibe ich *res adigit*"), but its correctness can be questioned. It is true that Amm. often uses the present tense in such opening phrases (e.g. 14.7.21 *puto nunc opportunum*, 23.4.1 *re ipsa admoneor*); there is, however, a parallel for the perfect tense in 16.7.4 *res monuit*. For *adigere* with inf. see the note ad 21.16.10. Cf. *ad has partes nos occasione magni principis devolutos* (22.8.1) at the beginning of the large digression on the Black Sea. As a synonym of *devolvi* (see the note ad 22.8.1) *prolabi* also occurs in 31.2.12 *quoniam huc res prolapsa est*. For the structure of the digression, see Signes, 1990.

ut in excessu celeri This certainly does not mean "en une sorte de digression rapide" (Fontaine), but 'as far as is possible in a rapid survey', 'taking into consideration the limitations of a necessarily brief digression'. For the variety of words which Amm. uses to express his aim of brevity see Emmett, 1981, 19–20; for *excessus* see the note ad 22.9.6; cf. also *excursu celeri* (29.4.4).

descriptionibus gentium curiose digestis Ethnography should play a prime part in a serious geographical survey. Therefore the author has meticulously arranged the relevant material. For *curiose* see the notes ad 20.11.9 and 22.12.8. A satisfactory study about Amm.'s sources for the digression on Persia is still lacking. Mommsen, 1881, thinks Amm. derived most of his information from Ptolemy's *Geographia* Bk. 6, and also Fontaine in his introduction to Amm.'s Bk. 23 (p. 57 f.) considers Ptolemy as Amm.'s main source. According to Dillemann, 1961, 137–8, Ptolemy's survey not only provided the bulk of Amm.'s information but also determined the structure of the digression; because of "les déformations de certains mots" (138) he is of the opinion that Amm. used a Latin edition of Ptolemy. See further Signes, 1990, 360–2.
Ptolemy was definitely not Amm.'s only source. Both Mommsen and Fontaine also mention Solinus as such, but Amm. must have used a variety of sources. The digression on Persia presents far more information, for instance on the history of the Arsacids and Achaemenids (§§ 2–9), than Ptolemy's enumeration of e.g. regions, villages, cities and rivers or the information Solinus provides. We may therefore agree with Brok, 1975, 55–6 in criticising Mommsen "dass die Behauptung, dass das Perserkapitel einfach ein Auszug ist aus Ptolemaeus Geographia, nicht haltbar ist". But Brok is going a bit too far by stating: "Vielleicht hat Ammian den Ptolemaeus überhaupt nicht eingesehen." However, we may agree with his remark: "wenn er die Geographia wohl zur Hand genommen hat, könnte das nur sein, um seine Quellen, die schon eine Anzahl Namen enthielten, mit einigen willkürlich gewählten Angaben zu ergänzen." It is hard to establish which other sources Amm. used for composing this digression, but Dio Cassius was most likely one of them (23.6.17–18). Autopsy and oral information will also have played a certain role in the preparation of this chapter.

in quibus aegre vera dixere paucissimi This tendentious phrase suggests the author's critical mind and shows his own wide reading, as a result of which only very few authors passed muster. In contrast to Clark and Seyfarth, Fontaine does not accept Petschenig's *in*; he takes *quibus* as an abl. instr., perhaps rightly, rendering it with "dans lesquelles". For *paucissimi* see the note ad 20.6.7.

ad scientiam proficiet plenam Amm. will have nothing to do with superficial learning, such as was e.g. provided by earlier writers on Gaul: *scriptores veteres notitiam reliquere negotii semiplenam* (15.9.2). His readers should be fully informed. For *proficere ad*, 'to contribute to', 'to be advantageous for', cf. the note ad 22.8.28.

quisquis enim affectat nimiam brevitatem The emphasis is on the adj., for on other occasions Amm. is not loath to pay at least lip-service to the need of conciseness: *evectus sum longius* (15.12.6), *prolati aliquantorsum longius quam sperabamus* (22.8.48), *evectus longius* (22.16.24). His ideal, however, is a "brièveté temperée" (Fontaine n. 130); cf. the programmatic phrase in 15.1.1 *tunc enim laudanda est brevitas, cum moras rumpens intempestivas nihil subtrahit cognitioni gestorum*. For *affectare* see the note ad *affectator* (21.16.4) and ad *affectare* (22.12.7). With this critical remark Amm. presumably refers to such surveys as are provided by Rufius Festus.

quid signatius explicet For *signatius*, 'exactly', see the note ad 22.15.11.

Hoc regnum quondam exiguum It is not immediately evident what Amm. means by *hoc regnum*, but it is likely that he refers to Persia in general. The history of Persia is not dealt with extensively. Amm. does not keep to chronology since he first reports the beginning and growth of the Parthian empire and only refers in § 7 for the first time to the Achaemenid kings. Whereas Amm. does refer to the Achaemenids and the Arsacids, he fails to mention the dynasty of the Sasanians; see also the note ad 23.3.2.

6.2

multisque antea nominibus appellatum ob causas, quas saepe rettulimus Amm. refers here to the predecessors of the Arsacid empire – Assyria, Media, the Achaemenid empire – which he mentions in the following sections. In none of the extant books does Amm. say anything about the reasons why Persia was called by various names; therefore he must have mentioned these in one of his lost books. Apart from references to passages now lost concerning the reign of specific emperors, Amm. at times refers more vaguely to his earlier reports; cf. e.g. 16.10.12 *praetereo memor ea me rettulisse, cum incidissent* (instances of Constantius' haughtiness), 19.2.3 *ut rettulimus saepe* (on the fear inspired by elephants), 28.4.6 *ut aliquotiens pro locorum copia fecimus* (the faults of the Roman aristocracy). In view of the often recurring wars with Persia which Amm. had to pay attention to, it is quite imaginable that he went into the question of the name more than once.

cum apud Babylona Magnum fata rapuissent Alexandrum As is noted ad 21.8.3, Amm. often refers to Alexander. Here he is only concerned with the date of his death as a chronological fact. The combinations of *fatum* (*-a*) with *rapere*, listed in TLL VI 1.362.66–7 do not all have the same meaning. The present instance can be parallelled by Ov. *Am.* 3.9.35 *cum rapiunt mala fata bonos*.

in vocabulum Parthi concessit Arsacis Cf. similar phrases in § 15 and 35, and 31.2.17; TLL IV 8.71 sqq. provides a list of occurrences of *concedere* denoting a change into another condition. Alexander the Great died at Babylon on 10 June 323. Amm. compresses chronology ruthlessly, since nearly a century had passed after Alexander's death before Arsaces appeared on the stage of history. It may well be that Amm. did not have a clear idea of the chronology since in § 3 he places the rising of Arsaces incorrectly during the reign of Seleucus Nicator.

obscure geniti For metrical reasons Clark did not trust this phrase and printed a crux after *geniti*. In view of 28.1.5 *obscurissime natus est*, 29.1.5 *obscurissime natum*, there is nothing wrong with the phrase as such. Cf. Iust. 41.4.6–7 *Erat eo tempore Arsaces vir, sicut incertae originis, ita virtutis expertae*. According to Str. 11.9.2 (515C) Arsaces was of Scythian origin (ἀνὴρ Σκύθης); he and his followers were Parni, nomads belonging to the tribe of the Dahae. Probably as a consequence of migratory movements in the north, Arsaces *cum suis* were forced to move from the river Ochus, along which they had lived. They consequently invaded (the satrapy of) Parthia. Hardly anything is known about Arsaces. The picture which Amm. paints of him in this and the following sections is clearly that of the good king; Fontaine n. 133 ad loc. See for Arsaces and the beginnings of Parthian rule: Iust. 41.4.6–5.6; Wolski, 1959, 1962, 1974 and 1976; Schippmann, 1980, 14–23; Sherwin-White/Kuhrt, 1993, 84–90; Wiesehöfer, 1993, 179–87.

latronum inter adolescentiae rudimenta ductoris Cf. Iust. 41.4.7 *solitus latrociniis et rapto vivere*. The phrase *inter adolescentiae rudimenta* simply means 'in his youth'; cf. the note ad 21.5.3.

in melius mutato proposito For *propositum*, 'mode of conduct', see the note ad 20.5.4.

clarorum contextu factorum aucti sublimius The two other instances of *contextus* in Amm. are entirely different. In 16.10.15 it denotes the enormous complex of Trajan's forum, which greatly impressed Constantius II; in 30.7.4 it is used for the 'addition' of Valentinian's personal virtues to his father's renown. TLL IV 4.694 sqq. suggests the meaning 'nexus, conexus'. Fontaine's "une suite ininterrompue" brings out the meaning convincingly. For *augere* denoting the increase of strength and status cf. 21.14.3 *quos multiplices auxere virtutes*, 22.11.4 *auctusque in damna complurium*.

6.3 *qui post multa...praesidiisque Macedonum pulsis* The early history and chronology of Parthian beginnings are problematic and difficult to unravel. The main sources – Str. 11.9.2 (515C) and Iust. 41.4.5 – are indistinct and contradictory. For a discussion of the views on chronology, see Altheim/Stiehl, 1970, 443–67; Will, 1979^2, 301 ff., esp. the notes; Bivar, 1983, 28–31; Frye, 1983, 206 ff.; Brodersen, 1986. The chronology as first put forward by Wolski, 1956–8 has won the acceptance of most scholars:

247   Arsaces king of the Parni and beginning of Arsacid era
245   Revolt of the satrap Andragoras against his Seleucid masters
239   Revolt of Diodotus and secession of Bactria from the Seleucid kingdom
238   Arsaces' invasion of Parthia.

Although it is often supposed that when Arsaces appeared on the historical scene, his power, thanks to a presupposed weak Seleucid rule, was immediately established and a great empire was forthwith founded – an opinion which is not only found in most scholarly literature but is also expressed by Amm. in this and the following section – reality must have been different. Str. 11.9.2 (515C) remarks that at the outset Arsaces was weak, that he and his successors were continually at war with those whose territory they had taken away, and that only later they became strong. The conquest of the satrapy of Parthia must have been a long process and the extension of Parthian power outside Parthia must have taken place only gradually. The domination of the Seleucid kings over their eastern satrapies was stronger than is often supposed. In spite of what Iust. 41.4.9 reports, Seleucus II's campaigns against the Parthians (231–227 B.C.) may well have been successful, since Str. 11.8.8 (513C) remarks that Arsaces fled from Seleucus II and withdrew to the country of the Apasiacae. Under Antiochus the Great the Parthians were vassals of the Seleucids as can be concluded from the satrapal headdress on Parthian coinage; see Sherwin-White/Kuhrt, 1993, 89–90; Drijvers, 1998. Only in the second century B.C. under Mithridates I (c. 171–139/8) and Mithridates II (c. 124/3–88/7) did the Parthians make great conquests and founded an empire.

Seleucus I Nicator (c. 358–281 B.C.) is also mentioned in 14.8.5 (*Nicator Seleucus... cum post Alexandri Macedonis obitum successorio iure teneret regna Persidis, efficaciae impetrabilis rex, ut indicat cognomentum*) and in 23.6.23 (*Seleucia, ambitiosum opus Nicatoris Seleuci*). Amm. is mistaken here, since it was not Seleucus Nicator, but Seleucus Callinicus (c. 265–225 B.C.) with whom Arsaces fought to gain independence for Parthia. Cf. Iust. 41.4.9: *nec multo post cum Seleuco rege, ad defectores persequendos veniente, congressus, victor* (i.e. Arsaces) *fuit: quem diem Parthi exinde solemnem, velut initium libertatis, observant*. The mistake may have been caused by Iust. 41.4.3 – provided Amm. used this text as his source – where Seleucus Nicator and Seleucus Callinicus are mentioned in the same passage (*Post hunc a Nicatore Seleuco ac mox ab Antiocho et successoribus eius possessi, a cuius pronepote Seleuco primum defecere*). For the phrase *post multa gloriose et fortiter gesta* cf. *post haec gloriose gesta* (17.12.20), *recordatio rerum gloriose gestarum* (17.13.26).

eiusdem Alexandri   See for this anaphoric use of *idem* the note ad 20.4.5.

cui victoriarum crebritas hoc indiderat cognomentum As in 22.8.33 (q.v.), Amm. expects his Roman readers to know enough Greek to understand this interpretation of the name *Nicator*.

tranquillius agens temperator oboedientium fuit et arbiter lenis He was the opposite of a tyrant and his quiet and mild ways won him the loyalty of his subjects. The rare word *temperator* occurs only here in Amm. It is open to doubt whether rendering it simply as 'ruler' is correct. Amm. uses the verb *temperare* to denote a moderating influence: e.g. *levioris ingenii, verum hoc instituto rectissimo temperabat* (25.4.16); see further the relevant note ad 20.11.28. In the present text he probably wants to say that Arsaces' own tranquillity preserved moderation among his subjects. This would also suit Fontaine's references to ideal kingship. For the substantive use of *oboedientes* denoting i.a. the subjects of rulers see the note ad 21.12.25.

6.4 *post finitima cuncta vi vel aequitatis consideratione vel metu subacta* Such alternative roads to subjugation are also mentioned in Livy, e.g. 28.43.14 *vi captas aut metu subactas*. As in 17.5.8 and 20.8.11, *aequitas* expresses the fair conditions when a conflict is peacefully solved. Alternatively, the phrase *aequitatis consideratione* could be taken to express respect for Arsaces' righteous conduct. Iust. 41.4.8 reports that Arsaces after having conquered Parthia also seized Hyrcania: *Non magno deinde post tempore Hyrcanorum quoque regnum occupavit*.

civitatum et castrorum castellorumque munimentis oppleta Perside Cf. Iust. 41.5.1–2: (Arsaces) *regnum Parthicum format, militem legit, castella munit, civitates firmat; urbem quoque nomine Daram in monte Apaorteno condit*. In 23.6.43 Amm. mentions the most important cities of the Parthians: *Oenunia, Moesia, Charax, Apamea, Artacana et Hecatonpylos*.

medium ipse agens cursum aetatis placida morte decessit However, Iust. 41.5.5 reports that Arsaces died at an advanced age as a renowned figure: *Sic Arsaces quaesito simul constitutoque regno non minus memorabilis Parthis quam Persis Cyrus, Macedonibus Alexander, Romanis Romulus matura senectute decedit*. The addition *placida morte* is necessary; death in middle age suggests foul play. Arr. *Parth*. 1.2 = Syncellus p. 521 (Bonn) = *FGrHist* 156 F 30a tells us that Arsaces was killed after having governed for only two years.

sententiis concinentibus This phrase also occurs in 21.12.4. See the note ad 20.4.1.

astris, ut ipsi existimant, ritus sui consecratione permixtus est The parenthesis prepares the ground for the unfavourable comments in the next sections.

The other instances of *consecratio* in Amm. concern oaths. TLL IV 379.33 mentions the present case in a list of passages where it denotes "apotheosis". For the use of *suus*, which here refers to the Agens rather than to the grammatical subject of *permixtus est*, cf. Kühner-Stegmann 1.604 and the note ad 20.5.4.

reges eiusdem gentis praetumidi The adj. is rarely used. There are three further instances in Amm.: 22.3.9 (q.v.) about Arbitio, 26.10.10 concerning autocratic behaviour and 27.9.7 about *latrones*. These passages illustrate the negative verdict passed on the Persian kings.

Solis fratres et Lunae Sapor gave himself this title in his letter to Constantius (17.5.3). There is no other source which mentions this title of the Parthian kings. Amm. attributed the titles of the Sasanians also to the Arsacid kings; Hartke, 1951, 46 n. 1; Dillemann, 1961, 137. This was all the easier for Amm. since nowhere in his work does he distinguish between the rule of the Parthians and that of the Sasanians; see the note ad 23.3.2.

6.5

utque imperatoribus nostris Thus Clark and Seyfarth. Fontaine, however, interprets V's *utque* as *ut quae*. This precludes the correlation *ut... ita*, and indeed Fontaine prints a full stop after *optata*. The interpretation of *quae...optata* as a relative clause, "avec antécédent très normalement inclus dans la relative", seems implausible, since this would imply that Amm. equates the arrogant title usurped by the Persian kings with the traditional Roman imperial name. He merely draws attention to the fact that, just as all emperors take the title 'Augustus', the Persian kings too followed in the footsteps of their founder.

Augusta nuncupatio This phrase means 'the official nomination as Augustus'. It also occurs in 26.2.10; cf. further 26.5.1 and 29.1.7. The verb is used in the same sense: *Augustusque nuncupatus* (26.2.3), *nuncupatum imperatorem* (26.7.17), *non Caesares sed Augustos germanum nuncupavit et filium* (27.6.16). For Roman emperors this nomination is 'delightful and welcome'; in other words, they are quite content with it, whereas the formerly low-born Parthian kings need an excessive increase in their status, the mere title 'Arsaces' not being suffient in their eyes. In contrast, cf. Iust. 41.5.8: *omnes reges suos hoc nomine* (Arsaces) *sicuti Romani Caesares Augustosque, cognominavere*.

abiectis et ignobilibus Presumably an instance of 'Synonymenhäufung' to emphasize the low origins of the Parthian royal stock; cf. *cum abiecto consorte* (14.9.6), *ut captivus...ignobilis* (21.9.7); *abiectus* concerns social, not moral order, as is clear from Lact. *inst.* 6.12.6 *non... domus illustribus debet patere sed humilibus et abiectis.*

felicibus Arsacis auspiciis Cf. 16.12.68, where Constantius' courtiers are said to ascribe everything *felicibus eius auspiciis*; the note ad loc. ("= conduct of the war, army command") is disputable. As in the present text, it more likely denotes the fortunate initiative taken by the ruler.

6.6 *numinis eum vice venerantur et colunt* For *vice*, 'as', cf. the note ad 21.5.9. As Hagendahl, 1924, 183 remarks, the two verbs are synonyms here. Outside this passage there is no evidence at all – pace Widengren, 1976, who thinks that the Arsacids were sacral kings – that the Parthian kings were venerated like gods or were sacrosanct, as the rest of the section suggests. However, the Sasanian kings were (cf. the *Res Gestae divi Saporis*), and it could well be that because of the divinity of the Sasanians, Amm. thought that the Arsacids were also venerated like gods. Fontaine n. 136 rightly does not accept that Amm. may have had Sal. *Hist.* 5.3 (*Adeo illis ingenita est sanctitas regii nominis*) in mind, as suggested by Seyfarth in n. 75 of his bilingual edition, since Sallust's remark concerns Mithridates of Pontus and not the Parthian kings.

ad nostri memoriam It is perhaps useful to quote V's text completely here: *ad nostri memoriam non nisi Arsacides issitus quam.* Fontaine agrees with the economical solution presented by Clark and Seyfarth, which, however, fails to convince where *nostri* is concerned. TLL VIII 681.5–12 provides a list of instances of *nostra memoria*, e.g. 29.1.37, which is the normal expression, in contrast to *nostri,* which cannot be parallelled and surely needs a congruent noun. Madvig and Novák suggested *aevi* and *temporis*, respectively.
The Parthian kings had to belong to the Arsacid house; Widengren, 1976, 237. Iust. 41.5.6 remarks that the memory of Arsaces was honoured by giving all subsequent kings the name Arsaces: *cuius memoriae hunc honorem Parthi tribuerunt, ut omnes exinde reges suos Arsacis nomine nuncupent*; Str. 15.1.36 (702C): τοιοῦτο δὲ καὶ τὸ παρὰ τοῖς Παρθυαίοις. Ἀρσάκαι γὰρ καλοῦνται πάντες.

in civili concertatione See the note ad 21.11.3 for *concertatio*, 'armed battle'.

vel privatum In contrast to *arma gestantem*, *privatus* here seems to mean 'unarmed'.

6.7 *Satisque constat* Sabbah 398–9 notes that in a historical context *constat* is used "pour rappeler une vérité admise".

hanc gentem... Propontidem et Thracias Without notifying his reader, Amm. in this section switches to an earlier period of Persian history, namely that of the

Achaemenids; the Achaemenid kings were responsible for extending Persian territory to the Propontis and Thrace. Cf. 17.5.5 (q.v.), where Sapor writes the following to Constantius: *ad usque Strymona flumen et Macedonicos fines tenuisse maiores meos antiquitates quoque vestrae testantur.* In 25.4.24 Amm. reports that, after Julian's defeat, the Persians claimed all territory as far as Bithynia and the Propontis: *cuncta petebantur a Persis, ad usque Bithynos et litora Propontidis.*

regna populis vi superatis compluribus dilatasse V's *suis* is an obvious example of dittography, which can be most satisfactorily repaired by Gelenius' *vi*, which is not a superfluous adjunct; other methods to subject peoples were mentioned in § 3. The Persians of old succeeded where, as the defector Antoninus pointed out at Sapor's winter quarters, their presentday successors, in spite of some partial successes, failed: *dilatasse decuerat regna* (18.5.7).

sed alte spirantium ducum superbia licenter grassantium For *alte spirare* see the note ad 22.3.12. As Seager 134 remarks, *superbia* "is a peculiarly barbarian trait". TLL VI 2200.56 notes that *grassari* as a synonym of *agere* is frequently used "in malam partem"; *licenter* means 'exceeding the standards of responsible behaviour'.

aerumnis maximis See the note ad 20.7.7 on Amm.'s predilection for *aerumna*.

Cyrum...filiorum Amm. refers here to Cyrus' fatal campaign against the Massagetae in 530 B.C., first described by Hdt. 1.204–214 and also related by later authors, such as D.S. 2.44.2; Str. 11.6.2 (507C), 11.8.6 (512C-513C); J. *AJ* 11.2; Iust. 1.8; Arr. *An.* 4.11.9, 5.4.5. See Dandamaev, 1989, 66–9. Hdt. 1.211–213 and other sources speak of only one son (named Spargapises) of Tomyris whereas Amm. speaks of *filii*. Hdt. locates the battle between Cyrus and Tomyris in the land of the Massagetae; Amm., however, thinks the fight took place on the European side of the Bosporus. It may be that Amm. confuses the campaigns of Cyrus and Darius, but it is also possible, as Fontaine n. 137 indicates, that Amm. follows a tradition also found in Amp. 13.1, where it is said that Cyrus *maiore parte Asiae subacta Europam quoque inrupisset, ni a Tomyri Scytharum regina victus oppressusque esset.* It could also be that Amm. locates the battle on the European side of the Bosporus because Tomi in Scythia was considered a foundation of Tomyris; Jord. *Get.* 10.62. For Tomyris, see Ziegler, 1937.

cum multitudine fabulosa As appears from 31.4.7, *fabulosus* expresses the general scepsis of later generations about the scale of the Persian attacks on Greece. However, the enormous surge of the Gothic tribes demands a reconsideration: *fides quoque vetustatis recenti documento firmata est* (31.4.8).

ad internecionem delevit Amm. evidently likes the phrase *ad internecionem* in combination with a verb meaning 'to destroy', since he uses it 8 times. Possibly he was inspired by Livy, who uses it 7 times.

6.8 *Dareus posteaque Xerxes Graeciam elementorum usu mutato aggressi* The change of elements refers to 'turning water into land', as Darius did by bridging the Bosporus during his Scythian campaign in 514 B.C. (Hdt. 4.83) and Xerxes by building a bridge across the Hellespont in 480 B.C. (Hdt. 7.33–36), and 'turning land into water' as he did when he had a canal dug through Mount Athos for the safe passage of his fleet (Hdt. 7.22–24); see also the note ad 22.8.2 and Fontaine n. 138.

cunctis paene copiis terra marique consumptis When writing these words Amm. may have had in mind the battles of Marathon (Hdt. 6.107–117), Salamis (Hdt. 8.40–97), Plataeae (Hdt. 9.16–88) and Mycale (Hdt. 9.90, 96–101). For *consumere*, 'to kill', see the note ad 20.11.12.

vix ipsi tutum invenere discessum Strictly speaking, this only applies to Xerxes' difficult and troubled retreat after the battle of Salamis (Hdt. 8.114–120). Darius did not personally participate in the expedition against Greece. For *discessus*, 'retreat', cf. 15.4.8 *discessu... veloci*, 16.12.2 *post ducis fugati discessum*.

ut bella praetereamus Alexandri Similar phrases occur in 23.1.1 (q.v.), 25.4.9, 30.7.7. See Pinkster, 1990, 34–5 on such pseudo-final clauses.

ac testamento nationem omnem in successoris unius iura translatam There never was any will of Alexander in which he designated his successor, i.e. Seleucus Nicator, although Amm. seems convinced that Seleucus was appointed by Alexander as his successor; see also 23.6.3: *Nicatore Seleuco, eiusdem Alexandri successore*. The will mentioned by Amm. is evidently to be considered as belonging to a later tradition; see Fontaine n. 139. It may have had its origin in 1 Macc. 1.6 and Curt. 10.10.5, where a will is mentioned according to which Alexander made arrangements for his succession and the division of his empire among his generals. However, Quintus Curtius does not believe in such a will himself: *Credidere quidam testamento Alexandri distributas esse provincias, sed famam eius rei, quamquam ab auctoribus tradita est, vanam fuisse comperimus*. In Late Antiquity even the (fictional) text of Alexander's testament was known; it is part of a work entitled *Incerti auctoris epitoma rerum gestarum Alexandri Magni cum libro de morte testamentoque Alexandri*. The testament can be found in ch. 115–123; its first words are: *Rex Alexander, Ammonis et Olympiadis filius, testamentum fecit*.

Quibus peractis transcursisque temporibus longis A very vague phrase in- 6.9
deed. Expressions similar to its first part occur in 16.12.67, 17.10.10, 21.8.1; in
each of these cases, however, it is fully clear what had been 'brought to comple-
tion'. This is the only instance in Amm. of transitive *transcurrere* with 'time'
as object. The nearest parallel is Gel. 5.10.7 *cum* (Euathlus)... *tempusque iam
longum transcurreret.*

nobiscum hae nationes subinde dimicarunt Curiously, after the singular *hanc
gentem* in § 7 and *nationem omnem* in § 8, Amm., perhaps remembering the
variety of the population of the Persian empire, now uses the plural (*hae
nationes*). Cf. for *nos* referring to the Romans *nobis obtemperantium* (20.7.1),
nulla nobis assuetudine cogniti (22.8.21, q.v.) and the phrase *nobis amicus*,
which occurs in 14.4.1, 18.2.8, 20.11.1, 25.7.12, 27.12.1. See also the note on
ad nostra (20.4.4). In the time of the Roman Republic and that of the Roman
(and Byzantine) Empire, the Romans fought many wars with the Parthians
and Sasanians, the first of which was fought by Crassus in 54/3 B.C. The
last conflicts took place in the first decades of the 7th century A.D; see the
chronological tables in Schippmann, 1980 and 1990. For the contacts between
Rome and Parthia, which began in 96 B.C. with the encounter between Sulla
and Orobazus on the Euphrates, see Ziegler, 1964; Wolski, 1976; Winter,
1988.

paribusque momentis... abiere victrices Cf. *pugnabatur paribus diu momentis* (16.12.43, q.v.), *aequis partes... discessere momentis* (31.16.5). At the end
of the sentence, the word order is c.c.; *victríces abiére* would have been less
satisfactory.

quantum ratio sinit Cf. comparable phrases in 15.4.1 (*quantum ratio patitur*), 6.10
27.9.3 (*cum adegerit ratio*). In these phrases *ratio* refers to the writer's "plan of
action" (OLD s.v. 10); cf. Rolfe's "my purpose" and Fontaine's "mon propos".

carptim breviter Predictably, Blomgren 16–7 does not support Clark's
predilection for *breviterque,* which also results in a regular cursus. However,
his argument that the two adverbs are synonymous is wrong: *carptim* refers
to the selection of interesting details, *breviter* to the scale of the exposition.

Persicum... mare I.e. the Persian Gulf, also called e.g. *Persicus sinus*, ὁ
Περσικὸς κόλπος, ἡ Περσικὴ θάλασσα, ὁ Περσικὸς πέλαγος in the sources,
e.g. Str. 15.2.14, 16.3.2 (765C-766C), Arr. *An.* 5.26.2, Plin. *Nat.* 6.108–9,
114. The Persian Gulf is *c.* 1000 km. long and 250–300 km. wide. Amm.'s
description of the Persian Gulf (§§ 10–12) is similar to that of Str. 16.3.2
(765C-766C). Strabo derived his information from Eratosthenes (Φησὶ δὲ περὶ
αὐτῆς Ἐρατοσθένης οὕτως, 16.3.2, 765C); see also Eratosth., Fragm. III B,

39 = Berger, 1880, 269 ff. Eratosthenes' knowledge concerning the Persian Gulf came from Androsthenes and Nearchus, two admirals of Alexander, who had both sailed around the Gulf, in 325 and 324 B.C. respectively; cf. Str. 16.3.2 (766C). Most descriptions of the Persian Gulf by ancient authors go back to these two admirals. See Herrmann, 1938.

ostia... angusta, ut ex Harmozonte... Maces With *ostia angusta* the modern Strait of Hormuz is meant. Cf. Str. 16.3.2 (765C): τὸ μὲν στόμα... εἶναι στενὸν οὕτως, ὥστ' ἐξ Ἁρμόζων, τοῦ τῆς Καρμανίας ἀκρωτηρίου, τῆς Ἀραβίας ἀφοράται τὸ ἐν Μάχαις. Plin. *Nat.* 6.98: *promunturium Carmaniae est, ex quo in adversam oram ad gentem Arabiae Macas traiectus distat LM passuum.* For its narrowness, see also Plin. *Nat.* 6.24, 6.152 and cf. 6.108 *Persicum introitu V mil. passuum latitudinis.* Sol. 54.6 mentions a distance of c. 75 km.: *inter Carmaniae promunturium et Arabiam quinquaginta milia passuum interiacent.* Amm. begins his description of the Persian Gulf in the south; he then describes the western coast (from the south to the north) and then the eastern coast (again from the south to the north). The promontory of Harmozon (i.e. Hormuz) is to be identified with Ras Kunari, just south of the estuary of the Tamaris; see Kiessling, 1912, 2391 f. The promontory of Maces is the modern Musandam peninsula (i.e. the modern state of Oman). Arr. *Ind.* 32.7 refers to it as ἄκρην, καλέεσθαι <δὲ> Μάχετα. Str. 15.2.14 (727C) mentions that sailing across the Strait of Hormuz takes no more than a day: τὸ δὲ στόμα τοῦ Περσικοῦ κόλπου οὐ μεῖζον διάρματος ἡμερησίου. The *incolae* are the people of the Μάχαι; Str. 16.3.2 (765C); Plin. *Nat.* 6.98, 152; Ptol. 6.7.14; Mela 3.79. For the Μάχαι, see Grohmann, 1930.

6.11 *quibus angustiis permeatis... Teredona porrigitur* Cf. Str. 16.3.2 (765C): ἀπὸ δὲ τοῦ στόματος ἡ ἐν δεξιᾷ παραλία περιφερὴς οὖσα κατ' ἀρχὰς μὲν ἀπὸ τῆς Καρμανίας πρὸς ἕω μικρόν, εἶτα πρὸς ἄρκτον νεύει, καὶ μετὰ ταῦτα πρὸς τὴν ἑσπέραν μέχρι Τερηδόνος καὶ τῆς ἐκβολῆς τοῦ Εὐφράτου. Teredon is also mentioned by Plin. *Nat.* 6.145 and Ptol. 5.20.5, 8.20.30. Its location cannot be exactly determined, although various suggestions (e.g. modern Abu Shahrein) have been made; see Weissbach, 1934 and Fontaine n. 144. Recently Potts, 1984 and 1990, 88–9 suggested that Teredon was near modern Basra.

Petschenig's emendation of V's *qua*, viz. *aequa* seems attractive, but his confident argument is less than convincing: "Da V *qua* hinter *extensa* hat, ist offenbar *aequa navigatio* richtig" (*Philologus* 50 [1891] 351). Fontaine, however, was convinced, but his optimistic rendering "s'y allonge aisément" does not seem to be supported by any parallel. Sen. *Her. O.* 589 *gradu... aequo* (about the Acheloüs' 'even flow') is not a parallel, since it concerns the water itself, not men's navigation on it. Walter's *aquarum* leaves *navigatio* without the qualifying adjective which it needs. If Heraeus' *vacua* without any addition could mean 'without obstacles', it would be plausible. As it is, Seyfarth's crux is inevitable.

ubi post iacturas multiplices pelago miscetur Euphrates Cf. Str. 16.3.2 (765C) in the preceding note and Str. 11.14.8 (529C), where it is also remarked that the Euphrates discharges itself into the Persian Gulf; also Sol. 37.6: *Euphratem defert in sinum Persicum*. Hdt. 1.180 remarks incorrectly that the Euphrates discharges itself into the Red Sea (ἐξιεῖ δὲ οὗτος ἐς τὴν Ἐρυθρὴν θάλασσαν). Mela 3.78 says that the Euphrates simply ceased to exist (*nusquam manifesto exitu effluit ut alii amnes sed deficit*); cf. Plin. *Nat.* 5.90 (*Euphrates... distrahitur in paludes*). Nowadays, before the Euphrates flows into the Persian Gulf, it first unites with the Tigris. This was not necessarily the case in Antiquity when the Persian Gulf extended more to the north and both rivers emptied therein without first uniting; cf. Birot and Dresch, 1956, 245–6, esp. fig. 40. As to the river's losses, Fontaine n. 144: "Les pertes de l'Euphrate sont dues à son utilisation pour les canaux d'irrigation dérivés de son cours principal." Apart from the diminution of its waters, alluvial deposits may also have contributed to these losses.

omnisque sinus dimensione litorea in numerum viginti milium stadiorum Cf. Str. 16.3.2 (765C-766C): περιέχει δὲ τήν τε Καρμανίων παραλίαν καὶ τὴν Περσῶν καὶ Σουσίων καὶ Βαβυλωνίων ἀπὸ μέρους, ὅσον μυρίων οὖσα σταδίων... τὸ δ᾽ ἐντεῦθεν ἑξῆς ἐπὶ τὸ στόμα πάλιν ἄλλοι τοσοῦτοι. Strabo's information is based on Eratosthenes (see the note ad § 10 *Persicum*); Plin. *Nat.* 6.108 *is qui ab oriente est, Persicus appellatur, $\overline{XXV}$ circuitu, ut Eratosthenes tradit*; Agathem. 3.12 (= *GGM* II, 474) Ἡ δὲ Περσικὴ θάλασσα κυκλοτερὴς οὖσα, συνάγουσα τὸ στόμα ἄκρῳ Καρμανίας καὶ Ἀραβίας, περίμετρον ἔχει μυριάδων δύο σταδίων; see also Berger, 1880, 274–6. In Solinus' version: *Persicus* (sinus)... *vicies et sexagies centena milia circuitu patens* (54.12) all proportions have been lost. The whole phrase is reminiscent of the description of the outline of the Black Sea: *omnis autem eius velut insularis circuitus litorea navigatio viginti tribus dimensa milibus stadiorum* (22.8.10, q.v.).

velut spatio detornato The verb means "to make by turning on a lathe" (OLD s.v.). Plin. *Nat.* 6.109 expresses the circular form – which does not quite tally with the geographical facts – in another way: *situm eius humani capitis effigie*.

ergo permeatis angustiis ante dictis With this phrase Amm. obviously returns to *quibus angustiis permeatis* in § 11. In the present text, however, the strait is passed in the opposite direction, on leaving the Persian Gulf. But what does *ergo* mean? It either confirms the preceding description: having sailed around the gulf, one leaves it, or it signals a return to the hidden main topic of Amm.,

6.12

viz. the coastline of the Indian Ocean; cf. the list of instances of *ergo* being used "post interruptam orationem" in TLL V 2.771.71 sqq.

ad Carmaniae sinum It is not clear to which sea Amm. refers here. It could be either the Gulf of Oman or the Arabian Sea, since both seas border on the region of ancient Carmania. Carmania is roughly identical with modern Luristan, Kerman and Makran, regions in southern Iran. For Carmania, see Kroll, 1919.

inde longo intervallo Clark, Seyfarth and Fontaine have all accepted Heraeus' addition of *inde longo*, which is plausible in view of 20.6.9 and 22.8.41. Amm. is obviously speaking about the sea passage along the coast of southern Iran and Pakistan.

Canthicus nomine...obnoxius sideri Amm. probably means the Gulf of Kachchh (*Canthicus sinus*), to the west of the peninsula of Kathiawar (India), and the Gulf of Khambhat (*Chalites sinus*), to the east of the same peninsula. See Fontaine n. 146.

praestrictis pluribus insulis...Indorum mari iunguntur oceano The main problem in this sentence is the subject of *iunguntur*. Fontaine's "on rejoint" is a free adaptation, Seyfarth ("die Buchten") and Rolfe ("those bays") are closer to the text, and interpret it correctly: TLL VII 2. 655.7 sqq. provides ample evidence of *iungi* in a geographical or topographical sense; see further the note ad 21.13.3 and cf. below in § 26 *His tractibus Susiani iunguntur*. Admittedly, *praestrictis pluribus insulis* would be more apt for a description of a ship's course – see for *praestringere*, 'to graze', the notes ad 20.3.5 and 21.7.2 –, but in describing the Aegean sea in 22.8.2 sqq., Amm. also uses the flow of the waters as the Agens. It is not known which islands Amm. means. In the *Periplus Maris Erythraei* 40 seven islands along the southern shore of the Gulf of Kachchh are mentioned; see Casson, 1989, 196. It is, however, uncertain if Amm. refers here to the same islands.

6.13 *utque geographici stili formarunt* From 27.4.2 *si veteres concinerent stili* it can be gathered that Amm. here uses *stilus geographicus* as a metonymia for a writer on geography. TLL incorporates the present instance of *formare* as an example of the meaning "fere i.q. delineare" (VI 1.1108.33–40). It is not clear whether or not Amm. had any particular geographers in mind. Fontaine n. 147 ad loc. tentatively suggests that Amm. may have given a resumé of Strabo's text for describing the northern frontiers of Persia ("Pour toute cette frontière nord, Ammien a-t-il résumé Strabon 11.6.1–2 (C 507)?"). This, however, is unlikely; as far as is known, Strabo's *Geography* was hardly or not at all known in ancient times as may be concluded from the fact that no references to it are made in the extant ancient sources; only in the sixth century was the *Geography* (re)discovered; Diller, 1975, 7 ff.

hac specie... ante dictus Presumably, *ante dictus* refers to *Persicum... mare* in § 10. From his remarks in this section, it seems that Amm. had no clear idea of the dimensions of Persia, as Seyfarth n. 81 of his bilingual edition already observed ("Der Autor gibt den Umfang Persiens durch Aufzählung einiger geographischer Merkmale an, hat aber keine klaren Vorstellungen von den wirklichen Verhältnissen."). Sundwall, 1996, 622 argues that Amm. in general "thought of the world as he describes it: with words", but tentatively infers from the present text that "Ammianus may have seen at least one map".

ab arctoo cardine Note Amm.'s careful variation of terms denoting geographical orientation: first *cardo* (cf. 15.11.7 *ab occidentali exordiens cardine*), then *plaga* (cf. 22.7.10 *ab australi plaga*), next *axis*, finally *frons*. He could also have used *latus*, as in *ex eoo latere* (22.8.5), *sidus*, as in 22.8.11 *sidus arctoum*, or *stellae*, as in *arctois obnoxiam stellis* (27.4.6).

Caspias portas I.e. the Caspian Gates, the modern pass of Sar-i-Darreh in the Elburz mountains between Teheran and Semnan. Ancient sources regularly refer to it: Str. 11.9.1 (514C), 11.13.7 (525C), 15.2.8 (723C); Plin. *Nat.* 6.43–4, Plb. 6.44.5, D.S. 2.2.3, Arr. *An.* 3.19.2, Sol. 47.1–2. For a map see Bosworth's edition of Arr. *An.* See also Standish, 1970.

Cadusiis A nation in northern Media on the shore of the Caspian Sea; e.g. Str. 11.6.1 (508C), 11.8.8 (514C), 11.13.3 (523C); Plin. *Nat.* 5.36, 48; Ptol. 6.2.2 and 5; Mela 1.13. See further Meier, 1940. Seyfarth n. 81 is wrong in stating that Pliny locates the Cadusii in northern Scythia.

Arimaspis hominibus luscis et feris Mythical, one-eyed people in northern Scythia. The griffins, the guardians of gold, lived among them, as a poem of Aristeas of Proconnesus related, according to Hdt. 3.116, 4.13 and 27. See Wernicke, 1896.

ab occidua plaga Amm. describes the western border of Persia from north to south.

Nifaten Mountain range near the Taurus, to be identified with the modern Tendürek Dagi. Str. 11.12.4 (522C), 11.14.2 (527C), 11.14.8 (529C); Plin. *Nat.* 5.98; Ptol. 5.12.1, 6.1.1; Mela 1.81. Plut. *Alex.* 31 locates this mountain range much too far to the south. See Weidner, 1937.

Albanos For the Albani, see the notes ad 18.6.22 and 23.5.16.

Scenitas Arabas, quos Saracenos posteritas appellavit See the notes ad 14.4.1 and 22.15.2.

Mesopotamiam sub axe meridiali despectat This is a strange remark, since Mesopotamia is situated to the west of the Persian heartland. For *despectare* as a geographical t.t., cf. *despectat oceanum* (22.15.8, q.v.).

orienti a fronte contrarius ad Gangen Amm. may have mistaken the Ganges for the Indus; see Fontaine n. 149.

pelagus... australe I.e. the Indian Ocean.

6.14 *quas vitaxae, id est magistri equitum, curant* For *curare* as a t.t. denoting duties of administration or command, cf. *dioecensin curans* (17.7.6), *civitatem curare* (26.7.4). Vitaxa – in Iranian bidaxs – is a title of Iranian origin which is found in various forms and in various languages from the first to the eighth century of our era. The title occurs e.g. five times in the *Res Gestae Divi Saporis* (ll. 11, 23, 25, 27 and 28). The title was mostly given to persons of foremost rank and indicates that its bearer functioned as second in rank after the king (at least in early Sasanian times). That the *vitaxae* were of very high rank becomes obvious from the fact that they could operate as *magistri equitum*, 'masters of the cavalry', especially if one knows that the Sasanian cavalry consisted for the greater part of nobles and men of rank. *Vitaxae* could apparently also function as (military) governors of provinces, if Amm. is to be believed. See for *vitaxae* Sundermann, 1990 and Fontaine n. 150.

recensere difficile est et superfluum Amm. uses the second term more often, when speaking about his selective treatment of facts, e.g. 20.5.4, 23.6.62, 27.2.11, 27.8.4.

Assyria... Gedrosia This enumeration of 18 regions corresponds with the contents of Bk. 6 of Ptolemy's *Geography*, except for some minor differences: Ἀσσυρίας, Μηδίας, Σουσιανῆς, Περσίδος, Παρθίας, Καρμανίας Ἐρήμου, Ἀραβίας, Ἀραβίας Εὐδαίμονος, Καρμανίας, Ὑρκανίας, Μαργιανῆς, Βακτριανῆς, Σογδιανῶν, Σακῶν, Σκυθίας τῆς ἐντὸς Ἰμάου ὄρους, Σκυθίας τῆς ἐκτὸς Ἰμάου ὄρους, Σηρικῆς, Ἀρείας, Παροπανισαδῶν, Δραγγιανῆς, Ἀραχωσίας, Γεδρωσίας. Although Arabia Felix is not mentioned in Amm.'s list, he discusses this region in 23.6.45–47. Amm.'s *Carmania maior* is Ptolemy's Καρμανία. In *Scythia infra Imaum et ultra eundem montem* the first three words have been inserted by Gardthausen. The suggestion by Blomgren 23 n. 1, *Scythia infra Imaum Scythia ultra etc.*, improves on this, since the error in the tradition is thus more easily explained as a case of haplography. After *montem* a comma should be printed. Cf. further 23.6.64: *Ultra haec utriusque Scythiae loca.* Sol. 55.1 also reports that Parthia was divided into 18 regions: *regna in ea duodeviginti dissecantur in duas partes. undecim quae dicuntur superiora... reliqua septem inferiora.*

Citra omnes propinqua est nobis Assyria The first three words seem to be a circumlocutory phrase for *proxima*. The description of Assyria is far longer than the discussions about the other Persian regions: 11 paragraphs for Assyria (§§ 15–25) and 50 paragraphs for the other 17 regions (§§ 26–74). This inequality may be due to several factors. First, Amm. knew Assyria from his own experience. Secondly, Assyria was the only region which played a role in Julian's campaign (see for these factors, Sabbah 527 n. 55). A third factor may have been the fact that Assyria, according to fourth-century sources, had been part of the Roman Empire, as the Roman province of Assyria during the reign of Trajan; see the note ad 23.3.1. Dillemann, 1961, 138 and 1962, 305 notes the surprising fact that, although Amm. had travelled through (parts of) Assyria, there is no trace of any "informations personelles" in these sections, as may be the case in his description of Egypt (see the note ad 22.15.1) or that of Thrace (27.4.2). Dillemann, 1961, 138–42 thinks that he can identify eight of Amm.'s sources on Assyria, some of which he used by way of intermediaries: Ptolemy, Diodorus Siculus, Quintus Curtius, Pliny, Dio Cassius, Strabo, Philostratus and the Historia Augusta; "Ainsi huit auteurs, sans compter les inconnus, ont fourni à Ammien la matière de son exposé" (p.142). However, Dillemann does not do justice to the complex matter of Amm.'s sources for his description of Assyria. A similarity between Amm. and one of the above-mentioned authors does not necessarily mean that Amm. used their work as a source. One exception must be made for the sections 17 and 18; it seems more than likely that Amm.'s information there goes back to Dio Cassius 68.27.

6.15

celebritate There seems to be no parallel for *celebritas* being used without any additional reference to density of population. Cf., however, *opportunam urbem et celebrem* (20.9.1, q.v.), *pagi... celebres* (22.8.24). The examples of *celebritas* in Cicero's *Epistulae* are of a different type; e.g. *odi enim celebritatem, fugio homines (Att. 3.7.1), sed nescio quo pacto celebritatem requiro (Att. 12.37.2)* refer to crowded conditions.

quae per populos... vocabulum Amm. refers to the time when Assyria, as an independent and powerful kingdom, was at its height, that is between the 14th and 7th century B.C. In his bilingual edition Seyfarth follows Clark in accepting Petschenig's *copiosos*, which is also printed by Fontaine. Petschenig, *Philologus* 51 (1892) 265, refers to 15.11.7 *civitatibus amplis et copiosis.* He might also have quoted Cic. *S.Rosc.* 6 *patrimonium amplum et copiosum.* However, *copiosa*, the third hand's correction in V is by no means impossible. Rolfe's "prosperous" is less opportune here; in contrast with the preceding phrase, Amm. now focusses on the large size of Assyria, which implies that *copiosus* means "extensive" (OLD s.v. 3); cf. *cum copiosa multitudine*. For this reason, Seyfarth's palinodia deserves support.

nunc omnis appellatur Assyria Cf. 23.6.23: *In omni autem Assyria*. Everywhere else (24.2.6, 24.8.4, 25.4.13, 25.6.8) Amm. just speaks of Assyria; *omnis Assyria* probably refers to Assyria with the inclusion of Babylonia and Adiabene. This may perhaps be concluded from the fact that Babylonia and Adiabene are not mentioned in the enumeration in section 14 above. Ptol. 5.20 and 6.1.1, for instance, does make a distinction between Assyria and Babylonia. For Adiabene as part of Assyria, see the note ad 23.6.20.

bitumen See the note ad 20.7.10 and below, ad § 23.

lacum nomine Sosingiten This lake is only mentioned by Amm. Probably Amm. means (as suggested by Dillemann, 1961, 139) lake Thospitis, the modern Lake Van; Ptol. 5.13.7 (λίμνην τὴν καλουμένην Θωσπῖτιν); Str. 11.14.8 (529C), 16.1.21 (746C); Plin. *Nat*. 6.128 (*Thospitis*). Strabo remarks that the lake, which contains soda, cleanses and restores clothes; for the same reason its water is unfit for drinking.

cuius alveo Tigris voratus The ancient authors were wrong in believing that the Tigris runs through Lake Thospitis; Plin. *Nat*. 6.128: *alterum deinde transit lacum qui Thespitis appellatur*; Str. 11.14.8 (529C): φέρεται δὲ δι'αὐτῆς ὁ Τίγρις ἀπὸ τῆς κατὰ τὸν Νιφάτην ὀρεινῆς ὁρμηθείς, Str. 16.1.21 (746C): διαρρεῖ δ' ὁ Τίγρις τὴν Θωπῖτιν καλουμένην λίμνην κατὰ πλάτος μέσην.

fluensque subterraneus percursis spatiis longis emergit Str. 11.14.8 (529C): κατὰ δὲ τὸν μυχὸν τῆς λίμνης εἰς βάραθρον ἐμπεσὼν ὁ ποταμὸς καὶ πολὺν τόπον ἐνεχθεὶς ὑπὸ γῆς ἀνατέλλει κατὰ τὴν Χαλωνῖτιν. According to Dillemann, 1961, 139 this passage was Amm.'s source; see, however, the note ad 22.6.13 for Strabo as an alleged source for Amm. Nevertheless, Strabo and others provide information on the subterranean course of the Tigris: Str. 16.1.21 (746C): περαιωθεὶς δ'ἐπὶ θάτερον χεῖλος κατὰ γῆς δύεται μετὰ πολλοῦ ψόφου καὶ ἀναφυσημάτων. ἐπὶ πολὺ δ'ἐνεχθεὶς ἀφανής, ἀνίσχει πάλιν οὐ πολὺ ἄπωθεν τῆς Γορδυαίας. Plin. *Nat*. 6.128: *Thespitis... rursusque in cuniculos mergitur et post xxii p. circa Nymphaeum redditur*. Iust. 42.3.9: *interiecto deinde aliquanto spatio, sub terras mergitur; atque ita post quinque et viginti millia passuum grande iam flumen in regione Sophene emergit*. For a discussion of these passages, see Dillemann, 1962, 40-7. For the subterranean course of the Tigris, see also Honigmann, 1937, 1011.

hic et naphta gignitur picea specie glutinosa, similis ipsa quoque bitumini   **6.16**
The adj. *piceus* occurs only here in Amm.; *picea specie* denotes the outward appearance of the substance (cf. the note ad *palustri specie* in 22.8.45) and *glutinosa* (cf. the note ad 20.11.25) its quality. Obviously it is a short description of oil. For oil in this region, see e.g. D.S. 2.12.1; Str. 16.1.15 (743C); Plin. *Nat.* 35.178. As a military man Amm. was probably interested in this liquid, since it could be used as a weapon; the inflammable matter carried by fire-darts, mentioned in 23.4.15, is likely to be naphta, bitumen or oil; cf. also 23.6.37–38 (*oleum Medicum*). See 24.2.3 for an oil well at Diacira. For the use of bitumen and oil in warfare, see also Veg. *mil.* 4.8 and 4.18. In 23.6.38 Amm. specifies naphta as a *vocabulum gentile*; see Huyse, 1993 for Iranian words in the *Res Gestae*.

si avicula insederit brevis For *brevis*, 'small', cf. *brevis...mus* (Ov. *Fast.* 2.574), *optimae breves* (apes) (Plin. *Nat.* 11.59).

praepedito volatu submersa If this is based on personal inspection, Amm.'s information provides us with a remarkable precedent of modern images of oil-polluted areas.

nullum...praeter pulverem exstinguendi commentum For *commentum*, 'device', 'strategy', see the note ad 20.6.6. In contrast to Amm.'s remark in 23.4.15 that oil cannot be extinguished by water but only by sand, Str. 16.1.15 (743C) says that this inflammable material can be put out by water.

This section is directly linked to the preceding text. A short digression only   **6.17**
starts in § 18, where it should be duly marked by the indentation which is out of place here.

In his pagis This vague phrase can only refer to the region where *naphtha gignitur* (§ 16).

hiatus quoque conspicitur terrae, unde halitus letalis exsurgens For *hiatus*, 'chasm', cf. *patentes terrae hiatus* (Liv. 7.6.4). Personal inspection by the author is not implied by *conspicitur*, since *conspici* means 'to be visible' (OLD s.v. 2b); cf. Nep. *Milt.* 7.3 *lucus, qui ex insula conspiciebatur*. The present tense means that the chasm existed in Amm.'s time. As to *halitus letalis*, in 19.4.6 such an exhalation is mentioned as a possible cause of the plague at Amida. See further the note ad 20.11.26 on the phenomenon in general.

quodcumque animal...consumit Cf. Lucr. 6.756–9, in the long description of the *loca Averna* and their dangers: *in Syria quoque fertur item locus esse videri,/ quadrupedes quoque quo simul ac vestigia primum/ intulerint, graviter vis cogat concidere ipsa,/ manibus ut si sint divis mactata repente*); cf. also Plin. *Nat.* 2.207–208: *spiritus letales aut scrobibus emissi aut ipso loci situ, mortiferi alibi volucribus tantum... alibi praeter hominem ceteris animantibus, nonnumquam et homini* and D.C. 68.27.2 καὶ τὸ στόμιον ἐθεάσατο ἐξ οὗ πνεῦμα δεινὸν ἀναδίδοται, ὥστε πᾶν μὲν ἐπίγειον ζῷον πᾶν δὲ πετεινὸν ἀποφθείρειν, εἰ καὶ ἐφ' ὁποσονοῦν ὀσφροιτό τι αὐτοῦ.

cum os eius... acerbitate fecisset The remarkable similarity to the excerpt from Dio Cassius' report on Trajan's campaign in the region continues: καὶ εἴπερ ἐπὶ πολὺ ἄνω ἐχώρει ἢ καὶ πέριξ ἐσκεδάννυτο, οὐδ' ἂν ᾠκεῖτο ὁ χῶρος. νῦν δὲ αὐτὸ ἐν ἑαυτῷ ἀνακυκλούμενον κατὰ χώραν μένει. In his bilingual edition Seyfarth had followed Clark in adopting Madvig's emendation *excessit si in latum*. Presumably his return to V's text implies his taking *excesserit* as an iterative subjunctive. Madvig, 1884, 265–6 had argued that, since the hypothetical apodosis denotes an unreal condition, an adequate protasis is needed, which he construed convincingly by his emendation. Another problem in V's text is that *latum* can only be taken with *os*, which seems a superfluous detail. It should be noted that for all its similarity Dio's description implies another assessment of the dangers involved: the ascending air is deemed very harmful too. Only the fact that it remains in the direct neighbourhood of the pit (ἀνακυκλούμενον, 'turning on itself') guards the surrounding areas from damage. TLL I 365.74–5 rightly presumes that *acerbitas* refers to the *odor acerbus* of the pit.

6.18 *simile foramen apud Hierapolim Phrygiae antehac, ut asserunt aliqui, videbatur* The adjective introduces a digression. Hierapolis in Phrygia (Ptol. 5.2.26) – not to be confused with the city of the same name in 14.7.5, 14.8.7 and 23.2.6 – was known for its hot springs out of which dangerous vapours were set free; Str. 13.4.14 (629C-630C); D.C. 68.27. Dio Cassius (and perhaps Strabo, but see for the acquaintance with his work the note ad 23.6.13) may belong to the *aliqui* to whom Amm. refers; they both have the same story about the lethal fumes at Hierapolis. For *videri*, 'to be visible' cf. Lucr. 6.756, quoted above in the note ad § 17 *quodcumque animal* and Caes. *Gal.* 2.18.3 *in aperto loco paucae stationes equitum videbantur*. Amm.'s use of *videri* may have been prompted by Dio Cassius' strong insistence on his personal visit to the Hierapolis spring: εἶδον ἐγὼ τοιοῦτον ἕτερον ἐν Ἱεραπόλει... οὐ μὴν καὶ τὴν αἰτίαν αὐτοῦ συννοῆσαι ἔχω, λέγω δὲ ἅτε εἶδον ὡς εἶδον καὶ ἃ ἤκουσα ὡς ἤκουσα. The past tense of *videbatur* contrasts with *conspicitur* in § 17 and is remarkably reminiscent of D.C.'s εἶδον.

noxius spiritus This is a variation of *halitus letalis* in § 17.

absque spadonibus solis Cf. Str. 13.4.14 (630C) οἱ δ' ἀπόκοποι Γάλλοι παρίασιν ἀπαθεῖς, D.C. 68.27.3 πλὴν τῶν ἀνθρώπων τῶν τὰ αἰδοῖα ἀποτετμημένων. Amm. regarded eunuchs as unnatural. He calls them sallow, disfigured and mutilated (14.6.17), and compares them with the Huns who slashed the faces of their children to prevent them growing beards (31.2.2). He also accused Semiramis, the first to castrate young males, of doing violence to nature (14.6.17 q.v.). For eunuchs see Hopkins, 1978, Guyot, 1980, Tougher 1997 and the notes ad 20.2.3 and 21.16.16.

rationibus physicis Cf. Dio Cassius' οὐ μὴν καὶ τὴν αἰτίαν αὐτοῦ συννοῆσαι ἔχω. See the note ad 20.11.26, where *rationes physicae* refers to the relevant doxographical tradition. Here it more probably denotes the learned analyses of the experts.

Amm. completely forgets to mention his main reason for adding this digression in the second degree, viz. the noxious potential of the spring which is being described: τοῦτο εὐόρκοις μὲν ἵλεών τε καὶ ἡδὺ ὕδωρ, ἐπιόρκοις δὲ παρὰ πόδας ἡ δίκη (Philostr. *VA* 1.6).

6.19

apud Asbamaei quoque Iovis templum in Cappadocia... numquam extra margines intumescit See Philostr. *VA* 1.6 for this section: Ἔστι δέ τι περὶ Τύανα ὕδωρ Ὁρκίου Διός, ὥς φασι, καλοῦσι δὲ αὐτὸ Ἀσβαμαῖον. The water of this well brings luck to honest people, whereas perjurers are punished with horrible diseases. Fontaine n. 157 refers to Plin. *Nat.* 2.232 and Plin. *Ep.* 4.30 for a phenomenon "fort analogue" to the one described here. However, the natural phenomenon described by both Plinys differs considerably from that referred to by Amm. Dillemann, 1961, 140 thinks that Philostratus may have been Amm.'s source for this story; Mommsen, 1881, 633 n. 6 doubts whether Amm. had a first-hand acquaintance with Philostratus' work. Fontaine n. 157 suggests that Amm. may have visited the spring at Tyana, which lay on the main road from Ephesus to Upper Mesopotamia.

amplissimus ille philosophus Apollonius This is high praise indeed; cf. *opinionum insignium auctor amplissimus Plato* (23.6.32) and *Thucydides est auctor amplissimus* (23.6.75). Apollonius was a pagan hero in late antiquity; cf. Dzielska, 1986 and the note ad 21.14.5.

magnitudine aquarum... intumescit For *inflare* denoting the rise of watery substances cf. TLL VII 1.1465.67–83. Amm.'s other example is *Euphraten nivibus patefactis inflatum* (18.7.9, q.v.). Wagner refers to a similar spring in ps. Arist., *De mirabilibus auscultationibus* 57.

6.20 *Intra hunc circuitum* For *circuitus* as a geographical t.t. denoting the perimeter of a territory or a sea 22.8.10 *omnis autem eius velut insularis circuitus* (q.v.), 23.6.13 *omnis circuitus ante dictus*.

Adiabena est Assyria priscis temporibus vocitata See the note ad 23.3.1 for Adiabene. Cf. Plin. *Nat.* 5.66: *Adiabene Assyria ante dicta*.

Onam Any other information about a river of this name is lacking. Fontaine has therefore ventured an emendation, viz. *Aboram*, the modern Khabour, which plays an important part in the preceding chapter (23.5.1, 4, 15, q.v.). See his n. 159, in which the emendation is elaborately explained.

numquam potuit Presumably the perfect tense indicates the reasons for changing the name in the past. It does not contrast a *fact* of the past with Amm.'s own times, in which, as becomes clear in the next section, two important rivers, which cannot be identified, were not crossed 'by a ford' either.

transire enim diabenin dicimus Graeci See the note ad 22.8.33 on the importance Amm. attached to his native language and on Seyfarth's predilection for V's transcriptions; cf. also Den Boeft, 1992, 12. Clark and Fontaine print διαβαίνειν.

6.21 *nos autem didicimus* For *discere*, "certiorem fieri" (TLL V 1.1335.15), "to be informed" (OLD s.v. 3) cf. 17.4.12 *discant, qui ignorant*, 18.10.1 *perfugarum indicio didicit*.

amnes sunt duo perpetui, quos transiimus, Diabas et Adiabas As in 22.8.29 (q.v.), the adjective means 'flowing without interruption', 'never drying out'. It seems rather drastic to disregard V's *sie* altogether. Eyssenhardt's suggestion *ipsi*, accepted by Fontaine, not implausibly emphasizes Amm.'s personal experience. According to Streck, 1905a and 1905b the Diabas and Adiabas are the rivers Dialas and Adialas, the modern Diyala and Adhaim. However, Dillemann, 1962, 305–8 seems to be right in refuting, mainly for geographical reasons, Streck's opinion. Dillemann suggests that these two rivers are to be identified with the Great and Little Zab. There is one problem with this line of reasoning, viz. that Amm. in 18.6.19 (q.v.) and 18.7.1 refers to the Great Zab as Anzaba and not as Diabas. Dilleman also argues that this passage in Amm. – including the reference to the two rivers which are so difficult to identify – is based on a lost part in book 58 of Dio Cassius. Considering that other passages in the account of the Persian expedition may also well go back to D.C., this is an interesting and worthwhile suggestion.

iunctis navalibus pontibus See the note ad 21.7.7.

ideoque intellegi Adiabenam cognominatam Fontaine regards *intellegi* as first person perfect ("j'ai compris"), but, apart from the fact that according to Neue-Wagener 3.416 and TLL VII 1.2096.72–5, *-g-* in the perf. stem is rare with this verb, the singular would be quite surprising after *nos didicimus* and *transiimus*. It is far more likely that *intellegi* is an inf.: the combination of a *quod*-clause and an inf. is remarkable, but not unique; cf. 18.6.16 *docetque, quod...ad Persas abierat profugus exindeque...se missum ad nostra* and Tac. *Ann.* 14.6.1. See further Ehrismann 67, where the examples, however, do not all belong to this class.

ut a fluminibus maximis Aegyptos Homero auctore et India For Homer who calls the Nile Aegyptos, see the note ad 22.15.3. India is of course named after the river Indus.

Euphratensis ante hoc Commagena Cf. 14.8.7 *Commagena, nunc Euphratensis* and the elaborate note ad loc., as well as 18.4.7 (with note). Commagene came under Roman rule for the first time in 18 A.D., was independent again between 38 and 72/3 under its king Antiochus, and was then incorporated into the province Syria; see Millar, 1993, 52–3, 81–2. As a consequence of Diocletian's provincial reorganization Commagene became the *provincia Euphratensis*; cf. Jones 1458.

itidemque Hiberia ex Hibero, nunc Hispania, et a Baeti amne insigni provincia Baetica Cf. Sol. 23.8: *Hiberus amnis toti Hispaniae nomen dedit, Baetis provinciae: uterque nobilis*. The Hiber is the modern Ebro; see e.g. Str. 3.4.7 (159C), 3.4.10 (161C), 3.5.9 (175C); Plin. *Nat.* 3.21. The Baetis is the modern Guadalquivir; Str. 3.1.6 (139C), 3.1.9 (140C), 3.4.12 (162C): ὁ δὲ Βαῖτις...εἰς τὴν Βαιτικὴν ῥεῖ; Plin. *Nat.* 3.9; Mela 3.5. The province Baetica was created by Augustus, either in 27 B.C. (D.C. 53.12.4–5) or during his tour of Gaul and Spain in 16–13 B.C. (Aug. *Anc.* 12); for a discussion of these dates see Richardson, 1996, 135–6. Baetica is the eastern part of the old province Hispania Ulterior. At the time of the creation of the new province it was already so thoroughly romanised that its administration was trusted to the Senate; Plin. *Nat.* 4.118.

In hac Adiabena Ninus est civitas Cf. 14.8.7: *Commagena...clementer assurgit, Hierapoli, vetere Nino, et Samosata civitatibus amplis illustris*. In 18.7.1 Amm. calls the city by its more common name of Niniveh: *Ninive, Adiabenae ingenti civitate*; see the note ad loc. For the foundation of Niniveh, which the Greeks and Romans believed to have been named after Ninus, see D.S. 2.3.2–4. Dillemann, 1961, 141 thinks that Amm.'s report on Ninus is based on Diodorus 2.1–4. However, it seems more likely that the foundation

6.22

of Niniveh by Ninus was common knowledge, so that Amm. did not need to consult Diodorus for this information.

quae olim Persidis regna possiderat For the *-i-* in the perfect stem of *possidere* see Neue-Wagener 3.415-6 and the note ad 19.2.8. The phrase refers to the Assyrian empire, of which, strictly speaking, Assur was the capital.

nomen Nini potentissimi quondam regis, Semiramidis mariti, declarans Cf. Iust. 1.1.4-10, where Ninus is described as the first king who made war on his neighbours and conquered an empire by subjecting the peoples of the entire East. In the Greek tradition Ninus is considered to be the (mythological) founder of the Assyrian kingdom; *FGrHist* 4 F 1 (Ctesias); see also D.S. 2.1 ff. See Drews, 1965 for Assyria in universal histories of classical authors. For Ninus as a principal figure in Greek novels, see Perry, 1967, 153-66; Reardon, 1989, 803-8; Stephens-Winkler, 1995, 23-71. Apart from the present text, Semiramis is mentioned by Amm. in 14.6.17 q.v., 23.6.23 and 28.4.9 (together with Cleopatra, Artemisia and Zenobia). Semiramis was only gradually identified as Ninus' wife in the literature of antiquity. Herodotus, who mentions her several times (1.184, 3.155) does not yet have this identification, whereas three centuries later D.S. 2.4.1, apparently following the earlier Ctesian tradition, calls her Ninus' wife: Ἐπεὶ δὲ μετὰ τὴν κτίσιν ταύτην ὁ Νίνος ἐστράτευσεν εἰς τὴν Βακτριανήν, ἐν ᾗ Σεμίραμιν ἔγημε τὴν ἐπιφανεστάτην ἁπασῶν τῶν γυναικῶν ὧν παρειλήφαμεν, as does Iust. 1.1.10 (*ipse decessit relicta... uxore Samiramide*). Fontaine n. 163: "La notice d'Ammien semble empruntée au tout début de l'abrégé de Trogue-Pompée par Justin." The legendary figure of Semiramis is based on the historical Assyrian queen Shammuramat (9th/8th century B.C.); Kuhrt, 1995, 491, 528, 609. The precise meaning of *declarans* is difficult to ascertan, since there is no clear parallel to the present phrase; *castrensium negotiorum scientiam plura declarant* (25.4.11) is a different case: Julian's military expertise is shown by many achievements. Presumably *declarans* means 'being a reminder (of the king's name)'.

Ecbatana et Arbala et Gaugamela Ecbatana is not situated in Adiabene but in Media; see 23.6.39 where Amm. mentions it as one of the Median cities. Fontaine n. 164 tentatively suggests that Amm. could have misread Sarbena for Ecbatana in Ptol. 6.1.5 (Γαυγάμελα, Σάρβηνα, Ἄρβηλα). On 1 October 331 Alexander defeated Darius at Gaugamela (modern Tell Gomel; Bosworth, comm. ad Arr. *An.* 3.8.7), 89 km. south of Arbela (Str. 16.1.3 [737C]; D.S. 17.53.4) and some months later, in the spring of 330, Alexander took the royal capital of Ecbatana. There is a resemblance between Amm. and D.C. 68.26.4: [Ἀδιαβηνὴ] ἔστι δὲ τῆς Ἀσσυρίας τῆς περὶ Νίνον μέρος αὕτη, καὶ τά τε

Ἄρβηλα καὶ τὰ Γαυγάμηλα, παρ᾽ οἷς ὁ Ἀλέξανδρος τὸν Δαρεῖον ἐνίκησε. See Dillemann, 1962, 307.

post discrimina varia proeliorum incitato Marte prostravit TLL V 1.1362.23-31 lists a number of instances of *discrimen* "c. genet. rerum periculosorum". Here *proeliorum* is best explained as a gen. inversus: 'after a varied series of dangerous battles'; cf. also *discrimine proeliorum emenso* (17.13.11), *inter prima discrimina proeliorum* (25.3.5). See the note ad 23.5.20 for *Mars*, 'battle'; *prosternere* expresses the inflicting of utter defeat, cf. 17.6.2 *prostravit acerrime multos*.

In omni autem Assyria multae sunt urbes Having dealt with *Adiabene*, Amm. now returns to Assyria in general, the subject of sections 15-19, which primarily sketches the natural surroundings. **6.23**

inter quas Apamea eminet, Mesene cognominata This Apamea should not be confused with other towns of the same name mentioned by Amm.; see the note ad 22.8.5. There are two towns of this name in this region, which are both mentioned by Pliny; *Nat.* 6.129 *(Apameam Mesenes oppidum)* mentions an Apamea in northern Mesopotamia, *Nat.* 6.146 *(Apameam, sitam ubi restagnatio Euphrathis cum Tigri confluat)* refers to an Apamea in southern Mesopotamia. Ptol. 6.1.3-6 does not mention an Apamea in Assyria. Since Amm. speaks of *Apamea...Mesene cognominata* and Pliny of *Apameam Mesenes oppidum*, presumably Amm. means the Apamea in northern Mesopotamia.

Teredon See the note ad 23.6.11.

Apollonia See Ptol. 6.1.6. Apollonia was a minor town about which hardly anything is known. It is therefore remarkable that Amm. mentions it.

Vologessia See Ptol. 5.20.6 (πρὸς δὲ τῷ Μααρσάρῃ ποταμῷ, Οὐολγαισία; for the Μααρσάρης ποταμός, i.e. the Naarmalcha, see 24.2.7); Steph. Byz. s.v. Βολογεσσιάς. *Tab. Peut.* 10.4: *Volgesia*. Pliny's Vologesocerta should probably be identified with Vologessia (Plin. *Nat.* 6.122: *Ctesiphontem...in Chalonitide condidere Parthi, quod nunc caput est regnorum, et postquam nihil proficiebatur, nuper Vologesus rex aliud oppidum Vologesocertam in vicino condidit*). Its Persian name is Valâshâbâd. The town was founded by the Parthian king Vologeses I (51-78 A.D.) as a centre of trade at a site some 5 kms. to the south-east of Seleuceia. It became indeed one of the important trading-posts on the commercial routes to the East; see Treidler, 1967 and esp. Maricq, 1959. It was still a major stronghold at the time of Julian's expedition. Curiously, Chaumont, 1974 distinguishes Vologesias and

Vologesocerta, placing the first on the Euphrates south of Babylon and the second near Ctesiphon. Matthews 156 identifies the unnamed *castellum* to which Amm. refers in 24.5.6–11 as Vologessia.

Babylon, cuius moenia bitumine Semiramis struxit Cf. Ov. *Met*. 4.57–8 *ubi dicitur altam/ coctilibus muris cinxisse Semiramis urbem* and see Bömer's note ad loc. For the use of bitumen in the construction of Babylon's walls, see e.g. Hdt. 1.179; Str. 2.1.31 (84C), 16.1.5 (738C-739C); Vitr. 1.5.8; Iust. 1.2.7 (*Haec Babyloniam condidit murumque urbi cocto latere circumdedit, arenae vice bitumine interstrato, quae materia in illis locis passim invenitur et terra exaestuata*); Curt. 5.1.16 (*Caverna ibi est ex qua fons ingentem bituminis vim effundit, adeo ut satis constet Babylonios muros ingentis operis huius fontis bitumine interlitos esse*), 5.1.25 (*Murus instructus laterculo coctili, bitumine interlito, spatium xxx et duorum pedum in latitudinem amplectitur*). For bitumen, see Forbes, 1955, 67 ff. For Semiramis' alleged role in this project, see the note below.

Curt. 2.9.9 tells us that only a small part of Babylon was inhabited in his time. Paus. 8.33.3 reports that nothing but the walls and the temple of Belus remained of Babylon. Str. 16.1.5 (738C) also remarks that Babylon was almost deserted. In Amm.'s time too, Babylon must have been an insignificant city, mainly known because of its rich history.

arcem enim antiquissimus rex condidit Belus Belus is Latin for Bel, who, historically speaking, was not a king. In fact, it is the title par excellence of the Babylonian city god Marduk. Marduk was venerated in Babylon as supreme god since *c*. 1800 B.C. Bel/Marduk was the Babylonian god of creation (Berossus, *Babyl.* 1.2.3–4). He embodied law and order which implied strong ties with the Babylonian kingdom; confusion between god and king may therefore have been easy. See for the cult of Bel/Marduk: Dhorme, 1949, 139–50, 168–70. The god resided in his temple, the so-called Esagila, which was a large complex in the centre of Babylon. As to the citadel mentioned by Amm., it is to be noted that other authors provide us with different information. Str. 16.1.5 (738C) mentions a pyramid built as a tomb for Belus, which was demolished by Xerxes; cf. D.S. 17.112.3. Curt. 5.1.24 tells us about Belus' residence which was still pointed out (*Belus, cuius regia ostenditur*). D.S. 2.9.4 mentions the temple of Belus, as does Paus. 8.33.3. These references to tomb, residence, citadel and perhaps temple are all references to the ziqqurat, the Tower of Babel. The ziqqurat was part of the Esagila to which also Marduk's temple belonged. See for a full account of the topography of Babylon with citations of relevant cuneiform and classical sources, Unger, 1970[2].

Amm.'s statement that the citadel of Babylon was founded by Belus and that the walls were built by Semiramis springs probably from the mingling of various traditions. According to the Greek (Ctesian) tradition, which is best represented by D.S. 2.7.2–11 and Curt. 5.1.24, Semiramis founded Babylon. Cf. Berossus, *Babyl.* 3.3.3, who censures the Greek historians for wrongly thinking that Babylon was founded by Semiramis; he, however, does not say who was responsible for the foundation of the city. There also was a tradition which attributed the foundation of Babylon to Belus; cf. Curt. 5.1.24: *Samiramis eam condiderat, non, ut plerique credidere, Belus.* Apparently Amm. compromised between these two traditions by attributing the foundation of the citadel to Belus, and the construction of the walls to Semiramis.

Ctesiphon Ctesiphon, situated on the left bank of the Tigris opposite Seleucia, was the capital of the Sasanian Persians until the Arabs conquered it in 637. Its conquest was the prime object of Julian's expedition (see Bk. 24). In the Greek and Roman sources it is first mentioned by Plb. 5.45.5 (ἡ καλουμένη Κτησιφῶν). Str. 16.1.16 (743C) calls it a village and informs us that it was the winter residence of the Arsacids: πλησίον (i.e. near Seleucia) δ' ἐστὶ κώμη, Κτησιφῶν λεγομένη, μεγάλη. ταύτην δ'ἐποιοῦντο χειμάδιον οἱ τῶν Παρθυαίων βασιλεῖς. Plin. *Nat.* 6.122 notes that it was the capital of the Parthians (*Ctesiphontem... condidere Parthi, quod nunc caput est regnorum*), as does Tac. *Ann.* 6.24.4 (*Ctesiphon sedes imperii*). Sol. 56.3: *in aemulationem huius urbis* (i.e. Babylon) *Ctesiphontem Parthi condiderunt.* For Ctesiphon, see the note ad 17.14.1. For *instituere* as a synomyn of *condere* or *fundare* (TLL VII 1.1987.50–1) cf. 15.9.7 *oppida... instituere non pauca.* Ctesiphon was captured several times by the Romans: in 116 by Trajan (D.C. 68.30.3; Eutr. 8.3.1; Zon. 11.22), in 165 by Verus' legate Avidius Cassius (D.C. 79.2.3; Eutr. 8.10.2; Zon. 12.2), in 197 by Septimius Severus (D.C. 75.9.2–5; HA *Sev.* 16.1–2; Zon. 12.9) and in 283 by Carus (Eutr. 9.18.1; HA *Car.* 8.1; Zon. 12.30).

quam Vardanes... specimen summum The information which Amm. provides on Ctesiphon is generally considered to be historically unreliable. Much is uncertain about the history of Ctesiphon. As appears from Str. 16.1.16 (743C) it was more than a mere village. This is also obvious from D.C. 40.20.3, where it is said that in 53 B.C. Crassus had the intention of conquering Ctesiphon. It must therefore have been a place of some importance in the first century B.C, so that Amm. cannot be right in calling the Parthian king Vardanes I (*c.* 39–45 A.D.) its founder. Possibly Pacorus, son of the Parthian king Orodes II (58/7-*c.* 39 B.C.) – and not king Pacorus (92/3–95/6 A.D., 113/4–114/5 A.D.) with whom Amm. may have confused him –, as part of his strategy, made Ctesiphon a fortified town for his campaigns against Syria and Asia Minor. In Amm.'s time it was said to be wellnigh impregnable: *civitas situ ipso inexpugnabilis defendebatur* (24.7.1).

The Greek name of the city may have originated by grecizing an indigenous name. See for this Honigmann, 1924, 1104. Κτησιφῶν is a Greek personal name, e.g. of the man who offered Demosthenes the well-known crown; cf. further such names as Ktesias, Ktesidemos, Ktesippos. For *specimen*, 'ornament', 'glory', cf. Apul. *Met.* 1.23.3 *specimen gloriosum*.

Seleucia, ambitiosum opus Nicatoris Seleuci I.e. Seleucia on the Tigris; Ptol. 5.18.8; Str. 16.1.5 (738C), 16.1.16 (743C), Plin. *Nat.* 5.88, 10.132 *Seleucia Parthorum*. It was situated on the right bank of the Tigris opposite Ctesiphon and was founded *c.* 300 by Seleucus Nicator as the capital of his kingdom, which it, however, never became. In 141 B.C. it was taken by the Parthian king Mithridates I (*c.* 171–139/8), but it seems to have retained its Graeco-Macedonian character and Greek population; Tac. *Ann.* 6.1; D.C. 40.16. In 116 Trajan captured the city and had it burnt; D.C. 68.30.2. In 165 it was destroyed again by fire, this time by Avidius Cassius, *legatus* of Lucius Verus; D.C. 71.2.3; HA *V* 8.3; Zon. 12.2. Plin. *Nat.* 6.122 mentions that it had 600.000 inhabitants; Eutr. 8.10.2 mentions that 400.000 people lived in Seleucia when L. Verus took it in 165 (*Seleuciam, Assyriam urbem nobilissimam, cum quadringentis milibus hominum cepit*). Ruf. Fest. 21 has the same number as Eutropius. For an elaborate description of Seleucia, see Matthews 140–3 and Hopkins, 1972 (esp. 149–63 for the history of Seleucia based on classical sources). Julian visited Seleucia, which by then had become a deserted city (24.5.3). Cf. the relevant note on 22.13.2 about *ambitiosus*.

6.24 *qua per duces Veri Caesaris, ut ante rettulimus, expulsata* This was a feat of Lucius Verus' *legatus* Avidius Cassius, *a quo contra fidem Seleucia, quae ut amicos milites nostros receperat, expugnata est* (HA *V* 8.2–3). For *per* as a synonym of *ab* cf. Szantyr 127; see also the note ad 22.8.12 for other examples in Amm. The expressions used by Amm. to refer to earlier passages in the *Res Gestae* are dealt with in the note ad 21.16.7. See further the note ad 22.9.6 on Amm.'s references to passages in the lost part of his work. For Blomgren 173 Amm.'s predilection for verba frequentativa is decisive in defending V's curious *expulsata*; TLL V 2.1812.55–66 lists only 4 examples of this verb, which seems out of place here. Admittedly, Müller's *expugnata*, chosen by Clark, is a shade too smooth, but Fontaine understandably accepts Petschenig's *expoliata*: "Seleucia wurde damals geplündert und niedergebrannt" (*Philologus* 51 [1892] 283).

avulsum sedibus simulacrum Comaei Apollinis Robert, 1969, 984 will have nothing to do with any 'eastern' interpretation of this deity: "Il n'y a aucun indice que cet *Apollo Comaeus* n'ait pas été porté à Séleucie du Tigre par ses adorateurs grecs lors du peuplement de la ville par des Grecs". In brief terms: it is "une importation macédonienne" (985). In Amm.'s text there is nothing to oppose this view.

post direptum hoc idem figmentum "Von Anfang an verbindet sich *idem* mit anderen Demonstrativa wie *hic, iste*" (Szantyr 188). All instances in Amm. of *hic idem* emphasize the identity of a person or thing mentioned in the preceding text, e.g. *ob hoc idem vitium* (16.8.10), *hac eadem nocte* (23.3.3), *in hac eadem regione* (24.5.2), *hic idem tribunus* (26.8.10). The same holds true in the present text: precisely the theft of this sacred object triggered off the fatal epidemic. For *figmentum*, 'portrait' or 'statue' see the note ad 22.9.6.

incensa civitate milites fanum scrutantes invenere foramen angustum Cf. τήν τε Σελεύκειαν διέφθειρεν ἐμπρήσας (D.C. 71.2.3), Τῷ Οὐολογαίσῳ συμβαλὼν ἥττησέ τε καὶ μέχρι Σελευκείας ἐδίωξε καὶ ταύτην ἐνέπρησε (Zon. 12.2). HA V 8.2 contains a different version of the events: *et nata fertur pestilentia in Babylonia, ubi de templo Apollinis ex arcula aurea, quam miles forte inciderat, spiritus pestilens evasit, atque inde Parthos orbemque complesse.*

ut pretiosum aliquid invenirent Contrary to the note in Seyfarth's app. crit., Blomgren 159 here concedes the necessity to add *ut* to V's text.

ex adyto quodam concluso a Chaldaeorum arcanis Since the Chaldaei are praised for their learning in the next section, it is probable that Amm. regards the closing of the rift in the inner part of the sanctuary as a wise and salutary measure, which was undone by the greediness of the soldiers, with catastrophic results. In view of *a, arcanis* should be taken as masc.: 'men among the Chaldaei who could be trusted to keep a secret'. See TLL II 434.55–75 for other examples of such an active sense of *arcanus*, viz. "qui celat vel tacet"; e.g. Plin. *Nat.* 7.178 *uti. . . aliquem ex arcanis mitteret.*

labes primordialis. . . polluebat et mortibus The general meaning of *labes* is defined in TLL VII 2.770.6–7 as "vitium vel res vitiosa integritatem destruens, contaminans, polluens". In 19.4.6 the term is used to denote the plague at Amida, but in the present text it refers to the age-old air which was liable to carry pathogenic germs. Curiously, *primordialis* is a word almost exclusively used by Christian authors. The hidden 'defect' was of course 'primordial', since it could not have been caused by anything else. Being exposed to outward influences, it then, like a womb, received the seeds of incurable diseases. It seems less likely that the *labes* itself 'generated' these diseases, as some translations suggest: rather it functioned as a fertile soil for them and then, presumably in the form of polluted air, spread them by way of contagion. Although pestilence and epidemics were never far away in the ancient world, the plague during Marcus Aurelius' reign stood out in its severity, wide extent and long duration. In 165 this plague, which is believed to have been some form of smallpox, was brought over from the eastern Mediterrean by Lucius

Verus' army. In 166 it had reached Rome. It kept raging until the 180s and reached large parts of the Roman world. In spite of its wide impact in terms of deaths and the subsequent disruption of social and economic life – especially established by Duncan-Jones, 1996 –, contemporary authors provide little information. Besides Amm., HA *MA* 13.3–6 is one of the main sources; see also Gilliam, 1961.

6.25 *Hic prope Chaldaeorum est regio* Amm. seems to have derived the reference to the *regio Chaldaeorum* from Ptol. 5.20; see for the territory of the Chaldaeans also Mela 3.76 and Plin. *Nat.* 6.145. The Chaldaeans were a nation which lived in Babylonia since at least the 9th century B.C. Some of their leaders were able to seize the Babylonian throne, like Nabopolassar who became king of Babylon in 626 B.C. and is considered the founder of the Neo-Babylonian empire. Chaldaeans also constituted the priestly class of Babylon. Hdt. 1.181, 183 mentions them as priests of Bel (Marduk); see also D.S. 2.29; Arr. *An.* 3.16.5. They were believed to have prophetic powers (D.S. 2.29.1–3; 17.112.2; 19.55.7–9) and to occupy themselves with divination, astronomy (e.g. Plin. *Nat.* 18.216) and astrology (e.g. D.S. 2.31.7–9). The various functions of the Chaldaeans sometimes confused classical authors, as for instance in Str. 16.1.6 (739C). Strabo calls them local philosophers who are concerned mostly with astronomy; he speaks of a tribe of Chaldaeans, of several tribes of Chaldaean astronomers and of a territory inhabited by Chaldaeans (in the neighbourhood of Arabia and the Persian Gulf). See further Koster, 1954 (with many references to classical sources), Camus, 1967, 166 ff., Rike, 1987, 71–2, 94.

altrix philosophiae veteris Amm. uses *altrix* two more times (15.5.38, 20.8.11) in a metaphorical sense. The respect for the wisdom and philosophy of early times, which is so characteristic of late antique thought, has perhaps been most clearly expressed by Plotinus when expounding his theory of the hypostases: καὶ εἶναι τοὺς λόγους τούσδε μὴ καινούς, μηδὲ νῦν ἀλλὰ πάλαι μὲν εἰρῆσθαι μὴ ἀναπεπταμένως ('explicitly'), τοὺς δὲ νῦν λόγους ἐξηγητὰς ἐκείνων γεγονέναι (*Enn.* 5.1.8); cf. also *Enn.* 3.7.1 Εὑρηκέναι μὲν οὖν τινας τῶν ἀρχαίων καὶ μακαρίων φιλοσόφων τὸ ἀληθὲς δεῖ νομίζειν. Before Plotinus, Numenius had preached the necessity to ἀναχωρήσασθαι ('go back') to the religious and philosophical knowledge of famous peoples. In his *Life of Pythagoras* 151 Iamblichus reports that the great sage, in his synthesis of divine philosophy and religion (τὴν θείαν φιλοσοφίαν καὶ θεραπείαν), borrowed from the Orphics, the Egyptian priests, the Chaldaeans etc. Τὸ τῆς φιλοσοφίας ἔργον ἔνιοί φασιν ἀπὸ βαρβάρων ἄρξαι is the very first phrase in Diog. Laert. The author then continues with these words: γεγενῆσθαι γὰρ παρὰ μὲν Πέρσαις Μάγους, παρὰ δὲ Βαβυλωνίοις ἢ Ἀσσυρίοις Χαλδαίους. See also D.S. 2.29 sqq. Amm.'s praise of the

Chaldaei may be intended as a contrast to their bad reputation in the Roman world; cf. e.g. *Cod. Theod.* 9.16.4 (25 January 357), which forbids to consult them.

ut memorant ipsi Dillemann, 1961, 142 thinks that Strabo may have been Amm.'s source for his information on the Chaldaeans (but see the note ad 23.6.13). However, *ut memorant ipsi* obviously implies the author's claim that he obtained his information from Chaldaean writings or from an oral Chaldaean source.

apud quos veridica vaticinandi fides eluxit This phrase is the expression of high praise. In 26.10.15 the adj. is characteristic of serious history in contrast to fables: *veridicae... antiquitates*; *fides* is used to denote the reliability of historical records in 22.16.13 and 23.5.20. The historian could hardly have put his respect for oracular lore in stronger terms. It is not likely that Amm. is referring to astrological accomplishments here, as Fontaine suggests in n. 171. In the digression on divination in 21.1.7-14 he does not pay any attention to this domain, which is not surprising in view of his general lack of real interest in it. More probably, the present text contains a reference to the *Oracula Chaldaica*, beloved by Julian, specifically as interpreted by his favourite philosopher Iamblichus. See for this Bouffartigue, 1992, 306-9; Smith, 1995, 91-113. For *elucere*, 'to manifest itself clearly', cf. *elucentis industriae iuvenem* (15.8.8). TLL V 2.426.3-4 suggests that in the present text "notio apparendi abit in eam q.e. oriri, nasci".

has easdem terras This probably refers to the *regio Chaldaeorum* and to Adiabene and Assyria which are mentioned by Amm. in sections 20-23.

hi, quos praediximus, et Marses et Flumen Regium et Euphrates After referring to the rivers in Adiabene mentioned in sections 20-21, Amm. turns to those which belong specifically to the region itself. His information is based on Ptol. 5.20.2: Διαρρέουσι δὲ τὴν χώραν ὅ τε Βασίλειος ποταμὸς καὶ ὁ... καλούμενος Μααρσάρες, ὃς τῷ μὲν Εὐφράτῃ συμβάλλει. Amm. and Ptolemy are obviously mistaken in distinguishing the Marses from the Fluvium Regium. Marses or Naarsares is seen as a rendering of Nar sarri, 'Royal River'. The Marses, however, is not a river but a royal canal; Fontaine n. 172. Plin. *Nat.* 6.123 calls it Narraga; see Weissbach, 1935; Dillemann, 1961, 153; Van der Spek, 1992, 236-7. Apparently Amm. was not aware of the fact that these were canals and not rivers. See Stol-Nissen, 1976-80 for canals in Mesopotamia. For the Euphrates, see the note ad 14.8.5.

qui tripertitus navigabilis per omnes est rivos Cf. the 7th-century author Theophylactus Simocatta, *Hist.* 5.6: διατέμνεται τρίχα τό τε οἰκεῖον ὄνομα ἀποβάλλει καὶ διαφόροις προσηγορίαις ὀνομάζεται. However, this author does not mention the navigability of the three branches.

insulasque circumfluens The islands in question cannot be identified, but were probably shaped by the circumfluent branches of the Euphrates.

arva cultorum industria diligentius rigans Remarkably, in this presentation of the facts the river is the Agens with human engineering causing the action. However, this instance of the abl. causae remains within Szantyr's definition: "ein Instrumental des Mittels, bei dem die ein Geschehen begleitenden äusseren oder inneren Umstände als Ursache der Handlung oder des Vorganges erscheinen". The river provided the fields with a supply of water 'thanks to the cultivators' diligent design'; *diligentius* is an example of comparativus pro positivo; see the note ad 20.4.16 *sublatius eminens*.

6.26 *His tractibus Susiani iunguntur* I.e. Susiana which is situated to the southeast of Mesopotamia and the north-east of the Persian Gulf. For *iungi* with dat. as a geographical t.t. cf. the notes ad 21.13.3 and 23.6.12.

Susa, saepe domicilium regum Susa was the capital of Elam. It became the first royal (winter) residence of the Achaemenids (e.g. Str. 15.3.2 [727C]); Darius I built his palace (Apadana) there. Xen. *Cyr.* 8.6.22 tells us that during the year Cyrus was in Susa for three months in the spring (and seven months in Babylon during the winter and two months in Ecbatana in the summer). During the reign of the Seleucid king Antiochus III it became a fully Greek city with a council, assembly and elected magistrates. Under the Seleucids and Parthians it was named Seleuceia-on-the-Eulaeus. Susa had a mixed population of Elymaeans, Persians, Syrians, Anatolians, Babylonians, Jews and Greeks. The city gradually decayed in the Sasanian period, esp. after Shapur II destroyed it and founded the city of Êrânsahr-Sâpûr near or at the same place; see Nöldeke, 1879, 58. For Susa in Achaemenid times, see Boucharlat, 1990; in Sasanian times, see Boucharlat 1987. See Harper et al., 1992 for the earlier periods and archaeological material from Susa.

Arsiana et Sele et Aracha Most probably Amm.'s Arsiana is the town of Tariana or Ταρείανα, which is mentioned by Ptol. 6.3.5 and 8.21.6; see Fontaine n. 174, who reads *Tareiana*, following Ptolemy ("tareiana ex Ptol. scripsi: tariana Wei. ariana Gar. arsiana codd., edd."). The French scholar adopts this practice throughout chapter 6 (cf. e.g. with respect to this same section his app. crit.: "oroatis ex Ptol. scripsi: oroates V, Cl. Rol. Sey. et vulgo" and "charax ex Ptol. scripsi: harax vulgo"). I. Opelt in *Gnomon* 55 (1983) 261 agrees ("ist dagegen nichts einzuwenden"), but R. Cappelletto in *RFIC* 107 (1979) 470–1 is, rightly, sceptical ("Sarebbe stato buon partito, dunque, mantenere anche per i toponimi quello stesso criterio di cauto conservatorismo (in questo caso suggerito da saggia prudenza) seguito dal F... .per la lingua di Ammiano"). Sele is also mentioned by Ptol. 6.3.5 (Σέλη). It is not quite clear which town Amm. means with Aracha. It is not mentioned by Ptol., who, however, does mention an Anouchtha (as second after Sele) and an Arakka (6.3.4); one of these two may be meant by Amm. There is a place with the name Aracha, but it lies 27 km. east of Palmyra (*CIL* 3, Suppl. 6719; cf. Ptol. 5.15.24: Ἄδαχα) and cannot be the same Aracha as the one mentioned by Amm. There is also an Arakia (the modern Khark), an island on the coast of Persis (Ptol. 6.4.8), which Plin. *Nat.* 6.111 calls Aracha. There is furthermore a place in Parthia by the name of Arakiana (Ptol. 6.5.2) which was situated near Apamea and Charax.

cetera brevia sunt   For *brevis*, 'small', cf. the note ad 23.6.16.

quibus praestant Oroates et Harax et Mosaeus   TLL X 2.907.5–6 lists this as an instance of *praestare* with the meaning 'to excell above'. The Oroates is the border river between Persis and Susiana, the modern Shūl. Str. 15.3.1 (727C) calls it the longest river in this part of the world; cf. also Arr. *Ind.* 39.9. It debouches into the Persian Gulf. See also Ptol. 6.3.1, 6.4.1 and 2; Plin. *Nat.* 6.111, 136; and Herrmann, 1942. In the case of Harax Amm. is mistaken since this is not a river but the town of Charax Spasinou at the northern coast of the Persian Gulf. The confusion may have been caused by Ptol. 6.3.2 where Charax is mentioned between the mouths of the rivers Tigris and Mosaeus; for Charax, see Weissbach, 1899. The Mosaeus is also mentioned by Ptol. 6.3.2 (Μωσαῖος). The mouth of this river, which also flows into the Gulf, is situated between the town of Charax and the mouth of the river Eulaios; see Weissbach, 1935.

per arenosas angustias, quae a rubro prohibent Caspium mare   From the viewpoint of modern geography this is a puzzling phrase. In Antiquity, however, *mare rubrum* not only indicates the modern Red Sea, but the sea around Arabia in general, part of the Indian Ocean and the Persian Gulf included (cf. e.g. Plin. *Nat.* 6.107–8). Perhaps Amm. specifically means the latter, which he calls *Persicum mare* in 23.6.10. In that case the phrase would be less problematical.

aequoream multitudinem inundantes   Clark's text is accepted by Seyfarth, whose rendering "und führen eine Menge Wasser herbei" is akin to the interpretation of *inundare* in the present text and 31.2.16 which is provided in TLL VII 2.248.28–30: "fere i.q. augere, sc. se infundendo". Petschenig's *aequorea multitudine*, which can also be derived from V, is perhaps easier to understand. Fontaine's ingenious *aequor ea multitudine inundantes*, "ils arrosent ainsi en foule le plat pays", poses some problems: three rivers can hardly be called a 'large number' and the only other instance in Amm. of *aequor*, 'plain' (31.4.6) occurs in a quotation from Verg. *G.* 2.106.

6.27 *At in laeva* Generally speaking, in this digression the author proceeds from west to east. Having reached Susiana, he now has to deal with regions on roughly the same degree of longitude and thus to turn to the north, which is on the *lefthand* side. Cf. the use of *dextra* and *laeva* in 22.8.2. Such terms are not used in relation to a map, but to the point of reference which the author has chosen for his description. See Sundwall, 1996, 633 sqq.

Media confinis Hyrcano panditur mari Cf. Ptol. 6.2.1: Ἡ Μηδία περιορίζεται ἀπὸ μὲν ἄρκτων μέρει τῆς Ὑρκανίας θαλάσσης κατὰ περιγραφὴν τοιαύτην. According to Strabo 11.6.1 (507C) the Hyrcanian Sea is the same as the Caspian Sea: καλεῖται δ' ἡ αὐτὴ θάλαττα (i.e. the Caspian Sea) καὶ Ὑρκανία. However, Plin. *Nat.* 6.36 and 46 (*Hyrcanis, a quorum litoribus idem mare Hyrcanium vocari incipit a flumine Sideri*) and *Tab. Peut.* X 5 – XI 2 make a distinction between both seas by calling one part of the same sea *mare Caspium* and another part *mare Hyrcanium*. Since Amm. refers to the Caspian Sea in the previous section and in this passage to the Hyrcanian Sea, it may well be that he also wants to make a distinction between the two gulfs. Str. 2.5.18 (121C) mentions the Caspian Sea as one of the four large existing seas which opens into the Northern Ocean (2.5.31 [129C]; 11.1.5 [491C]); cf. also Mela 3.44–45. However, Hdt. 1.202 already described it as an inner sea with no openings to other seas or oceans, as does Arist. *Mete.* 351a8 and 354a3 f. The Caspian Sea was also known as *mare Albanum* (Plin. *Nat.* 6.39) and *Scythicum mare* (Oros. 1.12.47). For a description of the Caspian Sea, see Str. 11.6.1 (507C). See further Herrmann, 1919.

quam ante regnum... legimus Asiae reginam totius Assyriis domitis Our main source for Media's supremacy in the seventh and sixth centuries is Hdt. 1.102 ff. The expansion and domination of Media took place under the reigns of the kings Phraortes – who, after he had conquered Asia (κατεστρέφετο τὴν Ἀσίην), marched against the Assyrians but without success (Hdt. 1.102) –, his son Cyaxares, who, after a temporary setback of Median power caused by the Scythians, managed to conquer Niniveh and thus Assyria (Hdt. 1.106), and Astyages. The Median empire was eventually incorporated into the Achaemenid empire by Cyrus I (559–529) after, according to Hdt. 1.130, 128 years of Median supremacy (Iust. 1.6.17 tells us that the Median empire existed for 350 years). In spite of Herodotus' report the history of Median hegemony is nebulous. In modern historiography serious doubt is expressed as to whether there ever was a Median state or empire; see Sancisi-Weerdenburg,

1988 and 1994; Kuhrt, 1995, 652–5. In this respect it is interesting to note that Strabo (11.6.2–3 [507C–508C]) already remarked that Herodotus' report is myth rather than history.

V's *legimus Asiae regna* has been dealt with in diverse ways. Valesius proposed to add *tenuisse*. Heraeus' *regnasse* is an even easier solution; the verb can be combined with a gen.; see for this Szantyr 83. Clark, however, chose Gelenius' *reginam*, tentatively suggesting the addition of *fuisse*. Neither Seyfarth nor Fontaine, who both also follow Gelenius, is convinced of the necessity of this addition. TLL VII 2.1129.28–42 indeed presents a list of instances of *legere* with two accusatives, but it seems that none of these concerns a clear fact of the past. As to *regina* in honour of a region, this might be possible. Amm. uses the term for Rome in 14.6.6; see further the evidence in Van Dam ad Stat. *Silv.* 2.2.12 *Appia longarum teritur regina viarum*. However, Heraeus' *regnasse* remains the most attractive proposal.

quorum plurimos pagos in Agropatenae vocabulum permutatos The information which Amm. provides here is questionable. Media Atropatene (the modern Iranian province Azarbayjan-e Sharqi) – situated to the north-west of Media proper and also called Little Media to distinguish it from the heartland of Media, Greater Media – only came into existence by the end of the 4th century B.C. (probably in 323). It was named after Atropates, satrap of Media under Darius and Alexander. After Alexander's death Atropates remained in power and in the wars which ensued after 323 he managed to gain independence for Little Media, which was thus eventually named after him. The name Media Atropatene is first attested by Str. 11.13.1 (522C-523C): ἡ δ' ἑτέρα μερίς ἐστιν ἡ Ἀτροπάτιος Μηδία, τοὔνομα δ' ἔσχεν ἀπὸ τοῦ ἡγεμόνος Ἀτροπάτου. Accursius' *Atropatenae*, accepted by Fontaine, is a plausible emendation. The area was regarded as independent under the Seleucids, Armenians, Parthians and Romans. See Schottky, 1989, esp. 35–53 for a detailed discussion of the creation of Media Atropatene; Sherwin-White and Kuhrt 1993, 77–8.

pugnatrix natio In Hdt. 1.103 the Median kings, especially Cyaxares, are called belligerent. 6.28

Parthos, quibus vincitur solis In the mid-second century B.C. the Parthians under Mithridates I made the first attempts to conquer Media. They eventually succeeded, probably after heavy fighting, *c.* 148 B.C. After the death of Mithridates I (139/8 B.C.) Media was probably lost again for the Parthians but was reconquered during the reign of Mithridates II (*c.* 124/3 – 88/7 B.C.); see Schippmann, 1980, 23 ff., 123–4.

regiones... formatas Str. 11.13.8 (525C) reports that the length and breadth of Media are approximately equal (τὸ δὲ μέγεθος πάρισός πώς ἐστιν εἰς πλάτος καὶ μῆκος).

celsitudines imminent montium, quos Zagrum et Orontem et Iasonium vocant Another instance of the gen. inversus, which occurs quite often in Amm.; see the note ad 20.6.7. The Zagros is a mountain range in north-western Iran (Kurdistan). It is also mentioned by Str. 11.12.4 (522C) and 16.1.1 (736C); Plin. *Nat.* 6.131; see further Treidler, 1967. The Orontes, which is also mentioned by Ptol. 6.2.4 is the 3745 m. high mountain massif south of Ecbatana; its modern name is Alvand. The Iasonium is a mountain range in south-east Media said to be named after the Argonaut Jason (Str. 11.13.10 [526C]); see also Ptol. 6.2.4 and 6: τὸ Ἰασόνιον ὄρος. It is again mentioned by Amm. in 23.6.39 (*Iasonio monte in terris sitae Syromedorum*).

6.29 *Coroni... montis altissimi* The modern Karen-Dagh; see Ptol. 6.2.4 (Κορωνὸς ὄρος); 6.5.1; 6.9.3.

frumentariis agris affluunt et vinariis Strabo (11.13.3 [523C], 11.13.7 [525C]) reports that most of Media, especially the northerly region, is high and cold, but that the region below the Caspian Gates (see for this pass 23.6.13 q.v.) consisting of low-lying lands, is very fertile. However, its soil does not produce good olives; they are dry and yield no oil.

pingui fecunditate laetissimi, fluminibus fontiumque venis liquidis locupletes Amm. goes out of his way to stress the prosperity of the people in question with traditional Roman agricultural terms. For *laetus* with abl., 'rejoicing in', cf. *laeta dolis* (Verg. *A.* 8.393). The abl. with *locuples* expresses that in which the riches consist; cf. a similar case in 23.6.45. Several of the rivers are mentioned in 23.6.40.

6.30 *praebent apud eos prata virentia fetus equorum nobilium* As could be expected, a wealth of emendations of V's *dent* has cropped up. Among these Gardthausen's *edunt* deserves close attention. The verb is used quite often "de terra, regione animantes proferente" (TLL V 2.85.19–43); cf. e.g. Cels. 5.27.10: Italy and comparable regions are healthier, *quod minus terribiles angues edunt*. Seyfarth's own solution *praebent* is not convincing. Phrases like *ver praebet flores* (Ov. *Rem.* 188) are not really comparable and *planities... nulla... latibula praebere sufficiens* (18.6.14) belongs to the class in which the verb has "locum, domum, latebras sim." as direct object (TLL X 2.383.67–384.5).

quibus, ut scriptores antiqui...Nesaeos appellant Several *scriptores antiqui* have passages on the Nesaean horses: Herodotus, Polybius, Arrian and Strabo. According to Hdt. 7.40 these horses were large and came from the Nesaean plain in Media; cf. also Hdt. 3.106, 9.20. As to the exact location of the Nesaean plain opinions differ; see Fontaine n. 180, Walbank ad Plb. 30.25.6 and Herzfeld, 1968, 8–9. Str. 11.13.7 (525C) says that these horses were used by kings (cf. Amm.'s *viri summates,* which means 'noblemen') because they were the best and largest. They were characteristically different from Greek horses and Strabo also mentions that some writers say that the breed did not come from Media but from Armenia. Plb. 10.27.1–2 calls them excellent horses and mentions royal stud-farms which supply the whole of Asia with these animals; see also Plb. 30.25.6. Arr. *An.* 7.13.1 mentions that there were originally 150.000 mares in the Nesaean plain but that in the time of Alexander there were only 50.000 left since most of them had been driven off by robbers; cf. D.S. 17.110.6 who mentions 160.000 and 6000. Str. 11.13.7 (525C) reports that there were 50.000 mares in this plain. As to *nosque vidimus*, on several occasions Amm. could have seen Sasanian noblemen riding these horses: during his service in the east under Ursicinus, at Amida, and, of course, during Julian's campaign.

abundat itaque civitatibus † quibus No doubt Madvig's *abundat itaque* is   6.31
closer to V's *abundantia que* than Haupt's *abundatque*, but his defense of *itaque*, viz. "propter soli fertilitatem ante descriptam" is somewhat laboured, even if *quibus* hides an adj. meaning 'rich' or 'prosperous'. One wonders whether Gelenius' *aeque* should not be preferred: having sketched Media's rich supply of corn, wine and fine horses, Amm. now reports that the region is 'equally' well supplied with cities. Several of these cities are mentioned by Amm. in 23.6.39. Str. 11.13.6 (524C) refers to some Greek cities in Media (Laodicea, Apamea, Heraclea and Rhaga), as well as to the metropolis Ecbatana (11.13.1 [522C]). Plb. 10.27.3 says that a ring of Greek cities was founded in Media by Alexander to protect the region from the neighbouring barbarians. That is probably also the reason why villages in Media were built *in modum oppidorum.*

utque absolute dicatur *Absolute* means 'in unambiguous terms' rather than expressing the briefness of the subsequent characterization, as some translators assume. See the relevant note on *absolutus* ad 21.16.18.

uberrimum est habitaculum regum This is probably a generalisation since only Ecbatana (mentioned by Amm. in 23.6.39) is known as a royal residence of the Medians, Persians, Macedonians and Parthians; Str. 11.13.1 (522C), 11.13.5 (524C), 16.1.16 (743C); Curt. 5.8.1. Hdt. 1.98 reports that it was founded by the first Median king Deiotes. Plb. 10.27.4–13 (see Walbank ad loc.) gives a description of Ecbatana and its royal palace; see also Chaumont, 1973, 216–7. Ecbatana has not yet been excavated.

6.32 Amm.'s long digression on Persia contains several specimens of what Sabbah has put into the following words: "il multiplie les digressions dans la digression" (527). The digression on the Magi is the longest and most important. It was indispensable for the author to pay due attention to an aspect of Persian life and religion which had fascinated the Graeco-Roman world since at least the 5th century B.C. There is a wealth of evidence about the varied ideas held about the Magi throughout the ages. This material can be consulted in Clemen, 1920 and especially Bidez-Cumont, 1938, who have incorporated the present digression as testimonium B21 (Tome II, 32–4). Although the particular theory of the latter-named scholars has met with considerable scepticism (see Nock, 1972 and Beck, 1991, 492–3) and is no longer shared by any expert, their collection of material remains a prime source of information. Recently Beck, 1991 and De Jong, 1997, 387–403 have dealt respectively with the pseudepigrapha published under the name of Zoroaster, to whom a decisive role is ascribed regarding the origin and development of the Magi's lore, and with the Magi as the priests of Persia. De Jong's survey is especially fruitful for understanding Amm.'s summary.

Herodotus is the first author who provides substantial evidence on the Magi, portraying them primarily as ritual specialists: ἄνευ δὴ μάγου οὔ σφι νόμος ἐστὶ θυσίας ποιέεσθαι (1.132). His general assessment is not negative, which deserves to be noted, since derogatory references to the Magi already appear in the 5th century B.C. A sort of easy equation between γοητεία and μαγεία developed, which, according to Diogenes Laertius 1.8, was even combated by Aristoteles ἐν τῷ Μαγικῷ. Throughout the ages comparable examples of respect occurred, but the negative reputation also persisted. In his *Apologia sive de magia*, Apuleius found it necessary to make a clear statement, which it is worthwhile to quote in its entirety: *Nam si, quod ego apud plurimos lego, Persarum lingua magus est qui nostra sacerdos, quod tandem est crimen, sacerdotem esse et rite nosse atque scire atque callere leges caerimoniarum, fas sacrorum, ius religionum, si quidem magia id est quod Plato interpretatur, cum commemorat, quibusnam disciplinis puerum regno adulescentem Persae imbuant – verba ipsa divini viri memini, quae tu mecum, Maxime, recognosce:* Δὶς ἑπτὰ δὲ γενόμενον ἐτῶν τὸν παῖδα παραλαμβάνουσιν οὓς ἐκεῖνοι βασιλείους παιδαγωγοὺς ὀνομάζουσιν. εἰσὶν δὲ ἐξειλεγμένοι Περσῶν οἱ ἄριστοι δόξαντες ἐν ἡλικίᾳ τέτταρες, ὅ τε σοφώτατος καὶ ὁ δικαιότατος καὶ ὁ σωφρονέστατος καὶ ὁ ἀνδρειότατος. ὧν ὁ μὲν μαγείαν τε διδάσκει τὴν Ζωροάστρου τοῦ Ὡρομάζου. ἔστι δὲ τοῦτο θεῶν θεραπεία. διδάσκει δὲ καὶ τὰ βασιλικά. *auditisne magian, qui eam temere accusatis, artem esse dis immortalibus acceptam, colendi eos ac venerandi pergnaram, piam scilicet et divini scientem, iam inde a Zoroastre et Oromaze auctoribus suis nobilem, caelitum antistitam, quippe qui inter prima regalia docetur nec ulli temere inter Persas concessum est magum esse, haud magis quam regnare* (Apul. *Apol.* 25.9–26.3). See the notes in Hunink's recent commentary.

Admittedly, Apuleius had an axe to grind, yet the quoted passage testifies to current opinion and shows that, however vague the information about them, the Magi were in the general public's bad books. In intellectual circles this was perhaps somewhat different. At the start of his survey of Greek philosophers, Diogenes Laertius polemizes with those who sought the beginnings of philosophy among the barbarians, i.a. the Persian Magi. Such a view is a late product of a far more positive tradition.

Amm.'s concise survey shows that he has chosen his stance within this tradition. In contrast to Apuleius, he refrains from any explicit criticism of misconceptions, and his abstinence from reporting even the slightest stain which from a Graeco-Roman point of view might taint the reputation of the Magi, is even more remarkable. Magic in its evil sense was legally banned in the Roman world; see for this Pharr, 1932. Some examples from the author's times in the *Codex Theodosianus*: *si quis magus vel magicis contaminibus adsuetus, qui maleficus vulgi consuetudine nuncupatur... fuerit deprehensus, praesidio dignitatis cruciatus et tormenta non fugiat* (9.16.6, 5 July 358), *quicumque maleficiorum labe pollutum audierit deprehenderit occupaverit, ilico ad publicum protrahat et iudiciorum oculis communis hostem salutis ostendat* (9.16.11, 16 August 389). Magic also occurs more than once in the *Res Gestae*, specifically as an object of legal prosecution; see for this Funke, 1967. It is notable that, whereas the laws use the terms *magus* and *magicus* to denote magic practices as well as *maleficus* and *maleficium*, Amm. never does so. He refers to magic with the phrase *artes nefandae* (14.1.2), *noxiae* (28.1.26), *pravae* (28.1.14), *secretae* (23.6.78, q.v.). He once mentions people who claimed to have been *clandestinis praestigiis laesi* (26.4.4). The words *magia* and *magus* occur only in the present digression. Obviously Amm. in his terminology implicitly departs from current usage: the Magi had nothing to do with magic.

There is another background to Amm.'s positive description. In the first centuries A.D. respect for traditions of the remote past had increased considerably. There are numerous instances of a conviction which is best expressed by τὸ πρεσβύτερον κάρρον (the Doric equivalent of κρεῖττον) τῶ νεωτέρω (Timaeus Locrus περὶ φύσιος 94 c). An important testimony in view of the present subject is Numenius fr. 1a (Des Places), where the philosopher emphasizes the need to ἀναχωρήσασθαι to at least Pythagoras, but not to halt there: ἐπικαλέσασθαι δὲ τὰ ἔθνη τὰ εὐδοκιμοῦντα, προσφερόμενον αὐτῶν τὰς τελετὰς καὶ τὰ δόγματα τάς τε ἱδρύσεις συντελουμένας Πλάτωνι ὁμολογουμένως, ὁπόσας Βραχμᾶνες καὶ Ἰουδαῖοι καὶ Μάγοι καὶ Αἰγύπτιοι διέθεντο. The idea that non-Greek peoples had better access to truth and wisdom, which had originated in the venerable past, is also voiced by Celsus:

ἔστιν ἀρχαῖος ἄνωθεν λόγος, περὶ ὃν δὴ ἀεὶ καὶ ἔθνη τὰ σοφώτατα καὶ πόλεις καὶ ἄνδρες σοφοὶ κατεγένοντο, "which has always been maintained by the wisest nations and cities and wise men" (Orig. *Cels.* 1.14, tr. Chadwick). Similar reflections induced Plotinus, having mastered Greek philosophy, καὶ τῆς παρὰ τοῖς Πέρσαις ἐπιτηδευομένης πεῖραν λαβεῖν σπεῦσαι καὶ τῆς παρ' Ἰνδοῖς κατορθουμένης (Porph. *Plot.* 3). To account for his preference for Indian wisdom, Apollonius of Tyana said that the people there were καθαρωτέραις ὁμιλοῦντες ἀκτῖσιν ('living in purer sunlight') and had a better grasp of the truth, ἅτε ἀγχίθεοι (Philostr. *VA* 6.11). Wisdom, and specifically reliable knowledge of the divine, have been preserved in the pure traditions of the eastern world. In his report on the Magi Amm. appears to be a moderate, but unequivocal supporter of such views on alien wisdom. He describes the Magi not as curious or dangerous performers of suspicious tricks, but as serious priests carrying out their duties with a knowledge of the divine and a ritual expertise which have sprung from an age-old tradition. This format had no room to spare for any negative evidence which the collection of Bidez and Cumont shows to have been amply available. In § 35 Amm. concludes his survey proper by stating that the Magi were highly esteemed *religionis respectu*. That is precisely his own position too. This survey may add precious little to our knowledge of the Magi or their image in the Graeco-Roman world, yet it provides essential evidence to those who want to define the author's own religious inclinations. His predilection for 'pure' forms of religion makes him respect *Christianam religionem absolutam et simplicem* (21.16.18, q.v.) and abhor Julian's cultic excesses (*superstitiosus magis quam sacrorum legitimus observator*, 25.4.17).

In his tractibus Magorum agri sunt fertiles Curiously, this important sector of Persian religion is almost casually introduced within the strictly geographical framework of the chapter. The Magi are a tribe, though a very special one, as will soon appear in Amm.'s description. Hdt. 1.101 mentions the Μάγοι as one of the six γένεα in Media. In Str. 15.3.1 (727C) they are one of the φῦλα living in Persia.

super quorum secta studiisque Amm. leaves the reader in no doubt about his opinion on the Magi: he considers their lore to be a serious 'school of thought', the accomplishments of which deserve to be explained to the reader.

quoniam huc incidimus Amm. uses this formula only here. For *incidere*, "to happen on a topic" (OLD s.v. 4b), cf. *imprudens huc incidi, iudices* (Cic. *Ver.* 4.43). Compared with other phrases expressing the suitability of a digression (see Emmett, 1981, 18–9) the present one is very flat.

pauca conveniet expediri The same phrase occurs in 22.14.7. See also the note ad 21.16.1 for some comparable phrases.

opinionum insignium auctor amplissimus Plato Amm. straightaway introduces a respected authority in order to emphasize the respectability of the Magi and their lore. Plato after all had produced 'excellent views'; for *opinio* denoting a philosophical or scientific theory cf. 17.7.11, 20.3.8, 20.11.30, 22.15.4 and 7. The choice of *amplissimus* as a further enhancement of Plato's status is connected with the supposed origin of his name; see the note ad 22.16.22 *sermonum amplitudine*.

hagistiam esse verbo mystico docet Not knowing what to do with the first part of V's *machagistiam*, Wagner implicitly suggested the emendation *hagistiam*, the transcription of ἁγιστείαν, a word which, however, is not to be found in Plato's authentic works. *Axiochus* 371 d τὰς ὁσίους ἁγιστείας is the only occurrence in the Platonic corpus. In a passage in Plato *Alcibiades I*, quoted by Apul. *Apol.* 25 (see the introduction to the present digression), the author reports that the education of 14-year-old boys is entrusted to the very best educators. The wisest among them μαγείαν τε διδάσκει τὴν Ζωροάστρου τοῦ Ὡρομάζου – ἔστι δὲ τοῦτο θεῶν θεραπεία (Plato *Alc*. 1.122 a). The last two words can be regarded as the equivalent of ἁγιστεία. Fontaine accepts Bidez and Cumont's emendation *magicam hagistiam*, which indeed accounts for V's *mac*, but seems to introduce a circular element in the definition ascribed to Plato. In Julian's *To the Mother of the gods*, ἁγιστεία is used several times to denote the sacred ceremonial rites of the goddess. A comparable meaning is feasible for the present text as well, corresponding with *verbo mystico*, which refers to the revelatory or initiatory character of the rites; cf. the notes ad 21.14.5 and 22.14.7.

divinorum incorruptissimum cultum This apposition functions as a further explanation of the hallowed term *hagistia*. The adjective occurs more often in Amm., but only here in the superlative. It is by no means merely an attempt to render ἁγι- in Latin, but stresses the purity of the Magi's ceremonial veneration of the divine, which has in no way been defiled by any superstitious influences. The use of the adj. *divinus* to denote religious cults and lore is of course quite normal. With *cultui divino* (18.10.4, q.v.) Christian worship is meant, whereas the phrase *intellegendi divini editionem multiplicem* (22.16.19, q.v.) refers to 'theological' knowledge. Here the use of the n.pl. lends a certain vagueness to the phrase: it is worship 'of the divine world'; cf. Tert. *anim.* 24.12 about the Platonic soul: *consciae divinorum*. Amm. obviously has no detailed knowledge concerning the identity of the deities worshipped by the Magi.

cuius scientiae... addidit Zoroastres With *scientia* Amm. adds a further detail to his reverent sketch of the Magi's lore. The term denotes systematic knowledge, e.g. *militaris rei* (22.7.9), *litterarum* (29.1.9), *iuris* (30.4.11), also in the domain of religion: *vaticinandi* (22.12.7, 25.2.8). The Magi perform their ceremonial duties on the basis of their expert knowledge. Its original scope had not been enriched by novelties of recent times, but in ancient, and therefore authoritative, periods many elements from the secret stores of wisdom of the Chaldaeans were opportunely introduced by no less an authority than Zoroaster. The author had no need to enlarge on the Chaldaeans, since he could assume that the beginning of § 25 was fresh in the readers' memory. In contrast to *a Chaldaeorum arcanis* (23.6.24, q.v.) *arcanis* is neutr. plur. here, denoting the secret lore of the Chaldaeans. The word *arcanus* is often used concerning secret rites, such as mysteries or magic, but it can also be used about deep religious or philosophic truths; cf. Quint. *Inst.* 1.12.15 (Plato) *Aegypti quoque sacerdotes adiit atque eorum arcana perdidicit*, Sen. *Ep.* 95.64 *Sicut sanctiora sacrorum tantum initiati sciunt, ita in philosophia arcana illa admissis receptisque in sacra ostenduntur*, Ambr. *fug. saec.* 2.5 (about a passage in Scripture) *lectionis arcana istius*. Like *temporibus priscis* (i.a. 20.6.9, q.v.), *priscis saeculis*, which also occurs in 14.8.9, 17.4.2, 22.8.14, denotes the remote past, usually in a purely matter of fact sense. Here, however, the phrase clearly adds to the value of the tradition. Remarkably, apart from *Bactrianus* Amm. does not provide any information about the famous Zoroaster. Did he deem this superfluous considering that his fame was widespread in the Graeco-Roman world? Or was he insufficiently informed himself? The answer to these questions depends on the interpretation of *qui* at the beginning of § 33. As to *Bactrianus*, see De Jong, 1997, 320 for other traditions about Zoroaster's nationality.

Hystaspes rex prudentissimus, Darei pater Again a telling adjective: Hystaspes may have been an eastern king, but he was a model of great wisdom, a worthy element in the Magi's spiritual pedigree. According to Hdt. 3.70 the father of Darius I was a satrap, not a king. As appears from the testimonia in Bidez-Cumont, 1938, II 359 sqq., later tradition usually gave him that title. There may be a confusion with Zoroaster's disciple king Vistaspa; see Bidez-Cumont, 1938, I 215; Colpe, 1994, 1059.

6.33 *qui cum superioris Indiae secreta fidentius penetraret* The translators have been convinced by the apodictic statement about *qui* in Bidez-Cumont, 1938, II 33: "non point Hystaspe, mais le fondateur de la secte des Mages,... et nulle part, on ne lit qu'Hystaspe ait passé pour le premier des Mages". Unfortunately, there is hardly any other evidence for Zoroaster's passage to India and, besides, Amm. is remarkably silent about the legendary founder of the Magi's lore. Moreover, *deinde* introduces a second phase after Zoroaster. Bidez-Cumont,

1938, II 359 rightly recant: "le *qui*, grammaticalement, devrait se rapporter à Hystaspes, et peut-être Ammien l'a-t-il ainsi entendu, ayant mal compris sa source". Presumably, *superior* in imitation of the names of Roman provinces means 'further inland'; for *secreta*, 'secluded regions' cf. 26.9.8 *nemorum secreta*, Suet. *Aug.* 94.5 *per secreta Thraciae*. In harmony with normal usage, *fidentius* expresses justified confidence; see the note ad 20.8.19.

cuius tranquillis silentiis praecelsa Brachmanorum ingenia potiuntur Since Alexander the Great's expedition knowledge of the Brahmans had spread in the Graeco-Roman world. Testimonia in Latin literature can be found in André-Filliozat, 1986. However, the most famous 'western' view is provided in the long passage in Philostratus' *Life of Apollonius of Tyana*, book 3, in which the author reports Apollonius' visit to the hill where the Brahmans lived, and his lofty conversations with them. This is the only instance in Amm. of *praecelsus* in a translated sense; cf. Symm. *epist.* 2.65 *praecelso animo tuo*. Yet one wonders whether the choice of the adjective hints at the Brahmans' art of levitation, referred to in 28.1.13 *dum studebat inter altaria celsius gradientes, ut quidam memorant, imitari Brachmanas*. In some occurrences of *potiri* "respicitur potius status possidendi, habendi" (TLL X 2.330.6 sqq.); cf. *cuncti enim caelites semper eodem statu mentis aeterna aequabilitate potiuntur* (Apul. *Soc.* 12).

eorumque monitu... eruditus In 26.1.8 Amm. mentions some famous Greek *periti mundani motus et siderum* of the past, but about Alexandria in his own days the author has to report the scarcity of students of astronomy (22.16.17). Apollonius took part in the Brahmans' discussions, αἷς ἀστρικὴν ἢ μαντείαν κατενόουν καὶ τὴν πρόγνωσιν ἐσπούδαζον (Philostr. *VA* 3.41). Obviously, Hystaspes had enjoyed the same privilege. The phrase *purosque sacrorum ritus* repeats *divinorum incorruptissimum cultum* in § 32, which now appears to stem from an excellent source. In view of the context it seems best to take *colligere* to refer to assembling facts, as in 15.9.2 *haec... collegit ex multiplicibus libris*. As becomes clear in TLL V 2.830.71–84 *erudire* with double acc. is quite rare. Kühner-Stegmann 1.299 and Szantyr 43 assume an analogy with *docere*.

aliqua sensibus magorum infudit After the restriction implied in *quantum colligere potuit* – not everything! –, this also mitigates the Indian influence on the Magi: only 'some' elements of Hystaspes' learned information were incorporated in their religious concepts.

cum disciplinis praesentiendi futura "Throughout the classical texts, the Magi are credited with extraordinary powers in the realm of divination" (De Jong, 1997, 397). Amm. leaves the reader in the dark as to the provenance of the Magi's mantic expertise. There can be no doubt that the author respected it since he explained its various aspects in an important digression, in which divination is called *doctrinae genus haud leve* (21.1.7).

6.34 *una eademque prosapia multitudo creata* A comparison with *illorum sanguine creatos* (Cic. *Agr.* 2.1) and *qua sitis stirpe creati* (Ov. *Met.* 3.543) makes clear that *una eademque prosapia* is an abl.: 'sprung from one and the same lineage'. This corresponds with the purity of the cult. They have grown considerably in number since their original *numerus... exilis* (§ 35), but their stock has not lost its integrity.

deorum cultibus dedicatur The plural of *cultus* does not often occur; see TLL IV 1330.33–49. Amm. may be using it here to emphasize the diversity of the individual cults; see the note ad *divinorum* in § 32.

si iustum est credi This is not an example of usual Latin idiom. It may well be a grecism: δίκαιόν ἐστι e.g. occurs several times in Herodotus, i.a. 7.235 δίκαιόν με σοί ἐστι φράζειν τὸ ἄριστον. Amm. presumably intends to express a slight, but polite doubt about the tradition in question. Concerning a different phenomenon, viz. shooting stars, in 25.2.5 he is less reserved, calling a spade a spade with *corpora enim qui credit caelitus posse labi, profanus merito iudicatur et demens*. Greek and Roman authors often note "that the Persians consider fire to be the most holy manifestation of the divine" (De Jong, 1997, 346).

sempiternis foculis Curiously, the adjective is transferred from the fire itself, which, as is often reported in the sources, was regarded as eternal: ἄσβεστος (Str. 15.3.15, 733C), αἰώνιος (Tat. *orat.* 17), *ardens perpetuo* (Cassiod. *hist.* 11.8.3); see further De Jong, 1997, 347. Valesius refers to Curt. 3.3.9 *Ignis, quem ipsi sacrum et aeternum vocabant, argenteis altaribus praeferebatur*, viz. every morning during a military campaign; cf. also Curt. 4.24.24. Xenophon reports that in the royal procession behind chariots in honour of Zeus and Helios πῦρ ὄπισθεν αὐτοῦ ἐπ' ἐσχάρας μεγάλης ἄνδρες εἵποντο φέροντες (*Cyr.* 8.3.12).

praeisse quondam Asiaticis regibus dicunt "Cette coutume passa – avec les idées qui s'y rattachaient – des Achéménides aux diadoques" (Bidez-Cumont, 1938, II 53). TLL X 2.596.62–4 rightly regards the Magi as subject of *dicunt*.

6.35 *huius originis* Cf. for *origo*, "stock", "line" (OLD s.v. 5b), *originis penitus alienae* (22.9.12), *regium illi genus et pace belloque clara origo* (Tac. *Hist.* 4.55.1).

Persicae potestates For *potestates*, 'officials', cf. 14.1.10 *celsae potestates*, 16.12.14, 23.5.15.

eratque piaculum aras adire vel hostiam contrectare Cf. Hdt. 1.132 ἄνευ γὰρ δὴ μάγου οὔ σφι νόμος ἐστὶ θυσίας ποιέεσθαι. With *piaculum*, 'sin', Amm. expresses this taboo in a Roman way; cf. 17.7.10, 25.9.2. The verb *contrectare* may have been deliberately chosen: τὰ κρέα ῥάβδοις λεπτοῖς ἐφάπτονται οἱ Μάγοι καὶ ἐπᾴδουσιν (Str. 15.3.14, [733C]).

conceptis precationibus Similar phrases to denote formal and sollemn utterances occur in 17.1.13, 19.12.4, 21.5.10, 25.9.11, 28.1.21, 29.1.31. The verb is used in this sense already in archaic Latin.

libamenta diffunderet praecursoria Cf. Str. 15.3.14 (733C) ἀποσπένδοντες ἔλαιον ὁμοῦ γάλακτι καὶ μέλιτι κεκραμένον. The other two instances of the adjective in Amm. are 15.1.2 and 31.3.6, in both cases with *index*, 'an informer arriving in advance'. In a ritual context it occurs in August. *Petil.* 3.56.68, where John the Baptist's baptism is called *lavacri praecursorium sacramentum*, 'a ritual anticipating (Christian) baptism'.

aucti... in amplitudinem gentis solidae concesserunt et nomen In view of *aucti* and *solidae*, both of which refer to physical existence, it seems better to regard *amplitudo* as denoting size rather than prestige. For *concedere in* see the note ad 23.6.2 *in vocabulum Parthi concessit Arsacis*, which makes it less likely that *nomen* means "renom" (Fontaine). Amm. says that only at the end of a long period of steady growth the family of priests had developed into a proper tribe with a specific name, viz. *Magi*. Seyfarth's "Sie wurden zu einer festen Stammeseinheit mit eigenem Namen" hits the nail on the head.

murorum firmitudine communitas Cf. *originis penitus alienae firmitudine communitas* (22.9.12). In the present text, however, *firmitudo* is not used 'de rebus incorporeis', but denotes material strength; for this reason the phrase can be regarded as an instance of genitivus inversus.

religionis respectu sunt honorati In view of *nullus existimationis respectus* (22.4.4), *humanorum respectu* (25.7.6), *sine respectu boni honestique* (27.11.4), *respectus* can be rendered by 'respect' here, *religionis* being a genitivus obiectivus: the Magi were honoured out of respect for their *religio*. It seems best to interpret this term here as denoting a clearly defined set of religious convictions and customs, as in the case of Christianity: 21.16.18 *Christianam religionem*; cf. also 18.10.4 and 22.5.3.

septem post mortem Cambysis regnum inisse Persidos Those who advocate 6.36
Amm.'s familiarity with Herodotus, will experience a bad moment here. As ap-

pears in Hdt. 3.70, not the Magi, but Darius and his Persian fellow-conspirators numbered seven. As becomes clear from Iust. 1.10, Pompeius Trogus gave the correct information. However, some consolation may be found in the fact that, as Lindenbrog notes, Valerius Maximus also mentions *septem magos* (9.2.ext. 6). For *inire* with *regnum* cf. Iust. 41.6.1 (Mithridates and Eucratides) *regna inierunt*.

antiqui memorant libri A somewhat vague category comparable to the *scriptores veteres* (15.9.2, 24.2.16) or *antiqui* (23.6.30, q.v.).

equino hinnitu sortiti ὅτευ ἂν ὁ ἵππος ἡλίου ἐπανατείλαντος πρῶτος φθέγξηται ἐν τῷ προαστίῳ αὐτῶν ἐπιβεβηκότων, τοῦτον ἔχειν τὴν βασιληίην (Hdt. 3.84); Darius' groom Oibares saw to it that his master's horse was the first. Ampelius' summary is very brief, but correct: *Darius rex unus ex septem Persis hinnitu equi regnum adsecutus* (13.3); cf. also Iust. 1.10.4.

6.37 *oleum...Medicum* Possibly the same kind of oil as described by Hdt. 6.119 who calls it ῥαδινακή.

quo illitum telum...pulveris consopitur Cf. 23.4.15 q.v. where practically the same words are used to describe the most efficient way of using this missile.

6.38 *oleum usus communis* In spite of its outward likeness to naphtha, this is not a curious product of nature, but a chemical compound made by human experts with normal olive oil as its raw material. Cf. Veg. *mil.* 4.8 *oleum, quod incendiarium vocant* (cf. also 4.18).

condiunt Usually the verb concerns food, wine or perfume. It occurs only here in Amm. In view of the following it probably expresses the process of the mixture maturing.

ad diuturnitatem servantes et coalescens TLL V 1.1644.45–65 lists a number of instances of *diuturnitas* without any addition, meaning "longum tempus". This is the only instance in which Amm. uses *coalescere* in its literal and material sense. Syntactically the phrase is an hybrid: *ad diuturnitatem* is an Adjunct, *coalescens* is a Praedicativum.

ex materia venenatur This repeats *herba quadam infectum*.

alia similis oleo crassiori species Only Clark's brilliant emendation *venenatur. alia* makes the sense of the phrase fully clear. It is by no means a superfluous addition. Amm. combats an error, testified to by Procop. *Goth*.

4.11.36 ἀγγεῖα δὲ θείου τε καὶ ἀσφάλτου ἐμπλησάμενοι καὶ φαρμάκου, ὅπερ Μῆδοι μὲν νάφθαν καλοῦσιν, Ἕλληνες δὲ Μηδείας ἔλαιον. The emphasis is on *alia*: naphtha and Medic (or Medea's) oil are different substances. Lindenbrog refers to Procopius without being able to understand Amm.'s purpose. See the note ad 23.6.16. It seems best to take *quam* as referring to *oleo crassiori*, its feminine form agreeing with *naphtham*. See for this type of agreement Kühner-Stegmann 1.37-8, Szantyr 443.

ut diximus In 23.6.16 Amm. indeed describes naphtha, without, however, mentioning the fact that the term is not a Greek or Roman one, but a *vocabulum gentile*.

Zombis et Patigran et Gazaca Zombis is also mentioned by Steph. Byz. p.297,13 (Meineke): Ζομβὶς, πόλις τῆς Μηδίας. It is not mentioned in this form by Ptolemy or any other classical author. Dillemann, 1962, 162, 302 identifies Zombis with the *mansio* Isumbo on *Tab. Peut.* X 8. It is probably the same as Strabo's Symbakè (11.13.2, 523C). According to a suggestion put forward by Dillemann and accepted by Seyfarth n. 102, Amm. mentions Zombis because he knew the place personally. Patigran may be the same as Bazigrabana which is mentioned by Isid. Char. 6 (*GGM* I 250) or Patansana which is referred to by *Tab. Peut.* X 4. See further Fontaine n. 195 and Herzfeld, 1968, 120 and 319 on these places. Gazaca is also mentioned by Str. 11.13.3 (523C) and Steph. Byz. p.194,15: Γάζαχα, πόλις μεγίστη τῆς Μηδίας; it is called Gazae and Phisganzaga by Plin. *Nat.* 6.42, 44. Ptol. 6.2.10 calls it Ζάζαχα. For a discussion on the name of the place as well as its location, which is uncertain but may have been near the village of Laylan, see Schottky, 1989, 15-21, 25-27; Weissbach, 1912.

6.39

opibus et magnitudine moenium conspicuae The translators unanimously render *moenia* with 'city walls'. This is of course possible, but the term could also refer to large buildings, as in 22.9.4 (q.v.), which would tally somewhat better with the economic prosperity expressed by *opibus*. See TLL VIII 1328.31 sqq.

Heraclia et Arsacia et Europos et Cyropolis et Ecbatana These towns are also mentioned by Ptol. 6.2.2, 14, 16, 17 but in a different order (Κυρόπολις, Ἐκβάτανα, Ἀρσακία, Ἡράκλεια, Εὔρωπος). Heraclia, Arsacia and Europos were Macedonian foundations. Heraclia lay near the town of Rhagae; see Str. 11.9.1 (514C). According to Str. 11.13.6 (524C) Arsacia and Europos were one and the same city, which was also known by the name of Rhagae: ʽ Ράγα, τὸ τοῦ Νικάτορος κτίσμα. ὁ ἐκεῖνος μὲν Εὐρωπὸν ὠνόμασε, Πάρθοι Ἀρσακίαν. In Parthian times the name of the city was apparently changed to

Arsacia. It is to be noted that, contrary to Strabo, *Tab. Peut.* XI 1-3 distinguishes between Arsacia/Rhagae and Europos; see further, Weissbach, 1920; Chaumont, 1973, 201–6. For the location of Rhagae: Marquart, 1901, 123–4. Cyropolis was founded by Cyrus and was according to Ptol. 6.2.2 situated between the rivers Cyrus and Amardus. For Ecbatana, modern Hamadan, see the note ad 23.6.31.

sub Iasonio monte   See the note ad 23.6.28.

Syromedorum   According to Ptol. 6.2.6 Syriamedia is the part of Media which borders on Persia. This may be the case, but according to Honigmann, 1932 it is more likely that with Syromedia a region in Media is meant which was once under the control of the Seleucids. In the same scholar's opinion "Ammianus Marcellinus setzt fälschlich *Ecbatana sub Iasonio monte in terris Syromedorum* an".

6.40   *Choaspes et Gyndes et Amardus et Charinda et Cambyses et Cyrus*   The Choaspes, the modern Karkheh, has its source east of Ecbatana and joins the Tigris close to the latter's debouchment; Plin. *Nat.* 6.130; Str. 15.3.4 (728C-729C). The Gyndes is the modern Diyālā (its upper course is named Sirwān) which joins the Tigris just south of Baghdad. Its source is the lake of Darbandi Khan; see further Streck, 1912. Both rivers, which in contrast to the others mentioned here by Amm., flow into the Persian Gulf, are already mentioned by Hdt. 1.188–189. Water of the Choaspes was taken by Cyrus on every journey, since the Great King only drank water from this river, because of its clarity and taste; e.g. Hdt. 1.188; Plin. *Nat.* 31.35; Sol. 38.4. For this reason the Choaspes was called royal; *Pan. Mess. (Corpus Tibullianum* 3.7 = 4.1.140) *regia lympha Choaspes*; Sol. 37.6 *nobilissimus amnis Choaspes*; see further Weissbach, 1899. Cyrus punished the Gyndes by dividing it into 180 canals because one of his sacred horses had drowned in this river; see Sen. *De ira* 3.21. The other four rivers all flow out into the Caspian Sea. They are mentioned by Ptol. 6.2.1, 2, although in a different order (from west to east): Καμβύσος, Κύρος, Ἀμάρδος, Χαρίνδα. The Amardus, which is identical with the modern Sefīd Rûd, is probably named after the nation of the Amardoi (see for them e.g. Str. 11.8.8 [514C]). The Charinda is not identifiable with any modern river. The Cambyses is to be identified with either the modern Alazani or the Iora which both flow through modern Georgia; Plin. *Nat.* 6.39; D.C. 37.3.5; Mela 3.41. The Cambyses joins the Cyrus, the modern Kura; Herrmann, 1919. The Cyrus/Kura is described by Str. 11.3.2 (500C) and is also mentioned by e.g. Plin. *Nat.* 1.6, 10; 6, 25, 26, 29, 39, 45, 52; Mela 3.41; Sol. 19.4–5. Amm. mentions this river again in 27.12.16–17.

Cyrus ille superior rex amabilis abolito vetere id vocabulum dedit   A contrary story is given by Str. 15.3.6 (729C) who relates that the Persian king assumed the name of the river Cyrus (in this case the Cyrus in Persis): ἔστι δὲ καὶ Κῦρος ποταμός, διὰ τῆς κοίλης καλουμένης Περσίδος ῥέων περὶ Πασαργάδας οὗ μετέλαβε τὸ ὄνομα βασιλεύς, ἀντὶ Ἀγραδάτου μετονομασθεὶς Κῦρος. See the note ad 21.9.2 for the other passages in which Amm. mentions Cyrus the Elder. As in the case of the Celtae (15.9.3), a remarkable re-naming after a king implies that the person in question must have been a beloved (*amabilis*) sovereign.

cum ereptum ire regna Scythica festinaret For *ereptum ire* see the note ad 22.2.2. Cyrus' Scythian campaign is dealt with in the note ad 23.6.7.

Per tractus... antiqua Having dealt with Media, Amm. turns to the south in order to describe the region which is called Persis in its original narrow sense (*antiqua*). *Expandere* can be used as a geographic t.t.; see the list in TLL V 2.1598.48–56, e.g. Mela 3.16 (Gallia) *ad ripas Rheni amnis expanditur*. For *confinia* see the note ad 21.12.22; Seyfarth's rendering "jenseits dieser Gebiete", viz. of Media, seems adequate. With *litoribus* Amm. refers to the coast of the Persian Gulf. It seems possible to regard *habitatur* as a grecism: cf. Hdt. 4.40 μέχρι δὲ τῆς Ἰνδικῆς οἰκέεται ἡ Ἀσίη. 6.41

Persis... minutis frugibus... iucundissima It should be noted that Amm. omits to report that Persis was the heartland of the Achaemenids. He also fails to mention that the Sasanians came from the same region (the town of Istakhr); this omission is not surprising (pace Fontaine n. 201) since Amm. nowhere in his work refers to them. Str. 15.3.1 (727C) reports that the seaboard of Persis is burning hot, sandy and not fertile, whereas the part above the coast produces everything and is excellent for the rearing of cattle; in this part there were also many rivers and lakes. The northern part of Persis is wintry and mountainous. For Persis, see Hinz, 1970; for its climate, Ganji, 1968 and for its vegetation, Bobek, 1968.

ante dictum... sinum I.e. *Persicus sinus*, first mentioned by Amm. in 23.6.10 q.v.

Batradites et Rogomanius et Brisoana atque Bagrada Amm. mentions these rivers in a north-west to south-east sequence. The river Batradites is probably the same, as Fontaine n. 202 already indicates, as the Oroates, the border river between Persis and Susiana (mentioned by Amm. in § 26); but according to Dillemann, 1961, 138 the Batradites and the Bagrada are one and the same river. The Rogomanius is also mentioned by Ptol. 6.4.2 (Ῥογομάνιος) and Arr. *Ind.* 39.6, who calls it Ῥωγονις; it is the modern Rûd-e-Helleh; Weissbach, 1920. The Brisoana is the same as Ptolemy's Βρισοάνας (6.4.2),

Arrianus' Βρίζανα (*Ind.* 39.7) and Pliny's *Brixa* (*Nat.* 6.136); it is to be identified with the modern Rûd-e-Mand; Weissbach, 1899. The Bagrada, further only mentioned by Ptol. 6.4.2, 8.3 (Βαγράδα), is the modern Nabend-Rûd; Tomaschek, 1896.

6.42 *incertum enim, qua ratione* See the note ad 21.7.6 for *incertum*-phrases. The present text is one of the rare cases in which *incertum* is followed by an interrogative clause. For the use of the indicative in interrogative clauses see the note ad 20.11.5 (*quales... pertulerat clades*).

Persepolis est clara et Ardea et Habroatis atque Tragonice These places are also mentioned by Ptol. 6.4.4–6: Περσέπολις, Ἄρδεα, Τραγονίκη, Ὀροβάτις πόλις. Persepolis was one of the main residences of the Achaemenid kings in Persis; it was built at the end of the sixth century by Darius I. It is referred to by many ancient authors; e.g. Str. 15.2.3 (728C), Ptol. 6.4.4, 8.21.13; D.S. 17.69 ff., 19.21 ff.; Arr. *An.* 7.1.1; Plin. *Nat.* 6.115, 123; Curt. 4.5.8, 5.4.33; Iust. 1.6.3, 11.14.10. The palace was destroyed by Alexander in 331 B.C.; Arr. *An.* 3.18.12; Str. 15.3.6 (729C-730C); D.S. 17.71–72; Curt. 5.7.3 ff.; Plut. *Alex.* 38. For Persepolis, see Schmidt, 1953–1970; Tilia, 1972–1978. It is remarkable that Amm., contrary to Ptol. 6.4.7, does not mention Pasargadae, the most important Achaemenid centre after Persepolis – built by Cyrus the Great (Str. 15.3.8, 730C) – in Persis. According to Ptol. 6.4.5 Ardea was situated to the south-east of Persepolis. Apart from Amm. only Ptol. 6.4.6 mentions Habroatis and Tragonice. Dillemann, 1961, 138 may be correct in suggesting that Habroatis is not the name of a place but a corruption of *Ab Oroatide* (for the river Oroates, see 23.6.26 q.v.); see, however, Fontaine n. 202.

Tabiana et Fara et Alexandria Tabiana is elsewhere only mentioned by Ptol. 6.4.8. It is possibly one of the *insulae duae parvae* of Plin. *Nat.* 6.99, between the debouchments of the Oroates and the Euphrates; the other island being Taxiana; Weissbach, 1934. It may then be identified with the modern island of Bannah. Fontaine's (n. 204) identification with modern Faylakah off the coast of Kuwait does not seem correct. Alexandria, which is also named Arakia (Ptol. 6.4.8: Ἀλεχάνδρου ἡ καὶ Ἀρακία; Plin. *Nat.* 6.11: *Aracha*), is the modern Khark, whereas Fara may be the same as Sophta (Ptol. 6.4.8: Σῶφθα), the little island near Khark; see Fontaine n. 204.

6.43 *His propinquant Parthyaei siti sub aquilone* At first sight *his* seems to refer to Persis or its cities, rivers and islands mentioned in § 41–2. In that case the geography is totally wrong. Parthia was not at all near Persis. Amm. may have been misled by the structure of Ptolemy's *Geographia*, in which Parthia is described immediately after Persis. Ancient Parthia corresponds with south-Turkmenestan and the modern Iranian province of Khorasan. However, *siti sub aquilone* may well be the counterpart of *per tractus meridianos expansa* (§ 41), Media being the region of reference for both. In that case *his propinquant* as a geographical expression would be comparable to *post haec confinia*, with *his*, like *haec*, functioning as an anaphoric pronoun referring to Media and its inhabitants.

This is the only time that Amm. uses the latinized Greek *Parthyaei* (Παρθυαῖοι) to designate the Parthians. Normally he uses the term *Parthi*. This could well be an indication that Amm. used a Greek source for this section.

Choatres fluvius This river is not mentioned by any other ancient author and is therefore hard to identify (Seyfarth n. 104 thinks that it is the modern Adschi-Su). If this river existed at all, it probably derived its name from the people of the Choatrae (Luc. 3.246) and/or the Παραχοάθρας ὄρος, either a mountain range between Media and Persis or another name for (a part of) the Taurus; Treidler, 1965. See further Fontaine n. 205.

potiora residuis For *residuus* as a synonym of *reliquus* see the notes ad 16.12.35 and 20.4.6.

Oenunia, Moesia, Charax, Apamea, Artacana et Hecatonpylos See Ptolemy's list of 25 Parthian places (6.5.2–4) of which Amm. mentions here only six in a different sequence from that of Ptolemy (Ptol.'s order: Οἰνουνία, Ἑκατόμπυλον Βασίλειον, Μυσία, Χάραξ, Ἀπάμεια, Ἀρτάκανα). Oenonia and Moesia are impossible to locate; Fontaine n. 206 suggests that, just as the other places mentioned, these were probably Macedonian or Seleucid foundations. It should be noted that Nisa, the only town founded by the Arsacids, is not mentioned (for Nisa, see § 54 and Chaumont, 1973, 211–5). Charax is situated in the Median region of Rhagiane between the town of Rhagae and the Caspian Gates (Plin. *Nat.* 6.43); it is also mentioned by Isid. Char. 7 (*GGM* I 251); see Tomaschek, 1899. Apamea, founded by Seleucus Nikator, is to be located in the area of Rhagiane south-east of the Caspian Gates; it is therefore called Apamea Rhagiane; Str. 11.13.6 (524C); Plin. *Nat.* 6.43; Isid. Char. 8 (*GGM* I 251); Ptol. 6.5.3. It can possibly be identified with modern Shahr-Khwar; Tomaschek, 1894. Artacana was a town in the south of Parthia near Carmania; possibly the modern Ardekan. Hecatonpylos, the modern Shahr-i Qumis, already existed in Achaemenid times but was refounded and renamed by Seleucus Nikator; App. *Syr.* 57, Curt. 6.2.14 (*urbs erat ea tempestate clara Hecatompylos, condita a Graecis*). When after 217 B.C. Tiridates expanded Parthian territory to the south-east coast of the Caspian Sea, he made Hecatonpylos the Parthian capital; Plin. Nat. 6.62 (*Parthiae caput*), 113; Plb. 10.28.7; Str. 11.9.1 (514C): Ἑκατόμπυλον, τὸ τῶν Παρθυαίων βασίλειον;

Curt. 6.2.15. See also Kiessling, 1912; Chaumont, 1973, 217–22; Colledge, 1977, *passim*.

a cuius finibus per Caspia litora ad usque portarum angustias stadia quadraginta numerantur et mille The distance from Hecatonpylos to the Caspian Gates (*portarum angustias*), the modern pass of Sar-i-Darreh (see the note ad 23.6.13), was according to Str. 11.9.1 (514C) 1260 stadia = approximately 225 km. (1 stadion = approx. 180 m.): εἰσὶ δ' ἀπὸ Κασπίων πυλῶν... εἰς δ' Ἑκατόμπυλον, τὸ τῶν Παρθυαίων βασίλειον, χίλιοι διακόσιοι ἑξήκοντα (στάδιοι). This differs from the distance of 133 Roman miles = approx. 196 km given by Plin. *Nat.* 6.44: *ipsum vero Parthiae caput Hecatompylos abest a Portis (Caspiis)* |CXXXIII| *p.* Amm.'s distance of 1040 stadia comes close to that given by Pliny, since 133 Roman miles is 1064 stadia. Cf. further Str. 11.8.9 (514C): ἀπὸ Κασπίων πυλῶν εἰς Ἰνδούς, εἰς μὲν Ἑκατόμπυλον χιλίους ἐννακοσίους ἑξήκοντά φασιν.

6.44 *feri sunt* "*Feri* and *feritas* refer almost exclusively to barbarians" (Seager 55).

eosque ita certamina iuvant... degeneres et ignavos In almost the same words this is also said of the Alans in 31.2.22: *utque hominibus quietis et placidis otium est voluptabile, ita illos pericula iuvant et bella. iudicatur ibi beatus, qui in proelio profuderit animam, senescentes enim et fortuitis mortibus mundo digressos ut degeneres et ignavos conviciis atrocibus insectantur.* The phrase *vitam* (or *animam*) *profundere* also occurs in 21.5.10 (q.v.), 24.4.28, 26.6.20, 26.10.13. For *morte fortuita*, 'natural death', cf. Plin. *Ep.* 3.9.5 *vel fortuita vel voluntaria morte*, Tac. *Ann.* 12.52.2 *morte fortuita an per venenum*. TLL VII 1.1856.6 sqq. provides a list of cases in which *insectari* means "hostiliter sequi, fere dicendo, scribendo sim.". See the note ad 22.9.1 for Amm.'s use of the word. More or less the same – love for warfare, no fear for death, contempt for cowardly behaviour – is said of Germans and Gauls; Tac. *Germ.* 12, 14; Luc. 1.460–2. For the Roman image of the Parthians, see Sonnabend 1986.

6.45 *Quibus ab orientali australique plaga Arabes beati conterminant* Amm. continues to follow the structure of Ptolemy's *Geography* by first describing the country of the Arabs and then Carmania (sections 48–49). Strictly speaking Amm. goes here beyond his own assignment of § 1 since the Arabs of the Arab peninsula were never part of the Persian realm (this also applies to the nations mentioned in the latter part of the digression). Seyfarth n. 106 in his bilingual edition rightly believes that *quibus* does not refer to the *Parthyaei* of the previous sections, but to the inhabitants of Persis, mentioned in § 41; see also Brok, 1975, 52. The expression *ab orientali australique plaga* poses a problem since the country of the 'happy' Arabs is situated to the southwest of Persis; *orientali* may occur because of the point of reference chosen by Amm. (see the note ad 23.6.27) or because of his lack of geographical knowledge.

The *Arabes beati* were the inhabitants of Arabia Felix. The ancients first only distinguished between *Arabia deserta* (ἡ ἔρημος Ἀραβία) and *Arabia felix* or *beata* (ἡ εὐδαίμων Ἀραβία). *Arabia felix/beata* covered the area south of *Arabia deserta* and was considered identical with the Arab peninsula; D.S. 2.48 f.; Str. 16.3.1 (765C), 16.4.2 (767C); Mela 3.79; Plin. *Nat.* 6.32. From Ptolemy we know that in his time Arabia was geographically divided into three parts: *Arabia felix, Arabia deserta* and *Arabia Petraea*. According to Ptol. 6.7.1, Arabia Felix borders in the north on Arabia Petraea and Arabia Deserta, in the west on the Red Sea, in the southeast on the Persian Gulf and the Strait of Hormuz, and in the south on the Erythraean Sea; see Grohmann, 1963, 4–5. The etymology of the name Arabia Felix is interesting, but strange. *Felix* renders Semitic *Jemen* or *taiman* which means "to the right", as well as "the south". The Greek and Latin words δεξιός and *dexter* can mean 'right' as well as 'happy'. Because of this latter meaning the region became known as Arabia Felix.

Amm.'s description of the fertility, the abundance of water, the wealth, climate, luxurious cities and residences of Arabia Felix in this and the next section recalls Strabo's description (16.4.2 [767C-768C]) of the southernmost parts of the Arab peninsula, i.e. the kingdom of Saba (roughly modern Yemen). Contrary to Amm., Strabo also correctly reports that a large part of Arabia Felix (= the Arab peninsula) was sandy and barren.

Arabia Felix was explored by the Romans during the reign of Augustus. In 26/5 B.C. the prefect of Egypt Aelius Gallus invaded the peninsula. However, the expedition ended in failure and since then the Romans made no other attempts to invade or conquer Arabia Felix. For Gallus' expedition see Str. 2.5.12 (118C), 16.4.22–24 (780C-782C), Wissmann, 1976 and Sidebotham 1986a. For information on the region in general, see e.g. Grohmann, 1963; Wissmann, 1964 and 1968. In 106 A.D. the Romans conquered the kingdom of Nabataea and incorporated it into the empire as the province of Arabia; Bowersock, 1983; Millar, 1993, 414 ff.

fetibus et palmite For *fetus* denoting "élevage" (Fontaine) cf. *binos gregum fetus* (*Pan.* 10.11.3) and for *palmes* referring to winegrowing cf. 14.8.1 *Isauria... uberi palmite viret.*

odorumque suavitate multiplici Cf. the similar pattern in *multiplici vertice dignitatum* (19.1.3), *dilationum ambage multiplici* (22.8.49), *multiplici telorum iactu* (23.5.8). In each of these cases a combination of genitivus inversus and enallage is involved. The quoted phrase could be rendered by 'a large variety of fragrant perfumes'.

magnaeque eorum partes mare rubrum latere dextro contingunt, laeva Persico mare collimitant From the north – Amm.'s point of reference – the Red Sea is indeed on the righthand side of the Arab peninsula, and the Persian Gulf is on the lefthand side. Note that in this case the *mare rubrum* is identical with the modern Red Sea whereas in § 26 q.v. *mare rubrum* indicates the sea around Arabia in general. For the various designations of *mare rubrum*, see Sidebotham 1986, Appendix A (The Terms "Erythra Thalassa" and "Rubrum Mare").

elementi utriusque Cf. *per elementum utrumque* (17.13.15, q.v.), *assuetum elementis ambobus* (22.15.15). The elements are of course land and water, both of which were used by the Arabs for transportation of their main export goods, namely frankincense, myrrh, and other aromatics and perfumes. Already Hdt. 3.107 knew that this region was known especially for these products. See Doe, 1971, 30–59 for trade in general between Arabia Felix and the West and the East; for the commercial contacts between Rome and Arabia Felix, see Sidebotham, 1986.

6.46 *diversoria regum ambitiosa nimium* For *ambitiosus* see the notes ad 14.7.6 and 22.13.2. As is pointed out in the note ad 21.16.3, *nimium* does not necessarily imply excess ('too splendid'): the quoted words mean "dimore regali molto fastose" (Caltabiano).

rivorum fluminumque multitudo perspicua Fontaine assumes a remarkable enallage with "quantité de rivières et de fleuves limpides". The adj. can indeed have the meaning 'transparent': *aquas...perspicuas ad humum* (Ov. *Met.* 5.587–8). Of the eight instances in Amm. only 17.5.11 *veritatem non obtectam praestrigiis, sed perspicuam* has this meaning, though in a figurative sense; *perspicua veritas* (24.7.5) could also be an example, but if this is so the meaning 'conspicuous', which fits all the other instances, is more likely. For enallage in Amm. see Blomgren 146–7 and the notes ad 20.6.6, 22.13.4 and 23.5.8. Although Fontaine's rendering is not entirely impossible, Seyfarth's "eine ansehnliche Menge" seems more feasible.

6.47 *abundet* The grammatical subject is implied in the preceding text: Arabia.

Geapolim et Nascon et Baraba Geapolis – also mentioned by Ptol. 6.7.29 (Γαία πόλις) – is situated west-north-west of Thaima in the upper part of the Arab peninsula along the caravan route from the Persian Gulf to the modern Gulf of Aqaba; Sprenger, 1875, 149; see also Tkaĉ, 1912. Nascos is called by Ptol. 6.7.35 Νάσχος μητρόπολις, by Plin. *Nat.* 6.154 *Nascus* and in 6.160 *Nesca*, and by Str. 16.4.24 (782C) Άσχα; it is to be identified with the modern Nashq; cf. Wissmann, 1976, 316 (map), 402–5; also Grohmann,

1935. Baraba is Mariaba, the capital of the kingdom of Saba; also mentioned by Plin. *Nat.* 7.160 and Ptol. 6.7.37 Μάρα μητρόπολις; Str. 16.4.24 (782C) calls it Μαρσίαβα. The aim of Aelius Gallus' expedition was to reach Mariaba: *In Arabiam usque ad fines Sabaeorum pro[cess]it exercitus ad oppidum Mariba* (Aug. *Anc.* 26); see Sprenger, 1875, 157–8; Wissmann, 1976, passim; Grohmann, 1930. Fontaine in his edition prints Mariba (*ex Plin. scripsi*); the Ammianean mss. give no occasion for such a reading.

Nagara et Maefen et Tafra et Dioscurida Nagara is Ptolemy's Νάγαρα μετρόπολις (6.7.37); Str. 16.4.24 (782C) calls it Ἀνάγρανα; it is the modern town of Najran; Sprenger, 1875, 158; Grohmann, 1935. Maefe is called Μαίφα μητρόπολις by Ptol. 6.7.41; cf. Sprenger, 1875, 162–3; Grohmann, 1930. Tafra is Ptolemy's Σάπφαρα μητρόπολις (6.7.41); cf. Plin. *Nat.* 6.104; Philost. *HE* 3.4 has Τάφαρον; see further Sprenger, 1875, 185; Grohmann, 1932 and Fontaine n. 211. The town of Dioscoris, situated on the island of the same name (the modern island of Socotra), is also mentioned by Plin. *Nat.* 6.153 and Ptol. 6.7.45 (Διοσκορίδος πόλις); Sprenger, 1875, 87–9.

insulas autem complures habet per utrumque proximas mare I.e. the islands in the Red Sea and the Persian Gulf; several of them are mentioned by Ptol. 6.7.47.

insignior tamen aliis Turgana est, in qua Serapidis maximum esse dicitur templum This island is probably to be identified with modern Masirah which lies to the south-east of the Arab peninsula off the coast of Oman; see Sprenger, 1875, 102; Grohmann, 1942. Ptol. 6.7.47 calls it Organa but incorrectly distinguishes it from *insula Serapidis*. Rolfe identifies Amm.'s Turgana with the island of Hormuz possibly because he considered Ptolemy's Organa identical with Arrian's Organa (*Ind.* 37.2); the latter is indeed to be identified with Hormuz. The fact that Turgana had a temple for Serapis underlines the importance of the commercial relations between this part of the world and Hellenistic and Roman Egypt; see for literature on this Fontaine n. 212.

Post huius terminos gentis Carmania maior verticibus celsis erigitur ad usque Indicum pertinens mare From the perspective of the region of the *Arabes beati* described above Carmania is on the other side of the Strait of Hormuz. It borders on Persis; see further the note ad 23.6.12. As to its high mountains, Amm. is correct; Carmania's highest mountain is the (modern) Kuh-e Hazaran (4420 m.). Ptol. 6.8.6 also reports that Carmania extended as far as the Indian Ocean. **6.48**

fructuariis arboreisque fetibus culta TLL VI 1.1370.30–1 regards this as an example of *fructuarius* meaning "ad fructum pertinens". For *fetus* cf. Verg. *G.*

1.55 *arborei fetus*, which according to Mynors ad loc. means "young, growing trees", Ov. *Met.* 10.664 *fetibus arboreis*, Col. 10.401, Cypr. *Demetr.* 3; *colere*, 'to till (land)' is of course normal, but the addition of an abl. denoting the type of cultivation seems unique; cf. *civitatibus culta* (§ 60). The phrase could be regarded as a condensation of *arboribus fructuariis aliisque arboreis fetibus*. Seyfarth's "besitzt Frucht- und Baumplantagen" conveys the meaning. Just as the passage on the fertility of Arabia Felix, these words recall Strabo (15.2.14, 726C). Arr. *Ind.* 32.4 also speaks about the fertility of Carmania.

obscurior TLL VI 1.1370.23–31 contains a small list of instances in which *obscurus* as a synonym of *ignobilis* is used about geographical entities, e.g. *urbs non obscura Marathos* (Mela 1.67).

caespitisque ubere This ultimately derives from Virgil's *ubere glaebae* (*A.* 1.531, 3.164) as a rendering of Homer's οὖθαρ ἀρούρης (*Il.* 1.141).

6.49 *Sagareus et Saganis et Hydriacus* These rivers are hard to identify but are probably identical with Ptolemy's Saganos, Saralos and Hydriakos (6.8.4, 7, 8). The Sagareus/Saganos is probably the modern Rûd Sangali which debouches at the entrance of the Strait of Hormuz. According to Herrmann, 1920 the Saganis/Saralos is the river which is now called Rûd-Rahig or Chor-Rahig. According to Kiessling, 1916 the Hydriacus is the modern Bahir.

sunt etiam civitates licet numero paucae Ptol. 6.8.13–14 mentions eleven cities in the heartland of Carmania: Πορτόσπανα, Κάρμανα μητρόπολις, Θάσπις, Νήπιστα, Χόδδα, Ταρσίανα, Ἀλεξάνδρεια, Σαβίς, Θρόασχα, Ὄρα, Κωφάντα. Only three of them are mentioned by Amm.

Carmana omnium mater et Portospana et Alexandria et Hermupolis Carmana, the capital of Carmania, is the modern town of Kerman. On the basis of the information which Ptolemy provides Fontaine n. 215 plausibly suggests that one should situate Portospana southwest of Kerman. Alexandria is also mentioned by Plin. *Nat.* 6.107 and may have been on the site of modern Gulash-gird; Tomaschek 1894. Fraser, 1996, 166–7 is of the opinion that this Alexandria cannot be identified. Hermupolis is not mentioned by any author except as (a) town(s) in Egypt (Str. 17.1.18–19 [802C], 17.1.22 [803C]; Ptol. 4.5.46, 60). It is not improbable that it is the same town as Ptolemy's Ἁρμουζα πόλις near the promontory of Harmozon (for which see 23.6.10 q.v.); see for other, but less likely, suggestions Fontaine n. 215 and Tarn, 1984[3], 482.

6.50 *Interius vero pergenti occurrunt Hyrcani* The same phrase occurs in 29.5.13 and 44. TLL VII 1.2214.72 sqq. lists the instances of *interius* as a geographical t.t., e.g. Mela 1.32 *interius et longe satis a litore*. The vague geographical expression may be an indication of Amm.'s lack of knowledge concerning the precise geography of the regions he describes. After his excursion to the southern regions of Arabia Felix and Carmania, he now returns again to the north. Hyrcania (modern Gurgan) lies in north Iran at the south-east corner of the Caspian Sea; it is bounded by the two mountain ranges of the Elburz and Kopet Dagh. On Hyrcania see the extensive article of Kiessling, 1916; and see further Berthelot, 1930, 167–73; Vogelsang, 1988; Sherwin-White/Kuhrt, 1993, 81–2.

quos eiusdem nominis alluit mare   I.e. the Hyrcanian or Caspian Sea; see the note ad 23.6.27.

apud quos glebae macie internecante sementes   If Salmasius' fine emendation, upheld by Valesius, is right, this is the only instance in Amm. of the rare verb *internecare*, which first occurs in Pl. *Am.* 189 *internecatis hostibus*. Str. 11.7.1 (508C) also mentions the barrenness of the region: ταῦτα μὲν οὖν τὰ χωρία λυπρά. See the note ad 23.6.51 for the fertility of Hyrcania.

vescuntur venatibus   For *venatus* denoting the hunted animals, the 'game', cf. Plin. *Nat.* 7.23 *venatu et aucupio vesci*.

immane quantum   This is an example of the category *immensum quantum* and similar phrases, described in the note ad 15.8.15. The present phrase occurs for the first time in Sal. *Hist.* 2.44; the other instances in Amm. are 23.6.78 and 24.4.2.

ubi etiam tigridum milia multa cernuntur feraeque bestiae plures   On tigers and other wild animals in Hyrcania, see Plin. *Nat.* 8.66; Mela 3.43; Lucr. 3.750; Verg. *A.* 4.367 (*Hyrcanaeque admorunt ubera tigres*); Sol. 17.4 ff.

quae cuiusmodi solent capi commentis, dudum nos meminimus rettulisse   One of the "incertae sedis reliquiae" in the list of references to lost books in Gardthausen's edition; cf. also Michael, 1880, 11, and 25.4.23. It is obvious that Amm. dealt with the subject somewhere. The tricks (*commentis*) used in the hunting of tigers, or rather their cubs, caught the Ancients' imagination, as is shown by passages in a variety of authors, e.g. Plin. *Nat.* 8.66, Mela 3.43, Sol. 17.4–7, Ambr. *hex.* 6.4.21, Claud. *rapt.* 3.263–268.

nec ideo tamen... ad plantandum   To prevent the reader from concluding   6.51
that the Hyrcani are mere nomadic hunters, Amm. hastens to add that they are not ignorant of agriculture as are the tribes described in 14.4.3, 22.8.42, 31.2.10. Str. 11.7.2 (508C-509C) also mentions the fertility of Hyrcania (Ἡ δ' Ὑρκανία σφόδρα εὐδαίμων). Amm.'s (and Strabo's) information seems to

contradict what has been said in the previous section, but other authors also mention Hyrcania's fertility; D.S. 17.75.4–7; Curt. 6.4.21 f.; *FGrHist* 134 F 3 f. (Onesikritos). The lower parts of Hyrcania, which consisted of loess-covered lands, could be very fertile provided they were properly irrigated. However, to the north, across the Gurgan and Atrek rivers, conditions were less favourable, with a more arid climate, as a consequence of which there was a scarcity of vegetation. The mountain slopes of the Elburz and Kopet Dagh were, and in some places still are, forested. See Kiessling, 1916, 456–9; Vogelsang, 1988, 122–3.

marinis mercibus plerique sustentantur Cf. Str. 11.7.2 (509C) for an opposite opinion: τῆς μέντοι προσηχούσης ἐπιμελείας οὐκ ἔτυχεν οὔτε αὐτὴ οὔτε ἡ ἐπώνυμος αὐτῇ θάλαττα, ἄπλους τε οὖσα καὶ ἀργός. However, in 11.7.3 (509C) Strabo mentions that by way of the river Oxus large quantities of Indian wares were brought down to the Hyrcanian Sea, and thence on that sea were transported to Albania and from there to the Black Sea. In general Hyrcania was an important junction of east-west traffic. During the Parthian period Hyrcania lay along the direct road from Mesopotamia to the Parthian capital of Nisa according to the *Mansiones Parthicae* of Isidorus Charax.

6.52 *Oxus et Maxera* The Oxus (Ptol. 6.9.2 Ὦχος), which (now) debouches into the Aral Sea, is the modern Amudar'ya. The Amudar'ya flows through ancient Bactria (cf. 23.6.57) and not through Hyrcania, as Str. 11.7.3 (509C) tells us (see the note above). However, it is believed that in antiquity a now dried-up branch of the Oxus was connected with the Caspian Sea; see Berthelot, 1930, 168–9; Herrmann, 1942; Olshausen, 1975; comm. Walbank ad Plb. 10.48.1; comm. Bosworth ad Arr. *An.* 3.29.2; see also Fontaine n. 219 and his carte II. This must be why Amm. (also) mentions the Oxus as a Hyrcanian river. The Maxera (Ptol. 6.9.2: Μαξήρας; Plin. *Nat.* 6.46: *Maziris*) is the modern Gurgan which debouches into the Caspian Sea. It should be noted that Amm. leaves ummentioned another main Hyrcanian river, namely the Socanda, the modern Atrek.

quos urgente...finitima populantur Amm. is the only ancient author who refers to this phenomenon.

habent etiam civitates inter minora municipia validas, duas quidem maritimas, Socanda et Saramanna Socanda is probably to be located at the debouchment of the Socanda (=Atrek) river; it debouches into the Caspian Sea; see Kiessling, 1916, 515. Saramanna is also mentioned by Ptol. 6.9.2 (Σαραμάννη πόλις); it is probably the same town as Strabo's Σαμαριανὴ (11.7.2 [508C]) and Pliny's *Maria* (*Nat.* 6.113) and lies in western Hyrcania at the Caspian Sea not far from Media; Berthelot, 1930, 168, thinks it should be identified with the modern town of Sari.

Asmurnam et Salen et his nobiliorem Hyrcanam Ptol. 6.9.7 mentions these cities in a different order: Ὑρκανία μητρόπολις, Σάκη (ἢ Σάλη), Ἄσμουρνα. Asmurna is situated south of the river Gurgan but its precise location cannot be determined; Ruge, 1896. The same applies to Sale; Berthelot, 1930, 171 wants to situate this town "à l'issue nord des Portes Caspiennes, sur la route de Saramané". Hyrcana may be the same as Arrianus' Ζαδράκαρτα, the capital of Hyrcania (*An.* 3.23.6) and Strabo's Κάρτα (11.7.2 [508C]).

Contra hanc gentem sub aquilone dicuntur Abii versari, genus piissimum, calcare cuncta mortalia consuetum This vague geographical expression does not allow us to locate the nation of the Abii, further than somewhere in the north. Amm. himself may not have known where exactly this people lived, but nor do other authors; Ptol. 6.15.3 (Ἄβιοι Σκύθαι) locates the Abii in the most northern parts of Scythia. Arr. *An.* 4.1.1 also identifies them as Scythians, more precisely as the Saca tribe which possibly lived in the Kyzyl Kum, the desert north-west of Samarkhand; see Bosworth ad loc. It may be that the Abii were not a real but a mythical nation, a poetic creation of Homer; *Il.* 13.6: Ἀβίων τε, δικαιοτάτων ἀνθρώπων. Abioi possibly means "those without violence" or "those with no (settled) livelihood", i.e. nomads; see further Janko ad loc. Str. 7.3.3 (296C) gives a rather strange explanation of their name; according to him Homer named them Abii because they lived apart from women and because of this he considered their life only half-complete. Homer's verse is given (in Greek) by Amm. in section 62 of this chapter (see the note ad loc.). For *calcare*, 'to treat as of no importance', see the note ad 23.5.11.

6.53

quos, ut Homerus fabulosius canit, Iuppiter ab Idaeis montibus contuetur The contents of this section do not mirror reliable historical evidence. It is the language of myth, the *fabulosa vetustas* (22.2.3, q.v.): "Omero canta con toni da leggenda" (Caltabiano). Seyfarth tries to bring out the comparative with "etwas sagenhaft", but it is far more likely that *fabulosius* is a case of comparativus pro positivo (see Hagendahl, 1921, 135 sqq., Szantyr 168–9), often, as in the present case, caused by the cursus. Amm. refers to the first verses of *Iliad* 13 where it is said that Zeus diverted his eyes from the Greeks and Trojans and set them upon i.a. the Abii.

Sedes vicinas post Hyrcanos sortiti sunt Margiani, omnes paene collibus altis undique circumsaepti Amm. proceeds further to the East, cf. § 50 *Interius vero pergenti occurrunt Hyrcani.* For *post* 'beyond' cf. 15.11.3 (the Marne and the Seine) *post circumclausum ambitu insulari Parisiorum castellum...consociati.* Elsewhere in Amm. *sortiri* has as its object either

6.54

a partner in marriage (18.6.16, 21.6.4 q.v., 24.1.10) or ruling power (above § 36). For *undique circumsaepti* cf. Sol. 48.2 (Margiana) *in faciem theatralem montibus clauditur*.

Margiana – modern southern Turkmenistan around the modern city of Merv (or Mary) – was surrounded, as Amm. reports, by mountains: in the west by the Kopet Dagh and in the south by the Barkhat Dagh. On its other sides it was mainly surrounded by desert; Str. 11.10.1–2 (515C-516C), Berthelot, 1930, 174 ff., Sherwin-White & Kuhrt, 1993, 82–4. It is to be noted that Amm. does not mention here the region of Aria (modern Herat in north-west Afghanistan). Other ancient authors mention Margiana and the adjacent Aria in one breath, e.g. Str. 11.10.1 (515C). Instead Amm. refers to Aria in 23.6.69 q.v. (*Ariani vivunt post Seres*), again following the order of Ptolemy's *Geography* (Ptol. 6.10: Margiana, 6.17: Aria).

et quamquam pleraque sunt ibi deserta aquarum penuria Part of Margiana was indeed barren, but another part of the region was made fertile by the water of the river Murghab (the ancient Margus). Str. 11.10.2 (516C) tells us that Antiochus I Soter, admiring the fertility of Margiana, enclosed a circle of 1500 stades and there founded the polis Antioch; Strabo adds that the land was well suited for growing the vine.

soli quaedam... The contents and the extent of the lacuna indicated here by Eyssenhardt can only be guessed at. V's reading *solique damsedi. asonion* has led to different efforts at emendation. The text printed in the editio princeps *sed quidem Sena, Asomon* is probably based on Ptol. 6.10, who mentions Sena among the cities of Margiana. The i of *sedi*, however, belongs without doubt to the next word, which must be Iasonion, also mentioned by Ptolemy in his description of Margiana. Therefore we may assume that the sentence as a whole followed the familiar pattern in this chapter: first the presence of cities is stated, then the names of the most important among them are given, as e.g. in § 26 *His tractibus Susiani iunguntur, apud quos non multa sunt oppida. inter alia tamen eminet* e.q.s. The same pattern is found in sections 42, 47 and 49. For that reason it seems likely that no other cities were mentioned here by name in the part of the sentence preceding Iasonion, Antiochia and Nisa. On the other hand, considering that in his descriptions of the other regions in this chapter Amm. mentions rivers as well as cities, it is likely that in the lacuna reference was made to the Murghab. Fontaine in his n. 222 suggests that the lacuna contained a reference to the fertility of this district in accordance with Strabo 11.10.2 (516C), which is quite plausible after the preceding *quamquam*. Plin. *Nat.* 6.46 also has a remark about viticulture in Margiana: *sola in eo tractu vitifera*.

Iasonion et Antiochia et Nisea Ptol. 6.10.3–4 mentions nine cities in Margiana including these three (Ἰασόνιον, Ἀντιόχεια Μαργιανή, Νίσαια ἢ Νίγαια). Iasonion is hard to locate; possibly it was situated at the junction where the river Kuskh joins the Murghab; Weissbach, 1916, Fontaine n. 223. Antiochia-Margiana was the capital of the Seleucid satrapy of Margiana. Plin. *Nat.* 6.47 says that the city was founded by Alexander and was given the name of Alexandreia. After its destruction it was founded for a second time by Antiochus I Soter and given first the name Syriana (or Seleucia, according to Sol. 48.3) and only later was it named Antioch. In contrast to Pliny, Str. 11.10.2 (516C) tells us that the city was first founded by Antiochus. Isid. Char. 14 (*GGM* I 253) calls the city Ἔνυδρος. See Tomaschek, 1894, Sherwin-White & Kuhrt, 1993, 82–3, Masson, 1982, 145 ff. Nisea, normally called Nisa, near modern Ashkhabad in Turkmenistan, was the capital of the Parthians; Isid. Char. 12 (*GGM* I 252) calls it Παρθαύνισα. It was possibly founded by Mithridates I (*c.* 171–139/8). A distinction has to be made between Old Nisa, the royal citadel, and New Nisa which represents the city; the latter is still unexcavated. (Old) Nisa provides the earliest, and until now the only, evidence of royal Arsacid (Parthian) architecture. It is a rich archeological site where i.a. 2000 ostraka were found containing 2758 archival texts, and art objects of clearly Hellenistic artistic forms. See Masson, 1982, 119–39; Wiesehöfer, 1994, 173–5; Invernizzi, 1998 (with extensive bibliographical references).

Proximos his limites possident Bactriani There is a note on *limes* ad 23.3.4. **6.55**
Bactria was bounded in the north by the Oxus river and in the south by the Hindu Kush. Sometimes Sogdiana, with which Bactria formed a satrapy in Achaemenid and Seleucid times, is also reckoned as belonging to Bactria; geographically, however, the regions are different, and Sogdiana is therefore to be considered as a separate geographical entity, as is done by Amm. There is little reliable information about Bactria's earliest history. It becomes clearer from the time of Alexander onwards. During the beginning of the Seleucid domination the Greeks colonised Bactria extensively. Around 230 B.C. the Seleucid satrap Diodotus managed to break away from Seleucid rule and a Graeco-Bactrian kingdom came into existence; Iust. 41.4.5–9. Bactria's efforts to remain independent suffered from setbacks – the Graeco-Bactrian kings were forced to acknowledge Seleucid supremacy during the reign of Antiochus III the Great – and the final secession from the Seleucid kingdom only took place in the second century B.C. Around 140 B.C. invasions by peoples from beyond the Oxus, among them the Tochari (see below § 57), ended the Graeco-Bactrian kingdom and obliterated the presence of the Greeks in Bactria. See Berthelot, 1930, 181–9; Tarn, 1984[3]; Part two ("Bactria before Alexander") of Holt, 1988; Sherwin-White & Kuhrt, 1993, 103–5, 107–11; for Bactria in Achaemenid times, see Briant, 1984, 45 ff. For the archaeology of Bactria, see Frumkin, 1970, passim; Masson, 1982, passim.

natio antehac bellatrix et potentissima Persisque semper infesta, antequam circumsitos populos omnes ad dicionem gentilitatemque traheret nominis sui Amm.'s information on the Bactrians is difficult both to assess and to verify with other sources. It seems natural to interpret the clause introduced by *antequam* as an explanation of the adverb *antehac* in the first part of the sentence. That, however, would lead to a very illogical statement: 'Bactria was a powerful enemy of the Persians before it subdued all its neighbours.' In all probability Amm. wants to say that Bactria was a powerful enemy before *Persia* subdued all its neighbours. That this is indeed what he means is evident from 31.2.13, where Amm. seems to refer to this sentence: (Halani) *nationes conterminas crebritate victoriarum attritas ad gentilitatem sui vocabuli traxerunt ut Persae*. Like the Halani, the Persians had forced their neighbours into accepting their superiority and even into adopting their name. If this interpretation is correct we have to emend the text of V and read either *Persidi* instead of *Persis* or *traherent* instead of *traheret*. This is how Selem ("sempre nemico dei Persiani, prima che questi riducessero...") and Veh ("immer mit den Persern verfeindet, bevor diese...") interpret this sentence. The next question is which period of Persian hegemony Amm. has in mind. The fact that in this section Arsaces is mentioned, who has been described in sections 2 – 6 of this digression as the founder of the Parthian empire in terms that resemble the present passage (§ 2 *Hoc regnum... in vocabulum Parthi concessit Arsacis* and § 4 (Perside) *assuefacta timori esse accolis omnibus, quos antea formidabat*) makes it practically certain that Amm. is thinking of the period of the Arsacids.

For the subjunctive following *antequam*, see the note ad 14.6.23. *Gentilitas* denotes different types of relationships: between families as in 14.1.1, between nations as here and in 31.2.13 quoted above, between sounds in 14.9.4 and 25.5.6. In 31.7.11 *Romani... voce undique Martia concinentes a minore solita ad maiorem protolli, quam gentilitate appellant barritum* it means "barbaro sermone" (TLL VI 1873.46–53).

quam rexere veteribus saeculis etiam Arsaci formidabiles reges In Iust. 41.4.8–9 Arsaces' fear of the Bactrian king Diodotus is mentioned twice.

6.56 *eius pleraeque partes ita ut Margiana procul a litoribus sunt disparatae* See § 54 above where it is reported that Margiana is surrounded by mountains and thus separated from the sea.

humi gignentium fertiles For *gignentia* "i.q. nascentia, τὰ γιγνόμενα, plerumque de herbis" (TLL VI 1992.35–59), cf. 23.6.68. Sal. *Jug.* 79.6 *loca... nuda gignentium* may have provided the model. Bactria was fertile because of its oases and extensive pasturage. Its great agricultural prosperity is also reported by Curt. 7.4.26, 30 and Str. 11.11.1 (516C). Bactria was also called "land of a thousand cities" (Iust. 41.4.6, Str. 15.1.3 [686C]) which is a sign of the land's prosperity.

pecus, quod illic...vescitur For the absolute use of *vesci* cf. 22.15.14 *in aridis...capreoli vescuntur* with the note.

membris est magnis compactum et validis The verb *compingere* with its derivatives belongs to Amm.'s favourites. For the present expression cf. his description of the Huns in 31.2.2: *compactis omnes firmisque membris* and the emperor Valens in 31.14.7: *figura bene compacta membrorum*. Ael. *NA* 4.55 reports that camels normally live for about fifty years but that those from Bactria live twice as long.

ut indicio sunt cameli Cf. 23.6.86 *idque indicium est aetheria...derivatione...hos oriri fetus*. *Indicio est* is less frequent than *indicium est* (TLL VII 1.1148.28), but not rare, e.g. Plin. *Nat.* 2.48 *spatio...consumi umbras indicio sunt volucrum praealti volatus*.

a Mithridate...visi Romanis In 74–73 B.C. Cyzicus was besieged by Mithridates VI Eupator (120–63 B.C.), king of Pontus. Amm.'s information that this was the first time the Romans saw camels may derive ultimately from Sal. *Hist.* 3.42. However, Sallust – and therefore Amm. – may be mistaken, as Plut. *Luc.* 11.6 already observed. Plutarch expresses his amazement about this piece of information and mentions the battle at Magnesia of 190 B.C. as the first occasion, in accordance with Livy 37.40.12. Since, however, Livy speaks of *cameli quos appellant dromadas* it could be that Sallust and Amm. refer to camels and Plutarch and Livy to dromedaries. That this is indeed the case seems to follow from Plin. *Nat.* 8.67: (camelos), *quarum duo genera, Bactriae et Arabiae, differunt, quod illae bina habent tubera in dorso, hae singula*, which is echoed in Sol. 49.9. Male camels that were to be used in warfare were castrated, the genital parts of female camels were cauterized: Ael. *NA* 4.55, Plin. *Nat.* 8.68, Sol. 49.12. Mithridates is also mentioned by Amm. in 16.7.9, 16.12.41, 25.9.8, 29.5.33.

gentes isdem Bactrianis oboediunt plures For *oboedire* used of peoples cf. **6.57** Cic. *Rep.* 3.41 *ut, qui adhuc voluntate nobis oboediunt, terrore teneantur*; TLL IX 2.137.61–75. For anaphoric *idem* see the note ad 20.4.5.

Tochari The Tochari were a nomadic people from central Asia. Str. 11.8.2 (511C) calls them Scythian nomads and Plin. *Nat.* 6.55 tells that they lived near the Scythians (*ad Scythas versi*). Amm. does not seem to be well-informed on the Tochari, since they were never subject to the Bactrians. It was just the other way round: around 140 B.C. the Tochari and other peoples invaded

Bactria, as a consequence of which the Graeco-Bactrian kingdom came to an end. Amm.'s mistake may have been caused by Ptolemy's mention in 6.11.6 of the Tochari in connection with Bactria. Ptolemy's Ταπούρεοι (6.14) are possibly identical with these Tochari.

ad Italiae speciem crebris fluminibus inundantur Although *species* is not at all rare in Amm., this prepositional phrase occurs nowhere else in the *Res Gestae*. It is used to introduce a comparison in Suet. *Aug.* 95 (about the halo) *circulus ad speciem caelestis arcus orbem solis ambiit*. That Italy had a great number of rivers is a recurring element in *laudes Italiae*, such as Plin. *Nat.* 3.41 *tot amnium fontiumque ubertas totam eam* (Italiam) *perfundens*, repeated in Sol. 2.2 *tot amnes, lacus tantos*, but, of course, first of all in Vergil's magnificent line (tot) *fluminaque antiquos subterlabentia muros* (G. 2.157). Presumably, Amm.'s association of Bactria with Italy was triggered by the opening lines of Vergil's *laudes*:

> *sed neque Medorum silvae, ditissima terra*
> *nec pulcher Ganges, atque auro turbidus Hermus*
> *laudibus Italiae certent, <u>non Bactra</u> neque Indi* (G. 2.136–8).

Inundantur suggests that Bactria owed its fertility to its rivers; cf. 22.15.9 (about the Nile) *inundatione ditissima*.

Artamis et Zariaspes... Oxi fluenta Amm. seems to follow Ptolemy closely, who in 6.11.3-4 mentions these rivers: Ἄρταμις, Ζαρίασπις, Δαργαμάνης, Ὦξος. His *ante sibi consociati* about the Artamis and the Zariaspes looks like a direct translation of πρότερον συμμίξαντες ἀλλήλοις in § 3. Ptolemy uses the same phrase again about the Dargamanes and the Ochus. Amm. varies the expression to *iuncti convenis aquis* (cf. the note ad 23.3.8 and for *consociare* 15.11.3 quoted ad § 54). The Artamis is the modern Ab-é-Khulm; Tomaschek, 1896. The Zariaspis is also called Bactrus, as is known from Str. 11.11.2 (516C) and Curt. 6.4.31, and is to be identified with the modern Balkh; Treidler, 1967, 2327. The Ochus which rose in the Indian mountains (Str. 11.7.4 [510C]) is probably to be identified with the modern Tedjen; Berthelot, 1930, 184. Ancient authors already had difficulty in identifying the Ochus; they were not certain about its course as appears from Str. 11.7.3 (509C), 11.11.5 (518C), Plin. *Nat.* 6.48, 31.75; see Sturm, 1937. The Orgomanes is perhaps the modern Herî-Rûd; Tomaschek, 1901. See also Fontaine n. 227 for a discussion about the identification of these rivers. For the Oxus see the note ad 23.6.52.

6.58 *his cedentes ut melioribus* Cf. 14.8.11 (Palaestina) *civitates habens quasdam egregias, nullam nulli cedentem*. For cataphoric *hic* cf. 16.12.32 *alios... his*

exhortationibus adiuvabat: "exsurgamus" e.q.s., 17.4.11 *cuius rei scientiam his interim duobus exemplis* (monstrabo), 21.14.4, 31.1.4.
It would help to print a colon after *melioribus*.

Chatrachartae... et Bactris These cities are also mentioned, be it with slight differences in the names, by Ptol. 6.11.7-9: Χαράχαρτα, Ἀλιχόρδα, Ἀσταχάνα, Μεναπία, Βάκτρα βασίλειον. Amm. made his own selection from the seventeen cities mentioned by Ptolemy in the section on Bactria. Their location is difficult to determine. Chatracharta at the confluence of the Ochus and Oxus is, according to Tomaschek, 1899, either modern Amûya/Amul or modern Andechûd; Berthelot, 1930, 187 thinks it is modern Tchardjoui. Alicodra in western Bactria is perhaps to be identified with Andechôd; Tomaschek, 1894. Berthelot, 1930, 186 wants to situate it much more to the east. Astatia is Ptolemy's Ἀσταχάνα (6.11.8). Tomaschek, 1896 thinks that it is either modern Astanâh near Andkhui in northern Afghanistan or modern Astîkhan; according to Berthelot, 1930, 188 it cannot be identified with any modern site. Also Curt. 7.4.31 and Str. 11.11.2 (516C) inform us that Bactra – named after the river Bactrus (also called Zariaspis) – was the capital of Bactria. It is modern Balkh. Bactra was initially named Zariaspa; Arr. *An.* 4.1.5, 4.7.1, Plb. 10.49.15, Str. 11.8.9 (514C): Βάκτραν...ἢ καὶ Ζαρίασπα καλεῖται, Str. 11.11.2 (516C); Plin. *Nat.* 6.48 calls it *Zariastes*. See also Treidler, 1967. Bactra was originally the designation for the whole of Bactria. Bactra was at a cross-roads of trade routes connecting China, India and the western world; Tarn, 1984[3], 114–6, 139–40; Holt, 1988, 28–9, 31–2.

unde regnum et vocabulum nationis est institutum In his note ad 17.13.27 *iam inde ab instituta gente* De Jonge drew attention to Amm.'s idiosyncratic use of the verb *instituere*. Here, Amm. seems to go one step further in coining the phrase *vocabulum instituere* for *nomen indere*. No parallels are to be found in the TLL.

...sub imis montium pedibus, quos appellant Sogdios Valesius' suggestion **6.59** for the lacuna: *Hinc Sogdiani agunt* is quite plausible, more so, in fact than Fontaine's *Sub <illis Sogdiani agunt> sub,* since there is no parallel for the use of *sub* with the name of a nation in Amm.
The region Sogdiana, also named Transoxiana, is bounded by the rivers Oxus in the south and Iaxartes in the north. It occupied the eastern part of modern Uzbekistan and Turkmenistan, the northern part of Tadzhiskistan and the southern part of Kirghizia. Sogdiana contained rich oases like the capital Marakanda (modern Samarkhand), but also deserts and mountains. The Σόγδια ὄρη (Ptol. 6.12.2) is such a mountain range of 525 km. which crosses Sogdiana. It is to be identified with what is now called the range of mountains of Hissar and Alaï; Kretschmer, 1929, 789; Berthelot, 1930, 192. Sogdiana is

mentioned by Hdt. 3.93 as part of the sixteenth satrapy of the Achaemenid empire. Its geography is described by Str. 11.11.3 (517C) – 11.11.5 (518C). See further Berthelot, 1930, 190–8; Kretschmer, 1929; Masson, 1982, 95 ff.

inter quos amnes duo fluunt navium capacissimi Valesius, evidently taking the *Sogdii montes* as the antecedent of *inter quos*, berates Amm. for his negligence in copying Ptolemy, who states that this mountain range lies between the two rivers: διατείνει δὲ ὄρη μεταξὺ τῶν δύο ποταμῶν καλούμενα Σόγδια (6.12.2). It seems more likely, however, that the relative refers to the inhabitants of Sogdiana who must have been mentioned in the lacuna, so that the meaning would be that the two rivers flow through the region of the Sogdiani. There is a note on *capax* ad 23.2.6 *ubi cum introiret. Navium* or *navigiorum capax* is found in Plin. *Nat.*, e.g. 3.21 and 3.51.

Araxates et Dymas Amm.'s Araxates is generally identified with the Iaxartes, the modern Syrdar'ya; but see below the note on *Oxiam nomine paludem*. Apart from being called Iaxartes (Arr. *An.* 7.16.3, Str. 11.6.1 [507C], 11.7.4 [510C], 11.11.5 [518C], Plin. *Nat.* 6.36, Ptol. 6.12.1) the river is also called Tanais (Arr. *An.* 3.30.7 and Bosworth ad loc., 4.1.3, Curt. 7.6.13, 25, Str. 11.7.4 [510C], Plin. *Nat.* 6.49); Herrmann, 1916. The Dymas, elsewhere only mentioned by Ptol. 6.12.3 (Δῆμος), is perhaps to be identified with the modern Chirchik; Fontaine n. 230. However, Holt, 1988, 22 suggests that the Dymas is identical with the Polytimetos, the modern Zeravshan; the latter is also mentioned by Str. 11.11.15 (518C), Curt. 7.10.1–3, Arr. *An.* 4.5.6, 4.6.7, Ptol. 5.14.2.

...iuga vallesque...decurrentes The simplest remedy for the lacuna between *Dymas* and *iuga* would be to insert *qui* as the subject for *efficiunt*. After the lacuna had come into being the word *fluvii* was probably added to make up for the lost subject, so that Gelenius had a good reason to omit it from his text. Transitive *decurrere* is found more often in Amm., e.g. 31.13.7 *solque sublimior decurso Leone*. For *praeceps* as an attribute of a river cf. 15.4.2 *inclinatione praecipiti funditur Nilus*. It is quite common in all periods of Latin; TLL X 2.417.6–28. The phrase *campestris planities* is found also in Col. 3.14.1 *campestris et uliginosa planities*. For *longe lateque diffusam* cf. 22.8.9 *quantum potest cadere sub aspectum late diffusum et longe* with the note.

Oxiam nomine paludem Amm. is the first ancient author who mentions the Oxia palus (= the Aral Sea). Furthermore, he is the only one who correctly reports that the Iaxartes debouches into this inner sea and not into the Caspian Sea as other authors had done. Herrmann, 1942, who apparently found the accuracy of Amm.'s information hard to believe, thinks that Amm.'s Iaxartes refers to the Oxus because of the fact that the ancient geographers knew that this river debouched into an inner sea, which can be identified with the Aral Sea.

Alexandria et Cyreschata et Drepsa metropolis Alexandria is Ἀλεξάνδρεια Ἐσχάτη; also mentioned by Arr. *An.* 4.1.3 (cf. Bosworth ad loc.), Curt. 7.6.25, Plin. Nat. 6.49, Ptol. 6.12.6; it was founded by Alexander for military and trading purposes. It is near the site of modern Khodzhent; see Fraser, 1996, 151–3. Cyreschata is called Κυρούπολις/Cyropolis by Arr. *An.* 4.3.2 and Curt. 7.6.16, τὰ Κῦρα by Str. 11.11.4 (517C) and Κυρεσχάτα by Ptol. 6.12.5. The city was founded by the Achaemenid king Cyrus *c.* 530 and demolished by Alexander the Great because of its frequent revolts; Str. *ibid.* It is either located at Ura-Tyube or, more probably, at modern Kurkat, 40 km. west of Khodzhent; see Bosworth ad Arr. *An.* 4.3.2. Drepsa is also mentioned by Ptol. 6.12.6 and 8.23.13: Δρέψα μητρόπολις. Probably it is the same place as Drapsaca mentioned by Arr. *An.* 3.29.1 (Bosworth ad loc.) and situated by him in Bactria and Strabo's Bactrian city Ἄδραψα (11.11.2 [576C], 15.2.10 [725C]). According to Tomaschek, 1905, it was situated in the region of the Drepsiani; Berthelot, 1930, 195–6 identifies it with Samarkhand. However, it seems now certain that it was situated on the site of modern Kunduz; Fontaine n. 231 and Holt, 1988, 20 n. 35.

His contigui sunt Sacae, natio fera The territory of the Sacae was situated **6.60** east of Sogdiana, south of Scythia; on the other sides it was bounded by the foothills of the Imavus mons; Ptol. 6.13.1. It may roughly be identified with modern Pamir. In Greek sources – e.g. Hdt. 7.64, Str. 11.8.2–05 (511C-512C) – the Sacae are identified as Scythians. Amm. evidently does not consider the Sacae as a Scythian tribe; cf. § 61. See for this people the extensive article by Herrmann, 1920; Briant, 1982, 181 ff. For *ferus* as a qualification of barbarian nations see the note ad 20.1.1 and Seager 55–6.

squalentia incolens loca solum pecori fructuosa, ideo nec civitatibus culta Amm.'s choice of words makes it clear that we are now leaving the civilised world; cf. his description of the Scythian nomads in 22.8.42. For *squalere* see the note ad 22.15.22. The description is inspired by Ptolemy's words in 6.13.2 Ἡ τῶν Σακῶν χώρα Νομάδων ἐστί. πόλεις δὲ οὐκ ἔχουσι, δρυμοὺς δὲ καὶ σπήλαια οἰκοῦσιν. For cities as ornaments of a country cf. 15.11.13 (Aquitania) *amplitudine civitatum admodum culta* and for the connection between the fertility of a region and the presence of cities cf. 14.8.1–2, 14.8.11 *ultima Syriarum est Palaestina per intervalla magna protenta cultis abundans terris et nitidis et civitates habens quasdam egregias* and the sections 29–31 of this chapter.

cui Ascanimia mons imminet et Comedus The former mountain range is also known as Ascatancas or Ascatacas (Ptol. 6.13.1: Ἀσχατάγχας). It constituted the northern boundary of the land of the Sacae; Tomaschek, 1896; Berthelot, 1930, 206 and fig. 5. The *Comedus* is the plateau named after the Sacaean tribe of the Komedai which lived in the Pamir region of Darwaz; Ptol. 1.12.7 τῆς τῶν Κωμηδῶν ὀρεινῆς, 6.13.2 ἥ τε εἰρημένη τῶν Κωμηδῶν ὀρεινή. See for the difficulties in identifying the *Comedus* Treidler, 1963, 36 ff.

praeter quorum radices et vicum... iter longissimum patet The famous Silk Route, for which see the note ad 22.4.5. For *radices* used of a mountain range cf. Var. *R* 3.14.2 *sub rupibus ac montibus, quorum adluant radices lacus ac fluvii*.

quem Lithinon pyrgon appellant This place was a σταθμός along the Silk Route to China. The only other source for this station is Ptolemy (1.11.4, 1.12.1 ff., 6.13.2), whose information goes back to Marinus of Tyrus. This geographer in his turn used the itinerary of Maès Titianus, a merchant from Damascus who *c*. 100 A.D. did business with the Chinese. See Treidler, 1963.

mercatoribus pervium ad Seras subinde commeantibus On the goods that were transported along the Silk Route in both directions see Raschke, 1978. There is a note on *subinde* ad 23.1.7. For the *Seres* see 23.6.64–69.

6.61 *Circa defectus et crepidines montium* Servius *A*. 10.653 explains *crepido* as *abrupti saxi altitudo*, so the difference between *defectus* and *crepido* must be that between gently sloping foothills and a mountain massif. *Defectus* in this sense is found again in 23.6.70. The only other instance, according to TLL V 293.9–11, is Heges. 3.9.5 *ab aquilone in defectu montis*. Madvig's *deiectus* printed by Fontaine is much more frequent (TLL V 402.59–71), but seems to refer to steep slopes and is therefore less suitable as a contrast to *crepido*.

quos Imavos et Apurios vocant Like Ptol. 6.13.1, Amm. when mentioning the *Imavus mons* is probably referring to the western part of the Himalaya and the eastern part of the Hindu Kush; Str. 15.1.11 (689C), Plin. *Nat.* 6.60; Berthelot, 1930, 205 and fig. 5. It constitutes the boundary between the Asian highland and the lower southern part of Asia; it also demarcates the borderline between *Scythia infra Imavum* and *Scythia ultra Imavum* (see lemma below). In his description of Scythia Ptol. speaks of τῶν Ταπούρων ὀρῶν (6.14.12), which may have prompted Gelenius' *Tapurios*. If we were absolutely certain that Amm. had consulted Ptolemy directly, V's *et Apurios* should be explained as a case of haplography and corrected accordingly. Since we are not, it cannot be excluded that the mistake was adopted by Amm. from an intermediate source. For that reason we should keep V's *Apurios*. The mountain range is to be identified with the modern Talasskiy Alatau.

Scythae sunt varii intra Persicos fines   Following Ptolemy, who distinguishes Scythia ἐντὸς from Scythia ἐκτὸς Ἰμάου ὄρους (Ptol. 6.14 and 6.15) Amm. speaks about *Scythia infra* and *ultra Imavum* (§ 14, cf. § 64). Heraeus' conjecture *varii* for V's *aura* is in accordance with *gentes variae* in the next section. The expression *intra Persicos fines* refers of course to the western side of the *Imavus mons*, i.e, the region which extended up to the western foothills of the Himalaya.

Asianis contermini Sarmatis Halanorumque latus tangentes   For the Sarmatae, see esp. 17.12 and 13; and in general Dittrich, 1984. It is not clear where exactly Amm. locates the Halani, but here he may follow Ptolemy 6.14.3 and 14.9 who reports that they live east of the Hyperboraean mountains near unknown territory. Amm. himself states in 31.2.17 that the Halani are divided between the two parts of the earth, i.e. Europe and Asia. It is evident that in this passage he refers to the Asian Halani. Amm. discusses this nation extensively in 31.2.12 ff.; see also the note ad 22.8.31.

velut agentes quodam secessu coalitique solitudine   For *coalitus* see the note ad 21.5.2. *Secessus* here probably means 'a remote corner', as in the last section of this digression *in Britannici secessibus maris*. Elsewhere *secessus* has the connotation of 'refuge', e.g. in 16.1.5, where it is said of Julian that he was *ut Erechtheus in secessu Minervae nutritus*; cf. also 27.12.11 *celsorum montium petivere secessus*. In 30.2.12 *in secessu* means 'in retirement'.

quas nunc recensere alio properans superfluum puto   It looks as though Amm. **6.62** draws back from the long lists in Ptol. 6.14, where no fewer than 37 Scythian peoples are enumerated. For the phrase *alio(rsum) properans* cf. 25.10.3.

illud tamen sciendum est   See for this expression the note ad 20.3.12.

inter has nationes paene ob asperitatem nimiam inaccessas homines esse quosdam mites et pios   The notion that the characteristic qualities of nations were to a large extent determined by their environment was widely held in antiquity. The view has found its classic expression in the Hippocratic treatise *Aër.* 12.24 on the differences between Europeans and Asians. Curtius Rufus, speaking about the Paropamisadae, who lived to the East of Bactria, remarks *locorum asperitas hominum quoque ingenia duraverat* (7.3.6). Thus peace-loving and just nations come as a surprise in these practically uninhabitable regions.

Iaxartae sunt The Iaxartae lived on the right bank of the Iaxartes river. Ptol. 6.14.10 gives a more exact location than Amm.: εἶτα Ἄορσοι, μεθ' οὓς Ἰαξάρται μέγα ἔθνος παρὰ τὸν ὁμώνυμον ποταμὸν μέχρι τῆς πρὸς τοῖς Ταπούροις ὄρεσιν ἐπιστροφῆς. Again Ptolemy's information may go back to the geographer Marinus of Tyrus. In his *orb. terr.* 929 Avienus, speaking about the *diri Iaxartae*, presents the Iaxartae in a less flattering light than Amm. Cf. also Priscus, 725 ff. and see Herrmann, 1916.

Galactophagi, quorum meminit vates Homerus in hoc versu This line, *Il.* 13.6, is quoted also by Strabo: 7.3.7 (300C), 7.3.9 (302C) and 12.3.26 (553C), who looks upon the names Γαλακτοφάγοι and Ἄβιοι as σημεῖα, 'significant characteristics', of the Scythians, in opposition to Apollodorus (*FGrHist* 244 F 157), who considered these peoples to be no more than poetical fabrications. Apparently Amm., following Ptol. 6.14.12, (Γαλακτοφάγοι Σκύθαι), considered them to be a real people. In modern editions of Homer Γαλακτοφάγων is printed with a small letter and taken as an adjective with the preceding Ἱππημολγῶν. See Janko ad loc. On the Abii see the note ad § 53.
Literal quotations from Homer are rare in the *Res Gestae*. The only other instance is 15.8.17, where Amm. tells us that Julian on his appointment as Caesar quoted *Il.* 5.83 ἔλλαβε πορφύρεος θάνατος καὶ μοῖρα κραταιή. The same quotation is found in Joh. Antioch. E 83 (fr. 176 Müller), which suggests a common source. The remaining references to Homer do not betray an intimate knowledge of his works. This confirms Fornara's statement (1992, 421 n. 11) "his recollection of Homer seems genuine enough, though not all citations are at first hand."

6.63 *vel potioribus iungit natura vel lapsu ipso trahit in mare* For *potior* 'greater' cf. § 25 above *potiores ante alios amnes* ("usu recentiore" according to TLL X 2.343.8). For *lapsus* cf. Cic. *Div.* 1.100 *si lacus* (Albanus) *emissus lapsu et cursu suo ad mare profluxisset*.

Rhymmus... et Iaxartes et Daicus According to Ptol. 6.14.4 and 5 the Rhymmus flows from the Rhymmian mountains into the river Ra (= Volga). It is identified by Berthelot, 1930, 222, with the western branch of the river Ural. Seyfarth n. 122 identifies the Rhymmus with the Malyy Uzen' and Bol Uzen' which both debouch into small lakes some 200 km. north of the Caspian Sea. For the Iaxartes see the note ad 23.6.59. Tomaschek, 1901, thinks that the Daicus is the Jajig, which is an old name for the river Ural. Berthelot, 1930, 222 however, supposes that the Daicus is to be located somewhere between the western mouth of the Ural and that of the Emba.

Aspabota et Chauriana et Saga Aspabota is mentioned by Ptol. 6.14.2 and 8.23.15 (Ἀσπαβώτα πόλις). It is situated in *Scythia intra Imavum* at the east coast of the Caspian Sea near the estuary of the Oxus and is to be identified with Kranovodsk; Tomaschek, 1896, Berthelot, 1930, 223-4. The other two cities are situated in the south-western part of *Scythia extra Imavum*; both are now in the modern Chinese province of Xinjiang Uyyur. Chauriana, also mentioned by Ptol. 6.15.4 (Χαύρανα), is most likely to be identified with modern Hotan; see Fontaine's note 237. About Saga Seyfarth n. 122 remarks: "Saga ist nicht zu identifizieren." It may, however, be the same place as Ptolemy's Σοΐτα (6.15.4). In that case it can be identified with modern Shache, which is also named Yarkant; Herrmann, 1929.

utriusque Scythiae For the two Scythias, see the note ad 23.6.61. **6.64**

in orbis speciem consertae celsorum aggerum summitates ambiunt Seras Amm. had used practically the same phrase in 21.10.3 q.v. The Seres – the name means 'Silk People' – are also mentioned in 14.3.3 q.v. and 31.2.15. For the Romans they represent the peoples living in the Far East; e.g. Hor. *Carm.* 1.12.56, 3.29.27, 4.15.23, Verg. *G.* 2.121, Mela 3.7, Sen. *Herc. Oet.* 668. The earliest reference to the Σῆρες is to be found in Apollodorus of Artemita (*FGrHist* 779 F 7) although it seems to have been Posidonius who first designated the Seres as the typical nation of the Far East. Seres is therefore not an *ethnikon* but a name for those eastern peoples who live in the lands where the silk comes from, i.e. the Chinese. When c. 100 A.D. the sea route to China was discovered another and more correct name for the Chinese and China came into being: Σῖναι or Θῖναι, a name probably derived from the Ts'in dynasty; Ptol. 7.3.1, 6. The *Periplus Maris Erythraei* 64 speaks of the land Θῖν and Cosmas Indocopleustes 2.45 ff. of Τζίνιστα. In geographical sources the term Seres is applied to peoples in northern China, more precisely in modern Xinjiang, and the term Sinae is used to designate the peoples in the south of China. In literary sources, like Amm.'s *Res Gestae*, the indistinct term of Seres was kept for indicating the Chinese: "Dasselbe gilt auch noch für Ammian... dessen Schilderung der hyperboreischen Existenz der Serer vom neuen geographischen Wissen des 2. Jh.n.Chr. nicht die geringste Notiz nimmt und der darum die Unterscheidung zwischen "Serern" und Chinesen fremd bleibt."; Dihle, 1984, 214. See also Janvier, 1984. The ancients' geographical knowledge of China was limited and speculative. Our main information comes from Ptolemy 1.11-14, 6.16, 7.3, 8.24. Additional information can be derived from Plin. *Nat.* 6.53-55, 6.88, Paus. 6.26.6 ff. and Mela 3.7. Ptolemy had a number of itineraries at his disposal, such as the one of Maès Titianus, mentioned in § 60, but not enough to present a reliable picture of China's geographical situation: "Die Topographie eines Landes nach solchen Quellen [i.e. itineraries] aufzuarbeiten, verspricht nur dann halbwegs zuverlässige Ergebnisse, wenn man über viele miteinander zu verknüpfende, sich gegenseitig stützende Itinerare verfügt"; Dihle, 1984, 210. It is likely that through contacts between the Roman and Chinese world knowledge about China increased in the 3rd and 4th centuries. However, no reflection of this is to be found in geographical and ethnographical descriptions of China and the Chinese. This is also true for Ammianus. As in his description of the Black Sea (22.8), he keeps to the literary traditions regarding China. This in spite of his use of Ptolemy, whose knowledge of China was very limited but more correct and up-to-date than that of Amm. See in general Ferguson, 1978, Poinsotte, 1979, Dihle, 1984 and Janvier, 1984. For Roman commerce with China, see Raschke, 1978.

The *celsorum aggerum summitates* are the mountains by which Serica was surrounded, esp. those in Mongolia, Chinese Turkestan and Tibet since not all of Serica/China was surrounded by mountain ranges. It has long been thought that Amm. includes the Chinese Wall in this phrase, probably as a consequence of misinterpreting the word *agger*, which Amm. uses several times to indicate a mountain range, as in 15.10.2 *aggeribus cedit Alpium Cottiarum,* 21.10.4 q.v., 27.4.3 and 31.8.1. The last sentence of this section *appellantur autem idem montes* e.q.s. proves that Amm. is thinking of mountains here.

ubertate regionum et amplitudine circumspectos The adjective *circumspectus* has different shades of meaning in Amm. It reinforces *cautela* in 14.2.7 *circumspecta cautela observatum est.* When used of colours (28.4.12) or precious materials (27.3.14) it means 'conspicuous'. Here it may be paraphrased as "cum admiratione spectatus, magnificus" (TLL III 1171.78–83), as in 14.6.6 *populique Romani nomen circumspectum et verecundum.*

nivosae solitudini cohaerentes Amm. seems to condense Sol. 50.1 *ab exordio huiusce plagae profundae nives, mox longa deserta,* which in its turn renders Plin. *Nat.* 6.53 *inhabitabilis eius prima pars...ob nives, proxima inculta saevitia gentium.* The reading *nivosae* (G), adopted by Seyfarth, is closer to V's *uosae* than Mommsen's *ignotae*, based on Ptol. 6.16.1 Ἡ Σηρική περιορίζεται... ἀπὸ δὲ ἄρκτων ἀγνώστῳ γῇ. The juxtaposition of snow and desolation suggests that Amm. follows Solinus here, rather than Ptolemy.

montes Anniba et Nazavicium et Asmira et Emodus et Opurocorra These five mountain ranges are also mentioned by Ptol. 6.16.2 (Ἄννιβα, Αὐξακίος, Ἀσμίραια, Ἠμωδός, Ὀττοροκόρρας), who even mentions three more (Κάσιος, τὸ Θάγουρον ὄρος, Σηρίχος). They constitute the western borderline of China from north to south. Since the geographical situation of the Chinese lands was not at all clear to the ancients it is very hard to identify their geographical indications of mountains, towns and rivers. The only help we have here are the coordinates given by Ptolemy, and they are often incorrect. The Anniba mountains may be identified with the modern Sayan mountains in southern Siberia. The Nazauicium is perhaps to be identified with the mountain ranges of the Tannu Ola, the Altai and the Hangayn Nuru; all three are in north-western Mongolia. The Asmira cannot be identified. This also holds true for the Emodus; even though Strabo (11.8.1 [511C], 15.1.11 [689C], 15.1.29 [698C] and 15.1.72 [719C]) and Pliny (*Nat.* 5.72.2, 6.21.1, 6.21.5, 6.24.8) mention a mountain Emodus, this cannot be the same as that of Amm. and Ptolemy; Ferguson, 1978, 586. Also the Opurocorra mountains are unidentifiable (Seyfarth n. 124). See Berthelot, 1930, 240–4 + fig. 6.

hanc itaque planitiem undique prona declivitate praeruptam A similar description of upland plains is found in 21.10.4 *prona humilitate deruptum.* Cf. also 15.10.4. *Hanc* loosely refers back to the preceding section 'the plain inhabited by these people', as in 23.4.2 *hac multiplici chorda* and 23.4.5 *hac medietate restium.*   **6.65**

terrasque lato situ distentas Cf. the digression on the Saracenes in 14.4.3 *errant semper per spatia longe lateque distenta* and the Halani in 31.2.18 *per solitudines... sine fine distentas.*

Oechartis et Bautis Ptol. 6.16.3: Οἰχάρδης, Βαύτισος. The Bautis is generally identified with the Huang-He or Yellow River; Tomaschek, 1899. Janvier, 1984, 300 prefers an identification with the Tsangpo river in Tibet. The Oechartis is harder to identify. Seyfarth n. 124 thinks it is the Tarim in Chinese Turkestan. Berthelot, 1930, 245–6 and in his wake Fontaine n. 240 think that the Oechartis can represent three different rivers, which are all three in northern Mongolia: the Selenga, the Yenisey and the Orchongol.

dispar est tractuum diversorum ingenium For *ingenium* in a geographical context cf. Mela 1.37 *Syrtis* (altera) *nomine atque ingenio par priori* and Flor. *Epit.* 1.33 (2.17.3) *ita undique... vallata est* (Hispania) *ut ingenio situs ne adiri quidem potuerit.*

hic patulum alibi molli devexitate subductum The phrase is partly repeated from 22.8.11. For *mollis* 'gently sloping' see TLL VIII 1380.13–28.

incolunt autem fecundissimam glebam variae gentes Amm. is here clearly writing about a part of the world about which his geographical knowledge and that of his sources leave much to be desired. Like Ptol. 6.16.4 he describes the country following the cardinal points. For the present phrase cf. Lucr. 1.21 *fecundas vertentes vomere glebas.*   **6.66**

Anthropophagi et Anibi et Sizyges et Chardi The Anthropophagi are also mentioned in 31.2.15: *Post hos Melanchlaenas et Anthropophagos palari ac-*

cepimus per diversa humanis corporibus victitantes, quibus ob haec alimenta nefanda desertis finitimi omnes longa petiere terrarum. Ptol. 6.16.4: ἔθνη Ἀνθρωποφάγων, Ἄννιβοι ἔθνος, Σίζυγες ἔθνος, Οἰχάρδαι. The Anthropophagi are Herodotus' Androphagi (4.106). These men-eaters are identified by Berthelot, 1930, 246 as the Ostiaci, a people living near the Yenisey river. See for the Androphagi/Anthropophagi, Tomaschek, 1894. The Anibi, a people from the mountains of the same name (see § 64) are located by Berthelot in northern Mongolia whereas Tomaschek, 1894 situates them more to the southwest, on the slopes of the Tyan Shan. The Sizyges are situated by Berthelot between the Sayan and Altai mountains; Herrmann, 1929, 419 however, considers them a Sacaean tribe which lived in the valley of the Alai mountains. The Chardi, or Oechardi, are no doubt to be located near the river Oechartis (see the note in the previous section), that is north-east of the Hangayn Nuruu mountains in Mongolia.

aquilonibus obiecti sunt et pruinis Cf. § 43 *siti sub aquilone colentes nivales terras et pruinosas* and 22.8.48 *quidquid. . . Pontici sinus aquilone caeditur et pruinis.*

exortum vero solis suspiciunt Cf. § 12 (oceano) *qui ferventem solis exortum suscipit omnium primus*, which makes one wonder whether instead of *suscipit* we should not read *suspicit*. The following words however, *ipse quoque nimium calens*, favour *suscipit*, since Amm. means that the eastern Ocean derives its heat from the rising sun.

Rabannae et Asmirae et Essedones omnium splendidissimi Ptol. 6.16.5: Ραβάνναι, ἡ Ἀσμιραία χώρα, Ἰσσηδόνες μέγα ἔθνος. The Rabannae are situated by Berthelot, 1930, 246 in the Selenga basin in northern Mongolia. Seyfarth n. 125 and Fontaine n. 243 for unexplained reasons locate them north-northwest of the Gobi desert. To the southeast of the Rabannae lived the Asmirae, possibly near modern Ulan Bator and the Keroulin basin (Berthelot); the name of this people probably has some connection with the Asmira mountains mentioned in section 64. Berthelot locates the Essedones in the Gobi desert. Although Amm. calls the Essedones *omnium splendissimi* (the qualification may have been prompted by Ptolemy's μέγα ἔθνος) next to nothing is known about them. Perhaps Amm. confused them with the Scythian Essedones (also named Issedoi or Issedones) which are mentioned by various sources; e.g. Hdt. 4.13, Plin. *Nat.* 4.88, 6.21, 50, Mela 2.2, 9, 13, Sol. 49.7, *Tab. Peut.* XI 3. These Essedones are located by Herrmann, 1916 east of the Ural and cannot therefore be the same as Amm.'s Essedones Sericae. *Splendidus* is rarely used of cities or countries. OLD 3b quotes *CIL* 2.6278.56 *in civitatibus splendidissimarum Galliarum* and cf. 15.11.12 *hae provinciae urbesque sunt splendidae Galliarum.*

Athagorae... et Aspacarae The Athagorae were situated in the region of the Helan Shan on the left bank of the Yellow River. The Aspacarae are supposed to have lived in the region of the upper course of the Yellow River between the mountain ranges of the Nanshan and the Bayan Har Shan. See Berthelot, 1930, 246.

Baetae vero australi celsitudine montium inclinati This people is difficult to place. It may be that they lived in Tibet. The Indians called them Bhôta. Their name may have been preserved in the Himalayan kingdom of Bhutan, as Fontaine n. 243 suggests; Tomaschek, 1899; Berthelot, 1930, 246. The only parallel quoted for this phrase in TLL VII 1.944.57–73 is Avien. *orb. terr.* 1012 *Lyciorum tenditur ora inclinata mari*. It is plausibly suggested in the TLL that in the present passage we should also read the dative *celsitudini* (G), for which we may compare 31.2.16 *parte alia... Halani sunt orienti acclines*.

urbibus... celebrantur The expression is comparable to *civitatibus culta* in § 60.

Asmira et Essedon et Asparata et Sera Ptol. 6.16.6–8 mentions fifteen cities in Serica including these four: Ἀσμιραία, Ἰσσηδὼν Σηρική, Ἀσπακάρα, Σήρα μητρόπολις. Like the *mons Asmira* (§ 64) and the people of the Asmirae, the town of Asmira is difficult to locate. Perhaps it was in Mongolia near Ulan Bator and the Keroulin river, the region where possibly the Asmirae were located. Tomaschek, 1896 and Seyfarth n. 125 locate it at the extreme east of the Tian Shan. As to Essedon Berthelot, 1930, 248 says that it was situated "à l'extrémité occidentale de la province de Kan-Sou, au bout de la Grande Muraille." It is possibly Yumen or Jiayuguan in the modern province of Gansu. Tomaschek, 1896, 1709 identifies Asparata with modern Xining, but according to Berthelot, 1930, 252–3 there are no certain data to identify Asparata with a modern site. Sera, also mentioned by Ptol. 1.11.1, 4; 1.17.5, 6.13.1, 6.16.8, 8.24.8, is considered to be the capital of Serica and "Endpunkt aller geographischen Kenntnisse im Osten" (Herrmann, 1923, 1661). Many modern places have been identified with Sera; see Herrmann 1923, who personally identifies Sera with Lanzhou, and Fontaine n. 244.

nitidae sunt Even more strained than *splendidus* is *nitidus* as a qualification of a city. The adjective is used in 14.8.11 for Palestine: *cultis abundans terris et nitidis*, where it denotes the fertility of the land.

utque hominibus sedatis et placidis otium est voluptabile, nulli finitimorum molesti **6.67** The sentence looks like a combination of on the one hand *utque illis otium est voluptabile, nulli molesti sunt* and on the other *ut homines sedati et placidi, nulli molesti sunt*. Contrast the Halani in 31.2.22 *utque hominibus* *quietis et placidis otium est voluptabile, ita illos pericula iuvant et bella.* This idyllic picture of the Chinese can also be found in Plin. *Nat.* 6.54 who speaks of *Seres mites* and Sol. 50.3 who uses the same expression. Mela 3.60 calls them a *genus plenum iustitiae*. The Syriac *Book of the Laws of Countries* (ed. H.J.W. Drijvers, Assen 1965, 41) reports that the Seres have laws which forbid killing and mentions furthermore that no murderer is to be found in their country. Avienus (*orb. terr.* 935), however, calls the Seres wild and bellicose, and Hor. *Carm.* 1.29.9 mentions the fame of their weapons (*doctus sagittas tendere Sericas arcu paterno*).

caeli apud eos iucunda salubrisque temperies For his description of the climate Amm. may well have used Sol. 51.1: *quibus temperies praerogativa miram aeris clementiam subministrat. Arcent sane adflatum noxium colles* e.q.s. Speaking about Arabia Felix Amm. had also mentioned their *sospitalis temperies caeli* (§ 43).

aeris facies munda A striking phrase. *Mundus* normally is used of food (16.8.8, 29.2.7, 29.5.37). Amm. probably means that the air is pure and clean, the opposite of what he tells us in 24.8.3 about the stifling atmosphere in Persia: *per eas terras vapore sideris calescentis muscarum et culicum multitudine referta sunt omnia earumque volatu dies et astrorum noctu micantium facies obumbratur.*

silvae sublucidae With this rare adjective Amm. evokes a pleasant broad-leaved forest, the opposite of the *horror silvarum squalentium* of 15.4.3.

a quibus arborum fetus aquarum asperginibus crebris velut quaedam vellera molientes ex lanugine et liquore mixtam subtilitatem tenerrimam pectunt 'Working' (or preferably, reading *mollientes*) 'softening the products of the trees from these forests with repeated sprinklings of water like a kind of fleece, they comb very fine, soft threads out of this material which consists of wool and moisture.' The genealogy of this highly bookish description of the production of silk is as follows. Amm. imitates Sol. 50.2: (Seres) *qui aquarum aspergine inundatis frondibus vellera arborum adminiculo depectunt liquoris et lanuginis teneram subtilitatem umore domant ad obsequium.* This is a characteristically laboured rendering of Plin. *Nat.* 6.54 *Seres lanicio silvarum nobiles, perfusam aqua depectentes frondium canitiem*, which in its turn is inspired by Verg. *G.* 2.120–1

> *quid nemora Aethiopum molli canentia lana*
> *velleraque ut foliis depectant tenuia Seres?*

Vergil's Ethiopians are a people living in the Far East (Nadeau, 1970), for whom Pliny has substituted the Seres. What these descriptions have in common is that they seem to represent the fabrication of silk as a purely vegetable process, comparable e.g. to the production of cotton ("Baumwolle"), unless we interpret the threads (*vellera*) that hang from the trees as threads spun by silk moths (*bombyces*). As André-Filiozat point out in their note ad Plin. *Nat.* 6.54, Pliny, in *Nat.* 11.78, uses very similar phrases in his description of the fabrication of Coan silk or *bombycina* and of the role of the silk moths in the process (*bombyces*). This would also explain the moistening of the leaves mentioned in Pliny, Solinus and Amm., which plays no part in the vegetable production of textiles, such as cotton, but is indispensable in processing the threads of the *bombyces*. Pliny writes in 11.78 *quae vero carpta sint lanicia, umore lentescere, mox in fila tenuari* ("tufts of wool plucked off are softened with moisture and then thinned out into threads", Rackham). The descriptions in Vergil, Pliny, Solinus and Amm. are therefore either totally wrong in that the authors confuse the fabrication of silk and cotton, or partly wrong in that they do not distinguish between Coan silk made from the threads of silk moths (*bombyces*) and Chinese silk made from the threads of silk worms.

In Greek sources on the Seres and silk production we also find the element of combing or carding leaves, ξαίνειν / *(de)pectere*, but without the detail that the leaves are moistened beforehand. Strabo 15.1.20 (694C) distinguishes σηρικά, which is produced ἐκ τινων φλοιῶν ξαινομένης βύσσου 'when silk is carded from certain barks' from cotton or wool (ἔριον), which blossoms on the branches of trees. Compare the version of Dionysius Periegeta, who says about the Seres in 754–5:

αἰόλα δὲ ξαίνοντες ἐρήμης ἄνθεα γαίης
εἵματα τεύχουσιν πολυδαίδαλα, τιμηέντα.

For a correct description of the way in which silk was produced by the Seres we have to wait until Pausanias, who in 6.26.6–8 explicitly contradicts Strabo before giving his version: οἱ μίτοι ('threads') δέ, ἀφ' ὧν τὰς ἐσθῆτας ποιοῦσιν οἱ Σῆρες, ἀπὸ οὐδενὸς φλοιοῦ, τρόπον δὲ ἕτερον γίνονται τοιόνδε. In Latin literature we find a comparable correction in Servius, who, when commenting upon *G.* 2.120–1, writes: *apud Aethiopiam, Indos et Seras sunt quidam in arboribus vermes* ('worms') *et bombyces* ('silk moths') *appellantur, qui in aranearum morem tenuissima fila deducunt, unde est sericum: nam lanam arboream* ('cotton') *non possumus accipere, quae ubique procreatur*. Distinctions like those made by Pausanias and Servius are unknown to Amm., who limits himself to outdoing Solinus and substitutes the recherché *arborum fetus* for *frondes*, *asperginibus crebris* for *aspergine* and *subtilitatem tenerrimam* for *teneram subtilitatem*. As the parallels quoted from Sol. 50.2 and Plin. *Nat.* 11.78 show, BAG's *mollientes* is clearly superior to V's *molientes*.

nentesque subtemina conficiunt sericum ad usus antehac nobilium Strictly speaking *subtemen* is the term for "the transverse threads woven in between the warp threads in a loom" (OLD). Amm. either expresses himself loosely and thinks about garments of pure silk (*holosericae*), or he means *subsericae*, clothing that is only partly made of silk. See for this distinction and the price of silk the note ad 22.4.5. *Ad usus* depends on *proficiens*. As Fontaine remarks in n. 247, Amm.'s criticism of the wearing of silk by common people is dictated by class consciousness. He does not condemn silk garments as being immodest, as Solinus (and many others) had done: 50.3 (*sericum*) *quo ostendere potius corpora quam vestire primo feminis, nunc etiam viris luxuriae persuasit libido*.

6.68 *ipsi praeter alios frugalissimi* This is Amm.'s own conclusion from the anecdote told in this section. The Seres are contrasted with Amm.'s Roman contemporaries whose *luxuria* he had criticised in the Roman digressions. See especially 14.6.9.

pacatioris vitae cultores See § 67 with the first note.

vitantes reliquorum mortalium coetus Pliny had compared the Seres to shy animals: *Nat*. 6.54 *feris similes coetum reliquorum mortalium fugiunt*.

cumque ad coemenda fila vel quaedam alia fluvium transierint advenae The river comes from Sol. 50.4 *primum eorum fluvium mercatores ipsi transeunt* (Seres). Plin. *Nat*. 6.88, quoted below, tells the same story also without mentioning the river by name. Elsewhere, however, in 6.55, directly after his remark on the *Seres mites*, Pliny says *primum eorum noscitur flumen Psitharas*, as did Solinus. Therefore the river Psitharas must have been the river on the border which Pliny had in mind. It seems likely that it is the same as the Ἀσπίθρας mentioned in Ptol. 7.3.2 as flowing across the border with India, tentatively identified by Treidler, 1959, 1412 as the Sinkiang. Fontaine n. 248 supposes that the Huang-He (Yellow River) is meant.

nulla sermonum vice... adventicium This is a typical 'Wanderanekdote', found for the first time in Herodotus about Carthaginian traders in Africa (4.196). For comparable stories told by modern travellers see How & Wells ad loc. Pliny has the following version: *Seras... nullo commercio linguae... fluminis ulteriore ripa merces positas iuxta venalia tolli ab iis, si placeat permutatio* (*Nat*. 6.88). The two stories are combined in Eustathius *Comm. Dion. Per.* 752 (=*GGM* II, 348). See also Mela 3.60 and *Periplus Maris Erythraei* 65. Amm.'s text is derived directly from Sol. 50.4 *nullo inter partes linguae commercio, sed depositarum rerum pretia oculis aestimantibus sua tradunt, nostra non emunt*. Just as in Solinus the *oculi* in all probability belong to both parties, thus in Amm. *aestimantur* applies both to the Chinese and to the foreign merchants. Solinus has changed Pliny's account. In Pliny the two parties exchange goods; according to Solinus the Seres disdain foreign articles. The reason may well be that Solinus misinterpreted Pliny's moralising comment *non aliter odio iustiore luxuriae quam si perducta mens illuc usque cogitet, quid et quo petatur et quare* ("hatred of luxury being in no circumstances more justifiable than if the imagination travels to the Far East and reflects what is procured from there and what means of trade are employed and for what purpose", Rackham) as the opinion of the Seres, who supposedly rejected the wares offered to them. Amm. probably thought that the Seres accepted only money and refused to buy foreign goods. For *gignentia* and *adventicius* see the notes ad 23.6.55 and 23.2.1 respectively.

Ariani vivunt post Seras This is clearly wrong; *post Seras* would imply that the Ariani lived to the east of the Seres, whereas in reality they lived to the west of them. As Fontaine points out in n. 249, the mistake may have been caused by the fact that Ptolemy's chapter on Aria (6.17) follows immediately after that on Serica (6.16). We have here another indication that Ammianus had only the vaguest of notions about the geography of the regions he is describing in these sections. Aria, named after the river Arias, now constitutes the region of Herat in eastern Afghanistan. In Achaemenid times it belonged to the 16th satrapy; Hdt. 3.93. The region is described by Str. 11.10.1 (515C-516C), who mentions its fertility in Str. 15.2.1 (720C), and by Plin. *Nat.* 6.93.

6.69

Arias...faciens lacum ingentem The Arias is the modern Harî-rûd/Tedzhen; Tomaschek, 1896. It is probably identical with the Orgomanes (= Dargamanes) mentioned in 23.6.57 q.v. and the Gordomaris in the following section; see Fontaine n. 227. Ptol. 6.17.2 calls it an important river (Διαρρεῖ δὲ τὴν χώραν ἀξιόλογος ποταμὸς καλούμενος Ἀρείας) but does not say explicitly that it was navigable. The lake may refer to the marshes in the frontier zone of Iran and Turkmenistan, into which the Arias flows after having been divided into various channels north-west of the town of Tedzhen; cf. Arr. *An.* 4.6.6 and Str. 11.11.5 (518C). See for an alternative opinion, Fontaine n. 249.

Vitaxa, Sarmatina et Sotira et Nisibis et Alexandria Ptolemy 6.17.4-8 mentions no less than 35 towns in Aria. According to Tomaschek, 1899, Vitaxa (Ptol. 6.17.4, 8.25.4: Βίταξα) is to be located on the northern slopes of the Kūh-e-Baba; it is questionable whether this is correct since this mountain range is a great distance from ancient Aria. Sarmatina and Nisibis are mentioned only by Ptolemy (6.17.1, if Σαρμάγανα is Amm.'s Sarmatina, and 6.17.7); these places cannot be identified with modern sites. Tarn 1984[3], 10 thinks that Nisibis was founded as a trading post from Antioch-Nisibis in Mesopotamia. Sotira is also mentioned by Ptol. 6.17.4 (Σώτειρα) and is evidently a Seleucid foundation. According to Herrmann, 1929, it was located on the southern shore of the Arian lake, but since it is not clear which lake went under that name, the information is not very helpful. Alexandria in Ariana (Ptol. 6.17.6: Ἀλεξάνδρεια ἐν Ἀρείοις) is also mentioned by e.g. Str. 11.10.1 (516C), Plin. *Nat.* 6.61 and Sol. 54.2. It was situated on the embankment of the river Arias (Plin. *Nat.* 6.93) and was built by Alexander near Artacoana, the capital of the Achaemenid satrapy of Aria. It is located within the area of the modern city of Herat; Fraser, 1996, 109 ff.

unde naviganti ad Caspium mare quingenta stadia numerantur et mille In ancient times it may have been possible to sail from Alexandria in Ariana to the Caspian Sea by way of the rivers Harî-rûd, Tedzhen and the now dried-up branch of the Oxus. The latter river debouched into the Caspian sea (see the note ad 23.6.52). The distance given by Amm. is definitely wrong. Strabo 11.8.9 (514C) gives a distance of 6400 stadia from the Caspian Gates to Alexandria in Ariana. This route was shorter than that by water, which makes Amm.'s figure even less trustworthy. For the dat. iudicantis in geographical indications cf. Szantyr 96.

6.70 *Paropanisadae* The Paropanisus (Ptol. 6.18.1: Παροπανισάδων θέσις) is the modern Hindu Kush and the Paropanisadae are the peoples living in and near this mountain range; see Arr. *An.* 4.22.4, 5; 5.3.2, 11.3; 6.15.3, 26; Str. 15.1.17 (691C), D.S. 17.82.1–5, Curt. 7.3.6, Plin. *Nat.* 6.92, Mela 1.13. Ptol. 6.18.3 mentions five of these peoples: Βωλῖται, Ἀριστόφυλοι, Πάρσιοι, Παρσυῆται, Ἀμβαῦται. The Paropanisus is called the Indian Caucasus by some authors: Arr. *An.* 5.3.3, Plb. 10.48.4, 11.34.11, Str. 11.5.5 (506C), 11.8.1 (511C), Dion. Per. 714, 113. See Herrmann 1949 and 1949a; Berthelot, 1930, 288–91.

ipsi quoque montium defectibus inclinati For *defectus/deiectus* see the note ad § 61. It is best taken as a dative, cf. § 66 *celsitudine montium inclinati* with the note.

quos… Gordomaris interluit fluvius a Bactrianis exsurgens The verb *inter-luere* is found for the first time in Verg. *A.* 3.420 (pontus) *arvaque et urbes / litore diductas angusto interluit aestu*. The Gordomaris is mentioned only by Amm. In all probability it is the same as the Orgomanes (= Dargamanes) in his description of Bactria (§ 57), and the Arias of § 69. Ptol. 16.8.2 reports that the sources of this river are in the Paropanisus: Ἐμβάλλουσι δὲ εἰς τήν χώραν ποταμοὶ ὅ τε Δαργαμάνης ὁ ἐπὶ τῆς Βακτριανῆς, οὗ ἡ θέσις τῶν πηγῶν εἴρηται. Amm. or his intermediate source may have misinterpreted Ptolemy here; Fontaine n. 251.

quibus clariores sunt Agazaca et Naulibus et Ortospana A curious phrase. It is tempting to read *e quibus*, but cf. *quis omnibus praestant* (§ 39), *amnes autem sunt hic ceteris notiores Sagareus* e.q.s. (§ 49) and *sunt et hic civitates… his*

210

cedentes ut melioribus Chatrachartae e.q.s. (§ 58). Ptol. 6.18.4–5 lists 16 cities in this region. Gazaca (Ptol. 6.18.4: Γάζακα ἢ Γαύζακα) is possibly modern Ghanzi; Kiessling, 1912. Naulibus (Ptol. 6.18.5: Ναυλιβίς) is in eastern Afghanistan, possibly "sur la route de Caboul à la vallée de l'Héri-roud"; Berthelot, 1930, 291. Ortospana is also mentioned by Str. 11.8.9 (514C), 15.2.8 (723C) and Plin. *Nat.* 6.61 (*Hortospanum*). Ptol. 6.18.5 and 8.25.7 calls it Κάρουρα ἡ καὶ Ὀρτόσπανα for which reason it is identified as modern Kabul; Stein, 1942, Tarn 1984³, 471–2.

unde litorea... duo milia et ducenta It is quite unbelievable that it was possible to sail from the Hindu Kush to Media. This again shows Amm.'s poor knowledge of the geographical situation in these regions. Moreover, the distance of 2200 stadia (= *c.* 407 km) is incredible in view of the more reliable information of Strabo: 6400 stadia (= *c.* 1184 km) from Herat to the Caspian gates; see the note ad § 69. Possibly Amm.'s figure is based on Str. 11.8.9 (511C), where the distance from the Arachotoi to Ortospana is given as 2200 stadia. For the Caspian Gates, see the note ad 23.6.13.

Drangiani collibus cohaerentes For this use of *cohaerere* cf. 22.15.2 (*Aegyptus*) *terrarum situ cohaeret immenso* and TLL III 1538.78–80. Ptol. 6.19 and Str. 11.10.1 (516C), 15.2.9–10 (724C) describe the region of the Drangiani. They were an eastern Iranian people, called Σαράγγαι in Hdt. 3.93, living in what is now southwestern Afghanistan in the basin of the Helmand river near the lake complex of Seistan into which the Helmand debouches. Their name seems to have been derived from this lake since in the Avesta 'zraya' (cf. Σαράγγαι) means lake; 'draya' (cf. Drangiana) in old Persian means sea. See for Drangiana, Tomaschek, 1905; Sherwin-White & Kuhrt, 1993, 80–1.

6.71

Arabium Ptol. 6.19.2: ποταμὸς ἀπὸ τοῦ Ἀράβιος ἐκτρεπόμενος. The principal river of Drangiana was not the Arabius but the Etymandros (modern Helmand). Like Ptolemy, Amm. seems to consider the Helmand as a branch of the Arabius, which was the main river of Gedrosia and identical with the Artabius mentioned by Amm. in § 73. As Fontaine n. 253 suggests, the lacuna may have contained a reference to the Ἄρβιτα ὄρη of Ptol. 6.21.2 (see the note ad § 73), where the Artabius/Arabius had its origin and after which the river was supposedly named.

Prophthasia et Ariaspe Ptol. 6.19.4–5 mentions eleven cities and villages in Drangiana; among them these two (Προφθασία, Ἀριάσπη). Prophthasia is also mentioned by e.g. Str. 11.8.9 (514C), 15.2.8 (723C) and Plin. *Nat.* 6.61. It was originally named Phrada but was given the name of Prophthasia by Alexander. It is identified with modern Farah; see Treidler, 1959 and Fraser, 1996, 123–30. Ariaspe was apparently the main city of the people of the

Ariaspi who are also known as the Εὐεργέται. The Ariaspi lived to the south of the lake complex of Seistan; see for them e.g. Arr. *An.* 3.27.4 (and Bosworth ad loc.), 4.6.6, Str. 15.2.10 (724C), D.S. 18.81; Gnoli, 1967, 47–51.

6.72 *Post quos exadversum Arachosia visitur* Arachosia is situated east of Drangiana, south of the Paropanisadae, north of Gedrosia and west of India; Ptol. 6.20.1. It can roughly be identified with the modern region of Kandahar in Afghanistan. The region was named after the river Arachos, the modern Arghandab. Arachosia was a satrapy of the Achaemenid and Seleucid kingdom; *c.* 250 B.C. it became part of the Indian empire of the Mauryas. See e.g. Str. 11.10.1 (516C), 15.2.9 (724C), Plin. *Nat.* 6.92, Arr. *An.* 3.8.4 (σατράπης Ἀραχωτῶν). It is not clear what Amm. means by *exadversum*, 'on the opposite side', an adverb he uses only here. It seems natural to think of a river, on the opposite side of which Arachosia begins. The Etymandros would be the perfect candidate. It is just possible that Amm. had Solinus in mind, who writes about the town of Arachosia in 54.2: *Arachosiam Erymandro amni impositam Samiramis condidit.*

dextrum vergens in latus Apart from § 45, where Amm. says about the Arabs that they *mare rubrum latere dextro contingunt, laevo Persico mari collimitant*, this is the only right/left reference in this digression. As Sundwall, 1996 has convincingly argued, this does not prove that Amm. used a map. If, as was suggested above, Amm. had the Etymandros in mind as the border river between Drangiana and Arachosia, the remark would make sense, since for someone facing north Arachosia lies to the right of that river. Cf. for similar expressions in the excursus on the Pontus Euxinus the note ad 22.8.30.

quam ab Indo...Arachotoscrenen appellant India is of course named after the Indus; see 23.6.21 q.v. The Indus was also called Sindus (e.g. Plin. *Nat.* 6.71: *Indus incolis Sindus appellatus*) or Σίνθος (*Periplus Maris Erythraei* 38); see further Wecker, 1916. This passage seems to be a translation of Ptol. 6.20.2: Ἐμβάλλει δὲ εἰς τὴν χώραν ποταμὸς ἀπὸ τοῦ Ἰνδοῦ ἐκτρεπόμενος, οὗ αἱ πηγαὶ ἐπέχουσι μοίρας... ἡ δὲ ἐκτροπὴ... τὸ δὲ κατὰ τὴν γινομένην ὑπ' αὐτοῦ λίμνην, ἥ τις καλεῖται Ἀράχωτος κρήνη. For that reason we must suppose that with *amnis multo minor* Amm. refers to the Arachos (after which Arachosia was named), despite the fact that this river is not a branch of the Indus but has its source in the region of Dasht-i-Nawar in the mountains some 30 km. east of Ghazni; nor does the Arachos debouch into a lake but in the Helmand river. The Arachotoscrene is to be identified with a depression at an altitude of some 3120 m. in the region of Dasht-i-Nawar where rainwater and melted snow assemble, and not with the lake of Ab-i-Istada as has long been thought; see Fontaine n. 255.

hic quoque civitates sunt inter alias viles Alexandria et Arbaca et Choaspa Ptol. 6.20.4–5 mentions thirteen cities and villages including these three: Ἀλεξάνδρεια, Ἀρβάχα, Χοάσπα. The last two occur only in Ptolemy and Amm. Alexandria is modern Kandahar. Isid. Char. 19 (*GGM* I 254) calls it the capital of Arachosia (Ἀλεξανδρόπολις, μητρόπολις Ἀραχωσίας), whereas Str. 11.8.9 (514C) leaves Alexandria unmentioned and speaks of Ἀραχωτοί; Plin. *Nat.* 6.61 speaks of *Arachosiorum oppidum* and Sol. 54.2 seems to deny Alexander's foundation and ascribes the founding of the capital of the Arachosians to Semiramis (*Arachosiam Erymandro amni impositam Samiramis condidit*). See Fraser, 1996, 132–40.

At in penitissima parte Persidos Gedrosia est The rare superlative *penitissima* **6.73** here does not mean 'close to the centre', as in the translation of Seyfarth ("Ganz im inneren Persiens"), but 'most remote', as in the translation of Fontaine ("la partie la plus reculée de la Perse"). A parallel for this meaning would be Gel. 9.4.6 *Scythas illos penitissimos*. Probably Gedrosia is given this qualification because it is the last of the regions listed in § 14. About the first region, Assyria, Amm. had said *Citra omnes propinqua est nobis* (§ 15). Gedrosia is therefore by contrast 'the remotest part of Persia'. Gedrosia, modern Beluchistan in Pakistan, was situated on the eastern edge of the Persian regions. For a more precise description of its geographical situation, see Ptol. 6.21.1. Gedrosia is described by Str. 15.2.3 (721C) and Arr. *An.* 6.22.5 ff.; see also Plin. *Nat.* 6.78, 94–95 and Kiessling, 1912.

dextra terminos contingens Indorum The Indians and India are mentioned several times in this chapter (§§ 12, 13, 21, 33, 64, 70, 72, 85) but unlike Strabo, Pliny, Ptolemy and Solinus, Amm. does not bother to describe this people and its country. One might argue that it falls outside his original aim – *situm monstrare Persidis* –, but the same is true for the *Arabes beati* and the *Seres* of whom he presents extensive surveys. The explanation for not including the Indians must be that in contrast to the *Arabes beati* and the *Seres*, they were not described in Bk. 6 of Ptolemy's *Geography*, Amm.'s direct or indirect source for this digression.

Artabio uberior flumine This expression is unique in the *Res Gestae*, but cf. e.g. Ov. *Tr.* 4.10.3 *Sulmo mihi patria est, gelidis uberrimus undis*. The river is called Ἄραβις by Ptol. 6.21.2. Plin. *Nat.* 6.97 calls it the Arbius (*flumen Arbium navium capax*). It is also mentioned by Arr. *Ind.* 21.8, 22.8; *An.* 6.21.3, 4; Str. 15.2.1 (720C), Curt. 9.10.6 and is to be identified with either the modern river Hab or the Porali; cf. Fontaine n. 257 who prefers an identification of the Artabius with the Girdar Dhor, also named the Hingol river. At the mouth of this river Ptol. 6.21.5 situates the town of Arbis which is supposed to have been founded by Alexander's admiral Nearchus; Plin.

Nat. 6.97: *oppidum a Nearcho conditum in navigatione.* The river was named after the Ἄρβιτα ὄρη mentioned by Ptol. 6.21.3, 7.1.28. The Indian people living in Gedrosia are known as Ἀράβιες (Arr. *Ind.* 21.8, 22.8, 10, 25.3), Ἀραβῖται (Arr. *An.* e.g. 6.24.4), Ἄρβιες (Str. 15.2.1 [720C]), Arbii (Plin. *Nat.* 6.95, 110), Ἀβρῖται (D.S. 17.100.4). Ptolemy speaks of the Ἀρβιτῶν κῶμαι (6.21.4). See Tomaschek, 1896.

ubi montes deficiunt Arbitani, quorum ex pedibus imis emergentes alii fluvii Indo miscentur For *deficere* cf. the note ad § 61 *Circa defectus.* Cf. Ptol. 6.21.3: Διατείνει δὲ διὰ μέσης τῆς Γεδρωσίας ὄρη καλούμενα Ἄρβιτα... ἀφ' ὧν εἰς τὸν Ἰνδὸν ἐμβάλλουσι τινες ποταμοί. The Ἄρβιτα ὄρη, also mentioned in Ptol. 7.1.28, are the modern Kirthar mountains.

mittentes nomina magnitudine potioris TLL VIII 1177.1–10 gives some parallels for *mittere* 'to give up', e.g. Var. *L.* 6.2 *verba ex verbis ita declinari scribunt, ut litteras alia assumant, alia mittant.* It is therefore not absolutely necessary to adopt G's *amittentes.* Something similar is reported in 15.11.17 about the Saône flowing into the Rhône: *Ararim, quem Sauconnam appellant inter Germaniam primam fluentem et Sequanos, suum et nomen asciscit.* For *potior* 'greater' see the note ad § 63.

praeter insulas Cf. Ptol. 6.21.6: Νῆσοι δὲ παράκειται τῇ Γεδρωσίᾳ Ἀσθαία..Κοδάνη. Asthaia is probably the modern Astola or Astalu Island off the coast of Pakistan; Tomaschek, 1896. Kodane is unknown.

Ratira et Gynaecon limen meliores residuis aestimantur Ptol. 6.21.2: ῾Ραγίραυα πόλις, Γυναικῶν λιμήν. Again Amm. makes a surprising selection from the thirteen cities and villages mentioned by Ptol. 6.21.2, 5. For instance it is to be noted that Amm. does not mention Παρσὶς μητρόπολις (Ptol. 6.21.5), the capital of Gedrosia. One may therefore wonder about the significance of the two cities mentioned here. Neither of them has an entry in the *RE.* Fontaine n. 258 thinks that both were situated on the coast in the region of Karachi and Korangi between the estuaries of the Ar(t)abius and Indus.

6.74 *orae maritimae spatia alluentia Persidos extremitates* This is a kind of hypallage, in which the form *alluentia* agrees with *spatia*, whereas its meaning goes with *mare*, as implied by *maritimae*: 'the length of the coastline of the seas that wash the furthest parts of Persia.' As becomes clear from what follows, the coasts at the extremities of Persia are the northern coast, constituted by the Caspian Sea, and the southern coast formed by the *mare rubrum*, i.e. the Red Sea, the Persian Gulf and part of the Indian Ocean; see the note ad 23.6.26.

per minutias See the note ad 23.1.1 about the disdain of the true historian for petty details. A good parallel for the present passage is 27.2.11 *nec historiam producere per minutias ignobiles decet*.

a proposito longius aberremus This phrase, which comes almost at the end of a very long and at times tedious digression, may strike the reader as rather ironical. The author, however, might defend himself by saying that Persia is a vast subject and that he has done his best to present his material *ut in discessu celeri* 'as well as was possible in a swift exposition'. For *propositum* see the note ad 20.5.4.

a Caspiis montibus per borium latus ad usque memoratas angustias In all probability Amm. refers to § 43 of this digression: *per Caspia litora ad usque portarum angustias*. The northern border of Persia is thus formed by the southern shore of the Caspian Sea, between the Caucasus in the West and the Portae Caspiae in the East. Alternatively, we may think of § 26 *arenosas angustias, quae a rubro prohibent Caspium mare*, 'the sandy tracts that separate the Caspian from the Red Sea'. This is how Sundwall, 1996, 632, n. 33 seems to take it. However, the clear distinction between the northern border (*per borium latus*) and the southern sea (*australe*) makes the former interpretation preferable. The adjective *borius* or *boreus* is found from Suetonius onwards (TLL II 2132.80) usually in connection with the northern celestial pole. The *Caspii montes* are generally identified with the Caucasus on the strength of Str. 11.2.15 (497C), who had his knowledge from Eratosthenes. Mela 1.109 and Plin. *Nat*. 5.99, however, seem to identify the *Caspii montes* with the modern Elburz.

novem milium stadiorum It is not known on which source Amm. based this information. Str. 11.8.9 (514C) comes closest with a distance of 7400 stadia. He reports that Eratosthenes stated that the distance from Mt. Caspius to the Cyrus river was about 1800 stadia and from there to the Caspian Gates 5600 stadia.

australe vero ab ostiis Nili fluminis ad usque principia Carmanorum The southern sea is the *mare rubrum* (see the note above). The words *ab ostiis Nili* may have been prompted by the fact that the most northern branch of the Red Sea is not that far away from the Nile delta. It is hard to conceive that Amm. really thought that the *mare rubrum* was connected with the mouths of the Nile; if so, he would have mentioned it in his earlier references to the Nile, especially in 22.15. For Carmania see 23.6.48–49.

quattuordecim milium stadiorum numero definitur It is not known how this distance was estimated and what the source for it was. The only time Amm.

mentions a distance in connection with the *mare rubrum* is in section 11 of this chapter, where he reports that the Persian Gulf is bounded by a shore of 20.000 stadia: *omnisque sinus dimensione litorea in numerum viginti milium stadiorum*. The 14.000 stadia mentioned here are perhaps the sum of the distances of the long shore of the Persian Gulf, estimated by Eratosthenes at 10.000 stadia (see the note ad 23.6.11), the southern coast of the Arab peninsula and the coast of the Red Sea. If so, a mistake has been made in adding up the various distances since 14.000 stadia (= *c.* 2600 km.) is too low a figure. It is highly questionable if Amm. had access to reliable figures. It is significant that in this respect even the *Periplus Maris Erythraei* has incorrect distances; see Casson, 1989, 278–82.

6.75 *Per has nationes dissonas et multiplices* As to *dissonas*, Rolfe renders the word with "of different tongues" (cf. Seyfarth's "verschiedener Sprachen"), but Fontaine opts for "discordants". This seems more appropriate, since the phrase lacks a specific defining element, as in e.g. 31.7.11 *interque varios sermonis dissoni strepitus* and Liv. 1.18.3 *gentes dissonas sermone moribusque*. Cf. TLL V.1 1506.58 sq.

sed ne generaliter corpora describamus et mores This is the only instance of *generaliter* in Amm. Fontaine's translation "une déscription trop générale" is not warranted by the parallels in TLL VI 1777.1–60. Since a general description is exactly what Amm. is going to give (*graciles paene sunt omnes*), this reading cannot stand. The easiest remedy is to read *ut* (BAG) instead of *ne*. Cf. for a similar transitional and introductory phrase 23.5.17 *sed ut a vetustate discedam*. Alternatively, a lacuna must be assumed with Petschenig. After the section on the physical appearance of the Persians, Amm. goes on to describe their customs in § 76–80, which makes *et mores* (BAG) instead of V's *et priores* practically unassailable.

graciles paene sunt omnes Cf. 24.8.1, where Amm., speaking of Persian prisoners, says that these naturally slender men (*graciles suapte natura, ut omnes paene sunt Persae*), were emaciated (*macie iam confectos*). TLL VI.2 2130 sq.

subnigri vel livido colore pallentes Amm. shares the predilection of physiognomists for composite adjectives with *sub-* (cf. 21.16.19 *subniger* and 22.16.23 *suffusculus* with the notes). As for skin colour, the fourth-century author of the treatise *de physiognomonia* says in § 79, after a general remark (*Colorum species in corporibus gentibus attributae sunt. Prout sunt igitur gentium ingenia, ita colorum similitudo noscenda est*): *Color niger levem, imbellem, timidum, versutum indicat* and: *color qui pallore deformatur, im-*

bellem, timidum eundemque tergiversatorem significat, si non aegritudo sit causa palloris.

caprinis oculis torvi In the passage about Persian prisoners just referred to (24.8.1), Julian calls those Persians *deformes illuvie capellas et taetras*. It is "the only application of the beast-metaphor to the Persians" (Wiedemann, 1986, 197, apparently not taking into account the present text), but should of course "not lead us to think that Amm. considered Persians to be animals". According to the Anonymus *de physiognomonia* 83, who quotes [ps.] Aristotle, goat's eyes are a sign of lust: *Idem dicit oculos caprinos libidini esse deditos: referri hoc ad caprum.* Cf. Serv. ad *Buc.* 3.8 *hircos id est capros libidinosa constat esse animalia* and see for the Persians' supposed wantonness the next section.

superciliis in semiorbium speciem curvatis iunctisque 'Curved in the form of half-circles.' Cf. *de physiogn.* 18 *Supercilia cum coeunt, tristem maxime hominem, sed et parum sapientem significant.* For *semiorbis* see the note ad 22.8.5.

non indecoribus barbis capillisque promissis hirsuti Procop. *Arc.* 7.8–9, speaking of novelties introduced by the factions of Blues and Greens, contrasts the different fashions in which Romans and Persians styled their hair, moustaches and beards: ἀπεχείροντο γὰρ αὐτὴν οὐδὲν ὁμοίως τοῖς ἄλλοις Ῥωμαίοις. τοῦ μὲν γὰρ μύστακος καὶ τοῦ γενείου οὐδαμῇ ἥπτοντο, ἀλλ' αὑτοῖς καταχομᾶν ἐπὶ πλεῖστον ὥσπερ οἱ Πέρσαι ἐς ἀεὶ ἤθελον.

gladiis cincti cernuntur Cf. J. *AJ* 18.45 (about Parthians) μαχαιροφορεῖν γὰρ ἔθος ἅπασιν.

quem Graecorum veterum morem abiecisse primos Athenienses Thucydides est auctor amplissimus True enough: Thuc. 1.6.1–3 Πᾶσα γὰρ ἡ Ἑλλὰς ἐσιδηροφόρει... ἐν τοῖς πρῶτοι δὲ Ἀθηναῖοι τόν τε σίδηρον κατέθεντο, but Amm. omits to mention that Thucydides regarded the new custom as a sign of effeminacy: ἀνειμένῃ τῇ διαίτῃ ἐς τὸ τρυφερώτερον μετέστησαν. Amm.'s implicit criticism of the Persians agrees more with Aristotle's *Pol.* 2.5.11 (1268 b 40), where the carrying of weapons by the Greeks of former times (ἐσιδηροφοροῦντό τε γὰρ οἱ Ἕλληνες) is cited as an example of oversimple and uncivilised laws (τοὺς γὰρ ἀρχαίους νόμους λίαν ἁπλοῦς εἶναι καὶ βαρβαρικούς) than with the idea expressed by Thucydides when quoted fully.
Thucydides' name occurs only twice in Amm.'s work, here and in 19.4.4 (the plague in Amida). See further the note ad 22.12.8 for a possible reference

to Thuc. 3.104 and cf. Fornara, 1992, 423-4. For *auctor est* + AcI, a phrase found often in historical prose, see Szantyr 359 and TLL II 1206.69 sqq.

6.76 *effusius plerique soluti in venerem* Amm. uses almost the same words concerning the Saracens in 14.4.4 (*incredibile est, quo ardore apud eos in venerem uterque solvitur sexus*). Cf. also Tac. *Hist.* 5.5.2 about the Jews: *proiectissima ad libidinem gens.* For *(ef)fusus* see the note ad 21.16.18.

aegreque contenti multitudine pelicum... pro opibus quisque asciscens matrimonia plura vel pauca Herodotus 1.135 had told the same story: γαμέουσι δὲ ἕκαστος αὐτῶν πολλὰς μὲν κουριδίας γυναῖκας, πολλῷ δ' ἔτι πλεῦνας παλλακὰς κτῶνται, as had Strabo 15.3.17 (733C): γαμοῦσι δὲ πολλὰς καὶ ἅμα παλλακὰς τρέφουσι πλείους. Cf. Sal. *Jug.* 80.6 about Moors and Numidians: *quia singuli pro opibus quisque quam plurumas uxores, denas alii, alii pluris habent, sed reges eo amplius.*
For *aegre* = *vix* cf. e.g. 14.8.2, 15.3.6 and see TLL I 943.48-60. *Matrimonia* is a clear example of abstractum pro concreto. See for this *figura* the notes ad 20.3.10 *exortus,* 21.6.6 *omnisque ordo* and 22.16.1 *quibus duas* and cf. Tac. *Dial.* 5.4 *asciscere necessitudines.*

puerilium stuprorum expertes This is in striking contrast to Herodotus 1.135: καὶ εὐπαθείας τε παντοδαπὰς πυνθανόμενοι ἐπιτηδεύουσι καὶ δὴ καὶ ἀπ' Ἑλλήνων μαθόντες παισὶ μίσγονται and Sextus Empiricus *P.* 1.152: παρὰ μὲν Πέρσαις ἔθος εἶναι ἀρρενομιξίαις χρῆσθαι, παρὰ δὲ Ῥωμαίοις ἀπαγορεύεσθαι νόμῳ τοῦτο πράττειν, but tallies with Curt. 10.1.26: *nec moris esse Persis mares ducere qui stupro effeminarentur.* In 31.9.5 Amm. condemns the Taifali in harsh terms for such practices: *hanc Taifalorum gentem... ac turpem obscenae vitae flagitiis ita accepimus mersam, ut apud eos nefandi concubitus foedere copulentur maribus puberes.*

caritas dispersa torpescit For *torpescere* 'to become paralyzed' cf. 14.6.23 (morbos) *ad quos vel sedandos omnis professio medendi torpescit.*

maximeque potandi aviditatem vitantes ut luem In remarkable contrast to Herodotus (1.133 οἴνῳ δὲ κάρτα προσκέαται and μεθυσκόμενοι δὲ ἑώθασι βουλεύεσθαι τὰ σπουδαιέστατα τῶν πρηγμάτων), who was "suivi en cela par tous les auteurs anciens" (Briant, 1996, 304, citing i.a. Hdt. 3.34, Plut. *Art.* 6.1, Ael. *VH* 12.1, Str. 15.3.20 [734C], Ath. 4.145 c, LXX Ju. 12.20, 13.1; cf. also Xen. *Cyr.* 8.8.10).

6.77 *sed venter unicuique velut solarium est* As Lindenbrog saw, the expression is ultimately derived from one of Plautus' lost plays, the *Boeotia*, quoted by Gellius 3.3.5: PARASITUS. *Ut illum di perdant primus qui horas repperit/ quique adeo primus statuit hic solarium,/ qui mihi comminuit misero articu-*

latim diem!/ nam me puero venter erat solarium. In *Variae* 11.46 Cassiodorus criticizes irregular meals as a sign of crudeness and inhumanity: *beluarum quippe ritus est ex ventris esurie horas sentire, et non habere certum, quod constat humanis usibus adtributum.*

quod inciderit, editur The subjunctive is iterative as in 30.4.17 *et si in circulo doctorum auctoris veteris inciderit nomen, piscis aut edulii peregrinum esse vocabulum arbitrantur.*

nec quisquam post satietatem superfluos sibi ingerit cibos Is this a veiled criticism of what Amm. had seen among his Roman contemporaries? Or a variation on the time-honoured maxim of μηδὲν ἄγαν? In any case it is a very general observation, without any specification as to the social class of the people spoken of.

According to Herodotus 1.133 the main dishes at Persian meals were few (σίτοισι δὲ ὀλίγοισι χρέωνται), but there were many sorts of desserts (ἐπιφορήμασι δὲ πολλοῖσι καὶ οὐκ ἀλέσι). Herodotus notes that this custom made the Persians say that Greeks were still hungry when they left the table, because they never had anything worth mentioning after the first course (καὶ διὰ τοῦτό φασι Πέρσαι τοὺς Ἕλληνας σιτεομένους πεινῶντας παύεσθαι, ὅτι σφι ἀπὸ δείπνου παραφορέεται οὐδὲν λόγου ἄξιον). If they had, Greeks would go on eating (εἰ δέ τι παραφέροιτο, ἐσθίοντας ἂν οὐ παύεσθαι) – as in fact happened, when a Greek by himself ate the meal which had been prepared for the satrap Ariobarzanes and nine other guests (Ath. 10.413 a-c, quoted, among other relevant texts, by Briant, 1996, 303). The special interest of Persians in desserts is also stressed by Xenophon in *Cyr.* 8.8.16 (ἀεὶ καινὰ ἐπιμηχανῶνται).

In *Cyr.* 8.8.9 Xenophon distinguishes between the Persians of old, who ate but one meal in the day (Καὶ μὴν πρόσθεν μὲν ἦν αὐτοῖς μονοσιτεῖν νόμιμον, ὅπως ὅλῃ τῇ ἡμέρᾳ χρῷντο καὶ εἰς τὰς πράξεις καὶ εἰς τὸ διαπονεῖσθαι) and the degenerated Persians of his own days, who did the same, but only seemingly (νῦν γε μὴν τὸ μὲν μονοσιτεῖν ἔτι διαμένει, ἀρχόμενοι δὲ τοῦ σίτου, ἡνίκαπερ οἱ πρωιαίτατα ἀριστῶντες μέχρι τούτου ἐσθίοντες καὶ πίνοντες διάγουσιν, ἔστεπερ οἱ ὀψιαίτατα κοιμώμεμοι). From a passage in Procopius (*Pers.* 1.14.34) one gets the impression that in the sixth century A.D. the custom of μονοσιτεῖν was still (or again) in use, at least in the army: αὐτοὶ μὲν σιτίοις ἐς δείλην ὀψίαν χρῆσθαι μόνον εἰώθασι, ʽΡωμαῖοι δὲ πρὸ τῆς μεσημβρίας. According to Strabo (15.3.18, [734C]), the daily food of young soldiers after their gymnastic exercises consisted of bread, barleycake, cardamum, grains of salt and roasted or boiled meat: ἡ δὲ καθ᾽ ἡμέραν δίαιτα ἄρτος μετὰ τὸ γυμνάσιον καὶ μᾶζα καὶ κάρδαμον καὶ ἁλῶν χόνδρος καὶ κρέα ὀπτὰ ἢ ἑφθὰ ἐξ ὕδατος.

For *ingerere* used of food see TLL VII 1.1549.26–45.

6.78 *immane quantum restricti* Amm. has a wide variety of adverbs or adverbial accusatives with *quantum*, such as *immensum* – (16.7.5, 16.12.61, 27.12.14, 29.6.1), *incredibile* – (17.12.17), *nimium* – (21.16.16, 22.9.4, 22.16.11). *Immane* – is found also in 23.6.50 and 24.4.2. Cf. Sal. *Hist.* 2.44 and see Szantyr 537. For *restrictus* cf. Tac. *Ann.* 15.48.3 *summum imperium non restrictum nec perseverum volunt.*

inter hostiles hortos gradientes nonnúmquäm et vinéta The hyperbaton of *vineta* is for the sake of the cursus (velox). For tetrasyllabic *nonnumquäm* cf. 14.5.5 *nonnúnquäm intepéscit*, 17.5.7 *urere nonnúnquäm et secáre* and 18.9.2 *nonnúnquäm foétens* and in general on the syllabication of *u* see Harmon 225–6.

secretarum artium In 29.1.7 (*motasque secretis artibus sortes*) and 30.5.11 (*asinum occidisse dicebatur ad usum artium secretarum*) the expression also refers to magical practices.

6.79 *nec stando mingens nec ad requisita naturae secedens facile visitur Persa* Amm. probably speaks from his own experience, although a reader is of course reminded of Hdt. 1.133 (σφι οὐκ ἐμέσαι ἔξεστι, οὐχὶ οὐρῆσαι ἀντίον ἄλλου) and Xen. *Cyr.* 1.2.16 (αἰσχρὸν δέ ἐστι καὶ τὸ ἰόντα που φανερὸν γενέσθαι ἢ τοῦ οὐρῆσαι ἕνεκα ἢ καὶ ἄλλου τινὸς τοιούτου). Cf. also Xen. *Cyr.* 8.8.11. Hes. *Op.* 727 μηδ' ἄντ' ἠελίου τετραμμένος ὀρθὸς ὀμείχειν e.q.s. is both a striking parallel to and an illuminating commentary on the present passage. See the notes of West ad loc. For the Persian taboo on urinating into a river see Hdt. 1.138 and Str. 15.3.16 (733C), with De Jong, 1997, 417–9. Plin. *Nat.* 28.69 observes that it was forbidden among the Magi to urinate on a person's shadow, presumably (so De Jong, 1997, 418) "because the shadow has a certain corporeal quality, and urinating on a person's shadow equals urinating on a person's body." De Jong, 1997, 418–9 also draws attention to the fact that the practice of urinating while standing is expressly condemned in several Pahlavi books (e.g. *AWN* 25.3, *MX* 2.39–41, *PhlRDd.* 11.3; cf. Williams, 1990, II, 144.4 for more references).

Stando is a perfect example of the use of the abl. gerundii as the equivalent of a present participle, for which see the note ad 20.4.22 *diu tacendo haesitantes*. It is neglected by Rolfe in his translation: "one seldom sees a Persian stop to pass water" (Hamilton's rendering is correct: "you will hardly ever see a Persian make water standing", as is that of Fontaine: "uriner debout").

6.80 *adeo autem dissoluti sunt* The ptc. *dissolutus* often has the overtone of effeminacy, as it does here as well as in 17.11.4 *caput digito uno scalpebat... ut dissolutum*. See TLL V 1.1501.66–75.

artuum laxitate vagoque incessu se iactitantes A very effective evocation of the swaggering Oriental. A well-mannered Roman walked modestly, cf. Sen. *Ep.* 40.14 *sapienti viro incessus modestior convenit* and Ps. Hil. *libell.* 11 p. 743 b *incessum* (viri) *esse simplicem, non iactatum aut fucatum.* For the rare substantive *laxitas* cf. 17.4.4 (Cambyses) *laxitate praepeditus indumentorum.* In this respect the Persians resemble the Gauls, who when drunk, *raptantur discursibus vagis* (15.12.4).

magis artifices quam fortes eminusque terribiles For *artifex* in general see the note ad 23.4.2 and for the meaning "master-schemer" (OLD) cf. 14.5.8 *in complicandis negotiis artifex dirus* and 27.9.2 *transferendaeque in alios invidiae artifex.* The battle-description in 25.1.17–18 may serve as an illustration of the phrase *eminus terribiles.*

abundantes inanibus verbis insanumque loquentes et ferum In 21.13.4 Amm. had presented a different picture of Persian nobles: *apud Persas nemo consiliorum est conscius praeter optimates taciturnos et fidos, apud quos silentii quoque colitur numen* (Justin 41.3.8 said of the Parthians that they were *natura taciti*). For *insanum loquentes* see TLL VII 1.1836.24. On *feritas* as a characteristic of barbarians see Seager 56 (who wrongly attributes the term *vesania* to this section).

magnidici et graves ac taetri The first adj. is rare. TLL VIII 104.42–5 quotes as the only parallels Pl. *Mil.* 923 and *Rud.* 515. For *graves Persae* Horace may have been the model: *Carm.* 1.2.22 *quo graves Persae melius perirent* and 3.5.4–5 *adiectis Britannis / imperio gravibusque Persis.* As regards *taeter*, in 22.8.42 the Scythians are said to live *ferarum taetro ritu*; in 24.8.1 captive Persians are called *deformes illuvie capellas et taetras.* Tacitus had used the adj. for the Jews (*Hist.* 5.8.2).

vitae necisque potestatem in servos et plebeios vindicantes obscuros Originally in Rome owners of slaves also had the absolute right to punish their slaves with death (cf. Wiedemann, 1981, 173, quoting Plut. *Cat. Ma.* 4.4 and D.Chr. 15.20), but in the course of time this right had been restricted (cf. e.g. *Cod. Theod.* 9.12.1). The summary execution of plebeians had been forbidden by the lex Valeria (traditionally dated to 509 B.C.), which brought legal recognition of the right of provocatio.

cutes vivis hominibus detrahunt particulatim vel solidas Procopius relates that once upon a time the Persian king Pacurius not only flayed Bassicius, a friend of the Armenian king Arsaces, but made a bag of his skin, filled it with chaff and suspended it from a high tree (Παχούριος δὲ Βασσιχίου μὲν τὸ δέρμα ἐκδείρας ἀσκόν τε αὐτὸ πεποιημένος καὶ ἀχύρων ἐμπλησάμενος ὅλον ἀπεχρέμασεν ἐπὶ δένδρου τινὸς ὑψηλοῦ λίαν, *Pers.* 1.5.28). However, his source for this, the History of the Armenians (ἡ τῶν Ἀρμενίων ἱστορία, *Pers.* 1.5.9), does not inspire much confidence. Neither does Tzetzes (*Chil.* 1.1.99–100), who mentions the death by flaying of the eunuch Petesaces in the time of the Median king Astyages.

That flaying was not considered to be a normal punishment in the Roman empire is clear from Amm.'s words and from the silence of the Theodosian Code on this issue. The fact that in the *passio s. Basilii presbyteri* 4 (BHG³ 242) the emperor Julian and some of his officers are accused of flaying alive the priest Basil of Ancyra (who miraculously recovered from this treatment), is one of the arguments against the reliability of this source (see Teitler, 1996, against Woods, 1992).

For the adverb cf. Sen. *Ep.* 24.14 *instrumenta excarnificandi particulatim hominis*. It is found also in 29.5.35, 31.7.2, 31.15.7.

nec ministranti apud eos famulo mensaeque astanti hiscere vel loqui licet vel spuere; ita praestratis pellibus labra omnium vinciuntur Seyfarth n. 137 points to Sen. *Ep.* 47.3 for a parallel: *at infelicibus servis movere labra ne in hoc quidem, ut loquantur, licet. Virga murmur omne conpescitur, et ne fortuita quidem verberibus excepta sunt, tussis, sternumenta, singultus*. Fontaine n. 268 (cf. n. 270 and 271), perhaps too ingeniously, sees in Amm.'s description of Persian customs here and in the following passages a veiled criticism of Roman norms and values: "Il se pourrait donc qu'ici – comme sans doute en bien d'autres passages de cette description critique du caractère et des moeurs des Perses, – Ammien vise indirectement des ecxès commis par son auditoire romain lui-même". The origin of the Persian custom, however, is perhaps to be sought in religious taboos. As De Jong, 1997, 420 observes, Amm.'s words may refer to the practice of eating 'in *bāj*' (MP *wāz*): "Zorastrians pray before and after meals. The prayers they say – known as *bāj* – are regarded as a single prayer; it is therefore not allowed to interrupt this prayer by talking during the meal. Similarly, it is considered a grave sin to speak while eating, both because it breaks the *bāj* and because it brings with it strong possibilities of polluting (the air and) the earth with pieces of undigested food, saliva and foul breath. The sin of breaking the *bāj* and speaking while eating is known as *drāyān-jōyisnīh*, usually translated as 'chattering while eating'. It is condemned in the strongest possible terms in many passages in the Pahlavi books" (see e.g. *PhlRDd* 20.4, *SnS* 5.2, *AWN* 23, *MX* 2.33–34). For *bāj* see Boyce-Kotwal, 1971.

Cf. further Menander Protector *exc. Rom.* 8 (ὁ δὲ Περσῶν πρεσβευτής... περιφρονήσας τὸν νόμον τῆς σιωπῆς τὸν ἰσχύοντα παρ' αὐτοῖς ἐν ταῖς ἑστιάσεσιν, ἐπιτροχάδην ἤρξατο διαλέγεσθαι, 'the Persian envoy began to discuss the matter rapidly, in defiance of the prevailing law in Persia which stipulates that there should be silence at dinner') and Theophylactus Simocatta

Hist. 5.5 (οὐ γὰρ εὐωχουμένοις θέμις τοῖς Πέρσαις διαλαλεῖν, 'it is a Persian custom not to talk at dinner').

Praestratis pellibus is not above suspicion. V's reading *prostratis* can be defended, as Fontaine does in n. 268, with a reference to 23.4.5 *fulmentum prosternitur ingens* (if that is the correct reading!). In any case, both with *prae-* and with *prostratis*, *pellibus* must refer to the bedding of the couches. In the light of the previous remarks about *bāj*, Valesius' note is highly interesting: *apud Persas labra famulorum... vincta fuisse pellibus, ita ut nec hiscere, nec loqui ac ne spuere quidem possent. Quod factum puto, ne famuli dapes, quas mensis inferebant, halitu suo inficerent.*

leges... contra ingratos et desertores Cf. Theophylactus Simocatta *Hist.* 2.5, **6.81** where mention is made of the Persian νόμος which forbade to readmit deserters into the city they had left (μὴ γὰρ οὖν εἰσοικίσασθαι τοὺς ῥιψάσπιδας Περσικὸν νόμον ἀνέχεσθαι). See also 24.5.3, quoted in the next note.

impendio formidatae For *impendio* see the note ad 20.7.1.

et abominandae aliae, per quas ob noxam unius omnis propinquitas perit In 24.5.3 Amm. gives an example of this practice (*corpora vidit suffixa patibulis multa necessitudinum eius, quem prodidisse civitatem Pirisabora rettulimus supra*), which is already found in Herodotus' account of Darius' measures against Intaphrenes (ἔλαβε αὐτόν τε τὸν Ἰνταφρένεα καὶ τοὺς παῖδας αὐτοῦ καὶ τοὺς οἰκηίους πάντας, 3.119). Cf. LXX *Es.* 8.12r σὺν τῇ πανοικίᾳ and Claudianus *in Eutr.* 2.478–9 (*rarus apud Medos regum cruor; unaque cuncto / poena manet generi*). For that matter, it was not an exclusively Persian custom, as Curt. 6.11.20 testifies: *legem Macedonum veriti, qua cautum erat ut propinqui eorum qui regi insidiati essent cum ipsis necarentur*. It was by no means unknown to the Romans either (cf. D.H. 8.80 καὶ ἐξ ἐκείνου τὸ ἔθος τοῦτο 'Ρωμαίοις ἐπιχώριον γέγονεν ἕως τῆς καθ' ἡμᾶς διατηρούμενον ἡλικίας, ἀφεῖσθαι τιμωρίας ἁπάσης τοὺς παῖδας, ὧν ἂν οἱ πατέρες ἀδικήσωσιν, ἐάν τε τυράννων ὄντες υἱοὶ τύχωσιν, ἐάν τε πατροκτόνων, ἐάν τε προδοτῶν, ὃ μέγιστόν ἐστι παρ' ἐκείνοις ἀδίκημα). Cicero condemned it (*ad Brut.* 1.15.11 *illud esse crudele, quod ad liberos, qui nihil meruerunt, poena pervenit*), but from Tac. *Ann.* 14.42–5 it is clear that in the first century A.D. it was still in use, at least as far as slaves were concerned (Tacitus relates that all 400 slaves of Pedanius Secundus were executed, when their master had been murdered by one of them).

parum alienis consiliis indigentes Like its counterpart *nimium*, for which see **6.82** the note ad 21.16.3, *parum* does not always imply excess ('too little'). Here *parum indigentes* is practically equivalent to *haud indigentes*. Cf. 14.1.6 about Gallus' spies: *homines quidam ignoti vilitate ipsa parum cavendi* and 28.4.2

about Olybrius' womanizing *vitium parum quidem nocens rei communi, sed in alto iudice maculosum*.

unde nostram consuetudinem rident, quae interdum facundos iurisque publici peritissimos post indoctorum collocat terga The personification *consuetudo collocat* is characteristic of the ornate style favoured by Amm. in his digressions. Cf. *finxit vetustas* in this same section and in general Den Hengst, 1992, 44–5. Perhaps the most remarkable word in this phrase is *interdum*. In itself its meaning is clear "at times" (Rolfe; note that the word is not rendered in Hamilton's translation). However, the situation as described here was quite common in the later Roman empire. Most judges were not chosen for their knowledge of the law and many of them were not learned in the law at all, but their inadequacy, as Jones 500 observes, "was to some extent remedied by the institution of assessors, or judicial advisors. Every magistrate with judicial duties had an assessor, and some had more" (see his n. 70 for evidence). If these assessors were lacking, there was ground for complaint, as can be inferred from Lact. *mort. pers.* 22.5 (*iudices militares humanitatis litterarum rudes sine adsessoribus in provincias inmissi*). Synesius' words in *De Regno* 20 (quoted by Wagner-Erfurdt) aptly illustrate the practice under discussion. However, that passage should be seen in its right context. Synesius' criticism (unlike that of Amm.'s Persians here) is not directed against the custom which made assessors sit behind magistrates and senators (νομίμων ἀνδρῶν ὀπίσω θακούντων), but against the fact that these magistrates and senators were barbarians.

As is clear from his wording (*ad iudicandum, ob iniquitatem iudicis* and *iudex alius*), Amm. here only speaks of judges, not, as in 30.4.2 (*iudicum advocatorumque pravitate*) e.q.s. of both judges and lawyers. The passage of Cicero (*de Orat.* 1.253) and Quintilian (*Inst.* 12.3.4), adduced as parallels by Fontaine in his n. 270, concern lawyers and are therefore, strictly speaking, not relevant.

nam quod supersidere corio damnati ob iniquitatem iudicis iudex alius cogitabatur The passage evokes Herodotus' report (5.25.1–2) of Cambyses' cruel treatment of Sisamnes, the father of Otanes, as a punishment for taking a bribe and perverting the course of justice. The anecdote is also handed down to us by Valerius Maximus (6.3 ext. 3), while Diodorus Siculus (15.10.1) tells a similar story (Diodorus transfers the event to the reign of Artaxerxes and speaks of more than one judge). If Zonaras 8.6 is to be believed, not only a Persian king was capable of the savagery mentioned here, but also Pyrrhus of Epirus.

For "anknüpfendes und adversatives *nam*" (Szantyr 505–6) see the note ad 22.8.8 and for a modern view Kroon, 1995, 152 sqq. The use of the frequentativum *cogitare* instead of *cogere* is very rare. Blomgren 171–3 discusses

Amm.'s predilection for frequentativa and mentions one parallel for *cogitare* with this meaning, viz. 15.5.16 (Silvanus) *in consilia cogitabatur extrema*.

aut finxit vetustas It may seem likely that Amm. here refers to Herodotus (so Sabbah 67), but it is by no means certain, given the fact that not only Herodotus, but also Valerius Maximus and Diodorus Siculus tell the anecdote.

militari cultu ac disciplina proludiisque continuis rei castrensis et armaturae Cf. for the terminology 14.11.3 (*per multiplicem armaturae scientiam agilitatemque membrorum inter cotidiana proludia exercitus consulto consilio cognitos*), 16.5.10 (*cum exercere proludia disciplinae castrensis philosophus cogeretur ut princeps*) and 21.6.7 (*artiumque armaturae pedestris perquam scientissimus*), with the notes.

6.83

quam saepe formavimus In a lost book, apparently. For *formare* in the sense of 'to describe' cf. § 13 *utque geographici stili formarunt*.

equitatus virtute confisi By stressing the importance of cavalry in the Persian army and depicting its infantry as a bunch of slaves (*turba tamquam addicta perenni servitio*), Amm. points to a fundamental and long-standing difference between the Roman forces and those of their eastern enemies (cf. Crump, 1975, 39–40). What Herodian (4.10.3) had said with respect to the time of the Parthians, applied to the Sasanian period too: εἶναι δὲ ῾Ρωμαίοις μὲν πεζὸν στρατὸν καὶ τὴν διὰ δοράτων συστάδην μάχην ἀνανταγώνιστον, Παρθυαίοις δὲ ἵππον τε πολλὴν καὶ τὴν διὰ τόξων εὔστοχον ἐμπειρίαν. It would seem, however, that "die Sasanidische Armee zählte mehr Fussvolk als die parthische" (Widengren, 1976, 296).

Julian was to find out on several occasions how dangerous the Persian cavalrymen were when they used their hit-and-run tactics (cf. 24.7.7, 25.1.18 and 25.3.2–4). On other occasions (cf. 24.6.8) he had to meet a frontal attack of the mail-clad horsemen (the cataphracts; see for them the note ad 20.7.2).

ubi desudat nobilitas omnis et splendor Hamilton's translation of *desudat* ("serve") is too flat. It is self-evident that *nobilitas omnis et splendor* served in the cavalry, rather than as foot-soldiers. What Amm. wants to stress is that, when they served as cavalrymen, "all the nobles and men of rank [had to] undergo hard service" (Rolfe).

It goes almost without saying that all the nobles were cavalrymen in the Persian army. The reverse, 'all the cavalrymen were nobles', is probably not true. The major part was perhaps not even free. Unfortunately this has to be deduced from evidence concerning the Parthians, because information about the social composition of the cavalry in Sasanian times is lacking ("Das Dienstmänner und Hörige der Vasallen immer noch das Gros der Truppen ausmachten, können wir aber bei der grossen Kontinuität zwischen Parther- und Sasanidenzeit getrost annehmen", Widengren, 1976, 296). Justin 41.2, speaking of the Parthians, says: *Exercitum non, ut aliae gentes, liberorum, sed maiorem partem servitiorum* ('serfs' rather than 'slaves') *habent... Hos pari ac liberos suos cura et equitare et sagittare magna industria docent*. He also informs us that in a certain battle *cum L milia equitum occurrerent, soli CCCC liberi fuere*.

pedites enim in speciem myrmillonum contecti iussa faciunt ut calones The last words (*iussa faciunt ut calones*) express the deprecation in this phrase, rather than the comparison with the *myrmillo* (a heavily armed gladiator with a rectangular shield, wearing a visored, Gallic helmet with the image of a fish for a crest; cf. Festus, p. 358 L). It is true that *myrmillo* can be used as an insult (cf. Cic. *Phil.* 6.13), but in 16.12.49 Amm. speaks appreciatively of Roman soldiers who covered themselves like these gladiators (*seque in modum myrmillonis operiens*). In 24.6.8 we catch a glimpse of the equipment of the Persian infantry: *manipuli... peditum contecti scutis oblongis et curvis, quae texta vimine et coriis crudis gestantes densius se commovebant*.
Authors as wide apart in time as Xenophon (*Cyr.* 2.3.14) and Agathias (3.23.1) testify to the hardships of the Persian *pedites*, whose contribution to warfare, although less highly thought of than that of the cavalry, was often considerable, e.g. during sieges (cf. 19.6.6 *duo tamen aggeres celsi Persarum peditum manu erecti*).

sequiturque semper haec turba tamquam addicta perenni servitio nec stipendiis aliquando fulta nec donis In the fourth century the Persian infantry consisted no doubt of peasant-soldiers, as it did in the time of Procopius (*Pers.* 1.14.25: τὸ γὰρ πεζὸν ἅπαν οὐδὲν ἄλλο ἢ ὅμιλος ἀγροίκων οἰκτρῶν). The conditions of service of these foot-soldiers will have been practically the same as in the days of Herodian, who relates that the Persians did not have a paid army like the Romans, nor permanent standing garrisons trained in military techniques, but were drafted into the army whenever the king gave the order (οὐ γὰρ δὴ μισθοφόροις χρῶνται στρατιώταις οἱ βάρβαροι ὥσπερ 'Ρωμαῖοι, οὐδὲ στρατόπεδα ἔχουσι συνεστῶτα καὶ μένοντα, πολέμου τέχναις ἐγγεγυμνασμένα, ἀλλὰ πᾶν τὸ πλῆθος τῶν ἀνδρῶν, ἔσθ' ὅπῃ καὶ τῶν γυναίκων, ἐπὰν κελεύσῃ βασιλεύς, ἀθροίζεται, 6.5.3; cf. 6.7.1 ὄχλος μᾶλλον ἢ στρατός).
For *nec stipendiis...fulta* cf. *Cod. Theod.* 7.22.11 *filii primipilarium...qui ingressi legitimos annos nullis stipendiis fulciuntur*. The model may have been Cic. *Rab. Post.* 43 *equitem Romanum...labentem excepit, corruere non sivit, fulsit et sustinuit re, fortuna, fide*.

praeter eas, quas abunde perdomuit In the course of his narrative Amm. mentions several of these *gentes* who fought with the Persians: Chionitae, Gelani, Albani, Cuseni and Segestani (cf. e.g. 17.5.1, 18.6.22 and 19.2.3).

sub iugum haec natio miserat De Jonge offers a long list of parallels for pluperfect indicative in the apodosis of an irrealis in his note ad 14.3.2.

ni bellis civilibus externisque assidue vexarentur The principal external adversary of the Persians in the third and fourth century was, as far as we know, the Roman empire. Civil wars and rebellions occurred sporadically during the long reigns of Sapor I (240-270) and especially Sapor II (309-379). In the intermediate period they were more frequent (see for the political history of Persia under the Sasanians Frye, 1983, but presumably Amm.'s remark is not only intended for the Sasanian period. Justin (42.4.16) called civil war among the Parthians endemic *(Parthiae... in qua iam quasi solemne est reges parricidas haberi)*, while Philo *(De spec. leg.* 3.17), speaking of Persians, but perhaps referring to Parthians, said: ἀεὶ γὰρ στρατείαις καὶ μάχαις εἰσὶ κτείνοντες καὶ κτεινόμενοι καὶ τοτὲ μὲν τοὺς πλησιοχώροις κατατρέχοντες τοτὲ δὲ τοὺς ἐπανισταμένους ἀμυνόμενοι, πολλοὶ δὲ πολλαχόθεν ἐπανίστανται. Cf. further Plut. *Luc.* 36.6 and above, section 6.

indumentis... lumine colorum fulgentibus vario Sextus Empiricus (*P.* 1.148) **6.84** regarded Persian clothes as unseemly for Greeks and Romans (Πέρσαι μὲν ἀνθοβαφεῖ ἐσθῆτι καὶ ποδήρει χρῆσθαι νομίζουσιν εὐπρεπὲς εἶναι, ἡμεῖς δὲ ἀπρεπές). Other ancient writers were not so negative, but many of them did express amazement at what they considered the strange and cumbersome Persian attire, which, according to Justin 41.2.4, in the course of time had become more luxurious than it had originally been *(vestis olim sui moris; posteaquam accessere opes ut Medis perlucida ac fluida;* cf. Xen. *Cyr.* 1.3.2, quoted below).
The clothes of the Persians (and of other oriental peoples) sometimes were adorned with gold or jewels. Cf. e.g. Curt. 3.3.13 (with Atkinson), about the body-guard of the Persian king: *illi vestem auro distinctam habebant manicatasque tunicas gemmis etiam adornatas*, and Hdn. 4.11.3, speaking of Parthians who welcomed Caracalla in one of their cities: ἐσθῆτί τε χρυσῷ καὶ βαφαῖς διαφόροις πεποικιλμένον. Especially the bright colours of the clothes *(lumine colorum fulgentibus vario)* caused quite a stir. Aelian (*NA* 5.21) compared them with the diverse colours of a peacock: ὑπὲρ τὴν τῶν Μήδων ἐσθῆτα καὶ τὰ τῶν Περσῶν ποικίλματα τὴν ἑαυτοῦ στολὴν ἀποδεικνύμενος, while Strabo (15.3.19, [734C]) observed that the colours changed with the seasons, at least in the case of the upper echelons of the Persian army: ἐσθὴς δὲ τοῖς ἡγεμόσι μὲν ἀναξυρὶς τριπλῆ, χιτὼν δὲ χειριδωτὸς διπλοῦς ἕως γόνατος, ὁ ὑπενδύτης μὲν λευκός, ἀνθινὸς δ' ὁ ἐπάνω·

ἱμάτιον δὲ θέρους μὲν πορφυροῦν ἢ ἀνθινόν, χειμῶνος δ' ἀνθινόν ("The garb of the commanders consists of three-ply trousers, and of a double tunic, with sleeves, that reaches to the knees, the under garment being white and the upper vari-coloured. In summer they wear a purple or vari-coloured cloak, in winter a vari-coloured one only", Jones).

Garments like the ones worn by Persians and Parthians could be rather annoying for anyone trying to run. This we learn from Hdn. 4.15.3 πρός τε τὸ φυγεῖν ἢ διῶξαι, εἰ δέοι, ὑπὸ τῆς περὶ τοῖς σκέλεσιν ἐσθῆτος χαύνως παρηωρημένης ἐμποδίζονται ("and furthermore, they are hindered from running away or pursuing, assuming this were necessary, by the loose folds of their clothes hanging around their legs", Whittaker). See also Hdn. 4.11.6 and Manil. 4.750–1 *laxo Persis amictu / vestibus ipsa suis haerens* ("loose-robed Persia, a nation hampered by its raiment", Goold).

inter calceos... et verticem The Persians wore tower-like hats on their heads and on their feet deep double shoes according to Strabo 15.3.19 (734C) (περὶ δὲ τῇ κεφαλῇ πίλημα πυργωτόν... ὑπόδημα κοῖλον διπλοῦν).

armillis uti monilibusque aureis et gemmis, praecipue margaritis, quibus abundant In his *Anabasis* Xenophon speaks of the wearing of necklaces and bracelets by Persian nobles (1.5.8 ἔνιοι δὲ καὶ στρεπτοὺς περὶ τοῖς τραχήλοις καὶ ψέλια περὶ ταῖς χερσίν and 1.8.29 καὶ στρεπτὸν δ' ἐφόρει καὶ ψέλια καὶ τἆλλα ὥσπερ οἱ ἄριστοι Περσῶν). Incidentally, in the *Cyropaedia* he claims that this was a Median rather than a Persian practice (1.3.2 ταῦτα γὰρ πάντα Μηδικά ἐστι, καὶ οἱ πορφυροῖ χιτῶνες καὶ οἱ κάνδυες καὶ οἱ στρεπτοὶ οἱ περὶ τῇ δέρῃ καὶ τὰ ψέλια τὰ περὶ ταῖς χερσίν, ἐν Πέρσαις δὲ τοῖς οἴκοι καὶ νῦν ἔτι πολὺ καὶ ἐσθῆτες φαυλότεραι καὶ δίαιται εὐτελέστεραι). Cf. Iust. 3.3.13 *illi* (sc. the so-called Immortals in the Persian army) *aureos torques... habebant*. Neither Xenophon nor Justin mentions pearls when speaking of necklaces or bracelets, but Chares of Mitylene, quoted by Athenaeus (3, 93 d), does: κατασκευάζουσι δ' ἐξ αὐτῶν ὁρμίσκους τε καὶ ψέλια περὶ τὰς χεῖρας καὶ τοὺς πόδας; περὶ ἃ σπουδάζουσιν Πέρσαι καὶ Μῆδοι καὶ πάντες Ἀσιανοὶ πολὺ μᾶλλον τῶν ἐκ χρυσίου γεγενημένων. Apparently for Persians pearls were still in use as ornaments in Late Antiquity, for Procopius *Pers.* 1.4.14 tells us that the Persian king Perozes (459–484) used to wear a pearl in his right ear (in an excursion Procopius relates the amusing story of how this exceptionally beautiful pearl came into the king's possession, *Pers.* 1.4.15–31). Cf. further the anecdote told by Amm. in 22.4.8, about the Roman soldier in Maximianus' army who found a *sacculum Parthicum, in quo erant margaritae* while pillaging a camp of the Persian king.

post Lydiam victam et Croesum In 547 or 546 B.C. (cf. Hdt. 1.84 ff.). Avienus in his *descriptio orbis terrarum* 1257–8 also sees a connection between the conquest of Lydia and the Persian craving for gold and jewels:

dives in his mos est iam longi temporis saecli
ex quo Maeoniam bello trivere cruento.

Cf. also Iust. 41.2.4, quoted above, but Rommel, 1930, 1686 is probably right in observing "(die) Beziehung zur Unterwerfung der Lydier ist natürlich Konstruktion".

super ortu lapidis huius Viz. the *margarita,* a feminine noun in Amm., as in most other Latin authors (the word is of oriental origin; sometimes we find *margaritum*); cf. TLL VIII 391.11 sqq.

6.85

In Latin the most extensive passage on the origin of pearls is to be found in Pliny's *Natural History* (9.107–124). Next in length is the passage in Solinus (53.23–27), whom Amm. has clearly followed, as the following notes will show. We can only guess at the reason why Amm. inserts this miniature digression on pearls here. Could it be a veiled allusion to the beginning of the hostilities between Persia and Rome during the reign of Constantine mentioned in 25.4.23 and told at greater length by Amm. in the lost books (*ut dudum rettulimus plene*)? It was part of the pagan and anti-Constantine tradition that Constantine provoked the hostility of Sapor II because of his greed. A philosopher, Metrodorus, had visited India and offered the emperor pearls which the king of India had given to him. Metrodorus told Constantine that he had sent part of the Indian king's gift along the land route through Persia and that they had been stolen during transport. That was the reason why Constantine haughtily reclaimed the stolen pearls as his property. The digression here, at the beginning of the actual campaign by Julian, might be a subtle reminder as to who was the real *auctor belli* and what had been his reasons for disturbing the peace between Rome and Persia.

apud Indos et Persas margaritae repperiuntur Amm. speaks in general terms, other authors are more specific as to the places in the East where pearls were to be found (see for such places in the West below, ad § 88). In *Nat.* 9.106 the elder Pliny gives the following survey: *Indicus maxime has* (sc. margaritas) *mittit oceanus... Indis quoque in insulas petuntur et admodum paucas* ("to procure them for the Indians as well, men go to the islands-and those quite few in number", Rackham). *Fertilissima est Taprobane* (i.e. Ceylon) *et Stoidis... item Perimula* (to be sought in the Street of Malacca), *promunturium Indiae. Praecipue autem laudantur circa Arabiam in Persico sinu maris Rubri*. Elsewhere in his work he also occasionaly mentions these places (e.g. in *Nat.* 6.81, 6.110 and 12.84).

According to Athenaeus 3.93 c, Chares of Mitylene, a companion of Alexander the Great, wrote the following: θηρευέται δὲ κατὰ τὴν Ἰνδικὴν θάλασσαν, ὡσαύτως δὲ καὶ κατὰ τὴν Ἀρμενίαν (this reading is disputed, cf. Rommel,

1930, 1688) καὶ Περσιχὴν καὶ Σουσιανὴν καὶ Βαβυλωνίαν. Strabo (16.3.7, [767C]) quotes another of Alexander's followers, Nearchus, who wrote about an (anonymous) island at the beginning of the Persian Gulf where many valuable pearls were found (λέγει δὲ καὶ ἐν ἀρχῇ τοῦ Περσιχοῦ παράπλου νῆσον, ἐν ᾗ μαργαρίτης πολὺς καὶ πολυτίμητός ἐστιν) – it must be the same island to which Arrian, also citing Nearchus, refers in *Ind.* 38.3: ὑπὸ δὲ τὴν ἔω ἐς ἄλλην νῆσον πλεύσαντες ὁρμίζονται οἰκεομένην· ἵνα καὶ μαργαρίτην θηρᾶσθαι λέγει Νέαρχος, κατάπερ ἐν τῇ Ἰνδῶν θαλάσσῃ, and it should perhaps be identified with the island mentioned, according to Ath. 3.93 d-e, by Isidorus Charax in his *Description of Parthia* (κατὰ τὸ Περσιχὸν πέλαγος νῆσόν φησιν εἶναί τινα, ἔνθα πλείστην μαργαρῖτιν εὑρίσκεσθαι).

Aelian in his *On Animals* first calls the *margarita* a nursling of the Red Sea (ὁ... μαργαρίτης θρέμμα μέντοι τῆς Ἐρυθρῆς θαλάττης καὶ οὗτός ἐστι, *NA* 10.13), but later (*NA* 15.8) also speaks of pearls from India: Ὁ δὲ Ἰνδὸς μάργαρος (ἄνω γὰρ εἶπον περὶ τοῦ Ἐρυθραίου), referring, as Pliny does, to the island and town of Perimula. As to the Red Sea, the author of the *Periplus Maris Erythraei* mentions pearls a couple of times (59 and 61, where the word πινιχόν is used instead of μαργαρίτης and the like; cf. also § 35). In Solinus the digression on pearls is part of his description of Taprobane.

permixtione roris anni tempore praestituto conceptae Amm., like Pliny and Solinus before him, poetically depicts the creation of pearls as the result of a kind of copulation during which sea-shells were inseminated with dew. Cf. Plin. *Nat.* 9.107 *Has (sc. conchas) ubi genitalis anni stimularit hora,... impleri roscido conceptu tradunt* and Sol. 53.23 *certo anni tempore luxuriante conceptu sitiunt rorem.* Later Isidorus (*Etym.* 16.10.1) followed suit: *gignitur autem de caelesti rore, quem certo anni tempore cocleae hauriunt.*

This version is of course rather fanciful, like the similar story of Aelian (*NA* 10.13), who openly says so: τίκτεσθαί γε αὐτὸν τερατολογοῦσιν ("they tell a marvellous story of how it is produced", Scholfield). A totally different tradition is represented by Tertullian. In his view pearls, despite their beautiful name, were nothing more than wastrels and warts: *Quodsi concha illa aliquid intrinsecus pustulat, vitium magis eius debet esse quam gloria. Et licet margaritum vocetur, non aliud tamen intellegendum quam conchae illius aliqua dura et rotunda verruca* (Tert. *cult. fem.* 1.6.2) – Tertullian's remark corresponds better to modern research than the remarks of Amm. and the other cited authors; cf. Cunningham in the *Encyclopaedia Britannica*: "the cause of pearl-formation is in most cases, perhaps in all, the dead body of a minute parasite within the tissues of a mollusc, around which nacreous deposit is secreted".

cupientes enim velut coitum quendam humores ex lunari aspergine capiunt densius oscitando Cf. Plin. *Nat.* 9.107 *pandentes se quadam oscitatione* and

Sol. 53.23 *velut maritum, cuius desiderio hiant: et cum maxime liquitur lunaris imber, oscitatione quadam hauriunt umorem cupitum.*

exindeque gravidulae edunt minutas binas aut ternas vel uniones Cf. Plin. *Nat.* 9.107 *gravidas postea eniti* (sc. conchas tradunt) and Sol. 53.23 *sic concipiunt gravidaeque fiunt.* As to the number of pearls, Aelian asserts that some shells contained as many as twenty (*NA* 10.13 εὑρεθείη δ' ἂν καὶ ἐν κόγχῃ μεγίστῃ μικρὸς καὶ ἐν μικρᾷ μέγας· καὶ ἡ μὲν οὐδένα ἔχει, ἡ δὲ οὐ πέρα ἑνός, πολλαὶ δὲ καὶ πολλούς· εἰσὶ δὲ οἳ λέγουσι καὶ εἴκοσι προσπεφυκέναι μιᾷ κόγχῃ).

uniones ideo sic appellatas, quod evisceratae conchulae singulas aliquotiens pariunt, sed maiores Pliny and other Latin authors often use *unio* merely as a synonym of *margarita* (so e.g. *Nat.* 9.109, 9.111 and Suet. *Nero* 31.2). In *Nat.* 9.112 he gives an explanation of the term which is in line with that practice. According to Pliny pearls vary so much in size, colour, weight etc., *ut nulli duo reperiantur indiscreti*: *unde nomen unionum Romanae scilicet inposuere deliciae, nam id apud Graecos non est, ne apud barbaros quidem inventores eis aliud quam margaritae.* This statement is clearly in disagreement with the present text, in which Amm. again follows Sol.: *numquam duo simul reperiuntur: inde unionibus nomen datum* (53.27). Isidorus *Etym.* 16.10.1 agrees with Amm.: *Ex quibus margaritis quidam uniones vocantur, aptum nomen habentes, quod tantum unus, numquam duo vel plures simul reperiantur.*

idque indicium est aetheria potius derivatione quam saginis pelagi hos oriri fetus et vesci, quod The use of the word *sagina* makes it practically certain that Amm. follows Solinus, who had written *de saginae qualitate reddunt habitus unionum... ita magis de caelo quam de mari partus habent* (53.24). Solinus imitated Pliny *Nat.* 9.107 *Ex eo quippe constare, caelique eis maiorem societatem esse quam maris.* **6.86**

guttae matutini roris isdem infusae claros efficiunt lapillos et teretes, vespertini vero flexuosos contra et rutilos et maculosos interdum Compared with Pliny and Solinus Amm. is verbose. Cf. Plin. *Nat.* 9.107 *inde nubilum trahi colorem aut pro claritate matutina serenum* and Sol. 53.25 *quotiens excipiunt matutini aeris semen, fit clarior margarita, quotiens vespere, fit obscurior.* Isid. *Etym.* 16.10.1 elaborates further: *meliores autem candidae margaritae quam quae flavescunt. Illas enim aut iuventus aut matutini roris conceptio reddit candidas; has senectus vel vespertinus aer gignit obscuras.*

minima autem vel magna pro qualitate haustuum figurantur casibus variatis Cf. Sol. 53.25 *quantoque magis hauserit, tanto magis proficit lapidum magnitudo*; Plin. *Nat.* 9.107 *si tempestive satientur, grandescere et partus.*

conclusae vero saepissime metu fulgurum inanescunt aut debilia pariunt aut certe vitiis diffluunt abortivis The corresponding passage in Solinus runs: *si repente micaverit coruscatio, intempestivo metu comprimuntur, clausaeque subita formidine vitia contrahunt abortiva; aut enim perparvuli fiunt scrupuli aut inanes* (53.25). The idea that thunderstorms and lightning had a baneful influence on germinating life can also be found in Arist. *HA* 6.2, 559 b and Plin. *Nat.* 10.152.

Remarkably, in Ath. 3.93 e we find a totally different story, derived from Isidorus of Charax, according to whom thunderstorms and heavy rainfall produce, not a few imperfect pearls, but in fact great quantities of the finest size and quality: φασὶ δ' ὅταν βρονταὶ συνεχεῖς ὦσι καὶ ὄμβρων ἐκχύσεις, τότε... πλείστην γίγνεσθαι μαργαρῖτιν καὶ εὐμεγέθη. Cf. Aelian *NA* 10.13 τίκτεσθαί γε αὐτὸν τερατολογοῦσιν ὅταν ταῖς κόγχαις ἀνεῳγμέναις ἐπιλάμψωσιν αἱ ἀστραπαί.

6.87 *capturas autem difficiles et periculosas* See for the various difficulties and dangers with which pearl fishers were confronted Ael. *NA* 10.20, Ath. 3, 94 b, Plin. *Nat.* 9.110 and Sol. 53.27; cf. Rommel, 1930, 1689–91.

amplitudines pretiorum Just as in modern times, pearls in Antiquity were very expensive indeed. Aelian assures us that pearls were so highly esteemed that many of those who traded in them became very rich (Ael. *NA* 10.13 καὶ πλούσιοί γε ἐξ αὐτῶν ἐγένοντο οὐ μὰ Δία ὀλίγοι οἷς ἐντεῦθέν ἐστιν ὁ βίος), while according to Pliny they were the most precious valuables in the world: *Principium ergo columenque omnium rerum pretii margaritae tenent (Nat.* 9.106). He cites some striking examples to prove his point (i.a. the pearls of Lollia Paulina, Caligula's wife, which, together with her emeralds, had cost 40 million sesterces, and those of Cleopatra, worth 10 million sesterces, 9.117–21), but he could have referred to others, e.g. Suet. *Jul.* 50, about the pearl of 6 million sesterces which Caesar presented to Servilia. Cf. further Ath. 3.93 b (quoting Androsthenes): αὕτη δ' ἐστὶ πολυτελὴς κατὰ τὴν Ἀσίαν καὶ πωλεῖται περὶ Πέρσας τε καὶ τοὺς ἄνω τόπους πρὸς χρυσίον and 3.93 d (quoting Chares): περὶ ἃ (sc. necklaces and chains made of pearls) σπουδάζουσι Πέρσαι καὶ Μῆδοι καὶ πάντες Ἀσιανοὶ πολὺ μᾶλλον τῶν ἐκ χρυσίου γεγενημένων.

circa devios scopulos et marinorum canum receptacula These sea-hounds ('sharks') are also mentioned among the dangers for divers by Plin. *Nat.* 9.110 *inter scopulos maior pars* (sc. concharum) *invenitur, in alto quoque comitantur marinis canibus* and Sol. 53.27 *inter scopulos aut inter marinos canes plurimum delitescant.* According to Aelian (*NA* 1.55 Κυνῶν θαλαττίων τρία γένη) and Oppian (*H.* 1.373–4 καὶ κύνες ἁρπακτῆρες ἀναιδέες; ἐν δὲ κύνεσσι / τριχθαδίη γενεή) there were three kinds of them. In Procopius' story of Perozes' pearl (*Pers.* 1.4.17–31) the fisherman who captured the precious gem himself fell victim to a shark (κύνα δὲ θαλάσσιον, § 19).

quod genus gemmae etiam in Britannici secessibus maris gigni legique licet dignitate suppari non ignoramus Fontaine n. 282 rightly points to Tac. *Ag.* 12.6 as the source for this piece of information: *Gignit et Oceanus margarita, sed subfusca ac liventia*. It looks as if Tacitus' *sed subfusca ac liventia* is shortened to *licet dignitate suppari* in Amm. However, since *suppar* in Amm. always means 'of almost equal standard' (15.8.12, 17.13.24, 22.15.10, 26.10.8, 31.2.21), the correction of Vm3 *dispari* is a decided improvement. The inferior quality of British pearls is mentioned also in Plin. *Nat.* 9.116 *In Britannia parvos atque decolores nasci certum est* and in Ael. *NA* 15.8 γίνεται δὲ καὶ κατὰ τὸν Ἑσπέριον ὠκεανὸν, ἔνθα ἡ Βρεττανικὴ νῆσός ἐστι; δοκεῖ δὲ πως χρυσωπότερος ἰδεῖν εἶναι, τὰς τε αὐγὰς ἀμβλυτέρας ἔχειν καὶ σκοτωδεστέρας ("though this kind has a more golden appearance, and a duller, duskier sheen", Scholfield). It does not occur in Solinus.

6.88

Apart from India, Persia (§ 85) and Britain (the Scotch pearl-fishery still existed in the nineteenth century), there were other places where pearls came from in Antiquity (cf. Plin. *Nat.* 9.115 *In nostro mari reperiri solebant crebrius circa Bosporum Thracium...Acarnania...Arabicis...circa Actium...in Mauretaniae maritimis* and Ael. *NA* 15.8 γίνεσθαι δέ φησιν Ἰόβας καὶ ἐν τῷ κατὰ Βόσπορον πορθμῷ, καὶ τοῦ Βρεττανικοῦ ἡττᾶσθαι αὐτόν, τῷ δὲ Ἰνδῷ καὶ τῷ Ἐρυθραίῳ μηδὲ τὴν ἀρχὴν ἀντικρίνεσθαι). Amm. no doubt knew this, and he could once again have demonstrated his knowledge (*non ignoramus*) by elaborating on it. But the time had come to bring the excursus on the origin of the pearls to a close. After all, it was only a digression within a digression and it should not be too long (*Restat, ut super ortu lapidis huius pauca succinctius explicentur*, § 85). Nobody who had read his learned excursus on Persia would regard him as an ignoramus.

Bibliography

This is not an exhaustive or selective list of handbooks, monographs and articles pertaining to the study of Ammianus Marcellinus. It only registers all publications referred to in the commentary after the manner described in section 3 of the *Legenda*. *RE*-articles are cited after the date of the second 'Halbband'.

Adler, M., 'Kaiser Julian und die Juden', in: R. Klein (ed.), *Julian Apostata*, Darmstadt 1978, 48–111 (translation of 'The Emperor Julian and the Jews', *The Jewish Quarterly Review* 5 [1893] 591–651).

Alföldi, A., 'Die Ausgestaltung des monarchischen Zeremoniells am römischen Kaiserhofe', *MDAI(R)* 49 (1934) 3–118 = *Die monarchische Repräsentation im römischen Kaiserreiche*, Darmstadt 1980^3, 3–118, cited as Alföldi, 1980^3.

Alföldi, A., 'Die Hauptereignisse der Jahre 253–261 n. Chr. im Orient im Spiegel der Münzprägung', *Berytus* 4 (1937) 41–68.

Alföldi, A., 'Some Portraits of Julianus Apostata', *AJA* 66 (1962) 403–405 = 'Einige Porträts des Kaisers Julian Apostata', in: R. Klein (ed.), *Julian Apostata*, Darmstadt 1978, 298–304, cited as Alföldi, 1978.

Al-Khalaf, M., and K. Kohlmeyer, 'Untersuchungen zu ar-Raqqa-Nikephorion/Callinicum', *MDAI(D)* 2 (1985) 133–162.

Altheim, F., and R. Stiehl, *Geschichte Mittelasiens im Altertum*, Berlin 1970.

Anderson, J.G.C., 'Pompey's Campaign against Mithridates', *JRS* 12 (1922) 99–105.

André, J., and J. Filliozat, *L'Inde vue de Rome. Textes latins de l'Antiquité relatifs à l'Inde*, Paris 1986.

Angeli Bertinelli, M.G., 'I Romani oltre l'Eufrate nel II secolo d.C. (le province di Assiria, di Mesopotamia e di Osroene)', *ANRW* 2.9.1 (1976) 3–45.

Arce, J., 'El historiador Ammiano Marcellino y la pena de muerte', *HAnt* 4 (1974) 321–344.

Austin, N.J.E., *Ammianus on Warfare. An Investigation into Ammianus' Military Knowledge*, Brussels 1979.

Avenarius, G., *Lukians Schrift zur Geschichtsschreibung*, Diss. Frankfurt, Meisenheim 1956.

Avi-Yonah, M., *The Jews of Palestine. A Political History from the Bar Kochba War to the Arab Conquest*, Oxford 1976.

Aziza, C., 'Julien et le Judaïsme', in: R. Braun and J. Richer (eds.), *L'empereur Julien. De l'histoire à la légende (331–1715)*, Paris 1978, 141–158.

Bacher, W., 'Statements of a Contemporary of the Emperor Julian on the Rebuilding of the Temple', *The Jewish Quarterly Review* 10 (1898) 168–172.

Bagnall, R.S., A. Cameron, S.R. Schwartz and K.A. Worp, *Consuls of the Later Roman Empire*, Atlanta 1987.

Baldini, A., 'Ammiano Marcellino (XXIII, 5, 2–3) e i Persiani ad Antiochia', *RSA* 19 (1989) [1992] 147–155.

Baldus, H.R., *Uranius Antoninus. Münzprägung und Geschichte*, Bonn 1971.
Barnes, T.D., 'Imperial Campaigns A.D. 285–311', *Phoenix* 30 (1976) 174–193.
Barnes, T.D., *The Sources of the* Historia Augusta, Brussels 1978.
Barnes, T.D., *The New Empire of Diocletian and Constantine*, Cambridge Mass. 1982.
Barnes, T.D., 'New Year 363 in Ammianus Marcellinus. Annalistic Technique and Historical Apologetics', in: J. den Boeft, D. den Hengst and H.C. Teitler (eds.), *Cognitio Gestorum. The Historiographic Art of Ammianus Marcellinus*, Amsterdam 1992, 1–8.
Barnes, T.D., 'Praetorian Prefects, 337–361', *ZPE* 94 (1992) 249–260.
Beck, R., 'Thus spake not Zarathustra: Zoroastrian Pseudepigrapha of the Graeco-Roman World', in: M. Boyce and F. Grenet, *A History of Zoroastrianism*, III, *Zoroastrianism under Macedonian and Roman Rule*, Leiden 1991, 491–565.
Behn, F., *Musikleben im Altertum und frühen Mittelalter*, Stuttgart 1954.
Bengtson, H., *Grundriss der römischen Geschichte mit Quellenkunde, I, Republik und Kaiserzeit bis 284 n. Chr.*, Munich 1982[3].
Bennett, J., *Trajan, Optimus Princeps. A Life and Times*, London 1997.
Béranger, J., 'Julien l'Apostat et l'hérédité du pouvoir impérial', *BHAC* 1970, Bonn 1972, 75–93.
Berger, H., *Die geographischen Fragmente des Eratosthenes*, Leipzig 1880.
Berthelot, A., *L'Asie ancienne centrale et sud-orientale d'après Ptolémée*, Paris 1930.
Berthold, R.M., *Rhodes in the Hellenistic Age*, Ithaca and London 1984.
Bickerman, E.J., *Chronologie*, Leipzig 1933 (repr. 1968).
Bidez, J., G. Rochefort and C. Lacombrade, *L'Empereur Julien, Oeuvres complètes*, Paris 1924–1972[3].
Bidez, J., and F. Cumont, *Les mages hellénisés. Zoroastre, Ostanès et Hystaspe, d'après la tradition grecque*, 2 vols., Paris 1938.
Bidez, J., *La vie de l'empereur Julien*, Paris 1930 (repr. 1965).
Birley, A.R., *The African Emperor Septimius Severus*, London 1988[2].
Birot, P., and J. Dresch, *La Méditerranée et le Moyen-Orient, II, La Méditerranée orientale et le Moyen-Orient. Les Balkans, l'Asie Mineure, le Moyen-Orient*, Paris 1956.
Bishop, M.C., and J.C.N. Coulston, *Roman Military Equipment. From the Punic Wars to the Fall of Rome*, London 1993.
Bivar, A.D.H., 'The Political History of Iran under the Arsacids', in: E. Yarshater (ed.), *The Cambridge History of Iran*, 3.1, Cambridge 1983, 21–99.
Blanchetière, F., 'Julien. Philhellène, Philosémite, Antichrétien. L'affaire du Temple de Jérusalem (363)', *Journal of Jewish Studies* 31 (1980) 61–81.
Bleckmann, B., *Die Reichskrise des III. Jahrhunderts in der spätantiken und byzantinischen Geschichtsschreibung. Untersuchungen zu den nachdionischen Quellen der Chronik des Johannes Zonaras*, Munich 1992.
Bloch, H., 'The Pagan Revival in the West at the End of the Fourth Century', in: A. Momigliano (ed.), *The Conflict between Paganism and Christianity in the Fourth Century*, Oxford 1963, 193–218.
Blockley, R.C., 'The Roman-Persian Peace Treaties of A.D. 299 and 363', *Florilegium* 6 (1984) 28–49.
Blockley, R.C., *East Roman Foreign Policy. Formation and Conduct from Diocletian to Anastasius*, Leeds 1992.

Blomgren, S., *De sermone Ammiani Marcellini quaestiones variae*, Uppsala 1937.
Bobek, H., 'Vegetation', in: W.B. Fisher (ed.), *The Cambridge History of Iran, I, The Land of Iran*, Cambridge 1968, 280–293.
Boeft, J. den, D. den Hengst and H.C. Teitler, *Philological and Historical Commentary on Ammianus Marcellinus XX*, Groningen 1987.
Boeft, J. den, D. den Hengst and H.C. Teitler, *Philological and Historical Commentary on Ammianus Marcellinus XXI*, Groningen 1991.
Boeft, J. den, 'Ammianus graecissans?', in: J. den Boeft, D. den Hengst and H.C. Teitler (eds.), *Cognitio Gestorum. The Historiographic Art of Ammianus Marcellinus*, Amsterdam 1992, 9–18.
Boeft, J. den, J.W. Drijvers, D. den Hengst and H.C. Teitler, *Philological and Historical Commentary on Ammianus Marcellinus XXII*, Groningen 1995.
Boucharlat, R., 'Suse à l'époque sasanide. Une capitale prestigieuse devenue ville de province', *Mesopotamia* 22 (1987) 357–365.
Boucharlat, R., 'Suse et la Susiane à l'époque achéménide. Données archéologiques', in: H. Sancisi-Weerdenburg and A. Kuhrt (eds.), *Achaemenid History IV. Centre and Periphery*, Leiden 1990, 149–175.
Bouffartigue, J., *L'Empereur Julien et la culture de son temps*, Paris 1992.
Boyce, M., and F. Kotwal, 'Zoroastrian *bāj* and *drōn*', *BSOAS* 34 (1971) 56–73 and 298–313.
Bowersock, G.W., *Julian the Apostate*, Cambridge Mass.-London 1978.
Bowersock, G.W., *Roman Arabia*, Cambridge Mass.-London 1983.
Braund, D.C., *Georgia in Antiquity. A history of Colchis and Transcaucasian Iberia, 550 BC – AD 562*, Oxford 1994.
Briant, P., *État et pasteurs au Moyen-Orient ancien*, Paris-Cambridge 1982.
Briant, P., *L'Asie centrale et les royaumes proche-orientaux du premier millénaire (c. VIIIe-IVe avant notre ère)*, Paris 1984.
Briant, P., *Histoire de l'empire perse de Cyrus à Alexandre*, 2 vols., Leiden 1996.
Brice, W., see S. Lloyd.
Brock, S.P., 'The Rebuilding of the Temple under Julian. A New Source', *PalEQ* 108 (1976) 103–107.
Brock, S.P., 'A Letter attributed to Cyril of Jerusalem on the Rebuilding of the Temple', *BSOAS* 40 (1977) 267–286.
Brodersen, K., 'The Date of the Secession of Parthia from the Seleucid Kingdom', *Historia* 35 (1986) 378–381.
Brok, M.F.A., *De Perzische expeditie van keizer Julianus volgens Ammianus Marcellinus*, Groningen 1959.
Brok, M.F.A., 'Demonstratie met een brandpijl', *Hermeneus* 46 (1975) 321–325 (cf. also 48 [1976] 66 for some slight corrections).
Brok, M.F.A., 'Die Quellen von Ammians Exkurs über Persien', *Mnemosyne* 28 (1975) 47–56.
Brok, M.F.A., 'Bombast oder Kunstfertigkeit. Ammians Beschreibung der *ballista* (23, 4, 1–3)', *RhM* 120 (1977) 331–345.
Brok, M.F.A., 'Ein spätrömischer Brandpfeil nach Ammianus', *SJ* 35 (1978) 57–60.
Browning, R., *The Emperor Julian*, Berkeley-Los Angeles 1976.

Caltabiano, M., *Ammiano Marcellino. Storie*, Milan 1989.

Cameron, A., *Circus Factions. Blues and Greens at Rome and Byzantium*, Oxford 1976.

Camus, P.-M., *Ammien Marcellin. Témoin des courants culturels et religieux à la fin du IVe siècle*, Paris 1967.

Casson, L., *The Periplus Maris Erythraei. Text with Introduction, Translation and Commentary*, Princeton 1989.

Češka, J., 'Ad Ammiani Marcellini libros XXII-XXXI a W. Seyfarth novissime editos adnotationes criticae', *Eirene* 12 (1974) 87–110.

Chalmers, W.R., 'An Alleged Doublet in Ammianus Marcellinus', *RhM* 102 (1959) 183–189.

Chalmers, W.R., 'Eunapius, Ammianus Marcellinus, and Zosimus on Julian's Persian Expedition', *CQ* 10 (1960) 152–160 (= 'Julians Perserzug bei Eunapius, Ammianus Marcellinus und Zosimus', in: R. Klein, ed., *Julian Apostata*, Darmstadt 1978, 270–284).

Chastagnol, A., *Les fastes de la préfecture de Rome au BasEmpire*, Paris 1962.

Chaumont, M.-L., 'Études d'histoire parthe, II. Capitales et résidences des premiers Arsacides (IIIe-I^e s. av. J.-C.)', *Syria* 50 (1973) 197–222.

Chaumont, M.-L., 'Conquêtes Sassanides et Propagande Mazdéenne', *Historia* 22 (1973) 664–710.

Chaumont, M.-L., 'Les villes fondées par les Vologèse: Vologésocerta et Vologésias', *Syria* 51 (1974) 77–81.

Chaumont, M.-L., 'L'Arménie entre Rome et l'Iran, I. De l'avènement d'Auguste à l'avènement de Dioclétien', *ANRW* 2.9.1 (1976) 71–194.

Chauvot, A., 'Parthes et Perses dans les sources du IVe siècle', in: M. Christol e.a. (eds.), *Institutions, société et vie politique dans l'empire romain au IVe siècle ap. J.-C.*, Rome 1992, 115–125.

Chuvin, P., *Chronique des derniers païens: la disparition du paganisme dans l'Empire romain, du règne de Constantin à celui de Justinien*, Paris 1990.

Clark, C.U., *Ammiani Marcellini rerum gestarum libri qui supersunt*, Berlin 1910–1915 (repr. 1963).

Clemen, C., *Fontes Historiae Religionis Persicae*, Bonn 1920.

Colledge, M.A.R., *Parthian Art*, London 1977.

Colpe, C., 'Hystaspes', *RAC* 16 (1994) 1056–1082.

Conduché, D., 'Ammien Marcellin et la mort de Julien', *Latomus* 24 (1965) 359–380.

Cornelissen, J.J., 'Ad Ammianum Marcellinum adversaria critica', *Mnemosyne* 14 (1886) 234–304.

Cornell, T.J., 'Ennius, Annals VI. A reply', *CQ* 37 (1987) 514–516.

Coulston, J.C.N., see M.C. Bishop.

Cracco Ruggini, L., *Il paganesimo romano tra religione e politica (384–394 d.C.). Per una reinterpretazione del* Carmen contra Paganos, Rome 1979 (*MAL* 23.1).

Cramer, W., 'Harran', *RAC* 13 (1986) 634–650.

Criniti, N., 'La nuova prosopografia dell' età tardo-imperiale Romana', *NRS* 58 (1974) 135–152.

Crump, G.A., *Ammianus Marcellinus as a Military Historian*, Wiesbaden 1975.

Cumont, F., 'La marche de l'empereur Julien d'Antioche à l'Euphrate', in: F. Cumont, *Études Syriennes*, Paris 1917, 1–33.

Cumont, F., see also J. Bidez.

Damsté, P.H., 'Ad Ammianum Marcellinum', *Mnemosyne* 58 (1930) 1–12.
Dandamaev, M.A., *A Political History of the Achaemenid Empire*, Leiden 1989.
Davies, R.W., 'The Roman Military Diet', in: D. Breeze and V.A. Maxfield (eds.), R.W. Davies, *Service in the Roman Army*, Edinburgh 1989, 187–206.
Demandt, A., *Die Spätantike. Römische Geschichte von Diocletian bis Justinian 284–565 n. Chr.*, Munich 1989.
Desnier, J.L., *Le passage du fleuve: de Cyrus le Grand à Julien l'Apostat. Essay sur la légitimité du souverain*, Paris 1995.
Dhorme, E., *Les religions de Babylonie et d'Assyrie*, Paris 1949.
Dihle, A., 'Serer und Chinesen', in: V. Pöschl and H. Petersmann (eds.), A. Dihle, *Antike und Orient. Gesammelte Aufsätze*, Heidelberg 1984, 201–215.
Dillemann, L., 'Ammien Marcellin et les pays de l'Euphrate et du Tigre', *Syria* 38 (1961) 87–158.
Dillemann, L., *Haute Mésopotamie Orientale et Pays Adjacents*. Contribution à la géographie historique de la région, du Ve s. avant l'ère chrétienne au VIe s. de cette ère, Paris 1962.
Diller, A., *The Textual Tradition of Strabo's Geography*, Amsterdam 1975.
Dittrich, U.-B., *Die Beziehungen Roms zu den Sarmaten und Quaden im vierten Jahrhundert n. Chr. (nach der Darstellung des Ammianus Marcellinus)*, Bonn 1984.
Dixon, K.R., see P. Southern.
Dodd, C.H., 'Chronology of the Eastern Campaigns of the Emperor Lucius Verus', *NC* 4 (1911) 209–267.
Dodgeon, M.H., and S.N.C. Lieu, *The Roman Eastern Frontier and the Persian Wars (AD 226–363). A Documentary History*, London-New York 1991 (repr. 1994).
Doe, B., *Southern Arabia*, London 1971.
Dohrn, T., *Die Tyche von Antiochia*, Berlin 1960.
Downey, G., *A Study of the Comites Orientis and the Consulares Syriae*, Princeton 1939.
Downey, G., *A History of Antioch in Syria from Seleucus to the Arab Conquest*, Princeton 1961.
Dresch, J., see P. Birot.
Drews, R., 'Assyria in Classical Universal Histories', *Historia* 14 (1965) 129–142.
Drijvers, H.J.W., *Cults and Beliefs at Edessa*, Leiden 1980.
Drijvers, J.W., 'Ammianus Marcellinus 23.1.2–3: The rebuilding of the temple in Jerusalem', in: J. den Boeft, D. den Hengst and H.C. Teitler (eds.), *Cognitio Gestorum. The Historiographic Art of Ammianus Marcellinus*, Amsterdam 1992, 19–26.
Drijvers, J.W., 'Strabo on Parthia and the Parthians', in: J. Wiesehöfer (ed.), *Das Partherreich und seine Zeugnisse – The Arsacid Empire: Sources and Documentation*, Stuttgart 1998, 279–293.
Drijvers, J.W., see also J. den Boeft.
Du châtiment dans la cité. Supplices corporels et peine de mort dans le monde antique (Table ronde organisée par l'Ecole française de Rome avec le concours du centre national de la recherche scientifique, Rome, 9–11 novembre 1982), Rome 1984.
Duncan-Jones, R.P., 'The Impact of the Antonine Plague', *JRA* 9 (1996) 108–136.
Dzielska, M., *Apollonius of Tyana in Legend and History*, Rome 1986.

Eadie, J.W., *The Breviarium of Festus. A Critical Edition with Historical Commentary*, London 1967.
Eckardt, K., 'Die armenischen Feldzüge des Lukullus', *Klio* 10 (1910) 72–115, 192–231.
Ehrismann, H., *De temporum et modorum usu Ammianeo*, Diss. Strasbourg 1886.
Elkeles, G., *Demetrios der Städtebelagerer*, Breslau 1941.
Elton, H., *Warfare in Roman Europe, AD 350–425*, Oxford 1996.
Emmett, A.M., 'Introductions and Conclusions to Digressions in Ammianus Marcellinus', *MPhL* 5 (1981) 15–33.
Emmett, A.M., 'The Digressions in the Lost Books of Ammianus Marcellinus', in: B. Croke and A.M. Emmett (eds.), *History and Historians in Late Antiquity*, Sydney 1983, 42–53.
Ensslin, W., 'Kaiser Julians Gesetzgebungswerk und Reichsverwaltung', *Klio* 18 (1923) 104–199.
Ensslin, W., *Zu den Kriegen des Sassaniden Schapur I*, Munich 1949 (SBAW, phil.-hist. Kl. 1947, no. 5).
Ensslin, W., '*Praeses*', *RE* Suppl. 8 (1956) 598–614.
Ensslin, W., 'Venustus 4', *RE* 8A (1958) 896.

Felix, W., *Antike literarische Quellen zur Aussenpolitik des Sāsānidenstaates. Erster Band (224–309)*, Vienna 1985.
Ferguson, J., 'China and Rome', *ANRW* 2.9.2 (1978) 581–603.
Filliozat, J., see J. André.
Finke, H., *Ammianus Marcellinus und seine Quellen zur Geschichte der römischen Republik*, Diss. Heidelberg 1904.
Fleury, Ph., 'Vitruve et la nomenclature des machines de jet romaines', *REL* 59 (1981) 216–234.
Fleury, Ph., *La mécanique de Vitruve*, Caen 1993.
Fleury, Ph., 'Traités de Mécanique', in: C. Nicolet (ed.), *Les littératures techniques dans l'antiquité romaine: statut, public et destination, tradition*, Geneva 1996, 45–75.
Fontaine, J., *Ammien Marcellin, Histoire, IV (Livres XXIII–XXV)*, 2 vols., Paris 1977.
Fontenrose, J., *The Delphic Oracle. Its Responses and Operations. With a Catalogue of Responses*, Berkeley 1978.
Forbes, R.J., *Studies in Ancient Technology, I: Bitumen and Petroleum in Antiquity. The Origin of Alchemy. Water Supply*, Leiden 1955.
Fornara, C.W., 'The prefaces of Ammianus Marcellinus', in: M. Griffith and D.J. Mastronarde (eds.), *Cabinet of the Muses. Essays on Classical and Comparative Literature in Honor of Thomas G. Rosenmeyer*, Atlanta 1990, 163–172.
Fornara, C.W., 'The Order of Events in Ammianus Marcellinus 23.5.4–25', *AJAH* 10 (1985) [1992] 28–40.
Fornara, C.W., 'Julian's Persian expedition in Ammianus and Zosimus', *JHS* 111 (1991) 1–15.
Fornara, C.W., 'Studies in Ammianus Marcellinus, II: Ammianus' Knowledge and Use of Greek and Latin Literature', *Historia* 41 (1992) 420–438.
Frankfort, Th., *Étude sur les guerres orientales de Trajan*, Brussels 1955.
Fraser, P.M., *Cities of Alexander the Great*, Oxford 1996.

French, D.H., 'A Road Problem. Roman or Byzantine?', *MDAI(I)* 43 (1993) 445–454.
Frye, R.N., *The History of Ancient Iran*, Munich 1983.
Frumkin, G., *Archaeology in Soviet Central Asia*, Leiden 1970.
Funke, H., 'Majestäts- und Magieprozesse bei Ammianus Marcellinus', *JbAC* 10 (1967) 145–175.

Gabba, E., 'I Cristiani nell' esercito Romano del quarto secolo d.C.', in: E. Gabba, *Per la storia dell' esercito Romano in età imperiale*, Bologna 1974, 75–109.
Gagé, J., 'Les Perses à Antioche et les courses de l'hippodrome au milieu du IIIe siècle ap. J.C. A propos du 'transfuge' syrien Mariadès', *BFS* 31 (1952–1953) 301–324.
Ganji, M.H., 'Climate', in: W.B. Fisher (ed.), *The Cambridge History of Iran, I, The Land of Iran*, Cambridge 1968, 212–249.
Garlan, Y., *Recherches de poliorcétique grecque*, Paris 1974.
Garzetti, A., *From Tiberius to the Antonines. A History of the Roman Empire AD 14–192*, transl. J.R. Foster, London 1974.
Gawlikowski, M., 'La route de l'Euphrate d'Isidore à Julien', in: P.-L. Gatier, B. Helly and J.-P. Rey-Coquais (eds.), *Géographie historique au Proche-Orient (Syrie, Phénicie, Arabie, grecques, romaines, byzantines)*, Paris 1990, 77–98.
Geffcken, J., *Kaiser Julianus*, Leipzig 1914.
Gelzer, M., 'Licinius 104', *RE* 13 (1927) 376–414.
Gelzer, M., *Pompeius*, Munich 1959².
Gilliam, J.F., 'The Plague under Marcus Aurelius', *AJPh* 82 (1961) 225–251.
Gilliam, J.F., 'Ammianus and the Historia Augusta: the Lost Books and the Period 117–285', *BHAC* 1970, Bonn 1972, 125–147.
Gnoli, G., *Richerche storiche sul Sistan antico*, Rome 1967.
Goebl, R., *Der triumph des Sasaniden Shapur über die Kaiser Gordianus, Philippus und Valerianus. Die ikonographische Interpretation der Felsreliefs*, Vienna 1974 (Denkschr.d.Oesterr.Akad.d.W., 116).
Gollancz, H., *Julianus the Apostate. Now translated for the first time from the Syriac original*, Oxford 1928.
Goossens, G., *Hiérapolis de Syrie. Essai de monographie historique*, Louvain 1943.
Graillot, H., *Le culte de Cybèle, mère des dieux, à Rome et dans l'Empire Romain*, Paris 1912.
Grainger, J.D., *Seleukos Nikator. Constructing a Hellenistic Kingdom*, London 1990.
Greenhalgh, P.A.L., *Pompey. The Roman Alexander*, London 1980.
Grohmann, A., 'Maipha', *RE* 14 (1930) 592–601.
Grohmann, A., 'Makai', *RE* 14 (1930) 614–615.
Grohmann, A., 'Μάρα μητρόπολις', *RE* 14 (1930) 1417–1418.
Grohmann, A., 'Tapharon', *RE* 4A (1932) 2253–2254.
Grohmann, A., 'Νάγαρα μητρόπολις', *RE* 16 (1935) 1574–1576.
Grohmann, A., 'Naskos', *RE* 16 (1935) 1792.
Grohmann, A., ''Οργάνα', *RE* 18.1 (1942) 1022–1023.
Grohmann, A., *Kulturgeschichte des alten Orients, 4. Arabien*, Munich 1963.
Guey, J., *Essai sur la guerre parthique de Trajan (113–117)*, Bucarest 1937.
Gundel, H., 'Ventidius 5', *RE* 8A (1958) 795–816.
Guyot, P., *Eunuchen als Sklaven und Freigelassene in der griechisch-römische Antike*, Stuttgart 1980.

Haehling, R. von, *Die Religionszugehörigkeit der hohen Amtsträger des Römischen Reiches seit Constantins I. Alleinherrschaft bis zum Ende des Theodosianischen Dynastie (324–450 bezw. 455 n. Chr.)*, Bonn 1978.

Hagendahl, H., *Studia Ammianea*, Diss. Uppsala 1921.

Hagendahl, H., 'De abundantia sermonis Ammianei', *Eranos* 22 (1924) 161–216.

Handius, F., *Tursellinus seu de particulis Latinis commentarii*, Leipzig 1829–1845.

Hanslik, R., 'M. Ulpius Traianus', *RE* Suppl. 10 (1965) 1035–1102.

Harmon, A.M., *The Clausula in Ammianus Marcellinus*, New Haven 1910 (Trans. Connecticut Acad. Arts and Sc. XVI, 117–245).

Harper, P.O., J. Aruz and F. Tallon, *The Royal City of Susa. Ancient Near Eastern Treasures in the Louvre*, New York 1992.

Hartke, W., *Römische Kinderkaiser. Eine Strukturanalyse römischen Denkens und Daseins*, Berlin 1951 (repr. Darmstadt 1972).

Head, C., *The Emperor Julian*, Boston 1976.

Heather, P., *Goths and Romans 332–489*, Oxford 1991 (repr. 1994).

Heckel, W., 'Demetrios Poliorketes and the Diadochoi', *PP* 39 (1984) 438–441.

Hengst, D. den, 'The scientific digressions in Ammianus' *Res Gestae*', in: J. den Boeft, D. den Hengst and H.C. Teitler (eds.), *Cognitio Gestorum. The Historiographic Art of Ammianus Marcellinus*, Amsterdam 1992, 39–46.

Hengst, D. den, see also J. den Boeft.

Herkommer, E., *Die Topoi in den Proömien der römischen Geschichtsschreiber*, Diss. Tübingen 1968.

Herrmann, A., 'Iaxartae', *RE* 9 (1916) 1180–1181.

Herrmann, A., 'Iaxartes', *RE* 9 (1916) 1181–1189.

Herrmann, A., 'Issedoi', *RE* 9 (1916) 2235–2246.

Herrmann, A., 'Kambyses 1', *RE* 10 (1919) 1810.

Herrmann, A., 'Kaspisches Meer', *RE* 10 (1919) 2275–2290.

Herrmann, A., 'Saganos' *RE* 1A (1920) 1733.

Herrmann, A., 'Sakai', *RE* 1A (1920) 1770–1806.

Herrmann, A., 'Sera', *RE* 2A (1923) 1661–1663.

Herrmann, A., 'Sizyges', *RE* 3A (1929) 419–423.

Herrmann, A., 'Soita', *RE* 3A (1929) 800–801.

Herrmann, A., 'Σώτειρα', *RE* 3A (1929) 1211.

Herrmann, A., 'Persischer Meerbusen', *RE* 19 (1938) 1030–1033.

Herrmann, A., 'Oroatis', *RE* 18.1 (1942) 1132.

Herrmann, A., 'Oxia palus', *RE* 18.1 (1942) 2004–2005.

Herrmann, A., 'Oxos', *RE* 18.1 (1942) 2006–2017.

Herrmann, A., 'Paropamisadai', *RE* 18.2 (1949) 1778.

Herrmann, A., 'Paropamisus', *RE* 18.2 (1949) 1778–1779 (cited as Herrmann 1949a).

Herrmann, A., 'Erdbeben', *RAC* 5 (1962) 1070–1113.

Herzfeld, E., see also F. Sarre.

Hinz, W., 'Persis', *RE* Suppl. 12 (1970) 1022–1038.

Hofmann, J.B., and A. Szantyr, *Lateinische Syntax und Stilistik*, Munich 1965 (repr. 1972), cited as Szantyr.

Holt, F.L., *Alexander the Great and Bactria: the Formation of a Greek Frontier in Central Asia*, Leiden 1988.

Honigmann, E., 'Hierapolis', *RE* Suppl. 4 (1924) 733–742.

Honigmann, E., 'Ktesiphon', *RE* Suppl. 4 (1924) 1102–1119.

Honigmann, E., 'Syromedia', *RE* 4A (1932) 1788.

Honigmann, E., 'Tigris', *RE* 6A (1937) 1008–1022.

Honigmann, E., and A. Maricq, *Recherches sur les Res Gestae Divi Saporis*, Brussels 1952 (Koninklijke Belgische Academie. Klasse der Letteren en der Morele en Staatkundige Wetenschappen, Verhandelingen, Verzameling in 8°, Tweede reeks, boek XLVII, fasc. 4).

Hopkins, C., *Topography and Architecture of Seleucia on the Tigris*, Ann Arbor 1972.

Hopkins, C., *The Discovery of Dura-Europos*, New Haven 1979.

Hopkins, K., 'Eunuchs in Politics in the Later Roman Empire', *PCPhS* 189 (1963) 62–80 (= *Conquerors and Slaves. Sociological Studies in Roman History*, I, Cambridge 1978, 172–196).

Hülsen, Chr., 'Almo', *RE* 1 (1894) 1589.

Humbach, H., and P.O. Skjaervø, *The Sassanian Inscription of Paikuli*, Wiesbaden 1978–1983 (3 parts in 4 vols.).

Huyse, Ph., 'Vorbemerkungen zur Auswertung iranischen Sprachgutes in den *Res Gestae* des Ammianus Marcellinus', in: W. Shalmowski and A. van Tongerloo (eds.), *Medioiranica* (Proceedings of the International Colloquium organized by the Katholieke Universiteit Leuven from the 21st to the 23rd of May 1990), Louvain 1993, 87–98.

Invernizzi, A., 'Parthian Nisa. New Lines of Research', in: J. Wiesehöfer (ed.), *Das Partherreich und seine Zeugnisse – The Arsacid Empire: Sources and Documentation*, Stuttgart 1998, 45–59.

Isaac, B., 'The Meaning of "limes" and "limitanei" in Ancient Sources', *JRS* 78 (1988) 125–147.

Isaac, B., *The Limits of Empire. The Roman Army in the East*, Oxford 1992^2.

Isaac, B., see also A. Oppenheimer.

James, S., 'Dura-Europos and the Chronology of Syria in the 250s A.D.', *Chiron* 15 (1985) 111–124.

Janvier, Y., 'Rome et l'Orient lointain: le problème des Sères. Réexamen d'une question de géographie antique', *Ktèma* 9 (1984) 261–303.

Johnson, M.J., 'The *Sepulcrum Gordiani* at Zaitha and its Significance', *Latomus* 54 (1995) 141–144.

Jones, A.H.M., *The Later Roman Empire 284–602. A Social Economic and Administrative Survey*, Oxford 1964 (repr. 1986).

Jones, A.H.M., see also PLRE I.

Jong, A. de, *Traditions of the Magi. Zoroastrianism in Greek and Latin Literature*, Leiden 1997.

Jonge, P. de, *Sprachlicher und Historischer Kommentar zu Ammianus Marcellinus* c.q. *Philological and Historical Commentary on Ammianus Marcellinus*, XIV-XIX, Groningen 1935–1982.

Kajanto, I., *The Latin Cognomina*, Helsinki 1965.

Keaveney, A., *Lucullus, a Life*, London 1992.

Kellum, B.A., *Sculptural Programs and Propaganda in Augustan Rome: the Temple of Apollo on the Palatine and the Forum of Augustus*, Ann Arbor 1982.

Kennedy, D.L., 'The Frontier Policy of Septimius Severus', in: W.S. Hanson and L.J.F. Keppie (eds.), *Roman Frontier Studies 1979*, Oxford 1980 (BAR Int. Ser., 71), 879–888.

Kettenhofen, E., *Die römisch-persischen Kriege des 3. Jahrhunderts n. Chr. nach der Inschrift Sahpuhrs I. an der Ka'be-ye Zartost (SKZ)*, Wiesbaden 1982.

Kettenhofen, E., 'The Persian Campaign of Gordian III and the Inscription of Sahpuhr I at the Ka'be-ye Zartost', S. Mitchell (ed.), *Armies and Frontiers in Roman and Byzantine Anatolia*, Oxford 1983 (BAR Int. Ser., 156), 151–171.

Kettenhofen, E., *Tirdād und die Inschrift von Paikuli. Kritik der Quellen zur Geschichte Armeniens im späten 3. und frühen 4. Jh. n. Chr.*, Wiesbaden 1995.

Kienast, D., *Römische Kaisertabelle. Grundzüge einer römischen Kaiserchronologie*, Darmstadt 1996[2].

Kiessling, A., 'Coniectanea Ammianea', *Index Scholarum in Universitate Litteraria Gryphiswaldensi* 6 (1874) 3–8.

Kiessling, E., 'Gazaka', *RE* 7 (1912) 887.

Kiessling, E., 'Gedrosia', *RE* 7 (1912) 895–903.

Kiessling, E., 'Hekatompylos 1', *RE* 7 (1912) 2790–2797.

Kiessling, E., 'Harmozeia', *RE* 7 (1912) 2390–2395.

Kiessling, E., 'Hydriakos', *RE* 9 (1916) 78–79.

Kiessling, E., 'Hyrkania', *RE* 9 (1916) 454–526.

Klein, W., *Studien zu Ammianus Marcellinus*, Leipzig 1914.

Klotz, A., 'Die Quellen Ammians in der Darstellung von Julians Perserzug', *RhM* 71 (1916) 461–506.

Kohlmeyer, K., see M. Al-Khalaf.

Koster, W.J.W., 'Chaldäer', *RAC* 2 (1954) 1006–1021

Kotwal, F., see M. Boyce.

Kretschmer, K., 'Sogdiana', *RE* 3A (1929) 788–791.

Kroll, W., 'Karmania', *RE* 10 (1919) 1955–1956.

Kroon, C., *Discourse Particles in Latin. A Study of nam, enim, autem, vero, and at*, Amsterdam 1995.

Krückmann, O., 'Osroëne', *RE* 18.1 (1942) 1589–1590.

Kühner, R. and C. Stegmann, *Ausführliche Grammatik der lateinischen Sprache, II, Satzlehre*, 2 vols., Hannover 1955[4], 1976[5].

Kuhrt, A., *The Ancient Near East: c. 3000–330 BC*, 2 vols., London-New York 1995.

Kuhrt, A., see also S. Sherwin-White.

Lambrechts, P., 'L'empereur Lucius Verus. Essai de réhabilitation', *AC* 3 (1934) 173–201.

Lane Fox, R., 'The Itinerary of Alexander: Constantius to Julian', *CQ* 47 (1997) 239–252.

Latte, K., *Römische Religionsgeschichte*, Munich 1960.

Lecker, M., see A. Oppenheimer.

Lee, A.D., *Information and Frontiers. Roman Foreign Relations in Late Antiquity*, Cambridge 1993.

Lendle, O., *Schildkroten. Antike Kriegsmaschinen in poliorketischen Texten*, Wiesbaden 1975 (Palingenesia X).

Lendle, O., 'Antike Kriegsmaschinen', *Gymnasium* 88 (1981) 330–356.

Lendle, O., *Texte und Untersuchungen zum technischen Bereich der antiken Poliorketik*, Wiesbaden 1983 (Palingenesia XIX).

Lepper, F.A., *Trajan's Parthian War*, London 1948.

Leumann, M., *Lateinische Laut- und Formenlehre*, Munich 1977.

Levenson, D., 'Julian's Attempt to rebuild the Temple: an Inventory of Ancient and Medieval Sources', in: H.W. Attridge, J.J. Collins and Th.H. Tobin (eds.), *Of Scribes and Scrolls. Studies on the Hebrew Bible, Intertestamental Judaism, and Christian Origins presented to John Strugnell on the occasion of his sixtieth birthday*, Lanham-New York-London 1990, 261–279.

Lévêque, P., 'De nouveaux portraits de l'empereur Julien', *Latomus* 22 (1963) 74–84 = 'Neue Porträts des Kaisers Julian', in: R. Klein (ed.), *Julian Apostata*, Darmstadt 1978, 305–317, cited as Lévêque, 1978.

Lewin, A., 'Dall' Eufrate al Mar Rosso: Diocleziano, l'escercito e i confini tardoantichi', *Athenaeum* 78 (1990) 141–165.

Lewy, Y., 'Julian the Apostate and the Building of the Temple', *Jerusalem Cathedra* 3 (1983) 70–96.

Liebeschuetz, W., 'Ammianus, Julian and Divination', in: M. Wissemann (ed.), *Roma Renascens. Beiträge zur Spätantike und Rezeptionsgeschichte* (Festschrift für Ilona Opelt), Frankfurt am Main 1988, 198–213.

Lieu, S.N.C., see M.H. Dodgeon.

Lightfoot, C.S., 'Trajan's Parthian War and the Fourth-Century Perspective', *JRS* 80 (1990) 115–126.

Linder, A., 'Ecclesia and Synagoga in the Medieval Myth of Constantine the Great', *RBPhH* 54 (1976) 1019–1060.

Lloyd, S., and W. Brice, 'Harran', *AS* 1 (1951) 77–111.

Löfstedt, E., *Beiträge zur Kenntnis der späteren Latinität*, Diss. Uppsala 1907.

Löfstedt, E., *Philologischer Kommentar zur Peregrinatio Aetheriae. Untersuchungen zur Geschichte der lateinischen Sprache*, Uppsala 1911.

Longden, R.P., 'Notes on the Parthian Campaigns of Trajan', *JRS* 21 (1931) 1–35.

Loriot, X., 'Les premières années de la grande crise du IIIe siècle: De l'avènement de Maximin le Thrace (235) à la mort de Gordien III (244)', *ANRW* 2.2 (1975) 657–787.

Luttwak, E.N., *The Grand Strategy of the Roman Empire. From the First Century A.D. to the Third*, Baltimore 1978^2.

MacCormack, S., *Art and Ceremony in Late Antiquity*, Berkeley-Los Angeles-London 1981.

MacDonald, D., 'The Death of Gordian III – Another Tradition', *Historia* 30 (1981) 502–508.

MacDonald, D., 'Dating the Fall of Dura-Europos', *Historia* 35 (1986) 45–68.

MacDermot, B.C., 'Roman Emperors in the Sassanian Reliefs', *JRS* 44 (1954) 76–80.

Madvig, J.N., *Adversaria critica ad scriptores Graecos et Latinos, III, Novas emendationes Graecas et Latinas continens*, Copenhagen 1884 (repr. Hildesheim 1967).

Malavolta, M., 'Interiores limites. Nota ad Amm. Marc. XXIII 5, 1–2', *MGR* 8 (1982) 587–610.
Marcone, A., see C. Prato.
Maricq, A., 'Vologésias, l'emporium de Ctésiphon', *Syria* 36 (1959) 264–275.
Maricq, A., 'Classica et Orientalia, VI: La province d'Assyrie créée par Trajan. A propos de la guerre parthique de Trajan', *Syria* 36 (1959) 254–263.
Maricq, A., see also E. Honigmann.
Marquart, J., *Eransahr nach der Geographie des Ps. Moses Xorenaci*, Berlin 1901 (Abh.d.Gesellschaft d.Wiss. zu Göttingen, Phil.-hist. Kl., N.F. 3,2).
Marsden, E.W., *Greek and Roman Artillery*, 2 vols, Oxford 1969 and 1971.
Martin, J., *Antike Rhetorik. Technik und Methode*, Munich 1974.
Martindale, J.R., 'Prosopography of the Later Roman Empire: addenda et corrigenda to volume I', *Historia* 23 (1974) 246–252.
Martindale, J.R., 'Prosopography of the Later Roman Empire: addenda et corrigenda to volume I', *Historia* 29 (1980) 474–497.
Martindale, J.R., see also PLRE I.
Mary, L., '"Navales pontes": logistique et symbolique chez Ammien Marcellin', in: L. Holtz and J. Cl. Fredouille (eds.), *De Tertullien aux Mozarabes. Mélanges offerts à Jacques Fontaine à l'occasion de son 70e anniversaire par ses élèves, amis et collègues*, I, Paris 1992, 595–612.
Masson, V.M., *Das Land der tausend Städte. Die Wiederentdeckung der ältesten Kulturgebiete in Mittelasien*, Munich 1982.
Matthews, J.F., 'The Historical Setting of the "Carmen contra Paganos" (Cod.Par.Lat. 8084)', *Historia* 19 (1970) 464–479.
Matthews, J.F., 'Symmachus and the Oriental Cults', *JRS* 63 (1973) 175–195.
Matthews, J.F., *The Roman Empire of Ammianus*, London 1989.
Mau, A., 'Carpentum', *RE* 3 (1899) 1606–1607.
Meier, G., 'Καδούσιοι', *RE* Suppl. 7 (1940) 316–317.
Mendelsohn, L., *Zosimi historia nova*, Leipzig 1887.
Meulder, M., 'Julien l'Apostat contre les Parthes: un guerrier impie', *Byzantion* 61 (1991) 458–495.
Meyer, M., 'Die Felsbilder Shapurs I.', *JDAI* 105 (1990) 237–302.
Mez, A., *Geschichte der Stadt Harran in Mesopotamien bis zum Einfall der Araber*, Strasbourg 1892.
Michael, H., *Die verlorenen Bücher des Ammianus Marcellinus*, Breslau 1880.
Millar, F., *The Roman Near East, 31 B.C.-A.D. 337*, Cambridge Mass.-London 1993.
Miltner, F., 'Pompeius 31 (Cn. Pompeius Magnus)', *RE* 21 (1952) 2062–2211.
Mommsen, Th., 'Ammians Geographica', *Hermes* 16 (1881) 602–636 (= *Gesammelte Schriften*, 7, Berlin 1909, 393–425).
Mommsen, Th., 'Das römische Militärwesen seit Diocletian', *Hermes* 24 (1889) 195–279 (= *Gesammelte Schriften* 6, Berlin 1910, 206–283).
Mommsen, Th., 'Bemerkungen zu einzelnen Stellen Ammians', *Gesammelte Schriften* 7, Berlin 1909, 426–429.
Montero, S., *Política y adivinación en el Bajo Impero Romano: emperadores y harúspices (193 D.C.- 408 D.C.)*, Brussels 1991.
Morosi, R., 'L'*officium* del prefetto del pretorio nel VI secolo', *RomBarb* 2 (1977) 103–148.

Morris, J., see PLRE I.
Mouterde, R., and A. Poidebard, *Le limes de Chalcis. Organisation de la steppe en haute Syrie romaine*, 2 vols., Paris 1945.
Müller, C.F.W., 'Zu Ammianus Marcellinus', *Fleckeisens Jbb*. 19 [107] (1873) 341–365.
Münzer, Th., 'Decius 15', *RE* 4 (1901) 2279–2281.
Musil, A., *The Middle Euphrates. A Topographical Itinerary*, New York 1927 (repr. 1978).

Nadeau, J.Y., 'Ethiopians', *CQ* 20 (1970) 338–349.
Naudé, C.P.T., '*Fortuna* in Ammianus Marcellinus', *AClass* 7 (1964) 70–88.
Neue, F., *Formenlehre der lateinische Sprache*. Dritte, sehr vermehrte Auflage von C. Wagener, Leipzig 1892–1905 (repr. Hildesheim 1985).
Nicasie, M.J., *Twilight of Empire. The Roman Army from the Reign of Diocletian until the Battle of Adrianople*, Amsterdam 1997.
Nilsson, M.P., *Geschichte der griechischen Religion, II: Die hellenistische und römische Zeit*, Munich 1974^3 (= 1988^4).
Nissen, H.J., see M. Stol.
Nock, A.D., 'Greeks and Magi', in: A.D. Nock, *Essays on Religion and the Ancient World*, ed. by Z. Stewart, Oxford 1972, II, 516–526.
Nöldeke, Th., *Geschichte der Perser und Araber zur Zeit der Sasaniden: aus der arabischen Chronik des Tabari*, Leiden 1879.
Norman, A.F., 'Magnus in Ammianus, Eunapius, and Zosimus: New Evidence', *CQ* 7 (1957) 129–133.
Norman, A.F., *Libanius. Selected Works*, I, The Julianic Orations, London-Cambridge Mass. 1969.
Novák, R., 'Kritische Nachlese zu Ammianus Marcellinus', *WS* 33 (1911) 293–322.

O'Connor, C., *Roman Bridges*, Cambridge 1993.
Olmstead, A.T., 'The Mid-Third Century of the Christian Era', *CPh* 37 (1942) 241–262 and 398–420.
Olshausen, E., 'Oxos', *Der kleine Pauly* 4 (1975) 388–389.
Oost, S.I., 'The Death of the Emperor Gordian III', *CPh* 53 (1958) 106–107.
Ooteghem, J. van, *Lucius Licinius Lucullus*, Brussels 1959 (Acad.Royale de Belg., Cl.des Lettres, Mém. 53,4).
Oppenheimer, A., in collaboration with B. Isaac and M. Lecker, *Babylonia Judaica in the Talmudic Period*, Wiebaden 1983.

Pack, R., 'Ammianus Marcellinus and the *curia* of Antioch', *CPh* 48 (1953) 80–85.
Parke, H.W., *Sibyls and Sibylline Prophecy in Classical Antiquity*, London-New York 1988.
Paschoud, F., *Cinq études sur Zosime*, Paris 1976.
Paschoud, F., Zosime, *Histoire Nouvelle*, II.1 (Livre III), Paris 1979.
Paschoud, F., '"Se non è vero, è ben trovato": tradition littéraire et verité historique chez Ammien Marcellin', *Chiron* 19 (1989) 37–54.
Perry, B.E., *The Ancient Romances. A Literary-Historical Account of their Origins*, Berkeley 1967.

Petit, P., *Libanius et la vie municipale à Antioche au IVe siècle après J.C.*, Paris 1955.

Petit, P., 'Les sénateurs de Constantinople dans l'oeuvre de Libanius', *AC* 26 (1957) 347–382 = 'Die Senatoren von Konstantinopel im Werk des Libanios', in: G. Fatouros and T. Krischer (eds.), *Libanios*, Darmstadt 1983, 206–247 (cited as Petit, 1983).

Pharr, C., 'The Interdiction of Magic in Roman Law', *TAPhA* 63 (1932) 269–295.

Pinkster, H., *Latin Syntax and Semantics*, London-New York 1990.

PIR^2, *Prosopographia Imperii Romani Saec. I. II. III*, E. Groag, A. Stein e.a. (eds.), Berlin ^{2}1933-.

PLRE I, *The Prosopography of the Later Roman Empire, I, A.D. 260–395*, A.H.M. Jones, J.R. Martindale and J. Morris (eds.), Cambridge 1971.

Poidebard, A., 'Coupes de chaussée romaine Antioche-Chalcis', *Syria* 10 (1929) 22–29.

Poidebard, A., *La trace de Rome dans le désert de Syrie: le limes de Trajan à la conquête arabe. Recherches aériennes 1925–1932*, 2 vols., Paris 1934.

Poidebard, A., see also R. Mouterde.

Poinsotte, J.M., 'Les Romains et la Chine. Réalités et mythes', *MEFR* 91 (1979) 431–479.

Potter, D.S., *Prophecy and History in the Crisis of the Roman Empire. A Historical Commentary on the Thirteenth Sibylline Oracle*, Oxford 1990.

Potts, D.T., 'Thaj and the Location of Gerrha', *Proceedings of the Seminar of Arabian Studies* 14 (1984) 87–91.

Potts, D.T., *The Arabian Gulf in Antiquity, II: From Alexander the Great to the Coming of Islam*, Oxford 1990.

Prato, C., and A. Marcone, *Giuliano Imperatore. Alla madre degli dei e altri discorsi*, s.l. 1987.

Price, J.J., *Jerusalem under Siege. The Collapse of the Jewish State 66–70 C.E.*, Leiden 1992.

Raschke, M.G., 'New Studies in Roman Commerce with the East', *ANRW* 2.9.2 (1978) 604–1361.

Ratti, S., 'La survie littéraire de Ventidius Bassus ou Le destin extraordinaire d'un muletier', *IL* 44.2 (1992) 40–47.

Reardon, B.P. (ed.), *Collected Ancient Greek Novels*, Berkeley 1989.

Reddé, M., *Mare nostrum. Les infrastructures, le dispositif et l'histoire de la marine militaire sous l'empire romain*, Paris 1986.

Regling, K., 'Zur historischen Geographie des mesopotamischen Parallelograms (mit einer Karte)', *Klio* 1 (1902) 443–476.

Richardson, J.S., *The Romans in Spain. A History of Spain*, Oxford 1996.

Ridley, R.T., 'Notes on Julian's Persian expedition (363)', *Historia* 22 (1973) 317–330.

Rike, R.L., *Apex Omnium. Religion in the Res Gestae of Ammianus*, Berkeley-Los Angeles-London 1987.

Robert, L., 'Εὔλαιος, ἱστορία καὶ ἀνθρωπωνυμία', *EEAth* (1962–1963) 519–529 = L. Robert, *Opera Minora Selecta*, II, Amsterdam 1969, 978–987.

Rommel, H., 'Μαργαρῖται', *RE* 14 (1930) 1682–1702.

Rostovtzeff, M.I., '*Res Gestae Divi Saporis* and Dura', *Berytus* 8 (1943) 17–60.

Rubin, Z., 'Dio, Herodian, and Severus' Second Parthian War', *Chiron* 5 (1975) 419–441.
Ruge, W., 'Asmurna', *RE* 2 (1896) 1703.
Russell, K.W., 'The Earthquake of May 19, AD 363', *BASO* 238 (1980) 47–61.
Rzach, A., 'Sibyllen', *RE* 2A (1923) 2073–2103.
Rzach, A., 'Sibyllinische Orakel', *RE* 2A (1923) 2103–2183.

Sabbah, G., *La méthode d'Ammien Marcellin. Recherches sur la construction du discours historique dans les* Res Gestae, Paris 1978.
Sancisi-Weerdenburg, H., 'Was there ever a Median empire?', in: H. Sancisi-Weerdenburg and A. Kuhrt (eds.), *Achaemenid History III. Method and Theory*, Leiden 1988, 197–212.
Sancisi-Weerdenburg, H., 'The Orality of Herodotus' *Medikos Logos* or: the Median Empire revisited', in: H. Sancisi-Weerdenburg, A. Kuhrt and M. Cool Root (eds.), *Achaemenid History VIII. Continuity and Change*, Leiden 1994, 39–55.
Sarre, F., and E. Herzfeld, *Archäologische Reise im Euphrat- und Tigris-Gebiet*, I, Berlin 1911.
Sartre, M., *L'Orient Romain. Provinces et sociétés provinciales en Méditerranée orientale d'Auguste aux Sévères (31 avant J.-C.-235 après J.-C.)*, Paris 1991.
Scala, R. von, 'Doxographische und stoische Reste bei Ammianus Marcellinus', in: *Festgaben zu Ehren Max Büdingers*, Innsbruck 1898, 117–150.
Schachermeyr, F., 'Moxoene', *RE* 16 (1935) 409.
Schippmann, K., *Grundzüge der parthischen Geschichte*, Darmstadt 1980.
Schippmann, K., *Grundzüge der Geschichte des Sasanidischen Reiches*, Darmstadt 1990.
Schlumberger, J., *Die Epitome de Caesaribus. Untersuchungen zur heidnischen Geschichtsschreibung des 4. Jahrhunderts n.Chr.*, Munich 1974 (Vestigia 18).
Schmidt, E.F., *Persepolis*, 3 vols., Chicago 1953–1970.
Schneider, R., *Griechische Poliorketiker*, Göttingen 1908 (Abh.d. Kgl. Gesellschaft d.Wiss.Göttingen, X 1).
Schottky, M., *Media Atropatene und Gross-Armenien in hellenistischer Zeit*, Bonn 1989.
Schramm, E., 'Μονάγχων und onager', *NGG* 2 (1918) 259–271.
Seager, R., *Pompey, a Political Biography*, Oxford 1979.
Seager, R., *Ammianus Marcellinus. Seven Studies in his Language and Thought*, Columbia 1986.
Seager, R., 'Perceptions of Eastern Frontier Policy in Ammianus, Libanius, and Julian (337–363)', *CQ* 47 (1997) 253–268.
Seeck, O., 'Zur Chronologie und Quellenkritik des Ammianus Marcellinus', *Hermes* 41 (1906) 481–539.
Seeck, O., *Regesten der Kaiser und Päpste für die Jahre 311 bis 476 n. Chr.. Vorarbeit zu einer Prosopographie der christlichen Kaiserzeit*, Stuttgart 1919 (repr. 1964).
Segal, J.B., 'Pagan Syriac Monuments in the Vilayet of Urfa', *AS* 3 (1953) 97–119.
Selem, A., *Le Storie di Ammiano Marcellino. Testo e Traduzione*, Turin 1965 (repr. 1973).
Seyfarth, W., 'Ein Handstreich persischer Bogenschützen auf Antiochia. Sprachliche und historische Rechtfertigung einer Stelle bei Ammianus Marcellinus XXIII, 5,

3', *Klio* 40 (1962) 60–64.

Seyfarth, W., *Ammiani Marcellini rerum gestarum libri qui supersunt*, adiuvantibus L. Jacob-Karau et I. Ulmann, 2 vols., Leipzig 1978.

Seyfarth, W., *Ammianus Marcellinus. Römische Geschichte. Lateinisch und Deutsch und mit einem Kommentar versehen*, II, Berlin 1983[5], III, Berlin 1986[3].

Sherwin-White, A.N., 'Lucullus, Pompey and the East', in: J.A. Crook, A. Lintott and E. Rawson (eds.), *The Cambridge Ancient History*, IX, *The Last Age of the Roman Republic, 146–43 B.C.*, Cambridge 1994, 229–273.

Sherwin-White, S.M., and A. Kuhrt, *From Samarkhand to Sardis. A new approach to the Seleucid empire*, London 1993.

Sidebotham, S.E., *Roman Economic Policy in the Erythra Thalassa, 30 B.C. – A.D. 217*, Leiden 1986.

Sidebotham, S.E., 'Aelius Gallus and Arabia', *Latomus* 45 (1986) 590–602 (cited as Sidebotham, 1986a).

Signes, J., 'El Excursus de los Persas de Amiano Marcelino (XXXIII, 6)', *Veleia* 7 (1990) 351–375.

Skjaervø, P.O., see H. Humbach.

Skutsch, O., 'Book VI of Ennius' Annals', *CQ* 37 (1987) 512–514.

Smith, R., *Julian's Gods. Religion and Philosophy in the Thought and Action of Julian the Apostate*, London and New York 1995.

Solin, H., and O. Salomies, *Repertorium nominum gentilium et cognominum Latinorum*, Hildesheim 1994[2].

Sonnabend, H., *Fremdenbild und Politik. Vorstellungen der Römer von Ägypten und dem Partherreich in der späten Republik und frühen Kaiserzeit*, Frankfurt 1986.

Southern, P., and K.R. Dixon, *The Late Roman Army*, London 1996.

Spek, R.J. van der, 'Nippur, Sippar, and Larsa in the Hellenistic Period', in: M. de Jong-Ellis (ed.), *Nippur at the Centennial*, Philadelphia 1992, 235–260.

Speyer, W., 'Gewitter', *RAC* 10 (1978) 1107–1172.

Sprenger, A., *Die alte Geographie Arabiens als Grundlage der Entwicklungsgeschichte des Semitismus*, Bern 1875 (repr. Amsterdam 1966).

Standish, J.F., 'The Caspian Gates', *G&R* 17 (1970) 17–24.

Steier, A., 'Löwe', *RE* 13 (1927) 968–990.

Stein, A., 'Mariades', *RE* 14 (1930) 1744–1745.

Stein, E., *Untersuchungen über das Officium der Prätorianerpräfektur seit Diokletian*, Vienna 1922 (repr. Amsterdam 1962).

Stein, O., ''Ορτόσπανα', *RE* 18.1 (1942) 1507–1508.

Stemberger, G., *Juden und Christen im Heiligen Land. Palästina unter Konstantin und Theodosius*, Munich 1987.

Stephens, S.A., and J.J. Winkler, *Ancient Greek Novels. The Fragments: Introduction, Text, Translation and Commentary*, Princeton 1995.

Stertz, S.A., 'Ammianus Marcellinus' Attitudes toward Earlier Emperors', *Studies in Latin Literature and Roman History*, ed. C. Deroux, II, Brussels 1980, 487–514.

Stiehl, R., see F. Altheim.

Stol, M., and H.J. Nissen, 'Kanal(isation)', *Reallexikon der Assyriologie* 5 (1976–1980) 355–368.

Stolte, B.H., 'De dood van keizer Gordianus III en de onbetrouwbaarheid van de Res Gestae Divi Saporis', *Lampas* 2 (1970) 377–384.

Streck, M., 'Diabas', *RE* 5 (1905) 300–301 (Streck, 1905a).
Streck, M., 'Dialas', *RE* 5 (1905) 319–320 (Streck, 1905b).
Streck, M., 'Gyndes', *RE* 7 (1912) 2091–2092.
Sturm, J., 'Ochos 2', *RE* 17 (1937) 1768–1770.
Sundermann, W., 'Bidaxš', *Encyclopaedia Iranica* 4 (1990) 242–244.
Sundwall, G.A., 'Ammianus Geographicus', *AJPh* 117 (1996) 619–643.
Swain, S., 'Macrianus as the "Well-Horned Stag" in the Thirteenth Sibylline Oracle', *GRBS* 33 (1992) 375–382.
Syme, R., 'Sabinus the Muleteer', *Latomus* 17 (1958) 73–80 = R. Syme, *Roman Papers*, I, ed. by E. Badian, Oxford 1979, 393–399.
Szantyr, A., see J.B. Hofmann.
Szidat, J., *Historischer Kommentar zu Ammianus Marcellinus Buch XX-XXI, Teil I: Die Erhebung Iulians*, Wiesbaden 1977; *Teil II: Die Verhandlungsphase*, Wiesbaden 1981; *Teil III: Die Konfrontation*, Wiesbaden 1996.
Szidat, J., 'Alexandrum imitatus (Amm. 24,4,27). Die Beziehung Iulians zu Alexander in der Sicht Ammians', in: W. Will and J. Heinrichs (eds.), *Festschrift für Gerhard Wirth zum 60. Geburtstag*, Amsterdam 1988, 1023–1035.

Tarn, W.W., *The Greeks in Bactria and India*, Chicago 1984^3 (Cambridge 1938^1).
Teitler, H.C., 'History and Hagiography. The *passio* of Basil of Ancyra as a historical source', *VChr* 50 (1996) 73–80.
Teitler, H.C., see also J. den Boeft.
Teixidor, V.J., 'The kingdom of Adiabene and Hatra', *Berytus* 17 (1967–1968) 1–11.
Thélamon, F., *Païens et chrétiens au IVe siècle. L'apport de l'"Histoire ecclésiastique" de Rufin d'Aquilée*, Paris 1981.
Thomas, G., 'Magna Mater and Attis', *ANRW* 2.17.3 (1984) 1499–1535.
Thompson, E.A., 'Ammianus' Account of Gallus Caesar', *AJPh* 64 (1943) 302–315.
Thompson, E.A., *The Historical Work of Ammianus Marcellinus*, Cambridge 1947 (repr. Groningen 1969).
Thrams, P., *Christianisierung des Römerreiches und heidnischer Widerstand*, Heidelberg 1992.
Tilia, A.B., *Studies and Restorations at Persepolis and other sites of Fars*, 2 vols., Rome 1972–1978.
Tkač, J., 'Gaia 3', *RE* 7 (1912) 480.
Tomaschek, W., 'Alexandreia 11', *RE* 1 (1894) 1390.
Tomaschek, W., 'Alikodra', *RE* 1 (1894) 1482.
Tomaschek, W., 'Androphagoi', *RE* 1 (1894) 2168–2169.
Tomaschek, W., 'Anniboi', *RE* 1 (1894) 2258–2259.
Tomaschek, W., 'Ἀντιόχεια Μαργιανή', *RE* 1 (1894) 2445.
Tomaschek, W., 'Apameia Rhagiane', *RE* 1 (1894) 2665.
Tomaschek, W., 'Arabis', *RE* 2 (1896) 363–364.
Tomaschek, W., 'Areios', *RE* 2 (1896) 623–624.
Tomaschek, W., 'Artamis', *RE* 2 (1896) 1305.
Tomaschek, W., 'Askatakas', *RE* 2 (1896) 1614–1615.
Tomaschek, W., 'Asmira', *RE* 2 (1896) 1702.
Tomaschek, W., 'Aspabota', *RE* 2 (1896) 1709.
Tomaschek, W., 'Aspakarai', *RE* 2 (1896) 1709–1710.

Tomaschek, W., 'Astakana', *RE* 2 (1896) 1773.
Tomaschek, W., 'Asthala', *RE* 2 (1896) 1789.
Tomaschek, W., 'Bagradas 2', *RE* 2 (1896) 2774.
Tomaschek, W., 'Bautai', *RE* 3 (1899) 174–175.
Tomaschek, W., 'Bautisos', *RE* 3 (1899) 175–176.
Tomaschek, W., 'Bitaxa', *RE* 3 (1899) 506.
Tomaschek, W., 'Charax 9', *RE* 3 (1899) 2121–2122.
Tomaschek, W., 'Chatracharta', *RE* 3 (1899) 2196.
Tomaschek, W., 'Chiliokomon', *RE* 3 (1899) 2278.
Tomaschek, W., 'Daïx', *RE* 4 (1901) 2016.
Tomaschek, W., 'Dargamenes', *RE* 4 (1901) 2215.
Tomaschek, W., 'Drangai', *RE* 5 (1905) 1665–1667.
Tomaschek, W., 'Drepsa', *RE* 5 (1905) 1698–1699.
Tougher, S.F., 'Byzantine Eunuchs: an Overview, with special Reference to their Creation and Origin', in: E. James (ed.), *Women, Men and Eunuchs. Gender in Byzantium*, London-New York 1997, 168–184.
Toumanoff, C., 'The Third-Century Armenian Arsacids. A Chronological and Genealogical Commentary', *Revue des Études Arméniennes* 6 (1969) 233–281.
Toynbee, J.M.C., *Animals in Roman Life and Art*, London 1973.
Treidler, H., 'Prophthasia', *RE* 23 (1959) 817–822.
Treidler, H., 'Psitharas', *RE* 23 (1959) 1407–1414.
Treidler, H., 'Πύργος Λίθινος', *RE* 24 (1963) 33–46.
Treidler, H., 'Παραχοάθρας ὄρος', *RE* Suppl. 10 (1965) 475–478.
Treidler, H., 'Οὐολογαισία', *RE* 9A (1967) 767–771.
Treidler, H., 'Zagros', *RE* 9A (1967) 2283–2285.
Treidler, H., 'Zariaspa', *RE* 9A (1967) 2326–2328.

Unger, E., *Babylon. Die heilige Stadt nach der Beschreibung der Babylonier*, Berlin 1970².

Veh, O., *Ammianus Marcellinus. Das römische Weltreich vor dem Untergang*, übersetzt von O. Veh, eingeleitet und erläutert von G. Wirth, Zurich-Munich 1974.
Vermaseren, M.J., *Corpus cultus Cybelae Attidisque*, Leiden 1977-..
Versnel, H.S., 'Two Types of Roman Devotio', *Mnemosyne* 29 (1976) 365–410.
Versnel, H.S., 'Self-sacrifice, compensation and the anonymous gods', in: O. Reverdin and J. Rudhart (eds.), *Le sacrifice dans l'antiquité*, Geneva 1981, 135–194.
Vogelsang, W., 'Some Observations on Achaemenid Hyrcania. A Combination of Sources', in: A. Kuhrt and H. Sancisi-Weerdenburg (eds.), *Achaemenid History III. Method and Theory*, Leiden 1988, 121–135.
Vogt, J., *Kaiser Julian und das Judentum. Studien zum Weltanschauungskampf der Spätantike*, Leipzig 1939.

Wagner, J., 'Provincia Osrhoenae. New Archaeological Finds Illustrating the Organisation under the Severan Dynasty', in: S. Mitchell (ed.), *Armies and Frontiers in Roman and Byzantine Anatolia*, London 1983, 103–129.
Wagner, J.A., *Ammiani Marcellini quae supersunt*, cum notis integris Frid. Lindenbrogii, Henr. et Hadr. Valesiorum et Iac. Gronovii, quibus Thom. Reinesii quasdam

et suas adiecit, editionem absolvit Car. Gottl. Aug. Erfurdt, 3 vols., Leipzig 1808 (repr. in 2 vols., Hildesheim 1975).

Waszink, J.H. (ed.), *Tertullianus De Anima*, Amsterdam 1947.

Waszink, J.H., 'Biothanati', *RAC* 2 (1954) 391–394.

Waters, K.H., 'The reign of Trajan, and its Place in Contemporary Scholarship (1960–1972)', *ANRW* 2.2 (1975) 381–431.

Webster, G., *The Roman Imperial Army of the First and Second Centuries A.D.*, London 1981².

Wecker, O., 'Indos', *RE* 9 (1916) 1369–1373.

Weidner, E.F., 'Nikephorion 2', *RE* 17 (1937) 309–310.

Weidner, E.F., 'Niphates', *RE* 17 (1937) 706–707.

Weinstock, S., 'Libri fulgurales', *PBSR* 19 (1951) 122–153.

Weis, B.K., *Julian. Briefe*, Griechisch-Deutsch, Munich 1973.

Weissbach, F.H., 'Brisoana', *RE* 3 (1899) 858.

Weissbach, F.H., 'Charax 10 (Χάραξ)', *RE* 3 (1899) 2122.

Weissbach, F.H., 'Choaspes 1', *RE* 3 (1899) 2354–2355.

Weissbach, F.H., 'Gazaca', *RE* 7 (1912) 886–887.

Weissbach, F.H., 'Iasonion', *RE* 9 (1916) 782.

Weissbach, F.H., 'Κάρραι', *RE* 10 (1919) 2009–2021.

Weissbach, F.H., 'Raga', *RE* 1A (1920) 125–127.

Weissbach, F.H., 'Rogomanius', *RE* 1A (1920) 1001.

Weissbach, F.H., 'Κιρχήσιον'(Circesium)', *RE* 11 (1922) 505–507.

Weissbach, F.H., 'Kyros 2', *RE* 12 (1925) 184–187.

Weissbach, F.H., 'Ταξίανα', *RE* 5A (1934) 75.

Weissbach, F.H., 'Teredon', *RE* 5A (1934) 584–586.

Weissbach, F.H., 'Μωσαῖος', *RE* 16 (1935) 343.

Weissbach, F.H., 'Narraga', *RE* 16 (1935) 1755–1756.

Weitzmann, K., *Age of Spirituality: Late Antique and Early Christian Art, Third to Seventh Century. Catalogue of the Exhibition at the Metropolitan Museum of Art, Nov. 19, 1977 – Febr. 12, 1978*, New York 1979.

Wernicke, K., 'Arimaspoi', *RE* 2 (1896) 826–827.

Westendorp Boerma, R.E.H., *P. Vergili Maronis libellus qui inscribitur Catalepton*, II, Assen 1963.

Whittaker, C.R., *Frontiers of the Roman Empire. A Social and Economic Study*, Baltimore 1994.

Widengren, G., 'Iran, der grosse Gegner Roms: Königsgewalt, Feudalismus, Militärwesen', *ANRW* 2.9.1 (1976) 219–306.

Wiemer, H.- U., *Libanios und Julian. Studien zum Verhältnis von Rhetorik und Politik im vierten Jahrhundert n. Chr.*, Munich 1995.

Wiedemann, Th., *Greek and Roman Slavery*, London 1981.

Wiedemann, T.E.J., 'Between Men and Beasts: Barbarians in Ammianus Marcellinus', in: I.S. Moxon, J.D. Smart and A.J. Woodman (eds.), *Past Perspectives. Studies in Greek and Roman Historical Writing*, Cambridge 1986, 189–201.

Wiesehöfer, J., *Das antike Persien von 550 v.Chr. bis 650 n.Chr.*, Munich-Zurich 1993.

Wilken, R.L., *John Chrysostom and the Jews. Rhetoric and Reality in the Late 4th Century*, Berkeley-Los Angeles-London 1983.

Will, E., *Histoire politique du monde hellénistique (323–30 av. J.C.), I, De la mort d'Alexandre aux avènements d'Antioche III et de Philippe V*, Nancy 1979².

Wille, G., *Musica Romana. Die Bedeutung der Musik im Leben der Römer*, Amsterdam 1967.

Williams, A.V., *The Pahlavi Rivāyat accompanying the Dādestan ī Dēnīg*, 2 vols., Copenhagen 1990.

Willrich, H., 'Demetrios 33', *RE* 4 (1901) 2769–2792.

Winter, E., *Die sāsānidisch-römischen Friedensverträge des 3. Jahrhunderts n. Chr. Ein Beitrag zum Verständnis der aussenpolitischen Beziehungen zwischen den beiden Grossmächten*, Frankfurt a. M. 1988.

Winter, E., 'On the Regulation of the Eastern Frontier of the Roman Empire in 298', in: D.H. French and C.S. Lightfoot (eds.), *The Eastern Frontier of the Roman Empire*. Proceedings of a Colloquium held at Ankara in September 1988, Oxford 1989 (BAR Int. Ser., 553), 555–571.

Wissmann, H. von, *Zur Geschichte und Landeskunde von AltSüdarabien*, Vienna 1964 (Oesterr.Ak.d.Wiss., Phil.hist.Kl., Sitzb. 246).

Wissmann, H. von, *Zur Archäologie und antiken Geographie von Südarabien. Hadramaut, Qataban und das Aden-Gebiet in der Antike*, Istanbul 1968.

Wissmann, H. von, 'Die Geschichte des Sabäerrreichs und der Feldzug des Aelius Gallus', *ANRW* 2.9.1 (1976) 308–544.

Wissowa, G., 'Devotio', *RE* 5 (1905) 277–280.

Wissowa, G., *Religion und Kultus der Römer*, Munich 1902 (1912², repr. 1971).

Wlosok, A., 'Aeneas Vindex: ethischer Aspekt und Zeitbezug', in: E. Heck and E.A. Schmidt (eds.), *Res humanae – res divinae. Kleine Schriften von A. Wlosok*, Heidelberg 1990, 419–436.

Wölfflin, E., 'Medietas, Mitte, Hälfte', *ALL* 3 (1886) 458–470.

Wolfram, H., *Geschichte der Goten. Von den Anfängen bis zur Mitte des sechsten Jahrhunderts. Entwurf einer historischen Ethnographie*, Munich 1979.

Wolski, J., 'The Decay of the Iranian Empire of the Seleucids and the Chronology of the Parthian Beginnings', *Berytus* 12 (1956–1958) 35–52.

Wolski, J., 'L'historicité d'Arsace Ier', *Historia* 8 (1959) 222–238.

Wolski, J., 'Arsace II et la généalogie des premiers Arsacides', *Historia* 11 (1962) 139–145.

Wolski, J., 'Arsace Ier, fondateur de l'état parthe', in: *Commémoration Cyrus, hommage universel III = Acta Iranica* 3, Leiden 1974, 159–199.

Wolski, J., 'Untersuchungen zur frühen parthischen Geschichte', *Klio* 58 (1976) 439–457.

Woods, D., 'The Martyrdom of the Priest Basil of Ancyra', *VChr* 46 (1992) 31–39.

Wright, W.C., *The Works of the Emperor Julian*, with an English translation, 3 vols., 1913–1923.

York Jr., J.M., 'The Image of Philip the Arab', *Historia* 21 (1972) 320–332.

Ziegler, K., 'Tomyris', *RE* 6A (1937) 1702–1704.

Ziegler, K.-H., *Die Beziehungen zwischen Rom und dem Partherreich. Ein Beitrag zur Geschichte des Völkerrechts*, Wiesbaden 1964.

Indices

I Lexical (Latin)

abiectus   137
absolute   167
absumere   123
accidentia   7
accidere   8
aculeus   77
acumen   63
ad internecionem   140
ad summam   125
aditus   78
adorare   52
adsurgere   71
adultus   23
adventicius   209
aedificium   72
aegre   218
aequitas   127, 136
aerumna   139
aerumnae   35
aetas   123
affectare   133
agger   202
agmen   40
alte spirare   139
altrix   160
altus   85
ambitiosus   9, 158, 184
ambulatorius   74
amplitudo   175
amplus   171
anhelare   40
anhelus   40
antesignanus   121
antiquitas   124
antiquus   110
apparitor   94
arcanum   172
arcanus   159
aries   69
armatus   71

armiger   51
artifex   62, 221
asciscere   81
assultus   10
attonitus   86
auctoritas   126
augere   134
avellere   93
axiculus   59
axis   145
bidental   108
bitumen   148
borius   215
brevis   141, 149, 163
calcare   104, 189
callidus   125
calones   33
campestris   196
canalis   61
canalis fundus   60
candor   109
capax   29, 196
cardo   145
carnifex   94
carpentum   50
carptim   58, 141
castellum   29, 83
catapulta   58
cautus   92
caverna   65
celebritas   147
chelonium   60
chorda   62
cilicium   67
circuitus   152
circumscriptus   58
circumspectus   202
claritudo   109
clarus   11
clavus   75

coagmentare 79
coalescere 176, 199
cochlea 62
cogitare 224
cohaerere 211
colere 186
colligere 173
colus 79
commentum 149
compaginare 55, 59, 75
compertus 11
competere 99
compingere 193
componere 60
concavare 79
concedere 133
concedere in 175
concertatio 68, 138
concinere 136
concludere 127
conclusio 127
condire 176
conficere 54
confinium 179
coniectare 127
consecratio 137
conserere 77
consiliarius 107
consociare 194
consopire 80
conspergere 47
conspicere 149
conspicuus 97
constare 109, 138
consuete 33
consultus 22
consumere 140
contemplari 105
contemplator 62
contextus 134
contrarius 104
contrectare 175
conturmalis 121
copiosus 147
crassatus 106
crebritas 73
crepido 198

cultus 174
cuneus 101
curare 48, 146
curate 30
curiosus 132
cursus 35
declarare 154
decurrere 196
defectus 198
deficere 214
deiectus 198
delere 94
depectere 207
despectare 146
destinatius 11
desudare 225
detrectare 76
deus 92
devolvere 131
devovere 122
diffundere 8
discere 152
discernere 102
discessus 140
discrimen 155
discurrere 128
displodere 69
disponere 17, 25, 112
dissolutus 220
dissonus 216
dissuadere 107
diuturnitas 176
diuturnus 16
divinus 171
documentum 84
dubitare 101
dubius 102
ductus 99
effusus 218
elucere 161
emetiri 46
enim 80
ereptum ire 179
ergo 143
erudire 173
evolare 23
exacerbare 86

exadversum 212
exceptus 29
excessus 131
excursatores 40
exercitualis 103
exhibere 95
exiguus 83
exitium 92
expandere 179
explicare 68
explicatio 69
expugnare 9
exsertus 72
exsultare 101
extentus 47
extremitas 63
faber 83
fabulosus 139
falx muralis 76
fatum 133
favorabilis 111
felicitas 99
felix 183
feritas 221
ferrum 59
ferus 182, 197
fetus 183
fidem implere 104
fidenter 92, 107, 173
fides 102, 161
fiducia 93, 110
figmentum 159
firmare 18, 47
firmitudo 175
flatus 102
flexus 63
formare 144, 225
fortuitus 182
fortuna 102
frons 145
fructuarius 185
frustrari (-e) 95
fulcire 226
fulgur 106
fulmentum 67
fundere 121
funis 65

fusus 218
generaliter 216
gentilitas 192
gestire 9
gibba 64
gignere 192, 209
glutinosus 149
gradilis 16
gradus 82
grassari 139
gravis 221
hagistia 171
harundo 78
helepolis 72
hiatus 149
honorate 117
ignarus 58
ignorare 58
illigare 61
imitari 86
immanis 101
immittere 86
immobilis 101
impendio 223
incautus 43
incertum (est) 180
incidere 170
inclinare 66
inconsultus 89
incorporare 68
incrementum 109
index 175
indicio est 193
inflare 151
ingenium 203
ingerere 219
inire 176
insectari 182
insidiosus 99
instar 71
instituere 157, 195
insularis 83
intempestivus 18
interius 186
interluere 210
internecare 187
internus 63

257

interpres 107
intueri 108
inundare 163, 194
invenire 67
isdem diebus 11
ita 91
ita demum 18
itaque demum 68
itus 25
iudex 24
iungere 144
iurisdictio 24
labes 159
laetus 166
languidus 78
lanx 71
lapsus 200
latus 145
legere 165
licenter 139
limes 41, 83, 191
litare 47
lituus 110
lixae 33
locuples 166
machinamentum 73
magicus 169
magnidicus 221
magus 169
maleficium 169
maleficus 169
malleolus 78
mandare 38
mare rubrum 184
margarita 229
medietas 66
meditamentum 73
medius 86
memoria 138
merere 92
metuendus 10
mimus 85
mitigare 125
mittere 214
mobilis 74
moenia 177
mollis 203

multifidus 79
multiplex 101
mundus 206
munimentum 83
myrmillo 226
nefandus 169
nervus 62, 63, 66
nimis 108
nimium 184, 223
nitidus 205
nomen 175
novus 23
nullus 4
numen 92
numerus 128
nuncupare 137
obire 119
oblique 103
obliquus 66
obnoxius 106
oboedientes 136
oboedire 193
obscurus 134, 186
observare 39
obtendere 67
offendere 32
onager 64
opimitas 49
opinio 171
oppugnare 9, 75
opus 72
orbis Romanus 121
ordinare 14
origo 174
ostendere 77
palea 33, 67
palmes 183
pari sorte 94
paries 78
parilis 42
particulatim 221
parum 223
patens 65
paucissimus 132
pax deum 91
pectere 207
pellis 51

penitus 213
per 158
percitus 63
perhibere 50
perrumpere 41, 114
Persis 112
perspicuus 184
piaculum 175
piceus 149
pietas 100
plaga 145
planities 196
plurifariam 79
polire 60
possidere 154
post 106, 189
posthabere 92, 124
potestas 175
potior 200, 214
potiri 173
potius 43
praecelsus 173
praeceps 23, 196
praecipere 8, 93
praecurrere 22
praefectianus 94
praerogativa 126
praesens 14
praestare 163
praesternere 223
praestringere 45
praesumere 126
praetendere 104
praetumidus 137
pravus 169
primordialis 159
priscus 172
privatus 3, 138
procedere 15
procinctus 17, 103
proculcatores 40
procursatores 40
producere 86
proeliator 127
proficere ad 132
profundere 182
prohibitorius 104

prolabi 131
promiscuus 25
promptus 82
propensus 119
properus 35
propinquitas 123
propositum 134, 215
prorumpere 102
prosapia 174
prosternere 155, 223
pueritia 98
pulsus 17
puteal 108
quadratus 60
quaeso 126
quassare 33
quatio 72
radix 198
rapere 133
ratio 71, 141
recens 84
reciprocus 72
recludere 72
reditus 25
regula 59
religiosus 37
remanere 93
remittere 18
repagulum 68
repellere 10
res cibaria 45
residuus 181
respectus 175
restis 66
restrictus 220
reverendus 104
ritus 37
robustus 49
rotabilis 63
rudimentum 134
saevus 15
sagina 231
saxeus 67
scaenicus 85
scientia 172
scorpio 64
scriptor 74

secessus 199
secretum 173
secretus 169
secus 126
secuto die 106
semiorbium 217
sequella 91
serenitas 111
serratorius 65
servare 43
sidus 145
signatus 133
significare 109
solvere 72
sors 103
sortiri 189
species 33, 149, 194
specimen 158
spiculum 78
splendidus 204
squalere 197
statio 51
stella 145
stilus 59, 66, 144
struppus 66
subinde 17, 198
sublimis 68
sublucidus 206
subtemen 207
subter 67
subtilis 62
summatim 58
superbia 139
supercilium 51
superfluus 146
superior 173
supinus 68
suppar 233
suspectus 83

taeter 221
tamen 103
temere 89
temo 59, 62, 66
temperator 136
tendere 29, 82
teres 60
tessera 23
testudo 75
tichodifros 73
tituli 15
tormen 46
tormentum 69
torpescere 218
tortor 63
trabea 2
transcurrere 141
tristis 91
trisulcus 77
tropaeatus 116
turma 40
ultra 92
ultro 92
unio 231
urguere 22
valere 78
vara 70
velut 38
venatus 187
vergere 106
vesci 193
vetustas 114
vibrare 17
Vicinus 41
vicis 138
vinculum 68
vitaxa 146
volumen 60

II Lexical (Greek)

αἰώνιος 174
ἄσβεστος 174
δίκαιόν ἐστι 174
ἑλέπολις 74

κεραία 60
κλιμάκιον 59
μαργαρίτης 230
οἴκημα 70

οὖθαρ 186
παροξύνειν 86
πινικόν 230

πλάστιγξ 71
ξαίνειν 207
χειροβαλλίστρα 59

III Syntax and Style

abl. causae 162
abl. gerundii 220
abstractum pro concreto 102, 218
accumulation of participle
    constructions 52
accusative of Goal 29
AcI-construction after decernere 12
adigere with inf. 131
adjectives as a substitute for the
    gen. 76
aliquid in a si-clause 109
anaphoric idem 10, 135
anaphoric pronouns 65
anastrophe 65
anknüpfendes nam 224
antequam with subjunctive 64, 192
asyndeton 22, 115
attendant circumstance expressed by
    perfect participle 52
auctor est + AcI 218
avoidance of certain verb forms 1, 14
brevitas 58, 131, 133
callidus with gen. 125
combination of a quod-clause and an
    inf. 153
comparativus pro positivo 87, 162, 189
composite adj. with sub- 216
cursus 82, 107, 220
dativus auctoris 104
dativus iudicantis 210
digressions, ornate style of – 224
dissuadere with AcI 107
distinction between pluperfect and
    perfect 16
emetiri, passive use of – 123
enallage 184
et 'and indeed' 3

et, at the beginning of a sentence 3
expressive pleonasm 65
facio, efficio ne 92
fate 93
first person plural, use of – 96
flowery style 57
frequentativa 158, 224
genitivus explicativus 126
genitivus identitatis 61, 62, 126
genitivus inversus 66, 166, 175
genitivus inversus and enallage 183
gerund substantivated 22
Grecism 86, 179
hic, anaphoric use of – 203
hic, cataphoric use of – 194
hypallage 66, 214
hyperbaton 67, 220
idem, anaphoric use of – 42, 193
idem, combined with other
    pronouns 159
indicative in the apodosis of an unreal
    condition 39
intueri, passive use of – 108
iterative subjunctive 68
memor with (a.c.)i. 128
oblique cases of is instead of sibi,
    se 11
orare with a passive infinitive 91
oratio obliqua, moods in subordinate
    clauses 109
passive use of a deponential verb 105
perfect instead of pluperf. 81
perfect instead of the pluperfect
    subjunctive 38
perfect passive forms with fui 68
perfect subjunctive, instead of imperf. or
    pluperf. 28
periphrasis 16

261

personificatio   64, 224
pluperfect indicative in the apodosis of an irrealis   227
posse + infin. used periphrastically   103
praecipere with inf.   93
pronomina, anaphoric use of –   61
pseudo-final clauses   140
quantum, adverbs with   220

repraesentatio   29
subjunctive in frequentative clauses   46
superlativus pro comparativo   106
suus, referring to the Agent   137
Synonymenhäufung   137
timere with AcI   123
transitional phrases   1
typifying   122
vacillation between -ibat and -iebat   38

IV Geographical Names

Abora   91, 152
Adiabas   152
Adiabene   36, 148, 152
Agazaca   210
Alexandria   173, 180, 186, 197, 209, 213
Alicodra   195
Almo   50
Amardus   178
Amaseia   44
Amida   30, 56, 75, 120
Anatha   54
Ancyra   50
Anniba   202
Antioch   xv, 87
Antiochia   128
Antiochia-Margiana   191
Anzaba   152
Apamea   136, 155, 167, 181
Apollonia   155
Aquileia   56
Arabia   183
Arabia beata   183
Arabia deserta   183
Arabia felix   146, 183
Arabius   211
Aracha   162
Arachos   212
Arachotoscrene   212
Arakia   163
Araxates   196
Arbaca   213
Arbala   154
Ardea   180

Aria   190
Ariaspe   211
Arimaspi   145
Armenia   106, 112
Arsacia   177
Artabius   213
Artacana   136, 181
Artamis   194
Artaxata   49
Asbamaeus fons   151
Ascanimia   198
Asculum Satrianum   122
Asmira   202, 205
Asmurna   189
Aspabota   200
Asparata   205
Assyria   30, 36, 115, 147
Astatia   195
Asthaia   214
Babylon   47, 156
Bactra   195
Bactria   188, 191
Baetica   153
Baetis   153
Bagrada   179
Bambyce   28
Banna   27
Bathna   27
Batnae   xv, 24, 27, 32, 49
Batnae (Osdroena)   xviii
Batradites   179
Bautis   203
Belias   45, 48
Belus   156

Beroea xv, 24, 26, 27
Bezabde 56, 78, 120
Brisoana 179
Busan 120
Caesarea 10
Callinicum xviii, 45, 48, 96
Canthicus sinus 144
Carmana 186
Carmania 146, 182, 185
Carmaniae sinus 144
Carrhae xviii, 35, 36, 45, 105
Carthage 50, 123
Caspiae portae 145
Caspian Sea 164
Caspii montes 215
Caspium mare 114
Centrites 44
Cercusium xii, xix, 37, 53, 82, 96
Chalcis 24, 27
Chalites sinus 144
Charax 136, 181
Charinda 178
Chatracharta 195
Chauriana 200
Chiliocomum 44
Choaspa 213
Choaspes 178
Choatres 181
Cilicia 26
Comedus 198
Commagene 28, 153
Corduene 44
Coronus 166
Ctesiphon xii, 45, 116, 157
Cyreschata 197
Cyropolis 177
Cyrrhus 26
Cyrus 178
Cyzicus 193
Daicus 200
Daphne 87
Davana xviii, 48
Diabas 152
Dioscoris 185
Doliche 26
Drangiana 211
Drapsaca 197

Drepsa 197
Dura xix, xx, 97, 100
Dymas 196
Ecbatana 154, 167, 177
Edessa 28, 32, 35
Emma 27
Emodus 202
Êrânsahr-Sâpûr 162
Essedon 205
Etymandros 211
Euphratensis 153
Euphrates 28, 54, 141, 143, 161, 180
Europos 177
Falerii 124
Fara 180
Fidenae 124
Ganges 146
Gaugamela 154
Gazaca 177
Gazae 177
Geapolis 184
Gedrosia 212, 213
Gindarus 114
Gordomaris 209, 210
Gynaecon limen 214
Gyndes 178
Habroatis 180
Harax 163
Harmozon 142
Hatra 116
Hecatonpylos 136, 181
Heraclea 167
Heraclia 177
Hermupolis 186
Hiber 153
Hierapolis xv, 26, 28
Hydriacus 186
Hyrcana 189
Hyrcania 187
Hyrcanian Sea 164
Iasonion 191
Iasonium 166
Iaxartes 196, 200
Imaus 146
India 213
Indus 146, 212
Isumbo 177

263

Lake Ulmia   44
Laodicea   167
Litarba   xv, 24
Lithinos pyrgos   198
Maces   142
Maefe   185
Maozamalcha   78
Marakanda   195
mare rubrum   163
Margus   190
Mari   35
Marses   161
Maxera   188
Media   164
Media Atropatene   44, 165
Megara   75
Mesene   155
Mesopotamia   30, 116, 146
Moesia   136, 181
Mons Amanus   114
Mosaeus   163
Moxoene   44
Munychia   75
Naarmalcha   155, 161
Naarsares   161
Nabataea   183
Nagara   185
Narraga   161
Nascos   184
Naulibus   210
Nazavicium   202
Nicomedia   106, 125
Nicopolis   26
Nifates   145
Nilus   153
Ninive   153
Ninus   28, 153
Nis(e)a   191
Nisibis   30, 49, 209
Numantia   123
Ochus   134
Oechartis   203
Oenunia   136, 181
Ona   152
Opurocorra   202
Oroates   163, 179, 180
Orontes   166

Ortospana   210
Osdroena   32, 116
Oxia palus   196
Oxus   188, 191
Palaestina   10
Paropanisus   210
Parthia   134
Pasargadae   180
Patigran   177
Perimula   229
Persepolis   180
Persicum mare   141, 163
Persicus sinus   141, 179
Persis   179
Petra   10
Phisganzaga   177
Phrygianum   49
Pirisabora   54, 57, 75
plain of Salmas   44
Pontus   193
Portospana   186
Prophthasia   211
Propontis   139
Psitharas   208
Ratira   214
regiones Transtigritanae   44
Reman   120
Resaina   117
Rhaga   167
Rhagae   177
Rhodus   74
Rhymmus   200
Rogomanius   179
Saba   183
Saga   200
Saganis   186
Sagareus   186
Salamis   74
Sale   189
Saramanna   188
Sarmatina   209
Scythia   139, 146
Sele   162
Seleuceia   155
Seleucia   158, 191
Sentinum   122
Sera   205

Sicyon   75
Singara   78, 120
Socanda   188
Sogdiana   195
Sosingites   148
Sotira   209
Strait of Hormuz   142
Susa   162
Susiana   162, 179
Syriamedia   178
Syriana   191
Tabiana   180
Tafra   185
Tamaris   142
Tanais   196
Taprobane   229, 230
Tarsus   26
Taxiana   180
Teredon   142, 155
Thaima   184
Thebes   75

Theodosiopolis   117
Thiltauri   27
Thospitis   148
Thrace   139
Tigris   20, 43, 148
Tomi   139
Tragonice   180
Turgana   185
Valâshâbâd   155
Veseris   122
Vitaxa   209
Vologesocerta   155
Vologessia   155
Zagros   166
Zai(u)tha   97
Zaitha   xix
Zariaspes   194
Zeugma   26
Ziata   29
Zombis   177

V   Names of Persons/Peoples

Abii   189, 200
Abraham   35
Aelius Gallus   183
Aethiopes   206
Alamanni   42
Alani   113
Albani   113, 145, 227
Alexander   24, 133, 140
Alexander the Great   111
Alypius   6, 9
Amardoi   178
Ambrose   49
Anatolius   111
Androphagi   204
Androsthenes   142
Anibi   203
Anthropophagi   203
Antiochus I   190
Antiochus III   162, 191
Antiochus of Commagene   153
Antiochus the Great   135
Antoninus   87

Antoninus Pius   116
Apasiacae   135
Apollo Comaeus   158
Apollonius   151
Apronianus   12, 19, 39
Aprunculus Gallus   18
Arabes beati   183
Arabes Scenitae   146
Arachosia   212
Aradius Rufinus   12
Ariani   209
Ariaspi   212
Aristobulus   4
Arsaces   21, 38, 45, 134–136
Arsiana   162
Artaxerxes   224
Artemisia   154
Asmirae   204
Aspacarae   205
Astyages   164, 222
Athagorae   205
Athanasius   42

Atropates 165
Avidius Cassius 116, 157
Baetae 205
Basil of Ancyra 222
Basilinna 14
Bito 56
Brahmani 173
Cadusii 145
Caecina 107
Callinicus 48
Callistus xiii
Cambyses 178, 224
Caracalla 35
Carinus 3
Carus 113, 157
Celsus 26
Chaldaei 160
Chardi 203
Chionitae 227
Choatrae 181
Claudius Mamertinus 3
Cleopatra 154
Clodius Albinus 116
Constantianus 53
Constantinus 3, 229
Constantius II 3
Crassus 35, 141
Craugasius 87
Cuseni 227
Cyaxares 164
Cyriades 88
Cyrus 139, 179
Dahae 134
Darius 139, 140, 176
Darius I 162, 172, 180
Decius 122
Deiotes 167
Demetrius Poliorcetes 74
Diocletianus 3
Diodotus 191, 192
Egeria 35, 54
Ephraem Syrus 4
Eratosthenes 141
Essedones 204
Eugenius 50
Eusebius (FGrH 101) 56
Eutropius xiii

Eutychides 16
Felix 14
Flavius Equitius 4
Flavius Sallustius 3
Flavius Victor 3
Galactophagi 200
Galerius 44, 105
Galli 50
Gallienus 48, 90
Gelani 227
Georgius 42
Gordiani 98, 117
Gordianus xix
Gordianus III 97, 112, 117
Goths 125
Gregorius Nazianzenus 4
Hadrianus 113, 116
Halani 192, 199
Helpidius 14
Hero 56
Hierocles 10
Homerus 200
Hystaspes 172
Iaxartae 200
Iberi 113
Iovianus xx, 44, 107
Iovinus 107
Iulianus 12, 14
Jason 166
Josephus 56
Jovian xii
Leontius 10
Libanius 25
Limigantes 125
Lucillianus 53, 54
Lucius Verus 158, 159
Lucullus 112, 113
Macae 142
Maès Titianus 198
Magi 168
Magnus of Carrhae 28
Marcus Aurelius 116
Marduk 156
Margiani 189
Mariades 87
Marinus of Tyrus 200
Mars 123

Massagetae   113, 139
Maximian   3
Maximianus Augustus   3
Maximianus Caesar   105
Maximus   104
Memorius   26
Merobaudes   43
Metrodorus   229
Misitheus   117
Mithridates I   135, 158, 165, 191
Mithridates VI   113, 193
Nabopolassar   160
Narse(u)s   105
Nearchus   142, 230
Nevitta   3
Ninus   154
Numenius   160
Octavianus   12
Oechardi   204
Oibares   176
Oribasius   xiii, 39
Orobazus   141
Orodes   157
Ostiaci   204
Pacorus   157
Parni   134
Paropanisadae   210
Parthi   17, 38, 112, 181
Parthians   137
Parthyaei   180
Persae   38, 112, 125
Pescennius Niger   116
Petesaces   222
Philagrius   xii
Philippus Arabs   99, 117
Philo   56
Phraates IV   35
Phraortes   164
Plato   151, 171
Plotinus   160
Pompeius   113
Pomponius Ianuarianus   3
Posidonius   201
Priscus   104
Procopius   38, 42, 45, 56
Pyrrhus of Epirus   224
Quadi   43

Rabannae   204
Rufinus   12
Rufinus Aradius   13
Sacae   197
Salutius   94, 111
Sapor I   87, 106, 227
Sapor II   162, 227
Saraceni   146
Saracens   21, 52, 82, 203, 218
Sarmatae   199
Sasanians   137
Scipio   123
Scythae   21, 31
Sebastianus   42, 45
Segestani   227
Seleucus   xii
Seleucus I   16, 48, 100, 134, 135, 140
Seleucus II   48, 135
Semiramis   151, 154, 213
Septimius Severus   54, 157
Seres   198, 201
Severus   115, 116
Sextus Claudius Petronius Probus   3
Sîn   35
Sinae   201
Sisamnes   224
Sizyges   203
Spargapises   139
Sulla   141
Symmachus   12
Tages   17
Theodosius   48, 50
Thucydides   151, 217
Tigranes   112, 113
Timesicles   117
Timesitheus   117
Tiridates   106, 181
Tochari   191, 193
Tomyris   139
Traianus   36, 54, 112, 115, 119, 157, 158
Valens   38, 43, 193
Valentinianus   38, 42
Valerianus   113
Vararanes   106
Vardanes   157
Vegetius   56

267

Ventidius 114
Venustus 12, 13
Verus 115, 116
Virius Nicomachus Flavianus 13
Vistaspa 172
Vitruvius 56

Vologaeses I 155
Vologaeses IV 116
Vologeses 155
Xerxes 53
Zenobia 154
Zoroaster 172

VI Military Matters

agmina 40
aries 56, 69
armiger 51
army, food supply of – 95
ballista 56, 58
castra praesidiaria 48
cataphracti 225
catapulta 58
cavalry, importance of Persian 225
chakhtour 55
comes rei militaris 42, 53
compulsory billeting 23
cuneus 101
decurio 40
excursatores 40
falx 76
fleet, use of – 54
helepolis 56, 72
kellek 55

limes 41, 83, 191
malleolus 56, 78
military inns 23
numerus 128
onager 56, 64
praefectianus 94
proculcatores 40
procursatores 40
scorpio 56, 64
siege warfare 56
speculatores 40
statio 51
testudo 75
tichodifros 73
tribunus 40, 53
tribunus stabuli 53
turma 40
turris ambulatoria 74

VII Various Topics

adoratio 52
Aelius Gallus 185
Africa, proconsulate of – 13
Alexander, will of – 140
alien wisdom 170
Ammianus
   and philosophy 104
   and the Greek language 152
   compresses chronology 133
   his sources for the Persan
      campaign xii
   joins Julian's army in
      Cercusium xii
   on the North-East frontier 44
   prides himself on his Greek

   origins 74
   sources of – 124
annua sollemnia 52
anti-Constantine tradition 229
Antioch, capture of – 89
Antiochenes
   attitude towards Julian of – 15
   reactions at Julian's death of – 25
   witticisms of – 24
Apollo, desctruction of his temple 39
apparitor 94
Arabic chronicles 87
astronomers 58
astronomy 173
Atargatis 28

autopsy 167
Bereshit Rabbah 76.6 88
biothanati 118
bitumen 156
Brahmans 173
canals in Mesopotamia 161
carpentum 50
cherry 113
China, contacts with – 202
Chinese
   a peace-loving nation 206
   a bellicose nation 206
   a frugal nation 208
Chronicle of Seert 90
chronology of the Persian
     campaign xv
cities, as ornaments of a country 197
civilitas 126
cohors 51
comes Orientis 13
comes sacrarum largitionum 15
conflation of sources 95
Constantine
   his provocation of the Persians x
   responsible for the war with
     Persia 229
Constantius' eastern policy 120
consul
   takes up office the 1st of
     January 15
   terms used by Amm. for his
     appointment 2
consularis 24
consulate, held by private persons 3
curiositas 2
Cybele
   Ammianus' interest in her cult 49
   attacks by Christian authors on
    – 50
   vitality of her cult 49
dates, exact 39, 106
death penalty 94
   forms of – 88
Dendrophori 50
determinism 92
devotio 122
digressions

introductions to – 58
   level of – 56
discipline, lack of – 124
divinatio 17
divination 106, 161, 174
doxographical tradition 151
dux Aegypti 42
Egyptian priests 160
Eratosthenes 141
Esagila 156
Eunapius, relation with Amm.'s
     account xiv
eunuchs 151
Eutropius, as a participant in the Persian
     campaign xiii
Eutychianus as a source for the Persian
     campaign xiii
extispicium 37
felicitas 99
fire, worship of – 174
first person plural, use of – 96
flaying 222
food supply 94
foreign auxiliaries 21
fortuna 121
fulgurales libri 108
fulmen consiliarium 18
fysici 58
Galli 50
genius 16
Gordianus, tomb of – xix, 97
guerilla warfare 52
haplography 119
haruspices 17
haruspicina 103, 108
henotheism 120
historiography, dignity of 2
Homer, quotations from – 200
imperial adlocutiones 111
imperial insignia 38
India, reason why it is not
     described 213
Italy, blockade of – 11
itineraries, use of – 201
Julian
   addiction to omina 47
   altering bad omens 47

269

Ammianus critical of – 9
and Alexander 111
and the Roman Senate 11
as interpreter of dreams and omina 38
attitude towards the Jews 5
civilitas 4
devotion to Cybele 49
disregard for omina x
interest in history 111, 124
motives for the Persian campaign ix
nomination for office 11
pietas 100
restless activity 8
restoration of the temple 4
strategy against Persia 45
lavatio 50
Libanius as a source for the Persian campaign xii
Liber Caliphorum 90
libri exercituales 18, 104
libri fulgurales 18
libri rituales 18
libri Tagetici 17
libri Tarquitiani 18
libri Vegonici 17
limes 191
lions 101
ludi Apollinares 84
Luna/Lunus 37
Magi 168
magical practices 220
Magnus of Carrhae as a source for the Persian campaign xiii
maps, evidence for the use of – 164, 212
Marathon, battle of – 140
Mars as a metonymy for warfare 123
Mater deorum 49
mimus 85
Misopogon 2
date of composition of – 14
modesty, declaration of – 58
moon cult 35
moon-temples in Carrhae 37
mors immatura 118

Mycale, battle of – 140
myrmillo 226
mythistoriae 2
names in divinatory practice 108
naphtha 176
nations, character and environment 199
Nesaean horses 167
nos, noster referring to Romans 141
officialis 94
oleum Medicum 176
omen impetrativum 48
omen oblativum 48
omina 38, 94
interpretation of – 16
opposition to the Persian campaign x, 1, 18, 19
oracula Chaldaica 161
orbis Romanus 121
Oribasius, as a source for the Persian campaign xiii
Orphics 160
Parthi and Persae used indiscriminately 38
Parthian kings
sacrosanctity of – 138
titles of – 137
pax deum 91
pearls 229
Persia
order of treatment 164
Rome's relations with – 115
Persian footsoldiers 226
Persians
beast metaphor applied to – 217
eating habits 222
proneness to sex 217
their customs 216
their physical appearance 216
personification of justice 118
phalerae 47
Philagrius, as a source for the Persian campaign xii
philosophers in Julian's entourage x
philosophy, respect for – 160
physiognomists 216
Plataeae, battle of – 140

praeses   26
praetorian prefect, office of –   94
prefecture of Rome   13
purple   38
quindecimviri sacris faciundis   19
references to lost books   133, 187
religion
   non-Greek peoples and –   169
   Persian –   168
Rufius Festus   133
Salamis, battle of –   140
Sasanian kings, sacrosanctity of –   138
Sasanians   179
scaenici ludi   85
scorched-earth policy   40
sea-hounds   232
Seleucus, as a source for the Persian campaign   xiii
Seneca as a source for Amm.   107
ship-bridge   31
Sibylline books   19, 39
Silk Route   198
smallpox   159
soldiers, mood of –   93
Strasbourg, battle of –   128
temple of Apollo on the Palatine   12
temple of Jerusalem, restoration of –   4
tessera   23
theologi   58
tigers   187
trade between Romans and Persians   49
Tyche, temple of –   16
urbs aeterna   11
vitaxa   146
Wanderanekdoten   208
wars between Romans and Parthians and Sasanians   141
ziqqurat   156
Zoroaster, and India   172
Zosimus, relation with Amm.'s account   xiv

VIII   Passages referred to (Latin)

Acta Arval.
   105 II 41   25
Ambrosius
   epist.
      18.30   50
      40   48
      40.12   4
   fug. saec.
      2.5   172
   hex.
      6.4.21   187
Amp.
   13.1   139
l'Année Epigraphique
   1964.231   100
Anon. de mach. bell.
   8   73, 77
   18   61
   18.1   61
   18.5   64
Anthologia Latina
   I 1   49
Apuleius
   Apol.
      25.9–26.3   169
   Met.
      1.23.3   158
      2.2   86
      5.25   51
      9.40   66
   Soc.
      12   173
Arnobius
   c. Gent.
      7.49   50
Augustinus
   C.D.
      1.23   107
      2.4   50
      4.20   121
   Petil.
      3.56.68   175
   s.dom.m.
      2.20.68   104

Augustus
  Anc.
    12   153
    26   185
    29.2   35
Aurelius Victor
  Caes.
    27.8   98, 99
    39.14ff   4
    39.35   105
Ausonius
  Prof.
    2.23   3
Avienus
  orb. terr.
    929   200
    935   206
    1012   205
    1257–8   228
B. Alex.
    2.5   74
Caesar
  Civ.
    2.9.4   76
    3.106.1   29
  Gal.
    1.25.1   126
    2.6.2   72
    2.18.3   150
    2.31.2   78
    3.14.5   77
    3.28.3   23
    7.73.6   60
Cassiodorus
  hist.
    11.8.3   174
  var.
    11.46   219
Cato
  R.R.
    156.5   46
    157.9   46
Celsus
    4.22.1   46
    5.27.10   166

Cicero
  ad Brut.
    1.15.10   84
    1.15.11   223
  Agr.
    2.1   174
    2.88   124
  Att.
    3.7.1   147
    10.8a.1   29
    12.37.2   147
  Cat.
    1.26   119
  de Orat.
    1.189   58
    1.253   224
    2.34   86
    3.2   85
  Div.
    1.2   109
    1.78   17
    1.92   107
    1.97   10, 47
    1.100   200
    1.102–3   108
    1.106   47
    1.127   69
    2.42–5   72
    2.115   102
    2.115–6   102
  Dom.
    138   86
  Fam.
    10.18.3   114
  Fin.
    2.61   122
    5.42   69
  Har.
    22   86
    25   86
    26   86
  Mil.
    10   18
  Mur.
    38   128
  N.D.
    2.12   107

3.48   37
Off.
   1.81   8, 18
   2.19   102
Phil.
   6.13   226
   11.9   119
Q.Rosc.
   20   86
Rab. Post.
   43   226
Rep.
   1.1   18
   3.41   193
S.Rosc.
   6   147
Tusc.
   1.8   122
   2.45   46
Ver.
   4.43   170
CIL
   2.6278.56   204
   3.12333   15
   3.7088   15
   3, Suppl. 6719   163
   5.8024   15
   6.1139   121
   6.1638   100
   6.1729   3
Claudianus
   Cons. Stil.
      2.340   2
   in Eutr.
      2.10   2
      2.478–9   223
   rapt.
      3.263–8   187
Codex Iustinianus
   3.42.6   117
   4.63.4   49
   6.10.1   117
   8.35.12   14
   12.37.1   55
   12.37.13   10
Codex Theodosianus
   3.1.3   14

7.4.6   55
7.4.30   10
7.22.11   226
9.12.1   221
9.16.1   17
9.16.4   17, 103, 161
9.16.6   169
9.16.9   103
9.16.11   169
12.1.55   10
12.13.6   52
14.4.3   12
16.10.1   103
16.10.9   103
16.10.14   50
16.10.20   50
Columella
   3.14.1   196
   10.401   186
Curtius Rufus
   2.9.9   156
   3.3.9   174
   3.3.13   227
   4.5.8   180
   4.24.24   174
   5.1.16   156
   5.1.24   156, 157
   5.1.25   156
   5.4.33   180
   5.7.3   180
   5.8.1   167
   6.2.14   181
   6.2.15   182
   6.4.21   188
   6.4.31   194
   6.11.20   223
   7.3.6   210
   7.4.26   192
   7.4.31   195
   7.6.13   196
   7.6.16   197
   7.6.25   196, 197
   7.10.1–3   196
   8.10.32   74
   9.5.19   78
   9.10.6   213
   10.1.26   218

10.10.5   140
Cyprianus
  Demetr.
    3   186
Dictys
  2.37   30
Digesta
  17.1.29.6   104
  19.2.19.9   104
  43.16.1.27   18
Ennius
  Ann.
    167 Sk.   102
Ephraem Syrus
  HcJul.
    4.3   14
Epitome
  27.2   99, 118
  27.3   97
Eutropius
  1.19.1   124
  7.5.2   114
  8.3.1   157
  8.3.2   36
  8.10.2   157, 158
  9.2.2   98, 118
  9.2.3   82, 83, 97, 99, 100
  9.18.1   157
  9.22.1   105
  9.25.1   105
  10.16.1   xiii, 42
Festus
  p. 358 L   226
Filastrius
  120.7   33
Florus
  Epit.
    1.6.4   124
    1.6.12   124
    1.31.4   123
    1.33   203
Frontinus
  Str.
    1.1.6   114
    2.2.5   114
    2.4.8   91

Fronto
  Aur.
    2. p. 80 (153N)   69
Gellius
  3.3.5   218
  5.10.7   141
  9.4.6   213
  15.4.4   114
Glossarii
  IV 68.44   86
  V 292.04   86
Gregorius Turonensis
  Franc.
    3.19   72
  glor. conf.
    76   50
Hegesippus
  3.5.2   85
  3.9.5   198
Hieronymus
  adv. Iovin.
    2.17   50
  Chron. s.a.
    371   13
  Comm. in Naum
    3.646   86
  epist.
    130.5   86
Historia Augusta
  Car.
    8.1   157
  Cc
    6.6   37
    7.3–5   37
  Gd
    26.3   98
    29–33   99
    33.4   119
    33.5   118
    34.2   83, 97
    34.3   100
  MA
    13.3–6   160
  OM
    1.4   2
  Pr.
    17.5   105

Sev.
  16.1–2   157
T
  2   87, 88
V
  8.2   159
  8.2–3   158
  8.3   158

Horatius
Carm.
  1.2.22   221
  1.12.56   201
  1.29.9   206
  3.5.4–5   221
  3.29.27   201
  4.15.23   201
Ep.
  2.1.168   86
S.
  1.2.44   33
  1.8.46   69

ILS
  751   15
  753   15
  8945   15

Isidorus
Etym.
  16.10.1   230, 231

Itala
Marc.
  10.25   65

Itinerarium Antonini
  p. 26   32
  p. 86   35

Itinerarium Egeriae
  18.2–3   31, 54
  19.1   32
  20.8   35

Iustinus
  1.1.4–10   154
  1.1.10   154
  1.2.7   156
  1.6.3   180
  1.6.17   164
  1.8   139
  1.10   176

  1.10.4   176
  3.3.13   228
  11.14.10   180
  41.2   226
  41.2.4   227, 229
  41.3.8   221
  41.4.3   135
  41.4.5   134
  41.4.5–9   191
  41.4.6   193
  41.4.6–5.6   134
  41.4.6–7   134
  41.4.7   134
  41.4.8   136
  41.4.8–9   192
  41.4.9   135
  41.5.1–2   136
  41.5.5   136
  41.5.6   138
  41.5.8   137
  41.6.1   176
  42.3.9   148
  42.4.16   227

Jordanes
Get.
  10.62   139

Juvenalis
  6.587   108

Lactantius
inst.
  5.9.20   58
  5.14.8   58
  6.12.6   138
mort.
  48.2   121
mort.pers.
  9.5   105
  9.7   105
  22.5   224

Livius
  1.18.3   216
  1.32.2   110
  2.12   122
  3.5.14   92
  4.34.3   124
  5.1–22   124
  5.16.10   128

5.27   124
7.6   122
7.6.4   149
8.9–10   122
9.16.17   110
9.41.16   71
10.28   122
21.1.5   52
21.8.10   60
21.11.7   74
22.43.1   89
24.31.4   92
25.37.10   118
25.38.5   38
28.43.14   136
36.32.9   92
36.44.2   66
37.40.12   193
38.7.4   72
39.13.12   80
45.8.7   102
per.
   20   124
   127–8   114
Lucanus
   1.156   72
   1.460–462   182
   3.246   181
   6.198–9   62
Lucretius
   1.21   203
   3.750   187
   5.1229   91
   6.86–9   72
   6.660   109
   6.756   150
   6.756–9   149
Macrobius
   Sat.
      1.5.13   13
      1.17.25   84
Manilius
   4.750–1   228
Mela
   1.13   145, 210
   1.32   186
   1.37   203

1.67   186
1.81   145
2.2   204
2.9   204
2.13   204
3.5   153
3.7   201
3.41   178
3.43   187
3.44–45   164
3.60   206, 208
3.76   160
3.78   143
3.79   142, 183
1.109   215
Nemesianus
   ecl.
      3.49   79
Nepos
   Milt.
      7.3   149
Orosius
   hist.
      1.12.47   164
      7.19.4   99
      7.20.1   99
      7.25.4   105
      7.25.10–11   105
Ovidius
   Am.
      2.5.51–2   77
      3.9.35   133
   Fast.
      1.59   123
      2.574   149
      2.55–58   xix, 82
   Met.
      2.195–6   79
      3.543   174
      4.57–8   156
      4.439–40   29
      5.587–8   184
      10.664   186
      14.329   50
   Rem.
      2.515   86
      188   166

Tr.
   4.10.03   213
Panegyrici latini
   2.31.4   22
   3.14.1–2   11
   5.18.4   83
   10.11.3   183
Panegyricus Messallae
   3.7   178
Persius
   2.27   108
Physiognomici
   18   217
   79   216
   83   217
Plautus
   Am.
      189   187
   Mil.
      923   221
   Persa
      625   108
   Rud.
      515   221
Plinius Maior
   Nat.
      1.6   178
      1.10   178
      2.43   72
      2.48   193
      2.194   17
      2.207–208   150
      2.232   151
      3.9   153
      3.21   153, 196
      3.41   194
      3.51   196
      4.88   204
      4.118   153
      5.36   145
      5.48   145
      5.66   36, 152
      5.72.2   203
      5.88   158
      5.90   143
      5.98   145
      5.99   215

      6.11   180
      6.21   204
      6.21.1   203
      6.21.5   203
      6.24   142
      6.24.8   203
      6.25   178
      6.26   178
      6.29   178
      6.32   183
      6.36   164, 196
      6.39   164, 178
      6.42   177
      6.43   181
      6.43–4   145
      6.44   177, 182
      6.45   178
      6.46   164, 188, 190
      6.47   191
      6.48   194, 195
      6.49   196, 197
      6.50   204
      6.52   178
      6.53   202
      6.53–55   201
      6.54   206–208
      6.55   193, 208
      6.60   198
      6.61   210, 211, 213
      6.62   181
      6.71   212
      6.78   213
      6.81   229
      6.88   201, 208
      6.92   210, 212
      6.93   209, 210
      6.94–95   213
      6.95   214
      6.97   213
      6.98   142
      6.99   180
      6.104   185
      6.107   186
      6.107–8   163
      6.108   142, 143
      6.108–9   141
      6.109   143

6.110	214, 229	31.35	178
6.111	163	35.73	77
6.113	181, 188	31.75	194
6.114	141	35.178	149

Plinius Minor
Ep.

6.115	180
6.119	48
6.122	155, 157, 158
6.123	161, 180
6.128	148
6.129	155
6.130	178
6.131	166
6.136	163, 180
6.145	142, 160
6.152	142
6.153	185
6.154	184
6.160	184
7.23	187
7.126	75
7.135	114
7.160	185
7.178	159
8.66	187
8.67	193
8.68	193
9.106	229, 232
9.107	230, 231
9.107–124	229
9.109	231
9.110	232
9.111	231
9.112	231
9.115	233
9.116	233
9.117–21	232
10.37	104
10.132	158
10.152	232
11.59	149
11.78	207
15.74	123
17.81	110
18.99	33
18.216	160
18.297	33
28.69	220

1.9.3	123
3.9.5	182
3.14.4	118
4.30	151

Prudentius
apoth.

439–440	19

Perist.

10.153	50
10.1006	50
1061	50

ps. Hilarius
libell.

11 p. 743 b	221

Quintilianus
Inst.

1.12.15	172
12.3.4	224

Rufinus
hist.

10.38	10
10.38–40	4, 9

Rufius Festus

14	36, 105
20	36
21	158
22	97–99, 118
25	105
28	42, 124

Rutilius Namatianus

2.52	19

Sallustius
Hist.

2.44	187, 220
3.42	193
5.3	138

Jug.

7.4	109
17.1	58
79.1	58
79.6	192

80.6   218
Seneca Minor
  Ag.
    247–8   102
  Cons. Polyb.
    14.5   123
  De ira
    3.21   178
  Ep.
    24.14   222
    40.14   221
    47.3   222
    79.10   97
    95.64   172
    118.9   18
    123.7   22
  Her. O.
    589   142
    668   201
  Nat.
    1.1.5   10, 64
    2.18–9   109
    2.24   109
    2.39.1   107
    2.57.4   72
    3.7.3   68
  Oct.
    598–600   118
Servius
  A.
    2.691   48
    4.386   118
    10.653   198
  Ecl.
    3.8   217
  G.
    1.43   23
    2.120–1   207
Sidonius
  epist.
    1.5.2   25
Silius
  13. 341/2   67
Sisenna
  hist.
    83   78

Solinus
  2.3   194
  17.4   187
  17.4–7   187
  19.4   178
  19.5   178
  22.12   68
  23.8   153
  37.6   143, 178
  38.4   178
  47.1–2   145
  48.2   190
  48.3   191
  49.7   204
  49.9   193
  49.12   193
  50.1   202
  50.2   206
  50.3   206, 208
  50.4   208
  50.2   207
  51.1   206
  52.37   69
  53.23   230, 231
  53.23–27   229
  53.24   231
  53.25   231, 232
  53.27   231, 232
  54.2   210, 212, 213
  54.6   142
  54.12   143
  55.1   147
  56.3   157
Statius
  Silv.
    2.2.12   165
Suetonius
  Aug.
    28.3   67
    29.3   39
    31.1   39
    49.1   51
    94.5   173
    95   194
  Cl.
    41.3   15

279

Dom.
  23.2   64
Jul.
  50   232
  89   119
Nero
  31.2   231
Tib.
  38   25
  48.1   125
Ves.
  4.5   9
Symmachus
  epist.
    2.65   173
    7.126   13
    9.112   2
Tabula Peutingeriana
  X 2   31
  X 3   35
  X 4   155, 177
  X 5 – XI 2   164
  X 8   177
  XI 1–3   178
  XI 3   204
Tacitus
  Ag.
    12.6   233
  Ann.
    1.80.1   24
    2.27.1   30
    2.27.2   107
    4.2.1   105
    6.1   158
    6.3.3   52
    6.3.4   102
    6.20.2   109
    6.24.4   157
    12.13   36
    12.52.2   182
    13.24.2   107
    13.36.1   23
    13.39.4   72
    14.6.1   153
    14.42–5   223
    15.2.4   38
    15.3.1   54

    15.18.1   116
    15.48.3   220
    16.22.3   30
  Dial.
    5.4   218
  Germ.
    12   182
    14   182
  Hist.
    1.2.1   15
    2.79–81   9
    3.17.1   110
    3.23.2   68
    4.26.3   73
    4.33.4   121
    4.34.2   52
    4.55.1   174
    5.1   9
    5.5.2   218
    5.8.2   221
    5.11   9
Terentius
  Hec.
    45   85
Tertullianus
  anim.
    14.5   65
    24.12   171
    57.1–05   118
  cult.fem.
    1.6.2   230
Tibullus
  2.1.63   79
Valerius Maximus
  3.3.1   122
  6.3 ext. 3   224
  9.2 ext. 6   176
Varro
  L.
    5.91   40
    5.148–9   122
    6.2   214
  R
    3.14.2   198
Vegetius
  4.20   76
  4.46   76

   mil.
      2.14   40
      3.3   40
      4.8   149, 176
      4.9.1   66
      4.14   71, 77
      4.16   74
      4.17   73, 76
      4.18   78, 149, 176
      4.22.4   64
      4.22.8   69
Velleius
   2.26.1   2
Vergilius
   A.
      1.2–3   29
      1.531   186
      2.492/3   72
      2.691   47
      3.164   186
      3.370   92
      3.420   210
      4.211–2   83
      4.367   187
      4.656   118
      5.529   86
      6.824   122
      7.254   103
      8.393   166
      8.426–8   60
      9.705–6   62
      11.896–7   15

      12.788   68
   Cat.
      10 (8)   114
   Ecl.
      1.17   107
   G.
      1.55   185
      1.286   104
      1.309   66
      2.106   164
      2.120–1   206
      2.121   201
      2.136–8   194
      2.157   194
      3.566   109
      4.86–7   80
Vitruvius
   1.5.8   156
   5.5.1   71
   10.10–12   58
   10.11.2   65
   10.11.7   60
   10.13.1–3   69
   10.13.2   70, 71, 76
   10.13.3   74, 76
   10.13.4   76
   10.16   74
   10.16.4   74, 75
Vulgata
   lev.
      7.17   68

IX Passages referred to (Greek)

Aeschylus
   Ag.
      689   74
   Pers.
      602   102
Aelianus
   NA
      1.55   232
      4.55   193
      5.21   227
      10.13   230–232

      10.20   232
      15.8   230, 233
   VH
      12.1   218
Agathias
   3.23.1   226
   4.25.1   105
Anonymus
   post Dionem
      (Müller FHG 4, p. 192)   87

Antiphon
   3.7   118
Appianus
   Mith.
      115   47
   Syr.
      57   48, 181
Aristoteles
   HA
      6.2, 559 b   232
   Mete.
      351a8   164
      354a3   164
   Pol.
      2.5.11 (1268 b 40)   217
Arrianus
   An.
      3.8.4   212
      3.8.7   154
      3.16.5   160
      3.18.12   180
      3.19.2   145
      3.23.6   189
      3.27.4   212
      3.29.1   197
      3.29.2   188
      3.30.7   196
      4.1.3   196, 197
      4.1.5   195
      4.3.2   197
      4.5.6   196
      4.6.6   209, 212
      4.6.7   196
      4.7.1   195
      4.11.9   139
      4.22.4   210
      4.22.5   210
      5.3.2   210
      5.3.3   210
      5.4.5   139
      5.11.3   210
      5.26.2   141
      6.15.3   210
      6.15.26   210
      6.21.3   213
      6.21.4   213
      6.22.5   213

      6.24.4   214
      7.1.1   180
      7.13.1   167
      7.16.3   196
   Ind.
      21.8   213, 214
      22.8   213, 214
      22.10   214
      25.3   214
      32.4   186
      32.7   142
      37.2   185
      38.3   230
      39.6   179
      39.7   180
      39.9   163
   Parth.
      1.2   136
Athanasius
   Hist. Arian.
      59   42
Athenaeus
   3.93 c   229
   3.93 b   232
   3.93 d   228, 232
   3.93 d-e   230
   3.93 e   232
   3.94 b   232
   4.145 c   218
   5.206 d   74
   10.413 a-c   219
   10.415 a   74
Athenaeus Mechanicus
   p. 27 Wescher   74, 75
Babrius
   95.16   102
Berossus
   Babyl.
      1.2.3–4   156
      3.3.3   157
Bito
   p. 52–6 Wescher   74
Chronicon Paschale
   s.a. 250   83
Chrysostomus
   De Laud. Pauli
      4   4

Exp. in Ps.
   110.4   4
Hom. in Acta Apost.
   41.3   4
Hom. in Mt.
   4   4
Jud.
   5.11   4
Jud. et gent.
   16   4
pan. Bab.
   1.17.22   14, 15
   2.22   4
   2.121   31
Cosmas Indocopleustes
   2.45   201
Dio Cassius
   36.16.1   113
   37.3.3–05   113
   37.3.5   178
   40.16   158
   40.17   35
   40.20.3   157
   48.39   114
   53.12.4–05   153
   62.20   36
   66.4–7   9
   66.9.4   2
   68.17.1   115
   68.26.4   154
   68.27   147, 150
   68.27.2   150
   68.27.3   151
   68.28   36
   68.30.2   158
   68.30.3   157
   71.2.3   158, 159
   75.9.2   105
   75.9.2–05   157
   75.9   54
   78.4–5   35
   79.2.3   157
Dio Chrysostomus
   15.20   221
Diodorus Siculus
   2.1   154
   2.2.3   145
   2.3.2–04   153
   2.4.1   154
   2.7.2–11   157
   2.9.4   156
   2.12.1   149
   2.29   160
   2.29.1–03   160
   2.31.7–09   160
   2.44.2   139
   2.48   183
   14.96.5   124
   15.10.1   224
   17.53.4   154
   17.69   180
   17.71–72   180
   17.75.4–07   188
   17.82.1–5   210
   17.100.4   214
   17.110.6   167
   17.112.2   160
   17.112.3   156
   18.81   212
   19.5.1   76
   19.7.2   76
   19.7.5   76
   19.21   180
   19.55.7–09   160
   20.45.5   75
   20.46.3   75
   20.48.1–03   74
   20.48.2–03   74
   20.58.1   74
   20.91.2–05   74
   20.91.2–08   74
   20.91.7   77
   20.91.5   76
   21.6.1   122
Diogenes Laërtius
   1.1   160
   1.8   168
Dionysius Halicarnassensis
   8.80   223
Dionysius Periegeta
   113   210
   714   210
   754–5   207

Euripides
  El.
    1147–8   102
Eratosthenes
  fr. III B, 39   141
Euagrius
  HE
    1.16   16
Eunapius
  fr.
    15 Blockley   xiii
    44 (Blockley)   43
  VS
    465   85
Eusebius Caesariensis
  HE
    6.34   99
Eusebius Historicus
  FGrH
    101, p. 481.9–21   78
FGrH
  134 F 3   188
  244 F 157   200
  4 F1   154
  779 F 7   201
GGM
  II, 348   208
  II, 474   143
Gregorius Nazianzenus
  Or.
    5.2   14, 15
    5.3–4   4
    5.4   7, 9
    5.8   112
    5.19   27
Herodianus
  3.9   54
  4.10.3   225
  4.11.3   227
  4.11.6   228
  4.13   35
  4.15.3   228
  6.2   38
  6.5.3   226
  6.7.1   226
Herodotus
  1.53   102

1.84   228
1.98   167
1.101   170
1.102   164
1.103   165
1.106   164
1.130   164
1.132   168, 175
1.133   218–220
1.135   218
1.138   220
1.179   156
1.180   143
1.181   160
1.183   160
1.184   154
1.188   178
1.188–189   178
1.202   164
1.204–214   139
1.211–213   139
3.34   218
3.70   172, 176
3.84   176
3.93   196, 209, 211
3.106   167
3.107   184
3.116   145
3.119   223
3.155   154
4.13   145, 204
4.27   145
4.40   179
4.83   140
4.106   204
4.196   208
5.25.1–02   224
6.107–117   140
6.119   176
7.22–024   140
7.33–036   140
7.40   167
7.59   53
7.64   197
7.89–100   53
7.142   103
7.235   174

8.40–097   140
8.114–120   140
9.16–088   140
9.20   167
9.90   140
9.96–101   140
Hippocrates
   Aër.
      12.24   199
Historia Acephala
   6   42
Homerus
   Il.
      1.141   186
      5.83   200
      13.06   189, 200
Iamblichus
   vit. Pyth.
      151   160
IGLS
   2.354   27
Iohannes Chrysostomus →
   Chrysostomus
Iohannes Lydus → Lydus
Iosephus
   AJ
      8.63–98   9
      11.2   139
      15.380–425   9
      18.45   217
      20.35   36
   BJ
      3.7   9
      3.211   71
      3.214–7   69
      3.215   71
      3.216   71
      3.230–1   73
      3.232   73
      6.220–270   9
      6.267   9
Isidorus Characenus
   3 (GGM I, 246–247)   51
   6 (GGM I 250)   177
   7 (GGM I 251)   181
   8 (GGM I 251)   181
   12 (GGM I 252)   191
   14 (GGM I 253)   191
   19 (GGM I 254)   213
Iulianus
   Ep.
      9   10
      10   9, 10
      25b   121
      28   14
      57 Wright   8, 21
      80   14
      89a   5, 6
      89b   5, 6
      98   xii, xv, 24, 27, 32
      98, 399 b   xv, 24
      98, 399 c   xvi
      98, 399 d   xvi, 27
      98, 400 a   xvii
      98, 401 b   xvii, 27
      98, 401 d   21, 82
      98, 401 d – 402 b   27
      98, 402 a   22, 30
      98, 402 b   55
      134   6
      204   5
   Gal.
      100 c   5
      148 c   5
      306 a   5
      306 b   5
   Mis.
      340 a   14
      342 b   86
      346 b   16
      360 c   128
      364 d   26
      365 c   14
      368 d   24
      370 b-c   26
   Or.
      7.223 b   26
      8   49
      8.20, 180 b   51
Johannes Antiochenus
   E 83 (fr. 176 Müller)   200
Libanius
   Ep.
      21   48

88   16
324   10
334   10
334 and 335   10
734   xii
764   14
802   xii, 27
802.1   xv
802.8   xii
811   xii, 24
825   13
836   26
838   24
1124   13
1219   13
1220.7–09   xii
1220.2   25
1256   24
1294   24
1343   13
1365   13
1374   13
1379   13
1380   13
1386   26
1395   9
1398   13
1400   13
1402.3   xii
1402.2   45
1434.2–06   xii, xiii
1456   24
1493   13
1508.6–07   xii, xiii
Or.
  1.13   25
  1.132   25
  12   15
  12.96   4
  14.36   14
  15   25
  15.16   87
  15.74   24
  15.86   26
  16   25
  16.53   26

17.19   119
17.22   3
17.37   25
18.169   21
18.177   17
18.211   128
18.213   22
18.214   xviii, 28, 30, 32, 37, 41–43, 55, 95
18.215   8, 43
18.255   124
18.260   42, 45
24.38   84
50.19   126
60.2–3   87

Lydus
  Mens.
    4.110   6
    4.118   42

Magnus
  (FGrH 225 F 1)   110, 111

Malalas
  Chron.
    8.13–14   16
    11.9   16
    12.295   88
    12.295–6   87, 88
    12.308   83
    13.328   27, 28, 90
    13.328–30 xiii
    13.328–329 8
    13.329   35, 36, 54, 83
    13.329–30 96
    13.330   53
    13.331   41
    13.329   42

Menander Protector
  exc. Rom.
    8   222

Novum Testamentum
  Acta
    16.10   96
  Mt.
    24.2   5

Numenius
  fr. 1a (Des Places)   169

286

Oppianus
  H.
    1.373–4   232
Oracula Sibyllina
  13.17   97
  13.18   99
  13.90   89
  13.119–128   89
  13.125–8   87
Origenes
  Cels.
    1.14   170
passio s. Bas. presb. 4 (BHG3 242)   222
Pausanias
  6.2.7   16
  6.26.6   201
  6.26.6–08   207
  8.33.3   156
Periplus Maris Erythraei
  38   212
  40   144
  59   230
  61   230
  64   201
  65   208
Petrus Patricius
  fr. 13   105
  fr. 14   105
PGM
  IV 1888   118
  IV 2578   118
  XII 107   118
Philo
  De spec. leg.
    3.17   227
Philo Mechanicus
  Bel.
    p. 95 Thévenot   74
Philostorgius
  HE
    3.4   185
    7.9   4, 9
    7.10   14, 15
Philostratus
  VA
    1.6   151

1.19   28
3.41   173
3.58   28
6.11   170
Photius
  Codex
    98 Henry 84 b 27 ff.   xiv
Plato
  Alc.
    1.122 a   171
Polybius
  2.32.9–10   93
  5.45.5   157
  6.25.1–02   40
  6.44.5   145
  10.27.1–02   167
  10.27.3   167
  10.27.4–13   167
  10.28.7   181
  10.48.1   188
  10.48.4   210
  10.49.15   195
  11.34.11   210
  30.25.6   167
Plotinus
  Enn.
    3.7.1   160
    5.1.8   160
Plutarchus
  Alex.
    31   145
    38   180
  Ant.
    33–4   114
  Art.
    6.1   218
  Cat. Ma.
    4.4   221
  Crass.
    19   35
    23.4   48
  Demetr.
    1.7   75
    20.7   74
    20.9   74
    20–21   74
    21.2   76

287

  39–40 75
  42.10 75
 Luc.
  11.6 193
  28.8 113
  36.6 227
 Mor.
  183 b 74
 Pomp.
  34.1–36.1 113
  36.1 114
Porphyrius
 Plot.
  3 170
Procopius
 Aed.
  2.6.2 82, 83
 Arc.
  7.8–09 217
 BP
  1.13.11 28
 Goth.
  1.21.8 70
  1.21.14 59, 61
  1.21.17 63
  1.21.5–12 69
  1.23.9–12 64
  4.11.36 176
 Pers.
  1.4.14 228
  1.4.15–31 228
  1.4.17–31 232
  1.5.9 222
  1.5.28 222
  1.13.11 28
  1.14.25 226
  1.14.34 219
  2.5.2 82
  2.7.2–04 xvi
ps. Arist.
 mirab. auscult.
  57 151
ps. Plato
 Axiochus
  371 d 171
Ptolemaeus
  1.11.1 205

  1.11.4 198, 205
  1.11–14 201
  1.12.1 198
  1.12.7 198
  1.17.5 205
  4.5.46 186
  4.5.60 186
  5.2.26 150
  5.12.1 145
  5.14.2 196
  5.15.24 163
  5.18.6 51
  5.20 148, 160
  5.20.2 161
  5.20.5 142
  6.1.1 145, 148
  6.1.2 36
  6.1.3–6 155
  6.1.5 154
  6.1.6 155
  6.2.1 164, 178
  6.2.2 145, 177, 178
  6.2.4 166
  6.2.5 145
  6.2.6 166, 178
  6.2.10 177
  6.2.14 177
  6.2.16 177
  6.2.17 177
  6.3.1 163
  6.3.2 163
  6.3.5 162
  6.4.1 163
  6.4.2 163, 179, 180
  6.4.4 180
  6.4.4–6 180
  6.4.5 180
  6.4.6 180
  6.4.7 180
  6.4.8 163, 180
  6.5.2 163
  6.5.2–4 181
  6.5.3 181
  6.7.1 183
  6.7.14 142
  6.7.29 184
  6.7.35 184

6.7.37	185	6.17.6	210
6.7.41	185	6.17.7	209
6.7.45	185	6.18.1	210
6.7.47	185	6.18.3	210
6.8.3	180	6.18.4	211
6.8.4	186	6.18.4–5	211
6.8.6	185	6.18.5	211
6.8.7	186	6.19	211
6.8.8	186	6.19.2	211
6.8.13–14	186	6.19.4–5	211
6.9.2	188	6.20.1	212
6.9.7	189	6.20.2	212
6.10	190	6.20.4–5	213
6.10.3–4	191	6.21.1	213
6.11.3–4	194	6.21.2	211, 213, 214
6.11.6	194	6.21.3	214
6.11.7–9	195	6.21.4	214
6.12.1	196	6.21.5	213, 214
6.12.2	195	6.21.6	214
6.12.3	196	7.1.28	214
6.12.5	197	7.3.1	201
6.12.6	197	7.3.2	208
6.13.1	197, 198, 205	7.3.6	201
6.13.2	197, 198	8.20.30	142
6.14	194, 199	8.21.6	162
6.14.2	200	8.21.13	180
6.14.3	199	8.23.13	197
6.14.4	200	8.23.15	200
6.14.5	200	8.24	201
6.14.9	199	8.24.8	205
6.14.10	200	8.25.4	209
6.14.12	198, 200	8.25.7	211
6.15.3	189	16.8.2	210

Res Gestae Divi Saporis 146
   l. 8   98
   l. 15   87
Septuaginta
   Es.
      8.12r   223
   Ju.
      12.20   218
      13.1   218
Sextus Empiricus
   P.
      1.148   227
      1.152   218

6.15.4	201
6.16	201, 209
6.16.1	202
6.16.2	202
6.16.3	203
6.16.4	203, 204
6.16.5	204
6.16.6–8	205
6.16.8	205
6.17	190, 209
6.17.1	209
6.17.2	209
6.17.4–8	209

Socrates
HE
    2.28.6   42
    3.17.6   26
    3.17.7–08   25
    3.20   9
    3.21   23
    3.21.1   23
    3.21.14   xiii
    3.20   4
Sozomenus
HE
    5.8   14
    5.8.4   15
    5.22   4, 9
    6.1.1   23, 32, 37
    6.1.2   8, 21, 36, 42
Stephanus Byzantius
    p.194,15   177
    p.297,13   177
    s.v. Βολογεσσιάς   155
Strabo
    2.1.31 (84C)   156
    2.5.12 (118C)   183
    2.5.18 (121C)   164
    2.5–31 (129C)   164
    3.1.6 (139C)   153
    3.1.9 (140C)   153
    3.4.7 (159C)   153
    3.4.10 (161C)   153
    3.412 (162C)   153
    3.5.9 (175C)   153
    7.3.3 (296C)   189
    7.3.7 (300C)   200
    7.3.9 (302C)   200
    11.1.5 (491C)   164
    11.2.15 (497C)   215
    11.3.2 (500C)   178
    11.4.8 (530C)   36
    11.5.5 (506C)   210
    11.6.1 (507C)   164, 196
    11.6.1 (508C)   145
    11.6.1–2 (507C)   144
    11.6.2 (507C)   139
    11.6.2–3 (507C–508C)   165
    11.7.1 (508C)   187
    11.7.2 (508C)   188, 189
    11.7.2 (508C–509C)   187
    11.7.2 (509C)   188
    11.7.3 (509C)   188
    11.7.4 (510C)   194, 196
    11.7.4 (510C)   194
    11.8.1 (511C)   203, 210
    11.8.2 (511C)   193
    11.8.2–5 (511C–512C)   197
    11.8.6 (512C–513C)   139
    11.8.8 (513C)   135
    11.8.8 (514C)   145, 178
    11.8.9 (511C)   211
    11.8.9 (514C)   182, 195, 210, 211, 213, 215
    11.9.1 (514C)   145, 177, 181, 182
    11.9.2 (515C)   134, 135
    11.10.1 (515C)   190
    11.10.1 (515C–516C)   209
    11.10.1 (516C)   210–212
    11.10.1–2 (515C–516C)   190
    11.10.2 (516C)   190, 191
    11.11.1 (516C)   192
    11.11.2 (516C)   194, 195
    11.11.2 (576C)   197
    11.11.3–5 (517C–518C)   196
    11.11.4 (517C)   197
    11.11.5 (518C)   194, 196, 209
    11.11.15 (518C)   196
    11.12.4 (522C)   145, 166
    11.13.1 (522C)   167
    11.13.1 (522C–523C)   165
    11.13.2 (523C)   177
    11.13.3 (523C)   145, 166, 177
    11.13.5 (524C)   167
    11.13.6 (524C)   167, 177, 181
    11.13.7 (525C)   145, 166, 167
    11.13.8 (525C)   166
    11.13.10 (526C)   166
    11.14.2 (527C)   145
    11.14.8 (529C)   143, 145, 148
    11.14.13 (530C)   36
    11.9.2 (515C)   134
    12.3.26 (553C)   200
    12.3.39 (516C)   44
    13.4.14 (629C–630C)   150
    13.4.14 (630C)   151
    15.1.3 (686C)   193

15.1.11 (689C)	198, 203	16.4.24 (782C)	184, 185
15.1.17 (691C)	210	17.1.18–19 (802C)	186
15.1.20 (694C)	207	17.1.22 (803C)	186
15.1.29 (698C)	203	Syncellus	
15.1.36 (702C)	138	715–6	87
15.1.72 (719C)	203	p.521	136
15.2.1 (720C)	209, 213, 214	Synesius	
15.2.3 (721C)	213	*De Regno*	
15.2.3 (728C)	180	20	224
15.2.8 (723C)	145, 211	Tatianus	
15.2.9 (724C)	212	*orat.*	
15.2.9–10 (724C)	211	17	174
15.2.10 (724C)	212	Theodoretus	
15.2.10 (725C)	197	*HE*	
15.2.14 (726C)	186	2.13–14	42
15.2.14 (727C)	142	3.9	14
15.3.1 (727C)	163, 170, 179	3.11–13	14
15.3.2 (727C)	162	3.12	14
15.3.4 (728C–729C)	178	3.13.14	15
15.3.6 (729C)	178	3.20	4, 9
15.3.6 (729C–730C)	180	3.21.1–4	8
15.3.8 (730C)	180	3.25.1	93
15.3.14 (733C)	175	3.26.2	32, 37
15.3.15 (733C)	174	3.28.1	25
15.3.16 (733C)	220	Theophylactus Simocatta	
15.3.17 (733C)	218	*Hist.*	
15.3.18 (734C)	219	2.5	223
15.3.19 (734C)	227, 228	5.5	222
15.3.20 (734C)	218	5.6	161
16.1.1 (736C)	36, 166	Thucydides	
16.1.3 (737C)	154	1.6.1–03	217
16.1.5 (738C)	156, 158	3.104	218
16.1.5 (738C–739C)	156	2.76.4	71
16.1.6 (739C)	160	Timaeus Locrus	
16.1.15 (743C)	149	94c	169
16.1.16 (743C)	157, 158, 167	Tzetzes	
16.1.19 (745C)	36	*Chil.*	
16.1.21 (746C)	148	1.1.99–100	222
16.1.27 (748C)	28	Vetus Testamentum	
16.3.1 (765C)	183	*Dan.*	
16.3.2 (765C)	142, 143	7.8	88
16.3.2 (765C–766C)	141, 143	*Gen.*	
16.3.2 (766C)	142	11.31	35
16.3.7 (767C)	230	24.4	35
16.4.2 (767C)	183	28.2	35
16.4.2 (767C–768C)	183	*Jb.*	
16.4.22–24 (780C–782C)	183	36.13	125

1 Macc.
  1.6   140

Xenophon
  An.
    1.5.8   228
    1.8.29 228
  Cyr.
    1.2.16 220
    1.3.2   227, 228
    2.3.14 226
    8.3.12 174
    8.6.22 162
    8.8.9   219
    8.8.10 218
    8.8.11 220
    8.8.16 219
  HG
    4.8.1   2

Zonaras
  8.5   122
  8.6   224
  11.22 157
  12.2   157–159
  12.9   157
  12.17 98
  12.18 99, 117
  12.23 87
  12.30 157
  12.31 105
  13.13.8 54

Zosimus
  1.18.2–03 117
  1.18.2–19.1 99
  1.27.2 87
  1.32.2 87
  1.34.1 83
  3.12.1 xv, xvii, 23, 27, 28
  3.12.2 xiv, xviii, 30, 32, 35
  3.12.3 xiv, 35, 82
  3.12.4 40, 41, 43
  3.12.5 36, 42
  3.13.1 35, 36, 42, 51, 82, 96, 97
  3.13.2 53, 91
  3.13.2–03 54
  3.13.3 36, 53, 95, 110, 111
  3.14.1 54, 91
  3.14.1, 3; 3.17.1 54
  3.14.2 xiv, 97, 100
  3.14.3 54
  3.16.2 54
  3.25.6 31
  3.32.4 118
  4.4.2 38, 42, 43
  4.23.1 43

X Passages referred to in Ammianus 14–22 and 24–31

14.1.2 169
14.1.6 223
14.1.8 98, 117
14.1.10 175
14.2.5 11
14.2.7 68, 202
14.2.9 23
14.2.11 10, 29
14.3.1 28, 30
14.3.2 32, 227
14.3.3 25, 32, 201
14.4.1 146
14.4.3 31, 203
14.4.4 218
14.5.1 1, 85
14.5.8 221

14.6.2 58
14.6.6 202
14.6.8 29
14.6.9 208
14.6.17 151, 154
14.6.19 85
14.6.23 192, 218
14.7.5 4
14.7.6 9, 184
14.7.9 119
14.7.21 131
14.8.1 183
14.8.3 26
14.8.5 135, 161
14.8.7 28, 32, 153
14.8.10 113

14.8.11　194, 197, 205
14.8.13　77, 116, 123
14.9.6　137
14.10.6　123
14.10.10　111
14.10.14　81
14.11.3　225
14.11.6　29
14.11.10　105
14.11.12　29
14.11.25–6　119
14.11.28　97
14.11.29　121
15.1.1　xii, 133
15.1.2　38
15.4.2　196
15.4.3　206
15.4.8　140
15.5.16　225
15.5.23　101
15.5.27　40
15.6.1　107
15.7.3　94
15.7.8　102
15.8.4　111
15.8.8　161
15.8.10　128
15.8.14　120
15.8.15　187
15.8.17　1, 200
15.9.2　132, 173
15.9.3　179
15.9.7　157
15.10.2　202
15.10.5　125
15.10.7　37
15.11.3　189, 194
15.11.6　24
15.11.7　145, 147
15.11.12　204
15.11.13　197
15.11.17　214
15.12.4　221
15.12.6　133
15.13.2　25
16.1.1　1, 2, 102
16.1.2　58

16.1.4　115
16.1.5　199
16.2.2　18
16.4.5　101, 127
16.5.4　8
16.5.10　225
16.5.12　12
16.5.14　40
16.7.4　58, 131
16.7.7　17
16.7.8–09　124
16.7.10　113
16.8.6　105
16.8.10　159
16.8.13　29
16.10.2　120
16.10.3　122
16.10.5　104, 111
16.10.6　28, 109
16.10.7　61
16.10.8　62
16.10.10　29
16.10.12　2, 4, 133
16.10.15　86, 134
16.10.17　109
16.11.4　43, 52, 112
16.11.6　103
16.11.9　60
16.12.2　140
16.12.8　111
16.12.9　112
16.12.13　110
16.12.16　22
16.12.18　18, 121
16.12.22　43
16.12.32　194
16.12.33　120
16.12.35　181
16.12.41　119
16.12.43　141
16.12.45　121
16.12.49　226
16.12.58　83
16.12.59　40
16.12.62　29
16.12.68　138
17.1.2　121, 127

17.1.8	79	18.6.10	84
17.2.1	101	18.6.14	166
17.4.4	221	18.6.16	153
17.4.11	195	18.6.19	152
17.4.12	152	18.6.20	44
17.4.13	93	18.6.22	145
17.4.15	109	18.6.23	53
17.4.16	123	18.7.1	153
17.5.5	139	18.7.9	151
17.5.6	30	18.7.10	48
17.5.8	136	18.8.2	40
17.5.11	184	18.8.5	31
17.5.15	104	18.8.10	33
17.6.2	155	18.9.3	26
17.7.6	146	18.10.1	152
17.7.7	125	18.10.4	171
17.7.9	17, 58	19.1.6	12
17.7.13	66	19.1.7	29, 62, 64
17.7.14	10	19.1.9	123
17.10.3	52	19.1.10	30, 37
17.10.9	50	19.2.1	118
17.11.3	123	19.2.3	133
17.11.4	220	19.2.8	154
17.12	199	19.4.2	104
17.12.8	82	19.4.4	217
17.12.10	52	19.5.1	75
17.12.20	135	19.5.4	83
17.13	199	19.5.5	119
17.13.1	41	19.5.6	64
17.13.6	40	19.6.1	29
17.13.10	125	19.6.6	226
17.13.11	155	19.7.7	63
17.13.15	184	19.7.8	127
17.13.19	47	19.8.2	33
17.13.25	111	19.8.6	33
17.13.26	135	19.8.7	61
17.13.27	195	19.9.9	121
17.13.28	40	19.11.1	84
17.14.1	157	19.12.14	118
17.14.3	38	19.7	56
18.1.1	101	20.1.1	2, 197
18.2.1–02	22	20.1.3	23, 128
18.2.13	33	20.2.3	104, 151
18.2.14	43	20.3.4	125
18.4.7	104, 153	20.3.5	106, 144
18.5.7	139	20.3.9	74
18.6.3	41	20.3.10	218

20.3.11	64	20.11.1	21, 106
20.3.12	71, 199	20.11.2	92, 124
20.4.1	136	20.11.3	43
20.4.2	38, 112	20.11.5	63, 91, 180
20.4.5	10, 42, 135, 193	20.11.7	11
20.4.6	55, 95, 181	20.11.9	67, 132
20.4.8	11, 76	20.11.11	87
20.4.9	24, 25, 112	20.11.11–15	69
20.4.12	82, 109	20.11.12	121, 140
20.4.14	11	20.11.13	76, 78
20.4.16	126, 162	20.11.15	62, 71, 72
20.4.17	87	20.11.19	68
20.4.18	42	20.11.22	45
20.4.19	108	20.11.24	22
20.4.22	220	20.11.25	149
20.5	111	20.11.26	78, 149, 151
20.5.1	9, 103	20.11.28	109, 136
20.5.3	112	21.1.3	126
20.5.4	134, 137, 215	21.1.6	38
20.5.7	24	21.1.7	106
20.5.8	71, 127	21.1.7–14	x, 161
20.5.9	22	21.1.8	92
20.5.10	9	21.1.10	17, 103
20.6.1	88	21.1.11	106, 109
20.6.2	128	21.2.2	47
20.6.3	78	21.2.3	7
20.6.6	78, 149, 184	21.4	xii
20.6.7	132, 166	21.4.2	xii
20.6.9	51, 172	21.4.7	18
20.7.1	32, 141, 223	21.4.8	85
20.7.2	225	21.5.1	8, 105, 110, 111, 126, 127
20.7.5	128	21.5.2	112, 127, 199
20.7.6	111	21.5.3	134
20.7.7	35, 139	21.5.4	120
20.7.9	62, 125	21.5.5	92
20.7.10	59, 78, 148	21.5.6	29, 121
20.8.1	1, 21, 31, 83	21.5.7	126
20.8.10	10	21.5.9	99, 127, 138
20.8.11	126, 136	21.5.10	182
20.8.15	18	21.5.12	87
20.8.17	126	21.5.13	23
20.8.19	38, 92, 107, 173	21.6.4	190
20.8.20	38	21.6.5	94
20.9.1	103, 147	21.6.6	40, 218
20.9.5	14, 64	21.6.7	44
20.9.8	14, 111	21.6.7–08	20
20.11	56	21.6.8	113

21.7.2	41, 114	21.16.10	131
21.7.3	103	21.16.11	116
21.7.6	180	21.16.16	151
21.7.7	31, 91, 152	21.16.18	167, 170, 175, 218
21.8.1	3, 91	21.16.9	126
21.8.2	33	22.1.1	2, 8, 121
21.8.3	133	22.1.2	14, 47
21.9.2	179	22.2.1	28
21.9.5	63, 71	22.2.2	179
21.9.6	23	22.2.3	189
21.9.7	137	22.3.1	3, 94
21.9.8	22, 127	22.3.2–3	3
21.10.3	201	22.3.7	15, 94
21.10.4	202, 203	22.3.9	137
21.10.6	26, 74	22.3.12	139
21.10.7	11	22.4.1	104
21.11.3	68, 138	22.4.2.	11
21.12	56	22.4.4	175
21.12.1	124	22.4.5	198, 208
21.12.4	136	22.4.6	124
21.12.5	48	22.4.7	124
21.12.7	93	22.4.8	105, 228
21.12.9	72, 102	22.5.3	80
21.12.9.	59	22.5.5	10
21.12.13	92	22.6.4	95
21.12.16	72	22.6.13	148
21.12.20	88	22.7.1	2, 15
21.12.22	179	22.7.3	18, 104
21.12.23	126	22.7.4	92
21.12.24	11	22.7.5	66
21.12.25	3, 136	22.7.8	8
21.13.3	144	22.7.9,	109
21.13.4	125, 221	22.7.10	52, 145
21.13.7	28	22.8.1	131
21.13.8	28	22.8.2	140
21.13.9	111	22.8.4	53
21.13.10	124	22.8.5	155, 217
21.13.13	81, 104, 121	22.8.8	224
21.14.2	28	22.8.9	196
21.14.3	93, 134	22.8.10	79, 83, 143, 152
21.14.5	151, 171	22.8.12	122, 158
21.15.2	24, 26, 94	22.8.13	63
21.16.1	4, 171	22.8.16	113
21.16.3	108, 184, 223	22.8.21	141
21.16.4	133	22.8.22	92
21.16.7	158	22.8.24	104
21.16.9	4, 90	22.8.28	132

22.8.29	152	22.15.14	193
22.8.30	212	22.15.21	43
22.8.31	199	22.15.22	63, 197
22.8.33	136, 152	22.15.28	74
22.8.37	59	22.16.1	218
22.8.38	113	22.16.10	106
22.8.40	51	22.16.11	125
22.8.42	104, 221	22.16.13	124
22.8.45	149	22.16.19	171
22.8.47	109	22.16.22	171
22.8.48	133, 204	22.16.24	133
22.9.1	127, 182	23.2.7	21
22.9.2	9	24.1.1	31
22.9.4	177	24.1.2	32
22.9.5	50	24.1.5	xx, 100
22.9.6	131, 158, 159	24.1.12	101
22.9.8	47	24.1.13	121, 125
22.9.10	38	24.2	73
22.9.12	174	24.2.7	155
22.9.13	26	24.2.10	76
22.10.1	8, 84	24.2.12	72, 109
22.11.1	11	24.2.13	63
22.11.2	94	24.2.18	75
22.11.4	14, 134	24.2.19	75
22.11.7	16, 92	24.3.4–07	112
22.11.11	109	24.3.9	33
22.12.1	8, 119, 120	24.3.14	79
22.12.2	103, 120	24.3.19	57
22.12.3	x, 18, 112	24.4.16	78
22.12.3,	1	24.4.23	14
22.12.6	23	24.4.25	78
22.12.7	16, 62, 133	24.4.28	62, 69
22.12.8	87, 132, 217	24.5.2	159
22.13.2	158, 184	24.5.3	223
22.13.3	46, 66, 124	24.5.5	101
22.13.4	184	24.5.6	51
22.13.5	17, 106	24.5.11	121
22.14.1	24, 126	24.6.8	226
22.14.2–03	25	24.6.11	121
22.14.3	24	24.7.1	157
22.14.7	62, 171	24.7.4	93
22.15.1	147	24.7.5	184
22.15.2	52, 146, 211	24.7.8	45
22.15.3	153	24.8.1	216, 221
22.15.4	123	24.8.3	206
22.15.8	146	24.8.4	44
22.15.11	133	24.8.6	45

25.1.13	29, 63	26.8.4	127
25.1.15	61	26.8.9	78, 125
25.1.17–18	221	26.8.10	159
25.2.1	40	26.9.8	173
25.2.5	174	26.10.10	126
25.2.6	64	26.10.15	161
25.2.7	17	27.2.11	215
25.2.8	91	27.3.1	103
25.3.3	121	27.3.8	78
25.3.5	125, 155	27.3.10	33
25.3.6	33	27.4.2	147
25.3.11	73	27.6.1	33
25.3.18	119	27.6.5	82
25.4.9	140	27.6.16	116, 137
25.4.11	154	27.8.7	79
25.4.13	128	27.9.2	221
25.4.16	136	27.9.7	29
25.4.17	170	27.10.10	37
25.4.23	x, 229	27.11.1	58
25.4.24	119, 139	27.11.4	175
25.4.26	xi	27.12.7	72
25.5.6	17	27.12.11	199
25.7.6	175	28.1.5	134
25.7.9	44	28.1.13	173
25.7.12	21, 45	28.1.14	169
25.8.5	116	28.1.20	37
25.9.12	26	28.1.26	169
25.10.1	xii, 103	28.2.10	53
25.10.3	199	28.2.14	94
25.10.4–05	26	28.4.2	223
25.10.11	17	28.4.6	133
26.1.1	83	28.4.9	126
26.1.2	104	28.4.14	58
26.1.8	173	28.6.2	105
26.1.14	120	28.6.23	76
26.2.10	137	29.1.5	126, 134
26.3.1	12	29.1.7	220
26.6.2	38	29.1.16	80
26.6.15	85	29.1.37	138
26.6.16	127	29.1.44	10
26.6.17	44	29.2.20	118
26.6.18	37	29.4.4	131
26.6.20	117	29.4.5	17, 124
26.7.4	146	29.4.6	124
26.7.13	41	29.5.38	127, 128
26.7.15	29	29.5.40	120
26.8.3	30	30.1.7	64

30.1.15	14	31.2.17	133, 199
30.1.22	47	31.2.18	203
30.2.9	118	31.2.22	182, 205
30.2.12	199	31.4.7	139
30.3.2	23	31.4.8	139
30.4.1	1, 85, 110	31.4.9	109
30.4.2	224	31.5.5	106
30.4.6	116	31.5.9	105
30.4.17	219	31.7.11	192, 216
30.4.19	127	31.7.13	125
30.5.11	220	31.9.5	218
30.5.13	43	31.10.7	121
30.7.4	134	31.10.13	121
30.7.5	123	31.10.18	72, 120
30.7.7	140	31.11.1	43
30.9.1	115	31.13.7	196
30.10.2	93	31.13.14	83
30.10.3	43	31.13.18	43
31.2.2	193	31.14.7	193
31.2.9	63	31.14.8	103
31.2.12	58, 131, 199	31.15.6	123
31.2.13	192	31.15.12	64, 69
31.2.15	201, 203	31.16.5	52, 141
31.2.16	205		

Printed in the United States
By Bookmasters